CONSUMER BEHAVIOR

CONSUMER BEHAVIOR

Todd Donavan
Colorado State University

Michael S Minor
The University of Texas - Rio Grande Valley

John Mowen
Oklahoma State University

With contributions by
Nese Nasif

CHICAGO
BUSINESS PRESS

CHICAGO
BUSINESS PRESS

CONSUMER BEHAVIOR

For product information or assistance, visit: www.chicagobusinesspress.com

ISBN 978-0-9971171-1-0

PREFACE

Managerial Applications

The key element that sets this book apart from other consumer behavior books is the use learning objectives in the form of managerial questions. As the first thing the reader sees in each chapter, these questions serve as the framework for the concepts that follow. The questions tackle issues that are commonly faced by marketing managers and/or public policy officials. In the process of answering the questions, the book provides students with the fundamental concepts necessary to understand the factors that influence consumer behavior.

Other consumer behavior textbooks do little to address managerial applications, place the applications at the end of each chapter, or locate them in stand-alone chapters. Instead, we use the questions at beginning of each chapter to place the managerial issues up front, and use them to guide the organization of the chapters.

The short case at the beginning of each chapter also serves to illustrate the application of the concepts that follow.

And to reinforce that managerial perspective throughout each chapter, we placed margin notes that call out and state *Managerial Principles* where ever they appear in the main body of the text.

Consumer Neuroscience

The concept and application of neuroscience in consumer behavior is significant. So much so that we've devoted an entire chapter to the subject. The chapter starts with the fundamentals of science and biology on which consumer neuroscience is based. From that foundation, the chapter introduces the applications of neuroscience in consumer behavior, as well as the implications and ethics of applying it.

Social Media

Every chapter includes boxed readings that highlight examples of the role of social media in consumer behavior and marketing.

Organization

Importantly, while the pedagogical approach is new, we retain a proven-effective chapter organization. The cover design reflects it. The "person" in the middle of each circle represents the individual consumer and the consumption choice he/she makes. This is what we cover in roughly the first half of the book. The outer circle represents the external influences (store atmospherics, family and peer influences, situational factors, demographics and lifestyle) that affect our decisions. This is, more or less, the overall theme of the second part of the book.

In Summary, our pedagogical approach provides an improved means of communicating the role of consumer behavior in making marketing management decisions. As a result, a course using this book will naturally follow the introductory course in marketing and fit well into a marketing curriculum. In addition, we worked hard to keep the material relevant to students with cutting-edge topics like the effects of Facebook or energy drinks on consumers. We also think students will be intrigued by the material in Chapter 15 as we take a simple, brief excursion into the world of consumer neuroscience.

Instructor Supplements

The comprehensive Instructor's Manual includes chapter outlines, along with answers to the end of chapter questions. The Test Bank provides multiple choice and essay questions for each chapter and includes a mix of descriptive and application questions. A PowerPoint deck provides an outline of the important topics in each chapter. Contact support@chicagobusinesspress.com to request the supplements.

BRIEF CONTENTS

Chapter 1 Introduction to Consumer Behavior   *1*

Chapter 2 Consumer Behavior and Developing Marketing Strategy   *23*

Chapter 3 Information Processing: Perceptual Processes   *51*

Chapter 4 Information Processing: Memory and Consumer Knowledge   *83*

Chapter 5 Motivation and Behavioral Learning   *111*

Chapter 6 Individual Differences: Personality, Self-Concept, and Psychographics   *141*

Chapter 7 Belief, Attitude, and Behavior Formation and Change   *169*

Chapter 8 Persuasive Communications   *201*

Chapter 9 Consumer Decision Processes   *231*

Chapter 10 Loyalty and Satisfaction   *269*

Chapter 11 Situational Influences   *303*

Chapter 12 Social Influences: Group, Dyadic, and Diffusion Processes   *329*

Chapter 13 Pop Culture   *361*

Chapter 14 Subcultures and Demographics   *387*

Chapter 15 Consumer Neuroscience   *415*

Chapter 16 The Dark Side of Consumer Behavior   *435*

Index   *455*

CONTENTS

Chapter 1   Introduction to Consumer Behavior   *1*

The History of Consumer Behavior   *3*

The Benefits of Understanding Consumer Behavior   *4*
Analyzing Consumers As a Foundation of Marketing Management   *5*
Public Policy and Consumer Behavior   *5*
Consumer Behavior and Altruistic Marketing   *5*

Why Study Theory?   *6*
The Personal Value of Consumer Behavior   *6*
The Decision-Making Perspective   *7*
The Experiential Perspective   *7*

The Three Perspectives   *7*
The Behavioral Influence Perspective   *8*

Benefits of Exchange   *9*
What Do We Exchange?   *10*

Dimensions of Exchange Relationships   *11*

Ethical Issues in Consumer Exchange Relations   *13*

An Organizing Model of Consumer Behavior   *15*
The Book's Organization   *17*
Summary   *18*
Key Terms   *19*
Review Questions   *19*
Discussion Questions   *20*
Endnotes   *21*

Chapter 2   Consumer Behavior and Developing Marketing Strategy   *23*

Introduction   *24*

**The Role of Consumer Behavior in
Marketing Research**   *25*
Qualitative Research Methods   *27*
Quantitative Research Methods   *28*

The Role of Consumer Behavior In Environmental Analysis   *29*
The Economic Environment and Consumer Behavior   *30*
The Natural Environment and Consumer Behavior   *32*
The Technological Environment and Consumer Behavior   *33*

The Role of Consumer Behavior In Market Segmentation   *34*
The Reciprocity between Consumers and the Environment   *34*
Characteristics of the Person   *35*

The Situation as a Segmentation Basis   *38*
Geographic Segmentation   *38*
Culture and Subcultures As a Basis for Segmentation   *38*
Segmenting Business Markets   *39*

The Role of Consumer Behavior in Product Positioning and Differentiation   *40*

The Role of Consumer Behavior in Marketing Mix Development   *41*
Product Development   *42*
Promotional Strategy Implications   *43*
Pricing and Distribution Applications   *44*

Using Consumer Behavior To Solve Marketing Problems   *45*
Summary   *46*
Key Terms   *47*
Review Questions   *48*
Discussion Questions   *48*
Endnotes   *49*

Chapter 3   Information Processing: Perceptual Processes   *51*

An Overview Of Information Processing   *52*
An Information-Processing System   *53*
The Exposure Stage and Information Processing   *54*
The Attention Stage and Information Processing   *56*

Changing a Product's Price or Features   *60*
The Study of Sensation   *61*
Preattention   *63*

Influencing Consumers Without Their Knowledge   *63*
Subliminal Perception   *64*

Maintaining Consumer Interest   *66*
Consumer Adaptation   *66*

Making Products Aesthetically Pleasing   *68*
Perceptual Organization   *68*
Perceptual Organization and Aesthetics   *70*

The Effects of Symbols   *71*
Semiotics   *72*
The Role of Expectations   *73*
Research   *75*
Environmental Analysis   *75*
Segmentation   *75*

Managerial Implications   *75*
Summary   *76*
Positioning and Differentiation   *76*
Marketing Mix   *76*
Key Terms   *78*
Review Questions   *78*
Discussion Questions   *79*
Endnotes   *80*

Chapter 4   Information Processing: Memory and Consumer
Knowledge   *83*

**Types Of Memory and Consumers' Responses To
Communications**   *84*
  The Multiple-Store Memory Model   *84*
  Memory-Control Processes   *89*

Consumer Knowledge and Brand Perceptions   *91*
  How Do Consumers Gain Knowledge?   *92*
  Knowledge and the Associationist School of Psychology   *93*
  Semantic Memory Networks   *96*

Keeping Consumers From Forgetting   *98*
  Creating Unique Ads   *99*
  Using Multiple Modalities   *99*
  Telling Incomplete Stories   *100*
  Time and Forgetting   *100*
  Market Research   *101*

Feelings and Memory   *101*

**The Managerial Implications of Memory and Cognitive
Learning**   *101*
  Environmental Analysis   *102*
  Segmentation   *102*
  Positioning and Differentiation   *102*
  Marketing Mix   *102*
Summary   *103*
Key Terms   *104*
Review Questions   *104*
Discussion Questions   *105*
Endnotes   *106*

Chapter 5   Motivation and Behavioral Learning   *111*

Motivated Behavior   *112*

Consumer Emotions   *114*
  Opponent-Process Theory   *115*

Consumer Psychological Needs   *116*
  McClelland's Theory of Learned Needs   *117*
  Maintaining Optimum Stimulation Levels   *118*
  The Motivation to Maintain Behavioral Freedom   *119*
  Perceived Risk and Consumer Motivation   *120*
  The Motivation to Attribute Causality   *122*
  The Managerial Implications of Motivation   *124*
  Classical Conditioning   *125*

Behavioral Learning and Consumer Behavior   *125*
  Operant Conditioning   *128*
  Vicarious Learning   *131*

Managerial Applications Analysis   *132*
  Research   *132*
  Environmental Analysis   *132*
  Segmentation   *133*

Positioning and Differentiation   *133*
Marketing Mix   *133*
Summary   134
Key Terms   135
Review Questions   135
Discussion Questions   136
Endnotes   137

Chapter 6   Individual Differences: Personality, Self-Concept, and
Psychographics   *141*

Personality, Self-Concept and Lifestyle   *142*

Understanding Personality   *143*
Psychoanalytic Theory   *144*
Trait Theory   *146*
How Are Traits Organized?   *150*
Do Brands Have Personality Traits?   *152*
Symbolic Interactionism and the Self   *153*

The Self-Concept And Marketing Strategy   *153*
Consumer Lifestyles   *155*

Lifestyle, Psychographic Analysis, and Marketing Strategy   *155*
Traditional Perspectives on Psychographic Analysis   *156*
The VALS Psychographic Inventory   *157*
The List of Values Approach   *159*

Managerial Implications Of Personality and Psychographics   *160*
Research   *160*
Environmental Analysis   *161*
Segmentation   *161*
Positioning and Differentiation   *161*
Marketing Mix   *161*
Summary   161
Key Terms   163
Review Questions   163
Discussion Questions   164
Endnotes   165

Chapter 7   Belief, Attitude, and Behavior Formation and Change   *169*

Consumer Beliefs   *170*
Consumer Attitudes   *172*
Behaviors and Intentions to Behave   *172*
The Direct Formation of Beliefs, Attitudes, and Behaviors   *173*

Forming Beliefs, Attitudes, and Behaviors   *173*
Hierarchies of Beliefs, Attitudes, and Behaviors   *175*

Predicting Consumer Attitudes Through Multiattribute Models   *176*
Attitude-Toward-the-Object Model   *177*
When Do Attitudes Predict Behavior?   *180*
The Behavioral Intentions Model   *180*
Persuasion: Attitude, Belief, and Behavior Change   *181*
The Decision-Making Approach to Attitude Change   *181*

Multiattribute Models and the Decision-Making Path to
Persuasion   *183*
The Experiential Path to Attitude Change   *185*
Balance Theory   *185*

Attitude Toward the Advertisement   *187*
The Behavioral Influence Route to Behavior Change   *188*
Ingratiation Tactics   *188*
The Foot-in-the-Door Technique   *189*
The Door-in-the-Face Technique   *189*

Managerial Implications–Responsive Marketing   *190*
Even-a-Penny-Will-Help Technique   *190*
Ethical Implications of the Techniques of Personal Influence   *190*
Research   *191*
Environmental Analysis   *191*
Segmentation   *191*
Positioning   *191*
Marketing Mix   *191*
Summary   *192*
Key Terms   *194*
Review Questions   *194*
Discussion Questions   *195*
Endnotes   *196*

Chapter 8   Persuasive Communications   *201*

Overview of Persuasion Communications   *203*
Source Characteristics   *205*

Source Credibility   *205*

Physical Attractiveness of the Source   *206*

Likability of the Source   *208*
The Impact of Sexually Suggestive Ads   *208*
Source Meaningfulness   *209*
Managerial Implications of Source Effects   *211*

Message Characteristics—Message Content   *211*
Developing Message Content   *212*

Message Characteristics—Message Structure   *220*

The Managerial Implications of Persuasive Communications   *222*
Research   *222*
Environmental Analysis   *222*
Segmentation   *223*
Positioning   *223*
Marketing Mix   *223*
Summary   *223*
Key Terms   *224*
Review Questions   *224*
Discussion Questions   *225*
Endnotes   *226*

Chapter 9   Consumer Decision Processes   *231*

Introduction   *232*
  The Decision-Making Perspective   *233*

**Alternative Perspectives on Consumer
Decision Making**   *233*
  The Experiential Perspective   *235*
  Behavioral Influence Perspective   *235*

Problem Recognition   *236*
  Internal Search   *237*

Consumer Search Behavior   *237*
  External Search   *239*
  How Much Search by Consumers?   *240*

Alternative Evaluation   *241*
  Judging Likelihood   *242*
  Judging Goodness or Badness   *245*
  Choice Under High- and Low-Involvement Conditions   *249*

The Consumer Choice Process   *249*
  Experiential Choice Processes   *254*

Impulse purchases   *255*
  Variety-Seeking Purchases   *256*
  Effects of Mood States on Choice   *256*
  Choices among Noncomparable Alternatives   *257*
  Choices among Stores   *257*

Managerial Implications—Responsive Marketing   *258*
  Research   *258*
  Environmental Analysis   *258*
  Segmentation   *258*
  Positioning   *259*
  Marketing Mix   *259*
Summary   *259*
Key Terms   *261*
Review Questions   *261*
Discussion Questions   *262*
Endnotes   *263*

Chapter 10   Loyalty and Satisfaction   *269*

The Qualities of a Satisfying Experience   *270*
  Product Use   *271*
  The Consumption of Performance   *272*
  Consumption Experience   *273*
  Cold Stone Creamery   *274*
  The Peabody Hotel   *274*
  Mood States and the Consumption Experience   *275*

**The Development of Post-Acquisition Satisfaction and
Dissatisfaction**   *275*
  Evaluating Product Performance and Quality   *277*
  The Development of Satisfaction and Dissatisfaction   *279*
  Measuring Consumer Satisfaction   *284*

From Satisfaction To Delight   *285*

Consumer Complaint Behavior   *285*
  Factors Influencing Complaint Behavior   *287*
  Corporate Reactions to Consumer Complaining   *287*

Product Disposition   *288*
  Complaints and Exit Behavior   *288*

Brand Loyalty   *289*
  Behavioral Approaches to Brand Loyalty   *290*
  Attitudinal Measures of Brand Loyalty   *290*
  Identifying Brand-Loyal Consumers   *291*
  Predicting Satisfaction and Loyalty   *292*
  Comparing Satisfaction and Loyalty   *293*

Managerial Implications   *293*
  Research   *294*
  Environmental Analysis   *294*
  Segmentation   *294*
  Positioning   *294*
  Marketing Mix   *294*

Summary   *295*
Key Terms   *296*
Review Questions   *296*
Discussion Questions   *297*
Endnotes   *298*

Chapter 11   Situational Influences   *303*

What We Mean By Consumer Situations   *304*

The Five Types of Situational Influence   *305*

Physical Surroundings: The Store Environment   *306*
  The Effects of Music   *306*
  The Effects of Crowding   *307*
  The Effects of Store Location   *309*
  The Effects of Store Layout   *309*
  Atmospherics: The Elements of Store Atmosphere   *309*
  Atmospherics in Service Settings   *311*

Social Surroundings   *312*
  Occasion-Based Marketing Opportunities   *313*

The Task Definition   *313*
  Gift Giving   *314*

Time As An Environmental Influencer   *316*
  Time As a Resource   *316*
  Time As a Product   *317*
  Time As a Situational Variable   *317*

Antecedent States   *318*
  The Effects of Temporary Mood States on Consumers   *318*

Usage Situation, Person, and Product Interactions   *319*
  Research   *321*
  Environment   *321*

Segmentation   *321*
Positioning   *321*
Managerial Implications of Situational Influences   *321*
Summary   *322*
Key Word   *323*
Review Question   *323*
Discussion Question   *323*
Endnotes   *324*

Chapter 12   Social Influences: Group, Dyadic, and Diffusion
Processes   *329*
Group Processes   *330*
Types of Groups   *330*
Brand Community Groups   *331*
How Groups Influence Consumers   *333*
Families And Households   *336*
The Demographics of Households   *336*
Childhood Consumer Socialization   *339*
Buying Behavior and Social Networks   *340*
A Model of Consumer Socialization   *340*
Dyadic Exchanges   *342*
Word-of-Mouth Communications   *342*
Service Encounters   *345*
Transmission Processes   *347*
Diffusion Processes   *347*
The Diffusion of Innovations   *348*
Diffusion through Social Networks   *350*
Research   *351*
Environmental Analysis   *351*
Segmentation   *351*
Positioning   *351*
Managerial Implications   *351*
Summary   *352*
Marketing Mix   *352*
Key Word   *354*
Review Question   *354*
Discussion Question   *355*
Endnotes   *355*

Chapter 13   Pop Culture   *361*
The Components of Culture   *362*
The Cultural Matrix   *364*
The Role of Consumer Goods in a Culture   *365*
Core Values   *366*
Consumer Research on Cultural Values   *367*
Rituals   *371*
Cultural Symbols   *373*
Examples of Pop Culture   *375*

Popular Culture   *375*

Fashion   *376*

   Fashion Trends   *377*

   How Pop Culture Develops   *377*

Managerial Implications of Popular Culture   *378*

   Research   *378*

   Environmental Analysis   *379*

   Segmentation   *379*

   Positioning and Differentiation   *379*

Summary   *380*

   Marketing Mix   *380*

Key Terms   *381*

Discussion Questions   *381*

Discussion Questions   *382*

Endnotes   *382*

Chapter 14   Subcultures and Demographics   *387*

The Many Cultures of the US   *388*

   Subcultures and Demographic Groups   *388*

   The Baby Boomers   *389*

Age Subcultures   *389*

   Generation X   *391*

   Millennials   *391*

Age and Information Processing   *392*

   The Elderly   *392*

Ethnic Subcultures   *394*

Race as a Subculture   *394*

   The Hispanic Subculture   *395*

   The Asian-American Subculture   *397*

   Comparing Anglo, African-American, and Hispanic Consumption   *397*

Regional Subcultures   *398*

   Portraying Minorities in Advertisements   *398*

   Geodemographics   *399*

   Should Companies Segment by Geography?   *400*

Social-Class Subcultures   *401*

   Social Class and Buying Behavior   *403*

   Psychological Differences among the Classes   *403*

   Social Class and Lifestyles   *404*

Other Subcultures   *406*

The Managerial Implications of Subcultures and Demographics   *406*

   Research   *406*

   Environmental Analysis   *406*

   Segmentation   *407*

   Positioning and Differentiation   *407*

   Marketing Mix   *407*

Summary   407
Key Terms   408
Review Questions   409
Discussion Questions   409
Endnotes   410

Chapter 15   Consumer Neuroscience   *415*
   Consumer Neuroscience   *416*
      Experimental Design in Consumer Neuroscience   *417*
      fMRI   *419*
   Techniques Used in Consumer Neuroscience   *419*
      EEG   *421*
      Why Use Consumer Neuroscience?   *423*
   Ethical Issues in Consumer Neuroscience Studies   *423*
      Consent, Privacy, and Confidentiality   *424*
      Protection of Consumer Interests and Autonomy   *425*
   Contributions of Consumer Neuroscience Studies   *426*
      Market Research   *427*
      Environmental Analysis   *427*
      Segmentation   *427*
   Managerial Implications of Consumer Neuroscience   *427*
   Summary   428
      Positioning and Differentiation   *428*
      Marketing Mix   *428*
   Key Terms   429
   Review Questions   429
   Discussion Questions   430
   Endnotes   432

Chapter 16   The Dark Side of Consumer Behavior   *435*
   Corporate Behaviors and The Dark Side of Consumer Behavior   *436*
      Deceptive Advertising   *436*
      Unfair Advertising   *437*
      Corrective Advertising   *437*
      Children's Advertising   *437*
   Dark-Side Behaviors Consumers Engage In   *438*
      Product Misuse   *439*
      Drinking and Driving   *440*
      Compulsive Behavior   *441*
   An Appropriate Role for The Corporation   *444*
      Succeeding in the Long Run   *444*
      Acquiring a Positive Public Image   *445*
   Dealing with Rumors   *446*
      Types and Causes of Rumors   *446*
   Managerial Implications   *448*
      Avoiding Government Regulation   *448*

Research   *448*
Environmental Analysis   *448*
Segmentation   *448*
Positioning and Differentiation   *449*
Marketing Mix   *449*
Summary   *449*
Key Words   *450*
Review Questions   *450*
Discussion Questions   *451*
Endnotes   *452*

Index   455

chapter

1

Introduction to Consumer Behavior

Learning Objectives:

1. What is consumer behavior?

2. Why study consumer behavior?

3. What is the role of theory in consumer behavior?

4. What are the research perspectives on consumer behavior?

5. How are the exchange processes beneficial to each party?

6. What is the role of ethics in consumer behavior?

7. How can we understand all the elements involved in consumer behavior?

Does social media help sell brands?

Many consumers select a brand based on other people's opinions or behaviors. One issue we address in consumer behavior is how others influence our behavior: social influence. With the tremendous growth of social media, we're beginning to see its influence on purchases. Let's look at a list of the top ten brands based on social media conversations.

1. Twitter
2. Apple
3. Facebook
4. Google
5. Walt Disney Company
6. LG
7. YouTube
8. Microsoft
9. Amazon.com
10. BBC[1]

This list is based on online conversations in blogs and on Twitter, Facebook, and other networks. The more a brand was discussed in a positive light, the higher the ranking it received. These brands are getting the most powerful form of marketing known to mankind: word of mouth. Consumers' attitudes and behaviors are often influenced as they read comments about brand experiences from their friends and acquaintances. Therefore, social media is becoming a powerful

force in marketing a brand. Understanding how consumers react to online conversations is a consumer behavior topic. If firms can facilitate a positive conversation about their brands, they'll be in a better position to gain future sales.

One goal of this book is to provide extensive applications of the concepts and theories of consumer behavior to similar decisions made by corporations, public-policy makers, and nonprofit organizations. Throughout this book, we'll address consumer behavior with an emphasis on social media's influence.

Another example of consumer behavior is the decision to undergo cosmetic surgery in order to feel more physically attractive. All of us have bought clothing, jewelry, or cosmetics for the same purpose, but surgery is a step beyond such purchases. Some brides spend upward of $6,000 a procedure for breast augmentation, liposuction, Botox, or Collagen for themselves and even members of the wedding party before the big day.[2] In 2010–2011, the E! network ran a reality show called *Bridalplasty* in which brides competed to win free plastic surgery. Have we gone too far in the pursuit of personal beauty? Indeed, some consumer actions can be truly bizarre.

In addition to investigating unusual buying activities, the study of consumer behavior is also critical for managerial decision making. In order to be successful, for instance, cosmetic surgeons must sell a product, and the marketing process requires an understanding of consumer needs and wants. By understanding their customers, practitioners can develop alternative plastic surgery products, from face-lifts to liposuction, breast augmentation, and hair implants.

Providers must also create promotional appeals that target the specific needs of their potential customers. Thus, when appealing to men, cosmetic surgeons may want to emphasize clients competing against younger rivals.

Providers can also use consumer behavior to market plastic surgery by identifying the personality traits of individuals who have these procedures done. They tend to be female and to have 1) a high concern for how others judge their attractiveness (the vanity view), 2) low health motivation, and 3) fairly materialistic leanings.[3] Clinics can develop promotions that emphasize how others will appreciate clients' beauty more, thus focusing on the vanity view. Or providers can focus on the materialism trait by emphasizing the body is the client's own personal object.[4]

Finally, the study of consumer behavior highlights concerns about ethics and social responsibility in the marketplace. For instance, while many cosmetic procedures may be safe in moderation, marketers may choose to de-market these procedures for ethical reasons. To protect society from too many surgical procedures, marketers can use a de-marketing strategy to discourage the behavior by focusing on associated risks, such as scarring, bleeding, nerve damage, as well as the potential risks of any elective surgery, including blood loss.

This book is organized around the theme of managerial questions, and a set of these questions, in the form of learning objectives (LOs), opens each chapter. In presenting these business questions and guiding them to resolve them as you read, we aim to show you how to solve relevant business problems in your work life.

THE HISTORY OF CONSUMER BEHAVIOR

Consumer behavior is a young discipline: its first textbooks were written in the 1960s. Its intellectual forefathers, however, are much older. For example, Thorstein Veblen talked about conspicuous consumption in 1899. In the early 1900s, writers began discussing how advertisers could use psychological principles.[5] In the 1950s, ideas from Freudian psychology were popularized by motivation researchers and used by advertisers. It wasn't until the articulation of the marketing concept in the 1950s, however, that the need to study consumer behavior was recognized.

The **marketing concept** embodies "the view that an industry is a customer-satisfying process, not a goods-producing process. An industry begins with the customer and his needs, not with a patent, a raw material, or a selling skill."[6] The recognition that an organization can exist only so long as it fulfills consumer needs and wants by thoroughly understanding its exchange partners (its customers) makes the study of the consumer essential.[7]

Consumer behavior, in turn, is the study of the buying units, which can be individuals or organizations, and of the **exchange processes** of acquiring, consuming, and disposing of goods, services, experiences, and ideas. This simple definition introduces a number of important concepts. First is the word *exchange*. A consumer inevitably resides at one end of an exchange process in which resources are transferred between two parties. For example, an exchange takes place between a doctor and patient—the physician trades medical services for the patient's money. In addition, parties can exchange other resources, such as material goods, services of all kinds, feelings, information, and status.

The "buying units" in an exchange also can be consumers or firms. Particularly in business-to-business marketing, a group of individuals in a buying center might make the purchase decision rather than a single person. Fortunately, the same basic principles apply to organizational buying behavior as to consumer buying behavior.

The definition of "consumer behavior" also reveals the exchange process is a series of steps, beginning with the acquisition phase, moving to consumption, and ending with the disposition of the product or service. When investigating the **acquisition phase**, researchers analyze the factors that influence the product and service choices of consumers. Much of the research in consumer behavior has focused on the acquisition phase. For instance, we know people may acquire a product for its symbolism, or the ideas and meanings it expresses to others about the buyer. Many sports fans eager to wear their team's paraphernalia after a big win are symbolically telling the social world they're affiliated with a winner.

When investigating the **consumption phase**, the researcher analyzes how consumers actually use a product or service and the experiences obtained from such use. In some service industries—restaurants, amusement parks, and rock concerts, for example—the consumption experience is the reason for the purchase. Brands such as Starbucks, Ritz Carlton, Great Wolf Lodge, and Pike Place Fish Market have discovered consumers are more satisfied when the marketer creates an experience rather than simply completes a transaction.

The **disposition phase** refers to what consumers do with a product once they have completed their use of it. The phase also addresses the level of satisfaction consumers experience after purchasing a good or service. For example, one critical problem physicians and patients face is increasing the level of satisfaction

SOCIAL MEDIA

Social Media to Target Wine Drinkers

To many individuals, wine is a high-status drink. In fact, wine drinkers can gain the status of connoisseur, or expert judge of quality. But not all individuals who enjoy wine are in the connoisseur category. This opens the door for a new product called Wines That Rock (WTR).

The makers of WTR realized consumers may be attracted to a wine associated with a successful musical act, so each WTR variety is named for a specific band or event. Names include the Police, the Rolling Stones, the Grateful Dead, Pink Floyd, and Woodstock. Fans are immediately attracted to the label. However, WTR doesn't simply slap a colorful label on bottles to sell the brand. Each variety of wine captures the essence of a band or Woodstock. WTR currently sells over 150,000 cases of wine per year.

Why are wine drinkers attracted to this brand? One reason is that WTR is the anti-wine, targeted at the anti-connoisseur. The company focuses on Sam's Club for distribution, and communication channels such as *Rolling Stone* magazine and social media such as Facebook to sell the brand—strategies other wine makers wouldn't even consider. With 17 million Pink Floyd fans on Facebook, WTR has a great opportunity to reach its target market. WTR offers these fans special deals by purchasing the brand through the social media Website. Consumer behavior seeks to understand the behavior of consumers and then

WTR's five varieties of wine appeal to certain music lovers.

use strategies to reach a target market. It appears that WTR understands the behavior of many consumers and has created a brilliant strategy.

How did WTR apply consumer behavior concepts to its branding? First, many consumers seek items that demonstrate their own personality and hobbies. WTR gives fans of these bands a great opportunity to showcase their loyalty. Second, consumers seek items that bring them joy. Some loyal fans of these bands will buy a bottle of WTR wine and perhaps never even open it—just having the bottle is satisfying. Finally, consumers can give this special product to someone else to express feelings of warmth, status, and comfort. By targeting a specific sub-segment of the wine market, WTR has demonstrated a keen understanding of consumer behavior.

with the results of the medical procedure. If consumers have unrealistic expectations, the anticipated outcomes aren't likely to occur and dissatisfaction will result. For the patient, unfulfilled expectations may result in a loss of self-esteem and possibly medical complications. From the surgeon's perspective, customer dissatisfaction is likely to increase the likelihood of patients filing lawsuits.

Finally, consumer behavior incorporates theories and concepts from all the behavioral sciences. When we study the acquisition, consumption, and disposition of products, services, and ideas, we're also exploring the disciplines of marketing, psychology, social psychology, sociology, anthropology, demography, and economics.

THE BENEFITS OF UNDERSTANDING CONSUMER BEHAVIOR

Understanding consumers and the consumption process provides a number of benefits. Managers can make better product decisions, marketing researchers can better analyze consumers, legislators and regulators can create more effective laws and regulations governing the purchase and sale of goods and services, and consumers can choose goods and services more wisely. In addition, the study of consumers can help us understand more about the general psychological, sociological, and economic factors that influence human behavior.

Analyzing Consumers As a Foundation of Marketing Management

Recall that **marketing** is "the process of creating, distributing, promoting, and pricing goods, services, and ideas to facilitate satisfying exchange relationships with customers and develop and maintain favorable relationships with stakeholders in a dynamic environment."[8] From this definition emerge two key marketing tasks. First, marketers attempt to satisfy the needs and wants of their target market. Second, they study the exchange processes in which two parties transfer resources. Putting these together, we recognize that for marketers to create a successful exchange, they must have an understanding of the factors that influence consumers' needs and wants.

Indeed, the principle of consumer-oriented marketing is when firms focus all activities around the consumers' point of view.[9] As Peter Drucker, the well-known management scholar, stated, "Marketing is the whole business seen from the point of view of its final result, that is, from the customer's point of view."[10] A cover story article in *Bloomberg Businessweek* suggested the importance of consumers in the digital age:

> *A Copernican revolution of sorts is under way. Executives used to imagine their companies as the center of a solar system orbited by suppliers and customers. The Internet is changing that—dramatically. Now, the customer is becoming the center of the entire business universe.*[11]

Public Policy and Consumer Behavior

Knowledge of consumer behavior can also assist in the development of public policy. As it pertains to consumer behavior, **public policy** means the development of the laws and regulations that affect consumers in the marketplace. In its legislative, regulatory, and judicial roles, the federal government often deals with consumer issues. For example, automobile gas consumption is highly regulated. Over the next few years, a company's fleet will be required to achieve specific standards: cars from 27.5 miles per gallon (mpg) to 37.8 mpg and trucks 23.5 mpg to 28.8 mpg by 2016.[12] Concern for our natural environment has greatly influenced our public policy on this issue.

Consumer *mis*behavior, sometimes called the dark side of consumer behavior, is a public policy area that investigates how consumers can act unethically, misuse products, and engage in behaviors that risk life and limb. While many consumers desire the quick pick-me-up offered by energy drinks, for example, the overuse of these products and their use in combination with alcohol has raised many concerns.

Consumer Behavior and Altruistic Marketing

Marketers also apply the ideas and concepts of marketing to nontraditional business areas. For instance, nonprofit groups, including political parties, religious organizations, and charitable groups, all engage in consumer research.

However, rather than market tangible products, they usually market intangible ideas. For example, the United Way promotes the idea that if thousands of individuals volunteer to help others through nonprofit organizations such as Big Brothers Big Sisters of America and the American Red Cross we can make the United States a better place to live.

Indeed, consumer researchers have recently argued that many of the most important problems society faces today are embodied in the choices consumers make, such as decisions to eat high-fat foods, smoke, drink and drive, take drugs, or use the services of prostitutes. Research by consumer behavior scholars can benefit society by finding ways to influence people to act more responsibly in their consumption of such goods and services. For instance, researchers recently identified how making consumer health goals more salient can help consumers make better decisions regarding food.[13]

The Personal Value of Consumer Behavior

A general knowledge of consumer behavior also has considerable **personal value**. It can help us become better consumers by showing us what's behind the consumption choices we and others make. It can assist us in the buying process by informing us of some of the strategies companies use to market their products. It can show us why product rumors start, why subliminal advertising messages are unlikely to influence buying, and why some product endorsers, such as the basketball players Michael Jordan and Shaquille O'Neal, can be effective even after their sports career has ended. Finally, being able to understand our own consumption motivations, as well as those of others, is satisfying and is part of being educated and self-aware.

WHY STUDY THEORY?

The study of consumer behavior provides three types of marketing information: (1) orienting, (2) factual, and (3) theoretical. The study of the consumer helps orient managers and public-policy makers so they consider the impact of their actions on consumers. The field also provides facts, such as the size of various demographic groups. In addition, the study of consumer behavior gives us theories. Table 1.1 provides a summary of why we should study consumer behavior.

Nothing is more practical than a **theory**, which is a set of interrelated statements defining the causal relationships among a group of ideas. Theories may be big or small, but all should have research support. Consumer behavior theories do have such support, as we'll see throughout the book, and that's why we can use them to understand and solve managerial and public-policy problems.

1. Analyzing consumers should be the foundation of marketing management. It assists managers to	**TABLE 1.1** Reasons for Studying Consumer Behavior
a. design the marketing mix.	
b. segment the marketplace.	
c. position and differentiate products.	
d. perform an environmental analysis.	
e. develop market research studies.	
2. Consumer behavior should play an important role in the development of public policy.	
3. The study of consumer behavior enables us to be better informed consumers.	
4. Consumer analysis provides useful knowledge of overall human behavior.	
5. The study of consumer behavior provides three pieces of marketing information:	
a. A consumer orientation	
b. Facts about human behavior	
c. Theories to guide the thinking process	

THE THREE PERSPECTIVES

A key feature of the field of consumer behavior is its research base, which draws research methods and procedures from psychology, sociology, economics, and anthropology. In this book, we organize research on consumer behavior into three perspectives to guide us in thinking about and identifying the factors that influence it: (1) the decision-making perspective, (2) the experiential perspective, and (3) the behavioral influence perspective.[14]

The Decision-Making Perspective

During the 1970s and early 1980s, researchers tended to view the consumer as a decision maker who first perceives a problem exists and then moves through a rational problem-solving process. The **decision-making perspective** thus portrays consumers as moving through a series of steps: problem recognition, search, alternative evaluation, choice, and post-acquisition evaluation. The roots of this approach are in cognitive and experimental psychology and economics.

Thinking back to the question of why people purchase cosmetic surgery services, the decision-making perspective focuses our attention on the steps through which consumer move when deciding which physician to hire to do cosmetic surgery. For example, in analyzing the choice process, researchers would attempt to identify the characteristics sought by consumers in their physician, such as his or her qualifications, bedside manner, explanation of risks, and price charged.

The Experiential Perspective

The **experiential perspective** on consumer buying proposes that in some instances, consumers don't make their purchases according to a strictly rational decision-making process. Instead, they sometimes buy products and services in order to have fun, create fantasies, and experience feelings.[15] Impulse- and variety-seeking purchases (in which consumers switch brands to lower boredom level and obtain stimulation) fall under this perspective. Another kind of experiential purchase is one in which consumers base their decision on a "how-do-I-feel-about-it" rule of thumb.[16] Many consumer services and products bought for leisure purposes have a strong experiential component, including going to rock concerts, symphonies, amusement parks, and movies. Even foods and drinks are now marketed with an experiential twist. Starbucks entered the coffee market and changed the entire industry. Its customers are entertained by the theatrics of the barista who "creates" the drink for them rather than simply filling customers' cups from a carafe. Starbucks' friendly cozy atmosphere also encourages guests to stay longer and experience the brand.

The roots of the experiential perspective are in motivational psychology, sociology, and anthropology. In particular, researchers who take an experiential perspective frequently use **interpretive research methods**. That is, they directly observe and record the activities or interest in them—or even participate.[17] Sometimes, they can be found recording the folklore and traditions of society in order to obtain an understanding of its members' consumption processes.[18] They also believe they themselves influence the data collection effort, focus on understanding rather than prediction, and assume reality is socially constructed.

The Behavioral Influence Perspective

The **behavioral influence perspective** says strong environmental forces propel consumers to make purchases without first developing strong feelings or beliefs about the product. In this instance, the consumer doesn't necessarily go through a rational decision-making process or rely on feelings when deciding to purchase a product or service. Instead, the action results from the direct influence on behavior of environmental forces, such as cultural norms, the physical environment, economic pressures, and sales promotion devices, such as contests.[19]

The behavioral influence perspective provides another viewpoint for understanding why people undergo cosmetic surgery. For example, strong group or social pressures might propel an individual to have his or her body pierced. The person may actually have a strong distaste for the procedure but still engage in the act because of the force of the situation.

In reality, most purchases will have some elements of each of the three perspectives. The purchase of a plastic surgeon's services, for instance, requires some level of decision making, such as when a consumer searches for information, evaluates alternatives, and makes a rational choice. However, it's also likely that an experiential process operates in which strong emotional elements drive the consumer to engage in actions that have a high level of symbolic meaning, such as having a face-lift to create a youthful image. Finally, as we've demonstrated with the body piercing example, strong pressures found in a social situation may also influence the behavior. In sum, it's useful to examine consumer behavior from each perspective to fully appreciate the impact of logical decision making, of feelings and emotions, and of environmental influencers on buying decisions.

BENEFITS OF EXCHANGE

Whenever a good, service, idea, or experience is transferred from one entity to another, an exchange takes place. Formally, we define **exchange** as "the provision or transfer of goods, services, or ideas in return for something of value."[20]

The idea that exchange is fundamental to marketing has been discussed for more than 50 years. In 1957, Wroe Alderson, one of the early founders of the field, said, "Marketing is the exchange which takes place between consuming groups and supplying groups."[21] Similarly, Armstrong and Kotler defined marketing as "Marketing consists of actions taken to create, maintain, and grow desirable exchange relationships with target audiences involving a product, service, idea, or other object."[22] The American Marketing Association has defined marketing as "the activity, set of institutions, and processes for creating, communicating, delivering, and exchanging offerings that have value for customers, clients, partners, and society at large."[23] In each of these definitions, the concept of exchange is central to defining the field of marketing.

Why is one person willing to give up something to receive something else in return? What will make two parties enter into an exchange? The basic reason for exchanging one good for another is that different people have different tastes and preferences. As economists tell us, consumers act to increase the total utility of the assortment of goods they possess by making exchanges. Thus, in economic terms, the fundamental principle driving the exchange is that people have different utility functions. Thus, if I have something that has lower value (a lower utility function) for me than it has for you, and if you have something that has lower value to you than to me, we have a basis for exchange.[24] Both parties profit from the exchange in this case because each receives something he or she values more highly than what was given up. In 2012, the television network A&E began the reality show *Barter Kings*. In each episode, the cast begins with a small item, such as a chair, and trades it up to another item. After a series of trades, the stars of the show end up with a much higher priced item, such as, believe it or not, an airplane. These exchanges demonstrate that both parties desire the product received more than the product given up.

What Do We Exchange?

Researchers have worked hard to identify what's exchanged between two people or two social units, such as a family and a firm.[25] Other types of resources exchanged include goods, services, money, status, information, and feelings. Table 1.2 provides examples of each of the six categories of resources.

TABLE 1.2

Examples of the Six Categories of Resources We Exchange[26]

1.	Feelings—expressions of affectionate regard, warmth, or comfort
2.	Status—evaluative judgment conveying high or low prestige, regard, or esteem
3.	Information—any advice, opinion, or instruction
4.	Money—any coin or token that has some standard of exchange value
5.	Goods—any product or object that has exchange value
6.	Services—any performance of labor done for someone else

Figure 1.1 is a diagram of the exchange process in which each party possesses certain resources. The resources input by one party represent his or her costs and become the outcomes received by the other party. Outcomes are derived not only from the resources exchanged but also from the experience of engaging in the exchange. Thus, each party may derive rewards or costs from the exchange process itself, in addition to those obtained from the goods, services, or money transferred.

FIGURE 1.1

Diagram of the Exchange Process

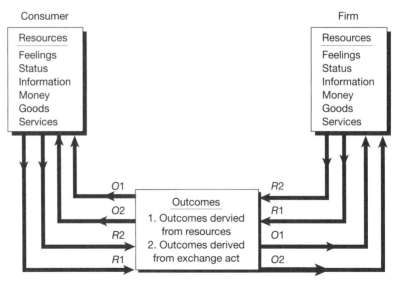

R1 and R2 = Resources input to exchange
O1 and O2 = Outcomes received from exchange

DIMENSIONS OF EXCHANGE RELATIONSHIPS

There are four dimensions that describe consumer exchange relationships: (1) restricted versus complex, (2) internal versus external, (3) formal versus informal, and (4) relational versus discrete (see Table 1.3.) Keep in mind these dimensions aren't mutually exclusive. An exchange can be complex, internal, and relational.

TABLE 1.3
Types of Exchange
Relationships

1. Restricted vs. Complex
    a. Restricted exchange—occurs between two parties
    b. Complex exchange—occurs among three or more parties
2. Internal vs. External
    a. Internal exchange—occurs within a group
    b. External exchange—occurs between groups
3. Formal vs. Informal
    a. Formal exchange—includes explicit written or verbal contracts
    b. Informal exchange—includes unwritten, unspoken social contracts
4. Relational vs. Discrete
    a. Relational exchange—creates long-term relationships
    b. Discrete exchange—constitutes a one-time exchange in which no relationships are formed

Restricted Versus Complex Exchanges The simplest type of exchange, called a **restricted exchange**, unites two parties interacting in a reciprocal relationship, such as a consumer and her stockbroker or a patient and his physician.[27] At the most complicated level is the **complex exchange**, in which three or more parties enact a set of mutual relationships. For example, in a car distribution channel, an automobile goes from a manufacturer (e.g., Ford Motor Company) to a dealer, which then sells the vehicle to a customer. Each party depends upon the others to supply resources. For example, even though car buyers and manufacturers are separated by a dealer, the consumer depends on the manufacturer to build a high-quality product. Similarly, the manufacturer depends on consumers purchasing its autos.

Internal Versus External Exchanges Some exchanges are **internal**, meaning they occur within a group, while others occur are **external** and occur between parties in separate groups. While consumer researchers have focused on developing an understanding of external exchanges, internal exchanges are also important. For example, should a Mexican restaurant produce its own salsa and chips (internal) or purchase the goods from an outside source (external)?

Formal Versus Informal Exchanges A **formal exchange** is outlined in an explicit, written or verbal contract. Formal exchanges are frequently external. An **informal exchange**, frequently internal, creates an unwritten social contract between parties, often reinforced by social norms and peer pressure.

One arena in which informal exchanges frequently occur is dating. From an exchange perspective, people have a set of characteristics, such as physical beauty, intelligence, money, a high-status occupation, and a good personality, that are the resources traded when they engage in romantic exchanges. Thus, we can argue that the dating process consists of men and women exchanging various resources.

So, how are these resources exchanged in an online setting? Online dating has changed the manner in which couples meet. Online daters are now able to screen out hundreds, if not thousands, of potential pursuers without the cost of a face-to-face interaction. There are currently around 60 million singles using either eHarmony or Match.com as their means to secure a date. Looking at online dating statistics, the resources that are most important on the first date are as follows: personality, 30%; smile and looks, 23%; sense of humor, 14%; and career and education, 10%. To increase their chance of going on a first date, men are most likely to lie about the following resources: age, height, and income. Women are likely to lie about weight, physical build, and age.[28] It appears that online daters are promoting, through their lies, various resources they deem important to the other person.

Relational Versus Discrete Exchanges   Exchanges are also categorized in terms of whether they're discrete or relational in nature. A **discrete exchange** is a one-time interaction in which money is paid for an easily measured commodity and doesn't include the creation of a relationship. In contrast, a **relational exchange** is a transaction that begins a long-term commitment in which trust and the development of social relationships play an important role.[29]

Relational exchanges have been equated to a marriage between buyer and seller. A relational exchange is ongoing, frequent, and often involves reciprocity. Thus, when viewed from a relational exchange perspective, transactions should be analyzed in terms of their history and anticipated future. Such transactions are noted for the social relations that occur as well as the benefits derived from the characteristics of the product or service obtained. Consumers will make long-term commitments with marketers to reduce overall transaction costs (e.g., by minimizing search costs), to lower risk, and to gain the positive feelings that result from interacting with someone who is liked. Table 1.4 depicts some of the characteristics of relational exchanges.

TABLE 1.4
Some Characteristics of
Relational Exchanges

1. Timing—long term. It reflects an ongoing process
2. Obligations—customized and detailed. Promises are made, and laws and regulations may apply.
3. Relationship expectations—conflicts are anticipated, but they are countered by trust and efforts to create unity.
4. Rewards—these are derived from economic and noneconomic means.
5. Communications—these are extensive through formal and informal means.
6. Cooperation—a great deal of cooperation is needed to maintain exchange.
7. Power—increased interdependence increases the importance of judicious application of power in the exchange.
8. Planning—there is a significant focus on the process of exchange. Detailed planning is required for future exchanges.

Examples of discrete and relational exchanges are found in restaurant transactions. A discrete exchange takes place when someone is traveling and stops in a restaurant. On the other hand, many consumers are loyal patrons to a local restaurant. Some consumers may visit the same restaurant every week or even daily to drink coffee. These customers often develop a strong personal relationship with the staff to the point the staff begins preparing the customers' "regular" order as they walk in the door. These regular customers are characterized as being in a relational exchange.

Examples of relational exchanges are found in both the industrial and the consumer sectors. For instance, a company producing a complex product—a jet aircraft, a submarine, or a large building—must contract with other corporations to supply specific components and services. In many industries, such as banking, high-tech, and manufacturing, the "personal touch" is the most important element of providing good service. Personal touch is showing commitment to the client and even remembering the customer's name. Personal touch is simply another term for what happens in relational exchanges. Table 1.5 is a summary of key elements found in relationship exchanges.

Social relations are particularly important in facilitating exchanges at home buying parties. Indeed, the term **market embeddedness** has been used to describe the situation in which the social ties between buyer and seller supplement product value to increase the perceived value of the exchange.[30] The importance of social relations has been recognized by companies such as Pampered Chef and Mary Kay. These companies frequently employ parties to sell their merchandise. At these parties, one finds a hostess, a demonstrator, and the invitees. Usually, close relationships exist within the group of invitees and between the invitees and the hostess.

1.	Relational exchanges become more important when services and products are complex, customized, and delivered over time.
2.	Relationships are more important when buyers are relatively unsophisticated.
3.	Relationships are more important when the buying environment is dynamic.
4.	Consumers make purchases partly for the product or service and partly for the feelings that result from the exchange.
5.	Trust and satisfaction with the past performance of the exchange partner influence perceptions of relationship quality.

TABLE 1.5
Summary of Some Key Findings Concerning Relationship Exchanges

ETHICAL ISSUES IN CONSUMER EXCHANGE RELATIONS

Within exchanges, the trust between the buyer and the seller is an extremely important element. One factor that influences the bonds of trust is the ethical conduct of the buyer and the seller. **Ethics** are the principles and standards that define acceptable conduct in marketing as determined by various stakeholders, including the public, government regulators, private interest groups, consumers, industry, and the organization itself.[31] Judgments of what is morally right or wrong are based on standards that:

Deal with serious human injuries and benefits, that May or may not be laid down by authoritative bodies that override self-interest, and that are based on impartial considerations.

Ethical judgments frequently involve a conflict between one's own self-interest and a standard of conduct. Thus, plastic surgeons are obligated to think first of their clients' interests, rather than their own. When making a decision that may have ethical implications, the person must use impartial considerations in reaching the decision. The decision should be based on moral guidelines and not on who's helped or hurt by the outcome of the action.

The problem faced by cosmetic surgeons in their relationship with patients illustrates an ethical dilemma. An **ethical dilemma** is defined as "a decision that involves the trade-off between lowering one's personal values in exchange for increased organizational or personal profits."[32] In sum, whenever consumers engage in exchange relationships, ethical principles are likely to come into play.

As a general statement, the following components occur in an **ethical exchange**:

1. Both parties will know the full nature of the agreement they are entering.
2. Neither party to the exchange will intentionally misrepresent or omit relevant information to the other.
3. Neither party to the exchange will unduly influence the other.[33]

There are ethical issues related to the resources being exchanged. First, one can identify the source of the resource (i.e., either the business firm or the consumer) and the recipient of the resource (i.e., either the consumer or the business firm). When one business extends resources to another business, it is engaging in **industrial marketing**. When a business sends resources to consumers, it is engaging in **consumer marketing**. In these two cases, ethical issues should influence the firm's actions. In particular, the firm must fulfill commitments made concerning its inputs to the exchange—service, product, and informational inputs must be performed as promised or implied.

Most discussions of ethics deal with industrial or consumer marketing. Such discussions typically focus on the firm's actions in such areas as misleading advertising, selling products that fail to comply with the claims made about them, producing unsafe products, exerting undue influence (e.g., bribery), and failing to disclose important relevant information (e.g., not telling a customer a product was used previously). In addition, consumers also have a responsibility to act ethically in their exchanges with firms and other consumers. Thus, if an acquaintance wishes to purchase your old car or lawn mower, you have an ethical duty to warn the person of safety problems, to avoid coercing the person to make the purchase, and to avoid misleading the person in terms of how it will perform.

Consumers should also act ethically in their dealings with business firms. For example, when consumers return products to a firm, they have an ethical duty to return the product in satisfactory condition. They also have a duty not to mislead the firm as to the reasons for the return. For example, is it ethical to purchase a dress, wear it on a single, special occasion, and then return it, claiming it simply didn't fit properly? Similarly, consumers should avoid the unethical act of **free riding**, which occurs when a person obtains a resource, such as information, from a firm and then fails to pay back resources in return. For example, a person may go to Best Buy to obtain product information and to identify satisfactory alternatives. If the person obtains product information from sales personnel and then uses the information to make a purchase on eBay or Amazon.com (hence, there's no personal service), the person is guilty of free riding. The consumer is acting unethically in such an instance because he or she had no intention of making a purchase. Real harm is done to the retailer because the consumer received informational and service resources while having no intention of buying. Reciprocity exists between consumers and businesses. When sufficient numbers of consumers act unethically, businesses will have to respond in some manner. If sufficient numbers of consumers engage in free riding, real harm results because full-service retail stores will either close their doors or become discount stores. Consumers will then lose an important source of marketplace information. Similarly, if too many consumers abuse return privileges, companies will be forced to institute no-return policies. In sum, ethical behavior is a two-way street. Consumers have a right to expect businesses to act ethically, and firms have a right to expect consumers to act ethically.

Within a firm, it's critical to develop a culture that emphasizes ethical core values.[34] Researchers have identified four rules that managers and consumers should follow to ensure their decisions are ethical.[35] By keeping these rules in mind when making decisions, an ethical culture can be developed in a firm. Although originally designed to apply to managers, these four rules have been slightly revised to apply to consumers as well:

1. The golden rule—act in a way you would expect others to act toward you.
2. The professional ethic—take only actions that would be viewed as proper by an objective panel of colleagues.
3. Kant's categorical imperative—act in a way such that the action taken under the circumstances could be a universal law of behavior for everyone facing those same circumstances.
4. The TV test—always ask, "Would I feel comfortable explaining this action on TV to the general public?"

AN ORGANIZING MODEL OF CONSUMER BEHAVIOR

To provide an overview of the broad field of consumer behavior, an organizing model is developed. Shown in Figure 1.2, the consumer behavior model has five primary components that form the field's core areas of study: the buying unit, the exchange process, the marketer's strategy, the individual influencers, and the environmental influencers.

In the model, buying units represent the customers of products, services, experiences, and ideas offered by marketers. Buying units may consist of an individual, a family, or a group that makes a purchase decision. In addition, buying units may be consumers (i.e., individuals and households) or organizations (for profit or nonprofit) making purchases. In sum, the principles of consumer behavior apply to business-to-business marketing as well as business-to-consumer marketing.

The term *marketer* is used extremely broadly in the model. A marketer could be a firm selling a good or service, a nonprofit organization, a governmental agency, a political candidate, or another consumer who wishes to sell or trade something. The marketer seeks to create an exchange with consumers by implementing a marketing strategy through which it attempts to reach its long-term customer and profit goals. A major focus of the text will involve identifying how an understanding of the exchange process, the individual influencers, and the environmental influencers can be used to develop marketing strategy.

FIGURE 1.2
An Organizing Framework
of Consumer Behavior

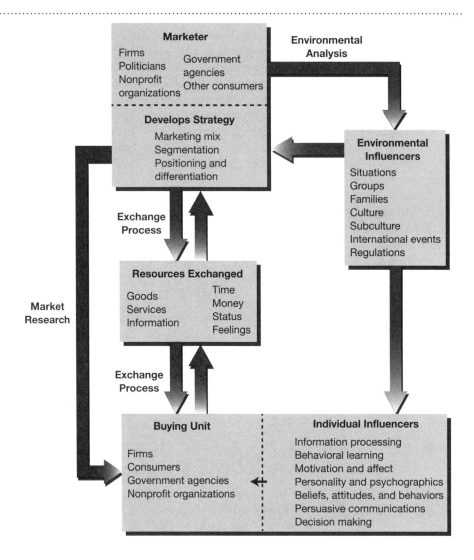

A **marketing strategy** can be defined as a process in which decision makers successfully allocate and coordinate marketing resources, tasks, and activities to implement the marketing concept and accomplish the organization's objectives. To implement strategy, marketers develop segmentation, positioning, and marketing mix objectives for a product. Segmentation refers to the division of the marketplace into relatively homogeneous subsets of consumers having similar needs and wants. Positioning involves influencing how consumers perceive a brand's characteristics relative to those of competitive offerings. In order to implement the segmentation and positioning objectives, the marketer develops a marketing mix strategy. The **marketing mix** consists of the product itself, as well as how it is priced, promoted, and distributed.

To develop a strategy, the marketer performs environmental analysis studies to anticipate the likely effects of the environmental influencers. In addition, market research is used to obtain information on individual consumers. Based on the environmental analysis and market research, managers develop their positioning and segmentation strategies, which are implemented through the marketing mix. Because consumer behavior findings and ideas have critical relevance to the development of marketing strategy, Chapter 2 of the text discusses how these concepts can be used by managers to market their goods, services, ideas, and experiences.

The model of consumer behavior connects the buying unit to both the individual influence factors and the environmental influencers. The **individual influence factors** represent the psychological processes that affect individuals engaged in acquiring, consuming, and disposing of goods, services, and experiences. The **environmental influencers** represent those factors outside of the individual that affect individual consumers, decision-making units, and marketers.

The individual influence factors and the environmental influencers lie on a continuum that moves from a highly micro to a broad macro focus. The continuum begins at the micro level by focusing on the individual and the most basic psychological processes involving perception and learning. As one moves along the continuum, the analysis moves to the study of personality, attitudes, persuasion, and, finally, consumer decision making. At this point, the emphasis changes from the study of the individual to investigations of the impact of situations and groups of people on consumer behavior. At the broadest levels of the continuum, consumer researchers examine how people in different nations and cultures acquire, consume, and dispose of goods, services, experiences, and ideas.

The Book's Organization

The major sections of the textbook are organized as follows. Part I acts as an overview of the field and is composed of two chapters. Chapter 1 defines the field and presents the organizing model of consumer. Chapter 2 identifies how knowledge of consumer behavior can be used to develop marketing strategy. Thus, it will discuss how consumer behavior concepts can be employed by managers of organizations to develop the marketing mix, segment the marketplace and position and differentiate products, perform environmental analysis, and conduct market research.

Next, Part II presents a set of chapters that cover factors that influence individual consumers. Individual consumer processes include information processing, motivation, personality and psychographics, attitudes, persuasive communications, and decision making. Finally, Part III considers the environmental influencers that affect buyers and sellers, which include consumer situations, group processes, culture, subcultures, and international and cross-cultural consumer behavior. The book concludes with a chapter that focuses on the dark side of consumer behavior and its public-policy implications.

We believe that if you focus on the research questions introduced at the beginning of each chapter of this book, you'll have the information required to gain an advantage in the marketplace. This advantage results because you have the knowledge to create exchanges that are mutually profitable for the consumer and for your organization. We hope the process is as enjoyable as it is lucrative.

SUMMARY

Consumer behavior is a broad field that studies the exchange processes through which individuals and groups acquire, consume, and dispose of goods, services, ideas, and experiences. The principles of consumer behavior are useful to business managers, government regulators, nonprofit organizations, and everyday people. For marketing managers, knowledge of consumer behavior has important implications for environmental analysis, for product positioning, for the segmentation of the marketplace, for designing market research studies, and for developing the marketing mix.

The high impact of consumer behavior on marketing management shouldn't be surprising. Modern marketing managers believe in the "marketing concept" and the idea that understanding consumer needs and wants will facilitate the exchange processes and achieve profits for the company and will satisfy consumers. As a result, marketing managers view the consumer as the focal point of the marketing effort.

Consumer behavior is an applied discipline. It borrows theories and knowledge from other fields, including anthropology, sociology, demographics, economics, and psychology. It is, however, a discipline in its own right. Consumer researchers are developing their own body of knowledge to supplement that obtained from other fields.

Central to the field of consumer behavior is the study of exchange processes. Exchange is the process through which something tangible or intangible, actual or symbolic is transferred between two or more social actors. It's the most basic element of the marketing function. For an exchange to take place, a number of elements must exist. In particular, the two parties must have the freedom to accept or reject the other's offer. When exchanges take place, resources are transferred between the parties. The resources that may be exchanged include goods, services, money, status, information, or feelings. Finally, exchanges may be restricted or complex, internal or external, formal or informal, and relational or discrete. Increasingly, marketers are focusing on creating relational exchanges. The term *market embeddedness* is used to describe the situation in which the social ties between a buyer and a seller supplement product value to increase the perceived value of an exchange.

An emerging area of study in consumer behavior is ethics—the study of the normative judgments concerned with what is morally right and wrong, good and bad. Such judgments deal with standards that pertain to serious human injuries and benefits, that may or may not be laid down by authority, that override self-interest, and that are based on impartial considerations. As applied to the field of consumer behavior, ethical issues pertain to actions engaged in by both businesses and consumers. Thus, consumers can, and do, act unethically, just as businesses.

In addition, three research perspectives on consumer acquisition behavior were identified. They are the decision-making perspective, the experiential perspective, and the behavioral influence perspective.

An organizing model of consumer behavior was developed in this chapter. It's composed of five primary elements: the individual influencers, the consumer environment, the exchange process, the buying unit, and the marketer. The textbook is organized around this model. Chapter 2 discusses how consumer behavior concepts can be employed by the marketer to develop marketing strategy and facilitate the exchange process with buyers. Part II of the text analyzes concepts related to the study of the individual influencers that impact buying units. Areas discussed in those chapters include information processing, behavioral learning, motivation and affect, personality and psychographics, attitudes, attitude change, persuasive communications, and consumer decision processes. Part III presents the environmental influencers that influence buying units and marketers. Chapters in Part III cover such areas as exchange/group and family processes and the effects of various consumer situations. In addition, Part III includes chapters on culture, the international environment, demographics and subcultures, economics, and the dark side of consumer behavior.

KEY TERMS

acquisition phase
behavioral influence perspective
complex exchange
consumer behavior
consumer marketing
consumption phase
decision-making perspective
discrete exchange
disposition phase
environmental influencers
ethics
ethical dilemma

ethical exchange
exchange
exchange processes
experiential perspective
external
formal exchange
free riding
individual influence factors
industrial marketing
informal exchange
internal

interpretive research methods
market embeddedness
marketing
marketing concept
marketing mix
marketing strategy
personal value
public policy
relational exchange
restricted exchange
theory

REVIEW QUESTIONS

1. Define the term *consumer behavior*. Why is consumption viewed as a process?
2. Identify the reasons why an understanding of consumer behavior acts as a foundation for the development of marketing strategy and planning.
3. How can the study of consumer behavior assist managers in environmental analysis?
4. How can the study of consumer behavior assist managers in product positioning and product differentiation?
5. How can the study of consumer behavior assist managers in the segmentation of the marketplace?
6. Through what means does consumer behavior assist the market research function?
7. In what ways can the study of consumer behavior provide consumers, managers, and public-policy makers with theories, facts, and an orientation?

8. What are the behavioral science fields from which consumer behavior may draw theories and concepts?

9. Draw a diagram of the consumer behavior model presented in the text.

10. Describe the three research perspectives that can be used to analyze the consumer purchase process.

11. Why is the concept of exchange fundamental to the understanding of marketing and consumer behavior?

12. Identify the basic prerequisites for exchange.

13. Identify the six categories of resources that are exchanged.

14. What is the definition of ethics?

15. What are the standards that should be used to judge whether an action is ethical?

16. Briefly describe the two broad levels of analysis from which consumer behavior may be analyzed—that is, the individual influencers and the environmental influencers.

DISCUSSION QUESTIONS

1. Consider the soft drink industry. Through what means do companies such as Coca-Cola, Pepsi-Cola, and Dr Pepper attempt to differentiate their products from those of other companies? (Think in terms of product characteristics and images.)

2. Define the concept of environmental analysis. What environmental factors may surface in the next ten years to influence soft drink consumption? (Hint: Think in terms of changes in the global marketplace and in demographics.)

3. Define the concept of market segmentation. From your knowledge of the automobile industry, try to identify different segments of customers auto manufacturers attempt to reach.

4. Consumer researchers are highly interested in the study of demographic trends. Identify three major demographic trends that may influence corporate market planning for marketers of golf clubs or of microwave ovens.

5. Identify three types of purchases you've made that were based mostly upon a careful, rational thought process. Briefly explain the nature of your thought process for each purchase.

6. Identify three purchases you've made that were based mostly upon a desire to obtain feelings and experiences. What feelings and experiences were you hoping to obtain from the purchases?

7. Identify three of your purchases that were made principally because of pressures from the environment. What was the nature of the pressure that encouraged each purchase?

8. Identify a relational exchange you have with a retailer or service provider. What are the characteristics of the exchange that allow it to be considered relational?

9. College students are in an exchange relationship with a university. Discuss the resources exchanged with the university. To what extent are the costs and benefits received by the university and by its students equitable? (For a discussion of equity theory, see Chapter 13.)

10. Identify an ethical dilemma students face. What factors should be considered when attempting to solve the dilemma?

ENDNOTES

[1] Ad Age, "Ad Age Social-Media Brand Ranking Top 10 – 2012," *Ranking the Brands*, SyncForce, 2015, accessed November 6, 2015, http://www.rankingthebrands.com/The-Brand-Rankings.aspx?rankingID=202&nav=category.

[2] "Some Brides Getting Plastic Surgery," *Health News*, March 13, 2011, accessed November 30, 2015, http://www.upi.com/Health_News/2011/03/13/Some-brides-getting-plastic-surgery/UPI-58231300058433/.

[3] John C. Mowen, Adelina Longoria, and Amy Sallee, "Burning and Cutting: Identifying the Traits of Individuals with an Enduring Propensity to Tan and to Undergo Cosmetic Surgery," *Journal of Consumer Behaviour* (Sept.–Oct. 2009): 238–251.

[4] Ibid., 249.

[5] Scott Ward and Thomas Robertson, "Consumer Behavior Research: Promise and Prospects," in *Consumer Behavior: Theoretical Sources*, eds. Scott Ward and Thomas Robertson (Englewood Cliffs, NJ: Prentice Hall, 1973), 3–42.

[6] Theodore Levitt, "Marketing Myopia," in *Modern Marketing Strategy*, eds. Edward Bursk and John Chapman (Cambridge, MA: Harvard University Press, 1964).

[7] Philip Kotler and Gary Armstrong (2014), *Principles of Marketing* (Upper Saddle River, NJ: Pearson), 7.

[8] William M. Pride and O. C. Ferrell, *Marketing 2012*, (Mason, OH: Cengage Learning, 2012).

[9] Philip Kotler and Gary Armstrong, *Principles of Marketing*, (Upper Saddle River, NJ: Pearson Education, 2014).

[10] Frank Houston, "The Marketing Concept, What It Is and What It Is Not," *Journal of Marketing* (April 1986): 81–87.

[11] Otis Port, "Customers Move Into the Driver's Seat," *Businessweek*, October 4, 1999, 103–106.

[12] Csaba Csere, "How Automakers Will Meet 2016 CAFE standards," *Car and Driver*, May 2010, accessed March 19, 2013, http://www.caranddriver.com/features/how-automakers-will-meet-2016-cafe-standards.

[13] Margaret Campbell and Gina S. Mohr, "Seeing Is Eating: How and When Activation of a Negative Stereotype Increases Stereotype-Conducive Behavior," *Journal of Consumer Research*, 38 (2011): 431–444.

[14] John C. Mowen and Michael S. Minor, *Consumer Behavior: A Framework* (Upper Saddle River, NJ: Prentice-Hall, 2001).

[15] Joseph B. Pine and James H. Gilmore, *The Experience Economy*, (Boston: Harvard Business School Press, 1999).

[16] Michel Tuan Pham, "Representativeness, Relevance, and the Use of Feelings in Decision Making," *Journal of Consumer Research*, 25 (1998): 144–159.

[17] Russell Belk, John Sherry, and Melanie Wallendorf, "A Naturalistic Inquiry into Buyer and Seller Behavior at a Swap Meet," *Journal of Consumer Research* (March 1988): 449–469.

[18] John Sherry, "Some Implications of Consumer Oral Tradition for Reactive Marketing," in *Advances in Consumer Research*, Vol. XI, ed. Thomas Kinnear (Ann Arbor, MI: Association for Consumer Research, 1984), 741–747.

[19] John C. Mowen and Michael S. Minor, *Consumer Behavior: A Framework* (Upper Saddle River, NJ, Prentice-Hall, 2001).

[20] William M. Pride and O. C. Ferrell, *Marketing 2012* (Mason, OH: Cengage Learning, 2012).

[21] Wroe Alderson, *Marketing Behavior and Executive Actions* (Homewood, IL: Richard D. Irwin), 1957.

[22] Armstrong, Gary, and Philip Kotler (2015), Marketing: An Introduction, Pearson, Upper Saddle River, New Jersey.

[23] "Definition of Marketing," AMA, July 2013, accessed March 8, 2013, www.marketingpower. com/aboutama/pages/definitionofmarketing.aspx.

[24] These ideas are based on the law of exchange articulated by Wroe Alderson, *Dynamic Marketing Behavior* (Homewood, IL: Richard D. Irwin, 1965).

[25] Madhu Viswanathan, Jose Antonio Rosa, and Julie A. Ruth, "Exchanges in Marketing Systems: The Case of Subsistence Consumer-Merchants in Chennai, India," *Journal of Marketing*, 74 (2010): 1–17.

[26] Gregory Donnenworth and Uriel Foa, "Effects of Resource Class on Retaliation to Injustice in Interpersonal Exchange," Journal of Personality *and Social Psychology*, 29 (1974): 785–793.

[27] Richard P. Bagozzi, "Toward a Formal Theory of Marketing Exchanges," in *Conceptual and Theoretical Developments in Marketing*, eds. O. C. Ferrell, Stephen W. Brown, and Charles W. Lamb, Jr. (Chicago: American Marketing Association, 1979), 32–39.

[28] "Online Dating Statistics," *Statistic Brain Research Institute*, accessed March 8, 2013, http://www. statisticbrain.com/online-dating-statistics/.

[29] John C. Mowen and Michael S. Minor, *Consumer Behavior: A Framework* (Upper Saddle River, NJ: Prentice Hall, 2001).

[30] Jonathan K. Frenzen and Harry L. Davis, "Purchasing Behavior in Embedded Markets," *Journal of Consumer Research* 17 (1990): 1–12.

[31] William M. Pride and O. C. Ferrell, *Marketing 2012* (Mason, OH: Cengage Learning, 2012.

[32] Gene R. Laczniak and Patrick E. Murphy, "Fostering Ethical Marketing Decisions," *Journal of Business Ethics* 10 (1991): 259–271.

[33] Manuel Velasquez, *Business Ethics: Concepts and Cases* (Englewood Cliffs, NJ: Prentice Hall, 1982).

[34] Anusorn Singhapakdi, Kenneth L. Kraft, Scott J. Vitell, and Kumar C Rallapalli, "The Perceived Importance of Ethics and Social Responsibility on Organizational Effectiveness: A Survey of Marketers," *Journal of the Academy of Marketing Science* 23 (1995): 49–56.

[35] Gene R. Laczniak and Patrick E. Murphy, "Fostering Ethical Marketing Decisions," *Journal of Business Ethics* 10 (1991): 259–271.

2

Consumer Behavior and Developing Marketing Strategy

Learning Objectives:

1. What are the managerial application areas to which consumer behavior concepts apply?

2. What's the role of consumer behavior in performing marketing research?

3. What's the role of consumer behavior in environmental analysis?

4. What's the role of consumer behavior in market segmentation?

5. What's the role of consumer behavior in product positioning and differentiation?

6. What's the role of consumer behavior in marketing mix development?

Coca-Cola Faces a Crisis . . . of Its Own Making

In 1972, Coca-Cola had a dominant market share in the soda industry with 18 percent of people exclusively drinking Coke and only 4 percent drinking Pepsi exclusively. But by the early 1980s, Pepsi began running a series of advertisements showing people blindly sampling small portions of the two brands. In these advertisements, most consumers preferred the taste of Pepsi. After running some head-to-head blind taste tests of their own, Coca-Cola found roughly 57 percent of consumers preferred Pepsi to Coke.[1]

Coke executives moved to make a big change to their brand. They directed their scientists to develop a new Coke to compete with Pepsi. The scientists developed a sweeter Coke. The new formula beat Pepsi in head-to-head blind taste

tests, so Coke introduced the new brand. The story should end here with Coke once again controlling a dominant portion of the soda market. However, the story did not end.

Shortly after the introduction of New Coke, Coke loyalists struck back. Thousands of loyal Coke drinkers demanded Coca-Cola bring back the original formula. Shortly thereafter, the company reintroduced the original formula as Coca-Cola Classic, while still selling New Coke. Today, Coke sells only the original formula.

One of the major mistakes Coca-Cola made was the manner in which the taste tests were completed. When consumers sample a soft drink in a sip test, the sweeter brand tends to rate higher than the less sweet brand. But when

drinking a soft drink with a full meal, the less sweet brand tends to win the competition. Coca-Cola failed to recognize this error.

Furthermore, Coca-Cola put all the blame for losing market share on the taste of the product. The company failed to recognize the competition was also positioning its brand as the youthful, energetic soft drink by using endorsers such as Michael Jackson to plug the product.

The problems encountered in the development of the **marketing strategy** of Coke illustrate the five strategy areas to which consumer behavior concepts apply and that we discuss in this chapter: research, environmental analysis, segmentation, product positioning, and marketing mix development. In the Coke example, the executives relied on flawed research by not realizing the taste tests were subject to interpretation. They failed to fully conduct an environmental analysis to understand there were thousands of customers who were loyal to the brand. In the segmentation and product positioning arenas, Coca-Cola should have tried to position its brand in a unique position rather than simply try to reformulate the brand to match the competition. Finally, Coke thought the market share drop was all due to a product issue, when there were other marketing mix issues, such as promotion, it could have addressed.

INTRODUCTION

As we saw in Chapter 1, an understanding of consumer behavior is critical for developing marketing strategy, whether in business, nonprofit, or governmental organizations. Also, remember the target market can be individual consumers, groups of consumers (e.g., families), and businesses. For example, Microsoft originally developed the Kinect motion sensing device for the consumer market purchasing the Xbox. Then, the company began an initiative to build products using the Kinect technology for businesses. One intriguing use is for surgeons. During surgery, physicians sometimes need to handle x-rays, computers, and other equipment that may not be sterile. Kinect technology allows them to use motion for accessing records and digitized x-rays, which saves surgeons from having to rescrub each time records are accessed.[2]

We conceptualize the development and implementation of marketing strategy as a cyclical process composed of five areas of focus, shown in Figure 2.1. You can remember the five areas by thinking of the words *responsive marketing* this way: **RESPonsive Marketing**. We say the strategy process is cyclical because it's ongoing and repeats over time.

The first two areas in the **marketing strategy cycle**, research and environmental analysis, go hand in hand. Identifying the expressed and latent needs and wants of consumers is central to implementing the marketing concept, and we identify these needs and wants through consumer research. Concurrently, and sometimes even before engaging in consumer research, organizations scan the environment to identify changes in consumer markets, to identify potential new markets, and to assess other environmental factors that affect strategy development, such as the effects of the economic, technological, and competitive environments on consumer behavior.

Then, based on marketing research and environmental scanning, managers take the third step in the cycle by segmenting the marketplace and identifying target markets. The fourth step in the cycle is the positioning of the brand,

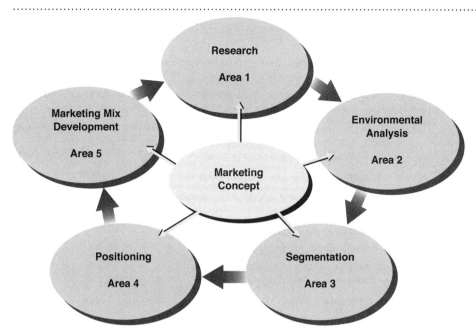

FIGURE 2.1
The RESPonsive Marketing
Strategy Cycle

followed by the development of the marketing mix. Table 2.1 briefly defines the five managerial application steps. After developing a basic understanding of them in this chapter, you'll be able to use the consumer behavior concepts discussed throughout the rest of the book to solve real marketing problems.

Managerial Applications Area	Definition
Research	Applied consumer research designed to provide management with information about factors that impact consumer acquisition, consumption, and disposition of goods, services, and ideas
Environmental analysis	Assessing the external forces that act on the firm and its customers and that create threats and opportunities
Segmentation	Subdividing the market place into distinct subsets of customers having similar needs and wants, each of which can be reached with a different marketing mix
Product positioning	The attempt to influence product demand by developing and promoting a product with specific characteristics that differentiate it from competitors
Marketing mix	The coordination of marketing activities involving product development and the promotion, pricing, and distribution of the product

TABLE 2.1
The Five Managerial
Application Areas of
Consumer Behavior
Concepts: RESPonsive
Marketing

THE ROLE OF CONSUMER BEHAVIOR IN MARKETING RESEARCH

Marketing research is a process in which we design and implement studies, analyze and interpret data, and report the results to management in order to develop an understanding of the factors that affect the acquisition, consumption, and disposition of goods, services, and ideas. Marketing research can be thought of as applied consumer research because, without a firm understanding of consumer behavior concepts, it's literally impossible to design a sound marketing research study. For example, marketing managers should perform research to know how satisfied their customers are with the firm's goods and/or services. However, unless marketing managers know which factors affect customer satisfaction (see Chapter 10), they can't know what questions to ask.

In addition to identifying the processes that impact buying behavior, consumer researchers provide many of the scales and instruments market researchers use. These instruments are used to measure myriad variables that impact the success of a marketing strategy. Following are some of the variables we measure in consumer research:

- how much attention consumers pay to advertisements and how well they remember them
- what customers believe and feel about a product
- how customers make buying decisions
- how satisfied customers are with a product
- the personality traits and psychographic characteristics that affect consumers' evaluation of products

Consumer research can even make a difference in determining whether regulators allow a product to be sold. For example, a number of years ago, Procter & Gamble Co. (P&G) began marketing its new manufactured fat substitute, Olestra. The product had huge sales potential for use in fried foods because it can't be absorbed by the human body, thus minimizing calorie gain and fat consumption from products such as potato chips. The downside, however, is that consuming it in large quantities can cause abdominal cramping and loose stools. Before letting P&G market the product, the US Food and Drug Administration (FDA) forced P&G to do marketing research to assess Olestra's effects on the gastrointestinal system. While some minor problems were found, the FDA gave its approval.[3] Interestingly, however, consumer response was tepid at best. P&G and Frito-Lay changed their advertising and packaging in order to minimize references to Olestra. This tactic worked, for a time period, however P&G has discontinued the product due to poor performance.

Consumer researchers use a variety of research methods, both qualitative and quantitative. There are six major forms of **qualitative research methods**:

- observational research
- ethnographic research
- focus groups
- depth interviews
- cognitive response collection

Quantitative research methods include the following:

- questionnaire research
- experimental research

A package of Ruffles Light potato chips, a product that featured the fat substitute Olestra.
Photo by John Mowen

- behavioral data collection
- neuroscience research
- secondary data collection

Quantitative and qualitative approaches differ in the extent to which the data they collect is converted into numbers for statistical analysis. For example, in qualitative research, we interpret the data to understand how our observations, field notes, text, and even photographs provide an understanding of consumers in the cultural, subcultural, and social contexts in which they live. In contrast, quantitative studies are organized so we can readily convert consumers' responses into numbers, such as a scale of 1 to 5 in a questionnaire. Because entire courses on research methods are taught in marketing, psychology, and sociology departments, we will only briefly discuss the research methods consumer researchers employ.

Qualitative Research Methods

In **observational research**, we unobtrusively observe consumers performing some sort of activity, such as shopping, using a product (say, dish detergent), or taking part in an event, such as a brand-sponsored community activity. For example, an observer may take field notes, photos, or even videos of members of a Porsche auto club who are interacting at a car rally.

While **ethnographic research** is a form of observational research, its goals are more ambitious than simple observational studies. That is, ethnographers seek to probe deeply so as to plumb the norms and values of the group, culture, or subculture under investigation. For example, one researcher used ethnographic research to understand the popularity of television shows focused on the occult, such as *Ghost Whisperer* and *Medium*. The researcher concluded, "The supernaturally oriented TV shows appeal . . . because they offer access to enchanted universes and provide explanations for mysterious phenomena." The researcher also noted that viewers of these shows believe science can't answer all their questions, so they turn to such programming.[4]

Depth interviews are one-on-one interactions between a researcher and a consumer. The goal is to probe deeply into the motivations behind a person's reactions to a product, advertisement, brand, company, or consumer activity (such as shopping). Depth interviews are based, in part, on psychotherapy, which emerged from Freudian psychology (see Chapter 5 on motivation). In this methodology, researchers record interviews and then interpret them to identify the internal drives that motivate the consumer.

Focus groups also emerged from clinical psychology and therapy groups. Organizations frequently use them to obtain consumer reactions to new products and newly designed print or television ads. Normally composed of eight to twelve consumers, focus groups are videotaped. Trained assistants then interpret the thoughts and feelings of the participants and code them into response categories, which may be converted into numbers for further analysis.

Finally, **content analysis** can identify themes found in written materials (e.g., books, advertisements, and websites), open-ended questions in questionnaires, and interviews. As with **cognitive responses**, the thoughts and themes can be categorized and turned into numbers for quantitative analysis.

Quantitative Research Methods

Perhaps the most common form of quantitative data collection is the **question-naire**, which asks consumers to respond to questions or statements using some type of scale. Questionnaires can be given via all sorts of means, including face-to-face interviews, mail, Internet, mall intercepts, and classroom settings. Table 2.2 lists a number of **questionnaire scales** consumer researchers use and provides an example of each.

TABLE 2.2
Examples of Scales Employed in Quantitative Research

Multiple choice	A question that has multiple possible answers from which the respondent must choose
	Example: What is your ethnicity? White Black Hispanic Asian Other
Likert scale	A statement to which people provide their level of agreement
	Example: Circle the extent to which you agree with this statement: "Toyota makes high-quality products."
	Strongly disagree disagree neutral agree strongly agree
Semantic differential	A series of items to which consumers respond on bipolar scales
	Example: Rate Apple products on the following scales
	Innovative 1 2 3 4 5 Not Innovative
	Expensive 1 2 3 4 5 Inexpensive
	Bad design 1 2 3 4 5 Good design
Likelihood scale	A scale that asks the respondent to indicate the likelihood something will occur
	Example 1: What is the likelihood a Prius is fast?
	Very low probability 1 2 3 4 5 Very high probability
	Example 2: How likely is it you will buy a Prius as your next car?
	Very low probability 1 2 3 4 5 Very high probability
Importance scale	A scale that assesses how important the respondent thinks something is
	Example: How important is it that your next car be fast?
	Very unimportant 1 2 3 4 5 Very important
Rating Scale	A scale that asks the respondent to rate an object on some feature
	Example: Rate the quality of service of Apple's website.
	very poor poor average good excellent

Note: The number of points used on a scale will vary depending on respondents' knowledge.

A second quantitative methodology is the **experiment**. Here, the researcher manipulates one or more independent variables and then measures consumer responses in the form of a dependent variable, such as a resulting behavior or a response to a scale. For example, suppose a researcher wanted to determine whether putting a Rolex print ad in color would affect consumer responses to it. Two ads would be created as the independent variables, one in black and white, the other in color. We might measure the dependent variable, consumer response, in terms of how many seconds the average consumer looked at each ad. We could also measure perceptions of the Rolex ad on various scales. For example, likelihood scales could ask, "How likely is it you will buy a Rolex?" Likert scales might ask respondents, "Rate your level of agreement with the following statements: 'I really like the message in the Rolex ad' and 'I really like the photograph in the Rolex ad.'"

Scientific devices can also collect data during experiments. For example, eye-tracking devices can measure the parts of an advertisement respondents are reading. Other devices may measure consumers' arousal levels via their blood pressure or heart rate.

In the field of **neuroscience**, researchers are studying the interior of the brain by using magnetic resonance imaging to measure blood flow and electro-encephalograms to monitor electrical activity. The idea is that such devices can assess consumer emotions about images, messages, products, and companies. For example, marketers at Frito-Lay who used neuromarketing techniques to test the colors of potato chip bags, which pictured potatoes and other "healthy" ingredients. They concluded that a matte-beige bag evoked less guilt than shiny, colorful bags. This finding was based on data indicating the matte-beige bag did not trigger activity in the anterior cingulate cortex, an area of the brain associated with feelings of guilt. As a result, Frito-Lay switched to the less colorful bag.[5]

A third quantitative method is to collect information about consumers from **secondary sources**, which is information obtained from a previous data collection effort. For example, census data that provides demographic information is a secondary data source. The scanner data routinely collected by retail establishments is another. Scanner data lets store managers identify the effect on sales of price promotions and point-of-purchase displays.

Finally, a vast amount of **online quantitative data** about consumers is being collected as they use the Internet. For example, Amazon.com tracks the books individual consumers purchase and recommends new books to them its software algorithms identify as similar to those previously purchased. Similarly, hundreds of marketing research firms now pay hundreds of thousands of dollars a year for information gleaned from Twitter users. For example, information contained in tweets has been used to predict the box office success of movies. As one researcher said, "[Twitter] is the ultimate customer research tool."[6]

THE ROLE OF CONSUMER BEHAVIOR IN ENVIRONMENTAL ANALYSIS

Environmental analysis consists of the assessment of external forces that act on the firm and its customers and how these forces create threats and opportunities. In large organizations, environmental analysis takes place in the market research department or the strategic planning group. In smaller organizations, the CEO and key staff members perform the analysis. Whatever their size, firms should monitor the seven key components of the external consumer environment on an ongoing basis. These environments are demographic, economic, natural, technological, political, competitive, and cultural. Table 2.3 lists these components and examples of the areas of consumer behavior that help us understand them.

The goal of environmental analysis is to understand the characteristics of the current environment, to predict changes in the environment, and to identify how these changes will influence consumers and the organization. For example, the publisher of this textbook, Chicago Business Press, must be able to predict changes in the number of consumers who are likely to read college textbooks

TABLE 2.3
Marketing Environments
and Their Consumer
Behavior Connections

Environment	Consumer Behavior Connection
Demographic	Study of population changes and subcultural values of various demographic groups based on factors such as age, sex, income, education, ethnicity, and geography
Economic	Study of factors influencing consumer economic sentiment and patterns of savings and spending
Natural	Study of how consumers react to changing weather patterns and to natural disasters, such as earthquakes, hurricanes, and diseases (e.g., flu and AIDS)
Technological	Study of the diffusion of technological innovations and consumer reactions to technological changes
Political	Study of the impact of laws, rules, and regulations on consumers
Culture and subcultures	Study of size, rituals, values, mores, customs, and norms and how they influence consumption behavior and market potential
Competitive	Analyses of the competition and of the way consumers perceive brands in comparison with each other

over the next five years. To make this estimate, researchers can obtain demographic data from the US Census Bureau to identify the number of consumers in the twelve- to sixteen-year-old age group, because many from this group will be in college within the next several years.

Among the seven external environments, four have particular relevance to the consumer behavior concepts we discuss in this book. These are the cultural, subcultural, demographic, and situational environments, which we will discuss in detail in Chapters 12 through 15. We briefly cover the remainder—the economic, technological, and natural environments—below.

The Economic Environment and Consumer Behavior

The economic environment consists of the set of micro and macro factors that affect consumer spending and saving. At the local, national, and international levels, the health of the economic environment influences the consumption patterns of millions of individuals and families. For example, when people are laid off from their jobs, it dramatically reduces their ability to make purchases. Because the US economy depends heavily on consumer spending, a rise in unemployment will cut spending and thereby affect the entire economy.[7] Similarly, long-term changes in the wealth of a nation can dramatically influence the lifestyle and well-being of its citizens. For instance, in the nineteenth century, Britain was the wealthiest country in the world. By 2009, its wealth had decreased and the standard of living of its population was rated as twenty-second in the world.[8]

The great recession of 2007–2009 dramatically influenced the consumption patterns of consumers throughout the world. For example, in the United States, the total amount of revolving credit fell for the first time since the 1960s, when records about credit were first kept. Two reasons for the decline were high credit card fees and the efforts of young adults to switch from credit to debit cards in order to decrease their debt.[9]

One area of economics, called behavioral economics, has particular relevance to consumer behavior. **Behavioral economics** is the study of the economic decisions individual consumers make and the behavioral determinants of those decisions. Although we can apply economic theories such as the law of demand at the individual level, traditional economists are most comfortable talking about people in the aggregate. (The law of demand states that an inverse relationship exists between the price of a product and the quantity demanded of that product). Behavioral economists take a radically different approach and analyze consumers individually. This bottom-up method, developed by George Katona, proposes we can assess the attitudes, motives, and expectations of individual consumers to make predictions concerning the population as a whole.

Behavioral economists have made four major contributions to the understanding of consumer behavior patterns. First, they originated and documented the idea the consumer sector of the economy can strongly influence the course of the aggregate economy. Part of the impetus for the development of behavioral economics was the recognition that the US economy had become consumer driven. Some estimates are that as much as 70 percent of the gross national product of the United States results from consumer spending. While some economists challenge this assertion, it's clear that if consumer income falls and/or the consumer savings rate increases, the demand for goods and services will fall, the production of goods and services will decrease, people will be laid off, and the economy will falter.[10]

Second, behavioral economists investigated the factors that influence the decisions of families to buy or save. Traditional economists tend to look at how such decisions affect the economy rather than identify the underlying reasons for spending and saving, such as consumers' confidence in the economy, their own anticipated financial prospects, and their propensity to be frugal. Indeed, a new frugality took hold in the United States during the recent Great Recession. In fact, one writer has proposed US consumers must now be frugal for an extended period in order to get their debt under control.[11]

The third contribution by behavioral economists was the development of a methodology for predicting aggregate economic activities based on consumer surveys rather than traditional econometric studies of the economy. In the survey approach, representative samples of consumers are interviewed to obtain information about consumer attitudes and expectations about their future buying behavior. Begun in 1946, surveys of consumer sentiment continue today at the University of Michigan Survey Research Center. In addition, other groups, such as the Conference Board, have developed their own indices of consumer confidence. Such indices are generally regarded as leading indicators of the future course of the economy. Thus, unexpected changes in the indices can have large effects on the stock market. Indeed, the depths of the Great Recession were illustrated as the Index of Consumer Sentiment fell from a high of about 110 points at the height of the economy in 2000 to a low of about 44 points in 2009.[12] Table 2.4 provides the five areas that are assessed by the Index of Consumer Sentiment.

| 1. An evaluation of the respondent's current financial situation |
| 2. Expectations of the respondent's financial situation in one year |
| 3. Expectations of the economy's overall financial situation in one year |
| 4. Expectations of the economy's overall financial situation over the next five years |
| 5. An evaluation of the economy's overall suitability for making major purchases. |

Each question has three basic responses: better, same, or worse.

TABLE 2.4
Areas Assessed in the Index of Consumer Sentiment[13]

The fourth contribution behavioral economists made was their study of the factors that bias consumer judgment and decision making. Working with psychologists in the field of behavioral decision theory, they are now influencing governmental policy and the study of the stock market. For example, economist Richard Thaler and Harvard law professor Cass Sunstein collaborated to write the book *Nudge*: *Improving Decisions about Health, Wealth, and Happiness*.[14] In it, they described various ways to nudge people to improve their decision making. For example, it's generally considered advisable for people to save for retirement by putting money in 401(k) retirement plans. A simple change such as forcing people to have to opt out of such a plan when starting a job, rather than having them opt in, substantially increases enrollments and savings.

The Natural Environment and Consumer Behavior

Features of the natural environment important to the marketer include the types and quantity of raw materials available, pollution, consumer fear of contracting deadly diseases, and various weather phenomena, such as hurricanes and drought. Each factor can influence consumption behavior.

Shortages of raw materials, such as oil, can dramatically influence the price of products and cause consumers to change their buying patterns. For example, in 2008, consumers in Mexico protested a tripling of the cost of tortillas—a food staple for the poor. The problem was a steep rise in corn prices resulting from the increased use of corn to make ethanol for automobiles. Some feared that hunger would result, as well as poorer nutrition for Mexico's poor.[15]

Another key raw material is water. In fact, some researchers propose water, not energy, is the world's greatest looming problem. China, for instance, has 75 percent less water per person than the average country around the world, and with China's explosive population growth, the problem will only get worse.[16]

The United States also faces critical water shortages—particularly in the Southwest. Indeed, the massive drought that occurred in 2012 even affected high school sports as giant cracks appeared in the parched earth, causing the cancellation of some football games.

Two other aspects of the external environment to consider are pollution and disease, which can go hand in hand. Pollution can degrade important waterways and coastlines and ruin industries. For example, pollution resulting from the Deepwater Horizon oil rig explosion in 2010 wiped out much of the fishing and tourism industry along the Gulf Coast for at least six months. And the impact of AIDS has changed the behavior patterns of sexually active people and encouraged the sale of condoms.

Weather is another component of the natural environment. Obviously, short-term cold snaps or rainy spells influence the purchase of clothing and other consumer goods. Droughts can result in the imposition of water restrictions, which will affect the sale of yard supplies. Hurricanes can change the buying patterns of thousands and millions of people as the lingering effects of Hurricane Sandy (also called Superstorm Sandy) on New York and New Jersey residents in 2012 illustrate. The possibility of further climate change is also influencing the behavior of millions of consumers. The marketing of green products has become a huge business, and a virtual subculture has emerged of consumers who are working to take themselves off the electric grid and lead a carbon-neutral lifestyle.

The Technological Environment and Consumer Behavior

Technological changes can dramatically influence the lifestyle of consumers and are an important source of new-product ideas. (Consumer lifestyle, or the way people live, is discussed in Chapter 14.) Examples of twentieth-century technologies that changed the way we live include automobiles, airplanes, televisions, radios, computers, the Internet, cell phones, the birth control pill, and numerous vaccines. In the first decade of the twenty-first century, the introduction of apps (i.e., applications) for smartphones had a large impact on consumers. By 2013, stores run by Google and Apple each offered more than 700,000 apps, and, somewhat unbelievably, consumers were estimated to spend more than two hours a day with apps.[17] Another new phenomenon of the early twenty-first century has been the increasing importance of social media (see the box about social media).

The effect of further technological advances in this century is the field of futurists. However, we can make some forecasts. For example, in 2010 synthetic life was created for the first time.[18] This advance opens up the possibility of humans creating designer life forms, which have the potential for curing disease and solving the world's energy problems as well as inviting abuse and misuse. Indeed, advances in the field of biotechnology are occurring at a rapid rate and harbor the potential for revolutionary changes, such as the creation of artificial organs and new life forms that result from combining the DNA of different organisms.

SOCIAL MEDIA

The Rise of Social Media Websites?

The rise of social media websites since the launch of Facebook in 2004 has been extraordinary. Literally, thousands of websites can be found. In March 2013, Wikipedia listed 198 active social media websites (excluding dating sites). There are, however, a limited number of sites that dominate the rest. Below is a listing of ten of these sites, along with a brief, tongue-in-check example of how each is used.

Name	Description
Facebook	Here's a photo of me eating pizza with my friends.
Twitter	I'm eating pizza with friends.
LinkedIn	I'm really skilled at chowing down on pizza.
Pinterest	Here's a pizza recipe.
Myspace	Here's a song about pizza.
Meetup	There's a pizza party at the Hideaway at 6:00 pm.
Deviant Art	Here's an oil painting of a pizza shaped like Abraham Lincoln.
YouTube	Here's a video of me putting an entire pizza in my mouth.
Ning	Join my pizza interest group.

An often-overlooked area of consumer research relating to technology is the investigation of the human-machine interface. The challenge is to produce machines and products that are user friendly. Apple's success at making computers more user friendly has been an important element in its success,

Shirts can
pick a tie
for you.

In Germany, smart dressing
rooms actually suggest
accessories, making shoppers
18% happier.
ibm.com/smarterplanet

IBM

In Germany, IBM is using sophisticated software to help consumers select clothing accessories.

for instance. The development of robots to assist the elderly and paraplegics is also a growth area. Long known for its technology, IBM is entering the consumer arena. For example, in Germany "smart dressing rooms" using IBM software are suggesting accessories to assist shoppers and making them 18 percent happier.

In sum, an important goal for the consumer researcher is to anticipate changes in the technological environment and then develop new products that provide the company with a first-mover advantage. In addition, the consumer researcher must predict how new technologies will influence the lifestyle and consumption patterns of consumers.

The Reciprocity between Consumers and the Environment

Just as the environment can influence consumers, so can consumers can influence the environment. We saw earlier in the chapter that changes in consumer spending and saving patterns can influence the economy. Similarly, the behavior of millions of consumers acting together can influence the natural environment. Many researchers believe one of the primary causes of the widening of the African deserts is people who allow cattle to overgraze and who cut down trees for firewood. Indeed, over 97 percent of climate scientists believe humans are changing the earth's climate with devastating results.[19] For example, rising ocean waters from the melting of glaciers and more severe storms from a warming ocean could force millions of people to move away from low-lying areas. Superstorm Sandy's arrival in New York and New Jersey in late 2012 vividly revealed the ocean there has risen nearly a foot over the past one hundred years.[20]

THE ROLE OF CONSUMER BEHAVIOR IN MARKET SEGMENTATION

Market segmentation is the division of a market into distinct subsets of customers having similar needs and wants, each of which we can reach with a different marketing mix. For segments to be useful to marketers, they should possess three characteristics: measurability, accessibility, and substantiality.

To measure a segment, a manager must be able to assess its characteristics, needs, and wants against various demographic, psychographic, attitude, and/or personality measures. For a market segment to be accessible, customers in it must be reachable via the marketing mix. That is, if a market segment can't receive promotional messages and the product itself, it's not a viable target. Finally, the segment must be substantial enough in size and income to generate sufficient sales for it to be managerially useful.

The advantages of market segmentation are two-fold. First, understanding the characteristics of a target market enables the manager to develop a positioning strategy for the product. Second, segmentation maximizes the manager's ability to tailor the marketing mix to the needs and wants of homogeneous subsets of customers. When these subsets have unique needs and wants not shared by larger groups, segmentation allows us to expand the total market potential for a general class of product. For example, when companies identified consumers' specialized needs and wants for fashion watches, diving watches, running watches, pocket watches, dress watches, and so forth, they increased the overall market potential for watches. If only one type of all-purpose watch were offered, total sales would be much lower than they currently are.

We identify segments by finding groups of consumers with similar needs and wants. A market segment for consumer goods might be composed of millions of people. For industrial goods, it might be hundreds or thousands of companies. A key problem for the manager is in identifying the **bases for segmentation**, the variables we can use to identify distinct groups of people or companies.

For consumer markets, four classifications of segmentation variables exist. These are the characteristics of the person, the nature of the situation in which the good or service may be purchased, geography, and the culture or subculture adopted by the consumer. These are summarized in Table 2.5.

Characteristics of the Person

The characteristics of people on which markets can be formed fall into four categories: demographic, behavioral, psychographic, and personality.

A Rolex Explorer watch targeted to an upscale segment of male consumers who seek a rugged and distinctive watch.

Demographic characteristics The **demographic characteristics** of interest to marketers include age, sex, income, religion, marital status, nationality, education, family size, occupation, and ethnicity. These descriptors have two important uses in the segmentation process. First, either singly or in combination, they can describe various subcultures whose members share certain values, needs, rituals, and behaviors. For example, by using a combination of education, occupation, and income, we can develop a measure of social class. Similarly, a combination of age, marital status, and number of children can tell us the stage of a family's life cycle. Thus, demographic variables help to identify the subcultures we can target with the marketing mix. (We'll discuss this further in Chapter 14.)

The second use of demographic variables is to describe consumers who are classified into segments via other means. For example, suppose the product manager of Coca-Cola wants to segment Coke drinkers into heavy, medium, and light users in order to target different promotions to each group. A large consumer survey is developed, and three thousand people are asked about how frequently they consume soft drinks and Coke Classic in particular. Suppose one thousand fall into the medium usage frequency. The marketing manager would like to target them for promotional messages and sales promotions (e.g., contests and coupons) to increase their consumption. The question is, how do you describe and reach this segment? The solution is to include in the consumer survey a series of questions that obtain demographic information. By knowing

TABLE 2.5
Bases for Segmenting the
Consumer Market

I.	Characteristics of the Person		
	A.	Demographics	
		1. Age	6. Education
		2. Sex	7. Family size
		3. Income	8. Occupation
		4. Religion	9. Ethnicity
		5. Marital status	10. Nationality
	B.	Consumption Behavior	
		1. Benefits sought	
		2. Demand elasticity	
		3. Brand loyalty	
		4. Usage rate	
		5. Other—purchase occasion, media usage	
	C.	Personality characteristics	
		1. Need for cognition	
		2. Tolerance for ambiguity	
		3. Propensity for taking risks	
		4. Connectedness vs. separateness	
	D.	Psychographic profile	
II.	Situation		
	A.	Task definition	
	B.	Antecedent states	
	C.	Time	
	D.	Physical surroundings	
	E.	Social surroundings	
III.	Geography		
	A.	National boundaries	
	B.	Regions	
	C.	State boundaries	
	D.	Urban/rural zones	
	E.	Zip code/census block	
IV.	Culture		
	A.	Cultural mores, customs, values, and norms	
	B.	Subcultural mores, customs, values, and norms	

the age, ethnicity, geographic location, sex, education, and income of the group, we can reach them through appropriate promotions in a cost-effective way.

Sometimes, companies will even tell a particular demographic group that a particular product is targeted to them. For example, in 2013, Ford introduced a new Lincoln MKZ and advertised it with the headline "Introducing the car for the 42-year-old, urban-dwelling businessman."

Demographic data are also important because they're readily available. The federal government collects a wealth of demographic data through the census. Magazines, newspapers, and television and radio stations collect demographic information about their audiences. Private research companies collect and provide demographic information about various groups of people. With such information, the marketing manager can make informed choices about the type of media to use to reach the target market as well as to make pricing and distribution decisions.

Behavior as a basis for segmentation Another approach to using demographic variables is **behavior segmentation**, which divides consumers into homogeneous groups based on various aspects of their buying behavior. Bases of behavioral segmentation include price elasticity, benefits sought, and usage rate.

The concept of segmenting on **price elasticity** is based on the economic principle that different groups of consumers may react differently to changes in the price of a good or service. Thus, customers who are price elastic will change their buying a great deal in response to price changes. In contrast, customers who are price inelastic show little change in buying patterns in response to price changes.

Airlines use price elasticity to charge more for tickets purchased close in time to the day of travel. The rationale is that individuals traveling on short notice tend to be price inelastic and willing to pay more for a ticket. Price-inelastic customers include those with higher incomes, business travelers, and those who are traveling because of an emergency. In contrast, price-elastic consumers are most typically vacationers who can make reservations well in advance of the trip.

Strategies based on price elasticity have a number of advantages for managers. First, they allow companies to increase their total sales and possibly increase the overall efficiency of their operations. For airlines, for instance, seats that wouldn't otherwise have been filled have occupants. Because the marginal cost of filling empty seats in a plane is minimal, the fares from such passengers go almost directly to the bottom line. Another plus is that, when done correctly, segmenting through price elasticity carries little risk that customers will infer the product has lower quality because it has a lower price.

Firms can also divide the market with **benefit segmentation**, which is segmentation based on the benefits consumers seek. For example, some consumers want a car that uses a minimal amount of gasoline. While others may be seeking the functional benefits of an all-terrain vehicle, such as a Jeep.

A final type of behavior we use for segmentation is **usage behavior** with respect to our product, which we can identify through market research as, say, light, moderate, and heavy. With this information, we can develop strategies to target one or more of the groups by manipulating the marketing mix. For example, in the sports industry, professional teams offer different packages based on the consumer usage. A heavy user of sports spectatorship may attend special events, such as opportunities to interact with the team and obtain autographs. A medium user may purchase seven NBA games a year. In this case, the professional team allows the fan to pick seven games among ten choices. The light user may attend only one game a year. In this case, the team may send out an e-mail message with a discounted offer to a game of user's choosing.

Introducing the car for the 42-year-old, urban-dwelling businessman.

Like individuals, no two journeys are alike. Which is why we've dramatically opened up our all-new 2013 MKZ to the world above with an available retractable panoramic glass roof. Giving you a whole new appreciation for the oddly shaped cloud, the inspiring steeple and the occasional neon cowboy. The sky just called shotgun. Get a panoramic look at the MKZ at Lincoln.com.

INTRODUCING
THE LINCOLN
MOTOR COMPANY

This ad for the 2013 Lincoln MKZ tells consumers the demographic target market for the car.

We can also identify usage behavior to help us segment based on brand loyalty. For example, we may want to use sales-promotion devices, such as coupons or rebates, to reach and influence users who switch between brands.

Psychographic and personality characteristics We can also segment markets based on consumers' psychographic and personality characteristics. **Psychographics** refers to the analysis of consumers' lifestyles, interests, activities, and opinions. **Personality** refers to the distinctive patterns of behavior, including thoughts and emotions, that describe how a person responds to the situations. (We'll discuss both topics more in Chapter 6.)

Of course, we can combine psychographic and/or personality segmentation with behavioral segmentation. That is, we first divide consumers into heavy, moderate, and light users of a brand and then analyze one or more of these usage segments according to members' psychographic and/or personality inventories. Based on the results, we can then design promotional messages and distribution and pricing strategies that will be most effective.

The Situation as a Segmentation Basis

Consumer situations are the temporary contexts—the time and place—within which a consumer buying activity occurs. For many types of products, segmentation by situation is the rule. For example, clothing and footwear have to be designed specifically for the physical surroundings (i.e., warm or cold weather; sun or rain) as well as for the task definition (e.g., party, sleep, casual). Research has shown situation strongly affects the choice of snack food, meat products, and fast-food chains.[21]

Consumers will purchase very different snack foods for a cocktail party than for a picnic. (We'll discuss consumer situations further in Chapter 11.)

Geographic Segmentation

For many products and services, geography is an important basis for segmentation. Managers can segment the market by region, by city, by county, or even by census block (i.e., groups of houses on a single street). Other means of geographic segmentation include population density and climate.

Researchers have combined the fields of geography and demography (the study of demographics) to create the new discipline of **geodemographics**. Companies are increasingly turning to geodemographics to assist them in segmenting the marketplace. In particular, geodemographic research allows the marketer to analyze the demographic characteristics of groups of people who live in particular census blocks or zip codes. The information is particularly useful for deciding where to locate a new business, such as a grocery store, fast-food restaurant, or golf course. (We will say much more about geodemographics in Chapter 14.)

Culture and Subcultures As a Basis for Segmentation

Culture is defined as the way of life of the people of a society. In contrast, a **subculture** is a subdivision of a national culture based on some unifying characteristic, such as social status or nationality. A subculture's members share behaviors that are somehow distinct from those of the national culture in which they live. For example, the United States, China, and Germany have distinctive national cultures. Yet, within each of these cultures, myriad subcultures coexist.

Culture is most clearly used as a segmentation variable in international marketing. In contrast, within the borders of a nation, marketers frequently target subcultures, usually described by demographic variables. Thus, particular religious groups (e.g., Mormons, Born Again Christians, and Jews) may be identified as targets for a marketing offering. Similarly, a product may be developed and promoted to carefully selected ethnic groups. For example, an insurance company may identify Asians or Hispanics for a particular type of insurance product.

Segmenting Business Markets

As with consumer markets, business markets can be divided into segments, but here, marketers have a great deal more information at hand. For example, the federal government has developed a system for categorizing all businesses into homogeneous groups. Called the **North American Standard Industrial Classification System** (NASIC), the database employs six-digit codes to classify businesses that produce the same type of product into groups. The NASIC system can assist industrial marketers in identifying potential new customers, estimating market potential, and identifying groups of companies likely to have similar product or service needs.

One strategy for segmenting industrial markets is to identify macro-bases and micro-bases.[22] Macro-segmentation identifies groups of companies with similar characteristics and buying situations. Characteristics on which we can segment organizations include size, geographical location, usage rate, and whether the company is centralized or decentralized. Segmenting based on the purchasing situation looks at whether the purchase is a new task, a modified rebuy, or a straight rebuy. Table 2.6 identifies a number of macro-bases for segmentation.

Segmentation Basis	Example
1. Characteristics of buying organization	
a. Size	Small, medium, large; can be based on overall sales
b. Geographic location	New England vs. Southwest
c. Usage Rate	Light, moderate, heavy
d. Buying structure	Centralized vs. decentralized
2. Product application	
a. SIC code	Varies by product
b. End market served	Varies by product
3. Characteristics of purchasing situation	
a. Type of buying situation	New task, modified rebuy, straight rebuy
b. Stage in decision process	Early vs. late stage

TABLE 2.6
Some Macro-bases of Segmentation of Industrial Markets

Source: Based on Michael D. Hutt and Thomas Speh, *Industrial Marketing Management* (New York: Dryden Press, 1995).

Micro-segmentation in industrial marketing identifies the characteristics of the decision-making units within each of the various macro-segments. Thus, it requires in-depth knowledge of the buying organization, such as its key decision criteria and the product and producer attributes its buyers seek. These could include quality of product, delivery reliability and speed, and supplier reputation.

THE ROLE OF CONSUMER BEHAVIOR IN PRODUCT POSITIONING AND DIFFERENTIATION

Through **product positioning**, an organization influences the way consumers perceive a brand's characteristics relative to those of competitive offerings. The goal of product positioning is to influence demand by creating a product with specific brand attributes and a clear image that differentiate it from competitors. **Product differentiation** is the process of manipulating the marketing mix so as to position a product in a manner that allows consumers to perceive meaningful differences between a brand and its competitors.

Product positioning and differentiation go hand in hand with segmentation. We identify a segment of customers and then develop and position a product so it fulfills the needs of that segment. For example, when Starbucks announced it would open coffee shops in Japan, the news sent shivers down the spines of Japanese coffee bar owners. Starbucks recognized the Japanese are the world's No. 3 coffee consumer. Japan represented an untouched market. Starbucks is positioned as an upscale, hip place to drink espresso, latte, mocha, and Seattle-style coffee. Because its image was highly differentiated from the mom-and-pop coffee bars in Japan, its earnings potential was extremely high

Companies can adopt two types of positioning strategies. In **specific positioning**, the company seeks to create strong linkages in consumers' minds among the product, its key attributes, and its benefits. In particular, market leaders will attempt to link attributes and needs in order to position their brand and create a strong product image. In this approach, other brands aren't specifically mentioned; however, the goal is still to differentiate the brand's qualities from the competitions' by emphasizing a key feature of the brand consumers seek. For example, Crest toothpaste has focused on the attribute-brand link of decay prevention.

The second approach to product positioning is **competitive positioning**, frequently employed by brands that aren't market leaders but that position themselves and their attributes in relationship to the market leader. These secondary brands will often use some type of comparative advertising.[23] (Chapter 9 discusses comparative advertising in more detail.)

How do marketers assess a brand's position? Perhaps the most common approach is to create **perceptual maps**, which show how consumers position various brands relative to each other on computer-generated graphs whose axes are formed by product attributes.

Figure 2.2 presents an example of a perceptual map developed by the authors that depicts the relative positions of automobile companies as seen by the second author of this book. The figure depicts automobile brands on two dimensions: price and expressiveness. Ferrari is shown as very high priced and very expressive. At the other extreme is Kia, which is low priced and conservative. The three brands shown for General Motors (GM)—Cadillac, Buick, and Chevrolet—are positioned far apart on the map, indicating they're well differentiated from one another.

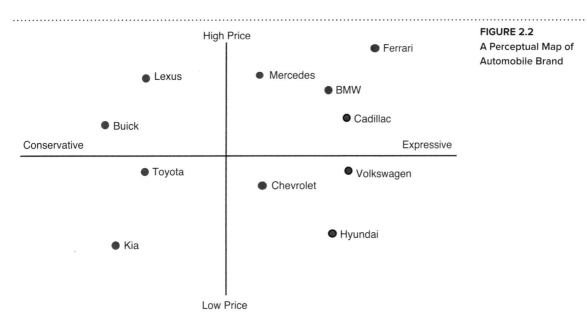

FIGURE 2.2
A Perceptual Map of
Automobile Brand

GM's recent decision to discontinue its Oldsmobile and Pontiac brands was a good one because, on a perceptual map, Oldsmobile was positioned very close to Buick and Pontiac was very close to Chevrolet. Because of this lack of differentiation, Oldsmobile and Buick were simply cannibalizing market share from each other, as were Pontiac and Chevrolet. By eliminating Oldsmobile and Pontiac, GM would lose relatively few sales and, at the same time, lower its costs.

Companies gain a number of benefits when consumers can differentiate one brand from others. Perhaps most important, product differentiation adds perceived value to the product, which helps increase the leverage of the various components of the marketing mix.[24] Thus, in the pricing area, brand differentiation can allow the company to command premium prices for a product. In the promotion area, product differentiation helps creative teams develop messages that promote only the brand advertised and not competitors as well. An example of a clearly differentiated brand using a claim effectively was Mercedes's unique selling proposition, "Engineered like no other car in the world." The company stands out for its engineering, and the claim was highly believable. Because of its ability to differentiate itself from other brands in the United States, Mercedes could price its cars significantly higher in the United States than in Germany.

THE ROLE OF CONSUMER BEHAVIOR IN MARKETING MIX DEVELOPMENT

The facts, theories, and concepts of consumer behavior directly affect the development of the marketing mix, which we generate to implement the positioning and segmentation strategy and to coordinate activities that create products and promote, price, and distribute them. Let's look next at how we apply consumer behavior to the four key applications of product, promotion, price, and distribution.

Product Development

As we've discussed, the term *product* is used very broadly to include physical objects, services, places, and organizations.[25] For almost any type of product, we can apply the principles of consumer behavior to four separate areas of the new-product development process: idea generation, concept testing, product development, and market testing.

Within the area of new-product development, consumer behavior concepts have perhaps their greatest impact on idea generation. For example, we study consumers' attitudes about existing products in order to identify their desires for particular product attributes (see Chapter 7 on attitudes). If consumers believe existing products fail to possess attributes they desire, a new-product opportunity may exist. For instance, for years, the toothpaste industry sold brands based on one of three attributes: cavity fighting (i.e., Crest), fresh breath (i.e., Close-Up), and teeth whitening (i.e., Rembrandt). Aquafresh decided the market wanted all three attributes at once and introduced Aquafresh in a clear pump tube that helped demonstrate to consumers all three attributes are present with the three colors (i.e. red, white, and blue), each one being one of the attributes. .

Concept testing is the pretesting of the product concept, the particular "consumer meaning that the company tries to build into a product idea."[26] For example, the product concept for a new car may be to build a car that drives itself and is powered only by electricity (i.e., Tesla). In order to determine whether a market exists for this concept, the firm can examine the consumer decision-making process (see Chapter 9) to determine the likelihood consumers will select this product over competitors.

After determining whether consumers are likely to select this product over competitive offerings, we can begin the product development process. Here, prototypes are developed, tested, named, and packaged. A variety of consumer behavior concepts are important in this phase. For example, we should be concerned with how consumers process information about the product. Does the packaging gain attention? (See Chapter 3.) Can consumers remember the name of the product? (See Chapter 4.)

When testing the product and packaging, we must also be concerned about the attitude formation process (see Chapter 7). Do consumers like the prototype product? Do they believe the claims made about it? Do they like the packaging?

After the product development phase has been concluded satisfactorily, marketers often move the product into **market testing**, placing it into limited distribution in order to identify any potential problems and to test the entire marketing mix. Meanwhile, marketers also take additional attitudinal measures to find out whether consumers are forming the expected beliefs, affective reactions, and buying intentions. In addition, marketers examine post-purchase satisfaction (see Chapter 12). Are consumers happy with the product after they purchase it? Are they rebuying it? Are they showing signs of developing brand loyalty? The manager will also want to know whether consumers are using the product in the expected situations. In general, the goal of the market test is to determine whether the marketing strategy is working.

Throughout the new-product development process, we must be concerned with the products and actions of competitors. Consumers don't perceive a brand in isolation, separate from competitors. Thus, assessment of how the product compares to competitive offerings is crucial. Moving into full-scale production would be a mistake if it were based on the finding that consumers rate our product as "good" on various attributes but rate competitors as "excellent" on the same attributes. Furthermore, we can't assume the competitive environment will remain constant while we develop our product. Instead, we're constantly trying to hit a moving target. Changes in the cultural, economic, and natural environments make the new-product development process exceptionally risky.

Promotional Strategy Implications

Consumer behavior concepts and principles form a basis for much of the manager's strategy for advertising, personal selling, sales promotion, and public relations. Let's look at these promotional activities in the context of consumer behavior.

Advertising Implications When developing advertising materials, we should think in terms of the kinds of ideas, images, and feelings creative people seek to evoke in consumers. One approach is to analyze the motivations, personality, and psychographic characteristics of the target market (see Chapter 6). Particularly for experiential products such as beer, perfume, and cigarettes, developing a theme and image for the product is crucial.

A classic example of an ad that targets an age subculture and its characteristics is a commercial for Budweiser beer shown during a recent Super Bowl. In the ad, a bridge has been washed out, and a Budweiser truck is stuck on the other side of a small town. A twenty-something male runs into a café yelling, "The bridge is out," and nothing happens. Then, he says, "But there's a Budweiser delivery truck on the other side." This galvanizes hundreds of people into action, and they run to the bridge to see the truck on the other side of the ravine. The first young man then says, "Everybody, lend a hand." The crowd is suddenly mobilized and builds a human bridge over which the truck drives. The comical idea of this impossible feat is targeted to members of Generation Y (born in the 1980s and 1990s), or millennials, many of whom are now in prime beer-drinking age. In addition, the ad evokes an important personality and lifestyle characteristic of Gen Y—the importance of social connections.

An understanding of the factors that increase the persuasiveness of communications is another particularly important area for advertisers. For example, the advertiser must have information about the type of message and endorser to use in order to influence consumers' feelings and beliefs. Should a fear appeal or humor be used in the ad? Would a celebrity endorser be the most effective source of information? Will comparative advertising work? These are the types of questions the knowledge of persuasive communications can answer for the marketing manager.

Personal Selling Implications Many decisions that are important in advertising also relate to personal selling. Knowledge of the way consumers form and change their attitudes can assist marketers in developing specific messages for the sales force, for instance. An analysis of any cultural or subcultural differences between the sales force and clients can also help the company avoid problems such as inappropriate statements or actions. For example, when dealing with more reserved and polite Chinese or Japanese clients, a manager doesn't want his or her sales force to push too quickly for decisions or behave too informally. (We discuss personal influence in Chapter 8.)

Sales Promotion Applications Sales promotion consists of all the supplementary promotional activities undertaken in addition to advertising and personal selling and includes personal selling, coupons, rebates, contests, sweepstakes, and dealer incentives.[27] Consumer behavior principles can influence planning in sales promotion application areas such as sales, coupons, and rebates . . . An important question when temporarily reducing the price of a product, for instance, is just how much to reduce it. Consumer research in the field of information processing and on the "just meaningful difference" is critical to answering this question. That is, if consumers don't believe the price reduction to be meaningful, it will decrease revenues because no additional sales occur and the normal level of sales will take place at a lower price.

Public Relations Public relations is a broad area that includes all nonpaid communications from the firm and focuses on the intersection of the corporation, consumers, and regulators. Consumer behavior research about attitude formation and change informs our knowledge of how to manage publicity about the firm and how to handle consumer questions and complaints. In particular, public relations managers must be concerned with the effects of negative publicity about the firm and its products, which can have a disproportionate impact on consumer attitudes. Public relations staff must constantly monitor print and electronic news media and consumer communications in order to quickly identify rumors and leaks about product recalls, firm disasters, corporate financial problems, illegal corporate activities, and complaints about company activities. For example, nongovernmental organizations (NGOs) may organize protests against a company for its anti-environmental behaviors. At the 2010 Winter Olympics in Vancouver, Canada, an NGO called the Pure Salmon Campaign held events in protest of salmon farming by a Norwegian company. The protestors alleged that farming salmon in huge fish nets threaten the wild salmon population, which was already in decline.[28] A public relations strategy that some companies are using is to partner with NGOs. An example of a healthy NGO-business partnership is the relationship of Walmart with the Environmental Defense Fund.[29]

The shared initiative focuses on five areas: global warming, fish farming, reducing packaging waste, alternative-fuel usage, and global factory operations. A business-NGO relationship must go beyond mere public relations, however, so it brings about actual changes in the company's products and their production.

In planning public relations strategy, the manager must anticipate how the public will perceive the message and the source. Training corporate officials to act as spokespersons for the company is an important task for companies with a high public profile.

Pricing and Distribution Applications

How will consumers react when companies raise or lower the price of a product? Principles of perception apply to this problem—unless the price change is greater than some threshold level, consumers may not notice a difference. Thus, if the price is being lowered, it should be lowered enough so consumers will perceive a change has occurred. In contrast, if the price is being raised, in most instances, the company would prefer the increase not be enough for consumers to perceive a difference. (We'll discuss pricing issues further in Chapter 3 on the price-quality relationship.)

Consumer behavior principles also apply to the distribution component of the marketing mix. That is, the extent to which consumers engage in search behavior should influence the intensity of a company's distribution efforts. If a product is bought under low-involvement conditions, it's unlikely consumers will engage in much search behavior before buying it (see Chapter 3 on involvement). Therefore, companies selling low-involvement products should seek to place the product in as many retail outlets as possible to make it available whenever a need arises it could fill. A classic example is the distribution strategy of soft drink companies—in particular, Coca-Cola Company. In most urban areas, a consumer can find a vending machine or retailer selling Coca-Cola within several hundred feet of wherever he or she stands.

Another consumer behavior area with application to physical distribution is geodemographics (see Chapter 14). Companies are concerned about where to place new retail outlets and distribution centers. Through geodemographic analysis, companies can assess the demographic characteristics of consumers in different geographical areas to inform their decisions. Analyzing population shifts among regions of the country can also pay dividends in lowering costs and matching the distribution of a product to growth areas. Geodemographics also helps with the placement of retail stores within cities and towns.

USING CONSUMER BEHAVIOR TO SOLVE MARKETING PROBLEMS

To develop managerial solutions to marketing problems, we need an understanding of consumer behavior concepts, of the RESPonsive Marketing cycle elements, and of ways to combine this information into a useful whole.

We can combine these ideas to form a three-step **marketing solutions analysis**:

1. Gather information and identify the problem or opportunity.
2. Identify the relevant consumer behavior concepts and how they apply to the problem or opportunity.
3. Develop a marketing strategy by systematically moving through the RESPonsive Marketing cycle and determining the consumer behavior concepts and their implications for each phase of the cycle.

In step 1 of the marketing solutions analysis, we gather as much information as possible about the case and carefully sift through it to identify the fundamental question, or questions, we need to answer. This step is important because the remainder of the analysis will flounder if we don't gather adequate information or correctly identify the problem or opportunity.

In step 2, we systematically identify the consumer behavior concepts relevant to problem or opportunity using each of the topic areas from the individual level of analysis (Part II of the text) and the environmental level (Part III). Key consumer behaviors for this analysis are found in bold letters in each chapter.

In step 3, we identify the marketing implications of the consumer behavior concepts. These implications will cover one or more of the five RESPonsive Marketing cycle elements (i.e., research, environmental analysis, segmentation, positioning, and marketing mix development). We examine the extent to which the various consumer concepts apply to each of the five managerial areas and develop marketing strategies from the concepts. After completing these three steps, we'll have a solution to our marketing problem.

Throughout the remainder of the book, we'll show you how to use consumer behavior concepts to develop marketing strategy. Indeed, whenever the question arises of how to apply consumer behavior concepts to designing marketing strategy, you should immediately think RESPonsive Marketing cycle. Then, you can systematically consider how the consumer concept applies to each of the components of the cycle and, from that answer, develop a strategic approach to solve the problem.

SUMMARY

What are the managerial application areas to which consumer behavior concepts apply?

Consumer behavior principles and research assist managerial decision making in five different but interdependent areas: research, environmental analysis, segmentation, product positioning, and marketing mix development. By following these steps, managers are better positioned to give customers the products they desire.

What's the role of consumer behavior in performing marketing research?

Marketing research is applied consumer research designed to provide management with information about factors that affect consumers, including acquisition, consumption, and disposition of goods, services, and ideas. Having a firm grasp of these factors helps us select what to measure and to avoid common pitfalls that can occur during the research.

What's the role of consumer behavior in environmental analysis?

Environmental analysis assesses the external forces that act on a firm and its customers and that create threats and opportunities. It investigates the demographic, cultural, situational, group, economic, natural, and technological environments.

What's the role of consumer behavior in market segmentation?

Market segmentation is the subdividing of a market into distinct subsets of customers with similar needs and wants—each segment can be reached with a different marketing mix. For segments to be useful, they should be measurable, accessible, and sustainable. The advantage of segmentation to a company is that the marketing mix can be tailored to meet the needs and wants of homogeneous subsets of customers, helping expand the total market potential for a general class of product. A number of factors have been identified on which people and companies can be grouped. Segmentation variables include the characteristics of the person, the nature of the situation in which the product or service may be purchased, geography, and the culture and subculture adopted by the consumer. Industrial markets are often segmented based on the NASIC database developed by the federal government.

What's the role of consumer behavior in product positioning and differentiation?

Product positioning and product differentiation are also key managerial application areas for consumer behavior concepts. Through product positioning, an organization influences the way consumers perceive a brand's characteristics relative to those of competitive offerings. The goal is to influence demand by creating a product with specific attributes and a clear image that differentiate it from competitors. Product differentiation is the process of manipulating the marketing mix so consumers perceive meaningful differences between a brand and its competitors. Positioning a product and segmenting customers go hand in hand. We identify a segment of customers and then develop and position a product so it fulfills the needs of that segment.

What's the role of consumer behavior in marketing mix development?

The final application area of consumer behavior concepts, marketing mix development, coordinates the activities in product development and the promotion, pricing, and distribution of the product. We use the term *product* very broadly to include physical objects, services, places, organizations, and so forth. Principles of consumer behavior apply to four areas of the new-product development process: idea generation, concept testing, product development, and market testing. Similarly, the principles apply to the four areas of promotional strategy: advertising, personal selling, publicity, and sales promotions.

In order to solve marketing problems, we use a three-step procedure. First, gather information and identify the problem or opportunity. Second, identify the relevant consumer behavior concepts and determine how they apply to the problem or opportunity. Third, develop a managerial strategy by identifying the managerial implications of each applicable consumer behavior concept.

KEY TERMS

bases for segmentation
behavioral economics
behavioral segmentation
benefit segmentation
cognitive responses
competitive positioning
concept testing
content analysis
culture
demographic characteristics
depth interviews
environmental analysis
ethnographic research
experiment
focus groups

geodemographics
market segmentation
market testing
marketing mix
marketing research
marketing solutions analysis
marketing strategy
marketing strategy cycle
neuroscience
North American Standard Industrial Classification System
observational research
online quantitative data
perceptual maps

personality
price elasticity
product differentiation
product positioning
psychographics
qualitative research methods
quantitative research methods
questionnaire
questionnaire scales
RESPonsive Marketing
secondary sources
specific positioning
subculture
usage behavior

REVIEW QUESTIONS

1. Identify the five key managerial strategy areas in which consumer behavior may be of assistance to managers.

2. Identify the six environmental areas in which consumer behavior information may be of assistance to managers. In addition, give two specific examples of useful consumer behavior information for each.

3. What do we mean by saying there's reciprocity between consumers and the environment?

4. Identify and give examples of two types of positioning.

5. What is a perceptual map? How can perceptual maps be used to help position products?

6. What three factors should be present for a market segment to be managerially useful?

7. Identify the bases for segmenting the consumer market.

8. What's meant by behavioral segmentation? What are three types of behavioral segmentation?

9. What are four areas of product development in which consumer behavior principles can assist managers?

10. Identify four ways consumer behavior concepts can assist in the development of promotional strategy.

11. Identify one example of how a consumer behavior principle can assist the manager in each of the following: sales promotion, public relations, pricing, and distribution.

12. What is a key area in which industrial and consumer markets may differ?

DISCUSSION QUESTIONS

1. Imagine you're a member of the planning department at GM's corporate headquarters. You have just been assigned the task of identifying the environmental factors that will likely influence consumer tastes and preferences over the next ten years. Outline the factors you'd consider in making such an analysis.

2. Identify a current example of specific positioning of a good or service in the marketplace. Then, identify an example of the competitive positioning of a good or service. How effective do you consider each of the strategies to be?

3. Using your personal knowledge and understanding of universities high school students in your region consider, develop a perceptual map the typical student might have of these universities. Of critical importance will be your identification of the map's vertical and horizontal dimensions.

4. Consider the automobile industry or some other major industry you know something about, such as cosmetics. Among the brands, identify

one that has a highly effective positioning strategy and one whose positioning strategy is poor. Discuss the rationale for your assessment.

5. Again, consider the automobile industry or some other major industry you know something about. Identify as many variables as you can on which the consumers in that industry can be segmented. Next, identify specific brands that target the various segments. Are there segments of the marketplace that haven't been adequately reached?

6. Imagine you work in the marketing department of a company that has developed a prototype of a new processed beef product. The product tastes and looks just like a high-quality piece of steak. However, it's made from beef chuck and costs about half as much as sirloin steak. Furthermore, it contains about half the calories and cholesterol of sirloin steak. Describe the RESPonsive Marketing issues your company would face in marketing the product to consumers.

ENDNOTES

[1] Malcolm Gladwell, *Blink: The Power of Thinking without Thinking* (New York: Little, Brown, 2005).

[2] Timothy Hay, "A New Game for Microsoft's Kinect," *Wall Street Journal*, March 19, 2013, B5.

[3] Raju Narisetti, "P&G Says Fake-Fat Olestra Gets Fewer Complaints than Expected," *Wall Street Journal*, July 25, 1996, B3.

[4] Wendy Martin, "Spirituality and the Supernatural on Television," *OnFaith*, July 18, 2008, accessed December 27, 2015, http://newsweek.washingtonpost.com/onfaith/guestvoices/2008/07/spirituality_and_the_supernatu.html.

[5] Laurie Burkitt, "Neuromarketing: Companies Use Neuroscience for Consumer Insights," Forbes, October 29, 2009, accessed December 27, 2015, http://www.forbes.com/forbes/2009/1116/marketing-hyundai-neurofocus-brain-waves-battle-for-the-brain.html.

[6] Robert Less Hotz, "Decoding Our Chatter," *Wall Street Journal*, October 1, 2011, C1, C2.

[7] Courtney Schlisserman, "Consumer Confidence in US Improves on Job Prospects," *BusinessWeek*, March 30, 2010, http://www.businessweek.com/news/2010-03-30/consumer-confidence-in-u-s-improved-in-march-on-job-prospects.html.

[8] Data refer to the year 2009. "World Economic Outlook Database: October 2010 Edition," *International Monetary Fund*, accessed October 6, 2010, https://www.imf.org/external/pubs/ft/weo/2010/02/weodata/index.aspx.

[9] Mike Shedlock, "Consumers Shun Credit Cards—Credit Card Usage Drops, Debit Card Usage Rises," *Mish's Global Economic Trend Analysis*, accessed December 27, 2015, http://globaleconomic analysis.blogspot.com.

[10] Kevin D. Williamson, "Seventy Percent: The Myth of the Consumer Recovery," *National Review*, September 27, 2010, accessed December 27, 2015, http://www.nationalreview.com/exchequer/247825/70-percent-myth-consumer-economy-kevin-d-williamson.

[11] Diane Brady, "Can the World Live with a Frugal American Consumer?" *Bloomberg Business*, January 29, 2009, accessed December 27, 2015, http://www.businessweek.com/careers/managementiq/archives/2009/01/can_the_world_l.html.

[12] Annalyn Censky, "Consumer Confidence Plunges to Lowest Level Since Great Recession," *CNN*, accessed March 4, 2013, http://money.cnn.com/2011/08/30/news/economy/consumer_confidence/index.htm.

[13] Jeff Dominitz and Charles F. Manski, "How Should We Measure Consumer Confidence (Sentiment)?" (working paper, Northwestern University Institute for Policy Research), http://www.ipr.northwestern.edu/publications/docs/workingpapers/2003/IPR-WP-03-10.pdf.

[14] Richard Thaler and Cass Sunstein, *Nudge: Improving Decisions about Health, Wealth, and Happiness* (New York: Penguin, 2009).

[15] Lorne Matalon, "Mexico's Poor Seek Relief from Tortilla Shortage," National Geographic, June 4, 2008, accessed December 27, 2015, http://news.nationalgeographic.com/news/2008/06/080604-mexico-food.html.

[16] Dexter Roberts, "China Faces a Water Crisis," *Bloomberg Business*, April 15, 2009, accessed December 27, 2015, http://www.businessweek.com/globalbiz/content/apr2009/gb20090415_032220.htm.

[17] Jessica E. Lessin and Spencer E. Ante, "Apps Bloom into Industry Set to Hit $25 Billion," *Wall Street Journal*, March 4, 2013, B10.

[18] John Lauerman, "Life Form Created with Man-Made DNA Offers Benefits, Dangers," Bloomberg Business, May 21, 2010, accessed December 27, 2015, http://www.businessweek.com/news/2010-05-21/life-form-created-with-man-made-dna-offers-benefits-dangers.html.

[19] William R. L. Anderegga, James W. Prallb, Jacob Harold, and Stephen H. Schneider, "Expert Credibility in Climate Change," *PNAS* 107, no. 27 (July 6, 2010): 12107–12109, accessed December 27, 2015, http://www.pnas.org/cgi/doi/10.1073/pnas.1003187107.

[20] "Sea Level Rise," *New York State Department of Environmental Conservation*, accessed December 27, 2015, http://www.dec.ny.gov/energy/45202.html.

[21] Russell W. Belk, "Situational Variables and Consumer Behavior," *Journal of Consumer Research* 2 (December 1975): 157–164.

[22] Michael D. Hutt and Thomas Speh, *Industrial Marketing Management* (New York: Dryden Press, 1981).

[23] Philip Kotler and Kevin Lane Keller, *Marketing Management*, 14th ed. (Upper Saddle River, NJ: Prentice-Hall, 2012).

[24] Thomas Robertson, Joan Zielinski, and Scott Ward, *Consumer Behavior* (Glenview, IL: Scott, Foresman, and Company, 1984).

[25] Philip Kotler and Kevin Lane Keller, *Marketing Management*, 14th ed. (Upper Saddle River, NJ: Prentice-Hall, 2012).

[26] Ibid., 231.

[27] Edmund Faison, *Advertising: A Behavioral Approach for Managers* (New York: Wiley, 1980).

[28] SeafoodSource Staff, "NGO Protests Farmed Salmon at Olympics," *SeafoodSource*, accessed December 27, 2015, http://www.seafoodsource.com/newsarticledetail.aspx?id=4294989192.

[29] "Walmart," *EDF+Business*, accessed March 3, 2013, http://business.edf.org/projects/walmart. Also see Brad Kenney, "NGOs and Business— Shared Goals, Mutual Trust," *IIP Digital*, accessed December 27, 2015, http://www.america.gov/st/energy-english/2008/March/20080312162449WRybakcuh0.8249105.html#ixzz16PuDZ8KB.

chapter

3

Information Processing: Perceptual Processes

Learning Objectives:

1. How can consumers be influenced to pay attention to messages?

2. How much should a product's price or features be changed?

3. Can consumers be influenced without their awareness?

4. How can marketers maintain consumer interest in their products?

5. What factors influence how aesthetically pleasing a product is?

6. How do symbols influence consumers?

The US Auto Industry and Six Managerial Questions

In 2000, 17.4 million vehicles were sold in the United States. By early 2008, the number had fallen to 15 million—a 14 percent reduction in sales.[1] Then, because of the great recession of 2008–2009, sales declined even further to 10.4 million.[2] In response, auto marketers reworked their strategies for influencing consumers to purchase vehicles. Six of these strategies reflect ideas found in this chapter.

Strategy 1: Auto marketers are increasingly turning to the Internet. How do they attract attention to their ads amidst the cacophony of competitive ads? General Motors (GM) solved the problem in one Internet ad that began with the GM logo flying across the computer screen, followed by a series of colorful cars doing figure eights. The unusual movement activated consumers' orientation reflex, which caused them to attend to the ad.

Strategy 2: Another problem concerned how much to lower the price of gas-guzzling vehicles in order to move them in sales promotions. In some instances, trucks listing for less than $30,000 were discounted by more than $8,000. Were discounts of over 25 percent necessary to sell the vehicles? The answer is yes, and the reason why is identified in the chapter.

Strategy 3: Some companies, such as BMW, may have tried to subliminally influence consumers. BMW produced a five-minute video for its new X6 crossover vehicle and showed it on *YouTube*. The video ends with two quick, metallic-sounding thumps that are synchronized to the display of the words *driving* and *pleasure*, which are shown in very, very small letters. Unless consumers focus hard on the words, they're unlikely to be consciously recognized. However, the

words may subliminally impact consumers. This chapter asks whether subliminal ads are effective and ethical to use.

Strategy 4: A decade ago, it took US car manufacturers about twice as long as the Japanese manufacturer Toyota to bring out a new model. If the appearance and/or performance of products and services aren't frequently changed, consumers will move on to newer products made by competitors. Japanese companies, such as Toyota, were using superfast computers in the design process. It wasn't until 2004 that GM acquired supercomputers, which decreased the design process to 15 months.[3] This allowed GM to more effectively compete against Toyota, particularly after its reorganization in 2010, by keeping consumers interested in its products.

Strategy 5: How a good feels, looks, and even smells influences purchases. Not only must a car's outside design be pleasing to the eye, its interior must also have good aesthetics. For example, many people buy a new car partly for that "new car" smell. Auto designers also pay particular attention to the design of the front of the car, which represents the car's head and shoulders and gives an expression to the vehicle. What's the expression of the exotic Japanese car shown in the nearby ad?

Strategy 6: Automakers have long used symbols to assist in the creation of brand images. For example, Jaguar employs a sinuous leaping cat as its symbol, which connotes a beautiful, fast, sleek vehicle. Similarly, the Ford Mustang employs the symbol of a wild horse as one component of the car's image. Understanding the perceptual processes that influence the meaning derived from symbols is critical to their effective use by managers.

AN OVERVIEW OF INFORMATION PROCESSING

Information processing is defined as the process through which consumers are exposed to information, attend to it, comprehend it, place it in memory, and retrieve it for later use. A critical component of the definition is the word *information*. **Information** represents content that's exchanged with the outer world as we adjust to it and make our adjustment felt upon it.[4] Information is obtained through each of the senses—that is, vision, hearing, taste, smell, and touch.

The information consumers receive is composed of raw stimuli, which include sound waves, light waves/particles, bits of chemicals, textures, temperature levels, and even the effects of gravity (i.e., through balance). The interpretation of and the meanings derived from these raw stimuli result from information processing. Importantly, different people may assign different meanings to exactly the same stimulus because their interpretation is influenced by their expectations and their general background. It's as though each person has a different lens through which he or she interprets the environment. One can't assume that two people who receive exactly the same information (e.g., in an advertisement) will perceive it and react to it similarly. For example, ask two avid fans of opposing basketball teams how well the game was refereed. Quite likely, the two will have very different views of the officiating because of the differences in the outcome in the game.

An Information-Processing System

Figure 3.1 presents a simplified diagram of the consumer information-processing system. The diagram shows three broad sets of factors influence how people process information: memory, level of consumer involvement, and perceptual processes.

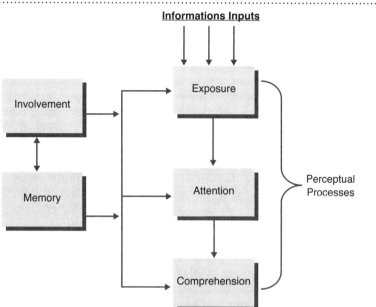

Informations Inputs

Exposure

Involvement

Memory

Attention

Perceptual Processes

Comprehension

FIGURE 3.1
A Model of Information Processing

Memory concerns how information is stored and retrieved for later use. Because memory processes play a large role in consumer behavior, Chapter 4 is devoted entirely to it. In the present chapter, we focus on how an understanding of perception assists managers in answering the six managerial questions.

Involvement is the level of the perceived importance of the information to a consumer. As the level of involvement increases, a person's motivation to process information also increases. Thus, at higher levels of involvement, a consumer will pay more attention to and think more about the subject of the information.

Perception is the process through which individuals are exposed to, attend to, and comprehend the information. The field of perception emphasizes the physiological and psychological processes through which raw stimuli (e.g., sound waves) are translated into something meaningful. Perception is composed of three stages. In the **exposure stage**, consumers receive information through their senses. In the **attention stage**, consumers focus on the stimulus and allocate cognitive processing capacity to it. In the **comprehension stage**, they organize and interpret the information in order to obtain meaning from it. Comprehension involves the process of making sense of stimuli so they may be understood.

With this background information on information processing, let's tackle the first managerial question—how can I get consumers to pay attention to my messages?

By understanding the exposure and attention stages of perception, marketers can understand how to get consumers to pay attention to what they have to say. The next two subsections discuss the exposure and the attention stages.

The Exposure Stage and Information Processing

As seen in the model presented in Figure 3.1, exposure to a stimulus is the first step in the processing of information. With information exposure, a consumer's sensory organs are activated and the entire mechanism of information processing can begin. In order to get consumers to pay attention to a communication, marketers must first expose them to the information. For example, some time ago, Nabisco slashed advertising spending on Planters Peanuts by 70 percent. Because of the drastic cut in ad spending, consumers weren't exposed to the charms of the Mr. Peanut character. The result was a reduction in sales from $60 million in 1993 to about $15 million in 1996.[5] Over the next decade, however, ad spending increased. By 2007, ads for Planters Peanuts were being placed on the major networks. With the increased exposure of the product, sales grew correspondingly. By 2011, the product's manufacturer, Kraft Foods, even updated the iconic character. Thus, the previously two-dimensional Mr. Peanut became more masculine, got a voice (via Robert Downey, Jr.), became three dimensional, and was given a gray flannel suit. Kraft was estimated to spend $30 million to $35 million on the print, Internet, and television campaign in 2011.[6]

One characteristic of consumer information processing in the exposure stage is consumers selectively choose the information to which they expose themselves. Thus, the concept of **selective exposure** represents the active choice of a consumer to have or not to have sensory contact with information. Selective exposure is of great interest to advertisers because this tendency of consumers to selectively screen information with which they come in contact can dramatically lower the effectiveness of advertising dollars. The effects of selective exposure are illustrated by events that take place when a wildly popular event, such as the Super Bowl, is televised. Sanitation supervisors at water departments have found that water consumption fluctuates dramatically during these events. Over a two- or three-minute period, water-holding tanks would be drained, and the system would be strained to capacity. Called the "flush factor," the sudden increase in water usage occurred during commercial breaks, when consumers left their televisions to rush to their bathrooms. The flush factor illustrates the point that consumers watching television will selectively avoid exposing themselves to commercials and attend to other matters.[7]

The old Mr. Peanut (left) and the new Mr. Peanut

The extent to which consumers engage in selective exposure to advertising has also been influenced by cable television. Television remote-control devices have proliferated with the influx of cable television systems. With such devices, consumers can rapidly and easily change from one channel to another. Called **zapping**, or channel surfing, in the industry, about 6 to 19 percent of consumers at any one time are zapping commercials by remotely switching channels. One study found consumers in 64 percent of homes with cable zap advertisements.[8] Another way to select away commercials is through zipping. **Zipping** occurs when consumers record TV shows and then zip past them through the fast forward control on their remote device. In 2012, Dish Network introduced the Hopper, which allows consumers to entirely bypass ads without having to go through the zipping process. Television networks responded with a series of lawsuits because the Hopper would destroy the advertising-supported television system.

Advertisers held a symposium on the zapping and zipping problems. The consensus was that an erosion rate of 59 percent occurs. Thus, about 4 of every 10 people watching a television program actually observe any one commercial. The response by professionals was that to reduce the audience-erosion problem, commercials would have to become more appealing. One executive commented that to prevent people from selectively avoiding commercials, ads would have to be made so well that people would want to view them.[9]

Technological innovations are making it increasingly easy for consumers to select what they are exposed to. For example, the National Football League and ESPN have channels that automatically switch to other network channels to games in which touchdowns are imminent. Similarly, companies are using mathematical modeling to develop software that allows consumers to sign up for alerts for baseball and football games "whenever their personal threshold for excitement is reached."[10]

In sum, in order to get consumers to pay attention to their messages, marketers must first create circumstances in which consumers are exposed to the information. This idea sounds very simple, but it's one managers frequently forget. This is how MSN.com became the leading Internet portal in 2007. At the time, most computers ran on Microsoft software. This software bundles the Windows Internet Explorer Internet search engine, which automatically sent buyers to the MSN.com website. Unless consumers changed the default setting, they were exposed to MSN.com. Similarly, commercials played in movie theaters prior to the beginning of a show attract involuntary attention. Theater operators, however, are extremely cautious about what kinds of ads to show for fear of aggravating customers. Corporations that own large numbers of theaters screen the ads to make sure they're appropriate and avoid a hard sell. As a result, the commercials shown tend to be highly lavish productions. Although the cost per thousand viewers is higher than for television advertising, theater advertising is claimed to be recalled three times better.[11]

The information technology revolution that connects consumers to each other (e.g., via Facebook, Twitter, blogs, Tumblr, etc.) has increased the amount and speed of information received. For example, when an earthquake occurred in Virginia in 2011, consumers at the epicenter of quake instantly sent out Twitter messages. As a result, individuals in New York learned of the quake 40 seconds before the first shock waves were felt there.[12]

Managerial principle 3.1
To get consumers to attend to a message, you must first expose them to it. While obvious, managers sometimes forget this important concept.

Social Media

Selective Exposure and Social Media

In 2013, 64 percent of retailers planned to increase ad spending on social media. Determining the return on the investment (ROI) in social media, however, is difficult. Why would they do this when the ROI is so uncertain?[13] One reason is that, because of their high level of involvement, consumers selectively expose themselves to messages sent through social media. As a result, many corporations added a social media component to the television ads shown in the 2013 Super Bowl. The following are some examples:

- Audi let users select one of three endings for its commercial.
- Doritos had a contest in which people created their own ads and then consumers voted on their favorite.
- Budweiser gave consumers a chance to name a baby Clydesdale.
- Coca Cola let consumers vote on the ending of a commercial.
- Pizza Hut ran a Facebook contest where the person who sent in the best video got to star in the Super Bowl ad.
- Lincoln started a Twitter campaign that asked consumers to tweet their most memorable road-trip stories.

A favorite ad was the Doritos funny "Goat 4 Sale," which featured a snack-loving man's relationship with his snack-loving pet goat. The totally crowd-sourced strategy featured the Doritos Crash the Super Bowl competition in which amateurs made hundreds of ads and consumers selected a finalist using Facebook. Similarly, prior to the Super Bowl, Audi asked consumers to select one of three endings for its ad. The one selected by consumers was seen on YouTube four million times following the Super Bowl game.[14]

In sum, using social media is a great way to induce consumers to expose themselves to ads and to build awareness and buzz about a product. This is critical when a thirty-second ad in the 2013 Super Bowl cost $3.8 million.[15]

The Attention Stage and Information Processing

When consumers pay attention to something, they allocate cognitive capacity to an object or task so information is processed consciously. Thus, **attention** is the amount of focus placed on and cognitive capacity allocated to a stimulus. When consumers attend to an advertisement, a public-relations piece of information, or a personal-selling communication, they're focusing their senses on the task. At the highest levels of attention, nothing else distracts from this focus.

Attention to information can occur either voluntarily or involuntarily. **Voluntary attention** happens when a consumer makes a decision to focus on a particular stimulus. Thus, when in a mall, a person can decide which store to enter. **Involuntary attention** occurs when there's something about the information or situation that causes a reflexive action in which the consumer, without thinking or conscious action, orients toward and focuses on the stimulus. Thus, in order to attract a consumer's attention, the marketer can use either of two broad strategies. Strategy 1 involves designing communications consumers want to experience voluntarily because the topic is important to them. Strategy 2 is to design communications that employ techniques to capture attention involuntarily. For example, as the demands of a task increase, such as driving a car fast, attention increases involuntarily. Similarly, if the information is very important to the consumer, he or she will focus attention on it voluntarily.[16] The next two subsections discuss voluntary and involuntary attention.

Attracting Voluntary Attention Common sense tells us consumers pay attention to the things that are important to them, and research supports this intuition. The concept of consumer involvement was developed to assess this motivational factor. **Consumer involvement** is the perceived personal importance and/or interest attached to the acquisition, consumption, and disposition of a good, service, or idea.[17] As involvement increases, consumers have greater motivation to attend to, comprehend, and elaborate on information salient to the purchase. The bottom line is that if consumers are highly involved in a particular product or issue, they're more likely to attend to communications relevant to that product or issue. Thus, if you want consumers to voluntarily attend to your message, it must contain information that's important and relevant to them.

Several factors influence the level of a consumer's involvement. They include: (1) the type of product under consideration, (2) the characteristics of the communication received by the consumer, (3) the characteristics of the situation within which the consumer is operating, and (4) the personality of the consumer. For example, as the product or service under consideration becomes more expensive, socially visible, and risky to purchase, a consumer's involvement in the purchase will increase. Similarly, communications such as fear appeals can also raise a consumer's involvement by arousing emotions.

Types of Consumer Involvement Researchers have identified two types of involvement.[18] **Situational involvement** occurs over a short time period and is associated with a specific situation, such as a need to replace a product that has broken (e.g., an automobile). In contrast, **enduring involvement** represents a longer commitment and concern with a product class. Thus, if a consumer consistently spends time thinking and reading about a product on a day-to-day basis, he or she is revealing enduring involvement. Based on the combination of situational involvement and enduring involvement, various involvement responses result. **Involvement response** refers to the level of complexity of information processing and the extent of decision making by a consumer.[19] Importantly, research indicates that the effects of situational involvement and enduring involvement add together. As a result, an even high number of involvement responses occur because the total level of involvement is equal to the enduring- and situational-involvement levels combined.[20]

Effects of High Involvement What happens when a consumer's involvement level increases? Evidence suggests that, under higher levels of involvement, consumers begin to process information in more depth. Along with the increased information processing, one sees a general increase in arousal levels, so consumers become more active and alert. The arousal may result in an increase in blood pressure, a change in brain wave patterns, a quickening of breathing, a slight sweating of the hands, and dilation of the pupils, among other things. One way of assessing the impact of an advertisement is to measure the arousal elicited when consumers view it. In order to assess arousal levels, market researchers employ devices that measure blood pressure, pupil dilation, brain wave patterns, and even the temperature of the eardrum.

As involvement increases, the amount of attention focused on a product or communication increases. Under high-involvement conditions, consumers also give more diligent consideration to information relevant to the particular decision.[21] This means consumers will think more about a decision when it is made under high-involvement circumstances. In addition, higher levels of involvement are likely to lead consumers to engage in a more extended decision process and move through each of the decision stages in a more thorough manner. Some authors have suggested the type of decision process diverges sufficiently in high- and low-involvement circumstances to warrant discussion of two categories of decision making—limited decision making in low-involvement circumstances and extended decision making in high-involvement circumstances.[22] We'll discuss high- and low-involvement decision making in Chapter 9.

When consumers are highly involved with a particular good, service, or idea, their attention shifts so that they seek out relevant information. In other words, consumers actively search out information that has personal relevance, and through the process of **selective attention**, consumers voluntarily focus attention on relevant information. For example, someone who's interested in buying a car, some furniture, or an expensive camera will actively seek information about the product. When reading newspapers, he or she will be on the lookout for advertisements and articles that deal with the product sought. Similarly, the individual interested in a particular brand of vehicle will notice the brand on the road more frequently. Conversely, if the marketing communication isn't perceived as matching a goal, the consumer will tend not to focus attention on it. Again, this is a major problem for advertisers on television, radio, and the Internet. Consumers may be exposed to the message but simply decide not to attend to the information contained in the communication because their involvement level is low.

Managerial principle 3.2
Gain attention by basing communications on issues and ideas about which the target market is highly involved.

In summary, the involvement concept is critical not only to understanding attention, it's also relevant to a number of other consumer topics. For example, a consumer's involvement level has important implications for understanding memory processes, decision-making processes, attitude formation and change, and word-of-mouth communication.[23] Consumer involvement will be discussed throughout the textbook.

Attracting Involuntary Attention   In addition to voluntary attention, attention can be placed upon a stimulus involuntarily. Involuntary attention occurs when a consumer is exposed to something surprising, highly positive, or highly negative. Such stimuli result in an autonomic response in which the person turns toward and allocates attention to it. This response, which the consumer can't control consciously, is called **orientation reflex**.[24] Because most communications to which consumers are exposed are unrelated to the immediate goals of the audience, marketers attempt to elicit the orientation reflex.

In order to elicit involuntary attention, marketers activate the orientation reflex by adroitly creating stimuli that surprise, threaten, reward, or violate the expectations of consumers. For example, consider a commercial for Travelers insurance company called "Lucky Rabbits Foot." The commercial begins with the line "This is Bailey, our first successful reattachment." Viewers then see a scientist in a white lab coat holding a rabbit. With uplifting music playing in the background, the commercial describes (tongue-in-cheek) how scientists are now successfully reattaching lucky rabbits feet to their rightful owners. The announcer says, "Thankfully, people everywhere have recognized that you don't need luck as long as you have the right insurance. We won't rest until every foot is returned to its rightful owner. Together, we can make a difference." The delightfully playful commercial violates expectations and surprises consumers. One can't help but be mesmerized by the artful silliness of the ad.

In addition to violating expectations, marketers can use movement to attract attention. Thus, on websites, highway billboards, and retail signs, one finds neon or LED lights that flash or give the appearance of movement.

Unusual sounds can also be effective. Television advertisers sometimes use distinctive nonverbal sounds to activate the orientation response. For example, ads for the financial corporation Shearson Lehman Brothers used a buzzing sound that grew louder as the commercial progressed. Executives claimed ad awareness increased by 50 percent with the use of the odd sound in the commercial. The ad agency that produced the commercial created the noise to mimic the sound of thinking in the ad campaign, which was called "Minds over Money." In another example, General Electric reported similar positive effects from its "beep ads" in which a symphony of peculiar beeps comes from digital kitchen appliances.[25]

Another stimulus factor that may influence attention is the size or magnitude of the stimulus. For example, all else equal, large-print advertisements are more apt to be attended to than small ones. Similarly, a loud television commercial is more likely to be processed than a quiet one. As the intensity of a stimulus (e.g., the volume of an ad) increases, the likelihood it will garner attention also increases. Advertisers, therefore, have an incentive to make their commercials as loud as possible without offending the consumer. Indeed, a common complaint by consumers is that television advertisements are louder than the programs they accompany. Although, by law, the maximum intensity of sound coming from a commercial can be no greater than that coming from a program, advertisers do take steps to create the sensation the loudness is greater, such as by recording the entire commercial near peak allowable sound levels.

Color can attract attention, particularly when it contrasts a sea of black and white print materials and consumers are in a low-involvement state.[26] Thus, graphic artists who employ the Gestalt principle of contrast increase the likelihood consumers will attend to an advertisement. Contrast occurs when a stimulus diverges substantially from surrounding background stimuli. A loud noise in a quiet room or a print ad with very little copy in a sea of verbose ads illustrates the concept of contrast. The De Beers print ad illustrates contrast in two ways. First, it's very simple, which will contrast with magazine copy. Second, the white letters and the glowing diamond stand out against the black background.

Attention is also influenced by the operation of two neurobiological systems.[27] First, the behavioral activation system (BAS) governs interest in achieving goals and obtaining

Managerial principle 3.3
Gain attention by creating stimuli that are large, colorful, move in some way, or create surprise.

This ad for diamonds by De Beers uses the contrast principle.

Managerial principle 3.4
Gain attention by creating stimuli that threaten or reward consumers.

rewards. When a stimulus activates the BAS, consumers focus attention on it in preparation to move toward it and embrace it. For example, most consumers view money as rewarding. As a result, communications that promise gaining wealth or saving money will attract attention. The second biological system is the behavioral inhibition system (BIS). It operates to help people avoid negative outcomes and negative stimuli. When the BIS is activated, it orients people toward the stimulus and creates a fight or flight response. Thus, if a consumer is afraid of something—perhaps getting skin cancer—the person will attend to communications that deal with this disease.

Finally, marketers can gain consumers' involuntary attention by placing ads in circumstances in which consumers have no choice but to attend to the information presented. In 2011, Facebook to become the most viewed website in the United States. The principle is the same, however. That is, when consumers go to their Facebook page, involuntary attention to ads occurs.[28] Table 3.1 summarizes how to elicit involuntary attention.

TABLE 3.1
How to Elicit Involuntary Attention

1.	Surprise the consumer.	5.	Increase the loudness of the sound.
2.	Make the stimulus move.	6.	Reward the consumer.
3.	Use color.	7.	Threaten the consumer.
4.	Increase the physical size.		

CHANGING A PRODUCT'S PRICE OR FEATURES

Consider the plight of a candy bar manufacturer such as Hershey Company. Suppose the price of chocolate suddenly skyrockets. Because chocolate is one of the costliest ingredients in the company's leading products, the sudden increase in price has a major impact on the company's profitability. One way of dealing with the problem is to increase price. But an increase in price may decrease demand for the product. Another option is to use less chocolate and substitute an artificial flavor for it. The problem here is consumers may not like the change in taste. Another option is to make the candy bar smaller and hope consumers can't tell the difference in size. Which option should the company select?

Similar issues are faced in numerous industries. For example, consider restaurants. When scientists discovered trans fats have negative health effects, public pressure forced restaurants to find a substitute for oil. The problem was one of taste—would the food taste as good? In addition, some large companies, such as McDonald's, use so much oil that finding adequate supplies of alternative oils was difficult. Similarly, consider the plight of auto manufacturers. In 2012, the price of gasoline approached $5.00 per gallon in some areas of the United States. As a result, auto companies had to decide whether to increase the mileage of their cars and trucks, a change that would increase manufacturing costs. For example, should GM spend an extra $100 per car to increase gas mileage from twenty-one miles per gallon to twenty-five miles per gallon, which would harm the car's performance? The answer to the question about changing a product depends on whether consumers can detect the difference and whether the difference is meaningful. These practical marketing questions can be answered by understanding concepts from the field of sensation.

The Study of Sensation

The study of **sensation** investigates how people detect and then react to the raw sensory information received through their sense organs. Thus, a manager at Hershey might want to know how much artificial flavoring can be added to a candy bar without consumers detecting it. Similarly, the manager might want to know how much difference in the amount of chocolate in a candy it takes before a consumer can detect a change in taste. The answers to these questions can be found by understanding two perceptual concepts—the absolute threshold and the difference threshold.

The **absolute threshold** is the level of intensity of a stimulus that can be detected 50 percent of the time. The **difference threshold**, which is also called the **just noticeable difference (JND)**, is the amount of change in the intensity of a stimulus that can be detected 50 percent of the time. The difference threshold has particular application to LO 3-2, which deals with consumer perceptions of differences, which we discuss below. The absolute threshold has application to LO 3-3 (influencing consumers without their awareness), which is discussed in the next section.

The Difference Threshold   As we just discussed, the just noticeable difference is the minimum amount of difference in the intensity of a stimulus that can be detected 50 percent of the time. The study of difference thresholds has important implications for marketing research, product development, and even pricing. For example, companies in the food industry are interested in creating products that give the optimum taste at the lowest cost.[29] In formulating products recipes, there's often a choice between two ingredients that may differ in price. The question is, will a change in ingredient create a just noticeable difference in the taste of the product?[30] For example, in 2013, the JND issue was faced by a chocolatier that made high-end cupcakes, cakes, and pies. Using high-quality ingredients (e.g., real butter), the chocolatier was losing money. The owner knew she'd have to either raise the price of her products or change to cheaper ingredients if she was going to stay in business. The situation had two key questions: (1) Would consumers perceive a taste difference if she used less expensive ingredients? and (2) Would an increase in price be sufficiently meaningful to decrease demand for her products?

One important aspect of the JND is it varies with the level of the stimulus. That is, as the absolute level of the stimulus increases, the size of the JND also increases. Discovered by the German scientist E. H. Weber, the relationship between the size of the stimulus intensity and the JND has become known as **Weber's law**, which states that as the intensity of the stimulus increases, the ability to detect a difference between the two levels of the stimulus decreases. Weber identified a formula that expresses these relationships:

$$JND = I \times K$$

I is the intensity level of the stimulus and K is a constant that gives the proportionate amount of change in stimulus level required for its detection.

The effects of the JND and Weber's law can be illustrated by an application to pricing. A rule of thumb retailers use is markdowns must be at least 20 percent before consumers recognize them.[31] This figure is equivalent to K, the constant in the equation for Weber's law. For example, if a diamond ring is priced at $5,000, it must be marked down by $1,000 for the sale to be meaningful (i.e., $5,000 × 0.20 = $1,000). In contrast, if the diamond were priced at $10,000, the markdown must be $2,000 for the sale to be effective. Thus, the JND increases in size proportionate to *K* as the dollar value of a purchase increases.

Information on absolute and difference thresholds may influence the packaging strategy of companies as well. Why does Campbell Soup Company package its pork and beans in a 20 3/4-ounce can while a major competitor uses a 21-ounce can? The reason may be consumers wouldn't notice the difference. Similarly, Bohemia lowered the quantity of beer in each bottle from twelve ounces to eleven. The cost savings was used to increase the ad budget and develop a fancier container. As a result, sales nearly doubled.[32]

On the other hand, the JND principle has been used to increase the size of portions as well as decrease them. After a twelve-month test, the candy company M&M/Mars found increasing the size of its candy bars increased sales by 20 to 30 percent. As a result, the company changed nearly its entire product line. The photo of canned peaches shows two cans of peaches that hold different quantities of the product while appearing to be the same size.

A Problem with Pricing and the JND   There can be a problem, however, in applying principles of sensation and perception, such as Weber's law, to consumer behavior issues. When applied to perceiving changes in taste, odor, sound, touch, or visual quality, the principles are appropriately used. In other cases, such as for pricing, the psychophysical processes don't match the problem being investigated. For example, Weber's law describes quite accurately the sensory impact of changes in the intensity of a stimulus, and it impacts the perception of taste, size, and smell. However, when applied to pricing, it's inappropriate to describe the processes in terms of a JND. The reason is the JND refers to the ability to detect a minimal level of change in stimulus. In contrast, the response to a change in price is based on perceptions of meaning rather than perceptions of sensations. Thus, from a sensory perspective, consumers can detect the 1-cent difference between a price of $5,000.00 and $5,000.01. However, the question is, is there a meaningful difference in price? The answer is no. In sum, the authors of this textbook prefer that, when applied to pricing issues, one shouldn't talk in terms of a JND. Rather, the phrase "just meaningful difference" (i.e., JMD) should be used.

An interesting example of the JMD occurred with the launch of the new iPad by Apple in 2012. Evolutionary, rather than revolutionary, the device included a number of changes, including better screen resolution and faster processing speed. On the other hand, the device's weight was increased by .11 pounds. The question was, would these changes be meaningful to consumers?

The JND and JMD concepts have important managerial implications. First, if you seek to raise the price of a product or

Two cans of peaches whose size difference falls within the JND.
Photo by John Mowen

change its composition so consumers don't notice the difference, the change should be within the JND or JMD. Second, if you want consumers to know you have a sale on the price of a product or have made a change you wish to advertise, the change in price or composition must be greater than the JND or JMD. For example, if you lowered the price of a product for a sale, you must decrease the price enough so it's meaningful to consumers and changes the level of demand for the product. If you make the mistake of insufficiently lowering the price, you'll simply decrease your profits because the quantity purchased won't change. Similarly, would the improvement in the resolution of the iPad screen and in the speed of its processor be sufficiently meaningful for consumers to invest in it when it cost $100 more than its predecessor?

As a final note, we should add that, practically speaking, it makes little difference to the marketing manager whether Weber's law is being applied correctly to pricing situations. Weber's law and its cousin, the just meaningful difference help the manager understand the relationship of the level of the stimulus to the amount of change required in the stimulus to make it noticeable—a concept that's critical to understanding how much to change a product or its price.

Managerial principle 3.5
When raising prices, keep the increase below consumers' JND.

Managerial principle 3.6
When lowering prices, make the increase greater than the target market's JMD.

INFLUENCING CONSUMERS WITHOUT THEIR KNOWLEDGE

A question that involves both practical and ethical issues concerns whether marketers can influence consumers without their knowing it. From a practical perspective, if marketers can employ techniques that surreptitiously influence consumer behavior, it will allow them to avoid public scrutiny—at least until they're caught. From an ethical perspective, is it moral to influence people without their awareness? An information-processing perspective provides two ways marketers either intentionally or unintentionally influence consumers— via preattention and subliminal perception. It should also be noted there are additional ways consumers can be influenced without their awareness—that is, through incidental learning and through behavioral learning processes. These will be discussed in Chapters 4 and 5.

Preattention

Researchers have discovered prior to consumers becoming consciously aware of something, it's processed in a preattention stage of information processing. In the preattention stage, people unconsciously and automatically scan the environment. Thus, **preattention** is an unconscious process in which consumers automatically scan the features of the environment. If a stimulus is sufficiently important or sufficiently strong, it will be automatically moved from preattention to attention. In the preattention stage, the information obtained is initially evaluated to determine whether it has sufficient importance to be further processed. If it does have sufficient importance, additional cognitive resources will be allocated to the stimulus, and the person will move into the attention stage of information processing.[33] In sum, preattention occurs between the time when the exposure stage occurs and when the consumer consciously attends to a stimulus.

One important finding is preattention processes can influence consumer feelings. In one research study, a pictorial ad was placed either to the left or the right of an accompanying editorial.[34] The consumer researcher found the respondents in the study liked the ad more when it was placed to the left of the editorial than when it was placed to the right of the editorial. The researcher proposed this occurred because the information contained in the ad would be transferred to the right hemisphere of the brain when the ad was placed to the left of editorial. The right hemisphere of the brain is responsible for forming holistic perceptions that directly impact emotions. While the respondents didn't consciously process the ad's placement, the effects of preconscious processing did influence their evaluations of the ad. In sum, the arrangement and placement of ads can influence consumer emotions without awareness.

Subliminal Perception

The term *subliminal* means below threshold. That is, when a stimulus is presented so its intensity is below an absolute threshold of awareness, consumers aren't consciously aware of it. As discussed earlier in the chapter, the absolute threshold is the lowest level at which a stimulus can be detected 50 percent of the time. This definition is different from that of the difference threshold. While the difference threshold deals with the amount of difference in the intensity of stimulus that's detectable, the absolute threshold deals with the absolute amount of the stimulus that's detectable. The absolute threshold is important to disaster officials as well as marketers. For example, how loud does a tornado or tsunami siren have to be for consumers inside a house to hear it? Knowing the absolute threshold can save lives. In a marketing context, an example would be, if I add a preservative to extend a product's shelf life, will consumers notice its taste?

The absolute threshold is also directly relevant to the controversial area of subliminal perception. **Subliminal perception** is defined as a process in which a stimulus is presented below the level of the absolute threshold yet subconsciously influences feelings and/or behaviors. Three types of subliminal stimulation have been identified: briefly presented visual stimuli, accelerated speech in low-volume auditory messages, and embedding or hiding sexual imagery or words in print advertisements.[35]

The controversial idea of subliminal advertising was highlighted in 1957, when audiences at a movie theater in New Jersey were exposed to messages presented briefly that said, "Drink Coca-Cola" and "Eat popcorn." The messages were superimposed on the movie and presented so quickly the audience didn't consciously realize they appeared. Although no evidence was presented, the marketing firm that created the messages claimed sales of the items increased dramatically. The media ran alarming headlines. The *New Yorker* magazine stated that people's minds had been "broken and entered." Others, however, saw potential in subliminal messages, and a radio stations began broadcasting subaudible messages that "TV's a bore."[36]

Does subliminal advertising work? According to one psychologist, the answer is "no, what you see is what you get."[37] He argues that subliminal stimuli are extremely weak and most certainly overridden by a host of other, more powerful messages. In addition, because people are generally in control of their overt responses to stimuli, they'll screen out attempts to affect undesired behavior.

Some evidence, however, has shown subliminal advertising can impact consumers. In one study, researchers investigated the effects of subliminal embeds on the ratings of ads by college students, who acted as simulated consumers. Two actual print ads were used, one for a popular cigarette and the other for a well-known scotch whiskey. After the stimuli were pointed out by the experimenters, students reported they could identify the representation of male genitals in the cigarette ad and the nude body of a woman in the liquor ad. A second version of each ad was created by having a professional photographer airbrush out the embedded material. Four other groups of students then evaluated the four ads. The results revealed the ratings differed between the control (airbrushed ads) and the embedded ads for the liquor advertisement having the female body, but not for the cigarette ad. A second study was run in which measures of autonomic arousal were taken. In this study, the students showed evidence of differences in arousal for both advertisements containing the embedded material.[38]

How does one explain the effects of subliminal advertisements? Two theories have been proposed.[39] **Incremental effects theory** states that a stimulus representation is gradually built in a person's nervous system over many presentations of a stimulus. At some point, the representation reaches a behavioral threshold and causes changes in the consumer's actions. However, the cause of the changes in actions is never recognized by the consumer.

The second theoretical approach is the **psychodynamic theory of arousal**. This theory assumes unconscious wishes to engage in some behavior may be activated by stimuli presented unconsciously. Thus, in the liquor advertisement, one must assume the students harbored an unconscious wish for sexual activity that was activated by the nude body embedded in the advertisement. The activation of this unconscious wish presumably influences the actual perception of the advertisement.

Absolut Vodka has fun with a subliminal embed.

In sum, research on subliminal perception indicates the idea shouldn't be dismissed. A recent article approached the issue from a neuroscience perspective. In the article, the researchers argued that subliminal perception isn't an either-or phenomenon. Rather, the cognitive awareness of stimuli is a continuum.[40] Thus, the focus of research should be on the effects of subliminal stimuli at various levels of awareness. Clearly, additional work is needed on the topic.

We conclude this section with a warning. Subliminal perception is controversial for two reasons. First, if subliminal persuasion is effective, it would be a way for unscrupulous marketers to clandestinely influence consumers. For example, were it possible for advertisers to embed in their thirty-second ads words whose sound is below the absolute threshold, these messages could covertly encourage consumers to purchase their products or, worse, engage in unethical or unlawful acts. Such actions would be deemed unethical by most people. The second controversial issue concerns whether subliminal perception actually impacts behavior. The authors of this text believe it's very unlikely subliminal stimuli can have a meaningful impact on behavior. The effects are too subtle, particularly when considered in relationship to the many overt means through which marketers can influence consumers.

Managerial principle 3.7
Subliminal perception has minimal impact on consumer behavior, and managers should avoid employing it for both practical and ethical reasons.

MAINTAINING CONSUMER INTEREST

Consumers can be fickle. A marketer may find customers are highly satisfied with a good or service and then discover many are defecting to competitors. The marketing term for this phenomenon is **spontaneous brand switching**. Consumers frequently switch brands, even when nothing indicates they're unhappy with the brand previously used. The phenomenon occurs most frequently with low-involvement products in which little difference exists between brands. The question for the marketer is, how can I inhibit spontaneous brand switching and keep customers interested in my product? One answer comes from an understanding of consumer-adaptation processes.

Consumer Adaptation

Everyone has experienced the process of **adaptation**. When first sitting in a hot bath, the steaming water may seem nearly unbearable. After a few minutes, however, the water will feel quite pleasant. The change in sensation didn't occur because the water got colder. It occurred because your nerve cells adapted to the water's temperature and no longer fired signals to the brain telling it the water was too hot. Adaptation occurs when an individual has repeated experience with a stimulus. Thus, **adaptation level** is the amount of the stimulus to which the consumer has become accustomed and represents a reference point to which changes in the level of the stimulus are compared. The adaptation level is related to spontaneous brand switching through its relation to the butterfly curve.

The Butterfly Curve   Have you ever wondered why fashions are constantly changing? Could it be because consumers enjoy seeing something different? The idea that something slightly different may be perceived more positively is supported by an effect called a butterfly curve. Illustrated in Figure 3.2, on the vertical axis is the degree of liking for a stimulus. The horizontal axis is the level of the stimulus and the position of the adaptation level. (The humps in the figure could look like the shape of a butterfly's wing.) The **butterfly curve** shows the preference for a stimulus is at its greatest level at points just higher or just lower than the adaptation level. Just to the right and left of the adaptation level, preference declines slightly because the person has become habituated to the stimulus. However, as the level of the stimulus moves too far from the adaptation level, the preference steadily decreases.[4]

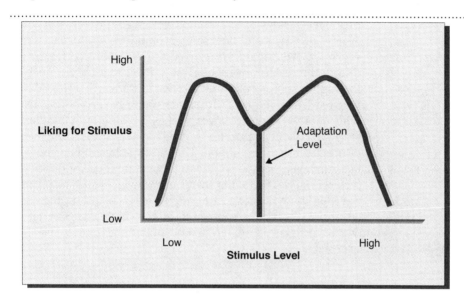

FIGURE 3.2
The Butterfly Curve

The butterfly curve nicely explains why fashion trends are constantly changing. Consumers quickly become adapted to a certain look, and the liking for it falls. Designers will then modify the current look in some relatively small way, and it will appear fresh and interesting because the stimulus has diverged from the adaptation level. The up-and-down movement of the hems of skirts over the years well illustrates the principle. Similarly, the widths of men's ties and lapels show the same tendency to change constantly.

The butterfly curve also suggests unusual fashion looks are adopted slowly because they are at first too far away from the adaptation level. For example, years ago, when Madonna first wore a bustier, the public was horrified. However, after several years, consumers adapted, and bustiers became familiar sights on dance floors and even in that fashion kingdom, the mall.

Similarly, many companies periodically change their logos and other corporate symbols to maintain a fresh look. For example, General Mills Inc. has frequently changed the look of its famous but fictitious cake-mix endorser, Betty Crocker. How was the new image of Betty Crocker chosen? As it turns out, a national contest was held and women were asked to send photos of themselves and write a statement saying how they embody the ideas of Betty. From the thousands of entrees, seventy-five photos were selected. All seventy-five photos were digitized and combined to form a multi-ethnic image. The resulting image reveals a somewhat familiar, though exotic, face. Take a second and consider where on the butterfly curve this stimulus resides.[42]

The ads using the Energizer Bunny keep changing in order to hold consumer interest.

Managerial principle 3.8
Keep people interested in your products by continually making incremental changes in the marketing mix.

So, how do you keep consumers interested in your product? Employ the ideas from adaptation and the butterfly curve. That is, you must make continual small changes to your product's contents, its packaging, and/or its promotion. Consumers quickly adapt to a certain look, style, or message. In order to keep a product fresh, marketers must continually vary the marketing mix. For example, while the formula for Ivory soap hasn't changed in more than 120 years, its packaging has undergone a series of revisions. Next, consider the product offerings of McDonalds, which continually introduces new products and new sales-promotions strategies. A few years ago, McDonald's improved the taste of its coffee. In addition, the restaurant regularly ties itself to a movie, such as the highly successful Shrek movies in the early 2000s. When you read this chapter, McDonald's will be promoting itself with another movie or sweepstakes of some type. Similarly, for years, the Energizer Bunny ads have used the same theme of the drum-banging rabbit. The message hasn't become boring, however, because of the highly creative use of dozens of different advertisements using humorous means to portray the idea the batteries last a long time. In addition, the company periodically improves the battery so its performance increases. The net result is a long-running advertising campaign that propelled the brand to become a leader in the marketplace.

MAKING PRODUCTS AESTHETICALLY PLEASING

Aesthetics is the field of study that deals with judgments and tastes concerning beauty. Marketers are increasingly recognizing the importance of aesthetics in the design and presentation of both goods and services.

The study of aesthetics is closely related to the process of perceptual organization, which occurs in the comprehension stage of information processing. As mentioned earlier in the chapter, in the comprehension stage, consumers first perceptually organize information and then interpret it in order to derive meaning. In the next subsection, we discuss interpretation processes and then show how they're critical for understanding the role of aesthetics in consumer behavior.

Perceptual Organization

In order to understand what makes a good, a store, or an advertisement aesthetically pleasing, one must have knowledge of how consumers perceptually organize information. **Perceptual organization** refers to the processes through which people perceive and make sense of the shapes, forms, figures, and lines in their visual world.

Much of the knowledge about perceptual organization comes from the efforts of the **Gestalt psychologists**. Active early in the twentieth century, these individuals identified the rules that govern how people make sense out of the disjointed shapes and forms to which they are exposed. **Gestalt** is the German word for "pattern" or "configuration." It denotes one of the basic principles of Gestalt psychology, which is the familiar phrase "the whole is greater than the sum of its parts." This is a simple but very powerful idea that has implications for performing market research. That is, it's impossible to understand completely how consumers perceive, interpret, and comprehend a product by obtaining evaluations of each of its individual components. Thus, an automobile is greater than the sum of its separate features. Porsche recognized this in the development of a new lightweight car. Their engineers recognized light cars are less safe. To solve the problem, they developed sophisticated computer programs that optimized the "whole vehicle rather than its separate parts."[43] Similarly, when measuring attitudes toward a car, one approach is to ask consumers to evaluate each separate feature of the car, such as its cost, its handling, its acceleration, and so forth. Gestalt psychologists would argue such a piecemeal approach fails to provide an understanding of how a consumer perceives the car as a whole.

Gestalt psychologists proposed a number of rules of perceptual organization, some of which are summarized in Figure 3.3. Many of the rules deal with how people decide what things go together. For example, the "rule of common fate" states that elements that move in the same direction are assumed to belong

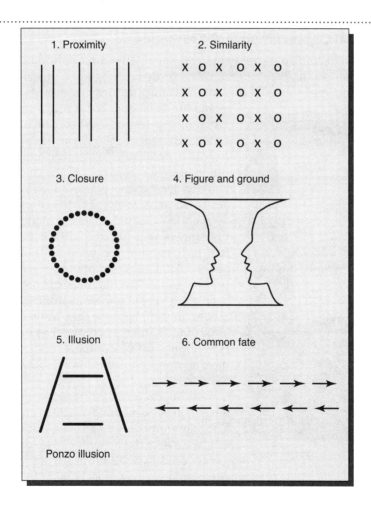

FIGURE 3.3
Rules of Perceptual Organization

to each other. Other rules apply to the problem of deciding what goes with what. These include rules of similarity, proximity, and closure.

Another area of Gestalt interest involves determining how people distinguish figure from ground in the visual world. Example 4 in Figure 3.3 illustrates figure-ground principles. At one moment, the reversible figure resembles two faces looking at each other. The next moment, it looks like a vase. The image switches back and forth because our brain can't decipher whether the figure is outside the lines (which causes two faces to be seen) or inside the lines (which causes a vase to be seen). In an advertising context, managers want their product to be the figure moving against the background of an ad because the figure attracts more attention than the background.

The Gestalt rules of perceptual organization are intentionally or unintentionally used by marketers to create print advertising, television advertising, package design, and even the design of buildings and spaces. When creating an ad, the artist will employ Gestalt principles to create the desired effect on the consumer. In particular, the artist should be attentive to the figure-ground concept. For the product to be noticed, it's important that it stand out from the background of the print ad. Similarly, if the goal is to associate the product with something else desirable—such as a popular celebrity endorser—the principles of proximity, closure, and common fate could be used.

Perceptual Organization and Aesthetics

Whether laying out advertisements, creating retail spaces, or building web pages, attention to aesthetics is critical. The aesthetic design of a product (i.e., how it looks, feels, and smells) represents a product feature that influences consumer buying behavior. For example, consider an automobile's features. When purchasing a car, consumers will consider features such as cost, handling, acceleration, comfort, and size. In addition, they'll consider how the car looks, how its seats feel, and even how it smells. Indeed, aesthetics are important to the design of goods as mundane as potato peelers and hammers. Consumers will pay more for a potato peeler that feels good in the hand and has a natural beauty to it. Even computers are being designed with aesthetics in mind. In particular, Apple has been able to command higher prices for its computers, in part, because they are more visually appealing than competitors. The aesthetic appeal of physical spaces has even been found to have an impact on consumers' satisfaction with a service.

An important question, however, concerns what makes something aesthetically pleasing. You have probably heard the phrase "Beauty is in the eye of the beholder." Gestalt psychologists would say the phrase is literally true, if perceptual organization is included as part of

The elegant lines of Apple Computer's products are in part responsible for the phenomenal success of the company.
Photo by John Mowen.

the eye. They argue principles of perceptual organization and, in particular, the concept of the "good figure" have a major impact on what people view as aesthetically pleasing. As a broad statement, a good figure is one that has order, stability, simplicity, and continuity. These ideas were supported by research on consumer reactions to logos.[44] Researchers found the logos people liked the most and were most easily recognized were harmonious, natural, and included repeated elements. Each idea is central to the concept of the good figure.

The idea of a good figure also applies to a ratio known as the **divine proportion**, or golden ratio. Since the time of the ancient Greek philosophers, artists have proposed beauty's found in the divine proportion, which is 1.618, an irrational number. How can one calculate the golden ratio? Look at the line shown in Figure 3.4. It's cut into two parts, A and B. The formula for the ratio, or phi, is a + b / a = a / b. Said another way, the point that cuts the line such that ratio of line A to line B is identical to the ratio of A to the entire line.

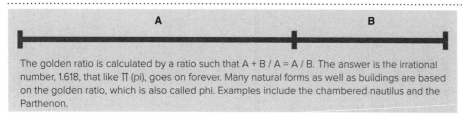

The golden ratio is calculated by a ratio such that A + B / A = A / B. The answer is the irrational number, 1.618, that like π (pi), goes on forever. Many natural forms as well as buildings are based on the golden ratio, which is also called phi. Examples include the chambered nautilus and the Parthenon.

FIGURE 3.4
The Golden Ratio

Philosophers and artists have proposed the divine proportion is highly pleasing to the eye. Many famous paintings (e.g., Salvador Dalí's *The Sacrament of the Last Supper*) and structures (e.g., the Parthenon in Greece) are argued to be based on golden ratio. Interestingly, the ratio is also found throughout nature (e.g., the curve of a chambered nautilus and the arrangements of seeds in sunflowers). It's also found in the angles of the Pentagon and the famous Fibonacci series of numbers (i.e., 1, 2, 3, 5, 8, 13, 21, etc.) created by adding the last two numbers to form the third. The wildly popular book and movie *The Da Vinci Code* prominently feature the Fibonacci series.

Consumer products are even designed around the golden ratio. For example, Twitter's creative director, Doug Bowman, designed its Flickr page around the golden ratio. Here's how he described it: "To anyone curious about #NewTwitter proportions, know that we didn't leave those ratios to chance. This, of course, only applies to the narrowest version of the UI. If your browser window is wider, your details pane will expand to provide greater utility, throwing off these proportions. But the narrowest width shows where we started, ratio-wise."[45]

Managerial principle 3.9
Aesthetically designed products and spaces increase positive feelings among consumers and can be created by adhering to Gestalt principles of organization.

THE EFFECTS OF SYMBOLS

As noted earlier, interpretation is the second component of the comprehension stage of information processing. In the **interpretation process**, people draw on their experiences, knowledge, and expectations to attach meaning to a stimulus. Understanding the factors that influence interpretation is critical for marketers. For example, researchers have found when people fail to correctly interpret an advertisement, they're less persuaded by it.[46]

The adroit use of symbols is one means by which marketers influence the interpretation process. How can a movie studio symbolically describe the amount of nudity on the cover of a DVD? The answer is to use symbols. For example, when the NC-17 video for the movie *Showgirls* was released, the video box showed a "curve of flesh running from a woman's head to her toes." On the box of an R-rated alternative, however, "the skin extended only through the model's cleavage."[47] The length of the curve symbolized the extent of nudity shown in the two versions of the film.

In this section, we analyze the effects of symbols from three perspectives. First, we discuss symbols from the perspective of the field of **semiotics**, which analyzes symbols and their meanings. Second, we discuss how marketers can employ symbols to influence the expectations of consumers. In turn, expectations strongly influence how consumers interpret stimuli. Finally, we discuss the price-quality relationship and how price can act as a symbol that sets expectations as to the quality of a product.

Semiotics

Researchers in the field of semiotics analyze how people obtain meaning from signs. **Signs** are the words, gestures, pictures, products, and logos used to communicate information from one person to another. Even nonverbal sounds can communicate meaning. For example, Harley-Davidson attempted to trademark the distinctive sound made by its motorcycles. The low, guttural growl of Harley bikes has been described as sounding like a growling animal saying, "Potato-potato-potato." The spokesperson for the company said, "A lot of owners tell us they buy a Harley just for the sound." Of course, the sound symbolizes much more than the motorcycle. It also stands for the Harley-Davidson image of macho, nonconformist, independent men and women. Competitors fought the petition in court because the possibility of trademarking sounds could open up a Pandora's box of problems. As one critic said, "How about Rice Krispies? Do you think you can trademark the snap, crackle, pop?"[48]

The discipline of semiotics has been studied in one form or another since before the time of Socrates.[49] Indeed, some have argued what sets the human species apart from others is its ability to adroitly use and manipulate symbols.[50] The field is highly relevant to the entire area of promotional strategy. It's through the use of various symbols or signs that information about a product or service is communicated to consumers.

The study of semiotics is an important aspect of the experiential perspective on consumer behavior. In order to understand how people emotionally react to symbols in the environment, one must gain an understanding of the shared meanings of various signs. Semiotics has relevance to a number of consumer behavior areas that will be discussed later in the book, including the use of Freudian symbolism in advertising, the utilization of symbols to express one's self-concept, and cross-cultural communications. Researchers have also found

The Eskimo Joe's logo symbolizes cold beer and good times.

meaning is, in part, determined by the cultural context within which the sign is embedded. Thus, a sign in one culture may have an entirely different meaning in another culture. For example, associating animals with products is done frequently and effectively in the United States. However, in some Asian cultures, the practice is viewed negatively. Advertisements by an optical company showing cute little animals wearing eyeglasses failed miserably in Thailand because animals symbolize a lower form of life among many people in the Thai culture.

The field of semiotics has particular importance in marketing communications. Marketing and advertising managers must be alert to the use of symbols and how their target market will interpret them. Indeed, researchers have described advertising as "the modern substitute for myth and ritual." In a comment on the culture of the United States, they proposed, "Advertising uses semiotics to give meaning to products for a culture whose dominant focus is consumption."[51]

The meaning of signs is learned early in life as a result of people's general acculturation. The ability to recognize the social implications of consumption choices is minimal among preschoolers. By the second grade, however, children can make inferences about what it means to purchase a Cadillac versus a Mercedes or buy a new, modern house versus an older, traditional house. By the sixth grade, these skills are almost fully developed. Interestingly, college students show the greatest extent of consumption stereotyping, which then weakens with age.[52]

Semiotics has particular application to the positioning of brands. For example, colleges and universities are currently working to refine and, in some cases, change their logos and mascots. As described in the university trade publication the *Chronicle of Higher Education*, universities are attempting to "create a catchy symbol that paints a thousand words about the college and entices people to buy shirts and notebooks bearing the emblem." As one college official said, "[A distinctive logo] sets an institution apart in the eyes of alumni, donors, and students." In addition to positioning a university, logos can bring in millions of dollars through the sale of T-shirts, hats, and other memorabilia. The use of the logos can also be licensed to vendors, typically for about $1.00 per use (i.e., $1.00 of the cost of a T-shirt goes to the university for the use of its logo.) When Villanova University updated its logo to a more-aggressive-looking wildcat, profits from licensing fees jumped nearly 600 percent.[53]

Managerial principle 3.10
Carefully select symbols to communicate the desired meaning to the appropriate target market.

The Role of Expectations

During and after attention to a stimulus, consumers interpret information to gain an understanding of what it means and how to react to it. In this interpretation phase, people retrieve knowledge about the stimulus from long-term memory, including expectancies of what may or may not happen and what's appropriate or inappropriate behavior. Importantly, these expectancies will differ from person to person. As noted earlier in the chapter, one problem for marketers is consumers may interpret the same stimulus differently. Classic illustrations of differences in interpretation can be found in cross-cultural marketing. For example, differences in the meaning of colors can be found throughout the world. Thus, yellow flowers create expectations of death in Mexico, whereas they create expectations of infidelity in France.[54]

Formally stated, **expectations** are a person's prior beliefs about what should happen in a given situation. The expectations may emerge from the effects of symbols or from the past associations a consumer has learned. For instance, expectations resulting from learned associations created problems for Adolph Coors Company Some time ago, the company decided to change the label on its flagship brand from "Banquet Beer" to "Original Draft." The change was made in response to Miller Brewing Company's successful new entry of "Genuine Draft" into the market. The problem was many Coors drinkers in the Southwest believed the change in the slogan to be associated with a changed taste of the beer. As one Coors executive explained, "We tried to convince them it was the same product, and they'd say, 'Oh, no it isn't.'" With a change in the label, Coors drinkers expected a change in the beverage. As a result of the expectation, they perceived a change in taste. When Coors changed the label back to the old version, a Coors distributor described customers as being elated and saying, "You brought it back just for me?" His response to each was, "You bet I did, old buddy."[55]

Managerial principle 3.11
Perform market research to identify the expectations consumers have regarding your product, and then change the marketing mix as necessary to influence these expectations.

Market researchers must be concerned with assessing the impact of consumer expectations on their evaluations of marketing stimuli. One study vividly illustrated how the perception of taste can be influenced by visual symbols that influence taste expectations. In the study, the color of vanilla pudding was made either dark brown, medium brown, or light brown by adding a tasteless and odorless food coloring. Respondents rated the puddings on a variety of scales. About 62 percent of study participants rated the dark-colored pudding to have the best chocolate flavor, even though there was no chocolate flavor associated with the product. The lighter-colored puddings were rated as creamier than the dark pudding. As the authors of the article stated, "It's the consumer's subjective perception of the product that counts, not the product's objective reality."[56] Other researchers have found coloring food in unexpected colors (e.g., dyeing potatoes blue) can make people physically ill.[57]

Expectations and the Price-Quality Relationship   An understanding of consumer expectations should also influence pricing strategies. As basic economic principles suggest, in most cases, the higher the price of a product, the less likely a consumer is to buy it. However, in some circumstances, consumers develop expectations of a **price-quality relationship**. Within a certain price range of a product, consumers may expect higher prices are indicative of greater product quality.[58] The price-quality relationship is probably learned over time through such aphorisms as "you get what you pay for." One summary of the evidence on the price-quality relationship gave the following occasions when price may be used to indicate the quality of a product:

1. The consumer has some confidence that price and quality are associated.
2. Real or perceived quality variations occur among brands.
3. Actual quality is difficult to judge through objective means or through brand name or store image.
4. Larger differences in price have a greater impact on perceived quality differences than smaller price differences.
5. The consumer is evaluating familiar rather than unfamiliar brands.[59]

Importantly, the more information consumers receive about a product's characteristics, the less price is used as a quality indicator. In addition, researchers have found perceived quality and perceived price combine to influence the perceived value of the brand. In this case, however, the higher the price of the product, the lower the perceived value. Thus, **perceived value** can be defined as the trade-off consumers make between perceived quality and perceived price when evaluating a brand.[60]

   In sum, in certain narrowly defined situations, a price-quality relationship is found in which consumers infer a product's quality from its price. However, a higher price will also lower the perceived value of a brand.[61] The implication for managers is that extreme care should be taken prior to raising prices as a means of increasing sales. A second implication is that the marketer should be highly attuned to adding symbols consumers interpret as indicative of quality if the plan is to use a high-price strategy. For example, adding gold or silver foil to the wrapping of a candy bar symbolizes exclusivity and high-end ingredients. When combined with a higher price, consumers are more likely to perceive a price-quality relationship and purchase the product.

Managerial principle 3.12
Raising the price of a product can increase the perception of quality, particularly if combined with the use of signs that symbolize quality.

MANAGERIAL IMPLICATIONS

The consumer behavior concepts that emerge from the study of perceptual processes have a number of managerial applications. They are identified within the RESPonsive Marketing principles.

Research

In order to assess the level of consumer involvement with a brand as well as determine the degree of exposure, attention, and comprehension of communications, marketing research is required. For example, when changing the size or composition of a food product, investigations into the JND are needed. Similarly, researchers can determine the meanings consumers derive from the symbols attached to products and organizations. Research can also identify the expectations consumers have regarding the characteristics of a product.

Environmental Analysis

It's critical to examine the competitive environment in order to understand consumer expectations and to set prices. For example, expectations are determined not only by what your company is doing but also by competitors' actions. So, if a competitor makes a significant improvement in a product's design, this will influence consumer expectations for your product's design as well. Similarly, while the price-quality relationship may allow you to charge premium prices for your product, if a competitor can demonstrate similar quality to your product at a lower price, your strategy won't work. An example is found in Hyundai Motor Company car sales. Because its vehicles are less expensive than competitors while, at the same time, having equal or better quality, Hyundai's US sales rose over 19 percent in 2010.[62]

Segmentation

Consumers' level of involvement with a product category is an important segmentation variable for marketers to consider. Markets can be divided into groups of consumers who are homogeneous with respect to their level of enduring involvement with a product. Based on their level of involvement, the degree of complexity of marketing communications, the distribution of the brand, and even the attributes and pricing of the brand may be influenced.

Positioning and Differentiation

The areas of semiotics and consumer involvement have implications for product positioning and differentiation. Within the domain of semiotics, the symbols and signs linked to a brand or organization provide meanings consumers interpret and comprehend. For example, the names given to brands frequently make use of symbols. Consider the following vehicle brand names: Mustang, Avalanche, Beretta, Tahoe, Avenger, Testarossa, and Viper. What meanings and images are associated with these symbols?

Products can also be positioned and differentiated based on the level of consumer involvement with the product category. For example, kitchen appliances are targeted to consumers with different levels of involvement with cooking. KitchenAid mixers costing in excess of $400 are promoted to people for whom cooking and baking are extremely important. Compare this with Black and Decker mixers costing less than $40.

Marketing Mix

Within the marketing mix, the concepts identified in the chapter have particular application to promotional strategy. Issues include how to induce consumers to be exposed to communications, to attend to the messages, and to comprehend the meanings in the desired manner. Messages such as fear appeals can be designed to influence the level of involvement of the target market. As described in the chapter, concepts from Weber's law have application to the pricing of products. The involvement level of consumers can influence strategies used to distribute brands. Concepts related to Weber's law and the JND can be applied to product development—particularly when changes in the size or composition of the product are considered.

SUMMARY

Information processing is the process through which consumers are exposed to information, attend to it, comprehend it, place it in memory, and retrieve it for later use. Several areas are closely related to the study of information processing. These include the study of consumer involvement and the processes of exposure, attention, comprehension, and memory. (Because of its importance, Chapter 4 will focus on memory processes.) In addition, the field of semiotics has strong relevance to the study of comprehension processes. By understanding these fields of study, you'll be able to answer the six managerial questions posed in the chapter by the learning objectives.

How can consumers be influenced to pay attention to messages?

In order to influence consumers to attend to messages, they first must be exposed to them. Exposure refers to the process through which consumers initially receive information through their senses. Advertisers must be concerned with how they can prevent consumers from selectively exposing themselves to commercials through zapping. An important aspect of the exposure process is the study of sensation. Sensations are the immediate impressions left by the firing of nerve fibers in response to the physical stimulation of the senses.

The study of attention is another important area of information processing. Voluntary attention involves the consumer in actively searching out information to achieve some type of goal. Through selective attention, consumers focus on stimuli that match their goals. Involuntary attention occurs when a consumer is exposed to something surprising, novel, or unexpected. Through the orientation reflex, people will focus attention on such a stimulus in order to comprehend its nature.

Consumer involvement refers to the level of perceived personal importance and/or interest evoked by a stimulus in a specific situation. Such situational involvement will change as the person, product, situation, and communications change. In contrast, enduring involvement refers to a longer-term commitment and concern with a product class. In order to gain consumers' attention, marketers should create messages that increase consumer involvement.

How much should a product's price and features be changed?

For consumer researchers, important aspects of the study of sensation include investigation of absolute and differential thresholds. An understanding of these areas will guide decisions as to how much to change a product's price or features.

Can consumers be influenced without their awareness?

Preattention is the process through which individuals unconsciously analyze information for its relevance and importance. Research has found preattention processes can influence consumers' feelings without their awareness. Through subliminal perception, marketers may be able to influence consumers. Subliminal perception occurs when consumers receive information that's below the absolute threshold. However, subliminal perception is likely to have minimal effects on consumers. In addition, there are serious ethical issues in its use.

How can marketers maintain consumer interest in their products?

A problem for marketers occurs when consumers spontaneously switch brands. This can occur when consumers become adapted to the product they've been using. The butterfly curve suggests marketers should frequently make small changes in their promotional strategy and products in order to keep consumers interested in their offerings.

What factors influence how aesthetically pleasing a product is?

Aesthetics concerns judgments and tastes regarding beauty. Knowledge of the comprehension stage of information processing provides marketers with information on how to make their product and their promotions more aesthetically pleasing. Comprehension refers to how consumers organize and interpret information. Perceptual organization refers to the process of how people make sense of the shapes and lines in the visual world. Knowledge of the Gestalt rules of perceptual organization and of how to create good forms will assist marketers in creating aesthetic products and communications. An understanding of the golden ratio is also an important component of understanding aesthetics. Marketers must recognize different people can perceive the same stimulus in quite divergent ways. Such perceptual differences can result from variations in expectancies and the particular ways in which different people organize information.

How do symbols influence consumers?

Marketers can use culturally defined symbols to influence consumers. The field of study devoted to understanding symbols and the meanings people obtain from signs is called semiotics. Signs are the words, gestures, pictures, products, and logos used to communicate information from one person to another.

KEY TERMS

absolute threshold	Gestalt psychologists	price-quality relationship
adaptation	incremental effects theory	psychodynamic theory of
adaptation level	information	arousal
aesthetics	information process	selective attention
attention	interpretation process	selective exposure
attention stage	involuntary attention	semiotics
butterfly curve	involvement	sensation
comprehension stage	involvement response	signs
consumer involvement	just noticeable difference (JND)	situational involvement
difference threshold	memory	spontaneous brand switching
divine proportion	orientation reflex	subliminal perception
enduring involvement	perception	voluntary attention
expectations	perceptual organization	Weber's law
exposure stage	perceived value	zapping
Gestalt	preattention	zipping

REVIEW QUESTIONS

1. Define the concepts of information and information processing.
2. Distinguish the concepts of exposure, attention, and comprehension stages.
3. What is meant by consumer involvement?
4. What are the types of consumer involvement? What happens when consumers are in a high-involvement state?
5. Briefly describe what happens during the exposure stage of information processing.
6. What does the study of sensation involve?
7. Can subliminal perception have an impact on consumers? Why or why not?
8. What are absolute and difference thresholds?
9. What's meant by the concepts of selective exposure and attention?
10. Define and give a marketing example of Weber's law. Why is it better to use the term *just meaningful difference* rather than *just noticeable difference*?
11. What's meant by adaptation level? How does it relate to the butterfly curve?

12. What are the two types of attention?
13. What happens during the comprehension stage of information processing?
14. What's the relationship between expectations and interpretation?
15. Identify five of the six principles of perceptual organization discussed in the chapter.
16. What's meant by the price-quality relationship?
17. What's meant by the term *semiotics*?

DISCUSSION QUESTIONS

1. Consumer involvement is influenced by the product, the situation, the communication received, and the person. Give two examples each of high- and low-involvement products, high- and low-involvement situations, and high- and low-involvement communications. Give an example of a case in which you are or were highly involved with a product and a specific acquaintance isn't or wasn't highly involved. How does this affect information processing for the two of you?

2. Select three products with different prices, ranging from less than $1 to thousands of dollars. For each product, indicate what you consider to be the JND for a sale price. To what extent do you find these JNDs exemplify Weber's law?

3. To what extent do you think clothing designers utilize the concept of the adaptation level? Would it make a difference in their behavior if they understood the concept of the butterfly curve? Explain.

4. Select three print advertisements. Identify how each one makes use of stimulus factors to gain your attention.

5. Using the same three advertisements, identify as many examples as you can of perceptual organization concepts used in the ads.

6. Look through magazines that contain cigarette and liquor advertisements. Find an example of the possible use of a subliminal message in an ad. In your opinion, was the subliminal message placed there deliberately?

7. Conduct interviews with five of your friends. In these interviews, identify cases in which these individuals have used price as an indicator of quality. To what extent do these cases match the occasions discussed in the chapter when price is most frequently used as an indicator of quality?

8. Watch a popular television show, such as *The Big Bang Theory*. Discuss how consumer products or services were used as symbols in order to help develop the plot of the show.

9. Go through one or more popular magazines and carefully examine the print advertisements. Identify three examples of symbols used in the ads.

ENDNOTES

[1] N. E. Boudette and N. Chirouzu, "Car Makers' Boom Years Now Look Like a Bubble," *Wall Street Journal*, May 20, 2008, 1, 17.

[2] "China 2010 Auto Sales Reach 18 Million, Extend Lead," *Bloomberg Business*, January 1, 2010, accessed January 10, 2011, http://www.bloomberg.com/news/2011-01-10/china-2010-auto-sales-reach-18-million-extend-lead-update1-.html. Downloaded January 10, 2011.

[3] J. N. Gartner, "Supercomputers Speed Car Design," *Wired*, April 26, 2004, http://www.wired.com/cars/coolwheels/news/2004/04/63185.

[4] N. Wiener, "Cybernetics in History," in *Modern Systems Research for the Behavioral Scientist*, ed. W. Buckley (Chicago: Aldine, 1968), 31–36.

[5] A. Markels and M. Murray, "Call It Dumbsizing: Why Some Companies Regret Cost-Cutting," *Wall Street Journal*, May 14, 1996, A1, A6.

[6] Stuart Elliott, "Mr. Peanut's New Look? Old School," *New York Times*, November 7, 2010, accessed December 29, 2015, http://www.nytimes.com/2010/11/08/business/media/08adco.html?_r=1&pagewanted=print.

[7] B. Whalen, "$6 Billion Down the Drain!" *Marketing News*, September 14, 1984, 1, 37.

[8] "Background on Zapping," *Marketing News*, September 14, 1984, 36.

[9] Ibid.

[10] Joshua Brustein, "Watching the Thrills (and Only the Thrills)," *New York Times*, March 13, 2011, 4.

[11] R. Alsop, "Coming Attractions: TV Ads at Movie Houses Everywhere," *Wall Street Journal*, July 3, 1986, 17.

[12] R. L. Hotz, "Decoding Our Chatter," *Wall Street Journal*, October 1, 2011, C1–C2.

[13] Zak Stambor, "Social Media Advertising Grows at the Expense of Other Channels, *Internet Retailer*, accessed March 7, 2013, http://www.internetretailer.com/2013/01/30/social-media-advertising-grows-expense-other-channels.

[14] Constantine von Hoffman, "Social Media Transforming Super Bowl Advertising," *CBS MoneyWatch*, accessed March 7, 2013, http://www.cbsnews.com/8301-505123_162-57566926/social-media-transforming-super-bowl-advertising.

[15] R. Grenoble, "Super Bowl Ads Spot to Cost Record $4 Million in 2013", Huff Post Business, Captured 1-4-2016, http://www.huffingtonpost.com/2013/01/04/cost-of-super-bowl-ad-2013_n_2410036.html

[16] D. Kahneman, *Attention and Effort* (Englewood Cliffs, NJ: Prentice Hall, 1973). This section relies heavily on ideas from this classic book.

[17] R. L. Celsi and J. C. Olson, "The Role of Involvement in Attention and Comprehension Processes," *Journal of Consumer Research* 15 (September 1988): 210–224. See also A. Greenwald and C. Leavitt, "Audience Involvement in Advertising: Four Levels," *Journal of Consumer Research* 11 (June 1984): 581–592. For a general review of the strength of involvement effects, see C. Costley, "Meta Analysis of Involvement Research," in *Advances in Consumer Research*, vol. XV, ed. M. Houston (Provo, UT: Association for Consumer Research, 1988), 554–562.

[18] M. Richins and P. H. Bloch, "After the New Wears Off: The Temporal Context of Product Involvement," *Journal of Consumer Research* 13 (September 1986): 280–285.

[19] M. Richins, P. H. Bloch, and E. F. McQuarrie, "How Enduring and Situational Involvement Combine to Create Involvement Responses," *Journal of Consumer Psychology* 1, no. 2 (1992): 143–153.

[20] Ibid.

[21] R. E. Petty, J. T. Caccioppo, and D. Schumann, "Central and Peripheral Routes to Advertising Effectiveness: The Moderating Role of Involvement," *Journal of Consumer Research* 10 (September 1983): 135–146.

[22] H. Krugman, "The Impact of Television in Advertising: Learning Without Involvement," *Public Opinion Quarterly*, 30, 583-596.

[23] J. W. Park and M. Hastak, "Memory-Based Product Judgments: Effects of Involvement at Encoding and Retrieval," *Journal of Consumer Research* 21 (December 1994): 534–547.

[24] Ibid.

[25] S. Siwolop, "You Can't (Hum) Ignore (Hum) That Ad," *Businessweek*, September 21, 1987, 56.

[26] P. S. Schindler, "Color and Contrast in Magazine Advertising," *Psychology and Marketing* 3, no. 2 (1986): 69–78. See also J. Meyers-Levy and L. A. Peracchio, "Understanding the Effects

of Color: How the Correspondence between Available and Required Resources Affects Attitudes," *Journal of Consumer Research* 22 (September 1995): 121–138.

[27] J. A. Updegraff, S. L. Gable, and S. E. Taylor, "What Makes Experiences Satisfying? The Interaction of Approach-Avoidance Motivations and Emotions in Well-Being," *Journal of Personality and Social Psychology* 91, no.4 (2004): 686–697.

[28] Alex Sherman, "Facebook Passes Google as Most Visited US Site," *Boston Globe*, January 1, 2011, accessed December 29, 2015, http://www.boston.com/business/technology/articles/2011/01/01/facebook_passes_google_as_most_visited_us_site/.

[29] D. Stipp, "A Flavor Analyst Should Never Ask, 'What's for Lunch?'" *Wall Street Journal*, August 3, 1988, 1, 10.

[30] B. Buchanan, M. Givon, and A. Goldman, "Measurement of Discrimination Ability in Taste Tests: An Empirical Investigation," *Journal of Marketing Research* 24 (May 1987): 154–163.

[31] R. L. Miller, "Dr. Weber and the Consumer," *Journal of Marketing* (January 1962): 57–61.

[32] J. Koten, "Why Do Hot Dogs Come in Packs of Ten and Buns in Eights or Twelves?" *Wall Street Journal*, September 21, 1984, 1, 26.

[33] C. Janiszewski, "Preattentive Mere Exposure Effects," *Journal of Consumer Research* 20 (December 1993): 376–392.

[34] Ibid.

[35] Ibid.

[36] T. E. Moore, "Subliminal Advertising: What You See Is What You Get," *Journal of Marketing* 46 (Spring 1982): 38–47.

[37] Ibid.

[38] W. Kilbourne, S. Painton, and D. Ridley, "The Effect of Sexual Embedding on Responses to Magazine Advertisements," *Journal of Advertising* 14, no. 2 (1985): 48–56.

[39] J. L. Saegert, "Why Marketing Should Quit Giving Subliminal Advertising the Benefit of the Doubt," *Psychology and Marketing* (Summer 1987): 107–120.

[40] Stephen Wiens, "Subliminal Emotion Perception in Brain Imaging: Findings, Issues, and Recommendations," *Progress in Brain Research* 156 (2006): 105–121.

[41] F. Hansen, *Consumer Choice Behavior* (New York: Collier Macmillan, 1972).

[42] S. E. Stewart, "My Years with Betty," *Wall Street Journal*, July 5, 1996, A6.

[43] "Make Mine a Porsche Lite," *Businessweek*, October 4, 1999, 6.

[44] P. W. Henderson and J. A. Cote, "Guidelines for Selecting or Modifying Logos," *Journal of Marketing* 62 (April 1998): 14–30. Similar findings were also obtained for typeface design. See P. W. Henderson, J. L. Giese, and J. Cote, "Impression Management Using Typeface Design," *Journal of Marketing* 68 (October 2004): 60–72.

[45] Brenna Ehrlich, "New Twitter Design Based on the Golden Ratio," *Mashable*, accessed December 29, 2015, http://mashable.com/2010/09/29/new-twitter-golden-ratio.

[46] D. W. Stewart, "The Moderating Role of Recall, Comprehension, and Brand Differentiation on the Persuasiveness of Television Advertising," *Journal of Advertising Research* 25 (March–April 1986): 43-47.

[47] Ibid.

[48] A. D. Wilde, "Harley Hopes to Add Hog's Roar to Its Menagerie of Trademarks," *Wall Street Journal*, June 23, 1995, B1.

[49] D. Mick, "Consumer Research and Semiotics: Exploring the Morphology of Signs, Symbols, and Significance," *Journal of Consumer Research* 13 (September 1986): 196–213.

[50] K. Boulding, *The Image* (Ann Arbor, MI: University of Michigan Press, 1956), 44.

[51] R. Zakia and M. Nadin, "Semiotics, Advertising, and Marketing," *Journal of Consumer Marketing* 4 (Spring 1987): 6.

[52] R. Belk, K. Bahn, and R. Mayer, "Developmental Recognition of Consumption Symbolism," *Journal of Consumer Research* 9 (June 1982): 4–17.

[53] J. L. Nicklin, "Marketing by Design," *Chronicle of Higher Education*, March 22, 1996, A33, A34.

[54] E. T. Hall, *The Hidden Dimension* (New York: Doubleday, 1966).

[55] M. Charlier, "Beer Drinkers in Texas, California Don't Swallow Change in Coors Label," *Wall Street Journal*, December 29, 1988, B4.

[56] G. Tom, T. Barnett, W. Lew, and J. Selmants, "Cueing the Consumer: The Role of Salient Cues in Consumer Perception," *Journal of Consumer Marketing* 4 (Spring 1987): 23–27.

[57] M. Tysoe, "What's Wrong with Blue Potatoes?" *Psychology Today* 19 (December 1985): 6, 8.

[58] Frank Kardes, Steven S. Posavac, Maria L. Cronley, and Paul M. Herr, "Consumer Inference," in *Handbook of Consumer Psychology*, ed. Curtis P. Haugtvedt, Paul M. Herr, and Frank R. Kardes (Mahwah, NJ: Erlbaum, 2008), 165–191.

[59] K. B. Monroe and A. R. Rao, "Testing the Relationship between Price, Perceived Quality, and Perceived Value." Paper presented at the Association for Consumer Research Annual Conference, Cambridge, MA, October 9–11, 1987.

[60] T. Z. Chang and A. R. Wildt, "Price, Product Information, and Purchase Intention: An Empirical Study," *Journal of the Academy of Marketing Science* 22 (Winter 1994): 16–27.

[61] It should also be noted that different consumers form divergent beliefs about the relationship between price and quality. For example, see K. H. Smith and N. Chinna Natesan, "Consumer Price-Quality Beliefs: Schema Variables Predicting Individual Differences," in *Advances in Consumer Research*, vol. 26, ed. E. Arnould and L. M. Scott (Provo, UT: Association for Consumer Research, 1999), 562–568.

[62] Timothy Cain, "Hyundai USA Sales Figures and Percentage Growth in 2010," *Good Car Bad Car*, accessed December 29, 2015, http://www.goodcarbadcar.net/2011/01/hyundai-usa-sales-figures-and.html.

4

Information Processing: Memory and Consumer Knowledge

Learning Objectives:

1. How do the types of memory affect consumers' responses to communications?

2. How does consumer knowledge influence brand perceptions?

3. How can marketers keep consumers from forgetting?

4. How do consumers' feelings affect memory?

Although Procter & Gamble (P&G) slit its traditional advertising budget by a whopping 14 percent in 2014, the company still spent $2.64 billion that year.[1] If consumers fail to remember the images and words from these communications, P&G's investment will have been wasted.[2]

A key factor hampering our memory of marketing communications is the sheer number of messages consumers receive each day. Estimates range from a low of 287 to a high of 5,000 messages per day.[3] Regardless of the actual number, the volume of messages creates information overload.

As important as the total number of messages we receive is the question of whether they contain negative information about a product. A classic example occurred when a US Department of Agriculture (USDA) employee gave the name "pink slime" to ammonia hydroxide-treated ground beef, an inexpensive filler made from leftover beef

trimmings that's chemically treated to ensure food safety. Ammonia hydroxide has been incorporated into hamburger meat for many years with no ill effects; it's considered a safe product for consumers. The product became an issue when the USDA planned to buy millions of pounds of it for school lunch programs and the name caused disgust among legislators and consumers alike. As a result, the purchase was halted, and grocery stores stopped carrying hamburger meat that included the product. But another effect of the controversy was the closing of multiple meat-packing plants. Thousands of jobs were lost, and the cost of hamburger, sausage, and ground beef increased. The disgust caused by the name pink slime overwhelmed its positive attributes, and one manufacturer filed a suit against ABC News for its coverage. As one comedian quipped, "Next to road kill, pink slime is my favorite."[4]

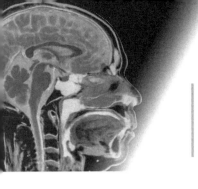

For marketing managers, the overloaded communication environment places a premium on understanding how concepts from the study of memory and **cognitive learning** can be used to develop effective marketing messages.

TYPES OF MEMORY AND CONSUMERS' RESPONSES TO COMMUNICATIONS

In the last chapter, we focused on three stages of perception—exposure, attention, and comprehension. Memory affects each of these stages. It allows consumers to anticipate and selectively expose themselves to the stimuli they might encounter. Similarly, memory influences attention processes by guiding a person's sensory system to focus selectively on particular stimuli. Finally, comprehension is affected by the expectations and associations elicited in memory by the stimuli encountered.

The way consumers remember marketing communications is a complex process. While there are a number of memory theories, a widely accepted approach is the multiple-store model, which provides an answer to the managerial question posed in our first learning objective.

The Multiple-Store Memory Model

Figure 4.1 presents the **multiple-store memory model**, which consists of three types of memory storage systems—sensory memory, short-term memory, and long-term memory.[5] As you can see in the figure, information is first registered in sensory memory, where the preattention stage occurs. Here, the person briefly and unconsciously analyzes a stimulus, such as an advertisement, to determine whether additional processing capacity should be allocated to it. If the stimulus is perceived to be related to the person's goals, cognitive capacity will be directed to it, and the information shifts to short-term memory. In short-term memory (i.e., working memory), people actively process information. Long-term memory is connected to short-term memory through encoding and retrieval processes. **Encoding** is the process of transferring information from short- to long-term memory for permanent storage. **Retrieval** is the process of accessing information stored in long-term memory so it can be utilized in short-term memory. In the next sections, the three types of memory are discussed.

FIGURE 4.1
Multiple-Store Memory
Model

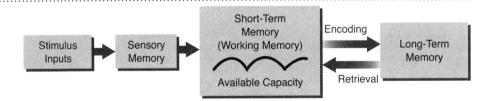

Sensory Memory We perceive sight, sound, touch, smell, or taste because a stimulus activates nerve fibers in our sensory organs—eyes, ears, skin, nose, tongue. The firing of the nerve fibers sends electrical impulses to the brain where the stimulus is very temporarily stored in sensory registers. Because short-term memory lasts for only a fraction of a second, the stimulus information will be quickly lost unless it's processed further.[6] The information stored in the sensory registers is monitored in the preattention stage. If the information is relevant to the person or activates an orientation reflex, it will be actively monitored in short-term memory.

Short-Term Memory **Short-term**, or **working memory**, is the site where information is temporarily stored while being processed. For example, when a consumer thinks about a TV commercial he or she has seen or actively attempts to solve a problem, these cognitive processes are occurring in short-term memory.

Just as the information contained in sensory memory is lost if not attended to, so is the information contained in short-term memory lost within about thirty seconds if not rehearsed.[7] **Rehearsal** occurs when a person repeats information to encode it into long-term memory. Another way such information is lost is through replacement by other information in the limited storage capacity of short-term memory.[8]

The limited capacity of short-term memory Short-term memory has a number of important characteristics. First, it has limited capacity. Psychologist George Miller, in his **Miller's law**, proposed the average person has the ability to process only about seven, plus or minus two, chunks of information at a time.[9] Think of a chunk as a single meaningful piece of information, which could be a single letter, a syllable, or an entire word. Some researchers have noted Miller may have been too optimistic about the capacity of short-term memory. Indeed, in consumer contexts, four bits of information, plus or minus one, may be a better estimate.

Short-term memory's limited capacity causes it to act as a bottleneck. If more information is received than the consumer can handle, some of it will be lost. This is what occurs in **information overload**, a reaction in which, in addition to being unable to process all the information, we experience a negative affective state and increased physiological arousal and focus our attention only on certain aspects of the incoming information. Other scientists think we can store far more memory, but the quality of these memories deteriorates, leaving us to "remember everything a little bit" rather than "a few things perfectly and others not at all."[10] In these circumstances, the consumer may simply make a random choice, not buy anything, or focus on the wrong product qualities when making a product-choice decision.

Information overload can occur in a number of circumstances, such as when consumers use the Internet. Another arena in which overload can occur is when a salesperson is explaining the characteristics of a complex product, such as the operation of the electronics

This ad for a cookbook from *Martha Stewart Living* illustrates Miller's law. Note the three chunks of information communicated about the burger: easy, flavorful, and meatless.

in a new car. The uninformed buyer can be overwhelmed with facts quite easily. In such cases, the consumer will become aroused and uncomfortable and, as a result, tend to focus on narrow aspects of the product, which may or may not be appropriate. Such overarousal and negative affect can lead to poor decisions and is often just the opposite of what the well-intentioned salesperson had in mind. Another occasion in which information overload can occur is when consumers make purchases in a culture in which they must speak a foreign language.[11] Under such circumstances, people can become too physiologically aroused and uncomfortable.

Involvement and short-term memory capacity   The level of involvement of a consumer in a product will influence the capacity of short-term memory.[12] In high-involvement situations, the consumer is likely to be physiologically activated to an optimal level, which expands the capacity of short-term memory to its maximum extent. In contrast, under low-involvement conditions, the arousal level is apt to also be low, so the consumer focuses relatively little memory capacity on the stimulus. Because consumers tend to be in a low-involvement state when exposed to commercials, advertisers limit the number of ideas in a message to three to five. Because copy points are analogous to chunks of information, this decision is consistent with the idea that in television, radio, and Internet advertising contexts, the cognitive capacity of consumers is quite low. The implication is direct—keep your messages simple.

Transferring information from short-term to long-term memory   One of the functions of short-term memory is to assist in the transfer of information to **long-term memory**, where information is permanently stored. As a person allocates more cognitive capacity to a stimulus, the likelihood of it being transferred to long-term memory increases. One way to allocate capacity to a stimulus is through rehearsal. An example of rehearsal is the silent repetition of a telephone number between the time we look it up and the time we dial it.

One research study investigated the effect of rehearsal on the ability of children ages four to nine years to recall advertised products.[13] When the children rehearsed the names of the products by saying them aloud, they were better able to recall information about the brands. The implication for advertisers is commercials that repeat information, such as by using jingles and slogans, may improve the transfer of information from short-term to long-term memory.

How long does it take to transfer a chunk of information to long-term memory? Researchers have found it depends on how the information is to be recalled from long-term memory. If the goal is to simply recognize we have seen a stimulus before, called a **recognition task**, it may take only two to five seconds for transfer. In contrast, if we're recalling the information without assistance at a later time, a **recall task**, the transfer time is longer—from five to ten seconds for a single chunk.

These differences in transfer times have important implications for managers. When developing messages, the marketer should consider whether the consumer will be in a recognition task or a recall task. In a recognition task, information is placed in front of a consumer. The goal of the person is to judge whether the information has been seen previously. In a recall task, the consumer must retrieve the information from long-term memory without assistance. Thus, in recognition tasks, memory recall is said to be aided, while in recall tasks, the retrieval of memories is unaided.

Grocery shopping is often a recognition task. An advertiser's goal is to provide verbal or visual information consumers will recognize. For example, for a low-involvement product, such as toothpaste or toilet paper, the shopper may merely scan the shelves for ideas on what to buy. If the shopper recognizes the product because of an advertisement and he or she liked the advertisement, the likelihood of a purchase will increase. As a consequence, the commercials used to advertise the brand won't have to be as long, be repeated as frequently, or attract as much attention in comparison with a situation in which the consumer must recall the information without the assistance of a package or a point-of-purchase display like the one shown here.

In other instances, unaided recall of a product name from memory is necessary. For example, suppose you're shopping, realize you're hungry, and decide to go to lunch. You know there are a number of acceptable restaurants in the area, and through unaided recall, you retrieve from memory the names of three and choose one. The set of acceptable alternatives a person can recall from memory is called the **consideration set**. If the name of a restaurant isn't retrieved from memory, it can't be selected. Because the time required to transfer information from short-term to long-term memory is longer when unaided recall is required, firms must go to greater lengths to promote their brand if recall memory is required rather than recognition memory.

A point-of-purchase display for locally brewed beer in a grocery store. PoP displays aid recall and recognition. Note how many displays surround checkout areas in grocery and convenience stores
Photo by John Mowen

Managerial principle 4.2
Adapt messages based on whether consumers are in a recall task or a recognition task.

Because short-term memory has a limited capacity, briefly stored information will be quickly replaced by new information. As a result, material received earlier may not be transferred to long-term memory. When consumers watch TV or read a magazine, they're bombarded by dozens of advertisements competing for attention. The problem of too many ads is called **advertising clutter**. Advertising clutter impedes the ability of consumers to move information from temporary storage in short-term memory to permanent storage in long-term memory.[14] Table 4.1 summarizes some important points concerning short-term memory, and the social media feature discusses how social media can overcome clutter.

1. Information is temporarily stored in short-term memory for up to 30 seconds.
2. It has a capacity of seven, plus or minus two, chunks of information in high-involvement situations.
3. It has a capacity of three to five chunks of information in low-involvement situations.
4. Information overload occurs if more information is received than can be processed there and the consumer's goal is to understand the message.
5. As involvement increases, consumers allocate more cognitive capacity to a stimulus and short-term memory increases in size.
6. Recall tasks require more time than recognition tasks to transfer information from short-term to long-term memory.

TABLE 4.1
Summary of Key Short-Term Memory Findings

Social Media

The Super Bowls, Clutter, and Twitter

Nowhere else is advertising clutter more pronounced than in the Super Bowl extravaganza. Lasting more than four hours, the broadcast can include sixty-five or more commercials lasting thirty seconds each and costing $5 million in broadcast fees. With this sheer mass of messages, it's extremely difficult for consumers to recall the product categories and brands being advertised.

We've seen in earlier chapters that marketers using social media can raise consumer involvement, increasing the likelihood consumers will expose themselves to and attend to the content of advertisements. Further, as involvement increases, the chances of a consumer remembering an ad increases. A key strategy of marketers that helps them stand out from the clutter is to induce consumers to use social media before the big game by viewing ads early on YouTube or entering contests on Twitter and Facebook. For example, in a recent year, Lincoln Motor Company hired talk show host Jimmy Fallon to run its "Steer the Script" campaign. Fallon tweeted his fans and asked them to help Lincoln create a Super Bowl commercial. Thousands of consumers told Fallon personal stories about their road trips. Lincoln used five of the tweets to create a thirty-second commercial, which was shown during the game.[15] Similarly, Pepsi held a contest in which consumers submitted photos of themselves in different dance poses using the hashtag #PepsiHalftime. Their inducement was a chance to be on stage with Beyoncé during her halftime show.[16]

All these efforts paid off. One organization counted 20.9 million Super Bowl-related tweets during the game, of which nearly three in ten were related to the commercials. Among the 52 national TV spots shown during the Super Bowl, half mentioned Twitter. .[17]

Long-Term Memory In contrast to short-term memory, long-term memory has an unlimited capacity to store information permanently.[18] We can store five types of information. First, semantic information consists of verbal meanings attached to words, events, objects, and symbols and the associations we make between them. Second, in episodic memory, we store information about life events and experiences. Third, long-term memory stores information we receive from our senses (vision, hearing, smell, taste, touch). Fourth, we store memories of procedures, such as dance moves, swimming strokes, and how to ride a bicycle. Finally, long-term memory holds memories of feelings and emotions.[19]

The permanent nature of long-term memory is illustrated by the enduring quality of brand names. For example, in 2006, Ford Motor Company discontinued production of the Taurus model because of poor sales. However, when Alan Mulally became the CEO of Ford, he brought back the name in a 2010 new car model. Mulally noted the Taurus name was well known and had positive brand equity.[20] One scholar-practitioner in marketing noted, "Bringing back well-known brand names could be a clever idea because so much of the marketing work is done. People's memory of old advertising campaigns and packaging is remarkably persistent."[21]

Pictures tend to be more memorable than words, particularly under low-involvement circumstances.[22] In one study, consumers received information about a brand's good value from the written copy in a print ad and information about its durability from the accompanying visual material . Thus, the visual material pertained to one characteristic of the brand (e.g., its durability) and the verbal material talked about another characteristic (e.g., its value for the money). The results of the study revealed the subjects recalled significantly more pictorial information than verbally presented information.[23] Thus, the saying "A picture's worth a thousand words" has some scientific support.[24]

Another study found if the words in a message are concrete and have high-imagery content, adding pictures isn't as important for making the message memorable. For example, *table* is a high-imagery word, while *future* is a low-imagery word. In the study, high- and low-imagery versions of advertisements were created with and without a photograph. The results revealed the photograph didn't enhance the recall of the message when high-imagery words were used, but it did when low-imagery words were used. We can draw two managerial implications from the research. First, advertisers should use high-imagery words whenever possible. Second, photographs can significantly increase recall when the words in the message have relatively low-imagery content.[25]

Researchers have also found visual material is more easily recognized if the objects to be remembered are perceived as interacting in some way. Thus, to increase the association between a product and an endorser, the advertiser should picture the endorser actually using the product in everyday scenes.[26] Table 4.2 summarizes the generalizations about the effects of the verbal and pictorial content of ads on memory:

The art on the box of Cap'n Crunch's Crunch Berries cereal illustrates the activation of picture memory and the effectiveness of an endorser (even if fictional) shown using the product.

1.	In general, pictorial content is recognized and recalled more readily than verbal content, particularly if the verbal material has low-imagery content.
2.	Verbal material is best recalled when it's processed under high-involvement circumstances.
3.	If consumers are engaged in high-involvement information processing, greater overall recall may result from giving different information about a product via verbal and pictorial means.
4.	Pictures are more effective if an endorser is shown interacting with the product.

TABLE 4.2
Effects of Verbal and Pictorial Information

Memory-Control Processes

It's crucial for consumer researchers to understand how people get information in and out of memory. **Memory-control processes** operate either consciously or unconsciously to influence the encoding, placement, and retrieval of information.[27]

Encoding   We saw earlier that the extent of rehearsal influences whether information is transferred from short-term to long-term memory. In addition, the way the information is encoded affects the speed of transfer and

Head & Shoulders illustrates a brand name that creates associations between the product and its use.
Photo by John Mowen.

the placement of the information in memory. During rehearsal, a consumer can simply repeat the stimulus over and over to move it to long-term memory. If the consumer also draws associations between the stimulus and information already in memory, however, the storage process is enhanced.[28] For example, the author of this chapter was having difficulty remembering the name of an acquaintance—Walter Coffee. However, when he associated the name with the visual cue of a large coffee cup, his memory problem was solved.

Researchers have found, when given new information on a topic, experts recall more information than novices. The difference is experts have already developed elaborate memory networks and knowledge structures into which they can place the new information, which allows it to be encoded more efficiently and makes the retrieval process easier. Their advantage also allows experts to better discriminate between important and unimportant information, which helps them make better decisions.[29] (Chapter 9 discusses decision-making processes.)

When developing brand names, marketers should consider how consumers encode information. Thus, if a product name closely matches the associations evoked by the product class, there's a proportional improvement in recall of the name. For example, compare the brand names Splenda and Head & Shoulders. Can you guess from its name that Splenda is an artificial, low-calorie sweetener? Because the name doesn't generate associations that link it to its product class, it will be more difficult to remember than the name Head & Shoulders, which immediately links to the product class of dandruff shampoo.

Managerial principle 4.3
When developing messages, employ concrete, high-imagery words.

Highly concrete names, which consumers can easily visualize, are better remembered because they can be encoded both visually and verbally and because they better relate to existing knowledge structures. In one study, respondents were given either high-imagery brand names using words (e.g., *ocean*, *orchestra*, *frog*, and *blossom*) or low-imagery brand names (e.g., *history*, *capacity*, *truth*, and *moment*).[30] The subjects recalled more of the high-imagery names. Automobile companies have a history of using high-imagery brand names, such as Jaguar, Mustang, and Viper.

Retrieval and Response Generation   The act of remembering something consists of the processes of retrieval and response generation. In the retrieval process, the individual searches through long-term memory to identify the desired information. In **response generation**, the person develops a response by actively reconstructing the stimulus.[31] The consumer doesn't access stored replicas of the encoded stimulus information. Instead, the person uses logic, intuition, expectations, and even advertisements to help reconstruct a memory from traces of stimuli.

A critical issue for advertisers is how to help consumers retrieve information about their brand from memory. One means is to provide consumers with retrieval cues on product packaging. We can create such **retrieval cues** by placing verbal or visual information from an ad on the product's packaging to assist consumers' memories during decision making.[32] This technique is frequently used by marketers in the promotion of children's cereals that feature animals in the ads and on the product boxes.

Another means marketers use to assist retrieval and response generation is employing music in advertisements. Research has shown people will recall sung messages better. Music acts as a very powerful retrieval cue that can substantially improve recall.[33] Some jingles can stay in consumers' heads for years. Mounds, the maker of Mounds and Almond Joy, brought back the "Sometimes You Feel Like a Nut" jingle because, even though the company hadn't played it for years, customers still remembered it. By bringing it back, the firm could also capture an entire new generation of consumers with its message. (When these jingles become annoyingly stuck in the brain, they're called ear worms.)

Advertising can assist consumers in reconstructing memories. That is, an advertisement that's seen after we've bought a product can actually influence our memory of the experience we've already had. Researchers have found, after seeing ads for a product, consumers may report more favorable product experiences than if they hadn't seen the advertising. These results strongly suggest advertisers should show scenes of satisfied consumers using a brand.[34] Not only will doing so influence expectations of future product performance, it'll also positively change consumers' recall of their own previous experience with the brand.

> **Managerial principle 4.4**
> Use advertising not only to inform consumers about promised future product experiences but also to influence memories of previous product experiences.

Other research revealed ads seen after experiencing a product can influence the recall of the feelings toward the product experience. These effects occurred without the awareness of the consumers.[35] Table 4.3 summarizes key points about the impact of long-term memory on consumer information processing.

1.	Long-term memory has an unlimited capacity.
2.	It's essentially permanent.
3.	Information can be stored in terms of words, input from the senses (e.g., vision and smell), episodes, emotions, and procedures (e.g., how to swim).
4.	Generally, visual memory is superior to semantic memory.
5.	The control processes of encoding and response generation influence what's stored in and retrieved from memory.

TABLE 4.3
Summary of Long-Term Memory Processes

CONSUMER KNOWLEDGE AND BRAND PERCEPTIONS

Stored in long-term memory is a person's knowledge about the consumption environment. **Consumer knowledge** is defined as the amount of experience with and information a person has about particular products or services.[36] As consumer knowledge increases, a person can think about a product across a greater number of dimensions and make finer distinctions among brands. For example, a consumer with large amounts of knowledge about wine can think in terms of a wine's color, bouquet, nose, acidity, and so on. A novice might think in terms of one dimension, such as how much he or she likes its taste.[37]

We can identify three types of consumer knowledge. Objective knowledge is the correct information about a product class a consumer has stored in long-term memory. Subjective knowledge is a consumer's perception of what or how much he or she knows about a product class. Objective and subjective knowledge are not highly correlated.[38] We find wide differences between how much people think they know and how much they really know. Indeed, the correlation between objective and subjective knowledge is only about $r = 0.37$.[39] The third kind of information is information about the knowledge of others. For example, product engineers sometimes fail to recognize consumers don't have sufficient knowledge to readily understand and use a product. For the product engineer using the product is easy because he or she developed it, while consumers without the knowledge may find the product extremely difficult to use. One example is the iDrive in BMW cars, a computer interface between the driver and the car that controls nearly everything, from heating to navigation to communications. Criticized for years as unintuitive and hard to use, it diminished the pleasure of driving BMW's otherwise high-quality cars. One person responded to a blog post about the iDrive in 2008:

> groan . . as a software professional with a user interface background I
>   assumed I could handle the idrive.
> what a trainwreck of an interface. It could be so much better.
> Software should be intuitively obvious to the occasional user. Not Idrive.
> PS my prior car, a lexus LS was so simple. I was warned but didnt heed.
> Software must be easier to use than not to use or people wont use it.
> Idrive needs a UI refresh. (and a touch screen wou be nice).[40]

Managerial principle 4.5
Match the complexity of a product's design to the level of the target market's product expertise.

For marketing managers, what are the implications of the study of consumer knowledge? As consumer knowledge increases, consumers become better organized; they're more efficient and more accurate in their information processing and recall information better. Managers should consider the extent of consumer knowledge when developing and promoting a product. For example, much more complex communications can be sent to consumers who are knowledgeable because they're less prone to information overload.

How Do Consumers Gain Knowledge?

Consumers obtain their knowledge through cognitive learning. Cognitive learning is the processes responsible for our forming associations among concepts, learning sequences of concepts (e.g., a list of names), solving problems, and having insights. It's an intuitive hypothesis-generating process in which we adapt our beliefs to make sense of new data.[41] Cognitive learning is an active process in which consumers seek to control the information obtained.[42]

We learn about the environment through both education and experience.[43] When **learning through education**, we obtain information through advertising, salespeople, and our own efforts to seek out data, such as by asking friends or searching online. In contrast, **learning through experience** is the process of gaining knowledge through actual contact with products. Overall, learning from experience is more effective because we're engaged in the learning experience and the information we obtain is more vivid, concrete, and salient.

The Gestalt Psychology Approach to Knowledge   Gestalt psychologists, who were active in the early twentieth century, made an important contribution to our understanding of cognitive learning and the way we gain knowledge.

They proposed people perceive the inputs from the environment as part of a total context. Furthermore, they argued humans aren't static organisms who respond automatically to inputs from the environment. Rather, the Gestalt psychologists focused on the active, creative nature of learning and action.[44] As one noted consumer researcher stated,

> *When we look at an automobile, we do not see glass and steel and plastic and bolts and paint. We see instead an organized whole, an automobile. And perhaps not even just an automobile but also comfortable transportation, prestige, status, and a symbolic sense of achievement. This is the familiar Gestalt dictum; the whole is different from, if not greater than, the sum of the isolated parts.*[45]

The work of the Gestalt psychologists has important implications for marketers. Market researchers tend to perceive products in terms of their individual characteristics, such as price, color, features, reliability, and so forth. In contrast, consumers tend to perceive the product as an integrated whole. In isolation, a particular color or style may be judged unacceptable. However, when seen in the overall context of a product, the characteristic could be quite satisfactory. Thus, when considered in isolation, colorful seats in a car might seem silly; however, in a sports car, they might fit quite well.

Another contribution of the Gestalt school is the idea consumers engage in problem-solving activities and have sudden bursts of insight and creativity. Many products or situations can activate the consumer so he or she begins problem-solving activities. For example, consumers are engaged in problem solving when purchasing an automobile, selecting among mutual funds for their retirement savings, or choosing which college to attend.

Problem solving and creativity are closely linked. We find creativity in numerous consumer activities, including cooking, crafts and hobbies, home-improvement tasks (e.g., painting a room or landscaping a yard), and the purchase of innovative products. One study investigated the effects of ambient noise on consumer creativity when purchasing innovative products. The results showed that increasing background noise from fifty decibels to eighty-five decibels harmed creativity and the likelihood of purchasing innovative products. The high level of noise decreased the extent of information processing and abstract reasoning.[46]

Creativity plays another role for consumers regarding advertising. Consumers who are creative like advertisements that are creative.

Knowledge and the Associationist School of Psychology

Yet another approach to cognitive learning is to analyze the associations consumers form between stimuli. Two discoveries by researchers working in the associationist school have important implications for consumer researchers—the serial position effect and the law of contiguity.

The Serial Position Effect The study of **serial learning** examines the way people put into memory and recall information in a sequential manner. For example, consider that, during a commercial break in a television show, viewers can be exposed to twelve or more advertisements. Does the position of an ad in that series influence how well it's remembered? A **serial position effect**

occurs when the order of presentation influences our recall of the information in the list. As you can see in Figure 4.2, researchers have found items at the beginning and end of the list are the most readily learned, while those in the middle are learned much less rapidly.[47] Recalling the material early in a list most easily is the **primacy effect**. Recalling the material at the end of the list is the **recency effect**.

FIGURE 4.2
The Seial Position Effect

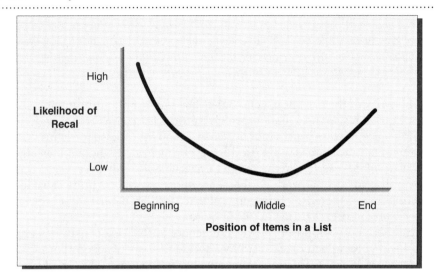

The serial position effect has two important implications for marketers. First, key information in an advertisement should be placed at the beginning or the end of the message. If important information is embedded in the middle of the communication, it will take more repetitions of the advertisement for consumers to learn the information. Second, advertisers should strive to have their commercials placed either at the beginning or the end of a series of ads.[48] The advertisements in the first and last position are called **bookend ads** and command higher prices because they are more likely to be remembered by consumers.

Managerial principle 4.6
Place advertisements and important information at the beginning or the end of a series of stimuli.

Research on the serial position effect indicates the commercial placed at the beginning of a series is recalled better than even an ad in the last position.[49] This finding was confirmed in a study investigating the recall of Super Bowl advertisements. Not only did consumers have better memories of commercials shown early in a pod of ads, but they also had better recall of ads shown earlier in the Super Bowl game itself. This finding provides strong evidence for the primacy effect on ads shown in a series.[50]

Messages can also appear simultaneously. For example, in a grocery store, we see all the various brands of milk in a dairy case at the same time. We see different brands on an Internet shopping page simultaneously. A recent study found consumers who were presented options sequentially expressed lower satisfaction with their choice than those who saw them simultaneously. The authors reasoned that consumers receiving the information sequentially tended to imagine a better option would always appear. In contrast, those who saw their options simultaneously focused on this set and didn't have to conduct "an eternal quest for the best."[51]

The Law of Contiguity In addition to studying how consumers learn lists of information, associationist researchers have investigated how consumers remember words or images that are paired with each other. They identified a principle called the **law of contiguity**, which states that things that are experienced together become associated.[52] The effect is called **paired-associate learning**. For example, three pairs of stimulus and response words might be Maytag-quality, Nike-Tiger Woods, and Volvo-crash protection. *Maytag*, *Nike*, and *Volvo* are the stimulus words, and *quality*, *Tiger Woods*, and *crash protection* the response words, respectively.

An important finding in paired-associate learning is learning speeds up when the stimulus and response items can be readily associated with each other and are familiar.[53] In particular, if we can develop mental images between stimulus and response words, learning is more rapid. Examples of effective word pairings are found in children's cereals, such as "Silly rabbit, Trix are for kids" and Tony-the-Tiger roaring, "Kellogg's Corn Flakes, they're great!" Table 4.4 summarizes the conditions under which paired-associate stimuli are most readily learned.

1. The stimulus and response words should be easily pronounceable.
2. The person should be familiar with the stimulus and response words.
3. The stimulus and response words should be meaningful.
4. The stimulus and response words should be easily associated.
5. Visual images should be created to link the stimulus and response words together.

TABLE 4.4
Conditions Maximizing
Paired-Associate Learning

Marketers instinctively use ideas from the law of contiguity to create cooperative advertising campaigns in which two distinct products are promoted together. For example, Intel invests hundreds of millions of dollars in cooperative ad programs with companies such as Dell, Toshiba, Lenovo, and Hewlett-Packard. Intel also has demanded at least 35 percent of the advertising be moved from traditional media (i.e., television and print) to online media. As one Intel executive said, "We're going where the consumers have gone."[54]

Another way marketers use the law of contiguity is to create brand names that suggest the product's use. For example, the names Head & Shoulders and Lean Cuisine identify the task the brand is designed to perform. Because the product's use and its brand name are associated, consumers' ability to recall the name increases. The brand name can even suggest specific attributes of the brand. DieHard connotes that the car battery, a Sears product, resists losing its charge. Research indicates suggestive names do increase the recall of the benefits such products claim, but recall is inhibited for benefits unrelated to the attribute. Thus, we would expect an attribute such as low price would be inhibited for a DieHard battery.[55]

The law of contiguity can also cause problems for marketers. When ads are positioned beside unflattering photos or news stories, the effect of the promotion may be reduced or even become negative. Most companies check carefully to ensure their television advertisements are not shown in conjunction with programs that could be offensive to their target market. Similarly, if a product endorser becomes controversial, it can create problems. For example, Gillette, Gatorade, AT&T, and Accenture stopped using Tiger Woods as an endorser when his marital problems became known in 2010.[56] Interestingly, however,

Managerial principle 4.7
Be sure to pair your product
with positive stimuli.

by 2013, the golfer's marital problems were behind him, and advertisers again flocked to hire him to associate their products with a winner.

Researchers have investigated whether corporate sponsorships of philanthropic organizations can mitigate the effects of negative publicity. For example, can an oil company's association with a positive stimulus, such as support of a children's hospital or an environmental group, reduce the effects of negative publicity, such as reports of an oil spill? Preliminary results indicate supporting an unrelated cause such as the children's hospital may minimize the negative publicity to a greater extent than supporting a related cause such as an environmental group.[57]

Semantic Memory Networks

Semantic memory consists of the network of meanings in the verbal material we have stored in long-term memory.[58] A few years ago, the author of this chapter decided to purchase a sports car. Figure 4.3 presents his semantic memory network for sports cars at the time. Networks are composed of a series of memory nodes representing the stored semantic concepts, lines showing the associations among the nodes, and the affective charge associated with the nodes. When a node is activated, information is recalled via spreading activation.[59] Thus, when the sports car node was activated, an impulse was created that spread to other linked nodes one after another. Each node activated represents a memory or a feeling that's experienced.

Looking at Figure 4.3, the sports car node was connected to five vehicles—Porsche 911s, Nissan Miata, Corvette, Audi A8, and Mustang. When the Porsche node was triggered, a spreading activation of nerve fibers occurred, activating other nodes, which triggered the firing of additional nodes. The activation of the sports car node first triggered the Porsche 911s node, which activated several key attributes of the vehicle: prestigious, expensive, reliable, and fast. In addition, a positive affective charge was activated for the Porsche. The Audi R8 was also activated. The attributes linked to it were cool looking, fast, and expensive. In addition, a negative affective charge was linked to it because of a previous bad experience with an Audi. You can trace the path of the spreading activation by looking at Figure 4.3. (Can you tell which sports car the author purchased? Check the "Notes" section to find out.[60])

Of course, different consumers possess divergent memory structures, and the activation of a semantic concept may result in quite different sets of associations. What's your semantic memory network for sports cars? Within the semantic memory network, a set of associations is connected to a brand's name. These links represent a consumer's **brand knowledge**, which is defined as a "brand node in memory to which a variety of associations have been linked."[61] As you can see in Figure 4.3, five types of information are stored and represent the brand knowledge of the consumer: brand name (e.g., Porsche), product category (e.g., sports car), brand features or attributes (e.g., fast, expensive, reliable), evaluative reactions to the brand and the ad (i.e., positive or negative), and advertisements and word-of-mouth information.

Managerial principle 4.8
Brand image results from the
semantic memory network
linked to the brand node.

Brand knowledge forms the basis for the brand image held by the consumer. If the brand node is linked to a negative attribute or concept, the image suffers. Thus, when the hamburger node was linked to the descriptor "pink slime," the product image was harmed. A similar situation befell BMW's Mini Cooper.

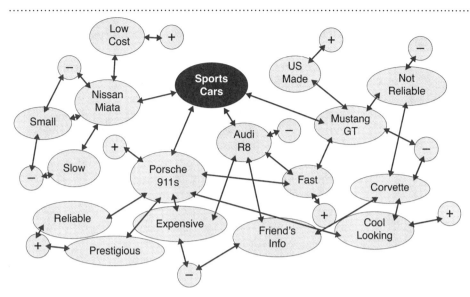

FIGURE 4.3
A Semantic Memory
Network for Sports Crs

In Europe, companies can pay to have their products linked to weather fronts and, thus, mentioned frequently on the weather news. In 2012, BMW bought the name of a low-pressure area and called it "Cooper." The idea was to promote the car's ability to get around in snow. Unfortunately, the weather front was one for the ages—temperatures fell to -22 degrees Fahrenheit and 250 people died. BMW had to scramble to apologize for choosing the unlucky linkage.[62]

Schemas   The total package of associations brought to mind when a node is activated is called a schema. Specifically, a **schema** is an organized set of expectations, beliefs, and feelings held by a person about an object. Said another way, schemas are "stored frameworks of knowledge about some object or topic and are represented by nodes in semantic memory."[63] The Porsche 911s schema consists of those associations activated when a particular person thinks about this car.

Researchers have found when new information is inconsistent with a schema, consumers engage in more diligent processing and, consequently, have improved memory about the stimulus. Thus, when consumers receive information that deviates from expectation, they allocate more cognitive capacity to it and process it in greater depth. In such circumstances, it's more likely the information will be transferred from short-term to long-term memory.[64]

Creativity in advertising results, in part, from violation of a schema. For example, a few years ago, the "Got Milk?" mustache campaign was identified as the No. 1 advertising campaign in the United States. Its highly memorable images portrayed attractive celebrities unexpectedly wearing a milk mustache. The ads drew attention and were highly memorable because they violated the schema of how celebrities should look.

One study tested the schema violation and memory ideas in a personal-selling situation.[65] Suppose a customer in a clothing store encounters a salesperson who interacts with the person in a different style. If the customer is surprised by the sales approach, he or she might pay more attention to the information and recall it better in the future. The study's results supported these

Caption: The duck on the label of this bottle of Duckhorn Vineyards acts as a prime to purchase the wine. *Credit: Photo by John Mowen.*

ideas. When the seller met expectations of the typical salesperson, product evaluations weren't affected by the quality of the arguments of the sales speech. However, when the salesperson violated the schema, subjects recalled more about the product from the arguments and had generally more positive attitudes about the product.

Priming   Priming occurs when a stimulus activates a node in the semantic memory network. The activation of the node can then influence a response to a later stimulus without our being aware of it.

The effects of priming are amazingly robust.[66] For example, one study found exposing consumers to a backpack increased the likelihood they'd cooperate with others. In contrast, exposure to a briefcase resulted in a higher likelihood of competitive actions. The authors reasoned cooperation is expected when backpacking, while briefcases are associated with business and competition.[67] Another study found people exposed to an Apple logo showed increased creativity in the use of a common object compared to people exposed to an IBM logo.[68] Interestingly, the effects of primes occur without the awareness of the consumer.

Sophisticated marketers can effectively employ primes to influence consumers to purchase their products. For example, some wine companies create "critter" wines that feature animals on their labels, such as frogs, penguins, or ducks. In one experiment, researchers found a respondent exposed to a particular animal would choose the wine whose label matched that animal—without being aware of why.[69] In sum, a marketer can use primes that have positive connotations and link those to a product.

KEEPING CONSUMERS FROM FORGETTING

If long-term memory is permanent, why do people forget? The answer is that, even though information has been placed in long-term memory, it can be difficult to retrieve. One study found respondents could recall the brand advertised in radio advertisements only 6 percent of the time.[70] Another study found respondents could recall less than 20 percent of the brands advertised in banner ads while browsing the web.[71] Such results are discouraging to advertising managers because the recall of ads is an important measure of advertising effectiveness. In order to improve recall, we must first understand why we forget.

Two factors that can cause problems in encoding, retrieval, and response generation are proactive interference and retroactive interference. When **retroactive interference** occurs, new material presented after old material has been learned interferes with the recall of the old material. That is, the learning of new material interferes with the retrieval or the response generation of the old material from memory. In **proactive interference**, material learned before the new material interferes with the learning of the new material. Such interference is an enormous problem for advertisers because of the many marketing messages consumers are exposed to each day.

Creating unique ads, using multiple modalities, and telling incomplete stories can all help advertisers minimize the effects of retroactive interference and proactive interference. Let's see how each of these strategies works.

Creating Unique Ads

Researchers have long known interference between bits of information to be learned increases as the similarity of their content increases.[72] If consumers see a series of messages making similar claims, confusion will result and learning will be impeded. Indeed, the confusion will grow proportionally to the degree the competing ads promote similar types of products or use similar adjectives to describe their performance (e.g., high quality, low cost, low maintenance). These effects have been found to be particularly strong for unfamiliar brands.[73] Of course, such confusion can provide important advantages for brands that are familiar to consumers. That is, consumers may mistakenly believe an ad for an unfamiliar brand is actually promoting the familiar one.

How can marketers decrease interference effects? Experiments have shown a unique item in a series of relatively similar items is recalled more easily.[74] This result, called the **von Restorff effect**, works because it minimizes the effects of retroactive interference and proactive interference. As a result, marketers go to great lengths to create unique, creative advertisements. A classic example is the ads for Coors beer that feature a silver colored, futuristic train roaring through snow in the Rocky Mountains. The train perfectly matches the nickname of Coors Light beer—"the Silver Bullet." Nike has also worked hard to develop unique ads that'll stand out from the advertising clutter. In one ad for its lightweight apparel, for example, a headless creature runs across a field.

Using the von Restorff effect increases the salience of information for consumers. **Information salience** refers to the level of activation of a stimulus (e.g., a brand name) in memory. Other strategies that increase the level of salience are using continuously high levels of advertising and cues such as point-of-purchase displays to remind consumers of a product. In addition, stimulus factors such as novelty, contrast, color, surprise, movement, and size can all act to make a stimulus salient. Generally, the more salient something is, the more likely it will be encoded into memory and later recalled. In sum, one of an advertiser's primary goals should be to make an advertisement highly salient to the consumer.

If one brand is highly salient to consumers, the recall of competing brands is reduced.[75] Thus, if a manager can develop the marketing mix so a brand is highly salient to consumers, recall of competing brands may decrease. The reason for this is, through retroactive interference, the presence of the salient brand in memory inhibits the recall of competitors.

Using Multiple Modalities

We can also reduce interference by providing information in both spoken and written forms, because the two forms are processed via different neural pathways.[76] In fact, we can enhance the encoding and retrieval of information generally by providing it in different modalities. Showing pictures of the product and even activating procedural memory by having the consumer experience the use of the product also help. For example, an auto salesperson should verbally go through the important attributes of the car, provide written information about it, show the client attractive photos of the vehicle, and have the customer experience the car by test-driving it.

Telling Incomplete Stories

Another factor that influences whether something will be forgotten is named after Bluma Zeigarnik, the Russian Gestalt scientist who discovered it. The **Zeigarnik effect** occurs when an individual is engaged in a task that's interrupted or not completed.[77] If we compare the recall of information in a task that's been interrupted with recall when the task has been completed, we will find material in the interrupted task is recalled better.[78] The Zeigarnik effect may explain, in part, the effectiveness of "soap opera ads," which, like TV soap operas, leave the story incomplete. One such ad was shown during the 2013 Super Bowl by Budweiser. The ad told a story of a man who raised a Clydesdale horse through sickness and health. Alas, however, the horse was taken away to pull the famous Budweiser beer wagon. Two years later, the man notices the Clydesdales will appear in a local parade. At the parade, he recognizes the horse, who also notices him. When the horse is unbridled, it gallops down a street and catches the man just as he's about to leave in his truck. In a tear-jerking scene, they nuzzle each other. Echoing the Zeigarnik effect, the story is incomplete as the audience is left to wonder what will happen to the obvious love affair between the man and his horse.

Time and Forgetting

Psychologists have found the operation of proactive interference and retroactive interference causes the recall of verbal information to decrease rapidly at first and then level off over time.[79] The rapid forgetting that occurs immediately after learning has been shown to occur after exposure to advertising as well. In a classic experiment, Hubert Zielske ran television advertisements for a product once a week for thirteen weeks.[80] At the end of the thirteen-week period, 63 percent of respondents could recall having seen the ad. Then no more ads were shown, and forgetting showed the same pattern as that found by psychologists. That is, forgetting occurred very rapidly at first and then leveled off. After twenty weeks, recall of the ads had dropped to less than 30 percent. By the time nine months had passed, only about 10 percent of those surveyed could remember the ads.[81]

Managerial principle 4.9
Forgetting can be impeded by creating unique ads, by activating multiple modalities, and by using spaced ads rather than massed ads.

In addition to giving one group of housewives one ad a week for thirteen weeks, another group was shown thirteen ads spaced four weeks apart over the course of a year. Respondents' ability to recall the ads increased slowly, but some 48 percent could remember them at the end of the year. The difference between the groups' levels of recall tells us if we want to quickly create awareness of a product, a high frequency of ads over a short period of time will be most effective, but rapid forgetting occurs thereafter. If the goal is to build long-term awareness of a product, messages should be pulsed so consumers see them regularly over a long period of time. Often, companies will combine the approaches and use a high-intensity campaign to introduce a product and then pulse regularly thereafter to maintain awareness.

FEELINGS AND MEMORY

One of the major themes of this text is, when investigating consumer behavior, the researcher must be concerned with experiential or affective processes. The term **affect** refers to the emotions and moods consumers may experience. A **mood** is a transient feeling state that occurs in a specific situation or time. It's not a personality variable because moods are temporary in nature, whereas personality is enduring over time. Similarly, moods are not emotions, which are more intense and attention getting.[82] Despite the short duration and mild intensity of moods, research suggests people are better able to recall information that has the same affective quality as their mood state. Thus, when people are sad, they're more likely to recall information that's sad. Conversely, when people are happy, they're more likely to remember happy information.[83] Additional research indicates, when compared with neutral moods, positive mood states enhance the learning of brand names.[84]

In one study, researchers asked consumers to think about happy, sad, or neutral past experiences to induce positive, negative, or neutral moods. Next, participants viewed a single print advertisement for a Mazda RX7 sports car. When the respondents were asked to form an impression of the car while reading the ad, the mood still affected their rating of the car forty-eight hours later. The researchers hypothesized that, when consumers read and evaluated the ad, their mood state influenced the way they encoded the information. Sad moods caused lower evaluations than neutral ones, and the highest ratings occurred when the subjects were in a positive mood state.[85]

A phenomenon called **flashbulb memory** occurs when consumers experience an emotionally charged, novel, and personal situation that vividly preserves the feelings, the people present, the location, and other details accompanying the event.[86] Some consumer situations in which flashbulb memory may take place include a special dinner with a special person, the experience of driving a brand new car for the first time after buying it, and the situation in which you learn of a catastrophe, such as where you were and what you were doing when you learned of the Boston Marathon bombing.

What can marketers learn from the case of flashbulb memory? In general, marketers should attempt to place consumers in a positive mood state when they're receiving information about a product or a service. A number of devices can be used to create these moods, such as humor in an advertisement, pleasant odors in a retail store, and an elegant meal for a client in a personal-selling situation.

THE MANAGERIAL IMPLICATIONS OF MEMORY AND COGNITIVE LEARNING

The principles and concepts of memory and cognitive learning have application to each of the five RESPonsive Marketing concepts. These are discussed below.

Market Research

Marketers should conduct research to identify the semantic memory network and schemas of the target market for their organization and brand and to evaluate consumers' recall and recognition of key advertising points. Marketers should assess the knowledge and engagement level of consumers in the target market to help determine how much information to transmit in messages and how complex to make the design of the product. Market research should also identify the affect associated with a brand or organization. If negative affective associations exist, they'll elicit other semantic memories with a similar affective charge.

Environmental Analysis

When marketing a brand, managers must carefully examine the competitive and communication environments. If the communications environment is cluttered with advertisements, brand managers must consider whether serial position effects are occurring. When advertising clutter is a problem—particularly if the clutter is caused by competitors—managers should make use of the von Restorff and Zeigarnik effects to improve the encoding and retrieval of information.

Segmentation

Different messages and potentially even different products can be targeted to consumers with divergent knowledge levels. Because involvement level affects the capacity of short-term memory, we can provide substantially more information to a high-involvement target market than to a low-involvement one.

Positioning and Differentiation

Organizations must identify and evaluate the way their target markets encode into memory the brand names of products, as well as the name of the organization. Assessing the semantic memory network of individuals in a target market helps us identify the schema they associate with our brand or organization. This, in turn, tells us how they see our brand positioning relative to that of other brands and what attributes they use to evaluate our brand. For example, if the schema for the Buick includes associations such as old-fashioned, grandfather, boxy, and boring, that has negative implications for the sale of the brand. Buick successfully repositioned its LaCrosse model as younger and hipper—a 2015 *Motor Trend* review used the word *sexy* four times when describing the car.[87]

Marketing Mix

The concepts in this chapter are particularly relevant to the product-development and promotional-strategy elements of the marketing mix. For example, the knowledge and involvement levels of the target market can influence the design of a product and the creation of promotional messages. Similarly, an understanding of the von Restorff and Zeigarnik effects guides managers in developing marketing communications, just as knowing about the serial position effect tells us whether to pay extra to purchase bookend ads. The law of contiguity is particularly important for the public-relations component of the promotional mix. That is, publicists must be on constant lookout for situations in which the brand or organization is paired with unfavorable information. Finally, if marketing research indicates a brand or organization is associated with stimuli having a negative affective charge, we must develop marketing communications that seek to change those feelings.

SUMMARY

In the model of memory presented in this chapter, information is input into sensory memory. If the information relates to the consumer's goals, it will be shifted into short-term memory for further processing. The more elaborate the processing in short-term memory, the greater the likelihood it will be permanently stored in long-term memory.

How do the types of memory affect consumers' responses to communications?

Short-term memory is characterized as having a limited processing capacity of seven (plus or minus two) chunks of information (i.e., according to Miller's law). If we receive more information than we can process, we experience information overload. As our involvement level with a product increases, so does the capacity of our short-term memory.

In encoding, we transfer information from short-term to long-term memory. The recall of information from long-term memory back into short-term memory is called retrieval. The likelihood we'll encode information into long-term memory increases as we spend more cognitive effort on the information through rehearsal or through a process of connecting the information with other knowledge stored in memory. Encoding is also enhanced if we can draw associations between the new information and other knowledge already held in memory.

The retrieval process is enhanced if cues are available to assist the consumer in recalling information. Verbal, visual, and other kinds of sensory information are stored in long-term memory. In addition, people can encode sequences of events in memory. Picture memory is superior to verbal memory, but we can enhance verbal memory for information such as people's names by linking the information to a visual image that depicts the name in some manner.

How does consumer knowledge influence brand perceptions?

Also encoded in long-term memory is a consumer's knowledge, consisting of his or her familiarity and expertise with a product or a service. Consumer knowledge has a number of characteristics, including the number of dimensions in which a person can think about something. Knowledge is also organized into the semantic memory. Semantic memory concerns how people store the meanings of verbal material in long-term memory. In semantic memory, concepts are represented by interconnected nodes. The activation of a node by a cue may result in a spreading activation, so information related to connected nodes is also recalled. This recalled information influences brand perception, which is one's thoughts and feelings about the brand.

How can marketers keep consumers from forgetting?

Retroactive and proactive interference can make it more difficult for us to encode information and retrieve it from memory. The von Restorff effect describes the fact we more easily recall a unique item in a series of relatively homogeneous items, avoiding some of the effects of interference. The Zeigarnik effect occurs when a task or story is interrupted, causing us to engage in deeper processing and form a stronger memory. Because people tend to forget information as time passes, marketers should consider pulsing information over time and making use of the serial position effect by placing their messages first or last in a series.

The cognitive learning theorists tackled the question of how people develop knowledge. One group, the Gestalt psychologists, emphasized consumers are active problem solvers who tend to perceive products and services in terms of the total environmental context. Another group, the associationists, proposed people gain knowledge because of the law of contiguity, which states things that are experienced together tend to become associated. If a product is linked with something negative, consumers may well make an unfortunate association.

How do consumers' feelings affect memory?

Brand evaluations can be influenced by a consumer's mood state when information is being received. In general, marketers should attempt to create positive consumer mood states to increase the chances consumers will recall positive information about the product or service.

KEY TERMS

advertising clutter
affect
brand knowledge
bookend ads
cognitive learning
consideration set
consumer knowledge
encoding
flashbulb memory
information overload
information salience
law of contiguity
learning through education
learning through experience

long-term memory
memory-control processes
Miller's law
mood
multiple-store memory model
paired-associate learning
primacy effect
priming
proactive interference
recall task
recency effect
recognition task
rehearsal

response generation
retrieval
retrieval cues
retroactive interference
schema
semantic memory
sensory memory
serial learning
serial position effect
short-term memory
von Restorff effect
working memory
Zeigarnik effect

REVIEW QUESTIONS

1. What are the three types of memory and how do they differ?

2. What happens when information overload occurs?

3. What's the difference between a recognition task and a recall task?

4. Compare the effectiveness of picture memory and word memory under high- and low-involvement conditions.

5. What's a memory network?

6. Define and give examples of memory-control processes.

7. Discuss what happens in short-term memory. What's the relationship between involvement and short-term memory?

8. How is information transferred from short-term memory to long-term memory?

9. Summarize what we know about long-term memory and knowledge processes.

10. Why does forgetting occur?

11. What's the relationship between time and forgetting?

12. What's the serial position effect?

13. What's the law of contiguity?

14. What's the relationship between affect and memory?

15. What's the difference between learning through education and learning through experience?

DISCUSSION QUESTIONS

1. Listen carefully to three television, radio, or Internet advertisements and identify the number of copy points in each. To what extent do you think consumers will remember these points? What factors might influence how well they do so?

2. Find three ads in a magazine. Identify the number of copy points in each ads. Compare the number of copy points in the print ads with the number you observed in the three ads you listened to in the previous question. What factors might account for any differences you found?

3. Describe two instances of consumer recognition tasks and two instances of consumer recall tasks. Do you find any differences in the advertising associated with the products you identified in each instance?

4. Relate the saying "A picture's worth a thousand words" to picture memory versus word memory. What are the implications for advertisers?

5. Draw a diagram of your memory network for fast-food restaurants.

6. Suppose you had to develop a name for a new tofu-based dessert that includes real fruit, has no cholesterol, and is safe for people who are lactose intolerant. Create several names and show how each utilizes the various memory-control processes in the chapter.

7. Go to a grocery store and identify as many examples as you can of point-of-purchase (POP) advertising that effectively helps the consumer associate national advertising with the brand on the store's shelves. What memory factors make the POP displays more or less effective?

8. Outline a fictitious ad for any product that makes use of the Zeigarnik effect.

9. Outline a fictitious ad for any product that makes use of the von Restorff effect.

ENDNOTES

[1] Nathalie Tadena, "P&G Cut Traditional Ad Spending by 14 Percent in 2014," *Wall Street Journal*, March 18, 2015, accessed December 2, 2015, http://blogs.wsj.com/cmo/2015/03/18/pg-cut-traditional-ad-spending-by-14-in-2014/.

[2] For more on memory effects in advertising, see H. Shanker Krishnan and Dipankar Chakravarti, "Memory Measures for Pretesting Advertisements: An Integrative Conceptual Framework and a Diagnostic Template," *Journal of Consumer Psychology* 8, no. 1 (1999): 1–37.

[3] Shari Worthington, "How Many Advertisements Do We See Each Day?" *What's Working in Marketing*, accessed January 6, 2016, http://blog.telesian.com/how-many-advertisements-do-we-see-each-day/.

[4] Bill Tomson, "Schools Can Opt Out of 'Pink Slime' Beef," *Wall Street Journal*, March 15, 2012, accessed January 3, 2016, http://www.wsj.com/articles/SB10001424052702304692804577283613 821625348; Joyce Russell, "'Pink Slime Is Making a Comeback. Do You Have a Beef with That?" *NPR*, accessed January 3, 2016, http://www.npr.org/sections/thesalt/2014/06/17/322911060/pink-slime-is-making-a-comeback-do-you-have-a-beef-with-that.

[5] For a discussion of memory processes, see Antonia Mantonakis, Bruce Whittlesea, and Carolyn Yoon, "Consumer Memory," in *Handbook of Consumer Psychology*, ed. Curtis Haugtvedt, Paul Herr, and Frank Kardes (New York: Lawrence Erlbaum Associates, 2008), 77–102. For a classic article on memory, see James R. Bettman, "Memory Factors in Consumer Choice: A Review," *Journal of Marketing* 43 (Spring 1979): 37–53. Researchers have also identified another type of memory that's called implicit memory. For a discussion of this concept, see Sarah L. Coates, Laurie T. Butler, and Dianne C. Berry, "Implicit Memory and Choice: The Mediating Role of Brand Familiarity," *Applied Cognitive Psychology* 20 (2006): 1101–1116.

[6] George Sperling, "The Information Available in Brief Visual Presentations," *Psychological Monographs* 74 (1960): 498.

[7] Herbert Simon, *The Sciences of the Artificial* (Cambridge, MA: MIT Press, 1969).

[8] Richard M. Shiffrin and R. C. Atkinson, "Storage and Retrieval Processes in Long-Term Memory," *Psychological Review* 76 (1969): 179–193.

[9] George A. Miller, "The Magical Number Seven, Plus or Minus Two: Some Limits on Our Capacity to Process Information," *Psychological Review* 63 (1956): 81–97. Note that researchers differ on the capacity of short-term memory. Some have argued it's limited to as few as three chunks of information. Others insist it can be as high as twenty chunks.

[10] Daniel Kahneman, *Attention and Effort* (Englewood Cliffs, NJ: Prentice Hall, 1973); James Devitt, "To Store More Memories, We Forget the Details," *Futurity*, accessed December 4, 2015, http://www.futurity.org/many-details-max-short-term-memory/.

[11] Claudia Dolinsky and Richard Feinberg, "Linguistic Barriers to Consumer Information Processing: Information Overload in the Hispanic Population," *Psychology and Marketing* 3, no. 4 (1986): 261–271.

[12] Daniel Kahneman, *Attention and Effort* (Englewood Cliffs, NJ: Prentice Hall, 1973).

[13] M. Carole Macklin, "Rehearsal Processes in Children's Recall of Advertised Products," in *Proceedings of the Division of Consumer Psychology*, ed. Wayne Hoyer (Washington, DC: American Psychological Association, 1986), 21–25.

[14] Tom J. Brown and Michael L. Rothschild, "Reassessing the Effect of Television Advertising Clutter," *Journal of Consumer Research* 20 (June 1993): 138–146. This important article found little evidence of the negative effects of clutter on the recognition of advertisements embedded in television programming. See Russell W. Belk, "Extended Self in a Digital World," *Journal of Consumer Research* 40 (October 2013): 477-500 for a treatment of "digital clutter."

[15] Bruce Horovitz, "Lincoln to Go a-Twitter with Super Bowl Ad" *USA Today*, January 8, 2013, accessed January 3, 2016, http://www.usatoday.com/story/money/business/2013/01/07/lincoln-social-media-tweets-super-bowl-commercial/1813871/.

[16] The URL for instructions on how to enter the contest was http://www.beyonce.com/news/pepsi-halftime-contest.

[17] "Super Bowl Ads: Facts and Figures," *Marketing Charts*, accessed January 3, 2016, http://www.marketingcharts.com/wp/television/super-bowl-ads-facts-and-figures-26588/.

[18] For a more detailed description of memory and memory-control processes, see James R. Bettman, "Memory Factors in Consumer Choice: A Review," *Journal of Marketing* 43 (Spring 1979): 37–53.

[19] Benton Underwood, "Attributes of Memory," *Psychological Review* 76 (November 1969): 559–573.

[20] "Ford CEO Alan Mulally Talks about the Return of the Taurus," YouTube video, 3:12, posted by "AutoInsiderNews," February 8, 2007, http://www.youtube.com/watch?v=uYlNOtqI8tc.

[21] Ronald Alsop, "Old Chewing-Gum Favorites Find There's Life After Death," *Wall Street Journal,* September 11, 1986, 37.

[22] Terry Childers and Michael Houston, "Conditions for a Picture-Superiority Effect on Consumer Memory," *Journal of Consumer Research* 11 (September 1984): 643–654.

[23] Terry Childers, Susan Heckler, and Michael Houston, "Memory for the Visual and Verbal Components of Print Advertisements," *Psychology and Marketing* 3 (Fall 1986): 147–150.

[24] Other research has found, however, the superiority of visual over verbal recall may not occur for preschool children. See M. Carole Macklin, "The Effect of Audio-Visual Information on Children's Product-Related Recall," *Journal of Consumer Research* 21 (June 1994): 154–164. For additional information on the persuasive effects of visual and verbal information, see Charles S. Areni and K. Chris Cox, "The Persuasive Effects of Evaluation, Expectancy, and Relevancy Dimensions of Incongruent Visual and Verbal Information," in *Advances in Consumer Research*, 21, ed. Chris Allen and Deborah Roedder John (Provo, Utah: Association for Consumer Research, 1994), 337–342.

[25] H. Rao Unnava and Robert E. Burnkrant, "An Imagery-Processing View of the Role of Pictures in Print Advertising," *Journal of Marketing Research* 28 (May 1991): 226–231.

[26] For a review of this literature, see Kathy Lutz and Richard Lutz, "Effects of Interactive Imagery on Learning: Applications to Advertising," *Journal of Applied Psychology* 62(August 1977): 493–498.

[27] James R. Bettman, "Memory Factors in Consumer Choice: A Review," *Journal of Marketing* 43 (Spring 1979): 37–53.

[28] R. N. Kanungo, "Effects of Fittingness, Meaningfulness, and Product Utility," *Journal of Applied Psychology* 52 (August 1968): 290–295.

[29] Elizabeth J. Cowley, "Recovering Forgotten Information: A Study of Consumer Expertise," in *Advances in Consumer Research*, vol. 21, ed. Chris Allen and Deborah Roedder John (Provo, Utah: Association for Consumer Research, 1994), 58–63.

[30] Kim Robertson, "Recall and Recognition Effects of Brand Name Imagery," *Psychology and Marketing* 4 (Spring 1987): 3–15.

[31] James R. Bettman, "Memory Factors in Consumer Choice: A Review," *Journal of Marketing* 43 (Spring 1979): 37–53.

[32] Kevin L. Keller, "Memory Factors in Advertising: The Effect of Advertising Retrieval Cues on Brand Evaluations," *Journal of Consumer Research* 14 (December 1987): 316–333.

[33] Wanda T. Wallace, "Jingles in Advertising: Can They Improve Recall?" in *Advances in Consumer Research*, vol. 17, ed. Marvin Goldberg and Gerald Gorn (Provo, UT: Association for Consumer Research, 1990), 239–242.

[34] Kathryn A. Braun, "Postexperience Advertising Effects on Consumer Memory," *Journal of Consumer Research* 25 (March 1999): 319–334.

[35] Elizabeth Cowley, "How Enjoyable Was It? Remembering an Affective Reaction to a Previous Consumption Experience," *Journal of Consumer Research* 34, (December 2007): 494–505.

[36] Joseph Alba and J. Wesley Hutchinson, "Dimensions of Consumer Expertise," *Journal of Consumer Research* 13 (March 1987): 411–454.

[37] For a different perspective on knowledge structures, see Robert Lawson, "Consumer Knowledge Structures: Networks and Frames," in *Advances in Consumer Research*, vol. 25, ed. Joseph W. Alba and J. Wesley Hutchinson (Provo, UT: Association for Consumer Research, 1998), 334–340.

[38] It's been noted that two types of consumer knowledge exist: objective knowledge (correct information about a product class stored in long-term memory) and subjective knowledge (the perception of what or how much a consumer knows about a product class). See C. Whan Park, David L. Mothersbaugh, and Lawrence Feick, "Consumer Knowledge Assessment," *Journal of Consumer Research* 21 (June 1994): 71–82.

[39] Jay P. Carlson, Leslie H. Vincent, David M. Hardesty, and William O. Bearden, "Objective and Subjective Knowledge Relationships: A Quantitative Analysis of Consumer Research Findings," *Journal of Consumer Research* 35 (February 2009): 864–876.

[40] Andy. "BMW iDrive Still Stucks," *Mobile Experience*, accessed January 3, 2016, http://themobileexperience.blogspot.com/2008/03/bmw-idrive-still-sucks.html. For a review of the 2015 iDrive, see Doug Newcomb, "BMW iDrive (2015)," *PCMag*, October 14, 2015, accessed January 3, 2016, http://www.pcmag.com/article2/0%2c2817%2c2469307%2c00.asp.

[41] Stephen J. Hoch and John Deighton, "Managing What Consumers Learn from Experience," *Journal of Marketing* 53 (April 1989): 1–20.

[42] For additional information on the transfer of consumer knowledge, see Jennifer Gregan-Paxton and Deborah Roedder John, "Consumer Learning by Analogy: A Model of Internal Knowledge Transfer," *Journal of Consumer Research* 24 (December 1997): 266–284.

[43] Stephen J. Hoch and John Deighton, "Managing What Consumers Learn from Experience," *Journal of Marketing* 53 (April 1989): 1–20.

[44] David Horton and Thomas Turnage, *Human Learning* (Englewood Cliffs, NJ: Prentice Hall, 1976).

[45] Harold H. Kassarjian, "Field Theory in Consumer Behavior," in *Consumer Behavior: Theoretical Sources*, ed. Scott Ward and Thomas Robertson (Englewood Cliffs, NJ: Prentice Hall, 1973), 120.

[46] Ravi Mehta, Rui (Juliet) Zhu, and Amar Cheema, "Is Noise Always Bad? Exploring the Effects of Ambient Noise on Creative Cognition," *Journal of Consumer Research* 39, no. 4 (December 2012): 784–799.

[47] Marvin Goldberg and Gerald Gorn, "Happy and Sad TV Programs: How They Affect Reactions to Commercials," *Journal of Consumer Research* 14, no. 3 (December 1987): 387–403.

[48] Frank R. Kardes and Paul M. Herr, "Order Effects in Consumer Judgment, Choice, and Memory: The Role of Initial Processing Goals," in *Advances in Consumer Research*, vol. 17, eds. Marvin Goldberg and Gerald Gorn (Provo, UT: Association for Consumer Research, 1990), 541–546.

[49] Rik G. M. Pieters and Tammo H. A. Bijmolt, "Consumer Memory for Television Advertising: A Field Study of Duration, Serial Position, and Competition Effects," *Journal of Consumer Research* 23 (March 1997): 362–372.

[50] Cong Li, "Primacy Effect or Recency Effect? A long-term Memory Test of Super Bowl Commercials," *Journal of Consumer Behavior* 9 (January–February 2010): 32–44.

[51] Cassie Mogilner, Baba Shiv, and Sheena S. Iyengar, "Eternal Quest for the Best: Sequential (vs. Simultaneous) Option Presentation Undermines Choice Commitment," *Journal of Consumer Research* 39, no. 6 (April 2013): 1300–1312.

[52] Horton and Thomas Turnage, *Human Learning* (Englewood Cliffs, NJ: Prentice Hall, 1976).

[53] Ibid.

[54] Stuart Elliott, "As Customers Flock to the Web, Intel Gives Chase with Its Ad Budget," *New York Times*, October 10, 2007, accessed December 5, 2015, http://www.nytimes.com/2007/10/10/business/media/10adco.html?_r=0.

[55] Kevin Lane Keller, Susan E. Heckler, and Michael J. Houston, "The Effects of Brand Name Suggestiveness on Advertising Recall," *Journal of Marketing* 62 (January 1998): 48–57.

[56] Michael McCarthy, "Gillette Ends Endorsement Deal with Tiger Woods," *USA Today*, December 24, 2010, accessed January 3, 2016, http://content.usatoday.com/communities/gameon/post/2010/12/tiger-woods-dropped-as-endorser-by-gillette/1.

[57] Erica Mina Okada and David J. Reibstein, "When !@#? Happens . . . Effects of Related and Unrelated Positive Associations on the Influence of Negative Secondary Associations," in *Advances in Consumer Research*, vol. 25, ed. Joseph W. Alba and J. Wesley Hutchinson (Provo, UT: Association for Consumer Research, 1998), 349–356.

[58] Claudiu Dimofte and Richard F. Yalch, "The Mere Association Effect and Brand Evaluations," *Journal of Consumer Psychology* 21 (January 2011): 24–37. For a classic article, see John Lynch and Thomas Srull, "Memory and Attentional Factors in Consumer Choice: Concepts and Research Methods," *Journal of Consumer Research* 9 (June 1982): 18–37.

[59] Alan Collins and Elizabeth Loftus, "A Spreading Activation Theory of Semantic Processing," *Psychological Review* 56 (1975): 54–59.

[60] The author purchased a Porsche 911s.

[61] Kevin Lane Keller, "Conceptualizing, Measuring, and Managing Customer-Based Brand Equity," *Journal of Marketing* 57 (January 1993): 1–22.

[62] Vanessage Fuhrmans, "Wather Deal Misfires for BMW's Mini," *Wall Street Journal*, February 6, 2012, B1, B7.

[63] Tom J. Brown, "Schemata in Consumer Research: A Connectionist Approach," in *Diversity in Consumer Behavior: Advances in Consumer Research*, vol. 19, ed. John F. Sherry, Jr., and Brian Sternthal (Provo, UT: Association for Consumer Research, 1992), 787–794.

[64] Michael J. Houston, Terry L. Childers, and Susan E. Heckler, "Picture-Word Consistency and Elaborative Processing of Advertisements," *Journal of Marketing Research* 24, no. 4 (November 1987): 359369.

[65] Mita Sujan, James Bettman, and Harish Sujan, "Effects of Consumer Expectations on Information Processing in Selling Encounters," *Journal of Marketing Research* 23 (November 1986): 346–353.

[66] Juliano Laran, Chris Janiszewski, and Marcus Cunha, Jr., "Context-Dependent Effects of Goal Primes," *Journal of Consumer Research* 35 (December 2008): 653–667.

[67] Aaron C. Kay, Christian Wheeler, John A. Bargh, and Lee Ross, "Material Priming: The Influence of Mundane Physical Objects on Situational Construal and Competitive Behavior Choice," *Organizational and Human Decision Processes* 95 (September 2004): 83–96.

[68] Grainne M. Fitzsimons, Tanya L. Chartrand, and Gavan J. Fitzsimons, "Automatic Effects of Brand Exposure on Motivated Behavior: How Apple Makes You Think Differently," *Journal of Consumer Research* 35 (June 2008): 21–35.

[69] Aparna A. Labroo, Ravi Dhar, and Norbert Schwarez, "Of Frog Wines and Frowning Watches: Semantic Priming, Perceptual Fluency, and Brand Evaluation," *Journal of Consumer Research*, 34 (April 2008): 819–831.

[70] Erica Riebe and John Dawes, "Recall of Radio Advertising in Low and High Advertising Clutter Formats," *International Journal of Advertising* 25, no. 1 (2006): 71–86.

[71] Peter J. Danaher and Guy W. Mullarkey, "Factors Affecting Online Advertising Recall: A Study of Students," *Journal of Advertising Research* 43, no. 3 (September 2003): 252–267.

[72] Charles E. Osgood, *Method and Theory in Experimental Psychology* (New York: Oxford University Press, 1964).

[73] Robert Kent and Chris T. Allen, "Competitive Interference Effects in Consumer Memory for Advertising: The Role of Brand Familiarity," *Journal of Marketing* 58 (July 1994): 97–105.

[74] Ibid.

[75] Ibid.

[76] Nader T. Tavassoli, "Language in Multimedia: Interaction of Spoken and Written Information," *Journal of Consumer Research* 25 (June 1998): 26–37; Mor Regev, Christopher J. Honey, Erez Simony, and Uri Hasson, "Selective and Invariant Neural Responses to Spoken and Written Narratives," *Journal of Neuroscience* (October 2, 2013): 15978–15988.

[77] Charles E. Osgood, *Method and Theory in Experimental Psychology* (New York: Oxford University Press, 1964).

[78] An interesting question concerns whether the interrupted story, or the inserted material causing the interruption, is recalled better. Research indicates the inserted material may actually be more salient. See Richard Harris, Ruth Sturm, Michael Klassen, and John Bechtold, "Language in Advertising: A Psycholinguistic Approach," *Current Issues and Research in Advertising* 9 (1986): 1–26.

[79] H. Ebbinghaus, *Memory*, trans. H. A. Ruger and C. E. Bussenius (New York: Teachers College, 1913).

[80] Hubert A. Zielske, "The Remembering and Forgetting of Advertising," *Journal of Marketing* 23 (January 1959): 231–243.

[81] The Zielsek findings have been replicated many times. For a review, see Hyden Noel and Beth Vallen, "The Spacing Effect in Marketing: A Review of Extant Findings and Directions for Future Research," *Psychology & Marketing* 26, no. 11 (November 2009): 951–969.

[82] Meryl Gardner, "Mood States and Consumer Behavior: A Critical Review," *Journal of Consumer Research* 12 (December 1985): 281–300.

[83] Patricia A. Knowles, Stephen J. Grove, and W. Jeffrey Burroughs, "An Experimental Examination of Mood Effects on Retrieval and Evaluation of Advertisement and Brand Information," *Journal of Academy of Marketing Science* 21 (Spring 1993): 135–142. See also Meryl Gardner, "Effects of Mood States on Consumer Information Processing," *Research in Consumer Behavior* 2 (1987): 113–135.

[84] Angela Y. Lee and Brian Sternthal, "The Effects of Positive Mood on Memory," *Journal of Consumer Research* 26 (September 1999): 115–127.

[85] Thomas S. Srull, "Memory, Mood, and Consumer Judgment," in *Advances in Consumer Research*, ed. Melanie Wallendorf and Paul Anderson (Provo, UT: Association for Consumer Research, 1987), 404–407.

[86] Harper Roehm, Jr. and Michelle Roehm, "Can Brand Encounters Inspire Flashbulb Memories?" *Psychology and Marketing* 25 (2007): 25–40; Jennifer Talarico, "Flashbulb Memories—Why Do We Remember Learning about Dramatic Events so Vividly?" *Medical Xpress*, accessed January 6, 2016, http://medicalxpress.com/news/2015-04-flashbulb-memories-events-vividly.html.

[87] Stefan Ogbac, "Ten Cool Facts about the 2017 Buick LaCrosse," *Motor Trend*, November 25, 2015, accessed January 6, 2016, http://www.motortrend.com/news/10-cool-facts-about-the-2017-buick-lacrosse/.

chapter

5

Motivation and Behavioral Learning

Learning objectives:

1. What is the process through which motivated behavior occurs?

2. What are the emotions consumers experience?

3. What are the psychological needs consumers experience?

4. How does behavioral learning influence consumer behavior?

Consumers and Their Dangerous Hobbies

Consumers are motivated do some strange things with their leisure time. For example, people jump out of perfectly functioning airplanes, possibly to plunge thousands of feet to their death. An estimated 22 people died while parachuting in North America in 2014.[1]

Interestingly, skydiving is *not* one of the five most dangerous sports. Which sports are the most dangerous? If you're talking about the number of people dying while playing a sport, golf and lawn bowling are at the top of the list. On the other hand, if you mean the number of injuries requiring an emergency room, basketball (522,817 visits), bicycling (510,905), and exercise and exercise equipment (466,162) are at the top of the list.[2] Interestingly, among high school and college athletes, cheerleading is particularly dangerous, with more than 25,000 injuries in 2010. Among these, 176 were catastrophic (e.g., serious head and neck injuries).[3] In fact,

the American Medical Association decided in 2014 that cheerleading should be designated a sport, which would increase safety measures and require better training for coaches.[4]

So, why do consumers engage in leisure activities that can result in a trip to the emergency room or even death? The answers lie in the closely related fields of motivation and behavioral learning. More specifically, a motivation for jumping out of a perfectly functioning airplane is found in the opponent-process theory, which is discussed in the next section of the chapter.

The fields of motivation and behavioral learning have practical importance because they help organizations understand and influence consumer needs, desires, and actions. Corporations spend tens of millions of dollars on research to understand how they can motivate people to purchase the full range of consumer goods and services, from automobiles

to clothing to medical services. On the other hand, on the dark side of consumer behavior, public-policy makers seek to determine what motivates people to consume cocaine, heroin, or other addictive drugs.

MOTIVATED BEHAVIOR

Motivation refers to an activated state that accompanies goal-directed behavior.[5] It consists of the "drives, urges, wishes, and desires that initiate the sequence of events leading to a behavior."[6] Motivation begins with the presence of a stimulus that spurs the recognition of a need. **Need recognition** occurs when an actual state of being diverges from a desired state of being. The stimulus may come from inside or outside of the consumer. For example, the stomach rumblings from hunger represent an internal state. An advertising message or a friend's comment about a product would come from outside the consumer.

How needs are recognized and behaviors result can be understood through a control theory approach.[7] From a control theory perspective, a consumer's motivational system functions like a heating, ventilation, and air conditioning system (HVAC). In an HVAC system, a desired temperature is set on the thermostat. In turn, the thermometer measures the actual temperature. If little difference occurs between the actual and desired temperatures, the thermostat tells the system to keep doing what it's doing. However, if the actual temperature diverges too much from the desired one, an interrupt occurs, and the thermostat tells the system to change what it's doing by either adding hot or cold air.

A person's motivational system works similarly. A hypothetical construct called a **comparator** functions like a thermostat and constantly monitors whether a difference occurs between a consumer's desired and actual states. As long as these states are close to each other, the comparator makes no changes in the person's ongoing behavior. If the actual and desired states are too far apart, however, the comparator recognizes a problem and an interrupt occurs. An **interrupt** describes the situation in which the comparator recognizes a need and physiological arousal, emotions are experienced. Also, when an interrupt occurs, the person engages in the cognitive appraisal of the situation and begins a decision-making process to find a solution to the problem.

Both internal and external stimuli influence the desired state and the actual state. There are three types of **internal stimuli**. One is a change in the person's physiological state, such as feelings of hunger. A second type is the personality traits and the self-concept that act as reference points for the desired and actual states. (Personality and the self-concept are discussed in Chapter 6.) For example, our self-concept may lead us to desire a higher-status car than the one we currently drive. Finally, psychological needs can influence the desired and actual states. Examples of psychological needs are McClelland's social, power, and achievement needs, which are discussed later in the chapter. Marketers are increasingly aware of the importance of focusing on the internal states of consumers. For instance, a relatively new field called sensory marketing has emerged in which managers engage consumers' senses to impact their actual state, desired state, feelings, and behaviors.[8] For example, a retailer (e.g., Saks Fifth Avenue) may use rugs and textiles to create soft surfaces that are experienced through the senses of touch and sight to create an upscale atmosphere.

External stimuli also influence the actual and desired states, and several types of external stimuli exist. They include marketing communications, the actions of other people (i.e., social stimuli), situations (e.g., a gift buying occasion, such as Valentine's Day), and the outcomes a person experiences (e.g., purchasing clothing in the wrong size). In addition, changes in stimuli associated with the senses affect consumers. For instance, the level of light is varied in restaurants and bars to influence their atmosphere. That is, as the level of lighting is lowered, people begin to sit closer together and talk in lowered tones. Similarly, the temperature has a huge impact on consumers. Obviously, as the temperature is lowered, people wear and buy more clothing. Interestingly, the temperature even influences the type of movies consumers watch. In cold weather, consumers watch more romance movies. Researchers argued that as the temperature goes down, people have a need for the psychological warmth provided by movies in the romance genre.[9]

A brief example illustrates the control theory approach for understanding consumer motivation. In early 2012, the price of gasoline soared. For many, the increased cost lowered the actual state of the availability of reasonably priced gas. This caused the comparator to perceive a sufficient gap between the desired and actual states to cause an interrupt. Because of the interrupt, emotions (e.g., anger at "Big Oil" companies), and cognitive appraisal were experienced. In the cognitive appraisal process, consumers had to decide whether or not to change their regular set of gasoline buying behaviors. Some consumers may have changed their behavior by driving less. Others may have purchased cars that were more fuel efficient, such as a hybrid. Finally, others may have changed their behavior by spending less money in other areas of their lives, such as by eating out less frequently. The drop in gas prices in 2015 influenced the opposite behavior. In fact, sales of pickups increase when gas prices are lower and passenger car sales increase when prices rise—every dollar of rise or fall in a gallon of gas influences truck or car sales by about 2 percent either way.

An understanding of the control theory approach to understanding motivation has important implications. Marketers can act to create need recognition by developing a product that has a new feature and then employ communications that raise consumers' desired state. For example, Samsung developed the Galaxy S 3 smartphone with the capability of transferring videos merely by touching two phones together. The company then developed advertisements showing people transferring videos. In one, an executive is shown leaving home for a business trip. He's in a cab with the window open. First, his kids are shown transferring videos to his phone by a simple touch. Then, his attractive wife says she has a video for him. They touch phones. Then, with an eyebrow raised, she suggests it would be better if he did not watch the video on the plane. What Samsung did is cleverly increase the desired state for smartphones (i.e., having the capability of transferring videos by touch), which helped make their solution to the problem a success.

There are two additional types of external stimuli: (1) conditioned and unconditioned stimuli and (2) reinforcers and punishers. The strong motivational impact of these external stimuli are readily observed in consumers, such as when a young child receives a present at Christmas (i.e., a positive reinforce) or is punished with a time-out for hitting a sibling. The types of external stimuli are discussed later in the chapter, when three types of behavioral learning are presented: classical conditioning, operant conditioning, and vicarious learning.

Managerial principle 5.1
Use the marketing mix to activate problem recognition by raising the desired state or lowering the perception of the actual state.

CONSUMER EMOTIONS

Emotions and **affect** designate the feelings and moods consumers experience. When need recognition is experienced and an interrupt occurs, affect is experienced in the form of negative emotions. Conversely, when a need state is fulfilled, positive emotions are felt.[10] In addition, when consumers experience a **reinforcer**, positive affect is felt. Conversely, when consumers experience a **punisher**, negative affect is felt.

As noted above, affect is used to denote the feelings, emotions, and moods experienced by consumers. Emotions are differentiated from moods by their greater intensity and psychological urgency.[11] Researchers have identified ten emotional states consumers can experience: interest, joy, surprise, anger, distress, disgust, contempt, fear, shame, and guilt.[12] (As a short exercise, reflect on times when you have felt strong emotions in a consumption context.)

Not only are emotions positive or negative, they also vary in the amount of physiological arousal associated with them. **Physiological arousal** refers to the extent to which a person's body is activated. Arousal can be measured by blood pressure, increases in breathing rate, and the level of skin conductance (i.e., how much a person sweats). Indeed, these are the measures polygraph tests use to evaluate whether someone is lying. In addition, as arousal increases people's eyes dilate, and brain wave activity changes. Finally, increased arousal also boosts the blood flow in the eardrum, which increases its temperature. Marketing researchers use these indicators of physiological arousal to assess consumer reactions to products and marketing communications. For example, one study found that as the length of relationship of consumers with a beloved increased, the amount of emotional arousal (as measured by skin conductance) decreased. The authors interpreted the results to indicate that as the length of relationship with a brand increased, the inclusion of the brand into the self-concept increased, but the level of arousal activated by the brand decreased.[13]

Figure 5.1 shows how the combination of different levels of arousal and affect result in four quadrants of emotions. Thus, emotions can be positive-high arousal (e.g., joy, delight, ecstasy, elation), positive-low arousal (e.g., calm, contented, serene, tranquil), negative-high arousal (e.g., anger, disgust, contempt), and negative-low arousal (e.g., fear, shame, guilt, depression).[14] Recent research found that how consumers defined "happiness" (i.e. positive affect) depended on whether their focus was on the present or the future. If focused on the

FIGURE 5.1.
Four Quadrants of Emotions

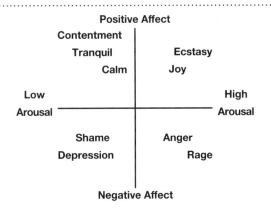

present, consumers defined happiness as calm (i.e., low in arousal), but if focused on the future, they defined it as excited (i.e., high in arousal).[15]

Consumer researchers are increasingly focusing on the study of the impact of affect and arousal on consumer behavior. For example, one recent study found that when the outcomes consumers experience are in the present rather than the future, feelings are relied upon more and weighted more heavily than arousal when making decisions. A classic example is the strategy of casinos to create positive affect for gamblers through the creation of an exciting, noise-filled environment. The positive affective state drives consumers to gamble more (and win in the present) than if they were in a negative affective state.[16]

Because emotions are physiological phenomena, they're accompanied by a cascade of hormones in the body. Importantly, our bodies have evolved such that systems are in place to maintain a balance. Some interesting effects result from the body's ability to maintain balance in emotions. Opponent-process theory explains these effects.

Opponent-Process Theory

A researcher made an interesting observation about the emotional reactions of parachutists. During their first free fall, before the parachute opens, they may experience terror. They yell, their eyes bulge, their bodies go stiff, and they breathe irregularly. Upon landing safely, they initially walk around stunned, with stone-faced expressions. Then they begin smiling, talking, gesticulating, and showing every indication of being elated. Why would someone who was terrified suddenly become elated? The answer is found in a theory of motivation called the opponent-process theory of acquired motivation.[17]

According to **opponent-process theory**, when a person receives a stimulus that elicits an immediate emotional reaction—positive or negative—two things occur. First, the immediate positive or negative emotional reaction is felt. Next, a second emotional reaction occurs opposite to the initial experience. The combination of the two emotional reactions results in the overall feeling experienced by the consumer. Because the second emotional reaction is delayed, the overall experience consists of the consumer first experiencing the initial positive or negative feeling. After some time period, however, this feeling gradually declines and the opposite feeling is felt. Likewise, the parachutists first felt extreme fear, but, after landing, the fear turned into its opposite emotion—elation.

Although opponent-process theory is quite simple, it has broad explanatory power. It can be used to account for a variety of consumer behaviors, such as drug addiction, cigarette smoking, running (i.e., runner's high), sauna bathing, and video game playing. For example, why do people endure the pain of running a marathon? The answer is that through the operation of opponent processes, the pain that accompanies the endurance run is followed by physiological pleasure. When combined with the positive reinforcement from family and friends, long-distance running can be an extremely positive experience.

Opponent-process theory also explains some aspects of the dark side of consumer behavior. For example, why do some consumers sink into debt from overusing credit cards? One explanation is that consumers make a purchase with a charge card to make themselves feel better. After the purchase, however, they begin to feel bad because of the negative rebound (as predicted by the theory). Further, the bills that inevitably arrive exacerbate the negative feelings. To combat

Giving away free samples in a grocery store acts to prime consumers to purchase more food.
Photo by John Mowen

the negative feelings, the consumer visits the local mall or clicks on a website to make another purchase. The vicious cycle results in major financial problems.

Priming   Another concept emerging from opponent-process theory is priming. **Priming** occurs when a brief exposure to a stimulus (e.g., food, playing a video game, or even a word or something in the situational context) influences a later response. An example is taste cravings. As Lay's potato chips famously pointed out in its slogan, "Betcha can't eat just one." The taste of the first potato chip activates the consumer such that the drive to consume additional chips is greater than the drive prior to eating the first one. The effects of priming can influence the consumption of drugs (e.g., cocaine and alcohol) as well as activate goals that are stored in memory.[18]

Marketers intuitively use principles of priming on a regular basis. For example, providing samples in a supermarket is a classic example of priming. One study found that providing free samples of doughnuts to grocery store shoppers resulted in consumers spending more than they had intended.[19]

Priming consumers with a small amount of a food product activates a physiological system, such as hunger. In addition, each of the other types of internal states can be primed. For example, the memories of consumers can also be primed, which in turn can impact the desired or actual state. For example, in one study, the researchers primed Asian consumers by frequently embedding the numeral 8 or the numeral 4 in a task in which they were asked to see how quickly they could respond to visual stimuli. In some Asian cultures, eight is considered to be lucky and four is unlucky. After doing the task, participants were introduced to an ostensibly different experiment in which they recorded their feelings, thoughts, and intentions. The results revealed that when the positive memories of being lucky were activated, the respondents were happier and felt luckier as compared with those primed by the unlucky number. In addition, exposure to the lucky number increased their willingness to participate in a lottery and the amount of money they would invest in different financial options. Thus, priming the lucky number 8 or unlucky number 4 influenced both their affect and their actual state of affairs—that is, "I feel lucky" or "I feel unlucky."[20]

In sum, the study of how feelings and emotions impact consumers is an important area for consumer and marketing researchers. But what are the internal needs that can activate positive and negative emotions? These are discussed in the next section.

Managerial principle 5.2
Influence consumers' actual and/or desired states through priming by providing a small experience with the product or with stimuli that activate concepts stored in semantic memory, including feelings, words, numbers, goals, and traits.

CONSUMER PSYCHOLOGICAL NEEDS

Psychologists and consumer researchers have identified a number of different types of needs. For example, a consumer researcher differentiated expressive from utilitarian needs.[21] **Expressive needs** involve desires by consumers to fulfill social, ego, and/or aesthetic requirements. Expressive needs are closely related to the maintenance of a consumer's self-concept. Expressive needs may be felt when outdated clothing fails to match a person's self-concept of being at the forefront of fashion. In contrast, **utilitarian needs** involve desires by consumers to solve basic problems, such as filling a car's gas tank or paying bills.

Much of the effort to understand needs has been performed by psychologists. Two well-known approaches to the identification of needs are Maslow's hierarchy of needs and Murray's social needs. Table 5.1 provides a list of the needs identified by Maslow and by Murray. Often, by the time students take a consumer behavior course, they have had the Maslow hierarchy presented in several other classes. Moreover, the research performed on these theories has been quite inconsistent. In particular, research hasn't confirmed the idea in Maslow's hierarchy that more basic needs must be fulfilled prior to the activation of more advanced needs. For example, young adults (including millennials) have been found to focus more on self-actualization needs than mature adults.[22] This finding is inconsistent with Maslow's concept that self-actualization is the last of the needs to be realized.

A. Maslow's Hierarchy of Needs

- Self-actualization
- Aesthetic needs
- Cognitive understanding
- Esteem needs
- Love belongingness
- Safety needs
- Physiological needs

B. Murray's List of Human Needs

Abasement	Harm avoidance
Achievement	Infavoidance
Affiliation	Nurturance
Aggression	Order
Autonomy	Play
Counteraction	Rejection
Defendance	Sentience
Deference	Sex
Dominance	Succorance
Exhibition	Understanding

TABLE 5.1

Needs Identified by Maslow and by Murray

SOURCE: A. H. Maslow, Motivation and Personality, 2nd ed. [New York: Harper :& Row, 1970]; and H. A. Murray, Exploration in Personality [New York; Oxford, 1938].

While the hierarchical structure of Maslow's theory has been criticized, the basic needs are very real. Consumers do exhibit each of his needs. Indeed, advertisers frequently seek to activate these needs in their marketing communications.

While the ideas from Maslow's hierarchy have received mixed reviews, other broad theories of motivation have received research support. In this section, we first describe McClelland's theory of learned needs. We then discuss four additional types of needs: the need to maintain an optimum stimulation level, the need for behavioral freedom, the need to avoid risk, and the need to determine causality.

McClelland's Theory of Learned Needs

Psychologist David McClelland identified four basic learned needs that motivate people: the needs for achievement, affiliation, power, and uniqueness/novelty.[23] Those with a high **need for achievement** seek to get ahead, to strive for success, and to take responsibility for solving problems. The **need for affiliation** reflects people's motivation to make friends, to become members of groups, and to associate with others. Those with a high need for affiliation tend to place the desire to be with others ahead of the need to succeed. The **need for power** refers to the desire to obtain and exercise control over others. The goal is to influence, direct, and possibly dominate other people. The need for power can take two directions according to McClelland. It can be positive, resulting in persuasive and inspirational power, or it can be negative, resulting in the desire to dominate and obtain submission from others. Finally, the **need for uniqueness** refers to desires to perceive ourselves as different and original.[24]

Some research has investigated the relationship between McClelland's ideas and consumer behavior. For example, a study investigated the motives for creating personal web pages. The results were consistent with McClelland's learned needs. That is, among the possible motive statements, 74 percent matched one of the learned needs. The two motives most frequently identified were the need for affiliation (i.e., through personal portrayal and social interaction) and the need for power (i.e., by conquering technology). Surprisingly, the need for uniqueness was identified as the predominant motive in less than 25 percent of the respondents and the need for achievement in less than 20 percent of the respondents.[24]

A clear prediction from McClelland's work is that products can be advertised with motivational themes derived from the four consumer needs he identified. The motivational characteristics of the target market are assessed via market research. Advertising themes are then developed to activate the motive, which in turn influences attitudes, beliefs, and behaviors.

Managerial principle 5.3
Identify how a product can fulfill one of Maslow's, Murray's, or McClelland's needs and activate the need via promotional activities.

Maintaining Optimum Stimulation Levels

Consumers are motivated to maintain an **optimum stimulation level**, which is a person's preferred amount of physiological activation or arousal. Activation may vary from very low levels (e.g., sleep) to very high levels (e.g., severe panic). Individuals are motivated to maintain an optimum level of stimulation and will take action to correct the level when it becomes too high or too low. If the arousal level is too high, the individual takes steps to lower it. Conversely, if activation is too low, the individual takes action to raise the stimulation level.

People who prefer higher levels of stimulation score high on a scale that measures sensation seeking and the need for arousal.[25] To maintain the high levels of stimulation they require, sensation seekers are more apt to engage in such activities as skydiving, mountain climbing, and high-stakes gambling. In addition, the desire to maintain an optimum stimulation level explains why consumers seek variety in their purchases, such as for restaurants, music, and leisure activities. Variety seeking occurs when a consumer selects a new brand or activity while still having a high degree of satisfaction with the current brand. Indeed, researchers have found consumers will even switch temporarily to less-preferred options just to create variety in their lives.[26]

The motive to maintain an optimum stimulation level has wide implications for marketers because a host of products and services act to arouse or depress a person's activation level. For example, various types of drugs lower arousal levels (e.g., sleep aids) or raise them (e.g., caffeine or amphetamines). The desire to maintain an optimum level of stimulation also accounts for some cases of spontaneous brand switching and variety-seeking among products.[27]

Many leisure activities strongly influence levels of arousal, including bungee jumping, whitewater rafting, and hunting. Indeed, the desire of some consumers to attend sporting events or to watch horror movies is influenced, in part, by the need for excitement. Similarly, some rides at amusement parks are built to scare their customers. Here is a description of the Tower of Terror in Queensland, Australia, which some describe as the scariest in the world.

> *The Tower of Terror has separated over eight million Australian rollercoaster riders from their lunches since its launch in 1997. Riders are catapulted out of a tunnel and up a vertical tower, reaching a top speed of 161 kilometers per hour in just seven seconds. At the top of the 115ft high tower they hang motionless and weightless for a split second before plummeting back to earth, into the tunnel and out to find the nearest sick bag.*[28]

The desire for hedonic experiences is closely related to the need to maintain an optimum stimulation level. For consumer researchers, **hedonic consumption** refers to the needs of consumers to use products and services to create fantasies, to gain feelings through the senses, and to obtain emotional arousal.[29] The feelings consumers seek to gain, however, may not be uniformly pleasurable. Particularly in their leisure activities, consumers may seek to experience a variety of emotions, such as love, joy, and even fear. At first thought, it seems odd that someone would seek out negative experiences such as fear. However, as mentioned earlier, roller coasters are built to create fear. Even their names are designed to instill fright, such as Screamer and the Beast. Similarly, horror movies are created to frighten and disgust people. In these cases of roller coasters and horror films, the underlying goal involves sensation seeking.

Managerial principle 5.4
Identify your target market's preferred level of stimulation and develop communications that link your product to the level that is sought.

The Motivation to Maintain Behavioral Freedom

Researchers have found that if the freedom to select a product or service is impeded, consumers respond by reacting against the threat. The motivational state resulting from the response to threats to behavioral freedom has been labeled psychological reactance.[30]

Reactance describes the motivational state of the person whose behavioral freedom has been threatened. A number of years ago, corporate managers the maker of Crayola crayons made a decision to retire eight colors from the popular sixty-four-crayon flip-top box and replace them with more contemporary colors. "Boring" colors, such as raw umber, maize, and lemon yellow were eliminated and replaced by "sexy" new hues, including wild strawberry, fuchsia, teal blue, and cerulean. Consumers reacted to the change with a boycott. In one protest march, protestors carried a coffin. One marcher said, "They call it a retirement. I call it a burial." First grader Ebony Faison said, "Whenever I draw me, I use raw umber. What color should I color now?"[31] For a year following the change, the company received more than three hundred calls and letters a month protesting the change. One spokesperson explained, "We were aware of the loyalty and nostalgia surrounding Crayola crayons, but we didn't know we hit such a nerve."[32]

Marketers intentionally use reactance principles to influence consumers. Thus, sharp restrictions of the supply of products can increase demand because their perceived value increases as a result of reactance. For example, researchers have found that one-day-only sales increase consumer desire to make purchases more than three-day-only sales. Similarly, companies will deliberately limit the supply of a popular brand in order to increase scarcity and thereby increase consumer desire for the item. For example, one Christmas season, Nike Inc. deliberately limited the supply of the Jordan Retro 11 Concord sneaker. Because of the sneaker's scarcity, long lines of consumers formed outside Foot Locker retail stores in an attempt to snap up the popular shoe. One 23-year-old New Yorker said he hoped to buy several pairs that he could sell for a profit in his neighborhood. Foot Locker is the largest retailer of Jordan sneakers. Its CEO said the strategy of making the shoes scarce was "choreographed months in advance."[33] Extremely high-priced products often use a scarcity appeal.

Two types of threats can lead to reactance. **Social threats** involve external pressure from others to induce a consumer to do something. Examples include pressing the consumer to buy a certain product, to go to a certain play, or to vote for a particular political candidate. If the pressure is too great, the consumer reacts against it, resulting in a boomerang effect. In such instances the consumer moves in the opposite direction intended by the person engaging in the social influence attempt. In the personal-selling area of marketing, the problem of the boomerang effect is great. Salespeople must take definite steps to persuade customers to buy their products. However, salespeople can't push too hard or they risk alienating the prospect. A time-tested strategy is to give customers information so they can persuade themselves the product is the right one to buy.

A second threat to behavioral freedom comes from impersonal sources. **Impersonal threats** are barriers that restrict the ability to buy a particular product or service. The barriers may result from a shortage of the product, from the possibility someone else will buy the product, or even from a rise in its price. In each case, something comes between the consumer and the purchase of the product. The consumer's likely reaction is to reevaluate the product and want it even more. When Blue Bell Ice Cream had to stop production in 2015 due to a *Listeria* contamination, some people in Texas proclaimed they now could eat no ice cream because as far as they were concerned, there was only one brand of ice cream in Texas. Even the decision to buy one product over another can result in the person's reevaluating the alternatives not chosen more positively.[34]

Managerial principle 5.5
Use promotional tactics that restrict the perceived supply of a product to increase its value to consumers.

For a consumer to experience reactance, three requirements must be met. First, the consumer must believe he or she has the freedom to make a free choice in a given situation. If the general ability to make a choice is unavailable, perhaps because alternative products are unavailable, reactance won't occur. Second, a threat to the freedom must be experienced. Third, the decision must be one that's of some importance to the consumer.[35]

Perceived Risk and Consumer Motivation

Perceived risk is defined as a consumer's perception of the overall negativity of a course of action based on an assessment of the possible negative outcomes and the likelihood those outcomes will occur.[36] As such, perceived risk consists of two major concepts: the negative outcomes of a decision and the probability these outcomes will occur.

Consumers are constantly faced with decisions that involve uncertainty and the possibility of negative outcomes. Indeed, almost any high-involvement decision a consumer makes has uncertainty. In general, consumers are motivated to be risk averse in their actions. However, exceptions to the rule exist. As discussed earlier, some consumers appear to seek risk, in part, to raise their activation levels to optimum levels.[31]

Types of Consumer Risks   The first discussion of the concept of perceived risk appeared in marketing literature in 1960.[38] Since that time, consumer researchers have sought to identify the various types of consumer risk. Table 5.2 identifies seven types of risk to which consumers may respond.[39] These are financial, performance, physical, psychological, social, time, and opportunity loss.

1. Financial—risk that the outcome will harm the consumer financially (e.g., will buying a car cause financial hardship?)
2. Performance—risk that the product won't perform as expected (e.g., will the car really accelerate faster than a Porsche 928?)
3. Physical—risk that the product will physically harm the buyer (e.g., will the car collapse in a crash?)
4. Psychological—risk that the product will lower the consumer's self-image (e.g., will I look like a soccer mom or dad rather than a cool hipster if I buy this car?)
5. Social—risk that friends or acquaintances will criticize the purchase (e.g., will my best friend think I'm trying to show him up by buying a Porsche?)
6. Time—risk that a decision will cost too much time (e.g., will buying a sports car cost me time because I have to tune it so frequently?)
7. Opportunity loss—risk that by taking one action, the consumer will miss out doing something else he or she would really prefer to do (e.g., by buying a Porsche 928, will I miss out on buying several expensive oil paintings?)

TABLE 5.2
Types of Perceived Risk

The promotional work of marketers is often geared toward lowering the perceived risk of consumers. Advertisements may be used to point out how a particular product or service may lower risk. For example, insurance advertising stresses the reduction of financial risk. Automobile manufacturers, such as Volvo, mention the reduction of physical risk when touting the safety of their brands. Many advertisements for personal-use products use a reduction-of-social-risk theme. Thus, products are available to help consumers ward off ring around the collar, bad breath, and dandruff, all of which can cause social embarrassment. Deodorant ads frequently use a social-risk theme. For example, by using the right deodorant, you can "Raise your hand, if you're Sure."

Factors Influencing the Perception of Risk   Researchers have found that a number of factors influence the amount of risk consumers perceive in a given situation. First, the characteristics of the individual consumer influence his or her perception of risk. Researchers have found the following personal characteristics to be associated with a greater willingness to accept risk: higher self-confidence, higher self-esteem, lower anxiety, and lower familiarity with the problem.

Second, the nature of the task influences risk perception. For example, researchers have discovered that voluntary risks are more acceptable to people than involuntary risks.[40] **Voluntary risks** include choosing to drive a car on a trip or choosing to go on a ski vacation. **Involuntary risks** include living in a home near a proposed nuclear power plant or undergoing surgery for a life-threatening condition. For voluntary activities, consumers perceive less risk than there really is. In contrast, consumers perceive more risk for involuntary activities than is actually present.

Third, the characteristics of the product or service can also influence perceived risk. In general, products or services whose use may result in highly negative outcomes are perceived as riskier. Factors associated with such negative outcomes include cost, social visibility, and the potential physical danger in its use.

Finally, risk perception may also be influenced by the salience of the potential negative outcomes. When negative outcomes resulting from product or service failures are highly salient, they're more available in memory, so consumers may erroneously perceive the product or service as riskier than it really is.[41] For example, in 2015, a Russian plane crashed in Egypt's Sinai Peninsula, killing all 224 people on board. The availability in memory of the tragedy increased the perceived risk of air travel in countries around the world.

Managerial principle 5.6
Assess the risk your target market perceives in your products, then take steps to reduce the perceived risk.

How to Reduce Perceived Risk   Because some degree of perceived risk is inherent in nearly all consumer decisions, individuals need ways to help them to make decisions with some confidence. One approach is to compare their perception of the amount of risk present to some criterion of how much risk is acceptable.[42] If the perceived risk is greater than the acceptable risk, the consumer is motivated to reduce the risk in some way or to forgo making the decision. What do consumers do to reduce the amount of perceived risk? In general, all the risk-reduction strategies involve taking steps to lower the perceived likelihood that negative outcomes will occur. Table 5.3 lists six risk-reduction strategies.

TABLE 5.3
Risk-Reduction Strategies

1.	Be brand loyal and consistently purchase the same brand.
2.	Buy through brand image and purchase a quality national brand.
3.	Buy through store image from a trusted retailer.
4.	Seek out information in order to make a well-informed decision.
5.	Buy the most expensive brand, which is likely to have high quality.
6.	Buy the least expensive brand in order to reduce financial risk.

The Motivation to Attribute Causality

As consumers move through their everyday lives, events happen that require explanation. The performance of a good or service may fall below expectations, a product endorser may strongly tout a brand of soft drink, a salesperson may flatter a customer's ego, or a company-related disaster may occur (e.g., the crash of an airliner). In each case, consumers try to understand the cause. They want to identify why the good or service brought dissatisfaction, why the endorser advocated buying the soft drink, why the salesperson was so ingratiating, and why the airliner crashed.[43]

The explanation of the processes through which people determine causality has been labeled attribution theory.[44] According to **attribution theory**, people attempt to determine whether the cause for action resulted from something internal or external to the person or object in question. For example, a consumer may ask whether an endorser recommended a product because he actually liked it (an **internal attribution**) or because he was paid to endorse it (an **external attribution**). Similarly, a consumer may ask herself why she bought a particular brand. If she attributes the purchase to something internal to the product (e.g., its good qualities), she may purchase it again. On the other hand, if she attributes the purchase to something external to the product (e.g., pressure from a salesperson or a temporary reduction in price), she may purchase another brand in the future. By identifying the cause for action, people gain control over their environment. Indeed, researchers have found that one reason people are attracted to the World Wide Web is that it gives them a sense of control.[45]

People make attributions as to the cause of an action to determine how to act in the future. Thus, if a consumer decides an endorser advocates a product merely because he or she is paid to do so, the consumer will attribute the cause of the message to an external factor (i.e., the money) rather than to an internal factor (i.e., the endorser's like for the product). Such an attribution will result in the message having little or no impact on the consumer's attitude toward the product. Because consumers tend to make external attributions to the endorsements of highly paid celebrities, companies may seek "virgin endorsers," who have not previously endorsed products. An example of a virgin product endorser is Alec Baldwin who became a spokesman for Capital One. What made this virgin endorser even more effective was that he donated his payment from Capital One to charities that support the arts.[46]

Consumers also make attributions as to the cause of the purchase of a brand. For example, if a brand is purchased when a large price discount is given, consumers reveal less brand loyalty because they attribute the purchase to the sale rather than to the quality of the product. Interestingly, however, if the consumer believes he or she was responsible for receiving the price discount, the attitude toward the brand increases, which results in repurchases and positive word-of-mouth communications.[47] One means for retailers to influence self-responsibility attributions is to give out cards that are punched each time the consumer makes a purchase. After ten purchases, the person gets a free cup of coffee, submarine sandwich, or whatever.

Attribution theory is actually composed of a family of theories, each of which explains how people determine causality in various situations. We'll examine two of them: the augmentation-discounting model of Harold Kelley and the fundamental attribution error.

The Augmentation-Discounting Model[48] The augmenting-discounting model is based upon the idea people examine the environmental pressures that impede or propel a particular action in order to determine the underlying cause for an action. Discounting occurs if external pressures could provoke someone to act in a particular way. That is, the actions would be expected given the circumstances. In this case, people believe the actions were caused by the environment rather than by the person's actual beliefs, feelings, and desires. In such circumstances, the person discounts the action as representing the other's real beliefs. In summary, the **discounting principle** states that the role of a particular cause in producing a given outcome is discounted if other plausible causes are also present. An example would be making the judgment the money paid to an endorser caused him or her to endorse a particular product.

What happens if a person moves against environmental pressures to do something? This is unexpected given the circumstances. As a consequence, the observer will infer that the person must have been highly internally motivated. The **augmenting principle** states that when a person moves against the forces of the environment to do something unexpected, the belief that the action represents the person's actual opinions, feelings, and desires is increased. An example of the augmentation principle would be a computer salesperson telling a prospective customer a computer made by a competitor was superior to one the salesperson sold. In such an instance, the salesperson would be moving against hisown best interests. Such an unexpected event augments the belief he really believed the statement. It would also increase the customer's trust in the salesperson.

One of the major difficulties faced by marketers is how to avoid having consumers discount their messages. Consumers recognize pressures exist to sell products and to make profits. Thus, when consumers watch advertisements on television or receive promotional messages, they tend to discount the messages and make external attributions. In general, consumers aren't particularly confident that promotional messages accurately describe product characteristics. For example, in one study, more than 59 percent of respondents found "statistical" claims in advertisements to be unbelievable.[49]

The Fundamental Attribution Error   The **fundamental attribution error** states that people have a systematic bias to make internal attributions for the cause of action of others. That is, when an individual or organization (e.g., an airline) engages in an action that results in an outcome, observers tend to believe the cause of the action was the person's or organization's true beliefs or policies. This occurs even when, in reality, the person or organization had no choice in the matter or the outcome was caused by purely external forces.[50]

The fundamental attribution error can have both positive and negative effects for corporations. On the positive side, it can benefit both salespersons[51] and celebrity endorsers.[52] That is, the bias causes consumers to believe the salesperson or the celebrity endorser strongly advocates the brand because of his or her true feelings (i.e., an internal attribution) rather than because of the money he or she receives (i.e., an external attribution). On the negative side, if a problem occurs in the provision of a service (e.g., a product is received late or a bad experience occurs in a restaurant), the fundamental attribution error increases the likelihood blame will be placed on the company rather than on external causes.[53]

The Managerial Implications of Motivation

In addition to the fundamental attribution error, researchers have identified a number of additional problems in how consumers make causal attributions. For example, a recent study found consumers have a bias to infer the causes of events from their consequences. Suppose a computer failure (an event) results in a highly negative consequence, such as job losses. In such a case, consumers will have a bias to infer a large cause, such as a widespread computer virus. On the other hand, if the computer failure resulted in a minimal negative consequence, such as an hour of lost time, consumers will infer a small cause, such as a failure of a cooling fan. Thus, while the event was the same (i.e., a computer

Managerial principle 5.7
Develop your marketing strategy so internal attributions are made for the purchase of a product and attributions external to the company are made for product problems.

failure), the perception of the cause changed depending upon whether the outcome was large or small.[54]

BEHAVIORAL LEARNING AND CONSUMER BEHAVIOR

Behavioral learning is the theoretical basis for the behavioral-influence perspective on consumer behavior in which environmental forces influence behavior directly. From the perspective of the control theory approach to motivation, behavioral learning occurs when external stimuli (i.e., environmental forces) and/or outcomes directly influence behavior without an interrupt, need recognition, or cognitive appraisal necessarily occurring. Importantly, however, emotions often accompany behavioral learning. Three behavioral learning theories are discussed in the following sections: classical conditioning, operant conditioning, and observational learning. Each of the theories has a strong motivational component. For example, emotions of consumers can be classically conditioned. In addition, through operant conditioning and vicarious learning, consumers can become highly motivated to obtain a reinforcer (e.g., money) or to avoid a punisher (e.g., a poorly performing product).

Classical Conditioning

Classical conditioning causes consumers to engage in a variety of behaviors, including responding more positively to advertisements, purchasing more in restaurants and grocery stores, and buying more with their credit cards. In classical conditioning, a neutral stimulus, such as a brand name, is paired with a stimulus that elicits a response. Through a repetition of the pairing, the **neutral stimulus** takes on the ability to elicit the response.

Russian physiologist Ivan Pavlov discovered the phenomenon while working with dogs. The dogs had the messy propensity to begin salivating profusely (the unconditioned response) each time meat powder (the unconditioned

SOCIAL MEDIA

What Motivates Consumers to Use Social Media?

Many of the motives identified in this chapter influence consumers' use of social media. The motive that has been most frequently identified in research studies is affiliation/social needs. The desires to belong, to be accepted by peers, to keep in contact with friends, and to make new friends all emerge from affiliation needs. Among the social media identified in Chapter 2, these needs are especially important for consumers using Facebook and Twitter. You should note that affiliation needs are found in the needs theories of Maslow, Murray, and McClelland.

The motives activated, however, also depend on the type of social media. For those who take the time and effort to create and pin photos to Pinterest, achievement motivation (identified by both Murray and McClelland), esteem needs (Maslow), exhibition needs (Murray), and aesthetic needs (Maslow) may be functioning. In addition to affiliation needs, motives for participating in Facebook may include the needs for play (Murray) and esteem (Maslow). Affiliation needs, as well as achievement in one's career, could also play a role in participating in LinkedIn. In sum, the extreme popularity and exponential growth of social media are readily explained by their appeal to numerous and varied motives.

stimulus, or UCS) was presented to them. The stimulus of the meat powder reflexively elicited the response of salivation. He discovered that when a bell rang before the dogs got the meat powder, salivation would occur even though the dogs hadn't received the meat powder. The bell represented a conditioned stimulus (CS) that elicited a conditioned response—the salivation. A variety of such stimulus-response linkages can be exhibited in people. For example, playing soothing music may elicit the response of relaxation.

Stated formally, **classical conditioning** occurs when a previously neutral stimulus (the CS) is repeatedly paired with the eliciting stimulus (the UCS). In the pairing, the CS needs to occur prior to the UCS, so it predicts the UCS. After a number of such pairings, the ability to elicit an unconditioned response is transferred to the CS. The response elicited by the CS is called the **conditioned response** (CR). Research on classical conditioning emphasizes that mere contiguity (or closeness in time) of the pairing of the CS with the UCS isn't enough to achieve classical conditioning.[55] Conditioning results from the informational relationship of the CS and the UCS. For the CS to provide information about the UCS, it must predict the occurrence of the UCS. Figure 5.2 depicts these relationships. For optimal conditioning to occur, the CS should slightly precede the UCS in time.[56] In the experiments by Pavlov, the ringing of a bell (the CS) preceded the presence of the meat powder (the UCS). After a number of such pairings, the mere ringing of the bell elicited the salivation (the CR).

FIGURE 5.2
The Classical Conditioning Paradigm

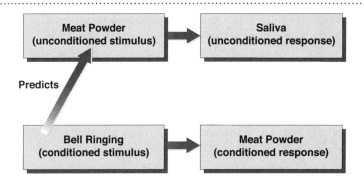

Researchers have found a variety of stimuli act to classically condition consumers. For example, music can influence consumers via a classical-conditioning process. In one experiment, the tempo of music played in a grocery was varied over a nine-week period. At various times, customers heard no music, slow-tempo music, or fast-tempo music. The study revealed significant differences in buying when slow- or fast-tempo music was played. When the pace at which customers moved between two points was measured, researchers found that those in fast-tempo conditions moved significantly faster than did those in the slow-tempo conditions. Interestingly, daily gross sales volume were 38 percent higher in the slow-tempo conditions.[57]

These results suggest shoppers may have been classically conditioned during their lives to respond to music in certain predictable ways. Thus fast-paced music, when played in a grocery store, causes customers to move faster. The fast pace then impedes buying. Similar findings have been obtained in a restaurant setting. The results revealed that when slow-tempo music was played, customers tended to stay longer at tables and to purchase more from the bar.

The estimated gross margin of the restaurant was significantly higher because of the increased bar sales.[58, 59]

In other studies, researchers found stimuli associated with spending money (specifically credit card insignias) may actually elicit spending responses. In the carefully controlled series of studies, one group of subjects was placed in a spending situation in which a MasterCard sign was in view. Another group of subjects was placed in the same situation, but the sign wasn't present. The presence of the sign caused respondents to make buying decisions to spend more quickly, to indicate that more would be spent on a clothing purchase and other consumer goods, to estimate they would give more to a charity, and to give more to a charity.[60] In explaining his results, the author proposed credit cards become paired with the buying act. For many people, the buying act takes on the properties of a UCS that elicits the UCR of positive feelings. Through many pairings of the credit card with the buying act, the credit card becomes a CS that elicits a CR of positive feelings. The positive feelings elicited by the credit card, in turn, make it more likely a person will spend money when the card s present.

The results of one study illustrate the importance of the CS preceding the UCS and of having those stimuli match up.[61] In the study, the UCS was a fictitious sports drink. In one condition, the UCS was Michael Jordan, who was a match with the sport drink because of his athletic prowess. In the other condition, the UCS was Pierce Brosnan. While equally liked by subjects in the experiment, Brosnan wasn't a match with the product because he's not known as an athlete. In addition, the celebrities were either paired with the sports drink so the drink predicted the showing of their photograph, or the photos were shown in a random order so no pairings occurred. The results revealed when Jordan was paired with the sports drink, the evaluations of the drink were significantly higher than when the photos of Jordan and the drink were shown randomly. This shows the CS must precede and predict the CR. In addition, the results revealed that conditioning didn't occur for Brosnan because he didn't match the product.

Alert readers will recognize neither Jordan nor Brosnan really represent an unconditioned stimulus. In reality, they were originally conditioned through their association with exciting, fun movies that acted as unconditioned stimuli. After they were conditioned, they became what are called secondary stimuli, which can cause classical conditioning to occur and thereby transfer their positive affect to a product.

It's also critical to avoid having a brand paired with stimuli that elicit negative affect. Competitors do this frequently. For example, in political campaigns, an opponent will link a candidate to some very negative event or person. Researchers have found evidence of the negative impact of having a product paired with a disliked celebrity. To develop a baseline evaluation, a music video was first assessed without an actor present. Then, it was paired with either a liked actor or a disliked actor. Predictably, the evaluation increased in the pairing with the liked actor and decreased in the pairing with the disliked actor.[62]

Research evidence shows consumers respond to a variety of stimuli in a manner consistent with classical conditioning.[63] The idea is to pair the brand name (the CS) with a UCS that elicits either a buying response (e.g., the credit card effect) or a positive affective response. By classically conditioning a brand name to elicit a positive affective response, the likelihood of consumers purchasing the brand increases. Examples of UCSs to which a brand can be paired

Managerial principle 5.8
In your marketing communications build positive affect toward your product by having it appear just prior to a positive emotion eliciting stimulus.

include beautiful people, music that's liked, stunning pictures, babies, and puppies. In sum, the use of classical conditioning principles is an important strategy for influencing consumers.

Operant Conditioning

Operant conditioning is a process in which the frequency of the occurrence of a behavior is modified by the consequences of the behavior.[64] Thus, when a consumer does something, such as buy a product, the consequences of the behavior will change the probability of it occurring again. If the behavior is positively reinforced, say, by the product performing well or by friends complimenting the person on his or her purchase, the likelihood of the purchase will increase. If the behavior is punished, say, because the product failed or because friends ridiculed the purchase, the likelihood of repurchase will decrease. Reinforcers and punishers are strong motivators that dramatically impact consumer behavior.

Operant conditioning is a sophisticated form of behavioral learning. The following sections delve into its key components.

Reinforcement and Influencing Behavior   Recall that a reinforcer is anything that occurs after a behavior and changes the likelihood that the behavior will be repeated.[65] Three types of reinforcers influence the probability of behavior reoccurring. First, a **positive reinforcer** involves placing an appropriate reward immediately after a behavior occurs. The reinforcer increases the likelihood the behavior will be repeated. Giving consumers a rebate of $2,500 if they purchase a particular brand of car is an example of a positive reinforcer.

A second type of reinforcer is a negative reinforcer. A **negative reinforcer** involves the removal of an aversive stimulus. That is, a behavior that results in the elimination of something negative is reinforced and is more likely to occur again in the future. An example of negative reinforcement is taking a pill (e.g., Excedrin) that relieves a headache. The behavior of taking the pill eliminates an aversive stimulus (the headache). Thus, the pill represents a negative reinforcer and, as a result, the behavior of taking the pill again is increased. One humorous example of the use of a negative reinforcer is a sign which reads, "Unattended children will be given an expresso and a free puppy."[66] In other words, recipients had to watch their children, or face the consequences.

A secondary reinforcer is the third type of reinforcer. A **secondary reinforcer** is a previously neutral stimulus that acquires reinforcing properties through its association with a primary reinforcer. Early in one's life, all reinforcers are of a primary nature. Such primary reinforcers are stimuli that are necessary for life and basic happiness, such as food, water, and soft touching. Over a period of time, previously neutral stimuli can become secondary reinforcers. The process occurs by pairing the neutral stimulus over and over with the primary stimulus. As a result of the pairing, the neutral stimulus takes on reinforcing properties similar to those of the primary stimuli. For example, money is a secondary reinforcer. That is, until it's paired with receiving primary reinforcers (e.g., getting things a person needs), it has no reinforcing value.

Managerial principle 5.9
Increase the likelihood consumers will repurchase your product by reinforcing them for their purchase.

In the marketing environment, most reinforcers are of a secondary nature. A product performing well, a reduction in price, and a friendly hello by a salesperson are all examples of secondary reinforcers. Even though they're secondary reinforcers, they still have a major impact on behavior.

Punishers Another operant-conditioning concept of importance to marketers is that of a punisher, which is any stimulus whose presence after a behavior decreases the likelihood of the behavior reoccurring. For a marketer, a key goal is to avoid punishing consumers for using the product or service being marketed. A great number of punishers discourage product purchases. Some examples include poor product performance, ridicule of the product by friends, irritating actions or remarks by a salesperson, or stock outages of a product.

A classic example of a punisher is found in the form of the rectangular ketchup packages given to consumers at the takeout windows of fast-food restaurants. The packages are extremely difficult to open, particularly when traveling in a car. In addition, the containers hold only a small dollop of ketchup—not nearly enough to adequately cover the order of french fries. (Some travelers deal with the problem by ripping the package open with their teeth, squirting the ketchup in their mouth, and then inserting the french fry into their mouth.) Because they're so hard to use, ketchup packets act as punishers for purchasing french fries. The result was that, overall, consumers purchased fewer and fewer fries at a drive-through. In response, Heinz developed a dip-and-squeeze package that holds more ketchup and is easier to use—and that will reinforce the purchase of french fries and the Heinz ketchup that goes with them.

> **Managerial principle 5.10**
> Carefully examine the stimuli that occur during and after a purchase to make sure no punishers are present that will inhibit future purchases.

Extinction and Eliminating Behaviors Once an operant response is conditioned, it will persist as long as it's periodically reinforced. However, if the operant response goes without reinforcement for an extended number of occasions, it will tend to disappear. This disappearance of a response due to lack of reinforcement is called **extinction**. Interestingly, immediately after the reinforcement ceases, the vigor of the response may actually increase. In humans, the reaction would probably be called anger. Suppose a salesman over the years has reinforced his customer for buying his product by taking him or her out to lunch each time the customer purchased the product. Suddenly, the salesman decides this is too expensive and quits providing the reinforcer. The initial reaction of the customer may be anger, and the eventual outcome could be the extinction of the buying response.

Schedules of Reinforcement A reinforcer doesn't have to be applied each time a particular behavior occurs in order to create a conditioned response. In these intermittent **schedules of reinforcement**, the behavior is reinforced after a certain number of repetitions or after a certain length of time has passed. One outcome of using schedules of reinforcement is the operant responses become more resistant to extinction. Thus, the reinforcer can be omitted for quite a number of cases and the behavior will persist.

Casinos employ schedules of reinforcement to provide rewards to gamblers. For example, slot machines employ a variable ratio schedule in which people win only after the one-armed bandits are fed coins an indeterminate number of times. This schedule of reinforcement results in gamblers becoming resistant to extinction. As a result, they will continue to gamble even though they're not winning.

Discriminative Stimuli **Discriminative stimuli** are those that occur in the presence of a reinforcer and don't occur in its absence. They're like signals that indicate whether or not a reinforcer will be present if a behavior is emitted. Because the discriminative stimulus is paired with the reinforcer, it increases the likelihood of the operant response occurring. Thus, a person learns to emit the operant response when the discriminative stimulus is present and not to emit the response when it's absent. There's nothing special about a discriminative stimulus. For example, the word *sit* has no particular impact on a dog until it's followed by a dog biscuit (if the animal does sit on the floor). If the word is consistently followed by a reward after the behavior has appeared, it will come to gradually elicit the instrumental response of sitting.

Managerial principle 5.11

Create discriminative stimuli that encourage purchases by creating distinctive logos, packaging, music, etc. that consumers associate with your product.

From an operant-conditioning perspective, the messages and information consumers receive about products and services act as discriminative stimuli.[67] Such information can signal the reinforcements that may result from a purchase. Discriminative stimuli are found in the logos, product packaging, brand names, and other symbols used by marketers. Similarly, a sale sign in a retailer's store window is a discriminative stimulus signaling the consumer can get a good deal on the merchandise.

FIGURE 5.3
The Operation of a
Discriminative Stimulus

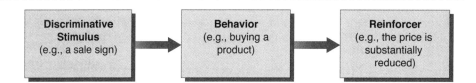

Shaping Consumer Responses Have you ever wondered how animal trainers are able to teach animals (e.g., dogs, killer whales, and elephants) to do bizarre tricks? Certainly, jumping through a hoop filled with fire isn't an instinctive behavior for the average killer whale. The process through which animals are taught such amazing tricks is **shaping**. Through shaping, totally new operant behaviors can be created by selectively reinforcing behaviors that successively approximate the desired instrumental response. Hobbes, a miniature poodle learned to leap to catch a Frisbee. His reward for returning with the Frisbee is the chance to play tug-of-war with the short-lived Frisbee. Some people will go to great lengths to train their dogs to do elaborate Frisbee tricks and then enter them into contests.

Companies strive to arrange contingencies to shape consumers. For instance, a car dealership might use the shaping process to encourage consumers to buy cars. First, the dealership might provide free coffee and doughnuts to anyone who visits. Next, the dealership could give $5 to a licensed driver who test drives a car. Third, the business might give a $500 rebate to the person for buying the car. Finally, the dealership can provide outstanding service to the customer when he or she brings in the car for maintenance. The ultimate behavior desired is repeat buying from the dealership. To obtain the behavior, the actions of the consumer that lead to a desired terminal behavior are selectively reinforced.[68]

Contingencies of Reinforcement The concepts of operant conditioning have wide application to consumer behavior and marketing management. Of particular importance is the analysis of the **contingencies of reinforcement**

being received by consumers when purchasing and using goods or services. This analysis refers to the study of all the reinforcers and punishers that accompany the purchase of a product. The relationship, or contingency, between when the reinforcers and punishers occur and the consumer's behavior influence the likelihood of that behavior occurring again. For instance, consider a consumer who goes into a fast-food restaurant. A variety of stimuli will act to reinforce or punish the consumer. Factors such as the cleanliness of the restaurant, the speed of service, the courtesy of the employees, and the quality and price of the food can act as either reinforcers or punishers. Managers must carefully analyze these contingencies of reinforcement to determine their motivational impact on customers. The careful examination of the contingencies of reinforcement is called **applied behavior analysis**.

Vicarious Learning

A third form of behavioral learning is **vicarious learning**. Also called **observational learning**, the theory describes the phenomenon in which

A shaping process was employed to teach the dog to catch and return a Frisbee.
Photo by John Mowen

people observe the actions of others to develop "patterns of behavior."[69] Thus, the observer assesses whether the target person is reinforced or punished for an action. If the person is reinforced for the behavior, the observer will tend to emulate the action. On the other hand, if the other person is punished for the action, the observer will avoid engaging in the action.

Three important ideas emerge from observational learning theory.[70] First, observational learning theorists view people as symbolic beings who foresee the probable consequences of their behavior. People anticipate the future and vary their behavior accordingly. Second, people have the ability to regulate their own behavior. Through this self-regulatory process, people supply their own rewards and punishments internally by feeling either self-critical or self-satisfied. Third, people learn by watching the actions of others and the consequences of these actions (i.e., by vicarious learning). Social-learning theorists particularly emphasize the importance of models in transmitting information through observational learning.

A **model** is someone whose behavior a person attempts to emulate. The effectiveness of a model has been shown to increase in the following instances:

1. The model is physically attractive.
2. The model is credible.
3. The model is successful.
4. The model is similar to the observer.
5. The model is shown overcoming difficulties and then succeeding.[71]

Managerial principle 5.12
Employ vicarious-learning principles in which positive models are shown enjoying the purchase of your product.

The ability of models to cause consumers to engage in new behaviors is particularly important for companies that introduce innovative products. For example, in order to broaden the appeal of its curved screen TVs, Samsung's ads pointed to the ability of the screen to "surround" the viewer in the action on the screen. . Modeling processes can also be used to inhibit undesirable behaviors, such as using drugs. Finally, models can be employed to increase the likelihood a previously learned behavior will occur.

A Caveat Although classical-conditioning, operant-conditioning, and observational-learning principles have major implications for managers and public-policy makers, a word of warning is in order. For example, both classical conditioning and operant conditioning work through multiple pairings of the response or behavior with a stimulus. However, in the real world of consumers, the pairings are often few in number, and it seems questionable that people can be conditioned with so few pairings. It's possible other theories, such as associative learning, can explain the findings in classical conditioning and operant conditioning. For the manager, however, the key issue concerns whether one can influence consumer behavior by implementing classical conditioning, operant conditioning, and observational learning procedures. The answer is a definite yes. For the manager interested only in obtaining results, the question of exactly what processes account for the behavioral change has little importance.

MANAGERIAL APPLICATIONS ANALYSIS

The principles and concepts of motivation have application to each of the five responsive marketing (RESPonsive Marketing) concepts. These are discussed next.

Research

Marketing research is required to measure the dominant motivational tendencies of the target market. In particular, analyses should be performed to assess a target market's dominant needs. For example, from the perspective of McClelland's social needs, is the target market focused more on the need for affiliation, power, or achievement? Similarly, what's the target market's need for arousal? Does the target market perceive a high degree of risk associated with the product category?

Environmental Analysis

As found in operant conditioning theory, the study of the contingencies of reinforcement involves examining the reinforcers and the punishers received by consumers purchasing a good or service. In this examination, managers must carefully analyze the nature of the environment in which the purchase is made. The analysis should include attention to the temperature, lighting, and smells in the retail store, the facial expressions (e.g., smiles and frowns) of sales personnel, and the time taken to serve consumers. These factors and more represent aspects of environmental stimuli that have reinforcing and punishing qualities.

The nature of the environment will also influence the perception of risk by consumers. For example, the threat of terrorism strongly impacts the tourism industry. Similarly, the natural environment affects tourism, which can lead to perceptions of risks, such as when a hurricane hits (e.g., Sandy in 2012) when a typhoon rocks a nation (e.g., the Philippines in 2013), or an avalanche kills climbers (e.g., Mount Everest in 2014).

Segmentation

The motivational needs of consumers can also be used to segment the marketplace. For example, marketers have recently recognized a segment of consumers with a high need for arousal seek extreme, high-risk vacations. Thus, companies are promoting adventures such as climbing Mount Everest, riding in a MIG 29 jet fighter, and rafting down white water rapids. Similarly, cereal brands target consumers with divergent motivational needs. Thus, Total targets those motivated to protect their bodies (the physical needs of Maslow) while Wheaties targets those motivated to achieve in sports.

Positioning and Differentiation

Concepts from this chapter have multiple applications to positioning and differentiation. From a motivation perspective, products can be positioned as fulfilling the needs arising from internal stimuli. For example, numerous fast-food restaurants are built around relieving hunger. Indeed, it's possible to position products as fulfilling any of the needs found in Maslow's hierarchy. Volvo has associated its cars with fulfilling needs for safety.

From operant conditioning, principles underlying the development of discriminative stimuli have direct application to positioning and differentiation. As described in the chapter, brand names, product logos, and various symbols can be employed that denote the brand and distinguish it from others. Such symbols can act to uniquely position the brand and differentiate it from competitors.

Marketing Mix

The study of motivation has particular relevance to the product and promotion components of the marketing mix. Products can be designed to fulfill the motivational needs of consumers. For example, if a segment of consumers places a high premium on risk avoidance, companies should offer extremely safe products (e.g., a safe car, such as Volvo). Other consumers may place a high value on affiliation. Products can then be developed that meet such desires, such as resorts that cater to college students during spring break.

Promotional messages can be designed to link a product to the motivational needs of a target market. For example, the web-based company Student City targets high need for arousal to college students with a number of recommended destinations and party packages for spring break. For the 2016 Panama City package, the company described the scene as follows:

> *There's always multiple pool and beach parties going on at the hottest spots. Home to Club La Vela, the largest nightclub in North America Crazy parties on the beach every day with DJs and MCs.*[72]

What Is the Process Through Which Motivated Behavior Occurs?

Motivation refers to an activated state leading to goal-directed behavior. A control theory model of motivation was presented that operates in a manner similar to the thermostat in one's home. Within the control theory motivation model, desired states are compared to actual states. When a comparator perceives a gap between the desired and actual states, an interrupt occurs and need recognition takes place. In turn, need recognition prompts cognitive appraisal and problem solving to occur. These processes then result in goal-directed behavior, outcomes, and changes in the actual state.

What Are the Feelings and Emotions Consumers Experience?

Accompanying a motivated state are feelings and emotions. These affective states are characterized by internal sensations, such as anger, distress, fear, interest, joy, and surprise. Opponent-process theory explains how strong positive or negative affect influences consumers and can lead to addictions. It also explains priming, which occurs when a brief exposure to a stimulus (e.g., food, playing a video game, or even a word or something in the situational context) influences a later response.

What Are the Psychological Needs Consumers Experience?

Two general theories of emotion that identified key psychological needs were presented—Maslow's hierarchy of needs, and McClelland's theory of learned needs. In addition, five mid-range theories of motivation were discussed: optimum stimulation level theory, motivation for hedonic experiences, the desire to maintain behavioral freedom, the motivation to avoid risk, and the motivation to attribute causality.

How Does Behavioral Learning Impact Consumer Behavior?

Behavioral learning is a process in which experience with the environment leads to a relatively permanent change in behavior. The study of behavioral learning is important because it's the foundation for investigating the behavioral-influence perspective on consumer buying. Three types of behavioral learning have been identified—classical conditioning, operant conditioning, and observational learning. Each of these theories has a strong motivational component.

In classical conditioning, a stimulus of some type elicits behavior, or an **unconditioned response**. In consumer behavior contexts, the behaviors of most interest are the positive and negative emotional responses that may be elicited by various stimuli. By pairing a previously neutral stimulus (the **conditioned stimulus**) with the eliciting stimulus (the **unconditioned stimulus**), the neutral stimulus gradually comes to elicit the response.

Operant conditioning occurs when an organism's behavior changes as a consequence of something happening after the behavior. Operants are the naturally occurring actions of an organism in the environment. In a consumer behavior setting, operants include activities such as purchasing a product or service, engaging in word-of-mouth communication, and tweeting about a poor service experience. From an operant-conditioning perspective, behavior is influenced by the reinforcers and punishers received after engaging in an action.

Marketers frequently attempt to arrange reinforcers and punishers to shape consumers. Shaping may create totally new behaviors. In a consumer setting, a salesperson may attempt to shape a person by using various sales promotion devices and social reinforcers (e.g., pats on the back). Of course, the ultimate behavior the salesperson wants to shape is a buying response. The technology of applied behavior analysis was developed to use operant-conditioning techniques to influence behavior.

The third behavioral learning theory is observational learning. Also called vicarious learning, the theory proposes that people develop patterns of behavior by modeling the actions of others. Observational learning theorists view people as symbolic beings who learn by observing others and the outcomes of their actions.

KEY TERMS

achievement motivation
affect
applied behavior analysis
attribution theory
augmenting principle
behavioral learning
classical conditioning
comparator
conditioned response
conditioned stimulus
contingencies of reinforcement
discounting principle
discriminative stimuli
emotions
expressive needs
external attribution
external stimuli
extinction

fundamental attribution error
hedonic consumption
impersonal threats
internal attribution
internal stimuli
interrupt
involuntary risks
model
motivation
need for achievement
need for affiliation
need for power
need for uniqueness
need recognition
negative reinforcer
neutral stimulus
observational learning
operant conditioning

opponent-process theory
optimum stimulation level
perceived risk
physiological arousal
positive reinforcer
priming
punisher
reactance
reinforcer
schedules of reinforcement
secondary reinforcer
shaping
social threats
unconditioned response
unconditioned stimulus
utilitarian needs
vicarious learning
voluntary risks

REVIEW QUESTIONS

1. Define the concept of motivation. Describe in a short paragraph the control theory model of motivation.
2. What are the seven needs identified by Maslow?
3. What are the three needs identified by McClelland?
4. Describe the opponent-process theory of motivation.
5. Define the concept of priming and how retailers can use it to increase buying.
6. Define the concept of optimum stimulation level. How would it impact consumers' choices of leisure activities?
7. What's meant by the term hedonic consumption? List four types of consumer goods/services that would be categorized as hedonic in nature.

8. Define the concept of reactance. What factors can cause reactance in consumers?

9. Define the concept of perceived risk. What are the seven types of perceived risk?

10. What occurs when consumers make an attribution? What's meant by the augmentation and discounting principles?

11. Define the concept of behavioral learning. What are the three types of learning consumer researchers discuss?

12. What's meant by observational learning? What are three important ideas that result from its study?

13. Define operant conditioning and describe its process.

14. Discuss the different effects of positive and negative reinforcers.

15. What's meant by extinction?

16. What's meant by a schedule of reinforcement?

17. How are discriminative stimuli used by marketers?

18. Give an example of how a marketer might be able to shape a consumer response.

19. What are the relationships among conditioned stimuli, unconditioned stimuli, conditioned responses, and unconditioned responses in classical conditioning?

DISCUSSION QUESTIONS

1. Imagine you're on an advertising team assembled to develop a campaign for a new running shoe. Develop three slogans that are based on needs identified by Maslow and McClelland.

2. How can a sausage company, a movie distributor, and an auto dealership use priming to influence consumers to purchase their products?

3. Discuss how your desire to achieve an optimum stimulation level impacts your choice of leisure activities.

4. Discuss how you could employ principles of reactance theory as a promotional strategy to increase the likelihood consumers will purchase an automobile.

5. Imagine you're the marketing director for a start-up company that sells a competitor to Apple's iPhone. What types of perceived risk may consumers perceive, and what steps can you take to minimize the perception of perceived risk?

6. Discuss how consumers' attributions for cause will influence their reactions to a company that has to recall a defective product.

7. Observational learning is an important means of socialization for children, teenagers, and adults. Consider the content of the popular television shows appearing in prime time. What patterns of behavior may people learn as a result of watching prime-time television? Are there public-policy implications that result from such an analysis?

8. What would you identify as the five major consumer reinforcers? To what extent can a salesperson use these reinforcers to influence the behavior of prospective clients?

9. Try to remember the worst experiences you've ever had in a restaurant. What were the various ways in which you were punished for eating there?

10. One problem many instructors face is how to get students to participate in classroom discussions. Develop a systematic plan in which reinforcers are applied to shape students into frequent classroom discussions.

11. Develop the outline of an advertising campaign for a new line of bath towels to include television commercials and point-of-purchase displays that make use of classical-conditioning ideas. Make sure you identify the conditioned stimulus, the unconditioned stimulus, the conditioned response, and the unconditioned response.

12. Visit a supermarket or a mall in your area. Take paper or electronic notes and record specific examples of how retail stores make use of behavioral learning principles to influence consumers. In which of the three types of behavioral learning did you find the most examples?

13. What social media do you use, and what are your motives for using each?

ENDNOTES

[1] "2014: North America," *Dropzone.com*, accessed November 9, 2015, http://www.dropzone.com/fatalities/2014/North_America/index.shtml.

[2] NEISS Data Highlights, *United States Consumer Product Safety Commission*, accessed November 9, 2015, https://www.cpsc.gov//Global/Neiss_prod/2014%20Neiss%20data%20highlights.pdf.

[3] "Cheerleading Ranks First in Catastrophic Sports Injuries," *US Sports Academy*, April 8, 2011, accessed November 9, 2015, http://ussa.edu/news/cheerleading-ranks-first-in-catastrophic-sport-injuries/; Frederick O. Mueller and Robert C. Cantu, "Catastrophic Sports Injury Research: Twenty-Ninth Annual Report, Fall 1982–Spring 2011," *University of North Carolina*, accessed November 9, 2015, http://www.unc.edu/depts/nccsi/2011Allsport.pdf.

[4] Lindsey Tanner, "AMA Officially Designates Cheerleading a Sport," USA Today, June 10, 2014, accessed November 9, 2015, http://www.usatoday.com/story/news/nation/2014/06/10/ama-cheerleading-sport/10272941/?siteID=je6NUbpObpQ-rWW.fLPn6hx0CeAeCuVlxw.

[5] Ernest Hilgard, Richard Atkinson, and Rita Atkinson, *Introduction to Psychology*, 6th edition (New York: Harcourt Brace Jovanovich, 1975).

[6] James A. Bayton, "Motivation, Cognition, Learning: Basic Factors in Consumer Behavior," *Journal of Marketing*, 22 (January 1958), 282–289.

[7] The model is adapted from the control theory model in John C. Mowen, *The 3M Model of Motivation and Personality* (Dordrecht, Netherlands: Kluwer Academic Publishers, 2000). Also, see John C. Mowen, Sojin Park, and Alex Zablah, "Toward a Theory of Motivation and Personality with Application to Word-of-Mouth Communications," *Journal of Business Research*, 60, (2007), 590–596.

[8] Aradhna Krishna, *Customer Sense: How the 5 Senses Influence Buying Behavior*, (New York: Palgrave Macmillain, 2013).

[9] Jiewen Hong and Yacheng Sun, "Warm It Up with Love: The Effect of Physical Coldness on Liking of Romance Movies," *Journal of Consumer Research*, 39, (August 2012).

[10] John P. Murray, Jr., and Peter A. Dacin, "Cognitive Moderators of Negative-Emotion Effects: Implications for Understanding Media Context," *Journal of Consumer Research*, 22, (March 1996), 439–447.

[11] Deborah J. MacInnis and Bernard J. Jaworski, "Information Processing From Advertisements: Toward an Integrative Framework," *Journal of Marketing*, 53 (October 1989), 1–23.

[12] Carroll E. Izard, *Human Emotion* (New York: Plenum Press, 1977).

[13] Martin Reimann, Raquel Castano, Judith Zaichkowsky, and Antoine Bechara, "How We Relate to Brands: Psychological and Neurophysiological Insights into Consumer-Brand Relationships," *Journal of Consumer Psychology*, 22 (January 2012), 128–142.

[14] Elizabeth C. Hirschman and Barbara B. Stern, "The Roles of Emotion in Consumer Research," in *Advances in Consumer Research*, vol. 26, ed. Eric J. Arnould and Linda M. Scott (Provo, UT: Association for Consumer Research, 1999), 4–11.

[15] Cassie Mogilner, Jennifer Aaker, and Sepandar Kamvar, "How Happiness Affects Choice," *Journal of Consumer Research*, 39 (August 2012), 429–443.

[16] Hannah H. Chang and Michel Tuan Pham, "Affect as a Decision-Making System of the Present," *Journal of Consumer Research*, 40 (2013).

[17] Richard L. Solomon, "The Opponent-Process Theory of Acquired Motivation," *American Psychologist*, 35 (August 1980), 691–712.

[18] Aner Sela and Baba Shiv, "Unraveling Priming: When Does the Same Prime Activate a Goal Versus a Trait," *Journal of Consumer Research*, 36 (October 2009).

[19] Sandon A. Steinberg and Richard F. Yalch, "When Eating Begets Buying: The Effects of Food Samples on Obese and Nonobese Shoppers," *Journal of Consumer Research*, 4 (March 1978), 243–246.

[20] Jiang, Yuwei, Angela Cho, and Rashmi Adaval, "The Unique Consequences of Feeling Lucky: Implications for Consumer Behavior," *Journal of Consumer Psychology*, 19 (2009), 171–184.

[21] Robert A. Westbrook, "Product/Consumption-Based Affective Responses and Postpurchase Processes," *Journal of Marketing Research*, 24 (August 1987), 258–270.

[22] Lynn Kahle, David Bousch, and Pamela Homer, "Broken Rungs in Abraham's Ladder: Is Maslow's Hierarchy Hierarchical?" in *Proceedings of the Society for Consumer Psychology*, ed. David Schumann (Washington, DC: American Psychological Association, 1988), 11–16: http://www.incentivesolutions.com/2014/09/12/millenials-maslows-hierarchy-needs/ accessed December 17, 2015.

[23] David C. McClelland, *Human Motivation* (New York: Cambridge University Press, 1987).

[24] George M. Zinkhan, Margy Conchar, Ajay Gupta, and Gary Geissler, "Motivation Underlying the Creation of Personal Web Pages: An Exploratory Study," *Advances in Consumer Research*, vol. 26 (Provo, UT: Association for Consumer Research, 1999), 69–74.

[25] Marvin Zuckerman, *Sensation Seeking: Beyond the Optimum Level of Arousal* (Hillsdale, NJ: Lawrence Erlbaum, 1979).

[26] Rebecca K. Ratner, Barbara E. Kahn, and Daniel Kahneman, "Choosing Less-Preferred Experiences for the Sake of Variety," *Journal of Consumer Research*, 26 (June 1999), 1–15.

[27] Satya Menon and Barbara E. Kahn, "The Impact of Context on Variety Seeking in Product Choice," *Journal of Consumer Research*, 22, (December 1995), 285–295.

[28] "Tower of Terror Roller Coaster—Yahoo Search Results," Yahoo, accessed November 9, 2015, https://search.yahoo.com/search?fr=mcafee&type=C110US80045D20150303&p=tower+of+terror+roller+coaster.

[29] Morris Holbrook and Elizabeth Hirschman, "The Experiential Aspects of Consumption: Consumer Fantasies, Feelings, and Fun," *Journal of Consumer Research*, 9 (September 1982), 132–140.

[30] Jack W. Brehm, *A Theory of Psychological Reactance* (New York: Academic Press, 1966). For a review of consumer research on reactance, see Greg Lessne and M. Venkatesan, "Reactance Theory in Consumer Research: The Past, Present, and Future," in *Advances in Consumer Research*, vol. 16, ed. Thomas K. Srull (Provo, UT: Association for Consumer Research, 1989), 76–78.

[31] Virginia Daut, "Roses Were Reds, Violets Blues, Till They Redid Crayola's Hues," *Wall Street Journal*, September 11, 1990, B1.

[32] Suein L. Hwang, "Hue and Cry over Crayola May Revive Old Colors," *Wall Street Journal*, June 14, 1991, B1. Consumers' votes in 2003 retired teal blue. See http://www.crayola.com/faq/another-topic/what-are-the-names-of-the-retired-crayon-colors/, accessed December 17, 2015.

[33] Dana Mattioli, "Nike's Footwork Yields Long Lines," *Wall Street Journal*, December 29, 2011, B1, B2.

[34] Darwyn Linder and Katherine Crane, "Reactance Theory Analysis of Predecisional Cognitive Processes," *Journal of Personality and Social Psychology*, 15 (July 1970), 258–264.

[35] Mona Clee and Robert Wicklund, "Consumer Behavior and Psychological Reactance," *Journal of Consumer Research*, 6 (March 1980), 389–405.

[36] G. R. Dowling, "Perceived Risk: The Concept and Its Measurement," *Psychology and Marketing*, 3 (Fall 1986), 193–210. For another discussion of problems in defining the concept, see James Bettman, "Information Integration in Consumer Risk Perception: A Comparison of Two Models of Component Conceptualization," *Journal of Applied Psychology*, 60 (1975), 381–385.

[37] For a discussion and model of perceived risk, see Grahame R. Dowling and Richard Staelin, "A Model of Perceived Risk and Intended Risk-Handling Activity," *Journal of Consumer Research*, 21 (June 1994), 119–134.

[38] Raymond A. Bauer, "Consumer Behavior as Risk Taking," in *Dynamic Marketing for a Changing World*, ed. Robert S. Hancock (Chicago: American Marketing Association, 1960), 87.

[39] The first five risks in Table 5-2 were identified by Jacob Jacoby and Leon Kaplan, "The Components of Perceived Risk," in *Advances in Consumer Research*, vol. 3, ed. M. Venkatesan (Chicago: Association for Consumer Research, 1972), 382–383. "Social risk" was identified by J. Paul Peter and Michael Ryan, "An Investigation of Perceived Risk at the Brand Level," *Journal of Marketing Research*, 13 (May 1976), 184–188. "Opportunity cost" was identified by William Zikmund and Jerome Scott, "A Factor Analysis of the Multi-dimensional Nature of Perceived Risk," *Proceedings of the Southern Marketing Association* (Houston, Texas: Southern Marketing Association, 1973), 1036.

[40] Baruch Fischhoff, Paul Slovic, and Sarah Lichtenstein, "Which Risks Are Acceptable?" *Environment*, 21 (January 1979), 17–38.

[41] Valerie S. Folkes, "The Availability Heuristic and Perceived Risk," *Journal of Consumer Research*, 15 (June 1988), 13–23.

[42] Donald Popielarz, "An Exploration of Perceived Risk and Willingness to Try New Products," *Journal of Marketing Research*, 4 (November 1967), 368–372.

[43] Brian K. Jorgensen, "Consumer Reaction to Company-Related Disasters: The Effect of Multiple Versus Single Explanations," *Advances in Consumer Research*, 21, ed. Chris Allen and Deborah Roedder John (Provo, Utah: Association for Consumer Research, 1994), 348–353.

[44] For a general review of the attribution process in consumer behavior, see Valerie Folkes, "Recent Attribution Research in Consumer Behavior: A Review and New Directions," *Journal of Consumer Research*, 14 (March 1988), 548–565.

[45] Michelle L. Peterman, Harper A. Roehm, Jr., and Curtis P. Haugtvedt, "An Exploratory Attribution Analysis of Attitudes Toward the World Wide Web as a Product Information Source," *Advances in Consumer Research*, ed. Eric J. Arnould and Linda M. Scott (Provo, UT: Association for Consumer Research, 1999), 75–79.

[46] Sheila Shayon, "Alert Alec Baldwin: Capital One Caught 'in Your Wallet,'" *Brandchannel*, July 25, 2012, accessed December 15, 2015, h http://brandchannel.com/2012/07/25/alert-alec-baldwin-capital-one-caught-in-your-wallet/. It should also be noted that Baldwin has promoted PETA, which doesn't represent a product.

[47] Robert M. Schindler, "Consequences of Perceiving Oneself as Responsible for Obtaining a Discount: Evidence for Smart-Shopper Feelings," *Journal of Consumer Psychology*, 7: 4 (1998) 371–392.

[48] Harold H. Kelley, "The Process of Causal Attribution," *American Psychologist*, 28 (February 1973) 107–128.

[49] Nancy Millman, "Product Claims Not Believable," *Advertising Age*, March 15, 1984, 1, 3.

[50] Lee Ross, "The Intuitive Psychologist and His Shortcomings: Distortion in the Attribution Process," in *Advances in Experimental Social Psychology*, vol. 10 (New York: Academic Press, 1977).

[51] Robert Baer, "Overestimating Salesperson Truthfulness: The Fundamental Attribution Error," in *Advances in Consumer Research*, vol. 17, ed. Marvin Goldberg et al. (Provo, UT: Association for Consumer Research, 1990), 501–507.

[52] Maria L. Cronley, Frank R. Kardes, Perilou Goddard, and David C. Houghton, "Endorsing Products for the Money: The Role of the Correspondence Bias in Celebrity Advertising," *Advances in Consumer Research*, vol. 26, ed. Eric Arnould and Linda M. Scott (Provo, UT: Association for Consumer Research, 1999), 627–631.

[53] John R. O'Malley, Jr., "Consumer Attributions of Product Failures to Channel Members," *Advances in Consumer Research*, vol. 23, ed. Kim Corfman and John Lynch (Provo: UT: Association for Consumer Research, 1996), 342–345.

[54] Robyn A. LeBoeuf and Michael I. Norton, "Consequence-Cause Matching: Looking to the Consequences of Events to Infer Their Causes," *Journal of Consumer Research*, 39 (June 2012).

55 Robert Rescorla, "Pavlovian Conditioning: It's not What You Think It Is," *American Psychologist*, 43 (March 1988), 151–160. Readers should recognize that a "cognitive revolution" has taken place in the understanding of classical conditioning. The idea that actions follow stimuli in a reflexive manner is no longer held by theorists. See Terence A. Shimp, "The Role of Subject Awareness in Classical Conditioning: A Case of Opposing Ontologies and Conflicting Evidence," in *Advances in Consumer Research*, vol. 18, ed. Rebecca Holman and Michael Solomon (Provo, UT: Association for Consumer Research, 1991), 158–163.

56 An excellent review of applications of classical conditioning and operant conditioning to marketing may be found in Walter R. Nord and J. Paul Peter, "A Behavior Modification Perspective on Marketing," *Journal of Marketing*, 410 (Spring 1980), 36–47.

57 Ronald E. Milliman, "Using Background Music to Affect the Behavior of Supermarket Shoppers," *Journal of Marketing*, 42 (Summer 1982), 86–91.

58 Ronald E. Milliman, "The Influence of Background Music on the Behavior of Restaurant Patrons," *Journal of Consumer Research*, 13 (September 1986), 286–289.

59 Elnora W. Stuart, Terence A. Shimp, and Randall W. Engle, "Classical Conditioning of Consumer Attitudes: Four Experiments in an Advertising Context," *Journal of Consumer Research*, 14 (December 1987), 334–349.

60 Richard A. Feinberg, "Credit Cards As Spending Facilitating Stimuli," *Journal of Consumer Research*, 13 (December 1986), 348–356.

61 Brian D. Hill, Sarah M. Stanley, and Randi Priluck, "Classical Conditioning and Celebrity Endorsers: An Examination of Belongingness and Resistance to Extinction," *Psychology and Marketing*, 25, (February 2008), 179–196.

62 Christian Schemer, Jorg Matthes, Werner Wirth, and Samuel Textor, "Does 'Passing the Curvoisier' Always Pay Off? Positive and Negative Evaluative Conditioning Effects of Brand Placements in Music Videos," *Psychology & Marketing*, 25 (October 2008), 923–943.

63 Terence A. Shimp, Elnora W. Stuart, and Randall W. Engle, "A Program of Classical Conditioning Experiments Testing Variations in the Conditioned Stimulus and the Context," *Journal of Consumer Research*, 18 (June 1991), 1–12.

64 This section on operant conditioning relies heavily on G. S. Reynolds, *A Primer of Operant Conditioning* (Glenview, IL: Scott, Foresman, 1968) [Publication info was missing, please verify]. (AU: Verified).

65 William Gaidis and James Cross, "Behavior Modification As a Framework for Sales Promotion Management," *Journal of Consumer Marketing*, 4 (Spring 1987), 65–74. Gordon Foxall has developed another view on the types of reinforcers in which he distinguishes hedonic from informational reinforcers. See Gordon R. Foxall, "The Behavioral Perspective Model of Purchase and Consumption: From Consumer Theory to Marketing Practice," *Journal of the Academy of Marketing Sciences*, 20 (Spring 1992), 189–198.

66 This sign is sold at http://www.sawdustcityllc.com/unattended-children-will-be-given-an-espresso-and-a-free-puppy/, accessed December 15, 2015..

67 Gordon R. Foxall, "The Behavioral Perspective Model of Purchase and Consumption: From Consumer Theory to Marketing Practice," *Journal of the Academy of Marketing Sciences*, 20 (Spring 1992), 189–198.

68 This example may be found in J. Paul Peter and Walter R. Nord, "A Clarification and Extension of Operant Conditioning Principles in Marketing," *Journal of Marketing*, 46 (Summer 1982), 102–107.

69 Albert Bandura, *Social Learning Theory* (Englewood Cliffs, NJ: Prentice Hall, 1977).

70 Ernest Hilgard, Richard Atkinson, and Rita Atkinson, *Introduction to Psychology* (New York: Harcourt Brace Jovanovich, 1975).

71 Charles C. Manz and Henry P. Sims, "Vicarious Learning: The Influence of Modeling on Organizational Behavior," *Academy of Management Journal*, 6 (January 1981), 105–113.

72 "Panama City Beach, Florida," *Student City*, accessed November 9, 2015, http://www.studentcity.com/trips-and-destinations/spring-break/panama-city-beach-florida/overview.

6

Individual Differences: Personality, Self-Concept, and Psychographics

Learning objectives:

1. How can marketers employ personality approaches to develop strategy?

2. How can marketers employ psychoanalytic theory to develop strategy?

3. How can marketers use trait theory to develop strategy?

4. How can marketers use an understanding of self-concept to develop marketing strategy?

5. How can marketers use lifestyle and psychographic analyses to develop marketing strategy?

Consumers and Their Bad Driving Habits

Two motorists became incensed with each other as they drove on an interstate highway. After several miles of acrimony, they pulled their cars off the road. One went to the trunk of his car and pulled out a powerful crossbow. He then fired a lethal arrow into the other man's chest.[1] Aggressive driving and its big brother, road rage, are forms of negligent consumer behavior. A market research firm estimated aggressive driving results in the deaths of at least 1,500 men, women, and children each year in the United States.[2] Aggressive driving behaviors are linked to half of all car crashes. It's the driver's legal responsibility to do everything to avoid being in a crash.[3]

Aggressive drivers can be male or female and come from every social class. Even celebrities have been known to lose their cool while driving, including actor Jack Nicholson. It's reported after he believed another driver had cut him off in traffic, at the next red light, the grabbed a golf club and repeatedly slammed the club onto the roof and windshield of the driver's Mercedes.[4]

Another type of driving, however, kills more people than aggressive or even drunk driving—distracted driving. In 2013, distracted driving led to the deaths of 3,154 people and injuries to 424,000 people. The most frequent cause of distracted driving is using a cell phone, which delays reaction time to a greater extent than driving drunk (i.e., at .08). Text messaging requires visual, manual, and cognitive attention, and we send 561 billion text messages monthly.[5] Distracted

driving can occur when drivers take their eyes off the road, their hands off the wheel, or their minds off what they're doing. Some common causes of distracted driving are texting, eating and drinking, grooming, using the navigation system, and watching a video. However, these distracters are mild in comparison to what some drivers do, such as change their clothes, have sex, and even play a guitar. The third author of this book (John Mowen) experienced firsthand an example of distracted driving when a guitar-playing cab driver serenaded him through the streets of Miami, Florida. The cabbie drove the car with his knees while he strummed his guitar—truly scary!

PERSONALITY, SELF-CONCEPT AND LIFESTYLE

Personality, self-concept, and psychographics represent three approaches for understanding individual differences among people in their acquisition, consumption, and disposition of goods, services, and ideas. **Individual difference variables** describe how one person varies from another in his or her distinctive patterns of behavior. As used in this book, individual-difference variables go beyond the mere measurement of demographic characteristics, such as age, gender, and marital status. Demographic data describe the characteristics of people, but they don't assess differences in distinctive patterns of behavior.

This chapter begins by discussing the concept of personality. **Personality** is defined as "the distinctive patterns of behavior, including thoughts and emotions that characterize each individual's adaptation to the situations of his or her life."[6] Personality has two key managerial uses. First, segments of consumers can be identified based upon their dominant personality characteristics. Second, marketing communications then can be developed that appeal to segments of consumers who possess these characteristics.

The next two sections discuss psychoanalytic theory and trait theory. These approaches to understanding individual differences represent the second and third learning objectives. Next, we analyze the self-concept, which is an important component of one's personality. The **self-concept** is defined as the "totality of the individual's thoughts and feelings having reference to himself as an object."[7] People have a strong need to act consistently with their self-concept of who and what they think they are.[8] In addition, they purchase products and services to build their self-image and to express themselves to others.

The last learning objective is built around the study of psychographic analysis. Through **psychographic analysis**, market researchers measure the lifestyles of consumers. **Lifestyle** refers to how people live, including their activities, interests, and opinions. In this chapter, we'll depart from some treatments of psychographics to show how the enduring dispositions to have certain activities, opinions, and interests can be conceptualized as personality traits.

The chapter concludes with the managerial implications of the concepts from personality, psychoanalytic theory, trait theory, the self-concept, and psychographics. These individual difference approaches apply to four of the responsive marketing (RESPonsive Marketing) strategy concepts—research, segmentation, positioning, and marketing mix development.

UNDERSTANDING PERSONALITY

The word *personality* comes from the Latin *persona*, which means "actor's face mask." As stated earlier, personality is the distinctive patterns of behavior, including thoughts and emotions,that characterize each individual's adaptation to the situations of his or her life.

The concept of personality has three essential characteristics. First, a person's behavior should show consistency across time. Second, the behaviors should distinguish groups of consumers from others. A personality characteristic can't be shared by all consumers. Third, personality measures assess dispositions to act. Researchers can't accurately predict an individual's behavior on one specific occasion from a single measure of personality. Thus, it's extremely difficult to predict how many cans of peas a person will buy by measuring personality characteristics. What can be predicted are enduring dispositions to engage in general classes of behaviors. For example, such enduring behavioral tendencies as aggressive driving, healthy diet, and bargaining proneness represent personality variables.[9]

Knowledge of personality is critical to marketing managers for two reasons. First, the dominant personality characteristics of a target market can be employed to develop messages to consumers—for instance, a personality characteristic of aggressive drivers is that they have a high need for arousal. That is, aggressive drivers actively seek out risk and enjoy feeling an adrenaline rush, which driving aggressively can provide. So, how do public safety officials appeal to these individuals so they drive more sanely (and safely)? One approach is to directly appeal to their arousal needs. For example, the text of a message might read as follows: "If you like to take risks, jump out of an airplane, but don't drive aggressively." We'll see more of this example later in this chapter.

A second important aspect of personality for managers is it can moderate (i.e., interact with) the effects of messages and situations on consumer behavior. As discussed further in Chapter 11, situational influencers are the temporary environmental factors that form the context in which a consumer activity occurs. One type of situation is the social context, which has been shown to interact with a personality characteristic that distinguishes people based on their tendency to conform to social pressures when making purchases. A personality scale called the **ATSCI** (attention to social comparison interaction) was developed to measure this disposition to conform to others.[10]

Figure 6.1 shows how ATSCI moderates the impact of the social situation to influence purchase behavior. In most circumstances, people go shopping with

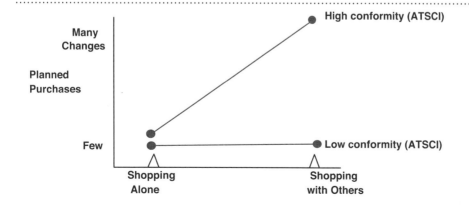

FIGURE 6.1
ATSCI Moderates the Effect of the Social Situation on Planned Purchases

plans to make certain purchases. Findings show the social situation interacts with the tendency to conform to others so as to impact the extent the consumer fails to make the intended purchases. As shown in the figure, a person who has a low tendency to conform will tend to make her desired purchases whether or not she shops alone or with a group. In contrast, a person with a high tendency to conform will make many more changes in purchase plans when shopping with a group than when shopping alone. Thus, the personality variable ATSCI interacts with the situation to influence the number of changes in planned purchases.

Psychoanalytic Theory

Sigmund Freud's **psychoanalytic theory of personality** strongly affected the understanding of our human makeup. Freud argued the human personality results from a dynamic struggle among inner physiological drives (e.g., hunger, sex, and aggression); a desire to follow laws, rules, and moral codes; and a desire for rationality. Furthermore, he proposed that individuals are aware of only a small portion of the forces that drive their behavior. From his perspective, humans have a preconscious, a conscious, and an unconscious mind. This idea that much of what propels humans to action is a part of the unconscious mind and not available for scrutiny revolutionized the understanding of the human personality.[11]

Freud's Approach to the Structure of the Personality According to Freud, the personality results from the clash of three forces—the id, the ego, and the superego. Present at birth, the **id** represents the physiological and primitive emotional drives that propel a person to action. These drives are completely unconscious and form a chaotic cauldron of seething excitations.[12] The id requires instant gratification of its instincts and operates on the **pleasure principle**. That is, the id functions to move a person to obtain positive feelings and emotions. The nearby photograph shows an image that would elicit the pleasure principle in many individuals.

The ego begins to develop as a child grows. The function of the ego is to curb the appetites of the id and help the person to function effectively in the world. As Freud stated, the **ego** stands for "reason and good sense while the id stands for untamed passions."[13] Freud viewed the ego as operating on the **reality principle**, which helps the person to be practical and to move efficiently through the world.

A photo that would elicit the pleasure principle in many individuals

The **superego** can be understood as the conscience or voice within a person that echoes the morals and values of parents and society. Only a small portion of it is available to the conscious mind. According to Freud, the superego forms during middle childhood through the process of identification. The superego actively opposes and clashes with the id, and one role of the ego is to resolve these conflicts. The focus on the conflict between the id and the superego is what classifies the psychoanalytic view of personality as a conflict theory. Thinking back to the crossbow story in the opening vignette, it's clear that when the crossbow-wielding motorist killed his hapless antagonist, neither the superego nor the ego was able to hold in check the emotions of the id.

Psychoanalytic Theory and Promotional Strategy Embraced by motivation researchers in the 1950s, psychoanalytic thought has had a major impact on marketing. Advertising firms hired psychoanalysts to help develop promotional themes and packaging to appeal to the unconscious minds of consumers. Psychoanalytic theory emphasizes the use of dreams, fantasy, and symbols to identify the unconscious motives behind a person's actions. Some marketing researchers use it still today to identify the symbols and fantasies that unconsciously propel people to buy. Indeed, much of the advertising today that employs an experiential orientation, as compared with a rational decision approach, seeks to provide consumers with pleasant fantasies involving the use of products.

According to psychoanalytic theory, the unconscious wishes of people are expressed through **symbols**. For example, phallic (male) and ovarian (female) symbols were thought to activate the release of **libido**, or sexual energy. Some writers have sold large numbers of books by sensationalizing the charge advertising agencies place phallic and ovarian symbols in advertisements to arouse sexual energy and thereby generate sales.[14] Phallic symbols are represented by figures that are long and cylindrical, whereas ovarian symbols are represented by figures that are round and receptive.

> **Managerial principle 6.1**
> To create positive affect, use fantasies in promotional materials that appeal to a product's target market.

According to psychoanalytic theory, people also have a death wish, which is symbolized in advertising by death masks. Death masks are facial covers that portray the contorted faces of people in unbearable pain. One author has argued that liquor advertisers place death masks in the ice cubes of liquor advertisements to activate the death wish of heavy drinkers.[15]

Do advertising agencies do this? The answer is a qualified no. A college professor asked advertising people if they ever deliberately embedded a subliminal message, such as a word, symbol, or sexual organ, in artwork for a client. Of those surveyed, 96 percent said they did not. When asked if they knew of anyone doing it, 91 percent said they did not.[16] Although the percentage admitting to awareness of the use of embedded symbols in ads was low, it's somewhat surprising anyone admitted to the practice at all. One has to ask, however, whether portraying the ideas symbolically has any impact on the observer given the open use of sex and violence in television, magazines, and the Internet today.

Psychoanalytic Theory and Consumer Research The psychoanalytic approach has affected marketing management through research methods that were derived from the approach. Psychoanalytic theorists developed projective techniques to identify the unconscious motives that spur people to action, which include projective techniques such as word association tasks, sentence completion tasks, and thematic apperception tests (TATs). (TATs are ambiguous drawings about which people are asked to write stories.) A therapeutic tool used by psychoanalysts is to have people lie on a couch and relax both physically and psychologically, which allows patients to lower their defenses and understand their unconscious motivations. Depth interviews evolved from this approach. **Depth interviews** are long, probing one-on-one interviews undertaken to identify hidden reasons for purchasing products and services.

Later, psychologists began to bring small groups of people together for group therapy (i.e., T-groups). T-groups led to the focus-group approach to market research. **Focus groups** employ long sessions in which small groups of consumers are encouraged to talk freely about their feelings and thoughts concerning a product or service.

An example of depth interviews is found in work the McCann-Erickson ad agency did a number of years ago. There, researchers asked this question: "Why weren't low-income women from the South responding positively to a new roach killer in a tray, which they believed was more effective and less messy than traditional products?" Psychologists performed depth interviews and asked the women to draw roaches. The women portrayed the roaches as male scavengers. One woman wrote, "A man likes a free meal you cook for him; as long as there is food, he will stay." Paula Drillman, the director of strategic planning at the ad agency, said, "Killing the roaches with a bug spray and watching them squirm and die allowed the women to express their hostility toward men and have greater control over the roaches."[17]

Managerial principle 6.2
Employ depth interviews and focus groups to identify hidden motivations for purchasing a good or service.

Trait Theory

In the trait theory approach, people are classified according to their dominant traits. A **trait** is a measurable characteristic in which one person over time consistently differs from other people. The various trait approaches to personality describe people in terms of their predispositions on a series of adjectives or short phrases. As such, a person's personality is depicted in terms of a particular combination of traits.

Identifying the traits of a target is important for the development of promotional strategy. Thus, advertising messages and images that are consistent with a trait will attract more attention and be perceived more favorably. For example, consumers who are higher in the need for arousal tend to be risk takers and enjoy an adrenaline rush. Red Bull energy drink targets these consumers with ads that activate the need for arousal, as shown in the nearby photo.

For the trait approach to be useful to marketers, the scale employed to measure a trait must be reliable and valid. **Reliability** is revealed when the scale is shown to be internally consistent (i.e., each question measures the same general construct) and gives similar results when an individual is retested after a period of time. **Validity** occurs when the scale measures the trait that it's designed to assess. Thus, if a trait is designed to assess a consumer's enduring disposition to drive aggressively, it's not valid if it assesses another characteristic, such as a propensity to gamble.

Think back to the previous chapter, which described the control theory model of motivation. Recall that internal stimuli impact the desired and actual states. Traits are one important type of internal stimuli that act as reference points for evaluating actual or expected outcomes. When marketing communications are congruent with consumers' traits, they'll pay more attention to the message and have a more positive attitude toward the mesage.[18]

Traits and the 3M Model of Motivation and Personality   More than four decades ago, researchers identified two problems with the trait approach.[19] First, the relationships between traits and consumer behaviors were considered to be weak and inconclusive. Such weak predictive ability occurs because

On the Cutting Edge

Are our personality traits influenced by our genes? It's beginning to seem so. For example, the 5HTT gene has been provisionally linked to aggressive, antisocial, and obsessive behaviors, including addictive consumption and food obsessions. The DRD4 dopamine receptor gene may be associated with novelty seeking, sensation seeking, and risky behavior. Other genes may make us more inclined to smoking and alcohol consumption. Currently, such proposed linkages are very preliminary, but these linkages may become clearer with time.

Source: Ning Wang and Michael S. Minor, "Genes, Social Behavior, and Consumer Behavior," working paper, 2015.

the traits are frequently borrowed from the psychological literature and don't assess enduring dispositions to engage in consumer related behaviors (e.g., distracted driving, bargaining, or compulsive buying). Second, researchers have developed a huge number of traits that have no organizing principle. However, the third author of this textbook (John Mowen) has developed an approach to personality that shows evidence of solving the two problems.[20] Called the **3M model of motivation and personality**, the approach shows promise in providing an organizational structure for understanding how traits affect behavior.

The 3M model solves the organizational problem by identifying four levels of traits based on their level of abstraction. Eight elemental traits are at the most abstract level. Table 6.1 identifies them. **Elemental traits** are the most basic underlying predispositions of individuals that arise from genetics and early learning history.

Traits	Examples
1. Openness to experience	innovative and creative
2. Conscientiousness	orderly, precise
3. Introversion	quiet, shy
4. Agreeableness	soft-hearted, kind
5. Emotional instability	moody, temperamental
6. Need for material resources	enjoys buying expensive things
7. Need for arousal	takes more risk than others
8. Need for body resources	focuses on own body and how it feels

TABLE 6.1
The Eight Elemental Traits of the 3M Model

At the next level are **compound traits**, which are predispositions to act that result from the effects of multiple elemental traits, a person's learning history, and the cultural environment. A few dozen compound traits are proposed to exist. Examples include need for learning, competitiveness, and need for activity. Importantly, both elemental and compound traits are cross-situational in nature. That is, they can influence behavior across a variety of different situations. For example, the compound trait of competitiveness influences the propensity of consumers to engage in such divergent situations as participating in sports, bargaining when shopping, and driving aggressively. Nike frequently seeks to activate competitiveness in its target market through its ads.

At the third and fourth levels of the 3M model are situational and surface traits. **Situational traits** are dispositions to act within general situational contexts. Dozens of situational traits exist. Examples include value consciousness, sports interest, product innovativeness, and health motivation. Situational traits are influenced by both elemental and compound traits, as well as learned dispositions to act within general situations.

Surface traits are the most concrete traits in the hierarchy. They are defined as enduring dispositions to act in context-specific domains. Surface traits are predicted by divergent sets of elemental, compound, and situational traits, as well as learned dispositions to act within context-specific situations. Examples of surface traits are aggressive driving propensity, distracted driving propensity, bargaining proneness, and compulsive buying likelihood. For example, think back to the discussion of distracted driving at the opening of this chapter. Research has shown the situational trait of health motivation is negatively related to the surface trait of distracted driving propensity. In other research, the situational trait of value consciousness was found to be predictive of the surface traits of coupon proneness, which assesses a general propensity to collect and use coupons when shopping, and bargaining proneness.[21]

Figure 6.2 presents the results of a study that employed the 3M model to investigate distracted driving propensity.[22] The figure includes the elemental traits, the compound trait of need for learning, the situational trait of health motivation, the surface trait of distracted driving propensity, and the demographic variable of gender. As can be seen, three elemental traits are positively associated with the need for learning: openness to experience, conscientiousness, and need for arousal. In turn, need for learning and need for body resources are positively related to health motivation. Finally, four traits are predictive of distracted driving: health motivation (negative relation), need for learning (negative relation), conscientiousness (negative relation), and need for arousal (positive relation). In addition, women are more prone to distracted driving.

FIGURE 6.2
The Trait Predictors of Distracted Driving

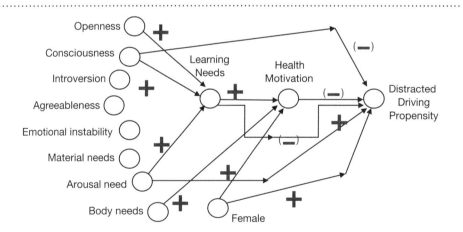

The 3M model accounted for over 26 percent of the variance in the enduring disposition to drive distractedly. These results confirm the proposal that a system of traits combines to create enduring dispositions to engage in consumer activities. Accounting for this high level of variance in distracted driving (i.e., 26 percent) reveals that personality traits, when used in combination with demographic variables (i.e., gender in this case), can meaningfully assist researchers and managers in understanding the motivations that lead to consumer actions.

In the introduction to the chapter, we asked whether aggressive drivers and distracted drivers are similar to each other. As it turns out, they share two traits. Both distracted drivers and aggressive drivers are higher in the need for arousal and lower in conscientiousness as compared with other drivers. There are differences between these two groups as well, however. Aggressive drivers are more frequently male, are higher in emotional instability, and are more hyper-competitive than distracted drivers. When combined with low conscientiousness and a high need for arousal, one can readily understand how this set of traits can lead to road rage on our highways.

Managerial principle 6.3
Use multiple traits in combination with demographic variables to understand the individual difference factors that affect consumer behavior.

Evolutionary Psychology and the Needs for Material and Body Resources

The 3M model departs from traditional approaches to personality by proposing there are basic needs for material resources and body resources. This idea emerged from evolutionary psychology, which proposes the human species survived, in part, because of a need to protect and enhance material and body resources. Thus, in order to survive, humans had a need for tools, clothing, shelter, weapons, and other material objects. The **need for material resources** is defined as an enduring disposition to collect and protect material resources. Similarly, a motivation to protect and enhance the body was essential to survival. The **need for body resources** is defined as the enduring disposition to protect and enhance the body.

Research on the need for material resources has shown it to be predictive of a variety of the more concrete traits in the 3M model hierarchy, including achievement orientation, competitiveness, impulsiveness, bargaining proneness, value consciousness (negative relation), tightwadism[23] (negative relation), compulsive buying, and product innovativeness. These findings are consistent with the idea that materialism has both positive and negative implications for consumers.[24] That is, higher levels of materialism have the positive effect of leading to greater amounts of achievement motivation and value consciousness. On the other hand, materialism can also lead to impulsiveness and compulsive buying. These ideas are also consistent with the proposal a person's level of material needs forms a component of the self-concept. In other words, "What we possess is, in a very real way, part of ourselves."[25] Indeed, William James stated in 1890 that we are the sum total of all our possessions.[26] The need for material resources can be exhibited at a very early age.

The need for body resources also has been found to be predictive of a number of compound and situational traits, including health motivation, competitiveness, value consciousness (i.e., people who seek to protect their body also seek to protect their finances), and sports interest.

Similar to the other elemental traits, including materialism, the level of the need for body resources forms a component of a person's self-concept. Interestingly, the various body parts differ in importance to a consumer's self-concept. This phenomenon has important practical implications. One major medical problem today is finding sufficient body parts for organ transplants. From a psychological perspective, transplanting body organs can be extremely traumatic for both the donor and recipient. Furthermore, decisions by next of kin to donate organs of a deceased person are made, in part, based on how sacrosanct the organs are perceived to be. Thus, organs important to the self-concept, such as the eyes and heart, are most frequently vetoed for donation.[27]

How Are Traits Organized?

Prior to the development of the 3M model, there was no way to arrange traits into an organizational structure. The 3M model, however, provides a structure in which traits can be placed into one of the four levels of the 3M model hierarchy. For example, the scale measuring ATSCI (i.e., attention to social comparison information), discussed earlier in the chapter, represents a compound level trait that's predicted by three of the elemental traits. Thus, consumers high in ATSCI are higher in agreeability and the need for material resources while being lower in openness to experience. Table 6.2 lists a number of traits investigated by consumer researchers and where they reside in the model's hierarchy.

TABLE 6.2

Examples of Traits and Their Location in the 3M Model

Elemental Traits	
Openness to experience	Emotional instability (neuroticism)
Conscientiousness	Material resource needs
Extroversion/introversion	Arousal needs
Agreeableness	Body resource needs

Compound Traits	
Need for learning/need for cognition	Altruism
Need for activity	Need for achievement
Competitiveness	Attention to social comparison information
Need for consistency	Impulsiveness
Need for uniqueness	Separateness-connectedness

Situational Traits	
Health motivation	Financial conservatism
Value consciousness	Superstitiousness
Leadership propensity	Volunteerism
Physical vanity view	Physical vanity concern

Surface Traits	
Aggressive driving	Healthy diet lifestyle
Distracted driving	Exercise lifestyle
Compulsive buying	Coupon proneness
Plastic surgery proneness	Tanning proneness
Gambling propensity	Stock investing propensity

As seen in Table 6.2, the trait need for cognition is at the compound level. The **need for cognition** measures the extent to which consumers have an intrinsic motivation to engage in problem-solving activities.[28] Consumers who consistently exert high effort are said to have a high need for cognition. Thus, those with a high need for cognition act as though they're in a high-involvement state. As a result, such people tend to think more prior to making a purchase.[29]

Researchers have also found consumers with a low need for cognition are influenced more by the characteristics of the source, such as his or her physical attractiveness and likability, than by the quality of the arguments in the ad.[30]

Separateness-Connectedness Another trait that resides at the compound level is **separateness-connectedness** (SC), which the extent to which people perceive their self-concept as autonomous and separate from other people (i.e., separated) or as interdependent and united with other people.[31] Connected people consider significant others as part of or as an extension of the self. In contrast, separated people distinguish themselves from others and set a clear boundary between "me" and "not me." Researchers have found SC differs across a number of demographic variables. For example, females have been found to have a more connected self-concept than males. Similarly, people from Asian cultures have a more connected self-concept than people from the United States, Canada, and Europe. Several Nike ads illustrate the use of a separateness theme as the female athlete eschews the pressure to conform to societies' idea of how the female body should look.

Other research has shown the SC trait moderates consumer responses to advertisements.[32] In the study, respondents first completed the SC scale. Two weeks later, they evaluated advertisements for the Discover credit card that employed either a separated or a connected theme. A portion of each the ads that illustrate how the connectedness and separateness themes were communicated follows:

- Connected theme: *Our marriage brings us together and it makes each "me" become part of the "us." Our family becomes our life. . . . We contribute to our relationship by our communal activities and joint decisions.*

- Separated theme: *Our marriage brings me and Chris together, but it doesn't make me lose my self-identify. I have a world of my own and I am keeping individuality and unique life style. . . . Be what you want, but always be you. Your credit card shouldn't be like someone else's.*

The results of the study revealed respondents scoring high on separateness rated the "individualistic" ad highly and the "communal" ad relatively lower. In contrast, respondents scoring high on connectedness rated the communal ad highly and the individualistic ad relatively lower.

> **Managerial principle 6.4**
> Use the key traits of a target market to develop promotional messages that are consistent with the traits and that lead to increased attention and positive affect.

Compulsive Buying as a Surface Trait Currently, a major societal problem in the United States involves consumers falling into debt and going bankrupt. While overspending can result from factors beyond a person's control (e.g., unexpectedly losing a job), the trait of compulsive buying can also result in poor money management. Compulsive buying is defined as the "chronic, repetitive purchasing that becomes a primary response to negative events or feelings."[33] As such, compulsive buying is part of the dark side of consumer behavior.

Consumer researchers have developed an instrument to measure the tendency to engage in compulsive buying.[34] The instrument can be used to screen consumers in order to identify those at risk for becoming compulsive buyers and encountering severe financial difficulties. Here are some of the questions on the instrument that successfully identified compulsive buyers:

- *Bought things even though I couldn't afford them.*
- *Felt others would be horrified if they knew of my spending habits.*
- *Felt anxious or nervous on days I didn't go shopping.*
- *Bought something in order to make myself feel better.*

A consistent pattern in which an individual answers yes to most of the questions indicates the person may be a compulsive buyer and should seek professional assistance. In the 3M model, compulsive buying is viewed as a surface trait. Work using the 3M model has found the following traits to be associated with compulsive buying: impulsiveness, emotional instability, need for material resources, low conscientiousness, and high agreeableness. These findings suggest counseling programs that assist people in becoming more conscientious, more emotionally stable, and less impulsive will help them overcome the buying addiction. In addition, the best way to minimize the harmful effects of materialism is to have the consumers cut up their credit cards.

Do Brands Have Personality Traits?

A component of a brand's image is its personality. Individuals with a particular personality will prefer brands whose perceived personality matches their own. In fact, researchers have found brand personality can be assessed with the same scales employed to measure a person's personality.[35]

What are some of the traits of brands? One study identified five dimensions of brand personality: sincerity, excitement, competence, sophistication, and ruggedness. Among these, sincere and exciting personalities were particularly important.[36] For example, the energy drink Red Bull has worked diligently to create an exciting/risk taking brand image. The personality traits of consumers will influence the choice of brands based on whether they match a brand's personality. For instance, consumers may buy a particular brand in order to project a desired image. Individuals in one study who were classified as "anxiously attached consumers" were influenced more than others by a brand's personality.[37] It's likely that brands can take on the same personality characteristics as those used to describe people. Thinking back to the elemental traits in the 3M model, brands can be positioned as high in body resources. A case in point is the Activia's ads touting its yogurt's digestive health benefits, which feature the actress Jamie Lee Curtis as a spokesperson.

Managerial principle 6.5
Employ marketing research to identify key traits of the target market, which can then be used to segment the market, position a product, and develop promotional strategy.

On the Managerial Use of Scales Measuring Personality Traits   Personality traits directly impact the responsive marketing (RESPonsive Marketing) application areas: research, segmentation, positioning, and the marketing mix component of promotional strategy. These ideas are illustrated in the work on the separateness-connectedness trait. Managers should first do *research* to determine whether it's possible to *segment* their target market based on the degree that it's high or low on the trait of separateness-connectedness. If the target market is found to be highly separated or highly connected, it's possible to *position* the brand on the personality trait. The marketing manager can then use various *promotional strategies* to match the theme of the marketing communications to the separated or connected target market. Thus, marketing communications could use a separated theme and position the brand as made for "individualists" and perhaps targeted to men. In contrast, a brand could be positioned as made for "those who are connected" and targeted to women.

THE SELF-CONCEPT AND MARKETING STRATEGY

The self-concept represents the "totality of the individual's thoughts and feelings having reference to himself as an object."[38] It's as though an individual turns around and evaluates just who and what he or she is. Because people have a need to behave consistently with their self-concept, the perception of themselves is one of the internal stimuli that acts as a reference for outcomes in the control theory model of motivation and behavior described in Chapter 5. By acting in a manner consistent with their self-concept, consumers can maintain their self-esteem and gain predictability in interactions with others.

At least eight dimensions of the self-concept have been identified (see Table 6.3). The actual self relates to how a person actually perceives himself or herself. The ideal self denotes how a person would like to perceive himself or herself.[39] The social self concerns how a person believes others perceive him or her. In contrast, the ideal social self relates to how a person would like others to view him or her. The situational self portrays how a person would like to act in various contexts. For example, at a sporting event, a person might want to be carefree. In contrast, when conducting a business deal, the person would want to be serious. The extended self denotes the impact of possessions on self-image. Researchers have also identified a self-perception called "possible selves." This perspective on the self refers to what a person perceives he or she would like to become, could become, or is afraid of becoming. Thus, the possible selves idea has a future orientation when compared with the other self-concept types.[40] Finally, as noted earlier in the chapter, the connected versus separated selves depict the extent to which people define themselves in terms of other people or groups with whom they are affiliated.

Managerial principle 6.6
Employ marketing research to identify the ideal self of the target market and then develop communications that link the product to the ideal self.

1.	Actual self—how a person actually perceives himself or herself
2.	Ideal self—what a person would like to be like
3.	Social self—how a person thinks others perceive him or her
4.	Ideal social self—how a person would like others to perceive him or her
5.	Situational self—a person's self-concept in a particular situation
6.	Extended self—the people and things that are important to a person
7.	Possible selves—what a person would like to become, could become, or is afraid to become
8.	Connected self—the extent a person defines himself or herself in terms of the connection with other groups or individuals

TABLE 6.3
Dimensions of the Self-Concept

Symbolic Interactionism and the Self

Proponents of **symbolic interactionism** view consumers as living in a symbolic environment, and how people interpret these symbols determines the meanings derived.[41] Within a society, people develop shared meanings as to what the symbols represent. Further, by linking themselves to these symbols, consumers can depict their self-concept to others. Indeed, managers seek to give brands strong personalities so consumers can appropriate the brand characteristics for themselves by purchasing the product. Because the brand meanings are shared, marketers are helping to construct the self-concept of consumers.[42]

The concept of the looking glass self is an important idea for symbolic interactionists.[43] A looking glass is a mirror, and the looking glass self is a metaphor that describes the idea people obtain signals about who they are by looking at how others react to them. It's as though we see reflections of ourselves in the faces and body language of others. Thus, we define ourselves, in part, based on how we perceive other people's reactions to us. For example, a woman may be shy and retiring as an office worker because that's how she believes her bosses and coworkers view her. In contrast, on the weekends, she may be a party animal as she moves from one bar to another. In part, she's using the reactions of others to determine her self-concept, which can diverge markedly from situation to situation. The Las Vegas Convention Bureau has used this idea in their advertising with the theme of "What happens here, Stays Here. "

Self-Concept and Product Symbolism   As noted by the symbolic interactionists, products may not be bought for their functional benefits, but for their symbolic value.[44] As such, possessions become an extension of the individual. A relationship may be found between a person's self-image and of certain products he or she buys. For example, if a young woman's perception of herself as attractive and exciting is thrown into doubt, she may buy products that symbolically portray her as exciting, such as perfume or a sexy blouse.

Products most likely to communicate one's self-concept to others have three characteristics.[45] First, they must have visibility in use so their purchase, consumption, and disposition are readily apparent to others. Second, the products must show variability—that is, some consumers must have the resources to own the product, whereas others don't have the time or financial resources to possess it. If everyone owned the product, it could not be a symbol. Third, the products should have personalizability, which refers to the extent a product denotes a stereotypical image of the average user. One can easily see how such symbolic products as automobiles or jewelry possess the characteristics of visibility, variability, and personalizability. Expensive men's watches, such as those by Rolex, exemplify a personalizable product.

Managerial principle 6.7
Develop your product and promotional strategy to maximize your product's personalizability.

The importance of recognizing the symbolic nature of products is depicted in Figure 6.3, which shows how the self is communicated to others via symbolic products. In the figure are three boxes. They represent a person's self-concept, an audience or reference group, and a product that acts as a symbol. In step 1 of the communication process, the consumer buys a product that may communicate his or her self-concept to the audience. In step 2, the consumer hopes the audience will have the desired perception of the symbolic nature of the product. In step 3, the consumer hopes the reference group views him or her as having some of the same symbolic qualities as the product.[46] Thus, consumers may be conceptualized as purchasing products to communicate symbolically various aspects of their self-concept to others. The theory consumers select products and stores that correspond to his or her self-concept has been called the self-congruity effect.[47]

The Self-Concept and Promotional Strategy   Whether in advertising or personal selling, companies should seek to enhance the consumers' self-image. American Express Corporation successfully used such a strategy. In 1980,

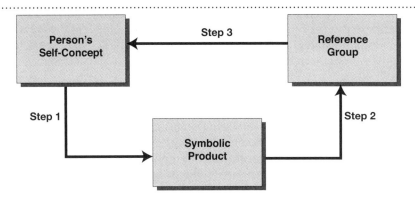

FIGURE 6.3
The Communication of Self to Others via Symbolic Products

Step 1: A person buys a product that's symbolic of himself or herself.
Step 2: A reference group associates the product with the person.
Step 3: The reference group attributes to the person the symbolic qualities of the product

US consumers owned slightly more than 100 million credit cards. By 2010, the number was almost 610 million, although ownership may be dropping, especially among millennials.[48] How can such an increase be explained?[49] One psychologist argued that owning a card enhances a person's self-esteem. He said, "The great modern nightmare is discovering that you're unrecognized, a nobody. With that card you can be surrounded by strangers, but you walk up and say, 'Look what I've got in my hand.'"[50] In its "Do You Know Me" campaign, American Express Corporation used this need to propel the company into a leader in the credit card industry.

LIFESTYLE, PSYCHOGRAPHIC ANALYSIS, AND MARKETING STRATEGY

A third approach identifying individual differences among consumers is to measure their lifestyles through psychographic analysis. Through psychographic analysis, consumer researchers describe segments of consumers in terms of how they live, work, and play. This section discusses these concepts, which are used frequently by marketing professionals.

Consumer Lifestyles

Lifestyle can be thought of as describing how people live. Lifestyle can refer to individuals, small groups (e.g., a sorority or fraternity), or an aggregation of people (e.g., a market segment). Historically, researchers have argued lifestyle denotes a set of ideas quite distinct from that of personality. That is, lifestyle relates to how people live, how they spend their money, and how they allocate their time. In contrast, personality describes the consumer from a more internal perspective. Thus, personality has traditionally delineated how consumers think, feel, and perceive the world.

From the perspective of the 3M model, however, lifestyle measures are conceptualized as surface traits. The lifestyle measure, or surface trait, can then be predicted by combinations of situational, compound, and elemental traits. Importantly, assessing lifestyle as surface trait simplifies market research. The reason is the researcher doesn't have to use measures that come from completely different sets of literatures (i.e., marketing, sociology, and psychology). It's important, however, to discuss psychographic analysis from the traditional perspective, as we do in the next section.

Traditional Perspectives on Psychographic Analysis

The term *psychographics* means different things to different researchers. The term itself connotes the idea of describing (graph) the psychological (psycho) makeup of consumers. In practice, however, psychographics is employed to assess consumers' lifestyles and factors associated with the lifestyles. Lifestyles are assessed by measuring consumers' activities, interests, and opinions (AIOs). Market researchers use psychographic research to describe a consumer segment so as to help marketing managers position products and develop the marketing mix. Traditional psychographic studies include questions to assess a target market's lifestyle, its personality characteristics, and its demographic characteristics. In sum, **psychographics** may be defined as the quantitative investigation of consumers' lifestyles, personality, and demographic characteristics. (Because the 3M model can assess all these factors, it fits the definition of a psychographic inventory.)

Psychographics and AIO Statements   In order to understand consumer lifestyles, psychographic researchers use questions called **AIO statements**. AIO statements describe the lifestyle of consumers by identifying their activities, interests, and opinions. Activity questions ask consumers to indicate what they do, what they buy, and how they spend their time. Interest questions focus on consumers' preferences and priorities. Opinion questions ask for consumers' views and feelings on such things as world, local, moral, economic, and social affairs. Table 6.4 lists questions representative of AIO items.

TABLE 6.4
Some Typical Questions Found in AIO Inventories

1. Activity Questions
   a. What outdoor sports do you participate in at least twice a month?
   b. How many books do you read a year?
   c. How often do you visit shopping malls?
   d. Have you gone outside of the United States for a vacation?
   e. To how many clubs do you belong?
2. Interest Questions
   a. In which of the following are you most interested—sports, church, or work?
   b. How important to you is it to try new foods?
   c. How important is it to you to get ahead in life?
   d. Would you rather spend two hours on a Saturday afternoon with your wife or in a boat fishing alone?
3. Opinion Questions (Ask the respondent to agree or disagree.)
   a. The Russian people are just like us.
   b. Women should have free choice regarding abortion.
   c. Educators are paid too much money.
   d. CBS Inc.™ is run by East Coast liberals.
   e. We must be prepared for nuclear war.

No hard-and-fast rules exist for developing AIO items. One dimension on which they frequently differ is their level of specificity. AIO questions may be highly specific and ask the respondent to provide information about his or her attitudes and preferences regarding a particular product or service. For example, a researcher for General Mills might be interested in consumer perceptions of Post Grape-Nuts cereal. The researcher might ask respondents to agree or disagree with the following highly specific questions:

- I find Grape-Nuts to be too hard to chew.
- Grape-Nuts remind me of the outdoors.
- When I eat Grape-Nuts, it makes me feel healthy.

On the other hand, AIO questions can be much more general. Some highly general questions researchers might ask consumers to agree or disagree with include the following:

- I consider myself an outdoor person.
- I believe in world peace.
- I think cities are where the action is.

Of course, researchers will have different purposes for asking the two types of questions. The highly specific questions give researchers information on what consumers think about the product and how that product relates to them. Products may be developed or changed and specific messages created from that information. Indeed, unique selling propositions may be formulated. A **unique selling proposition** is a quick, hard-hitting phrase that captures a major feature of a product or service. For example, General Mills, the maker of Wheaties, has used for many years the unique selling proposition "The Breakfast of Champions."

Consumer profiles can be developed from the responses to AIO questions. Such profiles provide an understanding of the general lifestyle of the targeted consumer segment. Based on the profile, advertisers can develop ideas for the themes of ads and for the setting within which to place an ad. For example, researchers investigated the psychographic characteristics of online shoppers.[51] The results showed three segments of online shoppers: risk-averse doubters, open-minded shoppers, and reserved information-seekers. These clusters of consumers could be predicted by their level of emotional stability, their willingness to buy, and their level of shopping pleasure on the Internet. Such knowledge suggests employing an advertising theme in which an attractive male is highly visible.[52]

The psychographic inventory receiving the most attention among corporations is **VALS** (Values and Lifestyles). More recently, consumer researchers have begun to address a second approach, called the LOV (List of Values) scale. These two inventories are discussed next.

Managerial principle 6-8
Employ psychographic analysis to develop lifestyle profiles of the target market. From such profiles, themes can be developed and used in marketing communications.

The VALS Psychographic Inventory

Perhaps the best-developed psychographic inventory of consumers is the **VALS lifestyle classification scheme**. Developed by the Stanford Research Institute (SRI), VALS has been widely used by US corporations to segment the market and to provide guidance for developing advertising and product strategy.[53] SRI has, in fact, developed two psychographic inventories. The first, called VALS, is based on motivational and developmental psychological theories—in particular, Maslow's hierarchy of needs theory. The second approach, called VALS 2, was developed specifically to measure consumer buying patterns. While firms have used both inventories, we will discuss only the VALS 2.

The goal of VALS 2 is to identify specific relationships between consumer attitudes and purchase behavior. It divides the American population into eight segments based on their self-identity and their resources. VALS 2 researchers identified three categories of self-identity orientation. Those oriented toward "principle" make consumer choices based upon their beliefs rather than feelings, events, or a desire for approval. Consumers oriented toward "status" make choices based on their perception of whether others will approve of their purchases. Finally, consumers oriented toward "action" make decisions based on desires for activity, variety, and risk taking.

The second dimension in the VALS 2 classification scheme is the resources of the consumer. These include financial, psychological, and physical resources. People with abundant resources are at one end of the spectrum, whereas those with minimal resources occupy the other end. Table 6.5 describes each of the eight categories of consumers identified by VALS 2.

TABLE 6.5
Descriptions of the VALS 2 Consumer Segments

1. Actualizers—high resources with focus on principle and action. Active, take-charge expression of taste, independence, and character. College educated, they compose 8% of the population. Median age is 43.

2. Fulfilleds—high resources with focus on principle. Mature, satisfied, well-informed people for whom image has little importance. Generally married with older children. Composing 11% of the population, their median age is 48, and they're college educated.

3. Believers—low resources with focus on principle. Traditional and moralistic, they live predictable lifestyle tied to family and church. Loyal to American products—noninnovative. High school educated, they represent 16% of the population. Median age is 58.

4. Achievers—high resources with focus on status. Successful, career-oriented individuals. Low risk takers, they respect authority and status quo. Highly image conscious, they buy expensive, expressive autos. College educated, they represent 13% of the population. Median age is 36.

5. Strivers—low resources with focus on status. Impulsive and trend conscious, these individuals seek social approval for actions. Money defines success for them. They frequently have some college education and represent 13% of the population. Median age is 34.

6. Experiencers—high resources with focus on action. Young, enthusiastic individuals who like sports and taking risks. Single and impulsive purchasers, they haven't yet completed their education. Representing 12% of the population, their median age is 26.

7. Makers—low resources with focus on practical action. Conservative and practical, they focus on family, working with their hands. High school educated, they represent 13% of the population. Median age is 30.

8. Strugglers—poor, with little education, they have few resources and must focus on living for the moment. Cautious but loyal shoppers, they represent 14% of the population. High school educated. Median age is 61.

Source: SRI International

Transport Canada used VALS 2 to survey travelers at Canadian airports. The results revealed that most of the travelers (37 percent) were actualizers. Actualizers have high incomes and buy products as an expression of their good taste, independence, and character. These characteristics suggested to the researchers that stores such as the Nature Company could do well in airports. As the researcher explained, "Actualizers are a good market for quality arts and crafts."[54]

A variety of research companies have developed their own psychographic inventories. Wilson Research Strategies, for instance, created an inventory that's based on sets of other-centered and self-centered values. A problem with assessing the utility of most psychographic inventories is they're proprietary instruments (i.e., not in the public domain) and restrict their access to consumer researchers. Therefore, their reliability and validity are difficult to assess.[55] It should be noted, however, the VALS 2 survey is available on the Internet (at www.strategicbusinessinsights.com/vals/presurvey.shtml). Interestingly, the majority of web users are classified as strivers in the VALS 2 typology.[56]

The List of Values Approach

A scale that shows promise of correcting some of the problems of VALS is the **List of Values (LOV) scale**. The goal of the LOV scale is to assess a person's dominant values.[57] Although not strictly a psychographic inventory (i.e., it doesn't use AIO statements), it has been applied to the same types of problems as the VALS inventories. Further, because it's available for public scrutiny, its validity and reliability can be assessed. The LOV assesses nine values.

1. self-fulfillment
2. excitement
3. sense of accomplishment
4. self-respect
5. sense of belonging
6. being well-respected
7. security
8. fun and enjoyment
9. warm relationships with others

When used for market research, demographic questions are added to the questions used to identify the nine values. The LOV scale has three dimensions. Questions regarding the first four items (i.e., self-fulfillment, excitement, sense of accomplishment, and self-respect) represent individual values of an internal nature. The second dimension (i.e., sense of belonging, being well-respected, and security) represents a focus on the external world. Thus, a person who worries a lot about crime and unemployment would tend to have a need for security. The third dimension consists of the last two items (i.e., fun and enjoyment and warm relationships with others) and reflects an interpersonal orientation.[58]

The LOV scale has received extensive testing and can differentiate consumers along the three dimensions of internal focus, interpersonal focus, and external focus. One study revealed consumers with an emphasis on internal values seek to control their lives. This desire for control extended to decisions such as where to eat and where to shop and was expressed by a need to obtain good nutrition and to avoid food additives by purchasing "natural" foods. In contrast, those with an external orientation tended to avoid natural foods, perhaps out of a desire to conform to society at large.[59]

SOCIAL MEDIA

Individual Differences and Social Network Use

Researchers have investigated individual differences in social network use from the perspectives of demographics and personality. From a demographic view, women and those ages eighteen to twenty-nine are the most active social network users. Interestingly, little differences are found among the various ethnic groups, except that African Americans are somewhat less likely to participate in social networks. Few differences are found among users based on education or household income.

Differences in demographics across various social media have been found. For example, men are more likely to visit LinkedIn than women. Similarly, those with post-graduate degrees were most likely to visit LinkedIn. Social media use is highest among lower (i.e., less than $30,000 per year) and higher income consumers (i.e., $75,000+ per year household income). Finally, about half of young adults use Instagram.[a]

Personality characteristics have been found to predict social media usage. Thus, extroverts and those open to experience were found to be more likely to participate in social networks. The finding that extroverts more frequently participate in social networks makes sense because they enjoy making friends and associating with others. An explanation for openness to experience is they enjoy novelty and new experiences, which participating in social networks encourages. Another finding is more active users of social networks tend to be lower in emotional stability. An explanation is because emotional instability has been linked to loneliness, these individuals participate in social networks to interact with others.[b]

a. Maeve Duggan, Nicole B. Ellison, Cliff Lampe, Amanda Lenhart, and Mary Madden, "Social Media Update 2014," *Pew Research Center*, accessed December 8, 2015, http://www.pewinternet.org/2015/01/09/social-media-update-2014/.

b. Teresa Correa, Amber Willard Hinsley, and Homero Gil de Zuniga, "Who Interacts on the Web?" *Computers in Human Behavior* 26 (2010): 247–253.

MANAGERIAL IMPLICATIONS OF PERSONALITY AND PSYCHOGRAPHICS

Individual difference variables have application to four of the responsive marketing strategy concepts—research, segmentation, positioning, and marketing mix development. First, marketing researchers can conduct studies to identify the individual difference variables that motivate consumers to action. Second, if different groups within the target market share similar personality, self-concept, and/or psychographic characteristics, they can become target segments. Third, by developing an understanding of a target market's personality, self-concept, and/or psychographic characteristics, managers can develop promotional messages that will tap into the group's needs and wants. Finally, companies can position brands based on a dominant individual difference characteristic of a target market. These ideas are discussed more fully below.

Research

Marketing research is required to measure the personality, self-concept, and psychographic characteristics chosen for investigation. Research should also be employed to test whether the messages designed to communicate positioning strategies are being interpreted by the target market in the desired way.

Environmental Analysis

Managers must recognize that the values of the dominant culture or subculture in which the target market resides will have an impact on their personality. In particular, culture and subculture can impact the compound and situational traits found in the 3M model. For example, individualism is an important part of the culture of the United States. This value can be measured by the compound trait of separateness-connectedness, discussed earlier in the chapter. Thus, the identification of the values of the dominant culture or subculture of the target market can provide managers with indications of what compound and situational traits to measure.

Segmentation

Segmentation represents the most important managerial use of the concepts described in this chapter. That is, the bottom-line purpose of investigating personality, self-concept, and psychographics is to provide an empirical means for identifying variables that break a heterogeneous population into homogeneous subgroups with similar needs, wants, wishes, and desires.

Positioning and Differentiation

By identifying the target market's dominant personality and psychographic characteristics, marketing managers can identify strategies to position and differentiate a product from competitors. For instance, if the target market has a dominant tendency to reveal a high need for arousal, the brand can be positioned by showing using or consuming the brand while doing exciting, thrilling, and risky activities. Mountain Dew advertising uses this approach to position and associate the brand with youth, enthusiasm, and daringness.

Marketing Mix

The study of personality, self-concept, and psychographics has clear implications for promotional and product strategies. Promotional strategy can be designed based on an understanding of the dominant personality, self-concept, and psychographic characteristics of the target market. Advertising and public relations themes and messages can be derived from the analysis. In addition, the identification of the dominant traits of the target market will have implications for product design. Suppose, for example, the target market is high in conscientiousness, low in need for arousal, highly emotionally stable, low in material needs, and low in openness to experience. For an automobile brand, this combination of traits suggests developing a very safe, inexpensive, reliable, and visually plain vehicle, such as the Toyota Camry.

SUMMARY

Marketing managers are interested in the study of personality, psychoanalytic theory, trait theory, self-concept, and psychographics because these concepts are particularly useful for segmenting markets, developing market research, creating promotional strategy, and positioning products.

How can marketers employ personality approaches to develop strategy?

Personality is defined as "the distinctive patterns of behavior, including thoughts and emotions, that characterize each individual's adaptation to the situations of his or her life." Although marketers can't expect to predict from personality profiles the specific brands purchased by consumers, it's possible to gain an increased understanding of the factors that motivate and guide their purchases. In particular, personality characteristics can be used to develop messages that appeal to a target market having a dominant personality characteristic. In addition, personality characteristics can interact with situational variables to influence specific market segments. Two different approaches to the study of personality were identified in the chapter—the psychoanalytic approach and the trait approach.

How can marketers employ psychoanalytic theory to develop strategy?

Psychoanalytic theory views the personality as resulting from conflict among the id, the ego, and the superego. It has had a major influence on marketers through its contribution to the motivation research. From psychoanalytic theory, the use of depth interviews and for focus groups emerged.

How can marketers use trait theory be used to develop strategy?

In the trait approach consumers are classified according to their dominant characteristics. A trait is a characteristic in which one person differs from another in a relatively permanent and consistent way. Trait theories describe people in terms of their predispositions on a series of adjectives or short phrases. As such, a person's personality is depicted in terms of a particular combination of traits.

The 3M model is an approach to understanding how traits influence consumer behavior. In the model, traits are arranged in a four-level hierarchy consisting of elemental, compound, situational, and surface traits. These sets of traits then influence the propensity of consumer feelings and behaviors. An example of an elemental trait is the need for arousal. An example of a compound trait is the need for learning. An example of a situational trait is health motivation. Finally, examples of surface traits are the tendencies to drive aggressively and distractedly.

How can marketers use an understanding of self-concept to develop strategy?

Self-concept is the totality of a person's thoughts and feelings with reference to himself or herself as the object. Many good and services are bought, in part, to reflect the self-concept of the consumer. As such, products become symbols representing the consumer's self to others.

How can marketers use lifestyle and psychographic analyses to develop strategy?

Psychographics is the quantitative investigation of consumers' lifestyles, cognitive styles, and demographics that can be used to assist marketing decision making. The goal of psychographics is to describe individual consumers in a way that helps managers to segment the marketplace, position products, and develop marketing mix strategy. Because of this highly applied purpose, marketing researchers borrow from any source possible those questions to be included in psychographic inventories.

As a broad statement, psychographic inventories contain questions that assess three aspects of consumers—their lifestyles, personalities, and demographic characteristics. Lifestyle refers to how people live, how they spend their money, and how they allocate their time. Generally, it's assessed by questions concerning a consumer's various activities, interests, and opinions. It concerns the overt actions and purchases of consumers. In contrast, personality refers to the characteristic patterns of thinking, feeling, and perceiving held by individual consumers. Demographic questions are also asked in psychographic inventories to further describe the characteristics of individual consumers.

One of the most frequently used psychographic inventories is called the VALS lifestyle classification scheme. In VALS 2, eight consumer segments were identified based on their self-identify and the amount of resources possessed. Numerous companies and organizations have used VALS to segment the market and to assist in the development of the marketing mix. Another approach relevant to performing psychographic analysis is the List of Values (LOV) scale, which is designed to assess the dominant values of a person.

KEY TERMS

AIO statements
ATSCI
compound traits
depth interviews
ego
elemental traits
focus groups
id
individual difference variables
libido
lifestyle
List of Values (LOV) scale
need for cognition

need for body resources
need for material resources
personality
pleasure principle
psychoanalytic theory of personality
psychographic analysis
psychographics
reality principle
reliability
self-concept
separateness-connectedness
situational traits

superego
surface traits
symbolic interactionism
symbols
3M model of motivation and personality
trait
unique selling proposition
validity
VALS
VALS lifestyle classification scheme

REVIEW QUESTIONS

1. Compare and contrast the concepts of personality and psychographics.
2. Discuss the structure of personality developed by Freud.
3. In what areas has psychoanalytic theory had an impact on marketing?
4. Describe what is meant by trait theory. What has been the major problem with the use of trait theory by marketers?
5. What are the four levels of traits identified in the 3M model? Give an example of a trait in each level.
6. What traits are predictive of the distracted driver?
7. To what types of consumer tasks might the concept of need for cognition be relevant? What types of consumer situations have been identified as ambiguous?

8. Define what's meant by self-concept. Identify five of the six types of self-concept.

9. Explain how consumers can communicate themselves to others via symbolic products.

10. A scale has been developed to measure product images and self-images. What are examples of the questions asked on the scale? What procedure must respondents go through in order to assess the relationship between product image and self-image?

11. Define consumer lifestyle and psychographics.

12. Provide three examples of questions that would be classified as obtaining psychographic information on activities, interests, opinions.

13. Outline the basics of the VALS II psychographic inventory.

14. Compare and contrast the LOV scale to VALS.

15. Can the 3M model be employed to assess the psychographic characteristics of a market segment?

16. What are the major managerial uses of personality, psychoanalytic theory, trait theory, self-concept, and psychographics?

DISCUSSION QUESTIONS

1. Consider your own preferences for types of automobiles (e.g., sports cars versus SUVs versus fuel-efficient cars). How do your preferences differ from those of your friends? Review the traits identified in the text. Identify traits that could explain why your preferences are different from those of others.

2. Go through a popular magazine and look carefully at the print advertisements. Identify two ads that possibly use Freudian symbolism. To what extent do you think people are influenced by these symbols?

3. According to Freud, one function of the superego is to create guilt. To what extent do advertisers attempt to use guilt as a mechanism to promote their products? Try to cite some specific examples.

4. Fantasy is a technique frequently used by marketers of perfumes, autos, and other products with a heavy symbolic emphasis. Develop a draft version of a print advertisement for a new perfume called Temptation. Develop the ad so it uses fantasy as a major theme.

5. In developing a trait profile of personality, it's important to develop surface traits that are closely associated with the consumer behavior in which you are interested. Develop a four-item surface trait scale that could be used to identify the characteristics of people who are heavy consumers of diet foods.

6. Go through a popular magazine, such as *Newsweek* or *Time*, and identify advertisements that use products as symbols of the self. Why are these products used to express self-concept to others?

7. Go to the internet and complete the VALS survey provided there. Its location as of December, 2015 was http://www.strategicbusinessinsights. com/vals/presurvey.shtml.

8. Look at the traits employed in the 3M model. What are your three most dominant traits? In what ways do these traits influence your choice of hobbies?

ENDNOTES

[1] James Perez, "Beware of Violent Aggressive Drivers!" Crime Watch, October 25, 2011, accessed November 9, 2015, http://blog.ctnews.com/crimewatch/2011/10/25/beware-of-violent-aggressive-drivers-2/.

[2] AAA Foundation for Traffic Safety, "Aggressive Driving: Research Update, April 2009," *AAAFoundation.org*, accessed April 1, 2013, https://www.aaafoundation.org/sites/default/files/AggressiveDrivingResearchUpdate2009.pdf.

[3] National Road Safety Association. http://nationalroadsafety.org/programs/speed-aggressionAccessed December 17, 2015,

[4] James Perez, "Beware of Violent Aggressive Drivers!" *Crime Watch*, October 25, 2011, accessed November 9, 2015, http://blog.ctnews.com/crimewatch/2011/10/25/beware-of-violent-aggressive-drivers-2/.

[5] "Facts and Statistics," *Distraction*, accessed November 9, 2015, http://www.distraction.gov/stats-research-laws/facts-and-statistics.html, and "Text Message Statistics," accessed December 17, 2015, http://www.statisticbrain.com/text-message-statistics/..

[6] Walter Mischel, "On the Future of Personality Measurement," *American Psychologist* 32 (April 1977): 2.

[7] Morris Rosenberg, *Conceiving the Self* (New York: Basic Books, 1979).

[8] Darrell Bem, "Self-Perception Theory," in *Advances in Experiential Social Psychology*, vol. 6, ed. L. Berkowitz (New York: Springer Press, 1965).

[9] John C. Mowen, *The 3M Model of Motivation and Personality: Theory and Empirical Applications to Consumer Behavior* (Boston: Kluwer Academic Publishers, 2000).

[10] William O. Bearden and Randall L. Rose, "Attention to Social Comparison Information: An Individual Difference Factor Affecting Consumer Conformity," *Journal of Consumer Research* 16 (March 1990): 461–471.

[11] A book that links psychoanalytic theory to personality is Paul J. Albanese, *The Personality Continuum and Consumer Behavior* (Westport, CT: Quorum Books/Greenwood Publishing Group, 2002).

[12] Sigmund Freud, "New Introductory Lectures," in *The Standard Edition of the Complete Works of Freud* vol. 22, ed. James Strachey (London: Hogarth Press, 1964).

[13] Ibid.

[14] Wilson Bryan Key, *Subliminal Seduction: Ad Media's Manipulation of a Not So Innocent America* (Englewood Cliffs, NJ: Prentice Hall, 1973).

[15] Ibid.

[16] Jack Haberstroh, "Can't Ignore Subliminal Ad Charges," *Advertising Age*, September 17, 1984, 42, 44. For some "subliminal" ads, see Jim Edwards, "The Ten Best Subliminal Ads Ever Made," accessed December 17, 2015, http://www.cbsnews.com/news/the-10-best-subliminal-ads-ever-made/10/.

[17] Ronald Alsop, "Advertisers Put Consumers on the Couch," *Wall Street Journal*, May 13, 1988, 17.

[18] Susan T. Fiske and Shelley, E. Taylor. *Social Cognition* (New York: Random House, 1984).

[19] Harold Kassarjian, "Personality and Consumer Behavior: A Review," *Journal of Marketing Research* 8 (1971): 409–418.

[20] John C. Mowen, *The 3M Model of Motivation and Personality: Theory and Empirical Applications to Consumer Behavior* (Boston: Kluwer Academic Publishers, 2000).

[21] Ibid.

[22] Sterling Bone and John C. Mowen, "Identifying the Traits of Aggressive and Distracted Driving: a Hierarchical Model Approach," *Journal of Consumer Behaviour* 5 (2006): 454–464.

[23] For research studies on tightwadism, see John L. Lastovicka, Lance A Bettencourt, Renée Shaw Hughner, and Ronald J. Kuntze, "Lifestyle of the Tight and Frugal," *Journal of Consumer Research* 26, (June 1999): 85–98 and Marcelo Nepomuceno and Michel Laroche, "Anti-Consumption and Personal Debt," in *NA—Advances in Consumer Research*, vol. 40, ed. Zeynep Gürhan-Canli, Cele Otnes, and Rui (Juliet) Zhu (Duluth, MN : Association for Consumer Research), 699–700.

[24] Kathleen S. Micken and Scott D. Roberts, "Desperately Seeking Certainty: Narrowing the Materialism Construct," in *Advances in Consumer Research*, vol. 26, ed. Eric Arnould and Linda M. Scott (Provo, UT: Association for Consumer Research, 1999), 513–518.

[25] Russell Belk, "My Possessions Myself," *Psychology Today* (July–August 1988): 50–52.

[26] William James, *The Principles of Psychology*, vol. 1 (New York: Henry Holt, 1890).

[27] Russell Belk, "Materialism: Trait Aspects of Living in the Material World," *Journal of Consumer Research* 12 (December 1985): 265–280.

[28] James W. Peltier and John A Schibrowsky, "Need for Cognition, Advertisement Viewing Time, and Memory for Advertising Stimuli," in *Advances in Consumer Research*, vol. 21, ed. Chris T. Allen and Deborah Roedder John (Provo, Utah: Association for Consumer Research, 1994), 244–250.

[29] Curtis P. Haugtvedt, Richard E. Petty, and John T. Cacioppo, "Need for Cognition and Advertising: Understanding the Role of Personality Variables in Consumer Behavior," *Journal of Consumer Psychology* 1, no. 3 (July 1992): 239–260.

[30] Curt Haugtvedt, Richard Petty, John Cacioppo, and Theresa Steidley, "Personality and Ad Effectiveness: Exploring the Utility of Need for Cognition," in *Advances in Consumer Research*, vol. 15, ed. Michael Houston (Provo, UT: Association for Consumer Research, 1988), 209–212.

[31] Cheng Lu Wang and John C. Mowen, "The Separateness-Connectedness Self Schema: Scale Development and Application to Message Construction," *Psychology and Marketing, Psychology and Marketing* 14 (March 1997): 185–207.

[32] Ibid.

[33] Ronald J. Faber and Thomas C. O'Guinn, "A Clinical Screener for Compulsive Buying," *Journal of Consumer Research* 19 (December 1992): 459–469.

[34] Ibid.

[35] Hazel H. Huang, Vincent-Wayne Mitchell, and Richard Rosenaum-Elliott, "Are Consumer and Brand Personalities the Same?" *Psychology & Marketing* 29, no. 5 (2012): 334–349.

[36] Jennifer L. Aaker, "Dimensions of Brand Personality," *Journal of Marketing Research* 34, no. 3 (1995): 347–356.

[37] Vanitha Swaminathan, Karen M. Stilley, and Rohini Ahluwalia, "When Brand Personality Matters: The Moderating Role of Attachment Style," *Journal of Consumer Research*, 35 (April 2009), 985–1002.

[38] Morris Rosenberg, *Conceiving the Self*, (New York: Basic Books, 1979).

[39] For an excellent review of the self-concept in consumer behavior, see M. Joseph Sirgy, "Self-Concept in Consumer Behavior: A Critical Review," *Journal of Consumer Research* 9 (December 1982): 287–300. See also Newell D. Wright, C. B. Claiborne, and M. Joseph Sirgy, "The Effects of Product Symbolism on Consumer Self-Concept," in *Diversity in Consumer Behavior, Advances in Consumer Research*, vol. 19, ed. John F. Sherry, Jr. and Brian Sternthal (Provo, UT: Association for Consumer Research, 1992), 311–318.

[40] Amy J. Morgan, "The Evolving Self in Consumer Behavior: Exploring Possible Selves," in *Advances in Consumer Research*, vol. 20, ed. Leigh McAlister and Michael L. Rothschild. (Provo, UT: Association for Consumer Research, 1993), 429–432.

[41] George H. Mead, *Mind, Self, and Society* (Chicago: University of Chicago Press, 1934).

[42] Mark Ligas and June Cotte, "The Process of Negotiating Brand Meaning: A Symbolic Interactionist Perspective," in *Advances in Consumer Research*, vol. 26, ed. Eric Arnould and Linda M. Scott (Provo, UT: Association for Consumer Research, 1999), 609–614.

[43] Charles H. Cooley, *Human Nature and the Social Order* (New York: Scribners, 1902).

[44] Sidney J. Levy, "Symbols for Sale," *Harvard Business Review* 37 (1959): 117–124.

[45] Rebecca H. Holman, "Product as Communication: A Fresh Appraisal of a Venerable Topic," in *Review of Marketing*, ed. Ben M. Enis and Kenneth J. Roering (Chicago: American Marketing Association, 1981), 106–119.

[46] Edward L. Grubb and Harrison Grathwohl, "Consumer Self-Concept, Symbolism, and Market Behavior: A Theoretical Approach," *Journal of Marketing* 31 (October 1967): 22–27. However,

the author conceived of these relations from the work of Fritz Heider on balance theory. See Fritz Heider, *The Psychology of Interpersonal Relations* (New York: John Wiley, 1958).

[47] Alexandra Aguirre-Rodriguez, Michael Bosnjak, and M. Joseph Sirgy, "Moderators of the Self-Congruity Effect on Consumer Decision-Making: A Meta-Analysis," *Journal of Business Research* 65, no. 8 (August 2012): 1179–1188.

[48] Tamara E. Holmes, "Credit Card Ownership Statistics," CreditCards.com, accessed November 11, 2015, http://www.creditcards.com/credit-card-news/ownership-statistics-charts-1276.php.

[49] Jeremy M. Simon, "Credit Card Ownership Sees First Jump Since 2008," *CreditCards.com*, access April 27, 2011, http://www.creditcards.com/credit-card-news/federal-reserve-new-york-household-debt-credit-Q4-2010.php#ixzz1Kk1eZf00. See also Charles McCoy and Steve Swartz, "Plastic Battle: Big Credit-Card War May Be Breaking Out to Detriment of Banks—American Express 13.5% Rate is Roiling the Industry; New Tax Law Plays Role—Do Consumers Really Care?" *Wall Street Journal*, March 19, 1987, 1, 24.

[50] See also Charles McCoy and Steve Swartz, "Plastic Battle: Big Credit-Card War May Be Breaking Out to Detriment of Banks—American Express 13.5% Rate is Roiling the Industry; New Tax Law Plays Role—Do Consumers Really Care?" *Wall Street Journal*, March 19, 1987, 1, 24.

[51] Stuard J. Barnes, Hans H. Bauer, Marcus Neumann, and Frank Huber, "Segmenting Cyberspace: A Customer Typology for the Internet," *European Journal of Marketing*, 41, no. 1–2 (2007): 71–93.

[52] Lynn R. Kahle and Larry Chiagouris, eds., *Values, Lifestyles and Psychographics* (New York: Psychology Press, 2014).

[53] For an in-depth discussion of VALS, see Arnold Mitchell, *The Nine American Lifestyles* (New York: Macmillan, 1983), 57.

[54] Rebecca Piirto, "VALS the Second Time," *American Demographics* (July 1991): 6.

[55] A number of researchers have noted that problems exist with the original VALS inventory. See John L. Lastovicka, John P. Murry, Jr., and Eric Joachimsthaler, "Evaluating the Measurement Validity of ATSCI Typologies with Qualitative Measures and Multiplicative Factoring," *Journal of Marketing Research* (February 1991): 11–23. See also Lynn R. Kahle, Sharon Beatty, and Pamela Homer, "Alternative Measurement Approaches to Consumer Values: The List Values (LOV) and Values and Life Style (VALS)," *Journal of Consumer Research* 13 (December 1986): 405–409; Sharon E. Beatty, Pamela Homer, and Lynn Kahle, "Problems with VALS in International Marketing Research: An Example from an Application of the Empirical Mirror Technique," in *Advances in Consumer Research*, vol. 15, ed. Michael Houston (Provo, UT: Association for Consumer Research, 1988), 375–380.

[56] http://www.strategicbusinessinsights.com/vals/presurvey.shtml, accessed December 17, 2015. [AU: This entry is incomplete. Please review and revise. Thanks.] AU: Done.

[57] Lynn R. Kahle, Sharon Beatty, and Pamela Homer, "Alternative Measurement Approaches to Consumer Values: The List Values (LOV) and Values and Life Style (VALS)," *Journal of Consumer Research* 13 (December 1986): 405–409.

[58] Pamela Homer and Lynn Kahle, "A Structural Equation Test of the Value-Attitude-Behavior Hierarchy," *Journal of Personality and Social Psychology* 54 (April 1988): 638–646.

[59] Lynn R. Kahle, Sharon Beatty, and Pamela Homer, "Alternative Measurement Approaches to Consumer Values: The List Values (LOV) and Values and Life Style (VALS)," *Journal of Consumer Research* 13 (December 1986): 405–409. See also Thomas P. Novak and Bruce MacEvoy, "On Comparing Alternative Segmentation Schemes: The List of Values (LOV) and Values and Life Styles (VALS), *Journal of Consumer Research* 17 (June 1990): 105–109. For another article that further explores the LOV scale, see Wagner A. Kamakura and Thomas P. Novak, "Value-System Segmentation: Exploring the Meaning of LOV," *Journal of Consumer Research* 19 (June 1992): 119–132.

7

Belief, Attitude, and Behavior Formation and Change

Learning Objectives:

1. How are my beliefs and attitudes related to my purchase behavior?

2. How can managers increase the likelihood consumers will buy?

3. How do consumers make decisions among different brands?

4. How does advertising cause behavior change?

Energy Drink Market Grows

The next time you walk into class, take a look around to see how many fellow students are enjoying an energy drink. Energy drinks combine ingredients such as caffeine, B vitamins, and exotic herbs to create a mixture designed to give a quick burst of energy to people on the go. The energy drink industry is growing rapidly. It targets active-lifestyle younger males.[1]

The energy drink industry became a serious category in 1997, when Red Bull was introduced in the United States.[2] By 2001, energy drink sales totaled $400 million, and the industry has continued growing by over 50 percent per year, now totaling more than $3.4 billion per year.[3] The dollar sales for energy drinks and shots from 2011 to 2015 totaled $13.5 billion in the United States alone.[4]

The energy drink market can be compared with the traditional soft drink industry. The top two brands in the industry are Coca-Cola and Pepsi, respectively. Importantly, they're positioned quite differently from each other. Pepsi is positioned as a "youthful" drink, while Coca-Cola is positioned around themes of "Americana" and "tradition." Each brand's positioning helps create specific consumer beliefs and attitudes toward the brand. By positioning themselves differently, both Pepsi and Coca-Cola have been able to sustain market dominance—the two combined own 30 percent of the soft drink market.[5]

In comparison with the traditional soft drink market, all the brands in the energy drink market tend to be positioned similarly. Thus, brands such as Red Bull, Monster, Rockstar, and Full Throttle position themselves around an edgy and high-intensity theme. Because the energy drinks all rely on the edgy, extreme image, consumers can't differentiate the

brands. As a result, the first mover, Red Bull, and Monster enjoy dominant market shares. Red Bull controls 43 percent and Monster controls 39 percent of the market, while the next five brands combined control 18 percent. (See Table 7.1.)

A question for the major brands is how to differentiate within the market without damaging consumers' attitudes and beliefs about the brand. Suppose you were the marketing director for Rockstar. In order to increase its market share, you could employ a strategy of being the low-price leader in the market. Consumers will undoubtedly appreciate a lower price. However, how will that strategy affect the consumers' attitudes, beliefs, and behaviors? The brand could be damaged by a lower price as low pricing is often associated with being cheap. A low-price strategy could change the consumers' attitudes and beliefs and, therefore, dilute the brand equity.

TABLE 7.1
Market Share of Energy Drinks[6]

Brand	Market Share
Red Bull	43
Monster	39
Rockstar	10
NOS	3
Amp	3
Full Throttle	1
Xyience Xenergy	1

This chapter discusses how consumers both form and change beliefs, attitudes, and behavior. The concepts of beliefs, attitudes, and behavior are closely linked. The generic phrase "consumer-attitude formation" is often used to describe the field. In fact, more has been written about consumer attitudes than any other single topic in the field of consumer behavior.[7] This chapter investigates the relationships among beliefs, attitudes, and behaviors.

CONSUMER BELIEFS

So, why do consumers choose to drink Red Bull or to drive a Ford Mustang over other brands? When consumers make a purchase decision, they consider the object, as well as their beliefs and attitudes. **Consumer beliefs** result from cognitive learning. They represent the knowledge and inferences a consumer has about objects, their attributes, and their benefits. **Objects** are the products, people, companies, and things about which people hold beliefs and attitudes. **Attributes** are the features or characteristics of an object. Finally, **benefits** are the positive outcomes objects provide to the consumer. Let's take, for example, the Ford Mustang and discuss it as an object. The car has a number of attributes, including sporty styling and a high-powered engine. One benefit may be that the individual gains status in his or her circle of friends by simply owning a Mustang.

The beliefs held by consumers about a product's attributes may not match reality, however. For example, halo effects can cause misperceptions about

SOCIAL MEDIA

Tracking Behavior with Social Media

Researchers worry consumption of energy drinks and shots may be hazardous to one's health. Most individuals who have an adverse reaction to the drinks and shots don't report it to the manufacturer or to the FDA. Consequently, researchers are selecting other means to uncover consumption behaviors. That's where social media comes into play.

Researchers recently tracked 91,143 energy drink conversations on Twitter, Facebook, and other forums. This allowed the researchers to identify actual behaviors without having to ask the consumers. Further, the data may be a more reliable assessment of actual behaviors because some consumers may be reluctant to admit any side effects they experienced. Thus, tracking social media gives us a look into any side effects.

The social media tracing discovered that in "4% of the conversations, the consumer drank a combination of more than one drink at a time." Four percent appears to be a low number of users taking multiple energy products at one time. Therefore, some may believe there's little harm being done. On a positive side, by using the social media forums, companies may be able to track behaviors in order to help inform and protect individuals.[8]

product attributes in the marketplace. A **halo effect** occurs when consumers assume because a product is good or bad on one product characteristic, it's also good or bad on another product characteristic. Thus, a consumer who believes the Mustang is the sportiest car may also believe it has the best safety system. Halo effects can even extend from a company's specific product to the company as a whole. For instance, consumers had a poor attitude toward Nike shoes due to allegations of the company using child labor in foreign countries. This low rating transferred to the entire brand. Consequently, consumers rated all Nike products lower than before. Consumers began to improve their attitudes and beliefs when Nike took a proactive stance in monitoring its subcontractors.

Attributes differ widely in their importance to consumers. **Attribute importance** is a person's assessment of the significance of an attribute for a specific good or service.[9] Researchers have found attribute importance is strongly influenced by the amount of attention directed to the specific feature of a product. That is, the greater the attention directed to an attribute, the more important it becomes. For example, Dyson has been promoting its brand of vacuum cleaners with the tagline "It is the only vacuum that does not lose suction." By doing so, Dyson has successfully drawn attention to that particular attribute.

Several factors have been found to influence attribute importance. Certainly, one factor consists of the dominant needs and the self-concept of the consumer. Thus, if a consumer has a self-concept that includes "ruggedness," the attribute of toughness in a truck could attract this person's attention. Second, advertising can influence the importance of attributes by directing attention to specific features of a product. For example, making the copy in an advertisement that pertains to an attribute highly concrete and vivid may direct attention to the attribute and increase its perceived importance. Certainly, for consumers, one of the most important attributes of a product is its price. Price doesn't necessarily mean the brand is more attractive. While we all want to save money on our purchases, in some cases, a higher price may make the product a status symbol.

Consumer Attitudes

Over the past 40 years, the term *attitude* has been defined in numerous ways. We employ the definition proposed by L. L. Thurstone, who was one of the originators of modern attitude measurement theory. Thurstone viewed an **attitude** as "the amount of affect or feeling for or against a stimulus."[10] This idea that attitudes refer to affect or a general evaluative reaction has been expressed by many researchers.[11] In sum, whereas beliefs are the cognitive knowledge about an object, in contrast, attitudes are the **affective feelings** people have about objects.

Attitudes are stored in long-term memory and serve four important functions for consumers.[12] First, the **utilitarian function** specifies people express feelings to maximize rewards and minimize punishments received from others. In this sense, the expression of an attitude is like an operantly conditioned response. For example, a salesperson might learn that making positive comments (i.e., expressing favorable attitudes) to a client is more likely to result in a sale (i.e., a positive reinforcer).

Attitudes can also serve an **ego-defense function** as well as a knowledge function. In their ego-defensive role, attitudes act to protect people from basic truths about themselves or from the harsh realities of the external world. An example would be smokers who hold positive attitudes toward smoking to defend themselves against the reality of what they're doing to their bodies. In their **knowledge role**, attitudes serve as guidelines to simplify decision making. For example, consumers may develop attitudes toward salespeople in loud jackets or retail stores with soft music and plush interiors. The knowledge function also helps explain the effects of brand loyalty. By remaining brand loyal and maintaining a positive attitude toward a product, consumers can simplify decision making by avoiding a long, drawn-out search process for information on alternative brands.

Finally, through the **value-expressive function**, consumers can express their central values and self-concept to others. In consumer settings, the value-expressive function can be seen in instances in which people wear clothing adorned with brand logos in order to make a statement about themselves.[13] Think about two individuals. One is wearing a Harley-Davidson black leather jacket and the other is a young street basketball player with his shorts hanging low on his waist. What does the particular clothing say about the two individuals?

Behaviors and Intentions to Behave

Consumer behaviors consist of all the actions taken by consumers related to acquiring, disposing, and using products and services. Examples of consumer behaviors include collecting information for a purchase, buying a product or service, providing feedback on a product or service to on a blog, and disposing of a product.

Prior to engaging in an action, people may develop behavioral intentions regarding their likelihood of engaging in the behavior. **Behavioral intentions** are defined as the intentions of consumers to behave in a particular way with regard to the acquisition, disposition, and use of products and services. Thus, a consumer may form the intention to search for information, to tell someone else about an experience with a product, to buy a product or service, and to dispose of a product in a certain way. Because they're highly predictive of actual behavior in high-involvement circumstances, measuring behavioral intentions is important to market researchers.

Now that we have clearly defined beliefs, attitudes, and behaviors, we'll move on to the second learning objective of this chapter: How can managers increase the likelihood consumers will buy?

FORMING BELIEFS, ATTITUDES, AND BEHAVIORS

Managers can increase the likelihood consumers will buy by understanding how consumers form beliefs, attitudes, and behaviors. Beliefs, attitudes, and behaviors may be formed in two distinct ways. The first is through direct formation in which a belief, attitude, or behavior is created without either of the other states occurring first. After a belief, attitude, or behavior is formed directly, the states build upon each other to create hierarchies of effects. **Hierarchies of effects** identify the order in which beliefs, attitudes, and behaviors occur. The next two sections discuss these processes.

The Direct Formation of Beliefs, Attitudes, and Behaviors

Disparate processes cause the direct formation of beliefs, attitudes, and behaviors, and these processes are directly linked to the three research perspectives on consumer behavior. First, beliefs are formed through the information-processing and cognitive learning activities of the consumer. Thus, information about the attributes of a product are received, encoded into memory, and later retrieved from memory for use.

Forming Attitudes Directly Three mechanisms explain how attitudes are formed directly: classical conditioning, the mere exposure phenomenon, and the influence of mood states. From a classical-conditioning perspective, an attitude is a conditioned emotional response that can be elicited by a conditioned stimulus.[14] The "hot" and "sexy" ads for the Go Daddy product illustrate the attempt to classically condition consumers so emotions are elicited by a brand.

Another method through which positive feelings may be formed is through repeated exposures with a stimulus. All else equal, through the **mere exposure phenomenon**, people's liking for something may increase simply because they see it over and over again.[15] The all-else-equal caveat is important: if the consumer perceives the stimulus negatively, the repeated exposures could lead to an increase in the dislike for the stimulus.[16] An interesting aspect of the mere exposure phenomenon is it doesn't seem to be cognitively based. The positive feelings created from repeated exposures can occur without the person consciously knowing or perceiving the object is familiar.[17] The ubiquitous Coca-Cola name is an example. One sees it repeatedly flashed on television, at baseball parks, in theaters, in restaurants, on buses, and elsewhere. The effect of mere exposure may be one of the factors making Coke the largest-selling soft drink in the world.

The mood of the consumer also has direct impact on attitude formation. Researchers have found when consumers are initially exposed to an object, their mood state at the time will impact the attitude formed. Thus, when consumers

Managerial principle 7.1
You can increase consumers' positive feelings toward a brand by merely exposing consumers to the brand. It's interesting that consumers don't need to even be aware of the exposure.

first learn about a new product, such as Blu-ray, their mood at that time will impact their evaluation of the product. A positive mood increases the evaluation, and a negative mood decreases it. When introducing consumers to new products, retailers should do everything possible to place consumers in a positive affective state.[18]

Creating behavior directly Traditionally, consumer researchers have viewed the behavior of buying a product or service as occurring after the formation of beliefs and attitudes. However, in certain circumstances behavior may be influenced directly without consumers first having developed strong beliefs or attitudes about the product. Behavior can be directly influenced when strong situational or environmental forces propel the consumer action. The design of the physical environment is an excellent example of how behaviors can be directly induced.[19] For example, the appropriate arrangement of aisles in a supermarket can move customers in desired directions, past high-margin food and nonfood items. Further, Paco Underhill suggests stores should be laid out to guide consumers to walk to the right. Consumers naturally walk to the right when shopping.[20] By designing a store in this format, consumers may increase their spending.

Operant conditioning can also be used to influence behavior directly. Shaping is an example of the direct influence of behavior through operant conditioning. For example, Chick-fil-A strives to increase sales by offering a number of opportunities to experience the brand. To shape consumer attitudes, the company gives free samples of their nuggets and other products to consumers passing by the restaurant. Chick-fil-A also ties in giveaways at their restaurant grand openings with their First 100® promotion. When the restaurant opens, the first one hundred customers who have complied with the official rules will

© CFA Properties , Inc. Chick-fil-A® Stylized is a registered trademark of CFA Properties, Inc.
Consumers camp out prior to a grand opening of a Chick-fil-A in order to win free food

receive free Chick-fil-A sandwich meals for an entire year. Consumers camp out in tents overnight in order to be one of the lucky first one hundred customers100®. In years past, the company has also offered a free original chicken sandwich to anyone who wears sports apparel to a Chick-fil-A restaurant on Labor Day, the opening weekend of college football.

Beyond free food offers, Chick-fil-A provides a top-of-the-line customer experience in the quick-service (i.e., fast-food) restaurant market. For instance, when consumers thank a Chick-fil-A team member for a free beverage refill, the employee is encouraged to reply, "My pleasure." Ultimately, Chick-fil-A desires repeat purchases from its customers. To gain that loyalty, the company selectively reinforces a number of consumer behaviors.

Managerial principle 7.2
To encourage consumers to repeat buying behaviors, you should positively reinforce the behavior with a positive outcome.

Hierarchies of Beliefs, Attitudes, and Behaviors

The second way behaviors, attitudes, and beliefs can be formed is indirectly through hierarchies of effects. The type of purchase process in which the consumer is engaged controls which hierarchy is implemented. Table 7.2 identifies four purchase processes. The four hierarchies are the high-involvement hierarchy, the low-involvement hierarchy, the experiential hierarchy, and the behavioral influence hierarchy.

Purchase Process	Hierarchy of Effects
High involvement	High-involvement hierarchy Beliefs-affect-behavior
Low involvement	Low-involvement hierarchy Beliefs-behavior-affect
Experiential/impulse	Experiential hierarchy Affect-behavior-beliefs
Behavioral influence	Behavioral influence hierarchy Behavior-beliefs-affect

TABLE 7.2
The Four Hierarchies of Effects

Decision-Making Hierarchies   The high- and low-involvement hierarchies represent the two forms of the decision-making hierarchies. In the **high-involvement hierarchy**, beliefs occur first, followed by attitude, which is, in turn followed by behavior.[21] As the amount of involvement in the decision increases, consumers increase their problem-solving activities and search extensively for information about alternative products. As a result, a large number of beliefs are formed about the alternatives. An affective charge is attached to each belief, and the sum of these charges creates the attitude. After the formation of beliefs and attitudes, behavior tends to occur.

In low-involvement circumstances, consumers first form beliefs about a product.[22] These beliefs are followed directly by the product's purchase. Only after the purchase does the consumer develop an attitude (affect) regarding the product.[23] Thus, the flow of events is quite different when consumers are involved in a low-involvement decision. In these cases, consumers aren't motivated to engage in extensive problem solving. Instead, they move through a limited decision process in which they consider only a few alternatives in a superficial manner. As a result, only a limited number of beliefs are formed about the product alternatives. Furthermore, because the alternatives aren't evaluated closely, consumers may not form any attitudes. In the case of energy drinks, the consumer may select Red Bull over other brands due to recognizing it more than other brands. In sum, when consumers have low involvement in a purchase, they tend to engage in limited problem solving and move through what's called a **low-involvement hierarchy** consisting of belief formation, then behavior, and finally attitude (affect) formation.[24]

Experiential Hierarchy The **experiential hierarchy** begins with a strong affective response. Behavior then results from the strong feelings. Finally, beliefs are developed in part to justify the behavior. Impulse purchases exemplify the experiential hierarchy. In an **impulse (experiential) purchase**, a strong positive feeling is followed by the buying act.[25] If questioned about the purchase, you'd be able to voice a series of beliefs. However, the belief statements you make may be to justify the decision.

Behavioral Influence Hierarchy In the **behavioral influence hierarchy**, strong situational or environmental forces propel a consumer to engage in an action without the person having formed either beliefs or affect about the object of the purchase. Thus, behavior is directly influenced without beliefs or attitudes intervening. When behavior is induced directly through the operation of environmental or situational factors, the hierarchy of effects begins with the behavior.

The study of beliefs and attitudes and their relationship to purchase behavior has major implications for promotional strategy. How companies promote a brand depends on the type of buying process the brands target market uses in buying products from its particular category. Table 7.3 summarizes some promotional strategies companies may use depending on the buying process involved.

TABLE 7.3
Some Promotional Strategies Based on the Type of Consumer Purchase Process

Buying Process	Possible Promotional Strategies
High involvement	Emphasize developing product-attribute and product-benefit beliefs through cognitive learning procedures. Can stress print advertising and personal selling. Help create affect through product demonstrations and advertising using classical-conditioning procedures.
Low involvement	Emphasize developing product-attribute beliefs through repetition of simple messages. Tie point-of-purchase displays to advertising, Place product and displays in high-traffic area.
Experiential/impulse	Emphasize the fun and positive feelings that can be obtained by experiencing the product or service. Emphasize creating affect through the classical conditioning of positive feelings toward the product.
Behavioral influence	Use sales-promotion techniques, such as sweepstakes, rebates, samples, or coupons.

PREDICTING CONSUMER ATTITUDES THROUGH MULTIATTRIBUTE MODELS

Consumers often face the task of choosing among various brands to purchase. This task isn't always easy, as many of the alternatives may have both good and bad attributes. When consumers choose among a number of brands, they often rely on their attitudes to make the selection. To answer the question posed in learning objective 7-3, we can study a number of topics that demonstrate how consumers choose among brands. We begin by investigating the multiattribute model. **Multiattribute models** describe how consumers combine their beliefs about product attributes to form attitudes about various brand alternatives, corporations, or other objects in high-involvement circumstances. Numerous multiattribute models have been developed.[26] In this chapter, two models will be presented. The first focuses on predicting the attitude a consumer forms toward a specific attitude object, such as a product, service, person, or idea. The second model focuses on predicting the behavioral intentions of consumers to perform some type of action, such as buying a product or service.

Attitude-Toward-the-Object Model

The **attitude-toward-the-object model**, or the Fishbein model, identifies three major factors that are predictive of attitudes.[27] First, a person's salient beliefs influence attitude formation about an object. **Salient beliefs** represent knowledge about the attributes of the object that's activated in memory when attention is focused on an object. The second factor of the attitude-toward-the-object model is the strength of the belief an object has a particular attribute in question. The strength of the object "attribute linkage" is usually assessed by asking a person this question: "How likely is it that object x possesses attribute y?" To measure strength of the belief, a ten-point scale is used. In the Mustang example, the researcher may ask, "Circle the number that represents how likely it is the Mustang is extremely sporty."

Extremely Unlikely   1   2   3   4   5   6   7   8   9   10   Extremely Likely

The third factor of the model is the evaluation of each of the salient attributes. The evaluation ratings provide an assessment of the badness or goodness of the salient attributes. For example, in the Mustang example, some consumers may evaluate "sporty" positively and some may evaluate it negatively (i.e., while sporty gives the vehicle a certain image, it also may create a negative associate with hybrid transportation). Researchers obtain evaluation ratings of the attribute by asking consumers how bad or good the attributes are. In the Mustang example, the researcher would ask consumers to rate the following two questions:

1. How bad or good is it for a vehicle to be extremely sporty?

   Very bad   –3   –2   –1   0   +1   +2   +3   Very good

2. How bad or good is it for a vehicle to be a hybrid?

   Very bad   –3   –2   –1   0   +1   +2   +3   Very good

In this example, different people will give divergent evaluations of the badness or goodness of the attribute of sporty. Some consumers may want a fuel efficient vehicle while others are much more interested in a vehicle that has greater sports car characteristics. On this attribute, ratings may range widely from –3 to +3.

When attempting to predict a consumer's attitude, information on the evaluation and strength of the salient beliefs is combined via an algebraic formula. Algebraically, the model is expressed as follows

$$A_o = \sum_{i=1}^{n} b_i e_i$$

where

A_o = the overall attitude toward object o

b_i = the strength of the belief of whether or not object o has some particular attribute I

e_i = the evaluation of the badness or goodness of attribute I

n = the number of beliefs

Table 7.4 presents a hypothetical example of the attitudes held by two market segments—"Macho Mikes" and "Enviro Ellens"—regarding three vehicles, a Ford Mustang, a Jeep Grand Cherokee, and a Toyota Prius. Macho Mikes are young males who are risk takers, like to participate in sports, and love to drink beer. Enviro Ellens are young, professional women who live in urban areas and

TABLE 7.4
Predicting the Attitudes of Two Consumer Segments

| | | Segment A: Macho Mikes | | | | | |
| | | Ford Mustang | | Jeep Grand Cherokee | | Toyota Prius | |
Attributes	e_i	b_i	$b_i \times e_i$	b_i	$b_i \times e_i$	b_i	$b_i \times e_i$
Sporty styling	−1	5	−5	7	−7	7	−7
Great handling	+1	5	5	6	6	8	8
Hybrid	−3	8	−24	2	−6	7	−21
Ruggedness	+3	7	21	9	27	4	12
Off-road capability	+3	7	21	9	27	1	3
Attitude score =			18		47		−5

| | | Segment B: Enviro Ellens | | | | | |
| | | Ford Mustang | | Jeep Grand Cherokee | | Toyota Prius | |
Attributes	e_i	b_i	$b_i \times e_i$	b_i	$b_i \times e_i$	b_i	$b_i \times e_i$
Sporty styling	+2	4	8	6	12	8	16
Great handling	+3	5	15	3	9	9	27
Hybrid	+3	1	3	2	6	7	21
Ruggedness	+1	7	7	7	7	5	5
Off-road capability	−3	9	−27	9	−27	2	−6
Attitude score =			6		7		63

Note: b_i = strength of belief (1 = extremely unlikely, 10 = extremely likely)
e_i = evaluation of badness/goodness (−3 = very bad, +3 = very good)
Attitude score = attitude toward the object

are very concerned about the environment. Let's assume members of each market segment evaluated the vehicles on five salient attributes: sporty styling, outstanding handling, whether it's a hybrid, ruggedness, and off-road capability.

In words, the attitude is predicted by first multiplying the belief ratings for each attribute by the evaluation of the attribute. For example, Macho Mikes gave an evaluation of +3 for off-road-capability. This number is multiplied by the belief rating of 7 for the Mustang to give 21. In contrast, for Enviro Ellen, the evaluation of off-road-capability is -3. This number is multiplied by the belief rating of 9 to give -27. The "belief x evaluation" scores are then added down the column for each object to provide an estimate of the attitude. Note the overall attitude score (i.e., 18 for Mustang by Macho Mikes) is virtually meaningless in and of itself. Only when compared with the scores for other alternatives does it take on meaning.

An inspection of Table 7.4 shows Macho Mikes prefer the Jeep Grand Cherokee (attitude = 47), followed by the Ford Mustang (attitude = 18) and the Toyota Prius (attitude = -5). In contrast, Enviro Ellens like the Prius the most (attitude = 63), followed by the Jeep Grand Cherokee (attitude = 7) and the Mustang (attitude = 6). Looking at the table, one finds the belief ratings of the two market segments were similar for the three autos. Both groups viewed the Jeep Grand Cherokee as rugged and possessing off-road capability. Both viewed the Ford Mustang as having good handling. What caused the extreme differences in the preferences of the two market segments was the wide variations in their evaluations of the attributes. Macho Mikes strongly desired ruggedness and off-road capability. In contrast, Enviro Ellens strongly desired sporty styling and great handling.

In sum, the attitude-toward-the-object model suggests three factors influence attitude formation: (1) the salient attributes, (2) the extent to which consumers believe the object possesses the attributes, and (3) the degree of positivity/negativity on which the attributes are evaluated. Marketing managers must know the salient attributes that consumers seek and the positivity/negativity of how they are rated. This knowledge will influence how the product is developed and how it's promoted. In particular, one important role of promotional messages is to influence beliefs concerning the extent to which an object possesses an attribute.

How does Fishbein's attitude-toward-the-object model deal with differences in the importance of the attributes? Interestingly, the Fishbein model makes no direct attempt to measure the importance of attributes. The omission of ratings of importance, however, has little impact on the ability of the model to predict attitudes. This occurs because the importance of an attribute is, in part, assessed by the evaluation ratings. That is, as the importance of an attribute increases, the evaluation ratings become more extreme.[28]

Managerial principle 7.4
Managers must understand not every brand attribute will be appreciated the same by all consumers. Obviously, this vehicle example demonstrates target markets seek different benefits.

Global Attitudes Versus Attitudes Toward the Object The measure of attitude obtained from a multiattribute model is an indirect measure of attitude. In other words, the researcher can estimate the level of consumers' attitudes toward an object by measuring the strengths of their beliefs about the attributes possessed by the object and their evaluations of the attributes of the object. In contrast, direct measures of consumers' global attitudes can be taken. Thus, a **global attitude measure** is the direct measurement of the overall affect and feelings held by a consumer regarding an object.

To measure global attitudes, researchers ask several questions on semantic differential scales. (Semantic differentials scales ask respondents to rate an object on various scales anchored by opposite meaning adjectives). For example, global attitudes regarding a Mustang might be phrased in the following manner: "Please describe your feelings about Mustang by circling the appropriate number on the scales."

Good   1   2   3   4   5   Bad   Positive   1   2   3   4   5   Negative

Whenever possible, market researchers collect data on global attitudes as well as sufficient information to predict the attitudes through an attitude-to-ward-the-object model. The results of the two estimates can then be compared. If global attitudes and predicted attitudes match closely, researchers can feel as though they have a good understanding of the factors influencing consumer attitude formation. In contrast, if predicted and global attitudes fail to correlate, additional research is required to identify what's happening.

When Do Attitudes Predict Behavior?

An important problem for consumer researchers involves explaining why the knowledge of consumer attitudes doesn't necessarily predict actual behavior. In fact, many consumer researchers are pessimistic about the ability of attitudes to predict overt behavior.[29] Recently, researchers have recognized the issue is one of knowing when attitudes predict behavior. A variety of factors have been found to influence the extent to which attitudes predict behavior.[30] The ability of attitudes to predict behavior increases in the following circumstances: consumer involvement is high, the attitude measure is reliable and valid, the attitudes are strongly held,[31] and situational factors don't intercede (e.g., interventions by other people, sickness, or promotional efforts of other brands).

The Behavioral Intentions Model

The behavioral intentions model, also called the **theory of reasoned action**, was developed by Martin Fishbein and his colleagues for the purpose of improving on the ability of the attitude-toward-the-object model to predict consumer behavior. It extended the basic attitude-toward-the-object model in several ways.[32] First, it proposed behavior results from the formation of specific intentions to behave. Thus, the model didn't attempt to predict behavior per se, but intentions to act. Researchers have found this model is superior to the attitude-toward-the-object model in predicting behavior.[33]

Managerial principle 7.5
Managers can better access the consumer's likelihood of behavior by asking him or her about how others feel about the behavior.

Second, the behavioral intentions model contained a new construct called the **subjective norm** (SN), which assesses what consumers believe other people think they should do. In other words, SN introduces into the formulation the powerful effects of opinion leaders and reference groups on behavior. For example, one study investigated the use of condoms by adults. The results revealed perceived normative pressure was, by far, the best predictor of condom usage. Pressure from socially important people was more important than other variables, such as AIDS knowledge, perceived susceptibility, and condom-use-outcome expectancies.[34] Other studies have shown the opinions of others influence a consumer's evaluations of a brand, particularly when the opinions are offered prior to when the consumer tries the brand.[35]

The third difference between the behavioral intentions model and the attitude-toward-the-object model involves the object to which attitudes are directed. Instead of assessing the consumer's attitude toward the brand itself, the behavioral intentions model assessed the consumer's attitude toward the overt behavior of purchasing the product. The key difference in assessing attitude toward behavior rather than attitude toward the object is the focus is on the consumer's perception of what the consequences of the purchase would be. When the consequences of the purchase are assessed rather than whether or not the product possesses certain attributes, the researcher has an enhanced ability to take into consideration factors that may act to impede intentions to behave. Considering the purchase of a sport utility vehicle, some consequences of the purchase might be: (1) buying the car would cause the person not to take a vacation, (2) buying the car would cause the person to have to deal with obnoxious salespeople, and (3) buying the car would involve the person in having to figure out how to get a loan. Attitude models that assess only the attitude toward the object can't account for these effects.

The Mere Measurement Effect Consumer researchers have found merely asking consumers about their purchase intentions influences their subsequent purchases. In one study of the mere measurement effect, which is also called the self-prophecy effect, researchers asked nearly five thousand consumers whether they intended to purchase a new car or computer.[36] Next, they determined whether the consumers actually made a purchase during the next six months. These results were compared to a control group of five thousand similar consumers who weren't asked the purchase intent question. The researchers found those who received the purchase intent question were significantly more likely to actually make the purchase, regardless of whether they said yes or no. These results provide a new reason for doing marketing research.[37] That is, the very act of asking behavioral intentions questions could increase the likelihood consumers will purchase a product.[38] Importantly, the research has been replicated in a variety of other settings.[39]

Managerial principle 7.6
Managers can increase the likelihood consumers will purchase a brand in the future by simply asking the consumer about a purchase intention.

Persuasion: Attitude, Belief, and Behavior Change

So far, we've discussed how beliefs, attitudes, and behavior are formed and how they may be predicted. In many instances, however, the goal is to persuade by changing preexisting attitudes and beliefs to influence consumer behavior. **Persuasion** is defined as the explicit attempt to influence beliefs, attitudes, or behaviors. Indeed, one might argue consumers rarely enter a situation with absolutely no preexisting attitudes and beliefs about an object. Because of previous experience, when a new product or service is introduced, consumers may already have an initial positive or negative feeling toward it. Thus, even when introducing new products, communicators are seeking to persuade consumers. Persuasion can be understood from the three perspectives on consumer behavior. We first look at the decision-making approach model.

The Decision-Making Approach to Attitude Change

An approach to understanding the persuasion process called the **elaboration likelihood model** (ELM) illustrates the decision-making path to belief, attitude, and behavior change.[40] In the ELM (depicted in Figure 7.1), the persuasion process begins when the consumer receives a message. Upon receiving the message, the consumer begins to process it. Depending on such factors as the message content, the nature of the consumer, and the consumer's situation, the person processes a communication with higher or lower amounts of involvement.

FIGURE 7.1

The Elaboration Likelihood Model of Persuasion

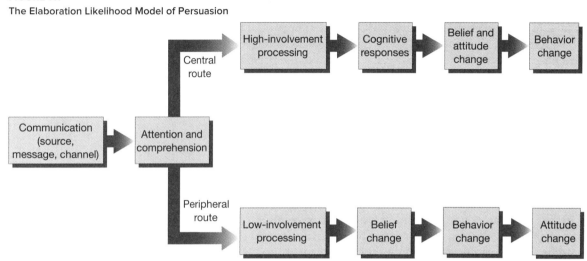

As described in Chapter 3, involvement refers to the perceived personal relevance of the information. Depending on the amount of involvement, belief, and attitude, change may take one of two routes. When high-involvement information processing occurs, the person is said to take the **central route to persuasion**. In contrast, when in low-involvement circumstances, the consumer is said to be engaging in the **peripheral route to persuasion**.

When attitude and belief change occur via the central route, the consumer attends more carefully to the message being received and diligently considers the communication and compares it to his or her own attitudinal position. If the consumer has the ability to process the information, he or she is likely to generate a number of cognitive responses to the communication.[41] (**Cognitive responses** are the favorable or unfavorable thoughts generated by consumers as a result of a communication.) Based, in part, on the extent to which the cognitive responses are supportive or nonsupportive of the message, belief change occurs. Following the change in belief, the consumer experiences attitude change, which leads to behavior change. When belief and attitude change occur through the central route, the effects are relatively enduring and predictive of behavior.[42] In these high-involvement circumstances, consumers employ central cues when evaluating the message. **Central cues** refer to ideas and supporting data that bear directly upon the quality of the arguments developed in the message.[43]

Managerial principle 7.7
To persuade high-involvement consumers, focus on the quality of the arguments.

In the peripheral route to persuasion, the low-involvement hierarchy of effects occurs. One finds minimal numbers of cognitive responses because the consumer isn't carefully considering the pros and cons of the issue. Instead, consumers use peripheral cues to determine whether to accept or reject the message. **Peripheral cues** include factors such as the attractiveness and expertise of the source, the mere number of arguments presented, and the positive or negative stimuli that form the context within which the message was presented (e.g., pleasant music). Two examples of using an attractive spokesperson are an ad for Prilosec and one for milk. Prilosec uses Larry the Cable Guy to promote the brand. Many consumers may find him attractive as a good-old-boy, common-man character. In the milk ad, Salma Hayek grabs readers' attention with the attractiveness of her beauty and as person others would like to get to know. Under low-involvement circumstances, beliefs may change, but it's unlikely attitudes or feelings are also influenced. If attitudes are formed, they're likely to be relatively temporary and unpredictive of behavior.[44]

You've probably heard the old aphorism "if you say something often enough, people will come to believe you." A phenomenon called the truth effect has direct bearing on the statement. The **truth effect** states that if something is repeated often enough, people who are in a low-involvement processing mode will begin to believe it. It occurs regardless of the actual truth value of the statement. In addition, it has been shown to more strongly impact elderly consumers than younger consumers.[45] Thus, the truth effect illustrates one type of peripheral cue that may act to persuade consumers in low-involvement conditions: the repetition of information.[46]

Are there individual differences in the route to persuasion? The ELM proposes consumers may chronically use either a central or peripheral route. A trait called the **need for cognition** measures the extent to which consumers chronically exhibit high- versus low-involvement processing of information.[47] Consumers who have a need to engage in high amounts of effortful cognitive activities are said to have a high need for cognition. Such people may tend to habitually evaluate argument quality and require a central route to persuasion. Other consumers may have a low need for cognition and require a peripheral route to persuasion. Information on a target market's need for cognition has importance for advertisers. More complex messages may be developed for consumers with a high need for cognition than for consumers with a low need for cognition.[48]

Multiattribute Models and the Decision-Making Path to Persuasion

The concepts underlying multiattribute models of attitude formation can be applied to help change the beliefs, attitudes, and behaviors of a target.

Persuasion and the Attitude-Toward-the-Object model Recall that in the attitude-toward-the-object model, an attitude results from three factors: (1) the salient attributes on which a person evaluates an object, (2) a rating of the evaluation of the goodness or badness of the various attributes of an object, and (3) a rating of the person's belief of the extent the object possesses each attribute. Each of these factors can be employed to change an existing attitude. First, communicators can attempt to change the perceived evaluation of an attribute. Another strategy involves introducing a new attribute rather than attempting to change the evaluation of an existing attribute. An example is found in an ad for Rembrandt Mouth Rinse that informed people the brand is alcohol free. Because the most popular mouthwash (i.e., Listerine) is almost 54 proof, or 27 percent alcohol, Rembrandt effectively added a reason for buying its product.

A third way of influencing attitudes through the attitude-toward-the-object model is to change the belief an object has a particular attribute. This is probably the easiest of the three approaches because a company can use a variety

Managerial principle 7.8
To increase the purchases of a low-involvement consumer, increase the number of arguments and use an attractive spokesperson.

Managerial principle 7.9
You can change the consumer's attitude toward a brand by introducing a new, salient attribute.

of methods to show the particular characteristic of the product has changed. A company could use demonstrations or trustworthy endorsers to show and explain the change.

The behavioral intentions model suggests additional approaches to attitude change. For example, marketers can influence perceptions of the consequences of a behavior. Thus, in the "Anti-Meth" campaign, advertisers identified at least one consequence of trying the drug even one time. That is, the drug is highly addictive and many who try it become addicted on their first exposure. By making salient this additional negative outcome of using meth, the campaign may have persuaded consumers not to engage in such behavior.

A second implication of the behavioral intentions model for attitude change involves the subjective norm component. The model explicitly considers the impact of other people on a consumer's intentions to behave. In the Anti-Meth campaign, researchers recognized the effect on teenagers' social connections in developing the advertising campaign. The subsequent advertisements portrayed the meth user as losing the current social connections in order to fit in with the dark social connections of the drug culture.

Table 7.5 summarizes the implications of multiattribute models for attitude change and behavior.

TABLE 7.5
Five Methods of Changing Attitudes: A Multiattribute Perspective

Method 1	
Change the perceived evaluation of the attributes.	
Advantage:	Can increase the attitude rating of a product or service without changing the product or service in the any way.
Disadvantage:	Very difficult to do because evaluation ratings are often tied to the consumer's self-concept.
Method 2	
Change the product-attribute beliefs.	
Advantage:	Easier to do because the company can use demonstrations or trustworthy sources to present the message. Beliefs about the extent to which products contain attributes are not usually connected to the consumer's self-concept.
Disadvantage:	May involve changing the product.
Method 3	
Add a new attribute for consideration.	
Advantage:	Beliefs and attitudes are easier to change when they are weakly held.
Disadvantage:	May involve changing the product or service. Requires extensive promotional efforts to get new information to target market.
Method 4	
Influence perceptions of consequences of behavior.	
Advantage:	Can identify consequences not previously recognized.
Disadvantage:	Target may not evaluate consequences as desired or may not perceive them to be likely.
Method 5	
Influence perceptions of reference group's reactions to behavior.	
Advantage:	Reference groups have a large impact on intentions to behave.
Disadvantage:	Motivation to comply may be very low.

The Experiential Path to Attitude Change

The persuasion process can also occur along an experiential path. When consumers follow the experiential path, attitudes are influenced directly, and beliefs about the object or behavior don't necessarily change beforehand. Two approaches have particular relevance to the experiential path to persuasion: balance theory and attitudes toward the advertisement.

Balance Theory

Researchers have found attitudes may be changed by creating cognitive imbalance within the target of persuasion. The objective is to make use of people's tendency to maintain cognitive consistency among the various ideas and concepts about which they think. **Cognitive consistency** is the name applied to the human desire to maintain a logical and consistent set of interconnected attitudes. Thus, by deliberately creating cognitive inconsistency, the skillful communicator can induce consumers to change their attitudes to bring their cognitive system back into balance. To explain the mechanisms behind the operation of cognitive consistency, it's first necessary to explain balance theory.

Balance theory specifies the relationships an observer (*o*) perceives between himself or herself, another person (*p*), and an impersonal object (*x*). In a consumer behavior setting, the observer represents the consumer, the other person might be a product endorser, and the impersonal object could be a brand. The observer, person, and object are called cognitive elements. Balance theory states that cognitive elements may form a system in which each is linked to the other. They're similar to the nodes found in a semantic memory network, as discussed in Chapter 4.

Figure 7.2 shows an example of a triad of elements forming a cognitive system. Two types of connections join the cognitive elements: sentiment connections and unit relations. **Sentiment connections** are identical in definition to the term *attitude* used in this text. Thus, sentiment connections are the observer's evaluation of other people and of other attitudinal objects. They're the positive or negative feelings the observer may have toward the other person

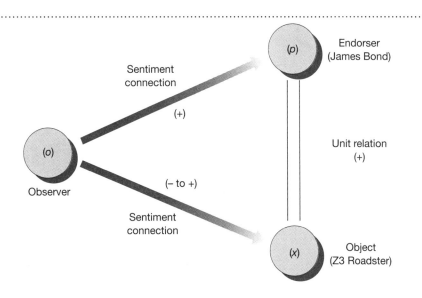

FIGURE 7.2
An Example of Cognitive Elements in a Balance-Theory Framework

and the object. Sentiment connections are given a positive or negative algebraic sign depending on whether the feeling toward p or x is positive or negative.

The second type of connection is called a **unit relation**, which occurs when the observer perceives the person and the object are connected to each other. The factors that govern whether a person perceives a connection are the same principles of perceptual organization discussed in Chapter 3. Thus, p and x would be perceived as having a unit relation through such principles as proximity, similarity, continuation, and common fate. As in the case of sentiment connections, the relationship between p and x may be either positive or negative. A positive unit relation indicates p and x are perceived as related and as forming a unit. A negative sign indicates the two elements are in opposition to each other. A zero (i.e., a 0) indicates no relation exists between p and x. In such a case, the observer wouldn't view the three elements as forming a unit, and no cognitive consistency forces would operate.

The basic premise of balance theory is people have a preference to maintain a balanced state among the cognitive elements of p, o, and x if they're perceived as forming a system. Fritz Heider defined the balanced state as a situation in which the cognitive elements fit together harmoniously with no stress for change. Such harmony occurs when the multiplication of the signs of the connections between the elements results in a positive value. As shown in Figure 7.3, a balanced state results from three positive signs or from two negative signs and one positive sign. An imbalanced state occurs when two signs are positive and one sign is negative or when all three signs are negative. As shown in Figure 7.2 of James Bond matched with the Z3Roadster, there are two positive connections; one between the Endorser (James Bond) and the object (Z3 Roadster) and one between the observer and the Endorser. For this example to remain in balance, the path between the observer and the object (Z3 Roadster) must also be positive.

Balanced states are preferred to unbalanced states. Further, if an imbalanced state is experienced, the person is motivated to change the signs of one

FIGURE 7.3

Examples of Balanced and Imbalanced States

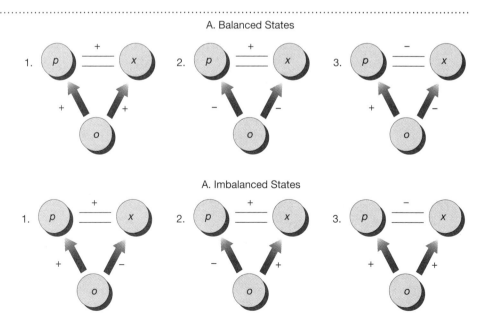

A. Balanced States

A. Imbalanced States

or more of the cognitive relations. Through a type of unconscious mental rationalization, the person comes to view one or more of the sentiment connections and unit relations differently.

Although companies may not realize they're using cognitive consistency procedures to change attitudes, one can identify numerous cases where their strategies employ principles of balance theory. Indeed, the use of celebrity endorsers to sponsor products fits balance model principles quite well. Companies strive to select endorsers who are viewed as positively as possible by consumers. From the perspective of balance theory, companies are attempting to maximize the strength of the sentiment connection between the observer (*o*) and the person (*p*). In addition, successful companies attempt to create a unit relation between the endorser (*p*) and the brand (*x*). Various ways of establishing this unit relation include hiring endorsers who are known experts in using the product; signing the endorser to long-term, exclusive contracts, so the celebrity is associated only with the company's brand and no others; and having the endorser consistently wear or use the product when in public view, so he or she is strongly associated with the product.

However, consumers don't always change attitudes as marketing managers plan. In general, one finds consumers change the sign of the weakest connection in an imbalanced cognitive system.[49] Thus, if consumers perceive a celebrity endorses a brand only for the money, a unit connection may not develop between the celebrity and the product. As a result, no attitude change will occur. It's possible celebrities who endorse many products, such as Michael Jordan, may gradually lose their effectiveness over time because no unit connection forms between the endorsers and the products they extol.

ATTITUDE TOWARD THE ADVERTISEMENT

A second approach to directly influencing brand attitudes without necessarily changing beliefs involves influencing consumer attitudes toward the advertisement. Researchers have found consumers develop attitudes toward advertisements just as they do brands.[50] In turn, these attitudes toward ads may influence attitudes toward the brand. An **attitude toward the ad** is a consumer's general like or dislike for a particular advertising stimulus during a particular advertising exposure.[51] Attitudes toward advertisements can result from a number of factors, including the content and imagery vividness of the ad, the mood of the consumer, the consumer's emotions elicited by the advertisement, and by consumers' like for the TV program in which the ad is embedded.[52] Evidence indicates these factors can influence attitude toward the ad under both high- and low-involvement conditions and whether or not the consumer is familiar with the brand.[53]

Researchers have found ads containing high levels of imagery strongly impact attitudes toward the ad.[54] Imagery refers to the extent an ad causes consumers to imagine their use of the product and to connect the ad to their own feelings and beliefs. Ads that employ concrete words, vivid verbal or pictorial images, instructions for consumers to imagine the use of the brand, and high levels of plausibility have been found to strongly impact consumers' attitudes toward the ad.

The combination of making an advertisement with vivid imagery and selecting the moment to run the advertisement can lead to great benefits. One of the most successful moments to run an advertisement is during the Super Bowl, which consistently ranks high on both ratings and share. Many consumers have very positive attitudes toward the clever advertisements during the game. So, do firms benefit from the positive attitudes of consumer? Two examples demonstrate how the positive attitudes can lead to benefits for the firm. For example, after Reebok's "Terry Tate, Office Linebacker" advertisement ran in 2003, the company's web traffic jumped more than 300 percent. In that same year, Cadillac saw its web traffic jump tenfold. [55]

Another beneficial impact of creating strong positive attitudes toward ads is it increases the time spent watching the commercial. Consumers have two direct means of controlling the time spent watching an ad. First, they can zap the ad by switching to a new channel. Second, they can zip the ad by fast-forwarding through programs already recorded. Researchers have found both zapping and zipping are reduced as the pleasure and arousal caused by an ad increase.[56] These findings reveal a firm should attempt to create ads that have positive emotional and informational qualities in order to reduce zapping and zipping.

The Behavioral Influence Route to Behavior Change

So far, this chapter has discussed the processes through which beliefs and attitudes are changed. As noted earlier in the chapter, through behavioral influence, our actions are affected without necessarily first influencing either beliefs or attitudes about the behavior. For example, the ecological design of buildings and spaces can strongly affect the behavior of people without them being aware of the influence. Similarly, strong reinforcers or punishers in the environment can induce people to take actions they'd prefer to avoid.

Behavioral influence techniques have been developed that cause people to comply with requests by making illicit use of strong norms of behavior. The techniques have been implemented by charities, by honest salespersons, and by everyday people. Unfortunately, the techniques also can be employed by unscrupulous individuals to gain their own illicit ends.

Ingratiation Tactics

Ingratiation refers to self-serving tactics engaged in by one person to make himself or herself more attractive to another.[57] In this case, attractiveness refers to the overall positivity or negativity with which one person views another. An ingratiator builds on the knowledge that as the attractiveness of one person increases, the likelihood of another complying with his or her wishes increases. It's a subtle way of obtaining increased power over another person. Of course, everyone attempts to make himself or herself more attractive to favored others. With ingratiation, however, the efforts are manipulative and calculating. A number of different ingratiation techniques are available for use, but the common denominator among all the tactics is the ingratiator subtly rewards the target in each case. The techniques include appearing to be similar to the target, conforming to the target's wishes, offering compliments and gifts, expressing liking,[58] asking advice, and remembering someone's name.[59]

Ingratiation tactics are effective methods of achieving increased power in a short-term relationship, such as a personal-selling situation. Indeed, one of the primary tactics of the skilled salesperson is to create a "close relationship" with the client. Work on ingratiation indicates it may be the most frequently used influence tactic.[60] Recent research suggests some buyers, who hold a self-orientation, may be more receptive to ingratiation tactics. Self-oriented individuals tend to be concerned with their own welfare and view the transaction only through their own lens rather than a relationship.[61] Ingratiation techniques may work more on these individuals due to their internal focus on the self.

A major problem can occur, however, if the ingratiator is caught in the attempt to manipulate the target. If the target recognizes he or she is being deliberately manipulated, the influence attempt is likely to boomerang, resulting in a loss rather than a gain of power. An ingratiator's dilemma, therefore, exists. The ingratiator can't be too obvious in his or her attempts to reward the target. On the other hand, for the approach to be successful, the target must be rewarded in some way.[62]

The Foot-in-the-Door Technique

An old saying exists that if a successful salesman can merely get his foot in the door, he can make the sale. The foot-in-the-door technique shows the adage has scientific support. A requester can increase the likelihood a prospect will say yes to a moderate request if the person can be persuaded first to say yes to a smaller request. Thus, by getting a prospect to let him in the door, the skilled salesman has persuaded him or her to capitulate to a small request. The task of selling the person the product then becomes that much easier.

The **foot-in-the-door technique** operates through a self-perception mechanism—that is, by complying to the first, small request, the prospect forms an impression he or she is the type of person who does such a thing. Later, when the second request is made, the person is more likely to agree to the request out of the need to be consistent with that self-perception.[63] The foot-in-the-door technique has been shown to influence people in a wide variety of settings. For example, in comparison with control groups, those who were first asked to do something very small, more frequently agreed to a larger request when asked—examples include giving blood, counting traffic for a fictitious safety committee, and completing market research surveys. Similarly, one study found people who were first contacted over the phone and asked a few short questions were more likely to complete a long written questionnaire later than were people who hadn't been contacted first on the phone.[64]

The Door-in-the-Face Technique

The **door-in-the-face technique** also involves making two requests. However, instead of being very small, the initial request is extremely large. In fact, it's so large no one would be expected to comply with it. After the respondent says gives an emphatic no to the first request, a second, smaller request is made. In comparison with control groups that don't receive an initial request, the two-step approach results in a greater degree of compliance to the second request. Areas for which the door-in-the-face technique have been found to increase the rate of compliance include asking people to complete marketing surveys, to take juvenile delinquents to the zoo, and to count automobiles for a traffic-safety committee.

The success of the door-in-the-face strategy operates through the norm of reciprocity.[65] The **norm of reciprocity** states that if a person does something for you, you should do something in return for that person. The norm helps to grease the wheels of society by ensuring efforts to help someone else won't go unrewarded. When the door-in-the-face strategy is implemented, the norm is illicitly invoked—that is, the requester makes the large request and never expects the person to comply with it. He or she then makes the smaller, more moderate request. The key to success is the requester must make it appear as though he or she has given up something when the smaller request is made. The target then feels he or she must return the favor. The only possible way of reciprocating the imaginary gift is to agree to the second request.

Even-a-Penny-Will-Help Technique

The foot-in-the-door and the door-in-the-face techniques are based on the norms to look good to others, to be self-consistent, and to reciprocate the concessions of others. The **even-a-penny-will-help technique** is based on the universal tendency for people to want to make themselves look good. Most often used in charity contexts, the approach operates by asking the target to give money and by tacking on the phrase "even a penny will help" at the end of the request. Because everyone has a penny, the person would look foolish saying no to the request. Thus, the person must say yes. The problem is the target can't simply give a penny because he or she would look completely foolish. Thus, the person tends to give whatever is normatively appropriate for the situation and the charity.

Research investigating the technique has found the total amount given to charities increases when the technique is used. Although individuals give slightly less money, on average, in comparison with those who didn't receive the request, the larger number of people giving something more than compensates for the slightly smaller individual contributions.[66] It's important to recognize the compliance tactic can be implemented in many ways in addition to merely using "even a penny will help." A market researcher could ask the respondent to complete a survey and add the phrase "even answering a question or two will help." A salesperson making a cold call could state, "Even two minutes of your time will be appreciated." The adaptations of the technique are limitless.[67]

Ethical Implications of the Techniques of Personal Influence

An important note should be added concerning the ethics of using the techniques of personal influence. Each of the four techniques has a Machiavellian element. In each case, the influencer attempts to manipulate another individual by engaging in a subtle subterfuge. In the case of the door-in-the-face technique, for example, the influencer lies to the respondent because the first request is a sham. This tactic is then in conflict with the critical principle that marketers and researchers should never lie to consumers. Fortunately, the ability to abuse the compliance techniques is self-limiting (i.e., if overused, consumers will readily identify them and turn against those who employ the tactics).

MANAGERIAL IMPLICATIONS–RESPONSIVE MARKETING

The principles and concepts derived from the study of attitudes, beliefs, and behavior formation and change have applications to each of the five responsive marketing (RESPonsive Marketing) concepts except for environmental analysis. These are discussed next.

Research

Market research is required to identify the salient attributes that are of high importance to consumers in a product category. It's also critical to perform research studies to compare your brand with competitors in terms of overall attitudes and in terms of the belief ratings of the extent it possesses key attributes. Other areas of research include identifying the involvement level of the target market and evaluating consumers' attitude toward the advertisements that are being developed. Finally, it's important to conduct research in order to identify the key benefits consumers are seeking in a product category.

Environmental Analysis

As a marketer, we must scan the environment to access consumers' beliefs and attitudes about our product and other brands. One key piece of information to gain is the importance of various attributes when choosing among the various brands. This information must be evaluated with our positioning in mind. For instance, consumers will often state "low price" is a key attribute when selecting a brand. While our environmental analysis may conclude price is the most important attribute, many consumers will still purchase the higher priced, differentiated brand.

Segmentation

The identification of important product attributes is the foundation of benefit segmentation. **Benefit segmentation** is the division of the market into homogeneous groups of consumers based on a similarity of benefits sought in a product category. Procter & Gamble has built huge market shares for many of its brands by establishing a strategy of focusing on how a product provides a benefit that fulfills one particular consumer need. For example, Crest toothpaste's dominant market share was built around providing one primary benefit—decay prevention. Similarly, Charmin toilet tissue has built its market share around providing the benefit of softness.

Positioning

By identifying the salient attributes that have high importance ratings and are given extremely positive evaluation ratings in the attitude-toward-the-object model, managers have a means of positioning and differentiating a brand. For example, Burger King differentiates its burgers from McDonald's with its "Be Your Way slogan." That is, having the ability to order a burger with the trimmings you want is an important attribute, and Burger King uses the slogan and backs it up with service to position and differentiate its brand.

Marketing Mix

The investigation of consumer beliefs, attitudes, and behaviors has particular relevance to product development and promotional strategy. First, after identifying the important product benefits, brands can be developed that have attributes that provide these benefits. Indeed, new product development should begin with an evaluation of the product benefits consumers seek and the attributes that provide them. Second, promotional strategy should be based around communicating to consumers the messages that evolve from the positioning strategy that emerges from the identification of key attributes. Other promotional issues that emerge include how to employ balance theory principles and behavioral influence techniques to persuade and influence consumers. Finally, it's important to work with the creatives on the advertising staff to fashion communications toward which consumers will have positive attitudes.

SUMMARY

How are my beliefs and attitudes related to my purchase behavior?

The study of the interrelationships among beliefs, attitudes, and behaviors is highly important to the marketing manager and the marketing researcher. Beliefs describe the knowledge a person has about objects, attributes, and benefits. An object, such as a particular brand, possesses various attributes and provides various benefits. Beliefs about the extent to which a brand possesses specific attributes and benefits may be formed from the exposure to and the processing of information obtained from advertising, from friends, or from experience with the product. Product attributes are the characteristics a product may or may not have. Product benefits are the positive and negative outcomes provided by the attributes.

Frequently, particular attributes may be extremely important to consumers. Managers should perform research to identify the attributes their target market considers to be important. These can be employed as part of a benefit segmentation strategy to position and differentiate a product. In addition, such considerations can influence both product design and promotional strategy. One attribute that's often extremely important to consumers is price. In some cases, a high price can serve a negative role and decrease the likelihood of purchasing a brand. In other instances, price can positively influence buying through the price-quality relationship.

Consumer attitudes represent the amount of affect or feeling a person holds for or against a stimulus object, such as a brand, a person, a company, or an idea. In high-involvement situations, attitudes may be formed because the consumer holds a number of beliefs about an object that are positive or negative in nature. Attitudes may also be formed through principles of classical and operant conditioning. The mere exposure phenomenon suggests positive feelings may result from repeated exposures to a previously neutral stimulus.

Consumption behaviors have been discussed in two ways. The first is through intentions to behave, which are the statements consumers give when asked about their likelihood to engage in some behavior, such as buying a product, supporting a political candidate, or visiting a retail store. Actual consumer behavior involves an overt consumer action to purchase a product or service, to visit a retail store, to surf the web for a product, to vote for a particular political candidate, and so forth.

Attitudes serve a number of different functions for consumers. Attitudes have a utilitarian function. In this case, people express an attitude in order to maximize rewards and minimize punishments from others. Attitudes can also serve a value-expressive function. Thus, by expressing an attitude, a consumer makes a statement to others about what he or she believes to be important and valuable. The ego-defensive function is the third use of attitudes. Here, consumers seek to maintain their self-concept by holding attitudes that protect them from basic truths about themselves or the external world. Finally, attitudes serve a knowledge function in which they help people understand a complex universe.

How can managers increase the likelihood consumers will buy?

Consumption behavior can result from a number of different processes that appear to be governed, in part, by the type of buying process in which the consumer is engaged. When the consumer is in a high-involvement situation, the standard learning hierarchy operates, in which behavior occurs after beliefs are formed and affect are created. In the low-involvement hierarchy, behavior appears to occur after a limited number of beliefs are formed. In such a situation, affect appear to play a minor role in influencing behavior and are formed only after the consumer purchases and uses the product. In the experiential hierarchy, affect occurs first, followed by behavior. Impulse purchases exemplify an experiential purchase. The behavioral influence hierarchy may be followed in situations where strong situational or environmental forces propel the consumer to engage in the behavior.

As managers understand whether the target market is in a high-involvement or low-involvement situation, they can be better informed to alter the promotional message to fit consumer needs. Further, managers who understand the behavioral influence hierarchy can adapt the environment to encourage customers to buy. For instance, the atmosphere at Starbucks encourages customers to stay longer and purchase more than one drink.

How do consumers make decisions among different brands?

Consumers must make purchase decisions based on the attributes the products offer. Consumers often use a multiattribute model to select between the various offerings. Multiattribute models attempt to predict consumer attitudes in high-involvement circumstances. In the attitude-toward-the-object model, information on the likelihood an object possesses an attribute and on the evaluation of the badness or goodness of the attribute are combined to predict an attitude. In the behavioral intentions model, intentions to behave are predicted by obtaining information on the attitude toward performing the behavior and on the subjective norm, which assesses what the consumer believes other people think he or she should do. Recently, researchers have found the mere attempt to measure behavioral intentions can influence the likelihood a consumer will purchase a brand.

How does advertising cause behavior change?

As we have discussed, consumers form attitudes toward brands and this attitude can affect the purchase decision. Attitudes toward brands, however, often develop from an attitude toward an advertisement. When consumers have a positive attitude toward an advertisement, this attitude often transfers to the brand. Likewise, if the consumer has a negative attitude toward the advertisement, the negative feelings are transferred to the brand.

The imagery shown in an advertisement strongly impacts the attitude toward the ad. Imagery is the extent the ad causes the consumer to imagine using the product. Further, showing the advertisement at the right time can greatly impact the consumer's attitude toward the brand. Placing an advertisement on the Super Bowl will reach a huge television audience. If the advertisement is interesting and portrays the brand in a positive light, the ad may very well increase the chances consumers will buy the brand.

KEY TERMS

affective feelings
attitude
attitude-toward-the-object
 model
attitude toward the ad
attribute importance
attributes
balance theory
behavioral influence hierarchy
behavioral influence techniques
behavioral intentions
benefit segmentation
benefits
central cues
central route to persuasion
cognitive consistency
cognitive responses

consumer behaviors
consumer beliefs
door-in-the-face technique
ego-defense function
elaboration likelihood model
even-a-penny-will-help technique
experiential hierarchy
foot-in-the-door technique
global attitude measure
halo effect
hierarchies of effects
high-involvement hierarchy
impulse (experiential) purchase
ingratiation
knowledge role
low-involvement hierarchy

mere exposure phenomenon
multiattribute models
need for cognition
norm of reciprocity
objects
peripheral cues
peripheral route to persuasion
persuasion
salient beliefs
sentiment connections
subjective norm
theory of reasoned action
truth effect
unit relation
utilitarian function
value-expressive function

REVIEW QUESTIONS

1. Define the concepts of belief, attitude, and behavior.
2. Why should researchers attempt to identify the importance of product attributes to consumers? What factors tend to influence attribute importance?
3. What's meant by the idea beliefs, attitudes, and behaviors may form into hierarchies of effects?
4. What processes account for how beliefs are directly formed?
5. What processes account for the direct formation of attitudes?
6. Identify three ways behaviors may be induced without the formation of strong attitudes or beliefs.
7. How do the hierarchies of effects differ in high- and low-involvement circumstances?
8. How do the hierarchies of effects differ in experiential versus behavioral influence processes?
9. What conditions limit the ability of attitudes to predict behavior accurately?
10. What's meant by a multiattribute attitude model?
11. Differentiate the attitude-toward-the-object model from the behavioral intentions model.

12. What are the four functions of attitudes identified by Katz (i.e., utilitarian, ego-defense, knowledge, value-expressive)?

13. Why would a market researcher want to assess consumer global attitudes?

14. According to the elaboration likelihood model, what are the two routes to persuasion? What factors cause a consumer to move through one route rather than another?

15. Through which of the routes of persuasion does attitude change tend to be more long lasting? Why?

16. According to the attitude-toward-the-object model, what are the three ways in which attitudes may be changed?

17. According to the behavioral intentions model, what are the means through which intentions may be changed?

18. What are the sentiment connections and unit relations of balance theory?

19. What are the three ways of forming a unit relation between an endorser and a product?

20. How may the attitude toward the ad influence attitudes toward the brand?

21. What's meant by ingratiation? What are the means of ingratiation?

22. How does the foot-in-the-door technique work?

23. How does the door-in-the-face technique work?

24. How does the even-a-penny-will-help technique work?

DISCUSSION QUESTIONS

1. List as many attributes as you can consumers may seek in an automobile. You should be able to identify at least ten attributes. Select five of these attributes and identify the benefits consumers may receive if the attributes are present in an automobile.

2. Consider the sports utility segment versus the family car segment of the car market. Rank in order the five attributes you think are most important for each segment.

3. Rough out a print advertisement that seeks to influence consumer beliefs about two attributes of a new energy drink. (You must create the new drink and identify its benefits.)

4. Describe the most recent commercial you've seen for an energy drink maker or a beer company. Which of the hierarchies of effects does the company seem to be assuming consumers are using? Why?

5. Go through magazines and identify a print advertisement that appears to view consumers as in a high-involvement state and for which a multiattribute model might describe attitude formation. Discuss how the advertisement attempts to influence your attitude by giving information on multiple attributes.

6. Interview five of your friends. Using the attitude-toward-the-object model, assess their attitudes regarding a local fast-food restaurant. What are the managerial implications of the exercise for the restaurant?

7. Consider the advertising for the following companies: Pepsi-Cola, Volvo, McDonald's, and IBM. Which of the ad campaigns would you consider to involve central routes to persuasion and which involve peripheral routes to persuasion? Why?

8. Identify two advertisements you have a positive attitude toward and two ads you have a negative attitude toward. Do your attitudes toward the ads influence your perceptions of the products?

9. Ingratiation is a device frequently used to influence others. Describe the various ingratiation tactics an automobile salesperson could use and their possible impact on customers.

10. You're working in the marketing department for a firm that does market surveys. Your boss tells you she wants to use the foot-in-the-door technique to increase the response rate to telephone interviewers. She asks you to develop the specific wording for telephone surveyors to use that incorporates the technique. The research in question involves a ten-minute survey on the use of dishwashing detergent. Write out the specific words the interviewers should use.

11. Repeat the exercise in question 11 using the door-in-the-face technique.

ENDNOTES

1 D. Gail Fleenor, "Energetic Sales?"*Progressive Grocer* 88 (November/December 2009): 80, 82.

2 Ibid.

3 Joseph Lord, "Energy Drinks' Sales Explode Despite Concerns," *News and Tribune*, January 5, 2007, accessed December 12, 2015, http://www.newsandtribune.com/news/energy-drinks-sales-explode-despite-concerns/article_74b9aee3-876e-5674-a07e-e2815cd80255.html.

4 "Dollar Sales of Energy Drink Beverages and Shots in the United States from 2011 to 2015 (in Billion Dollars), *Statista*, accessed December 10, 2015, http://www.statista.com/statistics/275525/us-dollar-sales-of-energy-drink-beverages-and-shots/.

5 Gary A. Hemphill, "US Soft Drink Sales Up Slightly in 2004, Beverage Marketing Corporation Reports," *Beverage Marketing*, accessed 2007, http://www. Beveragemarketing.com/news2uu.htm.

6 "Top Selling Energy Drink Brands," Caffeine Informer, November 10, 2015, accessed December 10, 2015, http://www.caffeineinformer.com/the-15-top-energy-drink-brands.

7 James Helgeson, Alan Kluge, John Mager, and Cheri Taylor, "Trends in Consumer Behavior Literature: A Content Analysis," *Journal of Consumer Research* 10 (March 1984): 449–454.

8 Elaine Watson, "What Can We Learn about Energy Drink Consumption Habits from Social Media?" *Food Navigator USA*, February 12, 2013, accessed December 10, 2015, http://www.foodnavigator-usa.com/Market/What-can-we-learn-about-energy-drink-consumption-habits-from-social-media.

9 Scott Mackenzie, "The Role of Attention in Mediating the Effect of Advertising on Attribute Importance," *Journal of Consumer Research* 13 (September 1986): 174–195.

10 The definition was found in Richard E. Petty, Thomas M. Ostrom, and Timothy C. Brock, eds., *Cognitive Responses in Persuasion* (New York: Psychology Press, 1981), 31.

11 Chris T. Allen, Karen A. Machleit, and Susan Schultz Kleine, "A Comparison of Attitudes and Emotions as Predictors of Behavior at Diverse Levels of Behavioral Experience," *Journal of Consumer Research* 18 (March 1992): 493–504. For a similar definition, see Darrel J. Bem,

Beliefs, Attitudes, and Human Affairs (Belmont, CA: Brooks/Cole, 1970). See also Martin Fishbein and Icek Ajzen, *Beliefs, Attitude, Intentions, and Behaviors: An Introduction to Theory and Research* (Reading, MA: Addison-Wesley, 1975). See also Phillip Zimbardo, E. Ebbesen, and C. Maslach, *Influencing Attitudes and Changing Behavior* (Reading, MA: Addison-Wesley, 1977).

[12] Daniel Katz, "The Functional Approach to Attitudes," *Public Opinion Quarterly* 24 (1960): 163–204. See also Sharon Shavitt, "Products, Personalities, and Situations in Attitude Functions: Implications for Consumer Behavior," in *Advances in Consumer Research*, vol. 16, ed. Thomas Srull (Provo, UT: Association for Consumer Research, 1989), 300–305.

[13] For an excellent discussion on the functions of attitudes and on the role of attitudes in consumer behavior, see Richard J. Lutz, "The Role of Attitude Theory in Marketing," in *Perspectives in Consumer Behavior*, ed. Harold Kassarjian and Thomas Robertson (Englewood Cliffs, NJ: Prentice Hall, 1991), 317–339.

[14] Elnora Stuart, Terence Shimp, and Randall Engle, "Classical Conditioning of Consumer Attitudes: Four Experiments in an Advertising Context," *Journal of Consumer Research* 14 (December 1987): 334–349.

[15] Robert Zajonc, "The Attitudinal Effects of Mere Exposure," monograph, *Journal of Personality and Social Psychology* 9 (1968): 2.

[16] Scott Mackenzie, "The Role of Attention in Mediating the Effect of Advertising on Attribute Importance," *Journal of Consumer Research* 13 (1986): 174–195.

[17] William Wilson, "Feeling More Than We Know: Exposure Effects without Learning," *Journal of Personality and Social Psychology* 37 (June 1979): 811–821.

[18] John Hadjimzrcou, John W. Barnes, and Richard S. Jacobs, "The Effects of Context-Induced Mood States on Initial and Repeat Product Evaluations: A Preliminary Investigation," in *Advances in Consumer Research*, vol. 23, ed. Kim P. Corfman and John G. Lynch, Jr. (Provo, Utah: Association for Consumer Research, 1996), 337–341.

[19] Walter Nord and J. Paul Peter, "A Behavior Modification Perspective on Marketing," *Journal of Marketing* 44 (Spring 1980): 36–47.

[20] Paco Underhill, *Why We Buy* (New York: Simon and Schuster, 1999).

[21] Michael Ray, "Marketing Communications and the Hierarchy-of-Effects," in *New Models for Mass Communications*, ed. P. Clarke (Beverly Hills, CA: Sage, 1973), 147–176.

[22] Herbert Krugman, "The Impact of Television Advertising: Learning without Involvement," *Public Opinion Quarterly* 29 (October 1961): 59–62. A variety of definitions of involvement have been proposed. For a good review, see John H. Antil, "Conceptualization and Operationalization of Involvement," in *Advances in Consumer Research*, vol. 11, ed. Thomas C. Kinnear (Provo, UT: Association for Consumer Research, 1984), 203–209.

[23] Richard W. Olshavsky and Donald H. Granbois, "Consumer Decision Making: Fact or Fiction?" *Journal of Consumer Research* 6 (September 1979): 93–100.

[24] For an excellent discussion of low-involvement decision making, see F. Stewart De Bruicker, "An Appraisal of Low-Involvement Consumer Information Processing," in *Attitude Research Plays for High Stakes*, ed. John Maloney and Bernard Silverman (Chicago: American Marketing Association, 1979), 112-130.

[25] Dennis W. Rook and Stephen J. Hoch, "Consuming Impulses," in *Advances in Consumer Behavior*, vol. 12, ed. Elizabeth C. Hirschman and Moris B. Holbrook (Provo, UT: Association for Consumer Research, 1985), 23–27.

[26] Numerous approaches to the study of attitudes exist. For a discussion of several of these, see Richard J. Lutz, "The Role of Attitude Theory in Marketing," in *Perspectives in Consumer Behavior*, 4th ed., ed. Harold H. Kassarjian and Thomas S. Robertson (Englewood Cliffs, NJ: Prentice Hall, 1991), 317–339.

[27] For a full discussion of the Fishbein model, see Martin Fishbein and Icek Ajzen, *Belief, Attitude, Intention and Behavior: An Introduction to Theory and Research* (Reading, MA: Addison-Wesley, 1975).

[28] Scott Mackenzie, "The Role of Attention in Mediating the Effect of Advertising on Attribute Importance," *Journal of Consumer Research* 13 (1986): 174–195.

[29] Allan Wicker, "Attitudes Versus Actions: The Relationship of Verbal and Overt Behavioral Responses to Attitude Objects," *Journal of Social Issues* 25 (Autumn 1969): 65.

[30] Robert Cialdini, Richard Petty, and John Caccioppo, "Attitude and Attitude Change," *Annual Review of Psychology* 32 (1981): 366.

[31] Linda F. Alwitt and Ida E. Berger, "Understanding the Link between Environmental Attitudes and Consumer Product Usage: Measuring the Moderating Role of Attitude Strength," in *Advances in Consumer Research*, vol. 20, ed. Leigh McAlister and Michael Rothschild (Provo, UT: Association for Consumer Research, 1992), 189–194.

[32] Icek Ajzen and Martin Fishbein, "Attitude-Behavior Relations: A Theoretical Analysis and Review of Empirical Research," *Psychological Bulletin* (September, 1977): 888–918. Readers should note the behavioral intentions model is now called the theory of reasoned action. I have retained the older name to emphasize its focus on predicting behavioral intentions.

[33] An example of an article finding the behavioral intentions model to be superior to attitude-toward-the-object model includes Michael J. Ryan and E. H. Bonfield, "Fishbein's Intentions Model: A Test of External and Pragmatic Validity," *Journal of Marketing* 44 (Spring 1980): 82–95. Readers should note work continues on behavioral intentions models. For a recent comparison of three models of behavioral intentions, see Richard Netemeyer, J. Craig Andrews, and Scrinvas Durvasula, "A Comparison of Three Behavioral Intentions Models: The Case of Valentine's Day Gift-Giving," in *Advances in Consumer Research*, vol. 20, ed. Leigh McAlister and Michael Rothschild (Provo, UT: Association for Consumer Research, 1992), 135–141.

[34] Martin Fishbein, Susan E. Middlestadt, and David Trafimow, "Social Norms for Condom Use: Implications for HIV Prevention Interventions of a KABP Survey with Heterosexuals in the Eastern Caribbean," in *Advances in Consumer Research*, vol. 20, ed. Leigh McAlister and Michael Rothschild (Provo, UT: Association for Consumer Research, 1992), 292–296.

[35] David B. Wooten and Americus Reed II, "Informational Influence and the Ambiguity of Product Experience: Order Effects on the Weighting of Evidence," *Journal of Consumer Psychology* 7, no. 1 (1998): 79–99.

[36] Vicki G. Morwitz, Eric Johnson, and David Schmittlein, "Does Measuring Intent Change Behavior?" *Journal of Consumer Research* 20 (June 1993): 46–61.

[37] The mere measurement effect was recently supported in research by Eric R. Spangenberg and Anthony G. Greenwald, "Social Influence by Requesting Self-Prophecy," *Journal of Consumer Psychology* 8, no. 1 (199): 61–89.

[38] Gavan J. Fitzsimons and Vicki G. Morwitz, "The Effect of Measuring Intent on Brand-Level Purchase Behavior," *Journal of Consumer Research* 23 (June 1996): 1–11.

[39] For a review, see David E. Sprott, Eric R. Spangenberg, and Andrew W. Perkins, "Two More Self-Prophecy Experiments," in *Advances in Consumer Research*, vol. 26, ed. Eric Arnould and Linda M. Scott, (Provo, UT: Association for Consumer Research, 1999), 621–626.

[40] Richard E. Petty, John T. Cacioppo, and David Schumann, "Central and Peripheral Routes to Advertising Effectiveness: The Moderating Role of Involvement," *Journal of Consumer Research* 10 (1983): 135–146.

[41] Richard Petty and John Cacioppo, "The Elaboration Likelihood Model of Persuasion," in *Advances in Experiential Social Psychology*, vol. 19, ed. Leonard Berkowitz (New York: Academic Press, 1986), 123–205.

[42] Robert B. Cialdini, Richard Petty, and John Cacioppo, "Attitude and Attitude Change," *Annual Review of Psychology* 32 (1981): 357–404.

[43] Recent research has been supportive of key elements of the ELM model. See Jong-Won Park and Manoj Hastak, "Effects of Involvement on Online Brand Evaluations: A Stronger Test of the ELM," in *Advances in Consumer Research*, vol. 22, ed. Frank R. Kardes and Mita Sujan (Provo, Utah: Association for Consumer Research, 1995), 435–439.

[44] John Cacioppo, Stephen Harkins, and Richard Petty, "The Nature of Attitudes and Cognitive Responses and Their Relations to Behavior," in *Cognitive Responses in Persuasion*, ed. Richard Petty, Thomas Ostrom, and Timothy C. Brock (Hillsdale, NJ: Lawrence Erlbaum, 1981), 31–54. See also Richard Petty, John Cacioppo, and D. Schumann, "Central and Peripheral Routes to Advertising Effectiveness." A number of studies have found evidence supportive of predictions made by the elaboration likelihood model. The work on the elaboration likelihood model is still relatively new, however, and several authors have noted it has weaknesses. See Charles Areni and Richard Lutz, "The Role of Argument Quality in the Elaboration Likelihood Model," in *Advances in Consumer Research*, vol. XV, ed. Michael Houston (Provo, UT: Association for Consumer Research, 1988), 197–203. See also Paul Miniard, Peter Dickson, and Kenneth Lord, "Some Central and Peripheral Thoughts on the Routes to Persuasion," in *Advances in Consumer Research*, vol. 15, ed. Michael Houston (Provo, UT: Association for Consumer Research, 1988), 204–208. Another recent article is

Paul W. Miniard, Deepak Sirdeshmukh, and Daniel E. Innis, "Peripheral Persuasion and Brand Choice," *Journal of Consumer Research* 19 (September 1992): 226–239.

[45] Sharmistha Law, Scott A. Hawkins, and Fergus I. M. Craik, "Repetition-Induced Belief in the Elderly: Rehabilitating Age-Related Memory Deficits," *Journal of Consumer Research* 25 (September 1998): 91–107.

[46] Scott A. Hawkins and Stephen J. Hoch, "Low-Involvement Learning: Memory without Evaluation," *Journal of Consumer Research* 19 (September 1992): 212–224.

[47] Curtis P. Haugtvedt, Richard E. Petty, and John T. Cacioppo, "Need for Cognition and Advertising: Understanding the Role of Personality Variables in Consumer Research," *Journal of Consumer Psychology* 1, no. 3 (1992): 239–260.

[48] Curt Haugtvedt, Richard Petty, John Cacioppo, and Theresa Steidley, "Personality and Ad Effectiveness: Exploring the Utility of Need for Cognition," in *Advances in Consumer Research*, vol. 15, ed. Michael Houston (Provo, UT: Association for Consumer Research, 1988), 209–212.

[49] M. J. Rosenberg, "An Analysis of Affective-Cognitive Consistency," in *Attitude Organization and Change*, ed. M. J. Rosenberg, C. I. Hovland, W. J. McGuire, R. P. Abelson, and J. W. Brehm (New Haven, CT: Yale University Press, 1960), 15–64.

[50] Andrew A. Mitchell and Jerry Olson, "Are Product Attribute Beliefs the Only Mediator of Advertising Effects of Brand Attitude?" *Journal of Marketing Research* 18 (1981): 318–332.

[51] Richard Lutz, "Affective and Cognitive Antecedents of Attitude Toward the Ad: A Conceptual Framework," in *Psychological Processes and Advertising Effects: Theory, Research, and Application*, ed. L. F. Alwitt and A. A. Mitchell (Hillsdale, NJ: Lawrence Erlbaum, 1985), 45–63.

[52] Kenneth R. Lord, Myung-Soo Lee, and Paul L. Sauer, "Program Context Antecedents of Attitude Toward Radio Commercials," *Journal of Academy of Marketing Science* 22 (Winter 1994): 3–15.

[53] Joseph Phelps and Esther Thorson, "Brand Familiarity and Product Involvement Effects on the Attitude Toward an Ad-Brand Attitude Relationship," in *Advances in Consumer Research*, vol. 18, ed. Rebecca H. Holman and Michael R. Solomon (Provo, UT: Association for Consumer Research, 1991), 202–209.

[54] Paula Fitzgerald Bone and Pam Scholder Ellen, "The Generation and Consequences of Communication-Evoked Imagery," *Journal of Consumer Research* 19 (June 1992): 93–104. For more information on the effects of pictures on information processing and brand preferences, see Carolyn L. Costley and Merrie Brucks, "Selective Recall and Information Use in Consumer Preferences," *Journal of Consumer Research* 18 (March 1992): 464–484.

[55] David Sweet, "Super Bowl Advertisers' Sites Get More Hits than Reebok's Office Linebacker," *Street and Smith's Sports Business Journal* 10 (February 2003): 16.

[56] James Boles and Scot Burton, "An Examination of Free Elicitation and Response Scale Measures of Feelings and Judgments Evoked by Television Advertisements," *Journal of Academy of Marketing Science* 20 (Summer 1992): 225–233.

[57] Edward E. Jones, *Ingratiation: A Social Psychological Analysis* (New York: Appleton-Century-Crofts, 1964).

[58] Michael J. Dorsch and Scott W. Kelley, "An Investigation into the Intentions of Purchasing Executives to Reciprocate Vendor Gifts," *Journal of Academy of Marketing Science* 22 (Fall 1994): 315–327.

[59] Daniel J. Howard, Charles Gengler, and Ambuj Jain, "What's in a Name? Complimentary Means of Persuasion," *Journal of Consumer Research* 22 (September 1995): 200–211.

[60] Lynnea Mallalieu and Corinne Faure, "Toward an Understanding of the Choice of Influence Tactics: The Impact of Power," in *Advances in Consumer Research*, vol. 25, ed. Joseph W. Alba and J. Wesley Hutchinson (Provo, UT: Association for Consumer Research, 1998), 407–414.

[61] Richard McFarland, Goutam N. Challagalla, and Tasadduq A. Shervani, "Influence Tactics for Effective Adaptive Selling," *Journal of Marketing* 70 (October 2006):103–117.

[62] Edward E. Jones and Harold B. Gerard, *Foundations of Social Psychology* (New York: John Wiley, 1967).

[63] Peter H. Reingen and J. B. Kernan, "Compliance with an Interview Request: A Foot-in-the-Door, Self-Perception Interpretation," *Journal of Marketing Research* 14 (August 1977): 365–369.

[64] Robert A. Hansen and Larry M. Robinson, "Testing the Effectiveness of Alternative Foot-in-the-Door Manipulations," *Journal of Marketing Research* 17 (August 1980): 359–364.

[65] John C. Mowen and Robert Cialdini, "On Implementing the Door-in-the-Face Compliance Strategy in a Marketing Context," *Journal of Marketing Research* 17 (May 1980): 253–258.

[66] Robert Cialdini and David Schroeder, "Increasing Compliance by Legitimizing Paltry Contributions: When Even a Penny Helps," *Journal of Personality and Social Psychology* 34 (October 1976): 599–604.

[67] For a single theoretical explanation of the four compliance techniques based on the availability valence hypothesis, see Alice Tybout, Brian Sternthal, and Bobby Calder, "Information Availability as a Determinant of Multiple Request Effectiveness," *Journal of Marketing Research* 20 (August 1983): 279–290. See also Edward Fern, Kent Monroe, and Ramon Avila, "Effectiveness of Multiple Request Strategies: A Synthesis of Research Results," *Journal of Marketing Research* 23 (May 1986): 144–152.

8

Persuasive Communications

Do Celebrities Really Influence Our Buying Behavior?

Tiger Woods jumped into the global spotlight at the age of 8 when he won his first tournament: the Optimist International Junior World.[1] Woods won 14 major golf championships by 2010, making him arguably the most successful golfer of all time. His golfing prowess turned him into an endorser extraordinaire. From 1996 through 2007, Woods earned a reported $669 million from endorsements alone.[2] At the same time, he became a beloved icon among consumers. Many consumers find Woods to be a persuasive endorser.

A measure of an endorser's persuasive power is the Q Score. The Q Score is the ratio of how appealing the endorser is among those who are familiar with him or her. From 2007 to 2009, Woods's Q Score ranked second among American sports celebrities, right behind the perennial leader Michael Jordan.[3]

In December 2009, many consumers changed their beliefs and attitudes toward Woods. The media announced Woods had cheated on his wife. The once iconic figure was suddenly tarnished. The 2010 Q Score ratings for athletes show Woods was no longer ranked second. In fact, he dropped completely out of the top ten list. (See Table 8.1 for that list.) In Chapter 7, we discussed the relationship among attitudes, beliefs, and behaviors. The change in consumers' attitudes and beliefs toward Woods negatively affected their behaviors in both sales and stock market values.

To illustrate this point, we conducted an event study to understand the impact on two firms that dropped endorsement deals with Woods: Gatorade and Gillette. An event study statistically analyzes the effect of information on stock prices. According to the efficient market hypothesis, stock prices are a reflection of all information about a firm. Any positive or negative information is immediately reflected in the stock price.

TABLE 8.1
Athlete Q Scores for 2009–2010[4]

	Athlete	2009 Q Score		Athlete	2010 Q Score
1	Michael Jordan	50	1	Michael Jordan	51
2	Tiger Woods	44	2	John Madden	41
3	John Madden	40	2	Shaun White	41
4	Magic Johnson	39	4	Peyton Manning	40
5	Nolan Ryan	37	5	Joe Montana	39
6	Joe Montana	35	5	Arnold Palmer	39
6	Cal Ripkin Jr.	35	7	Jerry Rice	38
6	Jerry Rice	35	7	Nolan Ryan	38
9	Arnold Palmer	31	9	Julius Erving	37
10	Brett Favre	26	9	Magic Johnson	37
			9	Apolo Anton Ohno	37

Figures 8.1 and 8.2 illustrate the stock market gains and losses of these two companies compared with leading competitors and the S&P 500 index. In Figure 8.1, PepsiCo is graphed against the S&P 500 index and Coca-Cola. PepsiCo is the parent company of Gatorade, which held an endorsement contract with Woods. Any changes in potential sales of Gatorade should be reflected in the stock price of PepsiCo. Coca-Cola was chosen because it's PepsiCo's major competitor. The graph begins with a zero starting point for the two firms and the S&P 500 index. The movement from zero represents the percentage accumulated change in the stock. We captured prices around a two-week window in December 2009. On approximately December 2, when the rumors of Woods's transgressions started to spread, PepsiCo was doing better than both Coca-Cola and the S&P 500. By December 11, the rumors were confirmed, illustrated by a dramatic change in the graph. PepsiCo suffered dramatic losses while Coca-Cola and the S&P 500 index had dramatic gains. The comparison with the index score is particularly compelling as it demonstrates the movement of PepsiCo relative to the market.

Figure 8.2 illustrates Procter & Gamble—parent company of Gillette—versus the S&P 500 and Johnson & Johnson. At the time, Woods held an endorsement deal with Gillette. In this illustration, the competitor (i.e., Johnson & Johnson), again, had a dramatic improvement compared with Woods's endorsed brand (i.e., Gillette) and the S&P 500. This event study gives us more insight into the impact endorsers can have on the endorsed firm's stock price.

FIGURE 8.1
Price History—PEP
(11/30/2009–12/15/2009)

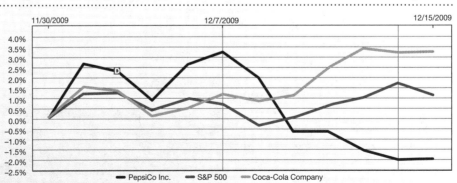

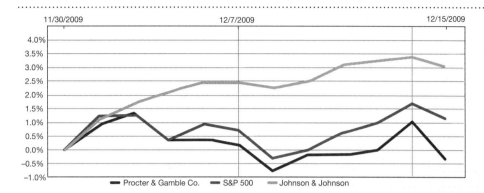

FIGURE 8.2
Price History—PEP
(11/30/2009–12/15/2009)

This opening vignette illustrates the importance of hiring the right endorser for our persuasive communications. In this chapter, we'll explore persuasive communications. Let's begin with an overview of the topic.

OVERVIEW OF PERSUASION COMMUNICATIONS

Communications are ubiquitous in society. Cell phones keep us in constant contact with friends and family. The media keeps us informed through radio and television commercials, print advertisements, billboards, packaging, and sales personnel. Each of these communication modes, including the cell phone, seeks to communicate with us and, ultimately, to influence us. For example, think about your friends calling you to convince you to go to a movie. Researchers estimate that, on average, American consumers receive from two hundred to five hundred commercial messages a day. Yet, they are aware of only 15 percent and actively process only 4 to 5 percent of the messages.[5] So how can we make these communication messages more effective?

A **communication** involves the use of a sign to convey meaning. A **sign** may be a verbalization, body language, words, a picture, an odor, a touch, or even the tone at which it is said. In fact, communication may have more to do with presentation than the actual words used. The persuasive ability of a source can be broken down into percentages based on their biggest impact. The actual words used account for 7 percent of the effectiveness in persuasive message, while the tone accounts for 38 percent and body language 55 percent. This information makes it imperative to select a source that will not only use the right words, but tone and body language as well.

An important point is that the meanings conveyed by signs are strongly influenced by culture. For example, within the youth subculture some choose to wear their pants down low which may symbolize their membership in the particular youth subculture. Many of us have grown to accept this behavior as a rite of passage for some youth. However, if you saw someone outside this membership group displaying that behavior, (say a 50 year old college professor), you might giggle and point.

Researchers have developed a **communications model** that depicts the relationships among the various factors that influence the effectiveness and impact of persuasive communications.[6] Figure 8.3 presents one version of this model. The model proposes that five separate categories of factors control the effectiveness of communications: source characteristics, message content, medium characteristics, contextual factors, and audience characteristics.

FIGURE 8.3
Communications Model

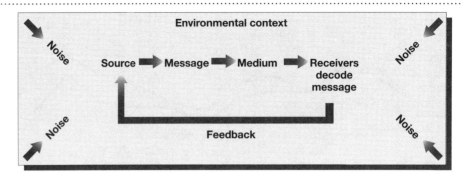

As shown in Figure 8.3, persuasive communications begin with a source of information that encodes and delivers a message. The message can be interpreted quite differently depending on the source. For instance, an advertisement promoting tourism in San Antonio, Texas, could be promoted by two different sources: the mayor of San Antonio or Matthew McConaughey, a popular actor who grew up in Texas. Consumers may interpret the ad featuring the mayor as biased and the ad with McConaughey as more honest and sincere. Consequently, consumers may view the ad with McConaughey as more persuasive.

The message is delivered through some medium, or channel of transmission. The medium could be face to face, print, radio, telephone, billboards, television, or the World Wide Web. The characteristics of the channel influence the interpretation of the message as well as how its information is processed. The classic example of this phenomenon is the presidential debate between John Kennedy and Richard Nixon. The story goes that Nixon was pale due to a recent hospitalization. When people watched the debate on television, they believed Kennedy won. The people who listened to the debate on the radio didn't see Nixon's apparent weakness and believed he won the debate. In this case, the medium used made a big difference in consumer attitudes.

Various characteristics of the audience can moderate the effects of persuasive communications. Personality, sex, intelligence, and involvement in the issue influence how receivers decode the information and react to the communication. Finally, the entire communications process takes place within a general environmental context. Various environmental stimuli may inhibit the communications process by distracting consumers, influencing their mood, or acting to create noise in the transmission of the message.

This chapter analyzes in detail two key factors that influence the effectiveness of the communication process: the characteristics of the source of information and the characteristics of the message that's communicated. Three other factors important to the communications process aren't discussed in the chapter: the context within which the message is delivered, the nature of the channel or vehicle through which the message is communicated, and the receiver. The receiver of the communication is an individual. Because individual differences in consumer behavior were discussed in Chapter 6, space limitations prohibit further analysis of this important topic. Because a communication begins with a source of information, this element of the communications model is discussed first.

Source Characteristics

Understanding the factors that influence the effectiveness of sources of information is extremely important to marketing managers and public-policy makers. For example, advertisers frequently hire endorsers to advocate a product or service. In one study that investigated 243 commercials, over 38 percent used some type of endorser.[7] The importance advertisers attribute to finding the "right" source is illustrated by the huge sums they're willing to pay celebrity endorsers. For example, Under Armour recently signed Kevin Durant of the Oklahoma City Thunder to a contract between $265 and $285 million for ten years.[8]

A **source** is an individual or character who's delivering a message, and **source characteristics** are the features that impact the effectiveness of a message delivery, including the source's credibility, physical attractiveness, and meaningfulness. The next several subsections discuss these source characteristics.

Social Media

Celebrities Get Paid to Tweet

Celebrity tweets are the new trend in sponsorships. For decades, companies have paid celebrities to endorse products in advertisements. However, today's communication streams have changed. Fewer people are watching network television or listening to the radio.

Firms are hiring celebrities to tweet about their brand. Companies that carefully select the right celebrity can reach millions of the celebrity's followers with a brand message. Celebrities receive $2,500 to $8,000 per tweet, depending on the number of followers they have. The companies gain from the traffic directed to their websites. For instance, CampusLIVE paid Lindsay Lohan $3,500 for one tweet to her 2.6 million followers, which led to the company receiving approximately 4,500 clicks on its website.[9]

SOURCE CREDIBILITY

Source credibility refers to the degree of a source's credence based on the perception of the expertise, trustworthiness, and selectivity of the source. Thus, the greater the expertise, trustworthiness, and selectivity of a source of information, the more likely an observer will perceive the source as credible. Figure 8.4 illustrates the components of source credibility. The credibility of the source has a large impact on consumer behavior. For example, we can consider two female celebrities as endorsers: Oprah Winfrey and Rosie O'Donnell. Oprah has high status in US society, while Rosie may be less credible due to some of her controversial remarks. Consider for a moment you're the CEO of Mercedes or Payless Shoe Source. Which of the two ladies would be a better choice as an endorser? What characteristics lead you to this conclusion?

Source expertise refers to the extent of knowledge the source is perceived to have about the subject on which he or she is communicating. **Source trustworthiness** refers to the extent the source is perceived to provide information in an unbiased, honest manner.[10] **Selectivity** refers to when the endorser gives careful consideration to which products to endorse. Attribution theory suggests that if consumers believe the endorser is merely endorsing the product for the monetary gains, the source isn't being selective. If the endorser is selective in

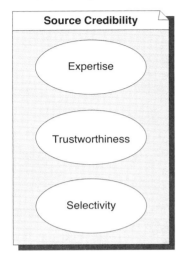

choosing what brands to endorse, perhaps consumers will view him or her as being more credible. Roger Federer is currently the world's most popular endorser, earning in excess of $58 million per year in endorsement deals.[11] However, just as other endorsers, Federer turns down many endorsement offers. Consequently, Federer is selective in picking brands.

Source expertise, trustworthiness, and selectivity make independent contributions to source effectiveness. The implication of this is that if someone is perceived as trustworthy, he or she can influence an audience even the audience also perceives him or her to have relatively little expertise or poor selectivity. For instance, a number of celebrities have successfully endorsed products despite the fact they have no expertise in the product category: Michael Jordan endorses Hanes, Peyton Manning endorsed Oreos, and Jack Black endorsed Apple's iPod. Similarly, even though someone may be perceived as untrustworthy, if perceived to be an expert as well, he or she will tend to have some persuasive ability.[12]

One important factor that influences trust is attributions made for the cause of the endorsement. If an endorser is perceived as presenting a message because of his or her own self-interest, trust will be substantially lower. These effects are magnified if multiple endorsers are used in an advertising campaign. If multiple trustworthy endorsers are employed to convey a message, attitudes are dramatically increased. Conversely, if multiple "untrustworthy" endorsers are employed, attitudes dramatically decrease. Thus, risks are run if the endorsers appear to be motivated primarily because they are paid rather than because they really believe in the product.[13] Advertising campaigns, such as for basketball shoes, beer, milk, and even insurance, have used multiple endorsers. For example, Geico, the low-cost insurance firm, has used a number of celebrity endorsers, including Little Richard, Burt Bacharach, and Verne Troyer (i.e., "Mini-Me" from the Austin Powers movies).

Another important positive effect of using credible endorsers is they reduce counter-argumentation. Advertisers realize consumers often develop their own thoughts in response to a message. These thoughts, called **cognitive responses**, may be positive regarding the message (i.e., support arguments), may be negative toward the message (i.e., counterarguments), or may concern the characteristics of the source (i.e., source derogations).[14] When a highly trustworthy and expert endorser is used, however, people lower their defenses and produce fewer cognitive responses. In particular, because highly credible sources inhibit counter-argumentation, they may be more persuasive than less credible sources.

PHYSICAL ATTRACTIVENESS OF THE SOURCE

Substantial research, as well as anecdotal evidence, suggests sources that are more physically attractive are more effective than less attractive sources.[15] In addition, people tend to form positive stereotypes about physically attractive people. One study found college men and women expected physically attractive people to be more sensitive, warm, modest, happy, and so forth. Indeed, the researchers summarized the results as "What is beautiful is good."[16]

Another study found individuals are viewed as more attractive simply because the individual is perceived to be an exerciser. In the experiment, participants evaluated a fictitious person who was an exerciser, a non-exerciser, or a control. Individuals who regularly worked out were rated as healthier and better looking than the non-exercisers. Further, the results demonstrated a **halo effect**. That is, the attractiveness feature also led to more positive ratings on personality dimensions. Exercisers were viewed as braver, happier, kinder, and more sociable than non-exercisers. This study demonstrates the source characteristics may be deeper than looks alone.[17]

This situation may be explained from a **social identity theory** perspective. An individual's identity is defined as his or her schema, or what is central about the individual.[18] When this schema overlaps with the schema of another entity, such as an endorser, then it's said the individual identifies with the entity. Identification can be real or aspirational. So, when a consumer aspires to be like the endorser, the consumer often purchases the items suggested by the endorser.

In the advertising arena, researchers have found attractive individuals are perceived more positively and reflect more favorably on the brand endorsed. For example, in one study, respondents were shown slides of either an attractive or an average-looking person who worked at the Cincinnati Zoo.[19] Respondents were asked to give their impressions of the presentation and of the person. In addition, they were asked if they would be willing to volunteer to assist the zoo. The results revealed that impressions of the slideshow were significantly more favorable when an attractive model was used. The effect was particularly strong for males who saw an attractive female. Males exposed to the attractive female were significantly more interested in attending a meeting about and in passing a levy to finance the zoo.

Physical attractiveness also interacts with other variables.[20] In one study, highly attractive and less attractive people endorsed either a coffee product or a fragrance. The results showed the sexy model produced greater intentions to buy the product when the product had a sexual appeal (i.e., when the product was the perfume). In contrast, if the product had nothing to do with attracting the opposite sex (i.e., the product was coffee), the unattractive source had more impact. Respondents in the study may have inferred physically attractive endorsers would know something about perfume but have little knowledge of coffee. These results indicate using physically attractive and sexy models may not be appropriate for some types of products, such as coffee.

These results illustrate the importance of matching the nature of the product with the characteristics of the endorser. This **match-up effect** (i.e., fit) states endorsers are more effective in changing attitudes, beliefs, and intentions when the dominant characteristics of the product match the dominant features of a source. These ideas explain the results of coffee and fragrance study. That is, because perfume is used to entice members of the opposite sex, a physically attractive source fits the product. In contrast, a characteristic of coffee is the difficulty of brewing a good cup, which isn't associated with physical attractiveness. Researchers have also found matching source and brand is particularly important when consumers are in a high involvement state.[21] Finally, another benefit of matching endorser to product is it leads to increased persistence in the attitudes consumers form as a result of the association.[22]

As discussed, the source characteristics of credibility (i.e., expertise, trustworthiness, and selectivity) and attractiveness affect purchase intentions. However, depending on the amount of fit between the endorser and the brand, this influence on purchase intentions may be strengthened or lessened. For example, Oprah Winfrey could endorse the shoe store DSW (Designer Shoe Warehouse) or Payless Shoe Source. Consumers should view her as a trustworthy spokesperson for both brands. However, because of her sophisticated,

Managerial principle 8.2

A good fit between an endorser and the brand will often increase consumer-purchase intentions.

high-class image, she has better fit with DSW than with Payless. In fact, if she chose to endorse Payless, some consumers may believe she's doing it simply for the money because the low-price brand doesn't fit her image.

The Impact of Sexually Suggestive Ads

How does sexually suggestive advertising affect consumer behavior? As one writer put it, "As our culture becomes increasingly sexualized, sexual discourse becomes more visible."[23]

Indeed, advertisers such as Victoria's Secret have turned up the steam a couple notches with hot underwear ads. In the United States, TV ads now regularly show models in their undergarments. As one ad researchers said, "Sex is everywhere. Advertisers are going to see what they can get away with on network TV."[24] Similarly, billboards for one brand of bras were placed in Great Britain, Germany, France and Italy that displayed a model clad in her underwear stretched sexily on a bed of grass. The billboard read, "Who said a woman can't get pleasure from something soft?" Such steamy ads have begun to draw protests. For example, a women's group in Mexico forced bra maker Playtex to put a dress on the model shown on billboards for Wonderbra.[25]

Academic research has shown sexy advertisements attract attention, enhance ad recall, and improve attitude toward the ad. However, responses to highly explicit ads can be negative. For example, one study found the presence of physically attractive, partially clad models positively influenced an automobile's image.[26] The same study also found if the erotic content of the ad was too high, it actually harmed **recall** of the ad when recall was measured a week after exposure to the ad.

Because of the increasing prevalence of male nudity in advertising, such as by the companies Hollister and Abercrombie & Fitch, researchers have begun analyzing its effects on consumer reactions. In one study, male and female respondents saw males in various states of dress (from fully dressed to suggestive to nude) modeling for body oil or a ratchet wrench set. The results paralleled the findings for female nudity—male consumers preferred ads in which the male models had on their clothes while females preferred suggestive and nude ads for the body oil product. However, when the wrench set was the product, full nudity turned off the women because the nudity had no relationship to the product, just as sexiness didn't sell coffee.[27]

Managerial principle 8.3
Use sexually suggestive advertising with the right audience and with the right product.

In sum, the following generalizations can be made about nudity in advertising. First, the nudity should be appropriate to the product. Second, increasing nudity draws attention to the ads and increases observers' arousal levels. Third, nude images decrease the cognitive processing of the brand and ad message because of distraction effects. Fourth, suggestive or nude models appeal more to the opposite sex.[28]

LIKABILITY OF THE SOURCE

Source likability refers to the positive or negative feelings consumers have toward a source of information. Likability is further defined as the degree of similarity in beliefs, attitudes, and behaviors between the source and the receiver.[29] You can think of likability with this question: Would I enjoy hanging out with this celebrity? If you answer yes, the endorser rates high on likability.

Endorsers are often selected based on a measure of likability captured in a Q Score, as mentioned in the chapter opening. Q Scores, which are taken annually on more than 5,000 celebrities, are a measure of the celebrity's likability among those who are familiar with the celebrity.[30] Likability alone is not enough to entice consumers. As discussed earlier, there should also be a match-up, or fit, between the endorser and the brand. For instance, Tim Duncan is an all-star NBA player for the San Antonio Spurs. Duncan is arguably a likable personality, although, compared with some other athletes, he's often called boring. Duncan fits well with any number of wholesome brands, such as Gatorade. However, if he decided to endorse a more "extreme" brand, such as Monster energy drink, consumers may believe his persona doesn't fit the brand. On the other hand, Olympic gold medalist Shaun White has a persona of being edgy and extreme. As such, White would likely be a good endorser for any extreme brand.

So, while likability is a key factor in selecting an endorser, fitting the brand is more important. Figure 8.5 illustrates the relationships among the attractiveness variables and customer behaviors.

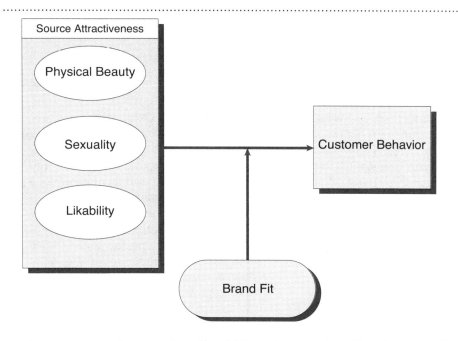

FIGURE 8.5
Source Attractiveness Model

To answer question two (i.e., Should I employ a highly attractive source?), we've discussed a number of key issues: physical attractiveness, sexual attractiveness, and likability. There's no Magic 8 Ball for selecting a good endorser. Firms must look at these characteristics individually and collectively to find the person who best fits the brand.

Managerial principle 8.4
Consumers are drawn to attractive endorsers. Attractiveness includes physical beauty, sexuality, and likability.

Source Meaningfulness

Sources of information also provide meanings to consumers. The connection between a source and a brand can transfer such meanings. The transfer of meaning from celebrity to product to consumer is diagramed in Figure 8.6. The figure presents a flowchart in which a celebrity plays a number of roles over his or her career.[31] Based on these roles, meanings become attached to the celebrity that are shared within a culture. As consumers buy the products endorsed by the celebrity, the meanings attached to the celebrity are transferred onto the consumer.

FIGURE 8.6
Transfer Meaning Model

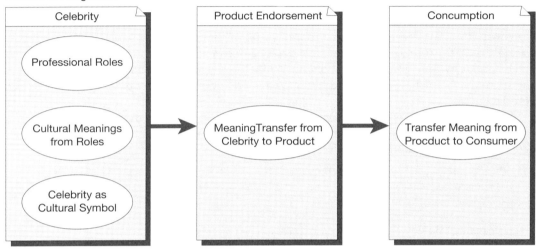

Let's take, for instance, Angelina Jolie, who's an Oscar-winning actress. Jolie is known for her roles in movies such as *Mr. and Mrs. Smith*, *Lara Croft: Tomb Raider*, and *Salt*. She's also known for her relationship with Brad Pitt and for her activism in encouraging others to adopt children from developing countries. Each of these roles, whether it be as an actress, a companion, or an advocate, is transferred to a brand she endorses and then to the consumer.

Two ads that transfer meaning to the consumer are endorsed by very different people: Drew Barrymore in one and Brett Favre and Dale Earnhardt Jr. in the other. Barrymore is known for her performance in *E.T. the Extra-Terrestrial* as a child and countless other movies over the years. By using Barrymore to endorse its makeup, Covergirl transfers her success to the buyer of Trublend products. In the second ad, athletes Favre and Earnhardt help transfer their success on the field or racetrack to Wrangler Jeans.

In sum, celebrities are cultural symbols. When a celebrity endorses a product in an advertisement, associations are formed so the culturally derived meanings may be transferred to the product. Finally, in the consumption phase, the meaning may be transferred from the product to the consumer. Thus, when consumers eat Oreos, some of the qualities of Peyton Manning may become symbolically attached to them.

Managerial principle 8.5
A celebrity's cultural meaning can be transferred to customers as they use the product the celebrity endorses.

Managerial Implications of Source Effects

A crucial decision for managers concerns what kind of source to use when developing advertising communications. The source of information is a vital component in delivering a message to an audience. The specific source used can also help a company position a product (e.g., consumers would perceive a brand promoted by Paris Hilton quite differently from a brand promoted by Kelly Clarkson). Careful market research studies should be performed to investigate audience reactions to the source and to track changes in reactions over time.

Finding a celebrity who's willing to make the endorsement and who's not already overexposed is difficult. In fact, the major advertising firm Ogilvy & Mather stopped using celebrities because of research showing the audience assumes the celebrity has been bought off.[32] Because of the problem of overexposure and the likelihood consumers discount the endorsement of celebrities, a premium is paid for the services of virgin endorsers.

One final managerial issue concerns whether hiring celebrity endorsers is worth it. One study investigated the impact of hiring a celebrity endorser on the stock price of companies. Interestingly, the research revealed that, while investors in the stock market sometimes reacted negatively to the hiring of a celebrity, overall, the action more frequently increased stock price. In sum, the market acts as though hiring celebrities will increase the profits of firms.[33] Table 8.2 provides an overview of key findings on the impact of source effects.

1.	Important source-effect variables include credibility, expertise, trust, selectivity, physical attractiveness, likability, meaning, and fit with the product.
2.	Source expertise has been found to have a greater impact on consumer responses than other source-effect variables.
3.	Sources with high credibility are more effective, enhance the advertiser's ability to use fear appeals, and inhibit the formation of counterarguments.
4.	In general, physically attractive people are more effective than less physically attractive people as sources.
5.	To maximize source effectiveness, the source and the product should be a good fit.
6.	Meanings derived from the characteristics of the source can be transferred to the product through their close association.
7.	The perceived characteristics and personality of the source interact with the nature of the product. Thus, in some circumstances, highly physically attractive or highly likable people may not be the most effective sources of information.

TABLE 8.2
Summary of Key Findings on Impact of Source Effects

MESSAGE CHARACTERISTICS—MESSAGE CONTENT

The effects of message content and construction on receivers have been intensively studied by researchers. **Message content** refers to the strategies that may be used to communicate an idea to an audience. Examples of such strategies include decisions of whether to use fear or humor in ads and whether to develop complex or simple messages. In contrast, **message construction** refers to the problem of how to physically construct a message. Answering the problem includes determining where to place information in a message to get maximum impact and how often to repeat information. Message content and message construction are highly relevant to differentiate brands from the

Social Media

The Changing World of News Gathering

As we discussed, a number of source characteristics play a role in persuading consumers. But what about the platform where the information is shared? The social media platforms of Facebook, Twitter, and so on have changed the landscape of how people get their news. Individuals are turning away from traditional media of television and radio and turning to many of these social media platforms. Facebook reports more than 1 billion users worldwide, and it manages 2.7 billion "likes" per day.

Social media has the power to change political outcomes. For instance, 37 percent of people ages eighteen to twenty-four years obtained information about the 2008 presidential election from social media. While social media may be quicker and more accessible than traditional media, it isn't necessarily more reliable. Forty-nine percent of people have heard false rumors on social media.[34]

With traditional media, reporters stake their reputation on credible storytelling. On the other hand, the individual creating or simply sharing a social media story often becomes anonymous as the story is passed along. A lie could be perpetuated to the point of becoming the "truth." So, as an author of this book, I ask you, how credible is information from social media?

competition. Issues in message content and construction are discussed in the sections that follow.

Developing Message Content

The logical first step in creating a message is to decide its content. That is, the sender must decide what signs to use to communicate meaning. Creating an effective message is an art. Next, we discuss ten approaches to developing message content. Table 8.3 summarizes these approaches.

TABLE 8.3
Types of Message Content

1.	*Rhetorical figure of speech*—using rhyme, puns, hyperbole, metaphor, irony, and paradox to increase interest and provide additional meaning to messages
2.	*Message complexity*—the decision of how much information to place in a message
3.	*Drawing conclusion*—the issue of whether to directly state the inference consumers are expected to obtain from the message (i.e., buy this product)
4.	*Comparative messages*—the question of whether to directly, indirectly, or not compare your brand to another brand
5.	*One-sided versus two-sided messages*—the issue of whether to present an audience with both sides of an issue
6.	*Fear appeals*—the decision of whether to develop a message that activates a fear response in consumers
7.	*Humor*—the decision of whether to employ humor in a message
8.	*Vivid versus abstract information*—the importance of using vivid and salient information in messages
9.	*Lectures versus dramas*—the decision of whether to persuade by having a source directly address the audience or by employing characters to indirectly address the audience by speaking to each other
10.	*Life themes*—the goal of developing messages around the critical values and goals that influence consumers at different stages of their lives

Using Rhetorical Figures of Speech The goal of rhetoric "is to discover the most effective way to express a thought in a given situation."[35] Examples of rhetorical figures of speech include rhyme, puns, hyperbole (e.g., exaggerated claims), metaphors, and irony. Issues of rhetoric are found in the development of all marketing messages, from advertisements to packaging to personal selling to public relations.

One reason to use rhetorical devices is to make otherwise dull prose more interesting. For example, consider the use of paradox. Paradox is a rhetorical figure of speech that refers to a statement that is self-contradictory, false, or impossible.[36] An example is when the insurance company Geico uses the tagline "It's so easy even a caveman can do it." Obviously, cavemen no longer exist, but this paradox gives the message some punch and humor.

It's important to recognize these rhetorical devices can be created visually as well as in verbal or written form. Absolut Vodka often uses metaphors to demonstrate its brand is hip and cool. Absolut is famous for mysteriously placing its unique bottle conspicuously in advertising images. For instance, one ad presented an egg frying on a hot, 110-degree sidewalk. The egg was in the shape of the unique Absolut bottle. In another campaign, the advertisement showed an overhead shot of a swimming pool. The pool was shaped like the Absolut bottle, and the logo was painted on the bottom of the pool.

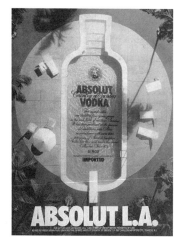

Message Complexity   From an information-processing perspective, for a message to have impact, the receiver must go through the exposure, attention, and comprehension stages. A factor that strongly influences comprehension is **message complexity**. If the information is too complex or, worse yet, presented in a garbled, confusing manner, receivers are less likely to comprehend and be persuaded by the information.[37]

Excessively high message complexity frequently results from attempts to place too much information in a communication. As noted in Chapter 4, consumers have a limited ability to process information. If too much information is given, they may become overloaded and react negatively. In the context of television commercials, the general rule is that no more than four major copy points can be communicated. If celebrity endorsers are used, even fewer bits of information can be processed by consumers because part of their cognitive capacity will be allocated to the endorser rather than to the message.[38]

A classic example of creating a simple message is the Wendy's tagline "Where's the beef?" That short and precise message told by an 81-year-old Clara Peller put Wendy's on the map. Another example is when Apple focused on the simplicity of its product in ads that featured an attractive man representing a Mac computer and a less attractive, clumsy man representing a generic PC brand. In the series of ads, Apple transformed a sometimes complex message of computer technology into a user-friendly tool. In one case, the PC man was having an Internet camera duct taped to his head. The Mac man explained that a camera comes standard on him. In this campaign, Apple kept every ad simple. Each ad stated a simple problem, such as attaching an Internet camera, and then offered an easy solution. This example also relates to the next issue of drawing conclusions.

Vivid versus Abstract Information   A well-established finding in psychology is that messages using vivid, concrete words tend to have greater impact on receivers than messages containing more abstract information.[39] **Vivid**

messages attract and hold attention. They also promote the receiver to use his or her imagination. As such, vivid messages are more likely to be placed into long-term memory and later recalled than more pallid information.

What makes information vivid? Three factors have been found to increase the vividness of messages. First, the extent to which the message has personal relevance, it will tend to have a greater impact. As the involvement level of the message increases, so, too, should its impact.

A second factor that increases the vividness of a message is concreteness. A concrete message gives a high degree of detailed, specific information about people, actions, and situations. Ivory soap used the tagline that its soap is 99 44/100 percent pure. While Ivory could easily claim 99 percent pure, by being so exact, Ivory tells the audience someone went to a great deal of work to verify the exact amount.

Managerial principle 8.6
Vivid messages remain in long-term memory longer than abstract messages.

Third, make the information as close as possible to the receiver in terms of time proximity, spatial proximity, and sensory proximity. Time proximity simply refers to using information that's as fresh and new as possible. For example, when a new product breakthrough occurs, managers should announce it as quickly as possible. Spatial proximity refers to the idea of placing information in a context that's linked as closely as possible to that experienced by the audience. Thus, if a product is targeted to one region of the country, television ads should be filmed in recognizable parts of that region. Sensory proximity refers to the concept of having the ideas in the message experienced firsthand by the audience or by someone else, such as an endorser, who can tell the audience what he or she experienced. One reason automobile salespeople are so eager to get you to drive a car is to have you obtain firsthand sensory experiences of the car.

Drawing Conclusions   Another question regarding the development of message content is whether the communicator should draw a conclusion for the audience. In a message, the communicator may generate a number of arguments that support a particular position. These arguments may logically build on one another and lead to an inference the audience should buy the product. Thus, an advertiser might state, "Our brand is built better, will last longer, and is priced lower than other brands." The conclusion could be drawn that the consumer should buy the product. However, the question is really this: Should the communication expressly draw the conclusion and tell the audience to go out and buy the product or let the audience draw the conclusion itself?

Managerial principle 8.7
Draw conclusions when the audience isn't highly involved or the message is complex.

Research on the effects of **drawing conclusions** indicates that whether or not to leave advertisements open-ended depends on the complexity of the message and the involvement of the audience.[40] If the message is relatively complex or the audience isn't involved in the topic, a conclusion should be drawn in the message. In contrast, if the audience is highly involved and the message is strong, without being too complex, it's better to let the audience make the inference.[41]

Comparative Messages   A **comparative message** is one in which the communicator compares the positive and negative aspects of his or her position to the positive and negative aspects of a competitor's position. The approach is frequently used by advertisers who may explicitly identify one or more competitors for the purpose of claiming superiority over them.[42]

Since the early 1970s, the Federal Trade Commission has encouraged the use of comparative advertising out of the belief that naming a competitor would assist consumers in evaluating a claim of superiority.[43] Comparative advertising is useful for small companies that are trying to enter a market, particularly if their claims are based on research done by independent third parties.[44] The opinion of many marketing managers was expressed by a Coca-Cola executive who said, "Comparative ads are good when you're new, but when you're the standard, it just gives a lot of free publicity to your competitors."[45] As an example, Red Bull shouldn't compare itself with, say, Amp or Full Throttle. However, both Amp and Full Throttle may find it advantageous to position themselves against the market leader.

Comparative ads can also be used to position and differentiate a brand. Consequently, in our energy drink example, comparative ads may be appropriate. By directly comparing a low-market-share product with the dominant brand, managers can anchor it close to the position of the dominant brand in a consumer's mind.[46] Using the product category of toothpaste, researchers found comparative advertisements were superior to noncomparative ads in anchoring a new brand closer to a dominant brand and in creating a clearer brand image. Thus, direct comparisons between an unfamiliar brand and a market leader act to reposition the unfamiliar brand so consumers perceive it to be more similar to the market leader.[47]

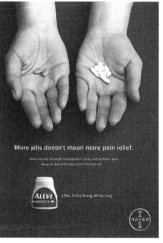

More pills doesn't mean more pain relief.

Two types of comparative advertisements have been identified. In **direct comparative advertisements**, one brand is compared specifically with another brand. An example is found in the ad campaign where Aleve compares itself to Tylenol. The message claims you can get just as much pain relief from taking two Aleve pills as to taking six Tylenol pills. This message was designed to show the benefits of Aleve over Tylenol. One ad uses great visuals of two hands holding the needed Aleve versus Tylenol to eliminate your pain.

In **indirect comparative advertisements**, the comparison brand isn't specifically mentioned. Rather, the ad compares the brand indirectly to "competitors." Deciding which type of comparative ad to use depends on the market share of the brand. One study found low-market-share brands should compare themselves directly to the market leader. In contrast, moderate-market-share brands should compare themselves indirectly to avoid mentioning the name of the competitor and confusing consumers. Finally, the results revealed market-share leaders should generally avoid comparative ads entirely.[48]

In sum, several conclusions can be drawn from the research on comparative advertising:

1. Comparative ads can be effective for low-market-share or new brands in reducing perceived differences with the leading brands.[49]

2. Moderate-market-share brands should use only indirect comparative advertising when comparisons are made to other moderate-share brands.

3. To differentiate its brand from another, a company should compare itself to the competitor on important attributes.

4. As a general statement, market leaders should avoid comparative advertising.[50]

One-Sided versus Two-Sided Messages Another communications issue concerns whether to present an audience with one or both sides of an issue. Research on the effectiveness of two-sided messages has shown it can be an effective persuasion technique. Presenting both sides of an argument gives the appearance of fairness and may lower the tendency of consumers to argue against the message and the source. Particularly in cases when the audience is unfriendly, when it knows opposition arguments exist, or when it's likely to hear arguments from the opposition, two-sided communications may be effective.[51] Because comparative ads frequently give information on both favorable and unfavorable aspects of a brand, they also represent two-sided messages.

Two-sided messages, however, aren't always the most effective. In some instances, giving only one side of an issue may result in the greatest attitude change. When the audience is friendly, when it's not likely to hear the other side's arguments, when it's not involved in the issue, or when it's not highly educated, one-sided messages may be more effective. In such instances, presenting the other side to a message may simply confuse the audience and weaken the effects of the arguments for the issue.[52]

Fear Appeals In a **fear appeal**, the communicator seeks to activate consumer anxiety by identifying one or more risks that can occur in the consumer environment. Each of the sources of risk identified in Chapter 5 can be employed to create fear appeals. For example, the risk of bodily harm has been used to generate fear by companies that sell the safety of burglar alarms and by auto manufacturers that advertise the crash protection of their cars. Insurance companies use the fear of financial risk. A variety of companies effectively use social risk. Various companies selling deodorants, dandruff shampoo, and laundry detergents have successfully used social risk fear appeals. By buying their products, consumers can avoid "awful" maladies such as ring around the collar, can raise their hand with the certainly of not having unsightly underarm sweat, and can scratch their heads without people snickering over their dandruff.

For fear appeals to be effective, researchers have found the message should contain one or more of the following types of information:

1. Give specific instructions on how to cope with and solve the problem.
2. Provide an indication that following the instructions will solve the problem.
3. Avoid giving high-fear messages to audiences that feel highly threatened and vulnerable to the threat.
4. Avoid giving high-fear messages to audiences that are low in self-esteem.

Managerial principle 8.8
When creating a fear appeal, be careful to not induce too much fear in consumers.

Recent research suggests at least a medium level of fear is necessary to change a person's behavior. An interesting finding points to television as the best medium to use to induce behavior change. Also the effects of both visual and audio sensations seem to work together to encourage a behavior change.[53]

Humor Like the use of fear appeals, the effectiveness of inserting **humor in messages** has been debated among marketing researchers. What is clear, however, is that humor is used frequently in advertisements. For instance, over half of the advertisements during the Super Bowl are humor based.

What makes something funny? One theory states humor results from incongruity or deviations from expectations.[54] For example, an advertisement from Cat's Pride for its Fresh & Light Kitty Litter shows a woman and her cat relaxing in a spa setting. The message goes on to say, "Relax. Lifting litter isn't the workout it used to be." The deviation from expectations is demonstrated by the cat relaxing with cucumber slices on its eyes.

A second humorous ad is demonstrated by Old Spice. Green Bay Packer Greg Jennings used Old Spice in a series of tongue-in-cheek ads related to controlling your smell.

Humor can result in unanticipated negative effects, however. First, humor can reduce the comprehension of the message. For example, one study compared the recall of ad content in humorous ads to that in serious ads. The results showed recall was significantly better in the serious ads.[55]

Second, using humor may shorten the life span of an ad. Particularly if the humor is of a gag type, it may quickly fade and lose its positive effects.

Third, humorous ads can also have unanticipated negative effects on various audiences. For example, ads for Budweiser beer were shown in Great Britain. In one, a truck driver for Chieftain Cement walks into a bar crowded with Native Americans. The driver has a ghostly pale face and is quite out of place in the bar. Just as the scene is about to turn ugly, the driver dunks his head into a pail of water. It turns out he's also Native American and was only covered with cement dust. The scene ends with the man gulping down a bottle of beer. While the English loved the ad, Native Americans hated it because it encouraged the stereotype of alcoholism among their group.[56] The ad executives were quite oblivious to the problem and astonished by the furor it caused.

Humor's negative effects are partly explained by findings that different audiences may react in diverse ways to the same humor message. Females may be more likely than males to react more negatively to the injection of humor in ads. Further, in our current culture, specific groups may react negatively to advertising based any number of issues, such as sex, race, national origin, personality, and social attitudes.[57]

Managerial principle 8.9
When using humor, know your audience!

Despite these potential negative effects, humor can influence attitudes and behaviors.[58]

One researcher investigated the effect of a large number of humor studies and found humor significantly enhances attitude toward the advertisement, attention toward the ad, and positive affect. There are three important findings in humor research. First, because humor places people in a good mood, it should lower counterarguments to the message. Second, humor can attract attention to an ad and increase its recall and comprehension. Third, the strongest effect of humor is it enhances the liking for the advertisement.[59] As described in the previous chapter, attitude toward the ad directly impacts attitude toward the product.

Two additional points are important for understanding the effects of humor on consumers. First, the humor should be related to the product or

Managerial principle 8.10
Humorous ads are best
employed to reinforce positive attitudes.

situation in some way. Second, the effects of humor interact with the prior
brand evaluation of consumers to influence attitudes.[60] A study created either
humorous or non-humorous ads for a pen. In addition, prior evaluations of
the pen were varied by giving fictitious *Consumer Reports* ratings of the pens.
Some respondents rated the pen very positively and others rated it negatively. After seeing the ads, respondents indicated their attitude toward the ad,
brand attitude, and purchase intentions. The results revealed that when the
ad was humorous and their prior evaluations were positive, their attitudes
and purchase intentions increased substantially. However, when the ad was
humorous and their prior evaluations were negative, their attitudes and purchase intentions plummeted. In contrast, the opposite pattern emerged for the
serious ads. When prior evaluations were negative, attitudes and purchase
intentions increased when a serious ad was used and decreased when a humorous ad was used. Figure 8.7 is a diagram of the effect of humor on product
evaluation.

FIGURE 8.7
The Effect of Humor on
Product Evaluation

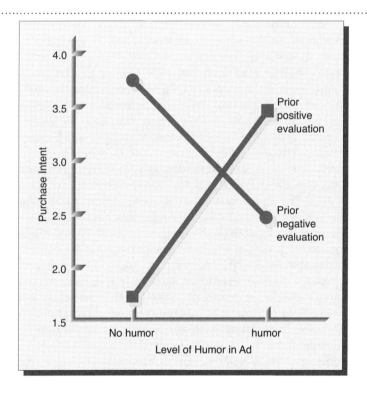

Lectures versus Dramas   A **lecture** occurs when a source speaks directly
to the audience in an attempt to inform and persuade.[61] It's like an oration in
which evidence is presented and arguments made. We frequently see lectures
in TV ads. Here, a source talks to the audience and gives information about
the product. In contrast to a lecture, in a **drama**, the characters speak to each
other and not to the audience. The viewer is an eavesdropper who observes an
imaginary setting that concerns a product or service.

When a person receives a lecture, facts are given, and the consumer recognizes a persuasion attempt is unfolding. In such cases, characteristics of the
source become extremely important, and the advertiser must be concerned

with the types of cognitive responses developed by the audience. Dramas work through a different mechanism. Because dramas are stories about the world, observational learning occurs. Viewers learn from the lessons revealed by the models in the communication. When a commercial drama rings true, the consumer is drawn into it and develops conclusions that may be applied to everyday life. As a result, fewer counterarguments emerge.

Lectures have the advantage of presenting information in a highly condensed form. However, they can frequently be dry and boring and spur counter-argumentation. In contrast, dramas have the potential to increase audience interest by creating emotional responses and by potentially transforming the meaning of using a product. **Transformational advertising** is the attempt to cause a consumer to associate the experience of using a product with a set of psychological characteristics not typically associated with the use of a product.[62] For example, an advertisement in which a woman is swept off her feet by an impassioned lover after getting the dishes squeaky clean is attempting to transform the experience of washing dishes. Normally, one doesn't associate sex with dishwashing. Such a commercial attempts to transform the experience by giving it a new psychological meaning.

When successful, transformational ads involve the audience emotionally in the advertisement. They change how the audience thinks and feels about the product or service advertised. The marketing of fragrances is largely based on attempts to transform the dabbing of something on one's skin into a romantic, sensual experience. In fact, one goal of such ads seems to be to transform a woman (man) into a gorgeous (handsome) creature having tremendous allure to the opposite sex.[63]

Researchers have begun the process of investigating the effects of dramas and lectures on consumer responses. In one study, respondents were shown ads for an automobile that employed either a lecture or a drama format. The lecture format resulted in more counter-arguments. In addition, respondents seeing the lecture ad revealed much less empathy and self-participation with the events in the ad.[64]

Researchers have found dramas are associated with the expression of greater amounts of feelings and less counter-argumentation. In addition, drama ads increase the respondents' perceptions of the authenticity of the commercial and their empathy toward the ad. In sum, respondents process lectures logically and dramas emotionally. Thus, effective lectures depended on the quality of the arguments overcoming the counter-argumentation that results. In contrast, effective dramas work to the extent they involve consumers emotionally and to the extent they seem authentic and create empathy.[65]

Life Themes **Life themes** represent critical values and goals that influence consumers at different stages of their lives. Life themes influence beliefs, attitudes, and behaviors because consumers interpret communications from within the perspective of their own lives.[66] Consider the copy in an advertisement for Georgia-Pacific that appeared in *Newsweek* magazine:

> *You've remade yourself a hundred times, searching for what would fit, and last. College kid, philosopher, James Dean wannabe. Now you're looking at an ad for vinyl siding and it is stirring you to imagine new ways of remaking your living space. Would you say your interests have evolved?*

The ad then identifies one of vinyl siding's key attributes: it's low hassle because it doesn't need to be repainted. Targeted to long-time homeowners (middle-class people at least fifty years old), the ad connects vinyl siding to their current life theme (i.e., wanting to minimize hassle and future costs when they live on a fixed retirement income). While the life theme appeals to older consumers, it's completely inappropriate for younger people.

From a managerial perspective, it's important to identify the life themes that influence the thinking of important market segments. By linking an advertisement to a life theme (e.g., freedom, achievement, or the avoidance of hassle mentioned above), consumers' levels of attention and involvement increase. In addition, more positive attitudes toward the ad will be created.

A final comment must be made about message content. There are many more types of messages than identified here. For example, advertisers can employ guilt appeals.[67] Even intentional silence in a TV ad represents a type of message.[68]

MESSAGE CHARACTERISTICS—MESSAGE STRUCTURE

While communicators must worry about message content, they must also be concerned with how the messages are structured. **Message structure** refers to how the source organizes the content of the message. For example, one major issue concerns where in the message important information should be placed. Another structural problem concerns how many times key pieces of information should be repeated in a message.

Primacy and Recency Effects   Primacy and recency effects refer to the relative impact of information placed either at the beginning or the end of a message. A **primacy effect** occurs when material early in the message has the most influence. A **recency effect** occurs when material at the end of the message has the most influence. The question is not trivial. Whether in a television commercial or in a formal presentation by a salesperson, the communicator wants to ensure each piece of information has the maximum impact on the receiver. In addition, primacy and recency effects can occur when a series of messages is received. For example, when a number of commercials appear in succession on television, do those at the beginning, middle, or end of the sequence have the most impact?

Some consistent findings are beginning to emerge on primacy and recency effects. First, over time, primacy effects have more impact than recency effects. The material heard early in the message tends to be persuasive for the simple reason that it's heard first.[69] Second, the primacy effect particularly occurs to a larger extent for verbal material, such as that in a radio advertisement, than for visual material found in a print ad.[70]

Managerial principle 8.11
Put your most important information at the beginning and at the end of the message.

One finding can be stated unequivocally, however. Material presented in the middle of a message is relatively poorly remembered and has the least impact. This finding may be one rationale for the plethora of fifteen-second commercials now on television. In the early years of TV, the majority of ads were one minute long. Because the material in the middle is lost, the advertisers might as well shorten the ads. Research on serial learning presented in Chapter 4 demonstrates the greater difficulty in retaining information placed in the middle of lists of material to be learned. Therefore, communicators should try to avoid placing the important parts of a message in the middle of a communication.

Repetition Effects In Chapter 5, we noted how the repetition of information is required for learning to take place. With this knowledge in mind, one must ask how many times the information should be repeated. Past research suggests as few as three exposures to an advertisement may be sufficient; however, with the abundance of messages through social media and other outlets, we suggest this number should be increased to around six.

Too much repetition will result in increasingly negative responses, a phenomenon called **advertising wearout**. Too much repetition can cause negative attitudes toward the ad. Recently, researchers found familiar brands are less susceptible to wearout than unfamiliar brands.[71] Advertising wearout was found in one study where members of church groups received one, three, or five exposures to an advertisement for a fictitious toothpaste during a one-hour television show. The results showed the number of counterarguments to the commercials increased as the number of repetitions increased.[72]

Sophisticated advertisers, however, rarely present the same commercial over and over. Instead, they create a series of ads that carry the same basic message. In one study, researchers tested such an approach by slightly varying the content of each ad. In this study, the number of positive cognitive responses increased and the number of negative cognitive responses decreased as the message was repeated.[73] The variations in ad execution substantially improved the recall of the ads that were repeated without causing wearout.[74] In addition, consumers were more resistant to attack ads by competitors.[75] Finally, researchers have found if exposures to repetitive ads are voluntary, distributed over time, made in the presence of ads by competitors, and made in the cluttered environment found in the real world, repetitive ads improve top-of-mind awareness and brand choice.[76]

Two-factor theory explains the effects of message repetition. The theory proposes that two psychological processes are operating as people receive repetitive messages. In one process, the repetition of a message causes a reduction in uncertainty and an increase in learning about the stimulus, resulting in a positive response.[77] However, in the other process, boredom begins to occur with each repetition. At some point, the tedium overtakes the positive effects and the receiver begins to react negatively to the ad. Two-factor theory suggests that, to avoid the negative effects of boredom, the communicator should vary the ad with each repetition. Figure 8.8 diagrams the relationships proposed by two-factor theory.[78]

Lists versus Narratives Another structural issue concerns whether the information in a print advertisement should use a list format (i.e., key points are bulleted) or a narrative format (i.e., a story is told in paragraph form). Research on the topic indicates attitude toward the messages were improved when the narrative form was used. For example, if a travel agency describes the experiences you'll have on a vacation, it's better to use a narrative than list the points in a bulleted format. The effect is particularly strong when negative information about the trip is included.[79]

Managerial principle 8.12
Change the message so it stays fresh and the audience pays attention to it.

FIGURE 8.8
Two-Factor Theory

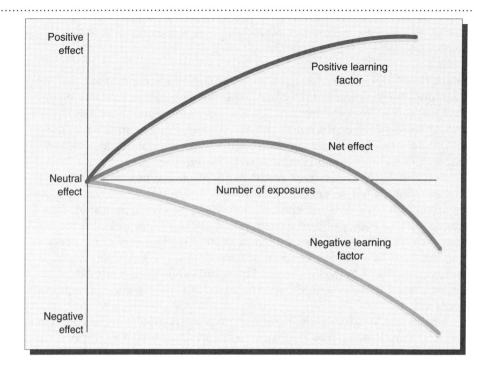

THE MANAGERIAL IMPLICATIONS OF PERSUASIVE COMMUNICATIONS

The principles and concepts derived from the study of persuasive communications have applications to responsive marketing (RESPonsive Marketing) cycle elements.

Research

Market research must be employed to identify in advance how a target market perceives the likability, credibility, and meaningfulness of sources. Research is also required prior to using strong fear appeals. In particular, the degree to which the audience feels threatened must be ascertained because members who feel too threatened will react poorly to strong fear appeals. Similarly, low self-esteem audiences react negatively to strong fear appeals. As a general rule, marketers should do pilot testing to identify how the target market responds to sources of information and to the messages developed.

Environmental Analysis

In order to decide which type of comparative advertisement to employ, managers need to analyze the competitive environment. If one's product is the brand leader, comparative ads should be avoided. In contrast, if your brand lags far behind the market leaders, the relationships suggest direct comparative ads are warranted. The regulatory environment should also be carefully examined when deciding on message content. In particular, different nations have different rules concerning the use of sexually explicit and comparative ads. Finally, the cultural and subcultural environments should be examined in order to identify potential reactions to the use of sexually explicit ads and the meanings attached to different celebrities who may be employed as message sources.

Segmentation

Divergent segments of consumers may require different sources of information and message content. For example, when targeting heterosexual men with sexually explicit advertising, female models should be employed. In contrast, females respond better when male models are employed. Similarly, consumers with higher levels of expertise on a topic can be given more complex messages than those with lower levels of expertise. Another example involves creating stronger fear appeals for high self-esteem consumers than for low self-esteem consumers. As a general statement, it's critical for marketers to develop a full understanding of the characteristics of divergent segments in order to select the best source, message, and channels to communicate most persuasively.

Positioning

The development of persuasive communications must be based on the positioning and differentiation strategies of the firm. For example, if the strategy is to position a brand as fun, exciting, and offbeat, advertisers should use a drama format in which attractive models are engaged in fun, exciting, and offbeat activities. Conversely, if the strategy is to position the brand as decreasing the risk of an important problem, a fear appeal message communicated by a credible source in a lecture format may be most appropriate.

Marketing Mix

The development of marketing communications is the major role of the promotional strategy component of the marketing mix. In particular, the selection of sources of information, messages, and channel through which the information flows is critical to advertising and public relations.

SUMMARY

How credible does an endorser have to be?

The general model of communications consists of a number of components, including source, message, medium, receiver, feedback, noise, and environmental context. In this chapter, three major source characteristics were identified. The first characteristic, source credibility, is the extent to which the audience perceives the sender to have expertise and trustworthiness. Highly credible sources have been found to produce greater attitude and behavioral changes in response to a communication. Highly credible sources may enhance the effectiveness of fear appeals and lower the counterarguments of audiences. However, for audiences already favorable to a topic, moderate credibility sources show some evidence of being more effective.

Should I employ a highly attractive source?

The second source characteristic is physical attractiveness. In general, research shows that physically attractive communicators are more successful than unattractive sources. However, managers should be careful not to mistake a sexually suggestive communicator for a physically attractive source. In some instances, using sexually suggestive ads can be counterproductive.

Likability, the third major characteristic, is the extent to which the source creates positive or negative feelings in the audience. Research evidence on the persuasive impact of likable and unlikable sources is mixed, and additional work is necessary before firm conclusions can be drawn on its impact.

How should the message be delivered?

Characteristics of the message are another important dimension of the communications process. Messages may have differential impacts depending on their content and on their structure. One content factor is the complexity of the message. Other content factors include whether conclusions are drawn, whether comparative messages are provided, whether the messages are one-sided or two-sided, whether fear appeals or humorous appeals are used, whether concrete or abstract information is included in the message, and whether a drama or lecture format is used.

How should the message be structured?

When studying message structure, the consumer researcher should focus on whether consumers may be influenced by primacy or recency effects. Another structural factor to consider is the amount of repetition required to influence the consumer. Repetition can enhance the consumer's memory toward the advertisement and brand. However, too much repetition can create boredom for the consumer and cause negative feelings toward the brand.

KEY TERMS

advertising wearout	indirect comparative advertisements	selectivity
cognitive responses	lecture	sign
communication	life themes	social identity theory
communications model	match-up effect	source
comparative message	message complexity	source characteristics
direct comparative advertisements	message construction	source credibility
drama	message content	source expertise
drawing conclusions	message structure	source likability
fear appeal	primacy effect	source trustworthiness
halo effect	recall	transformational advertising
humor in messages	recency effect	two-factor theory
		vivid messages

REVIEW QUESTIONS

1. Draw the communications model presented in the text. Briefly discuss each of the components of the model.

2. Identify six of the methods for varying message content presented in the text.

3. What are the reasons for and against using comparative advertisements?

4. When should a communicator consider using a two-sided message? A one-sided message?

5. What are the elements a message should have to be an effective fear appeal?

6. Identify the advantages and disadvantages of using humor in messages.

7. What are three factors that tend to make messages more vivid?

8. Identify a potential theoretical explanation for why advertising wearout occurs.

9. What are the basic source characteristics identified in the text?

10. What are the components of source credibility?

11. What are the benefits of using highly credible sources?

12. What are the benefits and liabilities of using sexually explicit ads?

13. What are the differential communications effects of lectures and dramas?

14. What is transformational advertising?

DISCUSSION QUESTIONS

1. Briefly describe a television ad, a print ad, and a billboard ad. Using the communications model, discuss each of the advertisements. (What source characteristics and message techniques are being used?)

2. Identify one excellent and one poor example of television ads that use celebrity endorsers. Discuss the factors that influence the effectiveness of the ads.

3. Write a television ad for your university. Create two versions—a lecture approach and a drama approach.

4. You're the account executive for an advertising firm working on developing a comparative advertising campaign for the Ford Mustang. The Mustang's major competitors are other so-called pony cars, such as the Camaro, Firebird, Eclipse, and Prelude. Sketch out a print advertisement that uses a comparative ad format. What things should you consider when developing the ad?

5. Identify three brands or types of products or services you believe should use one-sided messages in their advertising and three you believe should use two-sided messages. Explain your answers.

6. Go through magazines and find a print ad that uses a fear appeal. Critique the ad using the criteria that have been identified as necessary for the creation of good fear appeals.

7. While you're watching television, identify a commercial that uses humor. Discuss the effectiveness of the advertisement. What do you think were the advertising goals of the sponsors of the ad?

8. Write the copy for an existing print ad using highly concrete words and imagery.

ENDNOTES

[1] TigerWoods.com, accessed December 16, 2015, http://www.tigerwoods.com.

[2] Ron Sirak, "The Gold Digest 50, the Rich Get Richer: The Money on Tour Gets another Boost (and then There's That Tidy Retirement Fund). No Wonder Tiger's Approaching $1 Billion," *Golf Digest*, accessed January 7, 2011, http://www.golfdigest.com/magazine/2008-02/gd50.

[3] Terry Lefton, "Penalty Drop: Tiger Woods Plummets on Sports Q Scores List," *Street and Smith's Sports Business Journal*, accessed December 16, 2015, http://www.sportsbusinessjournal.com/article/65957.

[4] Ibid.

[5] Scott A. Hawkins and Stephen J. Hoch, "Low Involvement Learning: Memory without Evaluation," *Journal of Consumer Research* (September 1992): 212–226.

[6] C. I. Hovland and I. L. Janis, *Personality and Persuasibility* (New Haven, CT: Yale University Press, 1959).

[7] Terrence Shimp, "Methods of Commercial Presentation Employed by National Television Advertisers," *Journal of Advertising* 5 (Fall 1976): 30–36.

[8] Thomas Barrabi, "Top 10 Sports Endorsements Deals: Michael Jordan Still the No. 1 Richest Athlete Endorser after Kevin Durant Offer, *International Business Times*, August 21, 2014, accessed December 16, 2015, http://www.ibtimes.com/top-10-sports-endorsements-deals-michael-jordan-still-no-1-richest-athlete-endorser-after-1665548.

[9] "Celebrities Paid Thousands for Endorsement Tweets," *CBSNews*, accessed December 16, 2015, http://www.cbsnews.com/8301-31749_162-57319886-10391698/celebrities-paid-thousands-for-endorsement-tweets/.

[10] Readers should note that not all researchers define trust in the manner described here. In some cases, trust has been defined as including expertise within its bounds. That is, trust is defined in the same manner as I have defined credibility in the chapter. For an example, see Christine Moorman, Rohit Deshpande, and Gerald Zaltman, "Factors Affecting Trust in Market Research Relationships," *Journal of Marketing* 57 (January 1993): 81–101.

[11] Forbes, "The World's Highest_Paid Athletes, (2015) (Accessed December 23, 2015, http://www.forbes.com/athletes/list/#tab:overall_header:endorsements_sortreverse:true.

[12] Josh Wiener and John C. Mowen, "The Impact of Product Recalls on Consumer Perceptions," *Mobius: The Journal of the Society of Consumer Affairs Professionals in Business* (Spring 1985): 18–21.

[13] David J. Moore, John C. Mowen, and Richard Reardon, "Multiple Sources in Advertising Appeals: When Product Endorsers Are Paid by the Advertising Sponsor," *Journal of the Academy of Marketing Science* 22 (1994): 234–243.

[14] Peter Wright, "Cognitive Processes Mediating Acceptance of Advertising," *Journal of Marketing Research* 10 (February 1973): 5–62.

[15] Shelly Chaiken, "Communicator Physical Attractiveness and Persuasion," *Journal of Personality and Social Psychology* 37 (August 1979): 1387–1397.

[16] Karen Dion, E. Berscheid, and E. Walster, "What Is Beautiful Is Good," *Journal of Personality and Social Psychology* 24 (December 1972): 285–290.

[17] Kathleen A. Martin, Adrienne R. Sinden, and Julie C. Fleming, "Inactivity May Be Hazardous to Your Image: The Effects of Exercise Participation on Impression Formation," *Journal of Sport & Exercise Psychology* 22 (2000): 283–291.

[18] Jane E. Dutton, Janet M. Dukerich, and Celia V. Harquail, "Organizational Images and Member Identification," *Administrative Science Quarterly* 39 (1994): 239–263.

[19] Kathleen Debevec and Jerome Kernan, "More Evidence on the Effects of Presenter's Physical Attractiveness: Some Cognitive, Affective, and Behavioral Consequences," in *Advances in Consumer Research*, vol. 11, ed. Thomas Kinnear (Provo, UT: Association for Consumer Research, 1984),127–132. For additional information on the impact of attractiveness, see also Paul Speck, David Schumann, and Craig Thompson, "Celebrity Endorsements Scripts, Schema, and Roles: Theoretical Framework and Preliminary Tests," in *Advances in Consumer*

Research, vol. 15, ed. Michael Houston (Provo, UT: Association for Consumer Research, 1988), 69–76.

20 Michael Baker and Gilbert Churchill, "The Impact of Physically Attractive Models on Advertising Evaluations," *Journal of Marketing Research* 14 (November 1977): 538–555.

21 Amma Kirmani and Baba Shiv, "Effects of Source Congruity on Brand Attitudes and Beliefs: The Moderating Role of Issue-Relevant Elaboration," *Journal of Consumer Psychology* 7 (1998): 25–47.

22 Jaideep Sengupta, Ronald C. Goodstein, and David S. Boninger, "All Cues Are Not Created Equal: Obtaining Attitude Persistence Under Low-Involvement Conditions," *Journal of Consumer Research* 23 (March 1997): 351–361.

23 Feona Attwood, "Fashion and Passion: Marketing Sex to Women," *Sexualities* 8, no. 4 (2005): 392–406.

24 Pat Sloan, "Underwear Ads Caught in Bind over Sex Appeal," *Advertising Age*, July 8, 1996, 27.

25 Juliana Koranteng and Richard Bruner, "Sexy Bras Drawing Protests," *Advertising Age* (July 1996): 16.

26 M. Steadman, "How Sexy Illustrations Affect Brand Recall," *Journal of Advertising Research* 9 (March 1969): 15–19. See also Robert Chestnut, Charles LaChance, and Amy Lubitz, "The Decorative Female Model: Sexual Stimuli and the Recognition of Advertisements," *Journal of Advertising* 6 (Fall 1977): 11–14.

27 Penny M. Simpson, Steve Horton, and Gene Brown, "Male Nudity in Advertisements: A Modified Replication and Extension of Gender and Product Effects," *Journal of Academy of Marketing Science* 24 (Summer 1996): 257–262.

28 Stephen M. Smith, Curtis P. Haugtvedt, John M. Jadrich, and Mark R. Anton, "Understanding Responses to Sex Appeals in Advertising: An Individual Difference Approach," in *Advances in Consumer Research*, vol. 22, ed. Frank R. Kardes and Mita Sugan (Provo, UT: Association for Consumer Research, 1995), 735–739.

29 Jean-Charles Chebat, Michael Laroche, Daisy Baddoura, and Pierre Filiatrault, "Effects of Source Likability on Attitude Change through Message Repetition," in *Advances in Consumer Research*, vol. 20, ed. Leigh McAlister and Michael L. Rothschild (Provo, UT: Association for Consumer Research, 1993), 353–358.

30 Roobina Ohanian, "The Impact of Celebrity Spokespersons' Image on Consumers' Intentions to Purchase," *Journal of Advertising Research* (1991): 46–54.

31 Grant McCracken, "Who Is the Celebrity Endorser? Cultural Foundations of the Endorsement Process," *Journal of Consumer Research* 16 (December 1989): 310–321.

32 David Ogilvy, *Ogilvy on Advertising* (New York: Vintage Books, 1983).

33 Jagdish Agrawal and Wagner A. Kamakura, "The Economic Worth of Celebrity Endorsers: An Event Study Analysis," *Journal of Marketing* 59 (July 1995): 56–62.

34 "Are Social Networking Sites Good for Our Society," *ProCon*, accessed December 16, 2015, http://socialnetworking.procon.org/.

35 Edward F. McQuarrie and David Glen Mick, "Figures of Rhetoric in Advertising Language," *Journal of Consumer Research* 22 (March 1996): 424–438.

36 Ibid.

37 Alice Eagly, "The Comprehensibility of Persuasive Arguments as a Determinant of Opinion Change," *Journal of Personality and Social Psychology* 29 (1974): 758–773.

38 For more information on the impact of message complexity, see Tina M. Lowrey, "The Effects of Syntactic Complexity on Advertising Persuasiveness," *Journal of Consumer Psychology* 7, no. 2 (1998):187–206.

39 This section relies heavily on material found in Richard Nisbett and Lee Ross, *Human Inference: Strategies and Shortcomings of Social Judgment* (Englewood Cliffs, NJ: Prentice Hall, 1980).

40 Bertram Raven and Jeffrey Rubin, *Social Psychology* (New York: John Wiley, 1983).

41 Alan G. Sawyer and Daniel J. Howard, "Effects of Omitting Conclusions in Advertisements to Involved and Uninvolved Audiences," *Journal of Marketing Research* 28 (November 1991): 467–474.

42 Kanti V. Prasad, "Communications Effectiveness of Comparative Advertising: A Laboratory Analysis," *Journal of Marketing Research* 13 (May 1976):128–137.

43 Gerald Gorn and Charles Weinberg, "The Impact of Comparative Advertising on Perception and Attitude: Some Positive Findings," *Journal of Consumer Research* 11 (September 1984): 719–727.

44 William Wilkie and Paul Farris, "Comparison Advertising: Problems and Potential," *Journal of Marketing* 39 (November 1975): 7–15.

45 "Creating a Mass Market for Wine," *Business Week*, March 15, 1982, 108–118.

46 Cornelia Droge and Rene Darmon, "Associative Positioning Strategies through Comparative Advertising: Attribute versus Overall Similarity Approaches," *Journal of Marketing Research* 24 (November 1987): 377–388.

47 For a more detailed look at comparative ads, see Cornelia Pechmann and S. Ratneshwar, "The Use of Comparative Advertising for Brand Positioning: Association versus Differentiation," *Journal of Consumer Research* 18 (September 1991): 145–160.

48 Cornelia Pechmann and David W. Stewart, "The Effects of Comparative Advertising on Attention, Memory, and Purchase Intentions," *Journal of Consumer Research* 17 (September 1990): 180–191.

49 Gerald J. Gorn and Charles B. Weinberg, "The Impact of Comparative Advertising on Perception and Attitude: Some Positive Findings," *Journal of Consumer Research* 11 (September 1984): 719–727.

50 This conclusion was challenged in the following research: Paul W. Miniard, Michael J. Barone, Randall L. Rose, and Kenneth C. Manning, "A Re-Examination of the Relative Persuasiveness of Comparative and Noncomparative Advertising," in *Advances in Consumer Research*, ed. Chris T. Allen and Deborah Roedder John (Provo, UT: Association for Consumer Research, 1994), 299–303.

51 See, for example, the following studies: Russell Jones and Jack Brehm, "Persuasiveness of One- and Two-Sided Communications As a Function of Awareness: There Are Two Sides," *Journal of Experimental Social Psychology* 6 (1970): 47–56; Alan G. Sawyer, "The Effects of Repetition of Refutational and Supportive Advertising Appeals," *Journal of Marketing Research* 10 (February 1973): 23–33; and Michael Kamins and Henry Assael, "Two-Sided versus One-Sided Appeals: A Cognitive Perspective on Argumentation, Source Derogation on Argumentation, Source Derogation, and the Effect of Disconfirming Trial on Belief Change," *Journal of Marketing Research* 24 (February 1987): 29–39.

52 G. C. Chu, "Prior Familiarity, Perceived Bias, and One-Sided versus Two-Sided Communications," *Journal of Experimental Social Psychology* 3 (1967): 243–254. See also Cornelia Pechmann, "How Do Consumer Inferences Moderate the Effectiveness of Two-Sided Messages?" in *Advances in Consumer Research*, vol. 17, ed. Marvin E. Goldberg, Gerald Gorn, and Richard Pollay (Provo, UT: Association for Consumer Research, 1990), 337–341.

53 Marlize Terblanche-Smit and Nic S. Terblanche, "Race and Attitude Formation in HIV/Aids Fear Advertising," *Journal of Business Research* 63, no. 2 (February 2010):121–125.

54 Dana L. Alden, Wayne D. Hoyer, and Chol Lee, "Identifying Global and Culture-Specific Dimensions of Humor in Advertising: A Multinational Analysis," *Journal of Marketing* 57 (April 1993): 64–75.

55 Joan Cantor and Pat Venus, "The Effects of Humor on the Recall of a Radio Advertisement," *Journal of Broadcasting* (Winter 1980): 14.

56 Tara Parker-Pope, "British Budweiser Ads Rankle American Indians," *Wall Street Journal*, July 16, 1996, B1, B5.

57 Brian Sternthal and C. Samuel Craig, "Humor in Advertising," Journal of Marketing 37, no. 4 (October 1973): 12–18. See also Thomas J. Madden and Marc Weinberger, "The Effects of Humor on Attention in Magazine Advertising," *Journal of Advertising* 11 (March 1982): 4–14.

58 Martin Eisend, "A Meta-Analysis of Humor in Advertising," *Journal of the Academy of Marketing Science* 37 (2009):191–203.

59 Ibid.

60 Amitava Chattopadhyay and Kunal Basu, "Humor in Advertising: The Moderating Role of Prior Brand Evaluation," *Journal of Marketing Research* 27 (November 1990): 466–476. For another study on humor in advertising, see Stephen M. Smith, "Does Humor in Advertising Enhance Systematic Processing?" in *Advances in Consumer Research*, vol. 20, ed. Leigh McAlister and Michael L. Rothschild (Provo, UT: Association for Consumer Research, 1993): 155–158. This author found evidence that humor in an ad tends to lead to more peripheral processing, so the strength of ad claims aren't evaluated as closely as when more serious ads are employed. Thus, a more humorous ad positively impacted ratings only when weak claims were employed.

61 William Wells, "Lectures and Dramas." Paper presented at the Association of Consumer Research, fall 1987.

62 Christopher Puto and William Wells, "Informational and Transformational Advertising: The Differential Effects of Time," in *Advances in Consumer Research*, vol. 11, ed. Thomas Kinnear (Provo, UT: Association for Consumer Research, 1984), 638–643.

[63] For a model of transformational advertising, see Vanitha Swaminathan, George M. Zinkhan, and Srinivas K. Reddy, "The Evolution and Antecedents of Transformational Advertising: A Conceptual Model," in *Advances in Consumer Research*, vol. 23, ed. Kim P. Corfman and John G. Lunch, Jr. (Provo, UT: Association for Consumer Research, 1996), 49–55.

[64] Gregory W. Boller, "The Vicissitudes of Product Experience: 'Songs of Our Consuming Selves'' in Drama Ads," in *Advances in Consumer Research*, vol. 17, ed. Marvin E. Goldberg, Gerald Gorn, and Richard Pollay (Provo, UT: Association for Consumer Research, 1990), 321–326. For additional analysis of transformational ads, see John Deighton, Daniel Romer, and Josh McQueen, "Using Drama to Persuade," *Journal of Consumer Research* 16 (December 1989): 335–343.

[65] John Deighton, Daniel Romer, and Josh McQueen, "Using Drama to Persuade," *Journal of Consumer Research* 16 (December 1989): 335–343.

[66] David Glen Mick and Claus Buhl, "A Meaning-Based Model of Advertising Experiences," *Journal of Consumer Research* 19 (December 1992): 317–338.

[67] Robin Higie, June Cotte, Melissa Lunt Moore, "Believe It or Not: Persuasion, Manipulations, and Credibility of Guilt Appeals," in *Advances in Consumer Research*, ed. Eric J. Arnould and Linda M. Scott (Provo, UT: Association for Consumer Research, 1999), 288–294.

[68] Swee Hoon Ang, Siew Meng Leong, and Wendy Yeo, "When Silence Is Golden: Effects of Silence on Consumer Ad Response," in *Advances in Consumer Research*, ed. Eric J. Arnould and Linda M. Scott (Provo, UT: Association for Consumer Research, 1999), 295–299.

[69] Curtis P. Haugtvedt and Duane T. Wegener, "Message Order Effects in Persuasion: An Attitude Strength Perspective," *Journal of Consumer Research* 21 (June 1994), 205–218.

[70] H. Rao Unnava, Robert E. Burnkrant, and Sunil Erevelles, "Effects of Presentation Order and Communication Modality on Recall and Attitude," *Journal of Consumer Research* 21 (December1994): 481–490.

[71] Margaret C. Campbell and Kevin Lane Keller, "Brand Familiarity and Advertising Repetition Effects," *Journal of Consumer Research* 30 (September 2003): 292–304.

[72] George E. Belch, "The Effects of Television Commercial Repetition on Cognitive Response and Message Acceptance," *The Journal of Consumer Research* 9 (June 1982): 56–65.

[73] See the following study for research that supports this conclusion: Dena Cox and Anthony Cox, "What Does Familiarity Breed? Complexity As a Moderator of Repetition Effects in Advertising Evaluation," *Journal of Consumer Research* 15 (June 1988): 111–116. See also Arno Rethans, John Swasy, and Lawrence Marks, "Effects of Television Commercial Repetition, Receiver Knowledge, and Commercial Length: A Test of the Two-Factor Model," *Journal of Marketing Research* 23 (February 1986): 50–61.

[74] The encoding variability hypothesis also applies to the effects of repetition. See H. Rao Unnava and Robert E. Burnkrant, "Effects of Repeating Varied Ad Executions on Brand Name Memory," *Journal of Marketing Research* 28 (November 1991): 406–416. See also Robert Burnkrant and Hanumantha Unnava, "Effect of Variation in Message Execution on the Learning of Repeated Brand Information," in *Advances in Consumer Research*, vol. 14, ed. Melanie Wallendorf and Paul Anderson (Provo, UT: Association for Consumer Research, 1987), 173–176.

[75] Curtis P. Haugtvedt, David W. Schumann, Wendy L. Schneier, and Wendy L. Warren, "Advertising Repetition and Variation Strategies: Implications for Understanding Attitude Strength," *Journal of Consumer Research* 21 (June 1994): 176–189.

[76] Giles D'Souza and Ram C. Rao, "Can Repeating an Advertisement More Frequently Affect Brand Preference in a Mature Market?" *Journal of Marketing* 59 (April 1995): 32–42.

[77] L. McCullough and Thomas Ostrom, "Repetition of Highly Similar Messages and Attitude Change," *Journal of Applied Psychology* 59 (June 1974): 395–397.

[78] D. E. Berlyne, "Novelty, Complexity, and Hedonic Value," *Perception and Psychophysics* 8 (November 1970): 279–286.

[79] Rashmi Adaval and Robert S. Wyer, Jr., "The Role of Narratives in Consumer Information Processing," *Journal of Consumer Psychology* 7, no. 3 (1998): 207–245.

chapter

9

Consumer Decision Processes

Learning Objectives:

1. How do consumers make a purchase decision?

2. Do consumers always use a rational decision-making process?

3. What are the traditional rational steps consumers use to make a purchase decision?

4. Why don't we always buy the same thing?

Apple: From Niche Market to Market Leader

Apple, maker of the Mac computer, struggled for years to compete with companies selling PCs. The brand personality of Mac computer was viewed by many as a less sophisticated machine than the PC. Apple then introduced the iPod, the portable media player, in October 2001. The iPod quickly grew to a leader in the MP3 market. In fact, by October 2007, more than 119 million iPods had been sold worldwide, making it the leader in digital players.[1]

The success of iPod may have carried over to Apple's Mac computer. At the end of the first quarter 2008, Apple's quarterly profits rose to $1.05 billion, up 36 percent from the previous year's quarterly profits.[2] So, what led to this dramatic change? Apple's success may be a result of improving its image on critical decision steps. One argument for this dramatic shift is the change in consumer's decision-making process. A question remains as to how consumers decide among a plethora of competing brands. In this chapter, we'll discuss the steps consumers go through when making purchase decisions.

Is Social Media the Answer to All Business Success?

We have discussed social media throughout each chapter, and it appears that social media is the answer to all business success. Really? Let's consider two brands that have traveled very different roads in the social media market. Apple is viewed as either the No. 1 or No. 2 brand of 2015, depending on which metrics are used to evaluate brands.[3] But while Apple enjoys an outstanding position in overall brand standing, it really has a lackluster status in the social media world.[4]

On the other hand, we would expect a brand that wins accolades for its outstanding social media presence would be a big success. This second company has been praised for embracing social media and even sharing its social media experience with other companies. Unfortunately, social media success was not enough to help Kodak remain solvent.[5]

So, the moral of this story may be you can embrace social media all you want, but unless you make the products consumers want, consumers may not decide to buy your brand.

INTRODUCTION

FIGURE 9.1

A Generic Flowchart of the Consumer Decision-Making Process

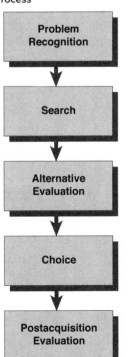

Prior to making an acquisition, consumers move through a decision process. **Consumer decision making** is the processes involved in recognizing problems, searching for solutions, evaluating alternatives, choosing among options, and evaluating the outcomes of the choice. Not only do consumers make decisions regarding which brand options to choose, they also decide what quantity of the good to purchase.[6] Consumers make decisions in order to reach goals, which include making the best choice among alternative actions, reducing the effort in making the decision, minimizing negative emotions, and maximizing the ability to justify the decision. Decision making is a constructive process. The approach taken by a consumer to make a decision is made on the fly and influenced by the problem's difficulty, by the knowledge and characteristics of the consumer, and by the characteristics of the situation.[7] It's critical for managers to identify the type of decision process employed by a target market because it will influence each of the managerial application areas.

The **generic decision-making model** identifies the stages through which consumers move when making decisions. It consists of five stages: problem recognition, search, alternative evaluation, choice, and post-acquisition evaluation. (The stages are diagramed in Figure 9.1). We will discuss all five stages as related to Apple. In the problem recognition stage, consumers recognize a need exists. In the case of Apple, consumers first recognize they need a computer. Perhaps their old computer is getting outdated or it's their first computer purchase. If sufficiently strong, the need may motivate the person to enter the second stage: the search for information. The search for information may be either extensive or limited depending on the involvement level of the consumer. In the third stage, consumers evaluate the alternatives they've identified for solving the problem. Alternative evaluation is synonymous with the formation of attitudes regarding the alternatives. Thus, material from Chapter 7 is particularly applicable to the evaluation stage. In the case of Apple, as consumers start liking the iPod, their overall attitude toward other Apple products (i.e., computers) may grow more positive.

Choice is the fourth stage. It involves deciding which alternative to select (e.g., which brand to choose, whether to spend or save, or from which store to purchase the product). Finally, in the post-acquisition stage, buyers consume and use the acquisition. In addition, they evaluate the outcomes of the consequences of the behavior and engage in the ultimate disposal of the waste resulting from the purchase. If the consumer of the Apple computer was satisfied, he or she may be inclined to purchase additional Apple products. The next chapter focuses specifically on such post-acquisition processes.

The generic decision-making process describes the steps in making choices employed by consumer. Businesses and organizations also use the process. For example, one researcher sent a questionnaire to more than two thousand purchasing managers of firms of varying sizes.[8] The dimensions she identified closely corresponded to the stages of the generic decision-making process.

ALTERNATIVE PERSPECTIVES ON CONSUMER DECISION MAKING

From the late 1700s through much of the 1970s, researchers viewed people as moving linearly through the generic decision-making process outlined in Figure 9.1. In the late 1970s, however, authors began questioning the concept that all consumer purchases result from a careful, analytical process. Some authors suggested that, in many instances, consumers may not engage in any decision making at all prior to making a purchase. As stated in one article, "We conclude that for many purchases a decision process never occurs, not even on the first purchase."[9] In addition, researchers recognized that many consumer behaviors don't merely involve the purchase of goods, such as automobiles and toothpaste. People also purchase experiences in the form of services, such as vacation excursions, rock concerts, theater tickets, parachuting, movies, art, novels, opera, casinos, and houses of ill repute.[10]

Due to the limitations of the traditional consumer decision process, researchers proposed alternative decision-making models that place different levels of emphasis on each of the stages identified in the generic flowchart. For these reasons, this textbook identifies three perspectives on consumer behavior: the traditional decision-making perspective, the experiential perspective, and the behavioral influence perspective. Each perspective defines a divergent type of decision process. Table 9.1 summarizes the acquisition process from the viewpoint of each of the three perspectives. Table 9.2 summarizes how the marketing mix of a firm changes depending on which of the three decision-making perspectives the target market is using. The following sections discuss in more detail the implications of the three perspectives for understanding consumer decision making.

The Decision-Making Perspective

The traditional **decision-making perspective** emphasizes the rational information-processing approach to consumer purchase behavior. It's closely related to the high-involvement hierarchy of effects approach to attitude formation discussed in Chapter 7. According to the approach, consumers move through

TABLE 9.1
Three Perspectives on Decision Making

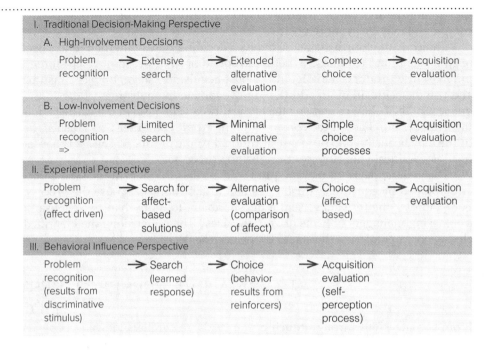

I. Traditional Decision-Making Perspective

  A. High-Involvement Decisions

Problem recognition	→	Extensive search	→	Extended alternative evaluation	→	Complex choice	→	Acquisition evaluation

  B. Low-Involvement Decisions

Problem recognition =>	→	Limited search	→	Minimal alternative evaluation	→	Simple choice processes	→	Acquisition evaluation

II. Experiential Perspective

Problem recognition (affect driven)	→	Search for affect-based solutions	→	Alternative evaluation (comparison of affect)	→	Choice (affect based)	→	Acquisition evaluation

III. Behavioral Influence Perspective

Problem recognition (results from discriminative stimulus)	→	Search (learned response)	→	Choice (behavior results from reinforcers)	→	Acquisition evaluation (self-perception process)

TABLE 9.2
Some Marketing-Mix Strategies for Products Bought via High- and Low-Involvement Decision Processes

I. High-Involvement Decision Processes

  A. Promotional strategy

    1. Sell the product via a skilled sales force.

    2. Utilize strong persuasive arguments in messages.

  B. Distribution strategy

    1. Utilize a more limited distribution system.

    2. Ensure distributors are trained to provide outstanding service.

  C. Pricing strategy

    1. Consider charging premium prices.

    2. Avoid use of frequent sales.

    3. Consider the policy of price bargaining with customers.

II. Low-Involvement Decision Processes

  A. Promotional strategy

    1. Place greater weight on mass advertising to create sales awareness.

    2. Use heavy amounts of message repetition.

    3. Utilize likable/attractive endorsers.

    4. Keep arguments in advertisements simple.

  B. Distribution strategy

    1. Utilize an extensive distribution strategy.

  C. Pricing strategy

    1. Attempt to be a low-cost producer.

    2. Consider using coupons and other price incentives to reach more price-conscious groups.

each of the stages of the decision process in a linear fashion, with high levels of information processing occurring.

In the 1970s, however, researchers recognized consumers don't always go through an extended decision process. Rather, under low-involvement conditions, limited decision making takes place, and less search behavior occurs.[11] Further, because the low-involvement hierarchy of effects is operative when limited decision making occurs, the alternative evaluation stage is largely absent from the decision process. Thus, in limited decision making, the choice among alternative brands is made in a relatively simple manner, and simplified decision rules are used.[12] In sum, the decision-making perspective evolved and considered high-involvement and low-involvement routes to making decisions.

The Experiential Perspective

In contrast to the decision-making perspective, the **experiential perspective** recognizes consumers as "feelers" as well as "thinkers." That is, they consume many types of products for the sensations, feelings, images, and emotions the products generate.[13] When problems are examined from the experiential perspective, managers focus on entertainment, arts, and leisure products rather than on more functional consumer goods. The experiential perspective recognizes that products carry subjective symbolic meanings for consumers.[14] In particular, products such as flowers, jewelry, perfume, and athletic team paraphernalia are bought largely for the meanings they provide.

There may be different meanings that are presented, depending on whether the product is purchased for oneself or for others. One recent study demonstrated that buying for others is related to the experiential perspective. Consumers tend to exhibit more self-control when buying personal products. But when it comes to buying for others, we tend to make more indulgent choices.[15] By being more extravagant in buying gifts for others, we create an enriched experience.

From an experiential perspective, problem recognition results from the realization a difference exists between actual and desired affective states. Similarly, the search process involves seeking information concerning the likely affective impact of various alternatives. In the alternative evaluation stage, the various options are evaluated based on their affective quality. Choice is based on affective criteria (e.g., which product will make me feel better?). Finally, post-acquisition evaluation is based on whether the outcome meets the emotional expectations of the consumer.

Behavioral Influence Perspective

When approaching problems from the **behavioral influence perspective**, researchers focus on the behaviors of consumers and the contingencies of the environment that influence the behaviors. For example, the physical environment can be used to induce behaviors from consumers. The use of textures, smells, and lighting can also create an atmosphere that elicits desired responses among consumers. Arranging aisles in a retail store to funnel consumers by desired products illustrates how the physical environment can impact behavior without changing beliefs or feelings about the action. Similarly, the mere arrangement of the containers of food products on shelves in a grocery store can affect consumer buying decisions independently of their beliefs and attitudes about the product alternatives.[16] Other researchers have found the volume of music should be considered in order to increase levels of food and drinks in restaurants. Specifically, guests consume more food and drink when the music is played at a relatively low volume.[17]

The discussion of the experiential and behavioral influence perspectives is controversial to some researchers. Indeed, arguments can be made that decision making occurs whenever consumers engage in a behavior. The experiential and behavioral influence perspectives are discussed, however, to emphasize the role of affect and environmental factors in causing consumer actions. A single-minded focus on belief formation and rational information processing fails to adequately capture the richness of consumer behavior.

The following sections discuss the first four states: problem recognition, search, alternative evaluation, and choice. Chapter 10 describes the final stage of the decision-making process: post-acquisition evaluation.

Managerial principle 9.1

As a manager, you must understand consumers don't always go through a rational decision process to make a purchase.

PROBLEM RECOGNITION

Problem recognition occurs when a discrepancy develops between an actual state of being and a desired state of being. (Note that the definition of problem recognition is identical to that of a need state discussed in Chapter 5). If satisfaction with the **actual state** decreases, or if the level of the **desired state** increases beyond a critical level, a problem is recognized that propels a consumer to action.[18]

A variety of factors may cause the actual state to decrease below acceptable levels. A person could run out of a product (e.g., gasoline or toothpaste), a product could wear out, or a product may simply go out of style. Similarly, the person could use the product and find it simply fails to meet expectations. Internal states of consumers, such as perceptions of hunger, thirst, or boredom, can decrease the perception of the actual state. Negative mood states can also lower the actual state. For example, the person could receive bad news, or a general situation could make the person uncomfortable (e.g., a consumer could be placed in a new social situation).

The desired state is influenced by factors that affect a consumer's aspirations and circumstances. Thus, such influences as culture, subculture, reference groups, and life-style trends can cause a person to change his or her desired state. For example, if a person joins an organization (e.g., a fraternity, a sorority, or a corporation), the pressures of the social group at the organization may change the person's perception of the appropriateness of wearing certain types of clothing. When a student graduates from college, a new set of dress requirements may be imposed. Thus, the desired state changes, and needs develop for nice suits, briefcases, and shoes that would be considered inappropriate in a college environment.

Because consumers have a capacity to think, plan, and dream, they can create new consumption visions. **Consumption visions** are defined as "self-constructed mental simulations of future consumption situations."[19] By being able to imagine themselves in new situations or owning new possessions, consumers may influence their own desired state. Of course, advertisers seek to encourage such consumption visions by showing off products and services in highly inviting ways.

Managerial principle 9.2

You can change a consumer's likelihood of making a purchase by promoting aspirational themes in your messages. This will change his or her desired state.

CONSUMER SEARCH BEHAVIOR

After a consumer identifies a problem, he or she begins a search process to acquire information about products that may eliminate the problem. **Consumer search behavior** is the actions taken to identify and obtain information on the means of solving a consumer problem.

Researchers have identified two types of consumer **search processes**—internal and external.[20] In **internal search**, consumers retrieve from long-term memory information on products or services that may help to solve a problem. Consequently, the long-term impacts of commercial advertisements often play a role in the decision process. The images consumers hold about Apple iPhone may be pulled from memory when making a computer purchase decision. In contrast, in **external search**, consumers acquire information from outside sources, such as friends, advertisements, the Internet, packaging, *Consumer Reports*, sales personnel, and so forth.

Managerial principle 9.3
Make sure you have a salient brand name because consumers often make a choice after searching for information internally.

In addition to distinguishing internal search and external search, researchers have also made the distinction between prepurchase search and ongoing search. **Prepurchase search** involves the information-seeking activities consumers engage in to facilitate decision making concerning a specific purchase in the marketplace that occurs because problem recognition has taken place. In contrast, **ongoing search** involves the search activities that are independent of specific purchase needs or decisions.[21] Ongoing search is found particularly among individuals who have built a hobby around a particular consumer product or activity. Thus, car, gardening, computer, and photography enthusiasts are constantly reading and studying because of their intrinsic interest in the topic.

Internal Search

Figure 9.2 identifies five categories into which a brand must fall.[22] In this figure, internal search is viewed as proceeding via a two-stage process. First, the consumer retrieves from long-term memory those products and brands of which he or she is aware. This **awareness set** is a subset of the total universe of potential brand and products available. At a minimum, a company wants its brand to be a part of the awareness set. If consumers are unaware of a brand, they're unlikely to ever consider it, unless they discover it in the external search process.

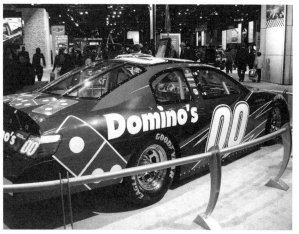

The importance of getting your brand into the awareness set is illustrated by Domino's Pizza. For years, Domino's struggled with being recognized on a national level. Typically, consumers who were aware of the brand lived within a three-mile radius of a franchise. When researchers asked consumers to name three pizza companies, only 7 percent of respondents had brand recall. Brand recall is critical to business success as many consumers won't trade with firms that aren't readily at the top of their mind. To change this situation, Domino's could invest in national television advertising or possibly sponsorship. Domino's invested in the IndyCar Series by sponsoring a car. In a three-year

FIGURE 9.2
Categories of Brands
Consumers May Retrieve
from Memory during Internal
Search

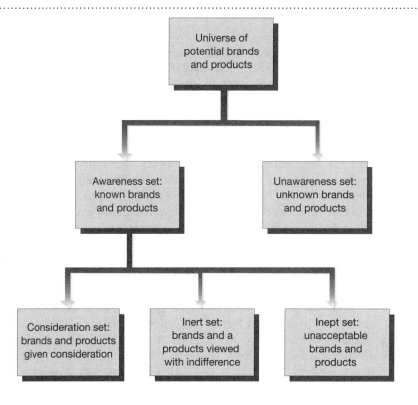

period, brand recall went from 7 percent to 87 percent.[23] Obviously, this strategy increased the number of customers who put Domino's in their awareness set.

After identifying the awareness set, the consumer separates the awareness group into three additional categories—the consideration set, the inert set, and the inept set. The **consideration set** consists of those brands and products that are acceptable for further consideration.[24] The **inert set** consists of the brands and products to which the consumer is essentially indifferent. The **inept set** consists of the brands and products the consumer considers unacceptable. Of course, the goal of a company is to have its brand placed in the evoked set.

An experience by one of the authors helps explain the consideration set. The next time you enter a convenience store, think about why you chose that particular store. Convenience store operators conduct intense research to determine the best location to place a store. Because most convenience stores have similar if not identical offerings, the location of the store is critical to business success. We can even point to examples of street intersections where two different convenience stores are located on two of the four corners.

So, do stores located across the street from each other cannibalize sales? We suggest that they don't cannibalize sales. Most of the traffic into convenience stores has a direct path to the store. This is opposed to having to cross traffic. Most consumers won't cross traffic to go to a convenience store. Consequently, the consideration set for a convenience store depends on what side of the street the store resides.

An example in the dining industry illustrates this point. In Wichita, Kansas, Pizza Hut built a store at an intersection where a Pizza Hut already existed. Rumors soon spread that the old store would be closed. Weekly revenue for the first store was around $32,000 per week. Once the second store opened, the weekly revenue for the "Pizza Hut intersection" rose to $45,000 per week. By building the second store, total revenues increased by 40 percent and customers did not have to cross traffic.

Researchers have made a number of findings about the size of the consideration set. First, the size of the consideration set is dynamic and may change as more information is added through external search.[25] Indeed, even the incidental exposure to a commercial may increase the chances a person adds the brand to the consideration set.[26] The size of the consideration set has been found to decrease as consumer satisfaction and brand loyalty increases. In forming consideration sets, consumers often seek to reduce the number of alternatives to a manageable size for the individual. The consumer can make the comparison task easier by reducing the number of alternatives in the consideration set.[27]

On the other hand, consumers engage in increased retailer search when the consideration set increases. This leads to an increase in the tendency to switch from one brand to another.[28] Factors associated with an increase in the size of the consideration set include consumers' education level, the size of consumers' families, the size of the awareness set, and the extent to which consumers recognize different brands can be used in different situations.[29]

How large are consumers' awareness and consideration sets? Researchers have found awareness set sizes ranged from a low of 3.5 for mouthwash to a high of 19.3 for laundry detergent. In general, consideration set size paralleled the size of the awareness set. Thus, for mouthwash, 1.3 brands were in the consideration set, whereas for laundry detergent, 5.0 brands were in the consideration set.[30] In general, the larger the awareness set, the larger the consideration set.[31]

Managerial principle 9.4
Remove any barriers that could place your brand in the inept set.

External Search

During external search, consumers solicit information from outside sources.[32] Table 9.3 identifies the basic types of information sought in external search. These include information about the alternative brands available, the evaluative criteria on which to compare brands, the importance of the criteria, and the performance of the brands on the attributes consumers are seeking.[33] Readers should be aware that the amount and types of information sought in external search can be derived directly from the concepts involved in attitude formation and change discussed in Chapter 7.

Measuring External Search It's important for managers to measure the extent consumers in the target market search because it directly impacts distribution strategies. That is, if consumers engage in little external search, extensive distribution is necessary, such as that found for soft drinks. Several approaches have been employed to measure the extent of external search. Some of these indicators include the number of stores visited, the number of friends with whom the person discusses the product, the number of buying guides consulted, the number of store employees with

TABLE 9.3
Types of Information Sought via External Search

1.	Alternative brands available
2.	Evaluative criteria on which to compare brands
3.	Importance of various evaluative criteria
4.	Information on which to form beliefs:
	• Attributes brands possess
	• Benefits various attributes provide

whom the consumer talks, and the number of advertisements the consumer sees, hears, or reads.

There's another approach to assessing the degree of external search. **Instrumentality of search** involves assessing the extent to which a person relies on or finds useful the various sources of information.[34]

Factors Influencing the Degree of External Search   Economists argue that consumers search as long as the marginal gains from search exceed the marginal costs of such a search.[35] From this viewpoint, consumers will continue searching only as long as the incremental gains that result from search are greater than the costs incurred to make the additional search.[36] The more costly it is for consumers to engage in external search, the less they will engage in the activity.

In general, consumers engage in heavy amounts of external search when in a high-involvement state and doing extensive problem solving.[37] In fact, this holds for both tangible and service goods. Researchers found in both "credence services" (e.g., life insurance or furnace repair) and in "experiential services" (e.g., fitness club or a Caribbean vacation), consumers engage in more search when involvement is high.[38] Research investigating the search process reported the following findings:

1. As time availability increased, search effort increased.
2. As perceived risk increased, total search effort increased.[39]
3. As attitudes toward shopping increased, total search effort increased.[40]
4. As education, income, and socio-economic status increased, external search increased.[41]

The characteristics of the market situation may also influence the amount of external search. Researchers have found that as the number of product alternatives available increases, greater amounts of search result.[42] Similarly, the number and proximity of available stores also influence the amount of external search. Consumers tend to engage in larger amounts of external search when stores are numerous and in close physical proximity to each other.[43] As one would expect, consumers engage in large amounts of external search when shopping in large malls, where a number of stores are in close proximity to each other. Thus, as search costs are reduced, search increases. It can be anticipated that because the use of the Internet decreases search costs, overall search will increase as increasing numbers of people buy products through the World Wide Web.

A recent summary of the literature discussed how product experience influenced the amount of search. The authors concluded that an inverted-U relationship exists. That is, at low levels of experience, little search occurs. As experience increases, search increases, but only up to a certain point. At high levels of experience, sufficient knowledge exists to make search unnecessary. Thus, at very high levels of product experience, relatively little search occurs.[44]

How Much Search by Consumers?

Research has shown consumers engage in surprisingly little external search, even when in extended problem-solving situations. For example, one study investigated the external search behavior for refrigerators.[45] The author found 42 percent of the respondents visited only one store. Furthermore, 41 percent considered only one brand. Another study found in 77 percent of the cases, consumers visited only one store when purchasing a small appliance.[46] Other researchers investigated the external search behavior for major appliances and automobiles. They concluded that "the amount of information sought by many buyers is small, even though information is accessible."[47]

Although consumers may visit few stores prior to purchasing appliances, one would expect them to engage in greater external search when options are easily compared, such as when shopping in a grocery store. In one study, shoppers were found to spend only 12 seconds in their selection process for each good purchased.[48] Immediately after they made a selection, they were asked to give the price of the brand selected. The researchers found only 59 percent of the shoppers claimed to have checked the price. Less than half were actually able to state the correct price, and 32 percent gave a price that was off by an average of 15 percent. In fact, when a product was selling for a reduced price, less than half were even aware of the sale. The authors reported that executives of leading packaged goods firms were surprised and concerned with these results. Consumers search very little, even in a grocery store. As a result, it's difficult to communicate with them via promotional strategy.

Why do consumers engage in so little information search? One reason is they may have engaged in extensive amounts of prepurchase search. Research indicates a majority of consumers exhibit high levels of pre-search decision activities.[49] Such pre-search activities may result from the passive, low-involvement reception of information from marketing communications. They may also result from consumers who have an enduring involvement with a product class and who consistently engage in high-involvement prepurchase search activities.[50] Finally, consumers may perceive they obtain few benefits in relation to the costs of additional search.

It should also be added, however, that consumer self-report surveys used to gather information may understate the actual amount of search by consumers. That is, when asked to describe their search process, many consumers forget all the steps they took in the search process.[51] Thus, consumers may actually be searching more than the data indicate.

> **Managerial principle 9.5**
> If you can simply get the consumer in your store, he or she will likely buy from you rather than comparison shop.

ALTERNATIVE EVALUATION

In the **alternative evaluation** stage of the acquisition process, the consumer compares the options identified as potentially capable of solving the problem that initiated the decision process. When the options are compared, consumers form beliefs, attitudes, and intentions about the alternatives under consideration. Chapter 7 identifies the concepts applicable to understanding the alternative evaluation stage of the generic decision process.

Consistent with the discussion in Chapter 7, alternative evaluation is influenced by the type of hierarchy of effects occurring. From a high-involvement decision-making perspective, alternative evaluation follows the standard learning model in which beliefs lead to affect formation resulting in behavioral intentions and behavior. In such instances, the multi-attribute models of attitude formation may be used to describe the evaluation process. In low-involvement situations, alternative evaluation consists of the formation of a few rudimentary beliefs about the options under consideration. Indeed, relatively little alternative evaluation tends to occur under low-involvement conditions. Strong affective reactions (i.e., attitudes) are viewed as developing only after behavior occurs.

From the experiential perspective, the evaluation process is viewed as affect driven. The focus isn't on belief formation but on affect creation. Thus, the researcher investigates what emotions are elicited by the acquisition that's about to be made. Finally, from the behavioral influence perspective, consumers are conceptualized as never consciously comparing alternatives. Table 9.4 summarizes the alternative evaluation process from the decision-making, experiential, and behavioral influence perspectives.

In the alternative evaluation stage, consumers consider the extent to which options possess various attributes. In addition, they begin to consider the importance and the goodness or badness of these attributes. Interestingly, when circumstances cause a person to have to exert greater effort to evaluate one alternative in comparison with another, negative affect occurs. For example, it may be more difficult to find information about the attributes of a particular brand. The result is people avoid choosing the option that required greater cognitive effort.[52] Through alternative evaluation, consumers gain the information needed to make a final choice, which is the next step in the decision-making process.

TABLE 9.4
Hierarchies of Effects and Alternative Evaluation

Hierarchies of Effect	How Alternatives Compared
High-involvement hierarchy	Beliefs about attributes are compared. Affective reactions are compared.
Low-involvement hierarchy	A limited number of beliefs about attributes are compared.
Experiential hierarchy	Affective reactions are compared.
Behavioral influence hierarchy	No internal comparison processes are recognized as occurring prior to behavior.

As noted, alternative evaluation occurs when consumers make overall assessments to compare and contrast options. When evaluating alternatives, consumers make two types of judgments: estimating the likelihood something will occur and valuing the goodness or badness of something. Judging probabilities and judging value are central to the alternative evaluation process.

Consumers also assess risk during the alternative evaluation stage. As noted in Chapter 6, risk perception is based on consumers' judgments of the likelihood negative outcomes will occur and of the degree of negativity of those outcomes. Thus, besides influencing consumer attitudes, judgments of likelihood and goodness or badness influence risk perception.

Because judging probability and value are central to the alternative evaluation process, the key question is this: How do consumers make these judgments of probability and value? There's good evidence people use judgmental heuristics to make such estimates. Judgmental heuristics are the simple rules of thumb people use to make estimates of probabilities and values. In the next two sections, we discuss some of the factors that influence judgments of probabilities and values.

Judging Likelihood

An entire area of research has developed around the topic of how people judge likelihood. When people say, "I think that," "Chances are that," or "I believe that," they are implicitly making a judgment of the likelihood something will occur. Probability judgments are made quite frequently in the consumer setting. For example, when people estimate the quality of a product, they're attempting to determine the likelihood the product contains the attribute of quality. Similarly, when people estimate the preferences of another person, they're evaluating the likelihood the other person has certain likes and dislikes.

Researchers have identified a number of judgmental heuristics consumers use to estimate probabilities. Three of these heuristics have particular relevance to consumer decision making. They are anchoring and adjustment, availability, and representativeness.

The Anchoring and Adjustment Heuristics When judging probability, people frequently start from an initial value and then adjust up or down to obtain the final answer. This process is called **anchoring and adjustment**. The problem with this heuristic is different starting points often result in different answers because the upward and downward adjustments are often insufficient. Thus, the starting point acts to distort the estimate.

One study found anchoring influenced probability estimates in predicting the preferences of spouses.[53] Husbands and wives must frequently estimate each other's preferences when making purchases. In this study, the husbands and wives were asked to predict their spouse's preferences for twenty new-product concepts. The results revealed both husbands and wives anchored heavily on their own preferences. That is, they tended to ask themselves what they would like and used that as the anchor, or starting point, for their prediction of their spouse's preference.

The interesting, and somewhat surprising, finding was that using one's own preference was the best strategy for estimating one's spouse's preference. When respondents attempted to adjust from their own preference, they tended to use criteria that were poor predictors of their spouse's preference. Thus, in many instances, using one's own reactions may be the best strategy for judging the likes and dislikes of others similar to you.

The fact that prior beliefs form anchors was found by other authors, who investigated how marketing research studies influence the beliefs of simulated market researchers.[54] In the study, MBA students assumed the role of assistant product managers at Campbell Soup Company. Participants were given information about consumer reactions to two commercials. This information was either consistent or inconsistent with their prior beliefs about which of the two commercials were superior. Results revealed that when the market research confirmed the students' prior beliefs, it tended to be rated higher and used in the decision making. However, when it was inconsistent with the students' prior beliefs, the market research was evaluated as poorly done and was less likely to be used.

Research on anchoring and adjustment in consumer behavior literature reveals that many consumers routinely use this heuristic device and, in some instances, it actually improves judgment accuracy. This is the case when the evaluators making the judgment are highly similar to the people they're assessing. However, if the evaluator is dissimilar to the target person, anchoring can lead to poor estimates.

The Availability Heuristic The **availability heuristic** states people assess the probability of an event by the ease with which the event can be brought to mind. Thus, the easier it is for people to recall an outcome, the more likely they are to think it will occur. In one classic demonstration of this effect, respondents were given lists containing the names of men and women. In half the lists, the men were more famous (hence, more available in memory and easily recalled). In the other half, the women were more famous. Respondents were asked to judge which of the lists contained more names of men and which had more names of women. In reality, both lists contained the same number of male and female names. The only factor that differed was how famous the males or females on the list were. Results showed that when the list contained names of famous males, respondents would estimate it contained more names of males, and, conversely, when the list contained names of famous females, respondents would estimate it contained more names of females. Because the names of the famous were easily recalled, subjects' estimates were influenced by the availability heuristic.[55]

One of the major goals of advertising is to make information about a product highly available in memory. So, if one company is more successful than its competitors in associating its brand with a positive attribute, it will have a strong competitive advantage. Even though competing brands may rate just as highly on one of the attributes, if consumers can't bring to mind the association, they'll rate the likelihood of the competing brands' possessing the attribute as low.[56]

Researchers have found one method of making an action or outcome available in memory is to induce consumers to imagine its occurrence. In one study, homeowners in a middle-class suburb were approached by a person selling cable television services.[57] In the information condition, the respondents were simply given factual details on the benefits of subscribing to the service, such as the costs and the programming available. In the imagination condition, respondents were given the same information, but additional words were inserted into the sales message that encouraged respondents to imagine the various benefits. For instance, the homeowners were asked to imagine how it would feel to be able to watch movies on the system. The results revealed respondents in the imagination condition rated the service as more likely to provide the benefits suggested. Further, homeowners in the imagination condition were more likely to subscribe to the service than were homeowners in the information condition.

Closely related to the availability heuristic is the hindsight bias. The hindsight bias states that people consistently exaggerate what could have been anticipated through foresight. So pervasive is this tendency that people often misremember their own predictions, exaggerating in hindsight what they know in foresight. Because information about what happened in the past is so available to memory, people assume these events must have been highly likely to occur.

The hindsight bias is responsible for the Monday morning quarterback phenomenon, in which armchair coaches second-guess the decisions made in the heat of battle during Sunday afternoon's game. In the consumer arena, this heuristic leads people to be highly critical of management for blunders they believe should have been anticipated.

The Representativeness Heuristic   The **representativeness heuristic** is a rule of thumb by which people determine the probability that "object A" belongs to "class B" by assessing the degree to which object A is similar to or stereotypical of class B.[58] Marketers frequently attempt to take advantage of this heuristic. For example, companies will bring out knockoff brands that have names and packaging similar to those of leading brands. KFC (Kentucky

Fried Chicken) has been so popular in China that a firm opened up a competing chicken restaurant called MFC. The goal of firms that create knockoffs is to convince consumers the knockoff brand performs like the national brand. To the extent consumers use the representativeness heuristic, the ploy will be successful. An interesting question is, are such practices ethical?

An offshoot of the representativeness heuristic known as the law of small numbers says people have a strong tendency to believe a sample is a true representation of a population even when the sample is extremely small. This heuristic is frequently found among marketing managers who observe focus groups. Because the opinions expressed in focus groups are so vivid and salient, managers often assume they must represent the views of the entire target market. However, everyone familiar with survey research knows one simply can't use a small sample of people to make predictions about a large population. The problem is the people in the focus group appear to represent the target group and, therefore, to depict all relevant aspects of the target group. Of course, this is an erroneous perception. Some companies have recognized this problem and don't allow their managers to observe focus groups directly.[59]

The law of small numbers may help explain the great influence of word-of-mouth communications. The reported experiences of others have a strong impact on consumers, even though the experience of one or two people is an extremely poor predictor of the experiences of millions of consumers. But from the perspective of a multi-attribute model, the representativeness heuristic (of which the law of small numbers is an offshoot) influences estimates of the probability an object has a particular attribute. Suppose a friend describes to you an occasion at a restaurant in which he found a long piece of hair in the lasagna he ordered. If his description is believable and you consider it representative of what can happen at a restaurant, it's likely to influence you strongly—that is, you'll probably form the belief the restaurant has a major problem with the attribute of cleanliness. Of course, your friend's experience represents only one observation; it could have been a unique event in an otherwise spotless kitchen. However, because of the representativeness bias, your evaluation of the restaurant will be highly negative.

The representativeness heuristic may explain why consumers sometimes behave atrociously. For instance, customers sometimes treat the people who dress up like cartoon characters and roam the grounds of Disneyland, Disney World, and Universal Studios as though they're indestructible "toons." Park visitors will punch them, taunt them, and even try to set them on fire. Consider Betina Becker. One day, dressed as Daffy Duck, she was walking around Six Flags Magic Mountain theme park, which lies just north of Los Angeles, California. Suddenly, a large man decided to show off for his wife and grandchildren by slugging Daffy in the ribs. However, unlike Daffy, who can come back from anything, Becker could not because the man had broken her ribs.[60]

Why do some consumers carry the representativeness heuristic to such ridiculous extremes? It seems these people see the cartoon character, place it in the "toon" category, and then treat the person inside the hot, sweaty suit as though he or she were an indestructible cartoon character rather than a human being.

Judging Goodness or Badness

In addition to judging the probability something will occur, consumers evaluate the **goodness or badness** of the potential outcomes of their decisions. As noted, earlier, the perception of the goodness or badness of the attributes of an object will influence a consumer's attitude toward the object. Two general classes of factors influence people's judgment of the goodness or badness of potential outcomes. The first concerns how consumers value the alternatives, and the second concerns how consumers relate the outcomes to the goodness or badness of the associations they have made between the outcomes and their memories. Each of these classes of factors is discussed in the paragraphs that follow.

Valuing Gains and Losses The **valuation of gains and losses** refers to an individual's psychological assessment of the goodness or badness of an outcome based on the level of the outcome in relation to some reference point or adaptation level. One approach to understanding how people value the goodness or badness of an object is prospect theory.[61]

According to **prospect theory**, how people psychologically interpret the goodness or badness of an option (i.e., a prospect) doesn't necessarily match any objective (i.e., psychological) or actual measure of its value. This difference between psychological and actual valuations is captured in a graph called the hypothetical valuation function, which is displayed in Figure 9.3. The hypothetical value function is defined as the relationship between the psychological valuation of gains and losses that may result from a course of action and the actual valuation of those gains and losses.[62]

FIGURE 9.3
Hypothetical Value Function

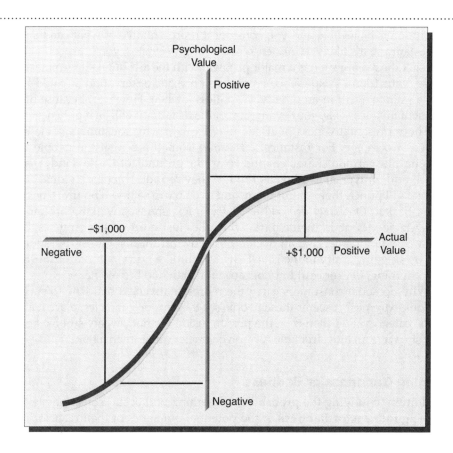

In Figure 9.3, the horizontal axis represents the actual value of a $1,000 bet. Thus, $1,000 is represented at the -$1,000 and +$1,000 points on the horizontal axis. The vertical axis represents the psychological value of the bet. The basic idea behind the hypothetical value function is psychological values don't necessarily match actual values. The curve shows how the psychological values are predicted to deviate from the actual values. (Note: If the psychological values precisely coincided with the actual values, there would be a straight line running diagonally through the origin of the curve). In the figure, the curve in the gain quadrant (i.e., the upper right part of the diagram) starts out steep and then flattens as it moves away from the origin. This shows that increasing gains have decreasing psychological value. It's consistent with the economic concept of decreasing marginal utility, which states each additional unit of something obtained brings proportionally less utility or satisfaction.

The hypothetical valuation function curve is steeper in the domain of losses (i.e., the lower left quadrant) than in the domain of gains. Thus, all else being equal, losses are weighted more heavily than gains. The curve also flattens out in the domain of losses so that each additional loss means less to the person.

Four managerial implications about how consumers value gains and losses can be deduced from the shape of the hypothetical value function:

1. Losses are given more weight than gains. Because the curve is steeper in the loss domain than in the gain domain, a loss of $1,000 will have a greater psychological impact than a gain of $1,000.
2. If people perceive they're in the gain domain, they'll tend to act conservatively.
3. If people perceive they're in the loss domain, they'll tend to take more risks.
4. The same decision can be framed from either a gain or a loss position.

Implications 1, 2, and 3 are directly related to consumers' risk-taking tendencies. In general, people like to avoid risk. However, if a person perceives he or she is already behind and in the loss domain, he or she will be much more prone to take risks. Consider the behavior of people who bet at horse races. As the end of the day approaches, gamblers increasingly bet on long shots. Why is this? Because they're in the loss domain (i.e., most gamblers have lost money by the end of the day). Because each additional loss has less psychological value, people are willing to take bigger risks to get even. For someone who has lost $100, the psychological value of gaining $100 and pulling even is much greater than the psychological value of losing another $100.

Framing and Prospect Theory As noted in implication 4, one of the key points of prospect theory is the same decision problem can be framed in different ways. **Framing** refers to whether a person perceives a decision as being made from a position of gain or a position of loss. That is, depending on the decision maker's reference point, the same decision dilemma may be framed as involving either a gain or a loss.[63] This phenomenon is analogous to describing a glass of water as either half empty or half full. If a decision problem is framed as involving a gain, risk aversion can be expected. Conversely, if a decision is framed as involving a loss, greater risk taking can be expected.[64]

One team of researchers demonstrated a framing effect in the risk-handling strategies of those selecting industrial vendors.[65] In this experiment, subjects were asked to respond to a written scenario describing a modified rebuy-purchase situation. They had to decide whether to award a contract to a vendor offering a certain guaranteed profit or to a vendor offering a fifty-fifty chance of either beating or falling below the guaranteed offer. The subjects were given a series of descriptions of various frames of reference they could use to make the decision. The results revealed subjects who framed the decision in terms of worst-case outcome (i.e., focusing on losses) or who calculated expected values tended to choose the risky option, while those who framed the decision in terms of factors that caused them to focus on gains (e.g., historical performance and guaranteed performance) tended to choose the conservative option.[66]

Another study found strong evidence that framing influences consumer preferences. In the experiment, respondents were asked to give their impressions of ground beef, which was described to them as being either 75 percent lean or 25 percent fat. Notice that, even though identical information was given to the consumers, the product was framed either positively or negatively. Ratings were taken on four scales: good-tasting/bad-tasting, greasy/greaseless, high quality/low quality, and fat/lean. In each instance, ratings differed significantly as a result of the framing manipulation. When the ground beef was framed as 75 percent lean, subjects rated it as significantly leaner, better-tasting, less greasy, and higher in quality than when it was framed as 25 percent fat.[67] This study shows that how information is framed in promotional messages can have a strong impact on how consumers value the goodness or badness of the information.[68]

The research on framing and prospect theory also has application to how consumers respond to changes in the price of a product. If a price change is framed as a change from the base price of the product, its impact won't be as great as it would if it were framed as a change from the zero point on the prospect theory curve. To see what this means, suppose the price of a $1,000 product is reduced by $90. If framed as a change in the base price of the product, the impact of this price reduction on the typical consumer will be small because of the shape of the value function curve. That is, in relation to $1,000, a $90 rebate is small change. However, if the price change is framed as a gain of $90—which makes it independent of the base price of the product—it will have a much larger psychological impact because the curve is much steeper as it passes through the origin of the hypothetical value function. In the second framing, the $90 feels like "found money" that can be used to buy something else.

Managerial principle 9.8
Frame small discounts as a gain and large discounts as a loss.

How can companies induce consumers to perceive a price reduction as a *gain* of *x* amount rather than as a *change* in the base price of the product? Many of the sales-promotion devices used by corporations are designed to do just that. Rebates are particularly good for framing the price change to the company's advantage. By mailing a consumer a $500 check after the purchase of a $15,000 car, the car company gets the consumer to think of the money as a gain of $500. If the price were merely reduced by $500 at the time of purchase, the consumer would interpret it quite differently. Psychologically, it's a large sum of money because the comparison is to getting nothing back.

Other sales-promotion devices, such as gifts, operate like rebates. For example, if a customer buys an expensive suit from a clothing store and the owner throws in one or two silk ties for nothing, the gifts will be valued independently of the cost of the suit. The customer will perceive the ties' $50 to $60 value as a gain rather than a reduction in the price of the $600 suit, and, as a result, it will have much greater psychological value. In general, sales-promotion devices such as rebates, gifts, and sweepstakes are more effective than a mere reduction in price because of the effects of framing.

THE CONSUMER CHOICE PROCESS

After engaging in an evaluation of the alternatives, the consumer's next step in the decision process is to make a choice among alternatives, such as among different brands, services, or stores. In addition to choosing between two brands of a particular product, consumers may also choose between noncomparable alternatives. For example, people may choose between going on an expensive vacation, purchasing a car, or building a swimming pool. So, how does the number of products offered affect the consumer? It has been argued that "choice overload" (i.e., being given a large number of choices) may lead to negative consequences, such as lower customer satisfaction.[69] In fact, researchers have found more choices benefit the consumer. Satisfaction didn't decrease significantly as the assortment size increased.[70] If we look at this finding from the perspective of a single firm, Apple should continue offering a variety of models (iPhones, iPods, etc.,) that compete against each other because consumers won't be negatively affected by the number of choices. This next section discusses the many types of choices—between brands, between stores, and between noncomparable alternatives.

How consumers go about making choices is strongly influenced by the type of decision process in which they are engaged. The choice process differs if consumers use a high-involvement approach as compared with a low-involvement approach. Similarly, if a consumer is using an experiential orientation, the choice process may be altered. (Of course, when behavioral influence is taking place, the consumer is considered not to be making any type of conscious, mentalistic choice). The next three sections discuss the choice process from the high-involvement, low-involvement, and experiential perspectives. Table 9.5 summarizes these approaches to the choice process.

Choice Under High- and Low-Involvement Conditions

The study of choice under high- and low-involvement conditions has focused on identifying the types of rules people use to decide which alternative to purchase and how they restructure the information they receive so they can make choices.[71] These investigations have identified two broad categories of choice models: compensatory and non-compensatory. Employed in high-involvement conditions, in compensatory models, high belief ratings on one attribute can compensate for low ratings on another attribute. The Fishbein attitude-toward-the-object model is an example of a compensatory model. Used in low-involvement conditions, in non-compensatory models, high ratings on one attribute may not compensate for low ratings on another attribute.[72]

An example is provided to illustrate the differences between the compensatory and non-compensatory model. Shown in part A of Table 9.6, the example involves a decision faced by a student acquainted

TABLE 9.5
Alternative Approaches to Predicting Choice

I. High-involvement choice
A.   Compensatory models
B.   Phased models
II. Low-involvement choice
A.   Conjunctive rule
B.   Disjunctive rule
C.   Elimination by aspects heuristic
D.   Lexicographic heuristic
E.   Frequency heuristic
III. Experiential choice processes
A.   Affect-referral heuristic
B.   Brand-awareness purchases
C.   Impulse purchases
IV. Noncomparable choice processes
V. Store choice

with the first author concerning which university he should attend. His consideration set consisted of four universities (i.e., brands)—Harvard, University of Florida, University of Texas, and his parent's alma mater, Colorado State University. In looking at these options, the student will make two types of judgments. First, he'll estimate the likelihood each school will perform as expected on each of the attributes on which it is being evaluated. Second, he'll value the goodness or badness of each of the attributes.

The table identifies the attributes on which the universities were evaluated, the evaluations of the goodness or badness of the attributes, the estimates of the likelihood the schools possessed the attributes, and the importance ratings of each of the attributes.

TABLE 9.6
Which University to Choose?

Belief Ratings and Consideration Set, Part A					
Attributes	**Evaluation Rating** e_i	**Harvard** b_i	**University of Florida** b_i	**University of Texas** b_i	**Colorado State University** b_i
Low tuition	+3	1(3)	4(12)	3(9)	7(21)
Number of friends attending school	+2	3(6)	3(6)	5(10)	8(16)
Extracurricular activities	+1	5(5)	7(7)	1(1)	5(5)
Athletic success	+3	6(18)	5(15)	9(27)	1(3)
		$\Sigma b_i e_i = 32$	$\Sigma b_i e_i = 40$	$\Sigma b_i e_i = 47$	$\Sigma b_i e_i = 45$

Belief Ratings and Consideration Set, Part B					
Attributes	**Importance Rating**	**Harvard**	**University of Florida**	**University of Texas**	**Colorado State University**
Low tuition	8	1	4	3	7
Proximity to home	9	3	3	5	8
Extracurricular activities	5	5	7	1	5
Athletic success	7	6	5	9	1

The next subsection discusses how a choice would be predicted in high-involvement circumstances. This is followed by a discussion of how a choice is predicted under low-involvement conditions.

High-Involvement Choice   Under conditions of high involvement, consumers have been found to act as though they're using a compensatory model. In **compensatory models of choice**, consumers are viewed as analyzing each alternative in a broad evaluative fashion so that high ratings on one attribute may compensate for low ratings on other attributes.[73] In such a process, all the information on the attributes of a brand are combined into an overall judgment of the preference for the brand. Such an evaluation is made for each of the brand alternatives. According to the compensatory model, the brand with the highest overall preference is then chosen. If a compensatory model is employed, an option isn't necessarily rejected because it has low ratings on any particular attribute. Thus, a consumer may rate a particular brand of automobile as poor in acceleration. However, because the car has high ratings on other attributes, and because judgment is based on a global evaluation, the brand could still be chosen. The Fishbein attitude-toward-the-object model discussed in Chapter 7 illustrates a compensatory model.

As shown in part A of Table 9.6, the student employed a high-involvement decision process in choosing a university. The Fishbein attitude-toward-the-object model should predict the selection. As seen in Table 9.6, the predicted attitude is computed in exactly the same manner as described in Chapter 7. The university with the highest rating was the University of Texas, with an overall attitude score of 47. The closest competitor was Colorado State University, with a rating of 45. The major reasons for the selection of the University of Texas were its athletic success and the number of friends attending the school. The belief ratings on these attributes compensated for the low rating on the low tuition attribute.

Low-Involvement Choice   In low-involvement circumstances, consumers have been found to act as though they use **non-compensatory models of choice**. In these models, high ratings on some attributes may not compensate for low ratings on other attributes. These non-compensatory models are also called **hierarchical models of choice**. They're hierarchical because the consumer is viewed as comparing alternatives on attributes one at a time. Thus, one attribute is chosen and all alternatives are compared on it. The person then moves to the next attribute and compares alternatives on it. The process continues in a hierarchical manner. For the decision maker, one advantage of the non-compensatory choice models is they're relatively simple to implement. When consumers are in a low-involvement situation, they're not willing to engage in the large amounts of information-processing effort required by a compensatory model.

The non-compensatory models are used as shortcuts to reach satisfactory decisions rather than optimal ones. Such a process has been called **satisficing** and depicts a goal of reaching a decision that's good enough rather than optimal.[74] The non-compensatory models have also been called heuristic models of choice. As noted earlier in the chapter, heuristics are simple rules of thumb people use to make satisfactory decisions rather than perfect ones. The use of heuristic choice models in low-involvement circumstances makes sense. In such cases, consumers are unconcerned with reaching optimal decisions; they merely want to make a decision that's good enough.

Several non-compensatory choice models have been identified using the conjunctive rule, the disjunctive rule, the elimination-by-aspects heuristic, and the lexicographic heuristics, as presented in part B of Table 9.6.[75] These are discussed next.

The conjunctive rule   In many instances, such as purchasing an energy drink, consumers are faced with a decision where a large number of brand alternatives are available. Clearly, it would be impossible to investigate each brand in detail, so a shortcut is needed to simplify the process. One such shortcut involves the use of the **conjunctive rule**, in which the consumer sets minimum cutoffs on each attribute he or she wishes to investigate. If the product fails to surpass the minimum cutoff level, the alternative is rejected. If the cutoff levels are set very stringently, it's possible only one alternative is left after all others are eliminated. More frequently, cutoff points are set lower so a number of alternatives remain. As such, the conjunctive rule is often used as an initial screening device to eliminate enough brands so a more complex decision approach, such as a compensatory model, can be applied to select from the remaining alternatives.

In the university example (part B of Table 9.6), belief ratings had to equal or surpass a cutoff of three or more to be considered. Using this rule, only the University of Florida had belief ratings that reached the cutoff on each attribute. Each of the remaining alternatives had at least one belief rating below the cutoff point. Therefore, based on the conjunctive model, the University of Florida would be selected.

The disjunctive rule   The **disjunctive rule** is similar to the conjunctive rule in that minimum standards are set for each attribute under consideration. Alternatives are then evaluated on the attributes. The disjunctive rule differs in that any alternative that surpasses the minimum cutoff on any attribute is accepted. Usually, the cutoff point is set very stringently. The alternative chosen by the disjunctive rule is the one rated extremely high on some attribute. It's as though the person is saying he or she wants an alternative that's great on some attribute.

In the university example, belief ratings had to reach the extremely high cutoff score of 9 for the alternative to be considered under a disjunctive model. The only school to have a 9 on any attribute was the University of Texas, which had a 9 on athletic success. If a disjunctive model were employed, the analysis would predict the student would select the University of Texas.

Note the key difference in the conjunctive and disjunctive models. Both set minimum standards for each attribute. However, in the conjunctive model, if a rating falls below the standard on any attribute, the alternative is rejected. In the disjunctive model, if a rating is above the cutoff level on any attribute, the alternative is accepted. Therefore, as one might expect, cutoffs for the disjunctive model are typically set higher than for the conjunctive model.

Elimination by aspects   According to the **elimination-by-aspects heuristic**, each alternative is thought of as a collection of aspects, or attributes. Choice occurs via a hierarchical process in which the alternatives are compared on the most important attribute. Alternatives not surpassing the cutoff on the attribute are eliminated. The decision maker then moves on to the next most important attribute and eliminates alternatives not surpassing the cutoff point. The process continues until only one alternative remains. The likelihood of choosing any one attribute on which to compare alternatives is based on its importance to the decision maker.

Suppose a cutoff point on the belief rating is set at 5. When the elimination-by-aspects heuristic is applied to the university example (see Table 9.6, part B), one predicts Colorado State University would be selected. On the most important attribute of proximity to home, only Colorado State and the University of Texas both equaled or surpassed the cutoff value of 5. On the second most important attribute, low tuition, Texas was eliminated. This left only Colorado State, which is the predicted choice.

The lexicographic heuristic   The **lexicographic heuristic** has strong similarities to the elimination-by-aspects approach. Both start with the consumer ranking the attributes in order of importance. The consumer then rates all alternatives on the most important attribute. At this point, the two approaches diverge. If a lexicographic model is used, the consumer then selects the alternative that's best on the most important attribute. If a tie occurs, the consumer moves on to the next attribute and selects the alternative rated best, and so forth. Thus, the lexicographic model uses a harsher standard of choice than the elimination-by-aspects model. The elimination-by-aspects model eliminates alternatives only if they fail to possess an attribute by not surpassing the cutoff point. In contrast, in the lexicographic model, an alternative is eliminated if it doesn't have the highest rating on the most important attribute. Only in cases of ties does one move on to the next most important attribute.

Looking again at the university example, consider which university the consumer is predicted to select. If the lexicographic heuristic is used, the analysis would predict Colorado State. On the most important attribute of proximity to home, it received the highest rating and all other options would be eliminated. One can readily see why the lexicographic model is non-compensatory. That is, an alternative could be eliminated merely because it didn't at least achieve a tie in the rating of the most important attribute.

Additional Choice Models Two additional choice models have been identified—the frequency heuristic and phased choice strategies.

The frequency heuristic According to the **frequency heuristic**, when consumers are in a low-involvement state, choice may be influenced by the "mere number of positive and negative attributes associated with a brand or by the mere number of dimensions on which one brand outperforms another."[76] When a frequency heuristic is used, consumers act as though they simply count the number of features on which one brand surpasses another. Little or no attention is allocated to the relative importance of the features.[77]

Commercials that use a **piecemeal report strategy** are employing the frequency heuristic. For example, auto companies have used comparative advertising in which their brand is selectively compared to a series of competitors on a number of attributes. The ad might state the vehicle has a trunk larger than a Mercedes, goes from zero to sixty miles per hour faster than an Audi, and has more leg room than a BMW. In fact, the car might be a very poor brand and be exceeded by its competitors on every other dimension. However, because the attributes on which it surpasses the competition are systematically selected, the illusion is created that it has a high frequency of positive attributes.

Phased strategies In a **phased strategy**, consumers sequentially use two non-compensatory models or use a non-compensatory model and then a compensatory approach. For example, a consumer first may use a conjunctive model to reduce the alternatives considered to three or four. The consumer could then use a lexicographic approach or even a Fishbein model to make the final choice. Such phased models are most likely used under high-involvement conditions.

Which Choice Models Do Consumers Use? One study asked respondents to make choices among various automobile alternatives after being given seven attributes on which to rate the cars.[78] Table 9.7 presents the results. The study found 60.7 percent of respondents used a lexicographic model. The next most frequently used was a compensatory model (32.1 percent). A phased strategy of using a conjunctive model to screen alternatives, followed by a compensatory approach, was used 5.4 percent of the time. These three strategies accounted for 98.2 percent of the choices. Although the researchers did use a simulated buying situation and used students as respondents, it does indicate consumers are likely to use non-compensatory models frequently in their decision making. It should be added, however, that the study didn't analyze the extent to which respondents used all the types of choice models. For example, it didn't analyze whether respondents used an elimination-by-aspects model or the frequency heuristic. More research is needed on this important issue.

TABLE 9.7

Frequency of Use of Choice Models in Brand Choice[79]

Choice Mode	Verbal Description	Percentage Using Approach
Conjunctive (non-compensatory)	I chose the car that had a really good rating on at least one characteristic.	0.6
Lexicographic (non-compensatory)	I looked at the characteristic that was most important to me and chose the car that was best in that feature. If two or more cars were equal on that feature, I then looked at my second most important feature to break the tie.	60.7
Multi-attribute (compensatory)	I chose the car that had a really good rating when you balance the good ratings with the bad ratings.	32.1
Phased (conjunctive—compensatory)	I first eliminated the cars with a really bad rating on any feature and then chose from the rest the one that seemed the best overall when you balance the good ratings with the bad ratings.	5.4
Other	(Category composed of several other types of heuristic models).	1.8

Experiential Choice Processes

From the experiential perspective, choice is viewed as resulting from consumers considering their feelings about alternatives; little emphasis is placed on the development of beliefs about attributes.[80] As a result, the purchase is made with little cognitive control and seems to happen in a largely automatic manner.[81] Several types of consumer choice can be categorized as experiential processes. These are discussed next.

The Affect-Referral Heuristic   When consumers employ the **affect-referral heuristic**, they base their choice on their overall emotional response to an alternative. Rather than examining attributes or beliefs about attributes, a holistic approach is used in which consumers choose the alternative toward which they have the most positive feelings. Affect-referral explains how consumers make brand-loyal purchases. As will be discussed in Chapter 10, consumers who express strong brand loyalty also reveal highly positive affect toward the brand. Thus, when making a purchase, they don't go through an extended or even a limited decision process. Rather, they simply refer to their feelings. In a similar manner, impulse purchases represent cases in which consumers base their decision on a strong affective response. Finally, affect-referral can cause consumers to postpone needed purchases. Some choices create trade-offs between attributes that produce a negative affective state. For example, people know they should buy life insurance, but the process makes them think about death and dying. This conflict produces a negative emotional state that causes the person to put off buying the insurance.[82]

The Effects of Brand Awareness　Brand awareness may also influence consumer choice through an affect-referral process. In particular, new brands face an extremely difficult problem in capturing market share because national brands are purchased, in part, because of the positive affect associated with them. One explanation for these effects is the mere exposure phenomenon discussed in Chapter 8. That is, because national advertising of a brand results in frequent exposure to it, consumers become familiar with it. The familiarity results in positive feelings when consumers are exposed to the brand. As a result, the more familiar brand is chosen. This phenomenon explains why incumbent politicians almost always win reelection. In this case, consumers are highly familiar with the "brand" the politician represents.

The effects of brand awareness were demonstrated in a study in which respondents chose among three brands of peanut butter. In the awareness condition, one of the peanut butters was a well-known national brand. In the unawareness condition, all three peanut butters were unknown regional brands. As might be expected, when the national brand was known, 93.5 percent of subjects chose it. Indeed, brand awareness was more important than the actual taste of the peanut butter. That is, the researchers varied the quality of the peanut butter independently of the brand name. When the good-tasting peanut butter was placed in the unknown brand's jar, only 20 percent selected it—even after they had sampled the alternatives that didn't taste as good. In contrast, when the tastier peanut butter was placed in the national brand's jar, 77 percent chose it.[83]

IMPULSE PURCHASES

An **impulse purchase** has been defined as a "buying action undertaken without a problem having been previously recognized."[84] An impulse to buy is accompanied by a sudden, powerful, persistent, and unplanned urge to buy something immediately. In addition, impulse buying is prone to occur with diminished regard for the decision's consequences.[85] Impulse purchases illustrate mindless reactive behavior. They're the antithesis of the rational consumption processes one finds in high-involvement purchases and to a certain extent in low-involvement purchases.[86] Impulse purchases occur frequently. Various studies have found as many as 39 percent of department store purchases and 67 percent of grocery store purchases may be unplanned.[87]

In one study of impulse purchases, researchers conducted depth interviews asking respondents to report on their feelings when they made purchases. One subject reported,

I was in Beverly Hills just walking around, not intending to buy, when I saw some shoes on sale. So I went inside and tried them on and they fit fine. At

that time, I thought about buying one pair, then I got the feeling I had to try everything. They were just calling to me. You suddenly feel compelled to buy something. It feels like getting an idea. It's a fast feeling, and if I don't get it right away, I'll think of reasons why I don't need it.[88]

In this case, strong positive feelings created a buying impulse that dominated all rational thought. The affective state led directly to a behavior without the person forming beliefs or thinking very hard about the purchase.

Social Media

How Are Stock Prices Related to Social Media?

The popularity of brands on Facebook relates strongly to its stock price. In a recent study, Arthur O'Connor found the correlation between the number of fan "likes" on Facebook is significantly related to the stock's price. The study demonstrated that impulse purchase products have a stronger relationship with stock price increases than non-impulse products. This finding suggests impulse brands should target social media as a promotional tool.[89]

Variety-Seeking Purchases

Variety seeking refers to the tendency of consumers to spontaneously buy a new brand of product even though they continue to express satisfaction with the previously purchased brand. One explanation of variety seeking is consumers attempt to reduce boredom by purchasing a new brand.[90] The theory of optimum stimulation has been proposed to explain this tendency to avoid boredom. Discussed more fully in Chapter 5, optimum stimulation theory posits if one's activation falls too low or moves too high, we take steps to change it.[91] The switching of brands may be a method of increasing stimulation by bringing something new into a consumer's life.

Recent research has suggested there are some commonalities and some differences between impulse buying and variety seeking. Individuals who are highly impulsive or who have a high optimum stimulation level engage in more impulse buying and variety seeking. However, the person's level of self-monitoring, (i.e., one's motivation to control one's impulses) affects these variables differently. Individuals with a high level of self-monitoring are more likely to seek variety, but they are less likely to buy impulsively.[92]

Effects of Mood States on Choice

Mood states influence whether a person uses a decision-making or an experiential approach to choice. One research team found people in a positive mood state responded more favorably to emotional appeals than to informational appeals. In contrast, people in negative mood states responded more favorably to informational appeals than emotional appeals. These findings were extended by the researchers to the choice process. They found when people were in negative moods, they tended to rely on an informational approach to product selection. When in positive moods, choice was more closely related to a focus on their feelings and fantasies about using particular brands.[93]

In the advertising arena, researchers discovered there should be a fit between the television program mood and the commercial mood when consumers view a television program. Specifically, when the program is happy, consumers have a more positive attitude toward positive commercials. On the other hand, if the program is sad, consumers have a more favorable attitude toward sad commercials. Consequently, the mood states of the commercial should fit the mood states of the programming.[94]

Choices among Noncomparable Alternatives

As noted earlier in the chapter, choices aren't always made among comparable alternatives. Rather than merely deciding which brand of digital camera to purchase, a consumer must sometimes decide how to allocate resources among the general alternatives. Should the consumer spend $600 to purchase a high-quality camera, new stereo speakers, or a new business suit? The traditional non-compensatory models are of little assistance here because they require the decision maker to form beliefs about alternatives on common attributes. What do consumers do when the alternatives have no attributes in common other than price?

In one study, subjects had to choose among non-comparable alternatives. The results demonstrated two trends.[95] First, subjects focused on using more abstract attributes in their comparison of alternatives. Thus, when comparing cameras to business suits, they would compare the alternatives on such attributes as necessity, stylishness, cost, and innovativeness. Second, the respondents shifted to a more holistic strategy in which overall attitudes toward the alternatives were compared. In addition to comparing each alternative on abstract attributes, the respondents evaluated each alternative separately to compare overall impressions of the products.[96]

The study of non-comparable alternatives is important because some of the most important decisions made by consumers involve very different product alternatives. For example, consumers may make a choice between purchasing an automobile or remodeling a kitchen. Similarly, an eighteen-year-old must make the choice between going to college or taking a job. A woman may be forced to choose between starting a family, concentrating on a career, or trying to do both.

Choices among Stores

Another area of research on choice concerns the store-selection process. A critical issue for retailers involves developing an understanding of the factors consumers use when selecting a story from which to purchase a product. The approaches to choice identified in the preceding sections are directly relevant to the issue. Using a decision-making perspective, retailers can identify the attributes people use to evaluate alternative stores, determine whether consumers are in high- or low-involvement states, and identify the appropriate choice model. Researchers have found consumers consider such attributes as the store's distance from the consumer's home, the overall prices of brands carried, and service.[97]

Another factor that influences store choice is the **context**. Context refers to those situational or extrinsic factors that dictate the options available to the decision maker.[98] Thus, the types of stores available, how many stores are available, and the presence of mail-order alternatives influence the nature of the choice process.

Other research on store choice has focused on the type of choice set used by consumers.[99] The research found consumers evaluate retailers based on the same types of sets discussed earlier (i.e., awareness, unawareness, inert, inept, and consideration). In addition, the research found new types of sets. For example, the **interaction set** consists of those stores where a consumer allows himself or herself to be exposed to personal selling. Such stores have an opportunity to sell that's not shared by those in the **quiet set**. Consumers may enter stores belonging to the quiet set, but they tend not to interact with any sales personnel.

MANAGERIAL IMPLICATIONS—RESPONSIVE MARKETING

Research

It's important to conduct appropriate research studies to identify the extent of external search in which consumers engage in the purchase of brands in a product class. This will have important implications for distribution strategies. In addition, it's even more important to determine the type of choice processes employed by the target market. Whether or not consumers engage in high-involvement, low-involvement, or experiential choice can impact both promotional and product strategy. For example, if market research reveals the target market employs a lexicographic choice model, it's critical to design and promote a product so it's perceived as the best on the most important attribute. Similarly, if consumers use a conjunctive choice process, it's critical to ensure the product exceeds a minimum cutoff level on each of the attributes.

Environmental Analysis

The nature of the consumer environment may have large effects on consumer search behavior. As a result, managers should evaluate the number of competing stores in a region. Interestingly, by placing one's store in close proximity to competitors, it lowers consumer search costs, resulting in higher traffic. Also, the number of competitors will affect the size of consumer consideration sets, which will affect internal search. Managers should also evaluate the impact of the consumer environment from a behavioral influence perspective. In particular, it's important to carefully assess the effects of the physical environment (e.g., the layout and atmospherics of stores) on consumers.

Segmentation

The extent of external search and the type of choice model employed by consumers can act as segmentation variables. For example, a strategy may be to focus on a high-involvement target market consisting of the early adopters in the product category. These individuals can be expected to engage in extended search processes, including pre-need search. In addition, they will likely employ a phased decision process that culminates in using a compensatory choice model. The approach to reach and influence these individuals will be very different from that employed to market a brand to consumers using either a low-involvement or experiential decision process.

Positioning

The analysis of problem recognition has direct relevance to positioning and differentiation strategies. As noted in the chapter, problem recognition and need recognition processes both result from a perceived discrepancy between an actual state and a desired state. Desired states represent benefits consumers seek. Thus, products can be positioned as fulfilling these benefits. For example, a consumer may have a desired state of protecting and enhancing the body. A product such as a sunscreen can then be positioned as performing this function by preventing sunburn and, potentially, skin cancer. Alternative evaluation processes also have relevance to positioning. That is, products can be positioned by identifying the attributes consumers perceive as extremely important. For example, in the university example, Colorado State University could be positioned based on its proximity factor.

Marketing Mix

As already described, identifying the attributes consumers rate as extremely important has implications for product and promotional strategies. Similarly, an understanding of the type of choice process employed by the target market will influence product and promotional strategies. For example, if the target market is found to employ a high-involvement choice model, it suggests managers don't have to be concerned about optimizing each of the features of the brand. Rather, the focus should be on identifying the attributes rated as most important by the target market and working to create strong beliefs the brand possesses these attributes. In addition, don't forget that price can be an attribute as well. For some product categories, price may be a relatively more important attribute than in others. In cases in which price is extremely important, managers must ensure their brands are priced competitively. Distribution and promotional strategies should be based, in part, on an understanding of the extent of consumer search. For example, if limited search occurs, the product must be promoted heavily and distributed widely.

SUMMARY

How do consumers make a purchase decision?

Consumer decision making involves the analysis of how people choose between two or more alternative acquisitions and of the processes that take place before and after the choice. A generic consumer decision process can be identified that consists of five stages: problem recognition, search, alternative evaluation, choice, and post-acquisition evaluation.

Do consumers always use a rational decision-making process?

Three divergent perspectives can be used to examine the consumer decision process. The dominant approach in consumer behavior has been the decision-making perspective. From this perspective, consumers are viewed as decision makers who make rational decisions regarding the products and services they buy. Researchers have identified two buying processes within the decision-making perspective. When consumers are highly involved in the purchase, they tend to engage in an extended decision-making process. In such high-involvement purchases, consumers are described as moving through each of the five stages of the action process in a sequential manner.

On the other hand, when consumers perceive little personal importance in the purchase, they move through a limited decision process. The search stage is minimized and the alternative evaluation stage may be largely skipped. In limited decision making, the choice process is much simpler than in high-involvement conditions.

From the experiential perspective, consumers are viewed as searching for products and services that elicit sensations, feelings, images, and fun. Some industries, such as the leisure industry, are based around creating experiences for people. The phenomena of impulse buying, variety seeking, and brand-loyal purchases also result, in large part, from consumers attempting to gain new and different experiences.

The third approach to consumer buying is the behavioral influence perspective. From this perspective, certain types of consumer behaviors are viewed as resulting from the effects of environmental forces rather than from consumers' beliefs or feelings. In effect, behavior is induced directly. Many of the phenomena of cultures, small groups, other people, and situations can be viewed as resulting from behavioral influence.

What are the traditional rational steps consumers use to make a purchase decision?

The traditional steps consumers use when making a purchase decision include problem recognition, search, alternative evaluation, choice, and post-acquistion evaluation. Problem recognition occurs when a sufficiently large discrepancy develops between an actual state of being and a desired state of being. A variety of factors can raise and lower the level of both states.

The consumer search process consists of those steps taken to acquire information about the products and services that may eliminate the problem identified in the first decision stage. Two types of search have been identified. Internal search consists of the consumer searching through long-term memory for information about brands that may eliminate the problem. External search involves the consumer seeking outside sources of information on what products may eliminate a problem. With alternative evaluation, the consumer compares the brands that may sufficiently satisfy their needs. This is followed by selecting among the alternatives, also known as choice. Finally, the consumer typically goes through a post-purchase evaluation of whether or not the choice was a good one.

Why don't we always buy the same thing?

Consumers often purchase a product on impulse due to a powerful urge to purchase the item. It's often a product the consumer hasn't purchased in the past, but the emotions the consumer is experiencing drives the individual to purchase it. Consumers also seek variety at times. A consumer may be perfectly satisfied with their usual brand, but perhaps they've grown bored with it. The consumer can reduce his or her boredom by testing a new product.

KEY TERMS

actual state
affect-referral heuristic
alternative evaluation
anchoring and adjustment
availability heuristic
awareness set
behavioral influence perspective
compensatory models of choice
conjunctive rule
consideration set
consumer decision making
consumer search behavior
consumption visions
context
decision-making perspective
desired state

disjunctive rule
elimination-by-aspects heuristic
experiential perspective
external search
framing
frequency heuristic
generic decision-making model
goodness or badness
hierarchical models of choice
impulse purchase
inept set
inert set
instrumentality of search
interaction set
internal search
lexicographic heuristic

mood states
non-compensatory models of choice
ongoing search
phased strategy
piecemeal report strategy
prepurchase search
problem recognition
prospect theory
quiet set
representativeness heuristic
satisficing
search processes
valuation of gains and losses
variety seeking

REVIEW QUESTIONS

1. Explain what's meant by the term consumer decision making.
2. Define the term consumer acquisitions. What are the types of acquisitions consumers may make?
3. Identify the stages of the generic consumer-decision process.
4. Identify the three alternative perspectives on consumer acquisitions. How do these perspectives differ from each other in explaining the factors that influence the consumer-decision process?
5. How does the movement of consumers through the stages of the decision process differ in high- and low-involvement conditions?
6. Contrast the experiential perspective with the decision-making view of consumer buying behavior.
7. Contrast the behavioral influence perspective with the decision-making view of consumer buying behavior.
8. Discuss the concept of consumer problem recognition. What factors tend to influence the consumer's actual state and the consumer's desired state?
9. Discuss the factors that cause consumers to engage in extensive problem solving and high amounts of external search.
10. From the perspective of an economist, what factors influence the amount of external search in which a consumer will engage?

11. Give three examples of how marketing mix strategies should differ under extended decision making versus limited decision making.

12. Identify three implications each for the experiential and the behavioral influence perspectives on managerial strategy.

13. Identify the categories of brands consumers may retrieve from memory during internal search.

DISCUSSION QUESTIONS

1. Identify a consumer purchase you've made in which you engaged in an extensive decision process. What were the steps you went through in selecting the brand to purchase? To what extent did this series of steps match the high-involvement decision process discussion in the chapter?

2. Identify a consumer purchase you've made that was based largely upon an experiential buying process. What were the steps you went through in selecting the product or service in this case? What were the types of feelings and experiences you were seeking from the purchase?

3. Attempt to identify a recent purchase or activity that resulted largely from behavioral influence. To what extent did you have any feelings about the action? To what extent did you engage in any extensive amounts of search for the product or service purchased? What environmental factor was most responsible for the purchase or action?

4. Try to identify a consumer purchase or action in which more than one of the purchase processes was involved. Which of the processes were operating simultaneously? Which of the processes tended to dominate the decision?

5. List as many as you can of the purchases of more than $5 you've made over the past several weeks. Categorize these as to whether they best fit into the high-involvement decision perspective, the low-involvement decision perspective, the experiential perspective, or the behavioral influence perspective. From which category did most of your purchases come?

6. To what extent do consumers characteristically use one of the purchase approaches more than others? To what extent do consumers show individual differences in their tendency to use one of the perspectives? For example, do some consumers tend to use a decision-making approach, whereas others tend to use an experiential approach in making their purchases?

7. How might advertising differ for products that are typically purchased under high-involvement conditions as opposed to products bought under low-involvement conditions?

8. Consider the product category of toothpaste. Identify your awareness set, evoked set, and inert set for the various brands of toothpaste you can recall. What could a company do to move its toothpaste from the inert set to the evoked set?

9. Why would a company that markets razor blades be interested in encouraging consumers to engage in problem recognition? How might a company that markets razor blades encourage consumers to engage in problem recognition?

10. Under what circumstances would a company want consumers to engage in large amounts of search behavior? Under what circumstances would a company want consumers to minimize their search behavior?

ENDNOTES

[1] Charles Gaba, "iPod Milestones," *Mac/PC Systems Shootouts*, accessed February 14, 2011, http://www.systemshootouts.org/?q=taxonomy/term/23

[2] Steve Dowling, "Apple Reports Record Second Quarter Results," *Apple*, accessed February 14, 2011, http://www.apple.com/pr/library/2008/04/23results.html.

[3] "Ad Age Social-Media Brand Ranking Top 10—2012," *Ranking the Brands*, accessed November 6, 2015, http://www.rankingthebrands.com/The-Brand-Rankings.aspx?rankingID=202&nav=category.

[4] Hayden Shaughnessy, "Does Apple's Success Prove Social Media Doesn't Really Matter," Forbes, September 21, 2012, accessed March 7, 2013, http://www.forbes.com/sites/haydnshaughnessy/2012/09/21/does-apples-success-prove-social-media-doesnt-really-matter/.

[5] Ibid.

[6] Brian Wansink, Robert J. Kent, and Stephen J. Hoch, "An Anchoring and Adjustment Model of Purchase Quantity Decisions," *Journal of Marketing* 35 (February 1998): 71–81.

[7] James R. Bettman, Mary Frances Luce, and John W. Payne, "Constructive Consumer Choice Processes," *Journal of Consumer Research* 25 (December 1998): 187–237.

[8] Michele D. Bunn, "Taxonomy of Buying Decision Approaches," *Journal of Marketing* 57 (January 1993): 38–56.

[9] Richard W. Olshavsky and Donald H. Granbois, "Consumer Decision Making—Fact or Fiction?" *Journal of Consumer Research* 6, no. 2 (September 1979): 98.

[10] B. Joseph Pine and James H. Gilmore, *The Experience Economy* (Boston: Harvard Business School Press, 1999).

[11] John C. Mowen and Michael S. Minor, *Consumer Behavior: A Framework* (Upper Saddle River, NJ: Prentice Hall, 2001).

[12] For an excellent discussion of low-involvement decision making, see Stewart De Bruicker, "An Appraisal of Low-Involvement Consumer Information Processing," in *Attitude Research Plays for High Stakes*, ed. John Maloney and Bernard Silverman (Chicago: American Marketing Association, 1979), 112–130.

[13] Meera P. Venkatraman and Deborah J. MacInnis, "The Epistemic and Sensory Exploratory Behaviors of Hedonic and Cognitive Consumers," in *Advances in Consumer Research*, vol. 12, ed. Elizabeth Hirschman and Morris Holbrook (Provo, UT: Association for Consumer Research, 1985), 102–107.

[14] B. Joseph Pine and James H. Gilmore, *The Experience Economy* (Boston: Harvard Business School Press, 1999).

[15] Juliano Laran, "Goal Management in Sequential Choices: Consumer Choices for Others Are More Indulgent than Personal Choices," *Journal of Consumer Research* 37 (2010): 304–314.

[16] Itamar Simonson and Russell S. Winer, "The Influence of Purchase Quantity and Display Format on Consumer Preference for Variety," *Journal of Consumer Research* 19 (June 1992): 133–138.

[17] Malcolm Sullivan, "The Impact of Pitch, Volume, and Tempo on the Atmospheric Effects of Music," *International Journal of Retail and Distribution Management* 30, no. 6 (2002): 323–330.

[18] Gordon C. Bruner and Richard J. Pomazal, "Problem Recognition: The Crucial First Stage of the Consumer Decision Process," *Journal of Consumer Marketing* (Winter 1988): 53–63.

[19] Diane M. Phillips, "Anticipating the Future: The Role of Consumption Visions in Consumer Behavior," in *Advances in Consumer Research*, vol. 23, ed. Kim P. Corfman and John G. Lynch, Jr. (Provo, UT: Association for Consumer Research, 1996), 70–75.

20 Janet R. McColl-Kennedy and Richard E. Fetter, Jr., "An Empirical Examination of the Involvement to External Search Relationship in Services Marketing," *Journal of Services Marketing* 15, no. 2 (2001): 82–98.

21 Peter Bloch, Daniel Sherrell, and Nancy Ridgway, "Consumer Search: An Extended Framework," *Journal of Consumer Research* 13 (June 1986): 119–126.

22 For information on the categories of brands consumers may retrieve from long-term memory, see F. May and R. Homans, "Evoked Set Size and the Level of Information Processing in Product Comprehension and Choice Criteria," in *Advances in Consumer Research*, vol. 4, ed. W. D. Perreault (Chicago: Association for Consumer Research, 1977), 172–175. See also Naeim Abougomaah, John Schlacter, and William Gaidis, "Elimination and Choice Phases in Evoked Set Formation," *Journal of Consumer Marketing* (Fall 1987), 67–73.

23 Fred M. H. Gregory, "The Money Moment," *Car and Driver* (June 2000): 167–173.

24 For an excellent discussion of the consideration set, see Allan D. Shocker, Moshe Ben-Akiva, Bruno Boccara, and Prakash Nedungadi, "Consideration Set Influences on Customer Decision Making and Choice: Issues, Models, and Suggestions," *Marketing Letters* (August 1991): 181–198.

25 John Howard and Jagdish Sheth, *The Theory of Buyer Behavior* (New York: John Wiley, 1969).

26 Stewart Shapiro, Deborah J. MacInnis, and Susan E. Heckler, "The Effects of Incidental Ad Exposure on the Formation of Consideration Sets," *Journal of Consumer Research* 24 (June 1997): 94–104.

27 Chakravarti, Amitav and Chris Janiszewski, "The Influence of Macro-Level Motives on Consideration Set Composition in Novel Purchase Situations," *Journal of Consumer Research* 39, no. 2 (2003): 244–258.

28 Rajan Sambandam and Kenneth R. Lord, "Switching Behavior in Automobile Markets: A Consideration-Set Model," *Journal of Academy of Marketing Science* 23 (Winter 1995): 57–65.

29 Ibid., 60.

30 Ayn E. Crowley and John H. Williams, "An Information Theoretic Approach to Understanding the Consideration Set/Awareness Set Proportion," in *Advances in Consumer Research*, vol. 18, ed. Rebecca Holman and Michael Solomon (Provo, UT: Association for Consumer Research, 1991), 780–787.

31 For more technical discussions of the factors that influence whether a brand enters the consideration set, see J. Wesley Hutchinson, Kalyan Raman, and Murali K. Mantrala, "Finding Choice Alternatives in Memory: Probability Models of Brand Recall," *Journal of Marketing Research*, 31, no. 4 (November 1994): 441–461. See also Andreas G. Lazari and Donald A. Anderson, "Designs of Discrete Choice Set Experiments for Estimating Both Attribute and Availability Cross Effects," *Journal of Marketing Research* 31 (August 1994): 375–383.

32 Sharon Beatty and Scott Smith, "External Search Effort: An Investigation Across Several Product Categories," *Journal of Consumer Research* 14 (June 1987): 84.

33 For an excellent review of the factors associated with the extent of external search, see Sharon Beatty and Scott Smith, "External Search Effort: An Investigation Across Several Product Categories," *Journal of Consumer Research* 14 (June 1987): 83–95.

34 Jeff Blodgett and Donna Hill, "An Exploratory Study Comparing Amount-of-Search Measures to Consumers' Reliance on Each Source of Information," in *Advances in Consumer Research*, vol. 18, ed. Rebecca Holman and Michael Solomon (Provo, UT: Association for Consumer Research, 1991), 773–779.

35 Arieh Goldman and J. K. Johansson, "Determinants of Search for Lower Prices: An Empirical Assessment of the Economics of Information Theory," *Journal of Consumer Research* 5 (December 1978): 176–186.

36 For a discussion of how children respond to the costs and benefits of search, see Jennifer Gregan-Paxton and Deborah Roedder John, "Are Young Children Adaptive Decision Makers? A Study of Age Differences in Information Search Behavior," *Journal of Consumer Research* 21, (March 1995): 567–580.

37 For a conceptual discussion of the factors that influence retail search processes, see Philip A. Titus and Peter B. Everett, "The Consumer Retail Search Process: A Conceptual Model and Research Agenda," *Journal of Academy of Marketing Science* 23, (Spring 1995): 106–119.

38 Janet R. McColl-Kennedy and Richard E. Fetter, Jr., "An Empirical Examination of the Involvement to External Search Relationship in Services Marketing," *Journal of Services Marketing* 15, no. 2 (2001):82–98.

[39] D. S. Sundaram and Ronald D. Taylor, "An investigation of External Information Search Effort: Replication in In-Home Shopping Situations," in *Advances in Consumer Research*, vol. 25, ed. Joseph W. Alba and J. Wesley Hutchinson (Provo, UT: Association for Consumer Research, 1998), 440–445.

[40] Sharon Beatty and Scott Smith, "External Search Effort: An Investigation Across Several Product Categories," *Journal of Consumer Research* 14 (June 1987): 83–95.

[41] N. Capon and M. Burke, "Individual, Product Class, and Task-Related Factors in Consumer Information Processing," *Journal of Consumer Research* 7 (August 1972): 249–257.

[42] D. R. Lehmann and W. L. Moore, "Validity of Information Display Boards: An Assessment Using Longitudinal Data," *Journal of Marketing Research* 17 (November 1980): 450–459.

[43] Stanton G. Cort and Luis V. Dominguez, "Cross-Shopping and Retail Growth," *Journal of Marketing* 14, no. 2 (May 1977): 187–192.

[44] Sridhar Moorthy, Brian T. Ratchford, and Debabrata Talukdar, "Consumer Information Search Revisited: Theory and Empirical Analysis," *Journal of Consumer Research* 23 (March 1997): 263–277.

[45] W. Dommermuth, "The Shopping Matrix and Marketing Strategy," *Journal of Marketing Research* 2 (May 1965): 128–132.

[46] J. Udell, "Prepurchase Behavior of Buyers of Small Appliances," *Journal of Marketing* 30 (October 1966): 50–52.

[47] Joseph W. Newman and Richard Staelin, "Prepurchase Information Seeking for New Cars and Major Household Appliances," *Journal of Marketing Research* 9, no. 3 (August 1972): 249–257.

[48] Peter R. Dickson and Alan G. Sawyer, "The Price Knowledge and Search of Supermarket Shoppers," *Journal of Marketing* 54 (July 1990): 42–53.

[49] Girish Punj, "Presearch Decision Making in Consumer Durable Purchases," *Journal of Consumer Marketing* 4 (Winter 1987): 71–82.

[50] Peter Bloch and Marsha Richins, "Shopping without Purchase: An Investigation of Consumer Browsing Behavior," in *Advances in Consumer Research*, vol. 10, ed. Richard Bagozzi and Alice Tybout (Ann Arbor, MI: Association for Consumer Research, 1983), 389–393.

[51] J. Newman and B. Lockeman, "Measuring Prepurchase Information Seeking," *Journal of Consumer Research* 2 (December 1975): 216–222.

[52] Ellen C. Garbarino and Julie A. Edell, "Cognitive Effort, Affect, and Choice," *Journal of Consumer Research* 24 (September 1997): 147–158.

[53] Davis, Harry, Stephen Hoch, and E. K. Ragdale, "An Anchoring and Adjustment Model of Spousal Predictions," *Journal of Consumer Research* 13 (June 1986): 25–37.

[54] Hanjoon Lee, Acito Acito, and Ralph Day, "Evaluation and Use of Marketing Research by Decision Makers: A Behavioral Simulation," *Journal of Marketing Research* 24 (May 1987): 187–196.

[55] Amos Tversky and Daniel Kahneman, "Availability: A Heuristic for Judging Frequency and Probability," *Cognitive Psychology* 5 (1987): 107–232.

[56] For more work on estimations based on information in memory, see Geeta Menon, Priya Raghubir, and Norbert Schwarz, "Behavioral Frequency Judgments: An Accessibility-Diagnosticity Framework," *Journal of Consumer Research* 22 (1995): 212–228.

[57] W. Larry Gregory, Robert Cialdini, and Kathleen Carpenter, "Self-Relevant Scenarios As Mediators of Likelihood Estimates and Compliance: Does Imagining Make It So?" *Journal of Personality and Social Psychology* 43 (1982): 89–99.

[58] Daniel Kahneman and Amos Tversky, "Subjective Probability: A Judgment of Representativeness," *Cognitive Psychology* 3 (1972): 430–454.

[59] Daniel Kahneman and Amos Tversky, "Choices, Values, and Frames," *American Psychologist* 39 (1984): 341–350.

[60] Christine Gonzalez, "This Daffy Duck Has Ribs, and They Can Really Be Broken," *Wall Street Journal*, August 2, 1993, 1, 4.

[61] Daniel Kahneman and Amos Tversky, "Prospect Theory: An Analysis of Decisions under Risk," *Econometrica* 47 (March): 263–291.

[62] For a review on prospect theory and framing, see Alice A. Wright and Richard J. Lutz, "Effects of Advertising and Experience on Brand Judgments: A Rose by Any Other Frame," in *Advances in Consumer Research*, vol. 20, ed. Leigh McAlister and Michael L. Rothschild (Provo, UT: Association for Consumer Research, 1992), 165–169. See also Donald J. Hempel and Harold Z. Daniel, "Framing Issues and Perspectives," in *Advances in Consumer Research*, vol. 20, ed. Leigh

McAlister and Michael L. Rothschild (Provo, UT: Association for Consumer Research, 1992), 273–279.

[63] Daniel Kahneman and Amos Tversky, "Choices, Values, and Frames," *American Psychologist* 39 (1984): 341–350.

[64] For a discussion of the impact of framing on direct-mail solicitations, see Gerald E. Smith and Paul D. Berger, "The Impact of Framing, Anchorpoints, and Frames of Reference on Direct Mail Charitable Contributions," in *Advances in Consumer Research*, vol. 22, ed. Frank R. Kardes and Mita Sujan (Provo, UT: Association for Consumer Research, 1995), 705–712. For a discussion of the impact of presentation format on framing, see James E. Stoddard and Edward F. Fern, "The Effect of Information Presentation Format and Decision Frame on Choice in an Organizational Buying Context," in *Advances in Consumer Research*, vol. 23, ed. Kim Corfman and John G. Lynch, Jr. (Provo, UT: Association for Consumer Research, 1996), 211–217. See also William D. Diamond and Abhijut Sanyal, "The Effects of Framing on the Choice of Supermarket Coupons," in *Advances in Consumer Research*, vol. 17, ed. Marvin E. Goldberg and Gerald Gorn (Provo, UT: Association for Consumer Research, 1990), 488–493. In addition, see John Mowen, Alan Gordon, and Clifford Young, "The Impact of Sales Taxes on Store Choice: Public Policy and Theoretical Implications," *Proceedings of Summer Educators' Conference* (Chicago: American Marketing Association, 1988).

[65] Christopher Puto, Wesley Patton, and Ronald King, "Risk Handling Strategies in Industrial Vendor Selection Decisions," *Journal of Marketing* 49 (Winter 1985): 89–98.

[66] In other research, the investigators found the framing of information about television sets influenced perceptions of risk. See Dhruv Grewal, Jerry Gotlieb, and Howard Marmorstein, "The Moderating Effects of Message Framing and Source Credibility on the Price Perceived Risk Relationship," *Journal of Consumer Research* 21 (June 1994), 145–151.

[67] Irwin Levin, "Associative Effects of Information Framing," *Bulletin of the Psychonomic Society* 25 (1987): 85–86.

[68] For additional research on the effects of framing, see Lauren G. Block and Punam Anand Keller, "When to Accentuate the Negative: The Effects of Perceived Efficacy and Message Framing on Intentions to Perform a Health-Related Behavior," *Journal of Marketing Research* 32 (May 1995): 192–203.

[69] Chernev, Alexnder, "When More Is Less and Less Is More: The Role of Ideal Point Availability and Assortment in Consumer Choice," *Journal of Consumer Research* 30, no. 2 (2003): 170–183.

[70] Benjamin Scheibehenne, Rainer Greifeneder, and Peter M. Todd, "Can There Ever Be Too Many Options? A Meta-Analytic Review of Choice Overload," *Journal of Consumer Research* 37 (2010): 409–425.

[71] Eloise Coupey, "Restructuring: Constructive Processing of Information Displays in Consumer Choice," *Journal of Consumer Research* 21 (June 1994): 83–99.

[72] For recent discussions of choice models, see Pratibha A. Dabholkar, "Incorporating Choice into an Attitudinal Framework: Analyzing Models of Mental Comparison Processes," *Journal of Consumer Research* 21(June 1994): 100–118. See also Maryon F. King and Siva K. Balasubramanian, "The Effects of Expertise, End Goal, and Product Type on Adoption of Preference Formation Strategy," *Journal of the Academy of Marketing Science* 22 (Spring 1994): 146–159.

[73] This section on noncompensatory models relies heavily on work by Peter Wright, "Consumer Choice Strategies: Simplifying Versus Optimizing," *Journal of Marketing Research* 11 (February 1976): 60–67. See also Dennis Gensch and Rajshekhar Javalgi, "The Influence of Involvement on Disaggregate Attribute Choice Models," *Journal of Consumer Research* 14 (June 1987): 71–82.

[74] Alan Newell and Herbert Simon, *Human Problem Solving* (Englewood Cliffs, NJ: Prentice Hall, 1972).

[75] Peter Wright, "Consumer Choice Strategies: Simplifying Versus Optimizing," *Journal of Marketing Research* 11 (February 1976): 60–67.

[76] Joseph W. Alba and Howard Marmorstein, "The Effects of Frequency Knowledge on Consumer Decision Making," *Journal of Consumer Research* 14 (June 1987): 14–25.

[77] Ibid.

[78] M. Reilly and R. Holman, "Does Task Complexity or Cue Intercorrelation Affect Choice of an Information-Processing Strategy? An Empirical Investigation," in *Advances in Consumer Research*, vol. 4, ed. W. D. Perrault, Jr. (Atlanta: Association for Consumer Research, 1977), 185–190.

[79] Adapted from M. Reilly and R. Holman, "Does Task Complexity or Cue Intercorrelation Affect Choice of an Information Processing Strategy?: An Empirical Investigation," in *Advances in Consumer Research*, vol. 4, ed. W. D. Perreault, Jr. (Atlanta: Association for Consumer Research, 1977), 189.

[80] Banwari Mittal, "A Study of Affective Choice for Consumer Decisions," in *Advances in Consumer Research*, vol. 21, ed. Chris T. Allen and Deborah Roedder John (Provo, UT: Association for Consumer Research, 1994), 256–263.

[81] P. Weinberg and W. Gottwald, "Impulsive Consumer Buying As a Result of Emotions," *Journal of Business Research* 10 (March 1982): 43–87.

[82] Mary Frances Luce, "Choosing to Avoid: Coping with Negatively Emotion-Laden Consumer Decisions," *Journal of Consumer Research* 24 (March 1998): 409–433. See also Mary Frances Luce, John W. Payne, and James R. Bettman, "Emotional Trade-Off Difficulty and Choice," *Journal of Marketing Research* 36 (May 1999): 143–159.

[83] Wayne D. Hoyer and Steven P. Brown, "Effects of Brand Awareness on Choice for a Common, Repeat-Purchase Product," *Journal of Consumer Research* 17 (September 1990): 141–148. Not all research is supportive of mere exposure effects. For example, see John W. Pracejus, "Is More Exposure Always Better?: Effects of Incidental Exposure to a Brand Name on Subsequent Processing of Advertising," in *Advances in Consumer Research*, vol. 22, ed. Frank R. Kardes and Mita Sujan (Provo, UT: Association for Consumer Research, 1995), 319–327.

[84] Dennis Rook and Stephen Hoch, "Consuming Impulses," in *Advances in Consumer Research*, vol. 12, ed. E. Hirschman and M. Holbrook (Ann Arbor, MI: Association for Consumer Research, 1985), 23–27.

[85] For a review and analysis of impulse purchasing, see James E. Burroughs, "Product Symbolism, Self-Meaning, and Holistic Matching: The Role of Information Processing in Impulsive Buying," in *Advances in Consumer Research*, vol. 23, ed. Kim P. Corfman and John G. Lynch, Jr. (Provo, UT: Association for Consumer Research, 1994), 463–469.

[86] Dennis Rook and Stephen Hoch, "Consuming Impulses," in *Advances in Consumer Research*, vol. 12, ed. E. Hirschman and M. Holbrook (Ann Arbor, MI: Association for Consumer Research, 1985), 23–27.

[87] "Industrial Retail Selling Strategies Designed to Induce Impulse Sales," *Beverage Industry*, June 3, 1977, 6ff.

[88] Dennis Rook and Stephen Hoch, "Consuming Impulses," in *Advances in Consumer Research*, vol. 12, ed. E. Hirschman and M. Holbrook (Ann Arbor, MI: Association for Consumer Research, 1985), 23–27.

[89] Arthur J. O'Connor, "The Power of Popularity: An Empirical Study of the Relationship between Social Media Fan Counts and Brand Company Stock Prices," *Social Science Computer Review* (2012): 1–7.

[90] M. Venkatesan, "Cognitive Consistency and Novelty Seeking," in *Consumer Behavior: Theoretical Sources*, ed. Scott Ward and Thomas Robertson (Englewood Cliffs, NJ: Prentice Hall, 1973), 354–384.

[91] P. S. Raju, "Optimum Stimulation Level: Its Relationship to Personality, Demographics, and Exploratory Behavior," *Journal of Consumer Research* 7 (December 1980): 272–282. For a review of variety seeking, see Leigh McAlister and Edgar Pessemier, "Variety Seeking Behavior: An Interdisciplinary Review," *Journal of Consumer Research* 9 (December 1982): 311–322.

[92] Piyush Sharma, Bharadhwaj Sivakumaran, and Roger Marshall, "Investigating Impulse Buying and Variety Seeking: Towards a General Theory of Hedonic Purchase Behaviors," *Advances in Consumer Research* 33 (2006): 388–389.

[93] Meryl Gardner and Ronald Hill, "Consumers' Mood States: Antecedents and Consequences of Experiential vs. Information Strategies for Brand Choice," *Psychology and Marketing* 5, no. 2 (1988): 169–182.

[94] Michael A. Kamins, Lawrence J. Marks, and Deborah Skinner, "Television Commercial Evaluation in the Context of Program-Induced Mood: Congruency versus Consistency Effects," *Journal of Advertising* XX, no. 2 (1991): 1–14.

[95] Michael Johnson, "Consumer-Choice Strategies for Comparing Noncomparable Alternatives," *Journal of Consumer Research* 11 (December 1984): 741–753. See also Barbara Kahn, William Moore, and Rashi Glazer, "Experiments in Constrained Choice," *Journal of Consumer Research* 14 (June 1987): 96–113.

[96] A topic related to choice comparability is decision difficulty. For a discussion, see Eloise Coupey and Carol W. DeMoranville, "Information Processability and Restructuring: Consumer

Strategies for Managing Difficult Decisions," in *Advances in Consumer Research,* vol. 23, ed. Kim Corfman and John G. Lynch, Jr. (Provo, UT: Association for Consumer Research, 1996), 225–230.

[97] James Bruner and John Mason, "The Influence of Driving Time upon Shopping Center Preference," *Journal of Marketing* 32 (April 1968): 57–61.

[98] Susan Spiggle and Murphy Sewall, "A Choice Sets Model of Retail Selection," *Journal of Marketing* 51 (April 1987): 97–111.

[99] Ibid.

10

Loyalty and Satisfaction

Learning Objectives

1. How do we create a satisfying experience for customers?

2. Why do customers complain?

3. How does disposing of a product affect customers?

4. How is satisfaction related to loyalty?

Exceptional Service Leads to Customer Satisfaction and Loyalty

The Ritz Carlton Hotel is renowned for its top-of-the-line customer service. By delivering exceptional customer service, the hotel benefits from high customer satisfaction and customer loyalty. To gain this satisfaction and loyalty, Ritz-Carlton empowers its employees to discover customer needs and then to satisfy them. Joseph Michelli tells a story of a Ritz Carlton employee overhearing that a guest's son was turning four years old during their hotel stay.[1] Additionally, the parents mentioned the child's love for Spider-Man. Without having to ask for permission to act, the employee ordered a Spider-Man cake to be delivered to the family's dinner table. Further, the cake was delivered by a man in a Spider-Man costume.[2] Obviously, the family's satisfaction and loyalty was enhanced by this employee going the extra mile to make their stay a good one.

Another example of the Ritz-Carlton culture of service is the use of its customer relationship management computer system, which the company named "Mystique."[3] Customers often have preferences for specific brands. When a Ritz-Carlton customer orders a Coca-Cola at the bar, for instance, the employee enters the request into the computer system. When this same customer stays at another Ritz-Carlton property, the room staff fills the guest's minibar with Coca-Cola to satisfy the customer's preference. Ritz-Carlton is one example of a firm that believes satisfaction and loyalty are key elements to long-term business success.

Chapter 9 discussed the first four stages of the consumer decision process: problem recognition, information search, alternative evaluation, and choice. This chapter focuses on the last stage of consumer decision making: post-acquisition processes. **Post-acquisition processes** refer to the consumption, postchoice evaluation, and disposition of goods, services, experiences, and ideas. During the

postchoice evaluation stage, purchase satisfaction or dissatisfaction may occur. Indeed, providing high levels of satisfaction is a major goal of most corporations, from local restaurants to Delta Airlines to General Motors.

Figure 10.1 presents a model of the consumer post-acquisition process, which encompasses five major topics: product usage or consumption, consumer satisfaction and dissatisfaction, consumer complaint behavior, the disposition of goods, and the formation of brand loyalty. During the consumption stage, consumers use and experience the product. This stage is followed by the development of consumer satisfaction or dissatisfaction. If consumers are dissatisfied with the product's performance, complaint behavior may occur. The final two stages of the post-acquisition process involve how consumers dispose of the goods they purchase and how brand loyalty and future buying intentions are formed.

FIGURE 10.1
A Model of the Consumer
Post-Acquisition Process

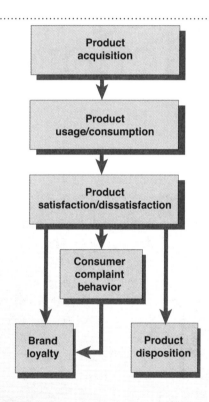

THE QUALITIES OF A SATISFYING EXPERIENCE

A consumer's **consumption experience** may be defined as the cognitions and feelings experienced by a person during the use of a product or service. In the following subsections, the three elements of the consumption experience will be discussed: product use, consumption of performance, and impact of moods and feelings on the overall consumption experience.

Product Use

Product use involves the actions and experiences that take place when a consumer is directly experiencing a good or service. The observation of how consumers use goods can lead to the development of new market offerings. For example, Boston Beer Company founder Jim Koch's strategy to discover new products came directly from the customer. To build the brand, he regularly visited with bar customers to discover the next great beer.[4]

Another area in which information on product usage can be important is in avoiding product liability problems. Companies must design a product so it's safe in the use for which it was designed. In addition, companies should take steps to anticipate unintended uses of their products and either design them for safe use or provide warnings they shouldn't be used in certain applications. For example, aluminum stepladders include warnings not to stand on the top of the ladder and to avoid use near electrical lines.

Marketers have identified three factors that are particularly important when assessing product usage.[5] First, the **consumption frequency** should be analyzed. Some products are used continuously (e.g., refrigerators and water heaters). Most products, however, are used discontinuously (e.g., dishwashers, medical services, toothpaste, and autos). In general, companies want consumers to use their products or service as frequently as possible (exceptions include efforts to reduce or eliminate the abuse of drugs).[6] An example of how firms are attempting to increase consumption frequency can be found in the coffee industry. Starbucks introduced its "Treat Receipts" promotion in an effort to increase consumption frequency. With this promotion, a customer who makes a purchase before 2:00 p.m. gets a large discount in the afternoon. By returning to any Starbucks after 2:00 p.m. with the receipt from the purchase made earlier in the day, the customer can buy a grande-sized beverage for $2, saving over 50 percent on a drink such as a Frappuccino.[7] This tactic offers a means to increase frequency as well as loyalty.

The **consumption amount** is the second issue for marketers to evaluate. In many cases, companies may develop strategies to increase the average amount of a product consumed. General Mills realized it could influence the consumption amount of its cereals via shelf placement. Because most people are right-handed, they naturally reach for cereals that are on the right side of a display. By putting larger packages toward the right, larger packages are more often bought.[8] Additionally, researchers discovered the shelf placement of dog treats can greatly impact sales. Retail anthropologist Paco Underhill found the primary target market for dog treats is twofold: senior citizens and families with small children. Both senior citizens and children may have difficulty reaching items on upper shelves. By placing the treats on lower shelves, sales increased dramatically.[9]

The **consumption purpose** is the third category researchers consider. A classic example of a company that has attempted to increase the number of purposes for which a product may be used is Arm & Hammer. A few of the many uses suggested for its baking soda include baking, brushing teeth, freshening a carpet, and serving as an antacid. Consumption purpose is closely related to what is called usage occasion. More will be said about usage occasions in Chapter 11.

Managerial principle 10.1
To better meet consumer needs, you must understand product use, consumption frequency, amount, and purpose.

Social Media

Ritz-Carlton Embraces Social Media

The luxury hotel brand Ritz-Carlton ranks #1 in social media within the hospitality industry. Ritz-Carlton receives almost four times more engagement than any other hotel chain. Back in 2009, the brand made a strategic decision to not target the large audience of unqualified fans, but rather the keen travel, luxury brand enthusiasts. The brand connects with past, present and future guests. The Ritz-Carlton does not use promotions and contests in these communications in the hopes of creating lasting relationships rather than short-term sales.[10]

The Consumption of Performance

Researchers argue our economy has evolved through a four-stage process of commodities, goods, services, and experiences.[11] **Commodities** are categories such as animals and minerals that are extracted from the natural world. By definition, commodities are fungible and can't be differentiated. Over time, we created **goods** that are differentiated by adding value to the commodities. In this sense, the commodities enabled goods. As our economic system developed, we created **services** by performing tasks for the customer. Finally, we developed experiences for the customer. **Experiences** are more memorable for the customer as we include acts of theater and surprise. Figure 10.2 displays the stages of the consumption of performance model. In the model, each stage enables the subsequent stage.

FIGURE 10.2
The Consumption of Performance Model
Model developed based on the work of Pine & Gilmore, "The Experience Economy". (1999).

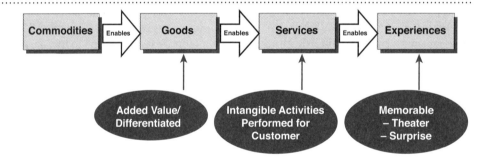

One vivid example of these stages is offered by B. Joseph Pine and James H. Gilmore. In years past, mothers purchased the commodities of flour, sugar, and chocolate to make a birthday cake from scratch. Companies such as Duncan Hines and Betty Crocker realized there could be money in combining these commodities for the customer, so they began selling the good of cake mixes in boxes. Over time, individuals started the service of baking the cake for the customer. Consumers can now purchase personalized cakes from professional cake makers or from almost any grocery store. An example of these specialized cakes is demonstrated on hit cable TV shows such as *Ace of Cakes* and *Cake Boss*, where bakers make elaborate cakes to fit their customers' specific requests.

In the last stage of this performance model, we find marketers creating experiences for the customer. Instead of just making a cake for the customer, we now offer all sorts of birthday experiences, such as attending a petting zoo or

Managerial principle 10.2
By creating a memorable experience, you increase the price customers are willing to pay.

a holding a theme party at a professional sports franchise. In these cases, the customer is an active participant in the consumption of performance.

Consumption Experience

Marketing researchers suggest people in Western society frame the consumption experience as though they were participating in a performance. Using naturalistic research methods borrowed from anthropology and sociology, researchers have investigated dramatic consumer performances such as sky diving and white-water river rafting.[12]

What does it mean to say consumers are participating in a performance? From a dramaturgical perspective, consumers and marketers act as though they're in a theatrical performance.[13] For example, when rafting down the Colorado River, the participants and their guide are actors. The boat, life vests, food, mosquito repellants, and so on are the props for the play. The Colorado River and the canyon form the stage. Within this backdrop, a story is told. In the first stage of the story, conflicting forces are introduced. For example, the participants ask themselves if they really want to participate in a white-water experience. During the second stage, tensions and emotions build as participants experience fear, hunger, and cold. In the conclusion, the conflict is resolved and emotions are released.

Marketers seek to script the exchange performance that occurs with customers. Indeed, consumers and marketers can be viewed as being in an "exchange play" in which each performs to a greater or lesser degree. For our purposes, a **consumer performance** can be defined as an event in which a consumer and a marketer act as performers or audience in a situation in which obligations and standards exist.[14] It's important to distinguish a performance from an **occurrence**. An occurrence happens as the result of an accident or act of nature. It's unplanned and doesn't arise from any obligation.

Table 10.1 distinguishes occurrences from three types of performances. In a **contracted performance**, the consumer and the marketer play only minimal roles. Contracted performances most frequently involve the purchase and use of low-involvement products, such as detergent, toothpaste, motor oil, or checking accounts.

1. *Contracted.* Both the consumer and the marketer have minimal interactions—occur with low-involvement goods.
2. *Enacted.* Both the consumer and the marketer have sufficient latitude to place blame for the outcome of the transaction—occur most frequently with high-involvement products.
3. *Dramatistic.* Both the consumer and the marketer know a show is occurring, and each party becomes concerned with the motives of the other—occur most frequently in the highest-involvement situations, such as skydiving or buying an automobile.

TABLE 10.1
Types of Consumer Performances

When the audience recognizes a satisfactory exchange depends on the performance of a person, an **enacted performance** takes place. Here, the exchange occurs in a manner in which the consumer or marketer can blame or give credit to the other for the outcome of the transaction. Enacted performances occur most frequently in service exchanges or with high-involvement goods. For example, the performance involved in being a passenger on an airline or a patient in the dentist's chair is enacted. Similarly, the purchase of a car involves both the consumer and the salesperson in a complex exchange in which blame or credit can be assessed by either party.

The third type of performance, **dramatistic performance**, occurs when both the consumer and the marketer know a show is occurring, and each monitors the other's role. The producer is putting on a show, and the consumer knows it. In a dramatistic performance, the stakes are large and the involvement levels of both the consumer and the marketer are quite high. In such instances, each actor is an audience to the other, and each becomes alert to the motives of the other in the performance, recognizing the actions of the other could be contrived. An example is a situation in which a consumer believes he or she has been wronged by a company and begins to complain. Another example is the performances that occur on a white-water rafting expedition or during skydiving, which also have a dramatistic flare. In other words, in both enacted and dramatistic performances, there's an element of theater, but in dramatistic performances, the marketer is deliberately trying to contrive an effect.

Cold Stone Creamery

In the 1950s, customers went to a malt shop and watched the server hand scoop ice cream into a stainless steel container followed by adding milk and chocolate. The items were then mixed to create a hand-made milk shake. Through the years, ice cream stores decided it was more cost effective to buy liquid soft serve and dispense ice cream from a machine.

At Cold Stone Creamery customers enjoy both the treats and the performance of making the treat.

One brand has brought us back to those good old days: Cold Stone Creamery. Cold Stone uses dramatic performance to engage its customers. They not only prepare shakes but a variety of hand mixed treats as well. Servers scoop up your choice of ice cream onto a cold stone surface where they add your choice of toppings, including cherries, pie crust, nuts, and more. The drama continues when you drop some change into the tip jar. The entire "cast" will sing you a song of appreciation.

The Peabody Hotel

The Peabody Hotel successfully uses dramatic performance to enhance the customer experience. Locations in Memphis, Tennessee, Orlando, Florida, and Little Rock, Arkansas, roll out the red carpet for their special guests: mallard ducks. At 11:00 a.m. each day, the duck master escorts a flock of ducks from the elevator down the red carpet. As the employee escorts the ducks to the indoor fountain, he entertains hotel guests with the story of how the ducks became part of the hotel. (In 1934, some intoxicated hotel guests played a prank on the hotel by capturing some ducks and placing them around the fountain. The hotel decided to include the ducks as part of its mystique). Today, the birds swim around the fountain until late afternoon each day. The drama performance continues at 5:00 p.m., when the duck master repeats the story and escorts the fowl to their rooftop home.

The metaphor of drama is particularly appropriate when purchasing services such as a hotel room at the Peabody. The dramaturgy metaphor may also hold for the purchase and use of goods. Indeed, a good can be described as merely the "frozen potential for performance."[15] Thus, consumers not only choose goods but also consume performances when they use the good. We even speak of a detergent or a car as performing well. At the extreme, building a house in which tens or hundreds of thousands of dollars are invested can take on the characteristics of a Greek tragedy.

The Peabody Hotel creates a unique brand positioning with its feathered guests

Mood States and the Consumption Experience

Moods are temporary positive or negative affective states. An important issue concerns the impact of the consumption experience on mood states. As discussed in Chapters 4 and 9, consumer mood states may have a strong impact on what's remembered and on which brand is chosen. Moods may be influenced by what happens during the consumption of a product. The mood state that's created during the consumption process may, in turn, influence the overall evaluation of the product.

One study investigated the impact of music on consumer mood states and subsequent product evaluations.[16] Respondents in the study either heard music they had rated very positively or very negatively. While listening to the music, they rated the taste of peanut butter. Premeasures indicated music rated positively influenced respondents to be in a more positive mood than those exposed to music rated negatively. Different groups of subjects rated one of three types of peanut butter, which in pretests were determined to taste very good, neutral, or very bad. The results revealed the type of music did not impact brand evaluations for the good- or the bad-tasting peanut butter. However, for the neutral-tasting peanut butter, brand evaluations were significantly higher when the music was liked than when it was disliked. In sum, consumer feelings about the consumption experience will affect their evaluations of the product independent of the actual quality of the product. Post-purchase evaluation of products is closely related to the development of feelings of satisfaction or dissatisfaction with the exchange process, which is the topic discussed next.

Managerial principle 10.3
Dramatistic performance engages the consumer by making the service memorable.

THE DEVELOPMENT OF POST-ACQUISITION SATISFACTION AND DISSATISFACTION

Consumers develop feelings of satisfaction and dissatisfaction during and after consuming a product or service. **Consumer satisfaction** is defined as the overall attitude regarding a good or service after its acquisition and use. It's a post-choice evaluative judgment resulting from a specific purchase selection and the experience of consuming or using it.[17] The word *satisfaction* comes from the Latin *satis*, meaning "enough." Hence, satisfaction takes on the meaning of

Managerial principle 10.4
Customer satisfaction is influenced by a number of factors, including emotions, overall exchange equity, expectations, performance, and attributions.

giving the customer enough. To put it more simply, satisfaction means meeting customer expectations.

From a managerial perspective, maintaining or enhancing customer satisfaction is critical. Three studies highlight the importance of customer satisfaction to the financial returns of firms. First, researchers in one study demonstrated customer satisfaction is a strong predictor of future growth in discretionary spending.[18] Firms can gain more profits as these satisfied consumers spend more of their income. In a second study, researchers found firms with higher customer satisfaction scores benefit from lower overall market risk.[19] In this case, firms that have lower risk due to less stock volatility are able to pass more profits on to their stockholders. A third study examined the satisfaction level of customers with Swedish companies. The results revealed, over a four -year period, an annual 1 percent increase in customer satisfaction resulted in an 11.4 percent increase in the companies' return on investment. The researchers found satisfied customers positively influence future cash flows. Thus, programs to increase customer satisfaction should be treated as investments.[20]

What factors contribute to feelings of consumer satisfaction or dissatisfaction (CS/D)? Figure 10.3 presents a model of CS/D. In the model, consumers are

FIGURE 10.3
A Model of Consumer Satisfaction or Dissatisfaction

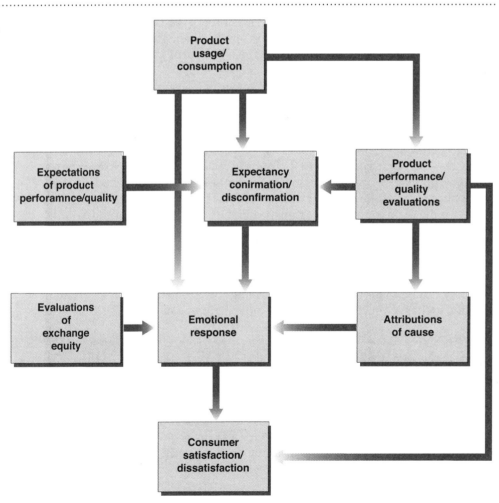

shown as consuming or using the good or service. Based on this experience, they evaluate its overall performance. This performance assessment has been found to be closely related to the ratings of the quality of the product.[21] These perceptions of product quality are compared to the consumer's expectations of the product's performance. An evaluation process then takes place in which consumers act as though they compare actual performance with expected performance. Based on that comparison (i.e., depending on whether expectations were confirmed), consumers will experience positive, negative, or neutral emotions. These emotional responses act as inputs into the overall perception of satisfaction or dissatisfaction.

In addition, the consumer's evaluation of the equity of the exchange will affect his or her level of satisfaction or dissatisfaction. Finally, attributions of the cause of the product's performance will also impact the attitude of satisfaction or dissatisfaction. The following sections discuss each of these ideas.

Evaluating Product Performance and Quality

Over the past twenty years, companies throughout the world have embraced the ideas that successful companies should continuously improve the quality of their products and that quality is defined by customers. **Product quality** is customers' overall evaluation of the excellence of the performance of a good or service.[22] A key issue in assessing perceived product performance concerns what aspects consumers use to make this assessment. Researchers in the services area have identified five dimensions on which consumers evaluate service quality. Part A of Table 10.2 details these dimensions.[23] Notice that four of the items are directly related to how the service personnel treat the customer.

Managerial principle 10.5
Your service personnel's attitudes and behaviors determine the customer's evaluation of service quality.

TABLE 10.2
Dimensions of Quality

Part A: Service

1. *Tangibles.* Include physical facilities, equipment, and appearance of personnel.
2. *Reliability.* The ability of personnel to perform dependably and accurately.
3. *Responsiveness.* Providing customers with prompt service.
4. *Assurance.* The knowledge and courtesy of employees, as well as their ability to inspire trust and confidence.
5. *Empathy.* The ability of employees to care and to provide individualized attention.

Source: A. Parasuraman, Valarie A. Zeithaml, and Leonard L. Berry, "SERVQUAL: A Multiple-Item Scale for Measuring Consumer Perceptions of Service Quality," *Journal of Retailing* 64 (Spring 1988): 12–36.

Part B: Product

1. *Performance.* Achievement of primary operating characteristics.
2. *Features.* The number of bells and whistles that supplement primary characteristics.
3. *Reliability.* Probability of failing or malfunctioning.
4. *Durability.* The life of the product.
5. *Serviceability.* Ease of repair and the speed, courtesy, and timeliness of personnel.
6. *Aesthetics.* How the product looks, feels, and sounds.
7. *Conformance to specifications.* Degree to which the product meets production benchmarks.
8. *Perceived quality.* A catchall category that includes the effects of brand image and other intangible factors that influence customers' perceptions of quality.

Source: David A. Garvin, *Managing Quality: The Strategic and Competitive Edge* (New York: Free Press, 1988).

The five dimensions identified in part A of Table 10.2 can be viewed as attributes on which consumers evaluate the overall performance of services. As applied to goods, however, they present a problem because, with the exception of the "tangibles" category, they focus exclusively on the interaction between employees and customers. What's needed is a set of dimensions that includes the concrete attributes consumers associate with goods. Such a set of dimensions has been proposed to assess product quality. These eight categories are listed in part B of Table 10.2. A careful analysis of Table 10.2 shows there's an overlap among the concepts identified in the service-quality and product-quality dimensions. We, the authors of this text, believe it's possible to combine these approaches to identify the following seven basic dimensions of quality:

1. *Performance.* The absolute level of performance of the good or service on the key attributes identified by customers. The extent to which the product or service is "done right." The number of attributes offered. The ability of employees to handle problems well. The quality of the information provided to the customer.

2. *Employee interactions.* The courtesy, friendliness, and empathy shown by people delivering the good or service. The overall credibility of the employees, including consumer trust in the employees and their perceptions of employee expertise.

3. *Reliability.* The consistency of the performance of the good, service, or store.

4. *Durability.* The product's life span and general sturdiness.

5. *Timeliness and convenience.* How quickly the product is received or repaired. How quickly information is provided or service is received. The convenience of the purchase/ service process, including acceptance of credit cards, operating hours, and parking.

6. *Aesthetics.* The physical appearance of the good or store. The attractiveness of the service presentation. The pleasantness of the atmosphere in which the product or service is received. The extent to which the design of the product is appealing.

7. *Brand equity.* The additional positive or negative impact on perceived quality that knowing the brand or store name has on the evaluation.[24]

Research is necessary to establish whether these seven categories fully represent the dimensions on which consumers evaluate quality. In particular, product aesthetics requires additional research. One exploratory study on product design did find consumers evaluated design in a gestalt (i.e., holistic) manner and did so largely unconsciously. Two factors seemed to be related to aesthetic preferences: proportion (i.e., the ratio of length and height of an object) and unity (i.e., the extent to which design elements appear to go together).[25]

Table 10.3 provides examples of how each of the seven categories can be applied to a good (e.g., an automobile) or a service (e.g., an elegant restaurant). A key question concerns how the dimensions of product quality are combined to form an overall impression of quality. We view the formation of overall product quality as a type of overall consumer belief. That is, we think consumers form beliefs about each of the product's quality dimensions and then sum up these beliefs to create an overall belief regarding the quality of the product. In effect, people act as though their perception of the overall performance quality of a product is formed via a type of multi-attribute model.

Product-Quality Dimension	Automobile Quality
1. Performance	Level of horsepower, handling, fit and finish, resale value, number of features (e.g., air bags, ABS breaking system, premium sound system, cup holders)
2. Employee interactions	Friendliness, helpfulness, empathy, credibility of service personnel
3. Reliability	Freedom from vehicle breakdown, consistency of personnel in providing expected levels of service
4. Durability	How long the car lasts before it wears out from use or before it becomes outdated technologically
5. Timeliness and convenience	The ability of the company to provide the vehicle and its service in a timely way, the convenience of the service provided.
6. Aesthetics	The attractiveness and functionality of the layout and style of the car.
7. Brand equity	The extent to which the vehicle's brand name results in customers believing is the restaurant's quality is high or low

Product-Quality Dimension	Restaurant Meal Quality
1. Performance	The degree to which the food is prepared according to standards of taste and temperature. The degree to which staff members know their jobs. The number of extra features provided with the meal (e.g., fresh flowers on the table, special breads provided as appetizers, free desserts)
2. Employee Interactions	The friendliness and helpfulness of the staff
3. Reliability	The consistency with which the restaurant provides a high-quality dining experience
4. Durability	The number of years the restaurant successfully pleases its customers
5. Timeliness and convenience	The ability of the staff to provide service in a timely way
6. Aesthetics	The atmosphere of the restaurant, the degree to which the food is pleasing to the eye, the physical attractiveness of the staff
7. Brand equity	The extent to which the restaurant's brand name results in customers believing is the restaurant's quality is high or low

TABLE 10.3
Consumer's Overall Evaluation of Service/Product Quality

The Development of Satisfaction and Dissatisfaction

A model critical for understanding and influencing CS/D is the expectancy disconfirmation model, which defines CS/D as the "evaluation rendered that the experience was at least as good as it was supposed to be."[26] Four additional approaches have been used to explain the formation of CS/D: equity theory, justice theory, attribution theory, and experientially-based affective feelings. In addition, the actual performance of a product has been found to impact CS/D.[27] This section discusses each of these approaches.

The Expectancy Disconfirmation Model (The Disconfirmation Paradigm)

The process through which CS/D is formed begins with the use of a product, as well as the use of other brands in the product class. Because of this usage behavior, as well as communications from companies and other people, consumers develop expectations of how the brand should perform. Consumers compare these performance expectations with **actual product performance** (i.e., the perception of the product's quality). If quality falls below consumers' expectations, **emotional dissatisfaction** will result. If it's above their expectations, they feel **emotional satisfaction**.[28] If performance is perceived as equal to expectations, consumers experience **expectancy confirmation**.[29] In fact, when expectations and actual performance coincide, evidence indicates consumers may simply not consciously consider their level of satisfaction with the product. Thus, although expectancy confirmation is a positive state, it often doesn't result in strong feelings of satisfaction. Strong satisfaction is apparently experienced only when actual performance is markedly superior to expected performance.

An example of the disconfirmation paradigm is found in a recent satisfaction study on movie sequels. The findings of the study demonstrate fans strongly support movie sequels in the early weeks of release. However, viewers quickly become less satisfied. The researchers attribute this finding to the expectation the sequel will be "fresh" and "new," when, in fact, sequels are often reconfigurations of the original movie.[30] Thus, the sequels don't necessarily live up to expectations.

Product expectations are the standard against which the actual performance of the product is assessed.[31] The level of performance expected of a product is influenced by the nature of the product itself, by promotional factors, by the effects of other products, and by the characteristics of the consumer. Consumers' prior experiences with the product, its price, and its physical characteristics all influence how they expect it to perform. Thus, if the product has a high price or has performed extremely well in the past, consumers will expect it to meet high performance standards.

How the company promotes the product through its advertising and the communications of sales personnel also influences performance expectations. A consultant with a market-research firm noted advertising hype can create expectations that are impossible to satisfy.[32] How a retailer chooses to organize items in a store is a form of promotion that can affect satisfaction. Research demonstrates high-knowledge customers are more satisfied when shelves are organized in an unexpected format.[33] The unexpectedness becomes a sense of newness, which engages the knowledgeable customers.

Consumers' expectations of performance are also influenced by their experience with similar products. For example, a key factor affecting consumer perceptions of the quality of medical services is the timeliness with which medical care is delivered. Physicians and hospitals have been slow to recognize consumers form their expectations of timeliness as much from their experiences with banks and restaurants as from their experiences with other medical facilities.

Finally, performance expectations are influenced by the individual characteristics of the consumer. Some consumers simply expect more of products than others do. Likewise, some consumers have wider latitudes of acceptance than others. Consumers with very narrow regions of acceptance are, of course, more easily dissatisfied than those with broad regions of acceptance.

Equity Theory and Consumer Satisfaction   Another approach to understanding consumer satisfaction is through equity theory. Researchers have found people analyze the exchange between themselves and other parties to determine the extent to which those exchanges are equitable, or fair.[34] **Equity theory** holds that people will analyze the ratio of their **outcomes** and **inputs** to the ratio of the outcomes and inputs of their partner in an exchange and experience feelings of inequity if they perceive their ratio is higher. The following equation shows these ratios:

$$\frac{\text{Outcome A}}{\text{Input A}} = \frac{\text{Outcome B}}{\text{Input B}}$$

The outcomes person A receives from an exchange divided by the inputs of person A to the exchange should equal the outcomes of person B from the exchange divided by the inputs of person B to the exchange.[35]

According to equity theory, the norm is each party to an exchange should be treated equitably. Therefore, satisfaction occurs when the ratios of outcomes and inputs for each party to the exchange are approximately equal. When the buyer believes his or her ratio of inputs to outcomes is worse than the seller's, the buyer experiences inequity, which leads to dissatisfaction.

Just what are a consumer exchange's inputs and outcomes? From the consumer's perspective, inputs are the information, effort, money, or time exerted to make an exchange possible. Outcomes for the consumer are the benefits and liabilities received from the exchange. Outcomes could consist of the good or service received from the marketer, the performance of the product, and the feelings obtained from the exchange.

A number of authors have investigated how equity theory can be applied to consumer behavior. One study looked at the exchange process between consumers and an airline.[36] For consumers, the inputs to the exchange consisted primarily of the money they paid for the ticket, and the outcomes consisted of the quality of the service they received and the speed with which the airline got them to their destination. The study revealed customers tended to be dissatisfied with the service if they perceived their inputs to be large because they paid higher-than-average fares. Also, customers revealed more dissatisfaction if they perceived outcomes were poor because flights had been delayed for two hours.[37]

Another study found people consider the outcomes of other consumers in determining their own satisfaction with a transaction.[38] Respondents in the study pretended to be automobile buyers. After the purchase, they learned another person had obtained either a better or worse deal on the same car. When the other consumer had received a better deal on the same car, the respondents were less satisfied with their own transaction and with the auto dealer than when the other consumer got a worse deal. This study shows factors other than the performance of the product may strongly influence feelings of satisfaction—specifically, the evaluation of the overall equity of the purchase transaction.

Note that the process equity theory proposes to explain CS/D is different from the process proposed by the expectancy disconfirmation model. In the expectancy disconfirmation model, CS/D results from the comparison of actual performance with expected performance. Equity theory, on the other hand, holds that satisfaction also results from comparing one's inputs and outcomes with others'.[39] What's the relative impact of equity versus expectancy disconfirmation on consumer satisfaction? In a study of more than four hundred new-car buyers, researchers obtained measures of satisfaction with the salesperson,

Managerial principle 10.6
Satisfaction is more than an evaluation of performance. Customers also consider fairness.

the degree of fairness in the transaction, and the inputs and outcomes of the salesperson and the buyer.[40] Buyers were self-centered—that is, they perceived a deal as fair when the buyer's outcome was high and the seller's inputs were high. Furthermore, perceptions of equity had a greater impact on overall satisfaction than did perceptions of expectation disconfirmation.

Equity theory has three managerial implications. First, marketers should ensure customers recognize all the inputs the company has added to the transaction. Second, as the authors of the new-car buyer study stated, "Equitable exchange from the point of view of the buyer may be seen as inequitable exchange by the salesperson."[41] Third, consumers do form judgments of equity, and these judgments may have a greater impact on satisfaction than expectancy disconfirmation. This combination of findings makes the salesperson's job extremely difficult because it forces the salesperson to manage impressions so buyers believe they're getting a great buy while the salesperson is giving up a great deal to make the sale. Unfortunately, the need to create such an impression encourages salespeople to use hype and false statements to make sales.

Regarding Justice, Product Failures, and Customer Satisfaction All customers encounter situations where the product or service doesn't live up to expectations. In such cases, firms need to develop strategies to address the consumer's perceived level of justice. Two specific areas of justice are distributive and interactional. In the context of a product or service failure, distributive justice is the perceived fairness of the outcome or recovery after a failure.[42] Interactional justice is the manner in which the problem is handled.[43]

An example can demonstrate the two types of justice. A customer buys a $600 vacuum that fails to work once her or she gets the product home. When the customer takes the machine back to the store, the employee could be very polite and apologetic or rude and unsympathetic. In the first case, the employee offered good interactional justice, while the rude employee was very low on offering interactional justice. To demonstrate two different levels of distributive justice, let's say the store could offer a replacement vacuum or to fix the vacuum at a cost to the customer. In the first case, the store offers acceptable distributive justice, while the second example is one of low distributive justice.

Managerial principle 10.7
When failures occur, you must treat customers with respect (i.e., interactional justice) and give them fair compensation (i.e., distributive justice).

Researchers have shown customer satisfaction during a failure is influenced by the level of both interactional justice and distributive justice. When a failure occurs, the customer is more satisfied when the employee offers high interactional justice in the form of being courteous and being able to correct the error immediately.[44] Further, customers are more satisfied when they receive a fair level of compensation: distributive justice.[45]

Relating Attribution Theory, Product Failure, and Consumer Satisfaction
The attributions people make can strongly influence their post-purchase satisfaction with a product or service. If a product fails (i.e., performance is below expectations), consumers will attempt to determine the cause of the failure. If they attribute the cause for failure to the product or service itself, they're likely to feel dissatisfied, but if they attribute the cause for failure to chance factors or to their own actions, they're not as likely to be dissatisfied.[46]

Managerial principle 10.8
When product or service failures occur due to an uncontrollable event (e.g., airline delay as a result of fog or ice), be sure to inform the customer of the cause of the failure.

One study investigating consumer satisfaction with airlines that were experiencing many delayed flights found satisfaction depended on the types of attributions consumers made.[47] When they attributed delays to uncontrollable factors such as fog or ice, they didn't tend to get angry. However, when they attributed delays to factors such as the actions of airline personnel, which the airline had control over, they were likely to feel angry and dissatisfied. In general, attributional processes are most likely to impact CS/D when consumer involvement in and experience with (i.e., knowledge of) the good or service is high.[48]

Actual Product Performance Researchers have found strong evidence actual product performance influences satisfaction independently of expectations, equity, and attributions. Even when consumers expect a product to perform poorly, they still feel dissatisfied when it does. A study investigating the effects of performance together with the impact of attribution, expectations, and equity on satisfaction with a stock market selection found performance influenced satisfaction independently of expectations.[49] Researchers have also found perceived product performance and quality directly influence CS/D, particularly when the product is unambiguous and easy to evaluate.[50]

Affect and CS/D CS/D may also be analyzed from an experiential perspective. The term **affect and CS/D** refers to the concept that the level of consumer satisfaction is influenced by the positive and negative feelings consumers associate with the product or service after purchase and during use. One researcher investigating the level of satisfaction with automobiles and cable television services after their purchase found two dimensions of affective responses: a set of positive feelings and a set of negative feelings.[51] These feelings were independent of each other. That is, consumers could simultaneously feel both positive and negative about a purchase. One can, of course, experience joy, interest, and excitement while also feeling anger, disgust, and contempt. For example, after purchasing a car, a consumer may feel excited and proud about the car while simultaneously being irritated and unhappy with the salesperson.[52]

The study also found measures of CS/D were directly influenced by consumers' feelings. Researchers discovered a relationship in which a purchase led to affective reactions that, in turn, led to feelings of CS/D.[53] Thus, in addition to the cognitive knowledge that expectancies were confirmed or disconfirmed, the feelings surrounding the post-acquisition process also appeared to affect satisfaction with a product. A similar pattern of results has been found in CS/D with restaurants and with automobiles. Affective responses predicted responses independently of customers' cognitive thoughts (i.e., beliefs about the server's attentiveness, friendliness, etc.). Particularly in high-involvement situations, such as the purchase of an automobile, customer satisfaction tends to have a strong emotional component.[54]

As can be seen in Figure 10.3, which diagrams the factors that influence CS/D, after the purchase and the use or consumption of the product, a series of cognitive and emotional reactions takes place in the consumer, including expectancy confirmation or disconfirmation evaluations, evaluations of the equity of the exchange, evaluations of actual product performance, and attributions of the cause of the outcomes.

Also note Figure 10.3 depicts emotions and attributions as interacting to influence consumer satisfaction or dissatisfaction. For example, if a product important to the consumer fails, the consumer is likely to have the immediate emotional response of anger. However, the anger is influenced by the attribution of cause made by the customer. If the person attributes the cause of the failure to factors beyond the control of the company, the dissatisfaction and anger felt is likely to be very mild. The extent of satisfaction or dissatisfaction, then, results from the manner in which the attribution of cause interacts with the emotional response to the product performance evaluations.[55]

Another recent finding is the level of satisfaction or dissatisfaction with a purchase tends to be magnified as the involvement level in the purchase situation increases.[56] Therefore, if outcomes exceed expectations, consumers will have higher levels of satisfaction if they're highly involved in the purchase. Likewise, if outcomes fall below expectations, consumers will have higher levels of dissatisfaction if they're highly involved in the purchase.

Measuring Consumer Satisfaction

Traditional measures of satisfaction have assessed consumers' overall evaluation of the product, as well as their evaluations of specific attributes. Likert scales are frequently used. That is, a statement is made and consumers are asked to indicate their level of agreement with it. For example, to assess overall satisfaction with an airline, a questionnaire might ask, "Overall, I was highly satisfied with the service provided by Delta Airlines." The following five-point scale could be used: Agree 1 2 3 4 5 Disagree.

A newer approach to satisfaction measurement is to use rating scales with which respondents evaluate the performance of a service or good on various dimensions. Thus, one question might be, "Rate the timeliness of how the airline service was provided," followed by this five-point scale: Very Bad 1 2 3 4 5 Very Good. Other questions would probe opinions about other characteristics of the service, such as customer-employee interactions, the aesthetics of the airplane (e.g., cleanliness), and the reliability of the service. Frequently, regression equations are developed to evaluate the ability of the attribute questions to predict overall satisfaction. This general approach can be used to evaluate satisfaction with virtually any good or service.

Researchers who use Likert and other rating scales to assess satisfaction treat satisfaction as though it were a type of attitude, a view that's validated by studies of airline services.[57] That being so, it seems likely customers will place different importance weights on the various attributes of a good or service. That is, some dimensions of the service will have a greater impact on overall satisfaction than others. For example, the study on airlines found punctuality and the quality of the meals served were extremely important in consumers' eyes. If the flight was delayed, not only did the importance of punctuality in predicting satisfaction increase but ratings were lower on other dimensions of the flight than they were if there was no delay in the flight. This finding illustrates a halo effect, which states extreme ratings on one dimension of performance will influence ratings on other dimensions of performance.

Recently, researchers identified a problem with traditional approaches to measuring satisfaction.[58] In self-reports of customer satisfaction, most respondents said they were satisfied. For example, the authors reported, across hundreds of different studies, on average, 65 percent of customers reported "high levels of satisfaction." These findings are important for managers. If the majority of customers state a high levels of satisfaction, a satisfaction score is virtually meaningless.

One way to correct this problem is to ask about dissatisfaction rather than satisfaction. Asking respondents to agree or disagree with a statement such as "I was highly dissatisfied with the product" counteracts the positivity bias and allows the manager to focus on areas of dissatisfaction.

Another recent line of thought has observed satisfaction doesn't necessarily translate into loyalty. Indeed, Frederick Reichheld, a well-known author on loyalty, may have coined the term *satisfaction trap*. Using data from the consulting firm Bain & Company, he notes between 65 and 85 percent of consumers who claim to be satisfied or very satisfied will defect.[59] The idea of consumer loyalty is discussed more fully later in this chapter.

FROM SATISFACTION TO DELIGHT

While most firms seek to make sure every customer is satisfied, research suggest these firms may benefit from seeking to delight customers. As discussed earlier in this chapter, satisfaction means meeting customer's expectations. If the customer receives only what he or she expects, there's potential for the competition to exceed expectations and steal your customers. Consequently, some researchers have suggested firms should attempt to exceed expectations and delight customers. Delight is a positive emotional state that results from one's expectations exceeded in a surprising degree.[60] Delight occurs due to unexpectedly or surprisingly pleasant features.[61] Tying this back to the expectancy disconfirmation model that was discussed earlier, delight is a surprisingly positive disconfirmation.[62]

To achieve delight, firms should look at a three-stage process of a must, a satisfier, and a delighter. Using a hotel setting, we can illustrate the three stages. When a consumer checks into a hotel, the room must be clean. A health club at the hotel could be a satisfier for many consumers. Finally, if the room has a scenic view of the ocean, the consumer may experience delight.

One concern firms have with delight is the raising of customer expectations. In other words, do customers grow to expect this level of performance the next time? While customers may raise their level of expectations, firms that embrace delight increase the level of dissatisfaction among their competitors' customers.[63] Consequently, firms may gain new customers as a result of embracing delight.

Managerial principle 10.9
Satisfaction shouldn't be our terminal outcome variable. Try to go beyond satisfaction and delight customers.

CONSUMER COMPLAINT BEHAVIOR

When consumers are dissatisfied with a product or service, what do they do about it? **Consumer complaint behavior** is a term that covers all the different actions consumers take when they're dissatisfied with a purchase.[64] Researchers have identified five common complaint behaviors, which are listed in Table 10.4.[65]

The first three behaviors—dealing with the retailer, not patronizing the brand or store and asking friends to also shun it, and complaining through third parties—are straightforward responses to product or service problems in which consumers either withdraw their business or seek some type of refund. The refund could be in the form of money or through a replacement product.

The last two behaviors are more far-reaching. Instead of merely withdrawing their own business (and perhaps that of friends and family), consumers who launch public boycotts are out to change marketing practices or to promote social change. Perhaps the most drastic behavior is the last: creating an entirely new organization to provide the good or service. Examples of such organizations are Consumers Union, food-buying co-ops (e.g. IGA grocery stores), credit unions, and the American Association of Retired Persons.

TABLE 10.4
Types of Complaint Actions

1.	Do nothing or deal with the retailer.
	a. Forget about the incident and do nothing.
	b. Definitely complain to the store manager.
	c. Go back or call retailer immediately and ask the manager to take care of the problem.
2.	Avoid using the retailer again and persuade friends to do the same.
	a. Decide not to use the retailer again.
	b. Speak to friends and relatives about your bad experience.
	c. Convince friends and relatives not to use the retailer.
3.	Take overt action with third parties.
	a. Complain to a consumer agency.
	b. Write a letter to a local newspaper.
	c. Take some legal action against the retailer.
4.	Boycott the organization.
5.	Create an alternative organization to provide the good or service.

Studies of consumer complaint behavior have shown a minority of dissatisfied customers actually take overt action against the company. For example, one study found, in a sample of 2,400 households, about one in five purchases resulted in some degree of dissatisfaction, but the buyer took action in less than 50 percent of these instances. The type of action taken by consumers depended, in part, on the type of product or service. For low-cost, frequently purchased products, less than 15 percent of consumers took any action when they were dissatisfied. But for household durables and automobiles, more than 50 percent of dissatisfied consumers took some sort of action. The product type that's most likely to produce action from dissatisfied customers is clothing. As many as 75 percent of those experiencing dissatisfaction with clothing took some form of complaint action.[66]

The models of consumer complaint behavior have identified two major purposes for complaining.[67] First, consumers complain in order to recover an economic loss. They may seek to exchange the problem product for another product or to get their money back, either directly from the company or store or indirectly through legal means. The second reason consumers engage in complaint behavior is to rebuild self-image. In many instances, the consumer's self-image is tied to the purchase of a product, so if the product performs poorly, the person's self-image is lowered. To restore self-image, the consumer may use negative word-of-mouth communications, stop buying the brand, complain to the company or the Better Business Bureau, or take legal action. The self-image maintenance aspects of consumer complaint behavior have been insufficiently studied by researchers and companies alike.

Factors Influencing Complaint Behavior

A number of factors have been found to influence whether consumers complain. As noted previously, one of them is the type of product or service involved. Another is the cost and social importance of the product. Some authors have suggested the likelihood of complaint behavior increases when any of the following occur:

- The level of the dissatisfaction increases.
- The attitude of the consumer toward complaining becomes more positive.
- The amount of benefit to be gained from complaining increases.
- The company is blamed for the problem.
- The product is important to the consumer.
- The resources available to the consumer for complaining increase.[68]

Previous experience with complaining is also associated with increased complaint behavior. People who have complained in the past know how to go about contacting appropriate authorities and are less bothered by the task than neophytes are.[69]

Attributions made by consumers relate to complaint behavior. When consumers attribute product problems to the company rather than to themselves, complaint behavior increases. Furthermore, if the problem is viewed as under the control of the company, complaining increases.[70] For example, if consumers attribute a problem with airline service to decisions purposely made by the company, they're much more likely to complain than if they believe the problem is beyond the company's control.

Researchers have been only partially successful in relating demographic factors to consumer complaint behavior.[71] In actuality, experience with complaining is a far better predictor of complaint behavior than any demographic factor.[72] Still, a modest correlation has been found between complaining behavior and age and income. Consumers who engage in complaining behavior tend to be younger and have higher incomes and more education.[73]

Investigations into the relationship between complaining and personality variables have found people who are more dogmatic, or close-minded, and self-confident are somewhat more likely to complain.[74] Consumers who value their individuality and a sense of independence also tend to complain more often than others. Perhaps these people make themselves feel important and different from others by complaining.[75]

Corporate Reactions to Consumer Complaining

Many consumer-oriented companies do make special efforts to track CS/D with their products and services. Firms often use consumer hotlines for this purpose. Procter & Gamble, Whirlpool, and 3M, for example, have used such toll-free numbers effectively. Many companies also advertise e-mail addresses to which customers can send complaints.

Public-policy makers take great interest in consumer complaint behavior. If they believe consumer complaints are too frequent in an industry, they're likely to develop regulations to ameliorate the problem. Managers, of course, prefer to avoid the encroachment of government—the mere possibility of government intervention can be a strong impetus to establish industry standards.

For instance, in Microsoft's battle with the US government over its anticompetitive stance, the company's competitors attempted to have Microsoft punished without increasing government regulation of the industry.

Managers should have mechanisms in place to handle complaints when they occur. The presence of toll-free numbers is one highly effective means of handling complaints. In addition, companies should establish a means of redress for legitimate consumer complaints.

When not at fault, companies should try hard to break the connection between themselves and the negative event. Several approaches are possible in these situations. First, the company can deny its involvement. Second, the company can deflect culpability by blaming someone else. Third, the company can explain the event and identify extenuating circumstances. In this third case, the company doesn't deny all responsibility. Rather, it encourages consumers to make a stronger external attribution for the event instead of blaming it completely on the company.

One interesting study analyzed company reactions to corporate complaints and, in addition, had consumers evaluate the types of excuses offered by the companies. Most companies attempted to avoid responsibility, an approach viewed negatively by consumers. Consumers gave the highest ratings to companies that sought to minimize the unpleasantness of an outcome for the consumer and gave a reason for the action.[76]

The authors of this study suggested companies use excuses strategically so that they accurately describe the causes and outcomes of the negative events that precipitated the complaints. The excuses provided by companies are an important source of information for consumers when they're deciding what course of action to pursue to correct a perceived wrong. Of course, consumers aren't always right, and companies aren't always wrong, so a courteous explanation sometimes can clear up a misunderstanding.

Complaints and Exit Behavior

Managerial principle 10.10
Treat every complaint as an opportunity! If you resolve the complaint in a satisfactory manner, you may gain a loyal customer.

Exit behavior refers to the consumer choice to either leave a relationship or to lower consumption levels of the good or service. Researchers investigating complaint behavior in the cell phone industry have found consumers who complain are more likely to leave a relationship and more likely to decrease their consumption levels of the good or service. In addition, they found the likelihood of complaining increased as the level of dissatisfaction increased. The researchers recommended a "get-it-right-the-first-time" attitude on the part of companies because, in many cases, it's simply not possible to appease a complaining customer. This recommendation is particularly important where the costs of obtaining new customers are high. In the cell phone industry, it costs $600 to obtain a new customer but only $20 to retain an existing one.[77]

PRODUCT DISPOSITION

Although disposing of acquisitions is a fundamental part of the consumer decision process, little research has been done in the area. Basically, a consumer has two alternative dispositional options after using a product for some period of time: keep it, or get rid of it permanently. [78] Each of these alternatives has sub-options. For example, if the decision is to keep the product, the consumer can continue to use the product, convert it to a new use (e.g., use an old toothbrush to apply shoe polish), or store it. Similarly, if the decision is to get rid of the product permanently, the consumer can throw it away, give it away, trade it, or sell it.

Disposing of goods can take on symbolic meaning, as possessions are partially responsible for creating our identity.[79] Our identity can be diminished when we dispose of goods. Take, for instance, a retired policeman who cherishes his police badge. He would feel a loss of identity if he simply discarded the badge. Possessions take on strong symbolic meanings as we age. In fact, we often find the elderly transferring symbolic goods to others as a means to strengthen family ties and create some immortality.[80]

A classic study investigated consumers' disposition decisions regarding six different products.[81] One clear pattern was the higher the value of the product, the more likely consumers were to dispose of the product in ways that maximized returns. Thus, refrigerators and stereo amplifiers were frequently sold, while toothbrushes were usually thrown away.

Product disposition can be extremely profitable. For some types of products, there's a thriving aftermarket that seriously cuts into sales of new products. For example, sales of used textbooks can severely lower the sales of new textbooks. Although students benefit in the short term by having to pay less for their books, in the long run, the cost of new textbooks is increased because fewer new books are sold, which increases the per-unit costs of production. Another enterprise based on product disposition is the used-car market. Hundreds of thousands of people make their living buying and selling used cars. And with publications such as *Consumer Reports* rating used cars, new-car buyers are beginning to make the resale value of a car one of the attributes they consider in the initial purchase decision. There are also large aftermarkets in used guitars and other musical equipment—sometimes, vintage equipment is worth more than a new equivalent.

Another product disposition issue is the handling of the garbage resulting from consumer purchases. Indeed, dealing with the environmental hazards posed by the mountains of waste we create each year in using products is a major public concern. Consumers have generally positive attitudes regarding programs to reduce waste, such as recycling, garbage reduction, and composting. Still, despite these positive attitudes, participation in programs to reduce waste varies widely.[82] Researchers investigating the factors spurring consumer intentions to reduce waste have found individual consumer attitudes predicted intentions to a greater extent than the opinions of other people. Moreover, the greater the individual's perception that a recycling action would have societal benefits, the stronger that individual's intention was to take the action.[83]

BRAND LOYALTY

Closely related to consumer satisfaction and consumer complaint behavior is the area of brand loyalty. **Brand loyalty** can be defined as the degree to which a customer holds a positive attitude toward a brand, has a commitment to it, and intends to continue purchasing it in the future. Brand loyalty is directly influenced by the satisfaction or dissatisfaction with the brand that has accumulated over time, as well as by perceptions of the product's quality.[84] Because it's from four to six times less costly to retain old customers than to develop new ones, managers should give top priority to creating strategies that build and maintain brand loyalty.[85]

The definition we have given of brand loyalty is based on two general approaches to understanding the concept: behavioral measures and attitudinal measures of brand loyalty.

Behavioral Approaches to Brand Loyalty

Behavioral approaches to brand loyalty measure consumers' actual purchase behavior regarding a product. The **proportion-of-purchases method** is the most frequently used measure of brand loyalty. In this approach, all the brands purchased within a particular product category are determined for each consumer and the proportion of purchases going to each brand is identified. Brand loyalty is then measured in terms of some arbitrary proportion of purchases going to a particular brand. For example, if more than 50 percent of the purchases went to a particular brand during some time period, that consumer would be said to be loyal to the brand.

The behavioral approaches make it clear that brand loyalty is not an all-or-nothing phenomenon. Instead, loyalty should be viewed as a continuum from complete loyalty to complete brand indifference. There are several types of loyalty besides undivided loyalty. In some cases, consumers have a divided loyalty between two brands. In other cases, they're largely loyal to one brand but occasionally switch to other brands, perhaps to break the monotony and raise their levels of arousal. In still other instances, customers are completely indifferent to distinctions between brands.[86] These different buying patterns, in which A, B, C, and D are different brands, may be portrayed as follows:

- Undivided loyalty: A A A A A A A A
- Occasional switch: A A B A A A C A A D A
- Switch loyalty: A A A A B B B B
- Divided loyalty: A A A B B A A B B B
- Brand indifference: A B D C B A C D

From the marketer's perspective, the problem with these behavioral measures of brand loyalty is they don't identify the reasons consumers purchase a brand. A particular brand could be purchased because of convenience, availability, or price. If any one of these factors changes, consumers might rapidly switch to another brand. In such instances, consumers can't be said to exhibit brand loyalty because implicit in the idea of loyalty is that the consumer has more than a passing infatuation with the brand.

Attitudinal Measures of Brand Loyalty

Managerial principle 10.11
Brand loyalty is more than simply repeat purchase behavior. The customer must also prefer the brand over other offerings.

The problems encountered in the behavioral measures of brand loyalty illustrate why distinguishing between brand loyalty and repeat purchase behavior is important. **Repeat purchase behavior** means the consumer is merely buying a product repeatedly without any particular feeling for it. The concept of brand loyalty, in contrast, implies a consumer has some real preference for the brand. In light of this distinction, another approach to assessing brand loyalty was developed, one based on the consumers' attitude toward the product, as well as their purchase behavior. According to this approach, consumers exhibit brand loyalty only when they actively prefer the product.[87]

With brand loyalty comes a commitment. **Brand commitment** has been defined as an emotional or psychological attachment to a brand within a product class.[88] Whereas brand loyalty has both behavioral and attitudinal components, brand commitment tends to focus more on the emotional component. In one study of consumers' brand commitment to soft drinks, researchers found commitment results from purchase involvement, which, in turn, results from ego involvement with the brand category.[89] According to the authors of the study, such ego involvement happens when a product is closely related to the consumer's important values, needs, and self-concept.

In sum, brand commitment occurs most frequently with high-involvement products that symbolize consumers' self-concepts, values, and needs. These products tend to be higher-priced consumer durables that possess greater perceived risk, although they may be such everyday emotion-laden products as soft drinks.[90] Some evidence indicates brand preferences are formed during childhood and adolescence, which suggests managers should begin targeting their customers early in their life.[91]

Identifying Brand-Loyal Consumers

One intriguing question for market researchers is whether there's a type of consumer who's brand loyal across various types of products. Research evidence so far indicates brand loyalty is a product-specific phenomenon. Consumers who are loyal in one product category may or may not be loyal in any other product category. Efforts to identify socioeconomic or psychological characteristics related to brand-loyal behavior have generally been unsuccessful.[92] However, two recent studies have identified situations that lead to demographic differences in loyalty. First, as we get older, we tend to be more brand loyal.[93] This loyalty may be a result of older consumers having more experience with products and they are simply sticking with their preferences. A second demographic variable of interest is gender. Marketers have used gender as a segmentation variable for decades. So, the question remains, how are women and men different when it comes to loyalty? Women tend to be more loyal to individuals, while men are more loyal to groups.[94] For example, women may be inclined to follow a stylist to a new hair salon, while men would be more loyal to the company (i.e., hair salon).

Another variable that does predict brand loyalty is store loyalty. Consumers who are loyal to particular stores also tend to be loyal to certain brands.[95] The connection here may be that consumers who repeatedly shop at the same stores may be forced to buy certain brands because they're the only ones available in these stores.

Firms may increase customer loyalty based on an association with a brand community. A brand community is a "specialized, non-geographically bound community, based on a structured set of social relations among admirers of a brand."[96] Countless brand communities engage customers around a brand. Some of the most famous brand communities are Apple, Harley-Davidson, Disney, and Jeep.

Membership in brand communities can be merely virtual in that members may never physically come together. Some communities interact psychologically. For instance, some connect online, often using Skype, Facebook, or Pinterest. Members of brand communities interact with each other by sharing emotional stories and experiences with the brand. Once consumers psychologically join a brand community, they become more deeply committed to the brand.

A deeper commitment to a brand leads to a number of positive outcomes to firms. These customers attend brand events more frequently, share positive word of mouth, and increase their brand preference.[97] Customers benefit from the brand community as they enjoy brand experience more by interacting with others.

It's important to remember marketing strategies involving sales-promotion devices may actually inhibit brand loyalty. If consumers purchase brands because of the sales promotion rather than because of the product's intrinsic positive qualities, they may get into the habit of buying only when there are sales promotions. One study found sales-promotion devices may cause even brand-loyal customers to switch brands. However, these researchers also found the likelihood the consumers would repurchase the new brand was low.[98] All the evidence points to the conclusion the quality of the product and the advertising of the brand are the key factors in creating long-term brand loyalty.

Predicting Satisfaction and Loyalty

Recent work in the brand experience arena demonstrates the relationship among four key concepts: brand experience, brand personality, satisfaction, and loyalty.[99] A brand experience is all the sensations, feelings, cognitions, and behavioral responses a consumer feels after interacting with the brand. Interactions may come in the form of packaging, communications, the brand's design, the brand's identity, and the environment. A consumer may view an advertisement for Nike and feel positive emotions and a drive to begin a workout program (i.e., behavioral intentions). In this case, the positive brand experience may motivate the consumer to purchase a Nike product.

A second element of the model is brand personality. A brand personality is defined as "the set of human characteristics associated with a brand."[100] Firms develop brand personalities for their products by carefully developing a brand identity. The Hurley brand can be described as hip, cool, youthful, and active, while the Mercedes brand can be described as older, sophisticated, and exclusive. There are five dimensions to brand personality, as Table 10.5 shows.

TABLE 10.5
Dimensions of Brand
Personality

Dimension	Description of Dimension
Ruggedness	Outdoorsy, tough
Sophistication	Upper class, charming
Competence	Reliable, intelligent, successful
Excitement	Daring, spirited, imaginative, up to date
Sincerity	Down-to-earth, honest, wholesome, cheerful

The personality of a brand affects both consumer satisfaction and loyalty. We can look at these personality dimensions to find unique customer reactions. For instance, sincere brands are more likely to encourage a strong relationship with the consumer. This relationship is analogous to a close personal friendship. Exciting brands are more similar to a short-lived fling.[101]

The relationship among the four concepts of brand experience, brand personality, satisfaction, and loyalty is presented in Figure 10.4. First, satisfaction leads to loyalty. This isn't a surprise, as consumers should be more loyal to a brand if they're satisfied. Second, brand personality plays a role in consumer satisfaction and loyalty. Customers are more satisfied with brands that have a unique personality. Finally, the brand experience influences the consumer's evaluation of brand personality, his or her satisfaction level, and his or her loyalty. Firms can benefit from this knowledge by developing a great experience for the customer and positioning the brand with a unique personality that's attractive to customers.

Managerial principle 10.12
You can increase customer loyalty through customer satisfaction, a desirable brand personality, and a good brand experience.

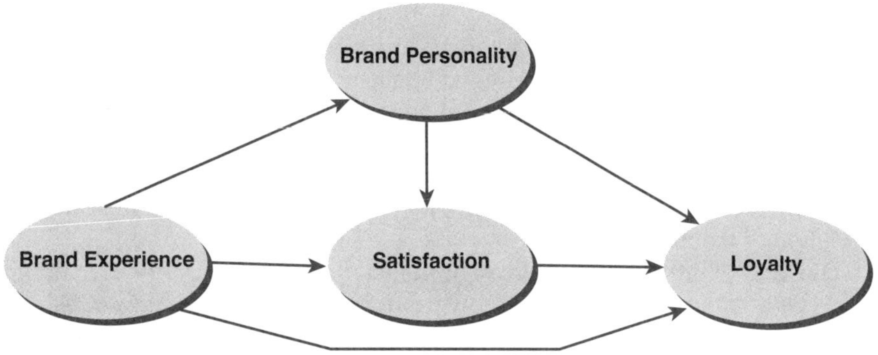

FIGURE 10.4
Brand Experience Model
Source: *J. Josko Brakus, Bernd H. Schmitt, and Lia Zarantonello, "Brand Experience: What Is It? How Is It Measured? Does It Affect Loyalty?* Journal of Marketing 73 (2009): 52–68.

Comparing Satisfaction and Loyalty

In the coming years, there may be an increasing emphasis on loyalty as opposed to satisfaction. As noted earlier, defection rates among even satisfied customers can be quite high. Thus, although satisfaction and loyalty are linked, the relation is asymmetric. Satisfaction is an unreliable determinant of loyalty. Richard Oliver, a leading scholar in the area of satisfaction, suggests there are several obstacles to loyalty, such as consumer idiosyncrasies (variety seeking and loyalty to multiple brands) and switching incentives (competitors may lure consumers away with enticing messages and incentives). He suggests, in fact, loyal customers are beyond satisfaction and even enduring preference—they're "determined defenders" in the face of enticing counteroffers from competitors.[102] From this perspective, satisfaction is a temporary, relatively passive state, and the burning question is how to convert this temporary state into enduring loyalty.

MANAGERIAL IMPLICATIONS

The consumer-behavior concepts that emerge from investigations of post-acquisition processes have application to each of the five RESPonsive Marketing areas. These are discussed in the following sections.

Research

One of the clearest applications emerging from this chapter is companies need to understand how they should deal with consumer complaints. Market research provides companies and marketers with tools for doing so.

As an exercise, perhaps evaluate your own behavior vis-à-vis satisfaction. Consider an occasion in which you've been most angry with a company as a result of a purchase of a good or service. What did happened to cause your emotions? What was the role of your own attributions in increasing or decreasing your anger? What specific actions could the company have taken that would have helped resolve your complaint?

Another area in which research would be helpful follows from the discussion of equity theory. Feelings of inequity may occur when consumers perceive the ratio of their outcomes to inputs is inferior to the retailer's, salesperson's, or manufacturer's outcomes to inputs.

Environmental Analysis

Scanning of the environment for threats from public-policy makers resulting from consumer complaints makes good business sense. When Coca-Cola found itself providing potentially dangerous products in Europe in 1999, failure to take dramatic action as quickly as possible resulted in a public relations fiasco (Chapter 16 discusses this further). A potential result even more damaging might have occurred, however, had public-policy makers stepped in to increase regulation of the industry.

The kind of information that can be gained by employing a toll-free hotline or a website can provide ideas for new products and improvements to existing products as well as forewarn of significant problems emerging that may result in either a sales drop or actions from policy makers.

Segmentation

Clearly, it would be good if one could identify more-loyal customers from those less loyal and make offers based on the differences between the groups. As this chapter points out, little can be determined in terms of a demographic profile of loyal customers. Nonetheless, research can possibly identify them, and different offers made, based on the reasons for their loyalty (or lack thereof).

Positioning

As discussed in this chapter, one way to position a brand is to offer outstanding customer service. Brands such as Ritz-Carlton are known for being the best in providing great customer service. While not every consumer will seek this treatment, there is a target market that will appreciate this type of positioning and thereafter seek out the brand.

Marketing Mix

Oliver's discussion of loyalty and satisfaction suggests competitors can (and do) provide persuasive messages and incentives to lure loyal—or potentially loyal—customers away. The elements of the marketing mix need to be employed in such a way as to blunt the impact of such enticing messages and offers from competitors.

How do we create a satisfying experience for customers?

While the previous chapter focused on the first four stages of the consumer's decision process, this chapter addressed the final stage: the post-acquisition process. One of the main topics of this chapter was the consumer experience. To create a satisfying consumer experience, marketers must analyze a number of factors, including product use, consumption frequency, amount, and purpose. These four factors help us understand the consumer's relationship with the brand and allow us to make appropriate changes to the marketing mix.

As our economy has moved from a focus on commodities to goods to services and, finally, experiences, marketers have made the consumption experience the focus of the exchange. Brands such as Starbucks, Cold Stone Creamery, and the Peabody Hotel focus on the experiential elements of the brand rather than simply the tangible aspects. In doing so, each brand works to include theater into the transaction, so the customer leaves with a memorable exchange.

The focus on memorable exchanges relates to another focus of this chapter: satisfaction. The word *satisfaction* comes from the Latin *satis*, meaning "enough." Hence, satisfaction has been defined as meeting customer's expectations. Customer satisfaction can be affected in a number of ways, such as the quality of the service or product. Service quality has been attributed to the five dimensions of tangibles, reliability, responsiveness, assurance, and empathy. On the other hand, product quality is determined by performance, features, reliability, durability, serviceability, aesthetics, conformance to specifications, and perceived quality.

A number of theories have been put forth to evaluate the levels of satisfaction and dissatisfaction. The expectancy disconfirmation model addresses the relationship between expected performance and actual performance to determine satisfaction. Equity theory uses the ratios of the inputs and outcomes of the parties involved to determine satisfaction. Attribution theory can explain satisfaction based on where the consumer attributes the success or failure. For instance, if the consumer attributes a failure to the self, he or she leaves satisfied. However, if the consumer attributes the failure on the exchange partner, he or she leaves dissatisfied.

Why do customers complain?

When consumers aren't satisfied with an exchange, some of them will take up some form of complaining behavior. These behaviors can range from doing nothing to complaining to the retailer to boycotting the retailer and encouraging others to do the same. While most of us experience dissatisfaction in numerous exchanges, very few of people actually take action. When we do take some form of action, it's done for two reasons: to recover an economic loss or to rebuild self-esteem. With so few consumers actually taking action and considering the reasons for the actions, firms need to recognize any complaint is an opportunity to rebuild the brand image and the relationship with the customer.

How does disposing of a product affect customers?

Once a product's usefulness is gone, consumers must decide how to dispose of the product. Products that have a symbolic meaning are often kept or passed to a family member or friend. Other items are sold at a profit. As we discussed early in the book, exchange occurs because the item being gained is worth more to the person than the item given away. Consequently, trading items can be a profitable means of disposing of goods.

How is satisfaction related to loyalty?

A concept closely related to satisfaction is brand loyalty. Brand loyalty has three components: the degree of positive attitude toward the brand, the level of commitment, and intentions to continue purchasing the brand. Loyalty isn't an all-or-nothing concept. Consumers often still buy other brands even when they show a degree of loyalty to one brand. However, firms that can encourage a strong degree of brand loyalty benefit from spending less to gain new customers.

The relationship among loyalty, satisfaction, brand experience, and brand personality and found loyalty was influenced by the consumer's brand experience, the brand's personality, and satisfaction. Consequently, to increase the chances a customer becomes loyal to our brand, we should look at the experience and the personality and create a satisfying experience.

KEY TERMS

actual product performance	consumption purpose	inputs
affect and CS/D	contracted performance	occurrence
brand commitment	dramatistic performance	outcomes
brand loyalty	emotional dissatisfaction	post-acquisition processes
commodities	emotional satisfaction	produce use
consumer complaint behavior	enacted performance	product expectations
consumer performance	equity theory	product quality
consumer satisfaction	exit behavior	proportion-of-purchases method
consumption amount	expentancy confirmation	repeat purchase behavior
consumption experience	experiences	services
consumption frequency	goods	

REVIEW QUESTIONS

1. Define what is meant by post-acquisition processes?
2. Explain consumption experience and define product use, frequency, consumption amount, and purpose.
3. How does the consumption experience differ between purchasing tangible products and purchasing experiences?
4. How does drama in a performance affect the consumer's engagement?
5. What contributes to your satisfaction and dissatisfaction when you make a purchase?

6. Describe the dimensions of service quality and product quality. How are the two sets of dimensions similar?

7. Explain the expectancy disconfirmation model.

8. Discuss the concepts of equity theory and satisfaction. What factors of the equity theory might lead you to be very satisfied or very dissatisfied?

9. What are some behaviors consumers engage in when they want to complain?

10. What events increase the likelihood consumers will complain?

11. How is loyalty different from satisfaction?

12. What factors lead to brand loyalty?

DISCUSSION QUESTIONS

1. List five things that might lead you to be satisfied with the purchase of a tangible product and five things that lead you to be satisfied with an experience. What are the similarities and differences between the two categories?

2. Write down the details of an experience you recently had where you walked away very satisfied and an experience where you walked away very dissatisfied. How could the firm in each example make sure you always walk away satisfied?

3. Starbucks transformed the coffee industry from the mundane to a theatrical experience. What other services could be transformed into an experience? What events would take place to change the service to an experience?

4. Describe an exchange you've experienced according to an equity theory perspective. Be careful to include all the inputs and outcomes for each party involved in the exchange.

5. Describe a situation where you've taken the initiative to complain to the company. How was the situation resolved?

6. What is it about you that makes you more likely or less likely to complain when a brand or company fails to meet your needs?

7. List five brands you have strong brand loyalty toward and five brands you're indifferent toward. What is it about each of these brands that makes you feel either loyal or indifferent?

8. Use Table 10.5 to come up with three products that rate high and three products that rate low on each of the brand personality dimensions.

9. Think about the brands you mentioned in the previous question. Do you have strong or weak brand loyalty with any of them? What role did the brand personality play in your loyalty evaluation?

ENDNOTES

1 Joseph A. Michelli, The New Gold Standard: The Ritz-Carlton Hotel Company (New York: McGraw-Hill, 2008).

2 Ibid.

3 Joseph Michelli, "Take It from Ritz-Carlton: Data Is Nothing Without the Personal Touches," Customer Think, accessed January 6, 2016, http://customerthink.com/data_nothing_personal_ritz_carlton/.

4 Sam Hill and Glenn Rifkin, Radical Marketing: From Harvard to Harley, Lessons From Ten That Broke the Rules and Made it Big (New York: HarperCollins, 1999).

5 Philip Hendrix, "Product/Service Consumption: Key Dimensions and Implications for Marketing" (working paper, Emory University, Atlanta, GA, August 1984).

6 Hendrix also identified consumption interval as a fourth factor. However, interval and frequency of usage are essentially identical. As a result, only frequency is identified here as one of the factors.

7 Emmaleigh R. Hall, "Starbucks Treat Receipts: Getting Even More for Your Money," Associated Content, accessed December 29, 2010, http://www.associatedcontent.com/article/5601582/starbucks_treat_receipts_getting_even.html?cat=22.

8 This anecdote was related to one of the authors by Jeanne Verkinnes, a General Mills employee, September 23, 1999.

9 Paco Underhill, Why We Buy: The Science of Shopping (New York: Simon and Schuster, 1999).

10 "The Ritz-Carlton Social Engagement Ranked Number One," accessed January 8, 2016, March 6, 2013, http://news.marriott.com/2014/07/the-ritz-carlton-social-engagement-ranked-number-one.html

11 B. Joseph Pine and James H. Gilmore, The Experience Economy: Work Is Theatre and Every Business a Stage (Boston: Harvard Business School Press, 1999).

12 Richard L. Celsi, Randall L. Rose, and Thomas W. Leigh, "An Exploration of High-Risk Leisure Consumption through Skydiving," Journal of Consumer Research 20 (June 1993): 8; Eric J. Arnould and Linda L. Price, "River Magic: Extraordinary Experience and the Extended Service Encounter," Journal of Consumer Research 20 (June 1993): 24–45.

13 Erving Goffman, The Presentation of Self in Everyday Life (New York: Basic, 1959).

14 This definition of performance was developed for the textbook and specifically designed to incorporate the notion that an exchange process is taking place. It borrows ideas from the work of John Deighton, "The Consumption of Performance," Journal of Consumer Research 19 (December 1992): 362–372.

15 John Deighton, "Consumption of Performance," Journal of Consumer Research 19, no. 3 (1992): 362–372.

16 Paul W. Miniard, Sunil Bhatla, and Deepak Sirdeshmukh, "Mood as a Determinant of Postconsumption Product Evaluations: Mood Effects and Their Dependency on the Affective Intensity of the Consumption Experience," Journal of Consumer Psychology 1, no. 2 (1992): 173–195.

17 Richard Oliver has distinguished satisfaction from attitude toward the object in his work. He argues attitude toward the product or brand represents a more generalized evaluation of a class of purchase objects. The approach taken in this text is attitudes occur at different levels of specificity. They can be highly abstract, such as one's attitude to his or her country, or highly specific, such as one's satisfaction with a specific purchase. All are affective reactions that range on a hedonic continuum from unfavorable to favorable. For an article using Oliver's approach, see Robert A. Westbrook and Richard L. Oliver, "The Dimensionality of Consumption Emotion Patterns and Consumer Satisfaction," Journal of Consumer Research 18 (June 1991): 84–91.

18 Claes Fornell, Roland T. Rust, and Marnik G. Dekimpe, "The Effect of Customer Satisfaction on Consumer Spending Growth," Journal of Marketing Research 47 (2010): 28–35.

19 Kapil R.Tuli and Sundar G. Bharadwaj, "Customer Satisfaction and Stock Returns Risk," Journal of Marketing 73 (2009): 184-197.

20 Eugene W. Anderson, Claes Fornell, and Donald R. Lehmann, "Customer Satisfaction, Market Share, and Profitability: Findings from Sweden," Journal of Marketing 58 (July 1994): 53–66.

21 J. Joseph Cronin and Steven A. Taylor, "Measuring Service Quality: A Reexamination and Extension," Journal of Marketing 56 (July 1992): 55–68. See also R. Kenneth Teas,

"Expectations, Performance Evaluation, and Consumers' Perceptions of Quality," Journal of Marketing 57 (October 1993): 18–34.

[22] This definition extends the definition of service quality to goods. See Valerie A. Zeithaml, "Consumer Perceptions of Price, Quality, and Value: A Means-End Model and Synthesis of Evidence," Journal of Marketing 52 (July 1988): 2–22.

[23] More-recent work on SERVQUAL is summarized in Valerie A. Zeithaml, Leonard L. Berry, and A. Parasuraman, "The Behavioral Consequences of Service Quality," Journal of Marketing 60 (April 1996): 31–46.

[24] Kevin Lane Keller, "Conceptualizing, Measuring, and Managing Customer-Based Brand Equity," Journal of Marketing 57 (January 1993): 1–22.

[25] Robert W. Veryzer, "Aesthetic Response and the Influence of Design Principles on Product Preferences," in Advances in Consumer Research, vol. 22, ed. Leigh McAlister and Michael L. Rothschild (Provo, UT: Association for Consumer Research, 1992), 224–228.

[26] H. Keith Hunt, "CS/D: Overview and Future Research Directions," in Conceptualization and Measurement of Consumer Satisfaction and Dissatisfaction, ed. H. Keith Hunt (Cambridge, MA: Marketing Science Institute, 1977), 455–488.

[27] Richard Oliver and Wayne DeSarbo, "Response Determinants in Satisfaction Judgments," Journal of Consumer Research 15 (March 1988): 495–507.

[28] R. B. Woodruff, E. R. Cadotte, and R. L. Jenkins, "Modeling Consumer Satisfaction Processes Using Viewer Satisfaction," Journal of Marketing 74: 108–121; Robert B. Woodruff, Ernest R. Cadotte, and Roger L. Jenkins, "Modeling Consumer Satisfaction Processes Using Experience-Based Norms," Journal of Marketing Research 20, no. 3 (August 1983): 296–304.

[29] R. L. Oliver, "A Cognitive Model of the Antecedents and Consequences of Satisfaction Decisions," Journal of Marketing Research 17 (November 1980): 460–69.

[30] Sangkil Moon, Paul K. Bergey, and Dawn Iacobucci, "Dynamic Effects among Movie Ratings, Movie Revenues, and Viewer Satisfaction," Journal of Marketing 74 (2010): 108–121.

[31] Robert B. Woodruff, Ernest R. Cadotte, and Roger L. Jenkins, "Modeling Consumer Satisfaction Processes Using Experience-Based Norms," Journal of Marketing Research 20, no. 3 (August 1983): 296–304.

[32] Patricia Sellers, "How to Handle Customers' Gripes," Fortune (October 24, 1988): 87–100.

[33] Cait Poynor and Stacy Wood, "Smart Subcategories: How Assortment Formats Influence Consumer Learning and Satisfaction," Journal of Consumer Research 37 (2010): 159–175.

[34] J. S. Adams, "Toward an Understanding of Inequity," Journal of Abnormal and Social Psychology 67 (1963): 422–436.

[35] The equity ratio shown has been criticized and is given primarily for pedagogical purposes. See John C. Alessio, "Another Folly for Equity Theory," Social Psychological Quarterly 43 (September 1980): 336–340.

[36] R. P. Fisk and C. E. Young, "Disconfirmation of Equity Expectation: Effects on Consumer Satisfaction with Services," in Advances in Consumer Research, vol. 12, ed. E. C. Hirschman and M. B. Holbrook (Ann Arbor, MI: Association for Consumer Research, 1985), 340–345.

[37] For other studies of equity in consumer behavior, see J. W. Huppertz, S. J. Arenson, and R. H. Evans, "An Application of Equity Theory to Buyer-Seller Exchange Situations," Journal of Marketing Research 15 (May 1978): 250–260.

[38] John C. Mowen and Stephen L. Grove, "Search Behavior, Price Paid, and the Comparison Other: An Equity Theory Analysis of Post-Purchase Satisfaction," in International Fare in Consumer Satisfaction and Complaint Behavior, ed. Ralph Day and H. Keith Hunt (Bloomington: Indiana University School of Business, 1983), 57–63.

[39] J. E. Swan and Alice Mercer, "Consumer Satisfaction as a Function of Equity and Disconfirmation," in Conceptual and Empirical Contributions to Consumer Satisfaction and Complaining Behavior, ed. H. Hunt and R. Day (Bloomington: Indiana University Press, 1982), 2–8.

[40] Richard L. Oliver and John E. Swan, "Consumer Perceptions of Interpersonal Equity and Satisfaction in Transactions: A Field Survey Approach," Journal of Marketing 53 (April 1989): 21–35.

[41] Ibid., 33.

[42] G. C. Homans, Social Behavior: Its Elementary Forms (New York: Harcourt, Brace, and World, 1961).

[43] R. J. Bies and J. S. Moag, "Interactional Communication Criteria of Fairness," in Research in Organizational Behavior, ed. R. J. Lewicki, B. H. Sheppard, and M. H. Bazerman (Greenwich, CT: JAI Press, 1986).

[44] Mary Ann Hocutt, Michael R. Bowers, and D. Todd Donavan, "The Art of Service Recovery: Fact or Fiction?" Journal of Services Marketing 20, no. 3 (2006):199–207.

[45] Mary Ann Hocutt, Goutam Chakraborty, and John C. Mowen, "The Impact of Perceived Justice on Customer Satisfaction and Intentions to Complain in a Service Recovery," in Advances in Consumer Research, vol. 24, ed. Merrie Brucks and Deborah J. MacInnis (Provo, UT : Association for Consumer Research, 1997), 457–463.

[46] Valerie Folkes, "Consumer Reactions to Product Failure: An Attributional Approach," Journal of Consumer Research 10 (March 1984): 398–409.

[47] Valerie Folkes, Susan Koletsky, and John Graham, "A Field Study of Causal Inferences and Consumer Reaction: The View from the Airport," Journal of Consumer Research 13 (March 1987): 534–539.

[48] T. N. Somasundaram, "Consumers' Reaction to Product Failure: Impact of Product Involvement and Knowledge," in Advances in Consumer Research, vol. 20, ed. Leigh McAlister and Michael L. Rothschild (Provo, UT: Association for Consumer Research, 1992), 215–218.

[49] Richard Oliver and Wayne DeSarbo, "Response Determinants in Satisfaction Judgments," Journal of Consumer Research 15 (March 1988): 495–507. See also David Tse and Peter Wilton, "Models of Consumer Satisfaction Formation: An Extension," Journal of Marketing Research 25 (May 1988): 204–212.

[50] Youjae Yi, "The Determinants of Consumer Satisfaction: The Moderating Role of Ambiguity," in Advances in Consumer Research, vol. 20, ed. Leigh McAlister and Michael L. Rothschild (Provo, UT: Association for Consumer Research, 1992), 502–506.

[51] Robert Westbrook, "Product/Consumption-Based Affective Responses and Postpurchase Processes," Journal of Marketing Research 24 (August 1987): 258–270.

[52] The finding that positive and negative dimensions of affect exist was also found by Haim Mano and Richard L. Oliver, "Assessing the Dimensionality and Structure of the Consumption Experience: Evaluation, Feeling, and Satisfaction," Journal of Consumer Research 20 (December 1993): 451–466.

[53] Laurette Dube-Rioux, "The Power of Affective Reports in Predicting Satisfaction Judgments," in Advances in Consumer Research, vol. 17, ed. Marvin E. Goldberg, Gerald Gorn, and Richard W. Pollay (Provo, UT: Association for Consumer Research, 1990), 571–576.

[54] Robert A. Westbrook and Richard L. Oliver, "The Dimensionality of Consumption Emotion Patterns and Consumer Satisfaction, Journal of Consumer Research 18 (June 1991): 84–91.

[55] This model is based, in part, on Lalita A. Manrai and Meryl P. Gardner, "The Influence of Affect on Attributions for Product Failure," in Advances in Consumer Research, vol. 18, ed. Rebecca Holman and Michael Solomon (Provo, UT: Association for Consumer Research, 1991), 249–254.

[56] Barry J. Babin, Mitch Griffin, and Laurie Babin, "The Effect of Motivation to Process on Consumers' Satisfaction Reactions," in Advances in Consumer Research, vol. 21, ed. Chris Allen and Deborah Roedder John (Provo, Utah: Association for Consumer Research, 1994), 406–411.

[57] Shirley Taylor and John D. Claxton, "Delays and the Dynamics of Service Evaluations," Journal of the Academy of Marketing Science 22 (Summer 1994), 254–264.

[58] Robert A. Peterson and William R. Wilson, "Measuring Customer Satisfaction: Fact and Artifact," Journal of the Academy of Marketing Science 20 (Winter 1992): 61–72.

[59] This line of thought is captured in Richard L. Oliver, "Whence Consumer Loyalty?" Journal of Marketing (1999): 33–44.

[60] Richard L. Oliver, Roland T. Rust, and Sajeev Varki, "Customer Delight Foundations, Findings, and Managerial Insight," Journal of Retailing 73 (Fall 1997): 311–336.

[61] Roland T. Rust and Richard L. Oliver, "Should We Delight the Customer?" Journal of the Academy of Marketing Science 28, no. 1 (2000): 86–94.

[62] Richard L. Oliver, "Processing of the Satisfaction Response in Consumption: A Suggested Framework and Research Propositions," Journal of Consumer Satisfaction, Dissatisfaction, and Complaining Behavior 2 (1989): 1–16.

[63] Roland T. Rust and Richard L. Oliver, "Should We Delight the Customer?" Journal of the Academy of Marketing Science 28, no. 1 (2000):86–94.

[64] This definition is highly similar to one developed by Jagdip Singh, "Consumer Complaint Intentions and Behavior: Definitional and Taxonomical Issues," Journal of Marketing 52 (January 1988): 93–107.

[65] The first three types of complaint actions were identified by William Bearden and Jesse Teel, "Selected Determinants of Consumer Satisfaction and Complaint Reports," Journal of Marketing Research 20 (February 1983): 21–28. The last two were identified by Robert O. Herrmann, "The Tactics of Consumer Resistance: Group Action and Marketplace Exit," in Advances in Consumer Research, vol. 20, ed. Leigh McAlister and Michael L. Rothschild (Provo, UT: Association for Consumer Research, 1992), 130–134.

[66] A. Andreason and A. Best, "Consumers Complain: Does Business Respond?" Harvard Business Review 55 (July–August 1977): 93–101.

[67] R. E. Krapfel, "A Consumer Complaint Strategy Model: Antecedents and Outcomes," in Advances in Consumer Research, vol. 12, ed. E. Hirschman and M. Holbrook (Ann Arbor, MI: Association for Consumer Research, 1985), 346–350.

[68] Diane Halstead and Cornelia Droge, "Consumer Attitudes toward Complaining and the Prediction of Multiple Complaint Responses," in Advances in Consumer Research, vol. 18, ed. Rebecca Holman and Michael Solomon (Provo, UT: Association for Consumer Research, 1991), 210–216; E. L. Landon, "A Model of Consumer Complaint Behavior," in Consumer Satisfaction, Dissatisfaction, and Complaining Behavior, ed. Ralph Day (Bloomington: Indiana University, School of Business, 1977), 20–22.

[69] See K. Gronhaug and G. Zaltman, "Complainers and Noncomplainers Revisited: Another Look at the Data," in Advances in Consumer Research, vol. 8, ed. K. Monroe (Ann Arbor, MI: Association for Consumer Research, 1981), 83–87.

[70] Valerie S. Folkes, Susan Koletsky, and John L. Graham, "A Field Study of Causal Inferences and Consumer Reaction: The View from the Airport," Journal of Consumer Research 13 (March 1987): 534–539.

[71] Kjell Gronhaug and Gerald Zaltman, "Complainers and Noncomplainers Revisited: Another Look at the Data," Journal of Economic Psychology 1 (June 1961): 121–134.

[72] Ibid.

[73] Michelle Morganosky and Hilda Buckley, "Complaint Behavior: Analysis by Demographics, Lifestyle, and Consumer Values," in Advances in Consumer Research, vol. 14, ed. Melanie Wallendorf and Paul Anderson (Provo, UT: Association for Consumer Research, 1987), 223–226.

[74] See J. Faricy and M. Maxio, "Personality and Consumer Dissatisfaction: A Multi-Dimensional Approach," in Marketing in Turbulent Times, ed. E. M. Mazze (Chicago: American Marketing Association, 1975), 202–208; W. O. Bearden and J. E. Teel, "An Investigation of Personal Influences on Consumer Complaining," Journal of Retailing 57 (Fall 1981): 3–20.

[75] Michelle Morganosky and Hilda Buckley, "Complaint Behavior: Analysis by Demographics, Lifestyle, and Consumer Values," in Advances in Consumer Research, vol. 14 (1987), 223–226.

[76] Donna J. Hill and Robert Baer, "Customers Complain—Businesses Make Excuses: The Effects of Linkage and Valence," in Advances in Consumer Research, vol. 21, ed. Chris T. Allen and Deborah Roedder John (Provo, UT: Association for Consumer Research, 1994), 399–405.

[77] Ruth N. Bolton and Tim M. Bronkhorst, "The Relationship between Customer Complaints to the Firm and Subsequent Exit Behavior," in Advances in Consumer Research, vol. 22, ed. Frank Kardes and Mita Sujan (Provo, UT: Association for Consumer Research, 1995), 94–100.

[78] J. Jacoby, C. K. Berning, and T. F. Dietvorst, "What About Disposition?" Journal of Marketing 41 (April 1977): 22–28.

[79] Helga Dittmar, "Meanings of Material Possessions As Reflections of Identity: Gender and Social Material Position in Society," in To Have Possessions: A Handbook of Ownership and Property, ed. Floyd W. Rudmin, Special Issue of the Journal of Social Behavior and Personality 6, no. 6 (1991): 165–186.

[80] Deborah Heisley, Deborah Cours, and Melanie Wallendorf, "Structural Dimensions of the Intergenerational Transfer of Possessions," in Proceedings (Nashville: Association for Consumer Research, Nashville, 1993).

[81] J. Jacoby, C. K. Berning, and T. F. Dietvorst, "What About Disposition?" Journal of Marketing 41 (April 1977): 23.

[82] J. A. McCarty and L. J. Shrum, "Recycling of Solid Wastes: Personal Values, Value Orientations, and Attitudes About Recycling As Antecedents of Recycling Behavior," Journal of Business Research 30 (May 1994): 53–62.

[83] Shirley Taylor and Peter Todd, "Understanding Household Garbage Reduction Behaviors: A Test of an Integrated Model," Journal of Public Policy and Marketing 14 (Fall 1995): 192–204.

[84] William Boulding, Ajay Kalra, Richard Staelin, and Valarie A. Zeithaml, "A Dynamic Process Model of Service Quality: From Expectations to Behavioral Intentions," Journal of Marketing Research 30 (February 1993): 7–27.

[85] Melanie Wells, "Brand Ads Should Target Existing Customers," Advertising Age, April 26, 1993, 47.

[86] A similar point was made by J. Paul Peter and Jerry C. Olson, Consumer Behavior and Marketing Strategy (Homewood, IL: Richard D. Irwin, 1990), 435.

[87] Jacob Jacoby and Robert Chestnut, Brand Loyalty, Measurement, and Management (New York: Wiley, 1978).

[88] Sharon E. Beatty, Lynn R. Kahle, and Pamela Homer, "The Involvement-Commitment Model: Theory and Implications," Journal of Business Research 16 (March, 1988):149–167.

[89] Ibid.

[90] Charles L. Martin and Phillips W. Goodell, "Historical, Descriptive, and Strategic Perspectives on the Construct of Product Commitment," European Journal of Marketing 25, no. 1 (1991): 53–60.

[91] Lester Guest, "Brand Loyalty Revisited: A Twenty Year Report," Journal of Applied Psychology 48 (April 1964): 93–97.

[92] See, for instance, Ronald Frank, William Massy, and Thomas Lodahl, "Purchasing Behavior and Personal Attributes," Journal of Advertising Research 9 (December 1969): 15–24.

[93] Raphaelle Lambert-Pandraud and Gilles Laurent (2010), "Why Do Older Consumers Buy Older Brands? The Role of Attachment and Declining Innovativeness," Journal of Marketing, 74: 104–121.

[94] Valentyna Melnyk, Stijn M. J. van Osselaer, and Tammo H. A. Bijmolt, "Are Women More Loyal Customers than Men? Gender Differences in Loyalty to Firms and Individual Service Providers," Journal of Marketing 73 (2009): 82–96.

[95] James Carmen, "Correlates of Brand Loyalty: Some Positive Results," Journal of Marketing Research 7 (February 1970): 67–76.

[96] A. M. Muniz, Jr. and T. C. O'Guinn, "Brand Community," Journal of Consumer Research 27 (March 2001): 412–432.

[97] Brad D. Carlson, Tracy A. Suter, and Tom J. Brown, "Social Versus Psychological Brand Community: The Role of Psychological Sense of Brand Community," Journal of Business Research 61 (2008): 284–291.

[98] Michael Rothschild, "A Behavioral View of Promotions Effects on Brand Loyalty," in Advances in Consumer Research, ed. Melanie Wallendorf and Paul Anderson (Provo, UT: Association for Consumer Research, 1987), 119–120.

[99] J. Josko Brakus, Bernd H. Schmitt, and Lia Zarantonello, "Brand Experience: What Is It? How Is It Measured? Does It Affect Loyalty? Journal of Marketing 73 (2009): 52–68.

[100] Jennifer L. Aaker, "Dimensions of Brand Personality," Journal of Marketing Research 34, no. 3 (1997): 347–356.

[101] Jennifer Aaker, Susan Fournier, and S. Adam Brasel, "When Good Brands Do Bad," Journal of Consumer Research 31 (2004): 1–16.

[102] Richard L. Oliver, "Whence Consumer Loyalty?" Journal of Marketing 63 (1999): 33–44.

chapter

11

Situational Influences

Learning Objectives:

1. What do we mean by consumer situations?

2. What are five types of situational influences?

3. What are the elements of physical surroundings that influence behavior?

4. How do our social surroundings influence our behavior?

5. What are the characteristics of gift-giving situations?

6. How does time influence consumption activities?

May I Warm That Coffee for You?

Can temperature affect our attitudes about global warming and investing—even our mood? Indeed, it can. In a study performed at Columbia University, US and Australian students who felt the current day was warmer than usual for the time of year were more likely to believe in and worry about global warming than those who thought it was cooler outside. Subjects were also more likely to believe in global warming when the room was made hotter. Respondents who had handled a warm cup of coffee were more likely to judge a hypothetical person as warmer and more sociable than did those who had handled a cold cup of coffee. As researchers at Ohio State University found, sunny days even influence the stock market positively

These are somewhat extreme examples of the subject of this chapter, temporary situational influences on consumer behavior, including weather, temperature, mood, time of day, and social setting.

WHAT WE MEAN BY CONSUMER SITUATIONS

The **consumer environment** is made up of those factors that exist independent of individual consumers and companies and that influence the exchange process. In Figure 11.1, the components of the consumer environment appear inside the dotted lines. The economic and cultural and cross-cultural environments are at the most macro level of our marketing analysis. As the arrows in the figure show, these factors influence both the subcultural and the regulatory environments, each of which, in turn, influences group and family processes. These, in their turn, affect the situational influences in each situation, as do individual consumer processes and the actions of the marketer.

Thus, it's at the most micro level of analysis within the consumer environment where we find temporary situational influences, such as mood and social setting. Situational influences affect the consumer or buying unit, the marketer, and the exchange process itself. Indeed, we can think of a marketing exchange as resulting from the interaction of the buyer, the marketer, and the situational influences at a particular time and place. This important interaction is called the **marketing triad**. All the other factors identified in the text, from individual consumer processes to environmental influences, come together to influence the triad's three parts.

FIGURE 11.1

The Consumer Environment and the Exchange Process

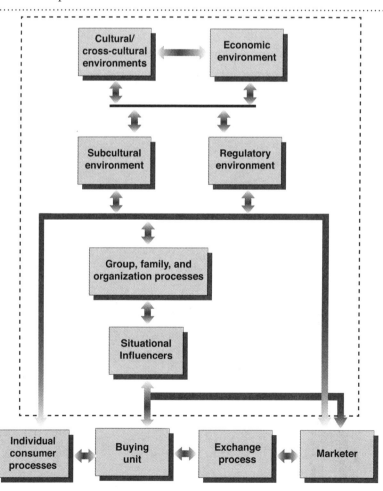

THE FIVE TYPES OF SITUATIONAL INFLUENCE

Consumer situations consist of the temporary environmental factors forming the context in which a consumer activity occurs. These five factors define the time and place of the action, explain why the action takes place, and influence consumer behavior. They're the physical surroundings, social surroundings, time, task definition, and antecedent (physiological) states—all of which are described in Table 11.1. (Note that consumer situations are relatively short-term events, so we distinguish their factors from longer-term influences, such as culture and personality.) Let's look at each of the five factors in turn.

1.	*Physical surroundings.* The concrete physical and spatial aspects of the environment encompassing a consumer activity.
2.	*Social surroundings.* The effects of other people on a consumer in a consumer activity.
3.	*Time.* The effects of the presence or absence of time on consumer activities.
4.	*Task definition.* The reasons that occasion the need for consumers to buy or consume a product or service.
5.	*Antecedent states.* The temporary physiological states and moods a consumer brings to a consumption activity.

TABLE 11.1
Five Types of Consumer Situations

Source: Russell Belk, "Situational Variables and Consumer Behavior," *Journal of Consumer Research* 2 (December 1975): 157–163.

Compare the food court at the mall with an elegant restaurant and you'll recognize why physical surroundings can have a major impact on consumers' experiences. In a convenience store, for example, designers attempt to create an atmosphere of safety by providing good lighting. If the physical surroundings are unpleasant, there's always another store down the road.

Social surroundings are also important, as we'll see in more detail in Chapter 12. When filling our car with gas, for example, we step out of our car and are relatively vulnerable. In this case, we may be concerned about avoiding unwanted social encounters. In a gym, the same situation may exist. Another situational element is time. For example, purchasing gas isn't typically a preferred pastime. The extent to which the time needed to complete this transaction can be shortened may influence the willingness of customers to use a certain gas station. Similarly, banks have experimented with being open on Sundays. Apple Pay and Android Pay, to some degree, also address the time element.

A fourth element is **task definition**, the reason or occasion we engage in a consumer action. Reasons can include needs, such as hunger, thirst, or having to buy a birthday present, as well as wants, including stopping for coffee on the way to work in the morning. A gas gauge nearing empty puts in motion the set of activities required to find a gas station, but gasoline retailers also try to increase the number of situational reasons for consumers to patronize them. Thus, many have added fast-food restaurants and convenience stores in order to satisfy the situational need of hunger. Similarly, when we are just browsing the web, we prefer a website that's prettier or more entertaining. But when we are looking to research a topic or make a purchase, we want a website that's more businesslike.[1]

Finally, we can think of antecedent states as the mood we bring to a consumption situation. Feelings of anger or exhaustion can easily influence our consumption behavior. The study of situations has important implications for managers because we can define products by the situations in which they're used. For example, wristwatches are positioned, and their purchasers are segmented, based partly on usage situations. A jogger may want a watch with a timing function for checking her pace or an activity tracker (e.g., Fitbit) to track her heart rate. A marketer can develop a product to fit the needs of that situation. Other situational factors might dictate the need for, say, a diamond watch, a sports watch, a waterproof watch, a fashion watch, a watch with a large face or numerals, a quartz or mechanical watch, and so on. Similarly, the marketer can create promotional materials that clearly position the product in reference to its situational use and to its competitors.

This chapter discusses each of the situational factors that may influence consumers, but we pay special attention to the influence of the physical environment, the effects of time, and the task definition. Social surroundings are discussed in more detail in Chapter 12. We cover antecedent states only briefly here because of their close relationship to mood, which earlier chapters have addressed. We begin with the physical environment.

PHYSICAL SURROUNDINGS: THE STORE ENVIRONMENT

Physical surroundings are the physical aspects of the environment in which a consumer activity occurs. Stimuli such as color, noise, lighting, weather, and the spatial arrangement of people or objects can influence consumer behavior through the sensory mechanisms of vision, hearing, smell, and even taste and touch. As such, retailers are particularly concerned about surroundings—perhaps their most important task is to manage the physical environment in order to influence consumers' behaviors, attitudes, and beliefs in a desired way. For example, if a retailer wants to present an upscale image, the surroundings must match and convey this image.

The perception of safety is another factor controlled, in part, by physical surroundings. Ample nearby parking, adequate outdoor lighting, and open spaces enhance shoppers' feeling of security. The presence of such physical attributes could increase nighttime shopping, particularly among the elderly, who are conscious of their perceived vulnerability to crime.

Researchers have investigated the impact of the physical environment on consumer perceptions and behavior in several retailing areas. These studies, which we look at next, have analyzed how music, crowding, store layout, store location, and store atmosphere affect buyers.

The Effects of Music

One component of the physical environment that's been shown to influence consumers in retail stores is background music. In one study, supermarket shoppers experienced either no music, slow-tempo music, or fast-tempo music over a nine-week period. The shoppers walked more quickly or more slowly depending on the tempo of the music and bought 38 percent more on a daily basis when slower music was played. No differences between the groups were found when customers were asked about their awareness of the music, suggesting it operated below their conscious level.

The second study obtained similar results in a restaurant environment. Fast- or slow-paced background music was randomly played on Friday and

Saturday nights over eight consecutive weekends in a medium-sized restaurant in the Dallas–Fort Worth, Texas, area.[2] The pace of the music influenced consumers to spend more or less time in the restaurant. In slow-tempo conditions, patrons took, on average, fifty-six minutes to complete their dinner. In contrast, patrons in the fast-tempo conditions took forty-five minutes to complete dinner. The increased time in the restaurant had no statistically significant impact on food sales; however, liquor sales went up significantly. Overall, the average gross margin per group was $55.82 in the slow-tempo and $48.62 in the fast-tempo conditions.

These studies demonstrate the physical environment can influence buyer behavior. However, we should not immediately generalize and say all retail businesses should play slow-paced music. There may be consumption situations in which fast music would be more appropriate. For example, restaurants that have low margins and depend on high volume must have a high occupant turnover rate. In this case, playing fast-paced music may speed up customers and make seats available for other customers more quickly.

Music is pervasive in the consumer environment. For example, when a customer is placed on hold on the phone, companies will frequently play music to fill the silence and help make the wait seem less negative. Surprisingly, however, research has found music rated as more pleasant does not make time seem to pass more quickly.[3] These results suggest playing appealing, peppy music while people wait on the phone or in line may prove counterproductive. Another study suggests louder music increases the perception that events are happening more quickly, but it also increases time duration estimates. So, keep the volume down.[4]

Research has also indicated music is more effective if it matches the general situational context of the purchase. For example, when a wine store played classical music rather than Top 40 selections, shoppers selected more expensive wines.[5] Clearly, the type of music should fit the situation.

The Effects of Crowding

Crowding occurs when we perceive our movements are restricted because of limited space. We can experience this sensation because there are too many people, too small a space, or a combination of the two. When consumers experience crowding, they may react by reducing their shopping time, altering their use of in-store information, or decreasing their communication with store employees.[6] Crowding can also increase shoppers' anxiety, lower their satisfaction, and negatively affect store image. Therefore, the perception of crowding has particular relevance to retailers, who must decide how to arrange their floor space and the way traffic flows through it.

Researchers have distinguished between the terms *density* and *crowding* (see Figure 11.2). **Density** describes how closely packed people are, while **crowding** refers to the unpleasant feelings that may result when a person perceives densities are too high and, as a result, feels control of the situation has been reduced below acceptable levels.

Although you might assume high density levels are always a negative, they can sometimes be perceived as beneficial. When consumers are seeking an experience such as being in a popular club or attending a critical sporting event, for instance, high levels of density may enhance the overall impact of the event.

FIGURE 11.2
The Effects of Density and
Crowding on Consumer
Behavior in a Retail Setting
Source: Figure based on
Michael K. Hui and John E. G.
Bateson, "Perceived Control
and the Effects of Crowding
and Consumer Choice on the
Service Experience," *Journal
of Consumer Research* 18
(September 1991): 174–184.

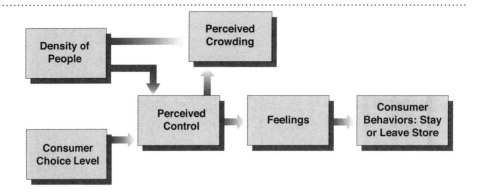

In any context, there's probably some optimum level of density. Dining out is uncomfortable if the restaurant is so full service is poor, but if the restaurant is nearly empty, the experience is equally negative. The optimum level of density is somewhere between the two extremes.

In a similar vein, people don't necessarily change their behavior just to limit crowding. Researchers in England found only 6 percent of a large sample of supermarket shoppers shifted their store visits from busy to quiet periods to avoid congestion. Other elements, such as the timing of shopping in relation to work and weekends, are probably more important.[7]

In some circumstances, consumers show the same kinds of behavior we observe in the actions of hysterical crowds, taking action as part of a crowd they'd never do alone. For three years in a row, for instance, impatient customers broke the hinges off the doors at the beginning of Black Friday sales in one Walmart store in New York. Just before an employee was trampled to death in 2008, other employees had been keeping back the crowd by physically holding the doors shut. At least one website keeps a running count of Black Friday deaths and injuries.[8] Apple, fearing similar crowd behavior, briefly halted the release of its highly anticipated iPhone 4s in China after a near-riot in Beijing.

The factors that cause normal consumers to evolve into crowds still aren't understood completely. In 1896, Gustav Le Bon suggested that people go into hypnotic trances when they are part of a mob, forming a collective mind. A more likely explanation is very large groups cause a high degree of physiological arousal, leading each member of the crowd to act on his or her dominant idea. Because a similar idea brought the group together, however, the individuals within the crowd are likely to share a tendency to act similarly and, in many instances, that dominant tendency is aggression. Each person in a crowd is inconspicuous, so individual responsibility is lost and the usual norms that control behavior don't apply. The result is an unruly, highly aroused group of people who aren't acting as individuals and aren't subject to the standard norms that control behavior. The result can be riots, runs on banks, panic buying of a product in short supply, and even deadly behavior at concerts. The firm Crowd Management Strategies publishes reports on trends in crowd safety issues, including a 2015 report on how the Paris attacks may affect concert safety procedures.

You may have heard the expression "the wisdom of the crowd," suggesting that, while individual members of a crowd may give wrong answers, on average, the crowd as a whole will have greater intelligence. Many firms are using this hypothesis to employ crowdsourcing of, for example, new product ideas and even start-up capital to good effect. [9] But the evidence for its validity is equivocal.

The Effects of Store Location

Real estate agents have a rule that the three primary factors influencing the value of a piece of property are location, location, and location. Those who study retailing echo this point, and location's contribution to store choice has been extensively researched.

Both actual distance and perceived distance can influence store selection. Research has shown consumers form individual cognitive maps of the geography of a city. Interestingly, consumers' mental maps of the locations of retail stores may not match the actual locations. Such factors as parking availability, merchandise quality, and the ease of driving to the shopping center can make the distance seem shorter or longer than it actually is. [10]

Image transference also influences our perceptions. That is, the image of larger anchor stores in a shopping center, whether upscale or discount, for example, affects the image of smaller stores in the center. And the image of a mall affects the image of the stores within it. [11] Small stores are better off located in a center with a department store as the anchor tenant rather than a discount store, unless the discount store is congruent with the smaller stores' image.

The Effects of Store Layout

Stores are designed to facilitate customer movement, present merchandise in its best light, and help create a particular atmosphere. The overall goal is to maximize profits by increasing sales through a cost-effective store design. These design elements affect online stores as well as brick-and-mortar locations.

Store layout can influence consumer reactions and buying behavior. For example, the placement of aisles influences traffic flow, and the location of items and departments relative to traffic flow can dramatically influence sales. One suggestion is all convenience foods—salad bar, deli, bakery, frozen entrees, frozen pizza, rotisserie chicken, and prepared meals—should be brought together for the upscale but harried consumer. [12]

The design of seating arrangements can dramatically influence communication patterns. Some have argued airport terminals are designed to discourage people from talking comfortably to each other. Chairs are bolted down and placed so people can't face each other and converse from a comfortable distance. Perhaps this antisocial arrangement is meant to drive people into airport bars and food courts, where space is arranged more comfortably—and where customers spend money. This concept has been taken to great lengths, with department stores and even casinos now making an appearance in airports: one designer describes the Pittsburgh International Airport, for example, as "a mall with planes parked around it." [13]

Atmospherics: The Elements of Store Atmosphere

A store's atmosphere delivers a message to consumers, such as, "This store has high-quality merchandise." **Atmospherics** is a more general term than store layout; it deals with all the ways managers can manipulate the design of the building, the interior space, the layout of the aisles, the texture of the carpets and walls, and the scents, colors, shapes, and sounds customers experience there. Even the arrangement of merchandise, types of displays, and poses of mannequins can influence consumers' perceptions of store atmosphere. These elements are pulled together well in the definition developed by Philip Kotler, which describes atmospherics as "the effort to design buying environments to produce specific emotional effects in the buyer that enhance his probability of purchase."[14]

Researchers have argued atmospherics influence the extent to which consumers spend beyond their planned levels in a store.[15] The store's atmosphere influences a shopper's emotional state—specifically, the levels of pleasure and arousal, which together induce the consumer to spend either more or less time on the premises.

Figure 11.3 diagrams these relationships. When the atmosphere arouses the consumer and positive emotions already exist, the buyer tends to spend more time in the store and has an increased tendency to affiliate with people, a situation that's likely to result in increased buying. In contrast, if the environment isn't pleasurable, increased arousal could lead to decreased buying. Research by psychologists has shown dominant tendencies are more likely to be activated when people become aroused. If the dominant tendency is to leave the store, then increased arousal tends to increase the desire to leave.

FIGURE 11.3
Atmospherics and Shopping Behavior
Source: Adopted from a discussion in Robert Donovan and John Rossiter, "Store Atmosphere: An Environmental Psychology Approach," *Journal of Retailing* 58 (Spring 1982): 34–57.

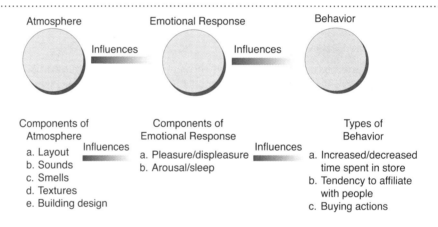

Because the atmosphere of a retail store influences emotional responses, the study of atmospherics is linked directly to the experiential perspective on consumer behavior. However, we can also understand atmospherics from a behavioral influence perspective. In particular, the layout of buildings and the design of traffic corridors in cities, malls, and stores directly influences consumers' movements, often without affecting either beliefs or feelings. As Winston Churchill said, "First we shape our buildings and then they shape us."[16]

A variety of other studies have found a building's atmosphere influences its inhabitants. Some researchers have suggested increasing the number of windows and, therefore, the amount of sunlight entering a space, can actually improve mood states. Walmart once opened a prototype store in Lawrence, Kansas, in which half the departments were illuminated by skylights, the other half by artificial light. Sales were higher in the areas with natural light, and employees in the areas with artificial light tried to have their departments moved to those with skylights.

Atmosphere becomes increasingly important as the number of competitors increases, as differences in product features and price decrease among the competitors, and as the market becomes segmented on lifestyle and social-class differences. A retail store can use atmosphere as a tool to differentiate itself from others and to draw specific groups of consumers for whom its atmosphere is attractive. Next, we look at the way atmospheric strategies interact with the senses.

Smell All five senses come into play with atmospherics, including the olfactory, or sense of smell. A study found shoppers return more often to scented stores and perceive goods sold there to be of better quality than in unscented stores. The intensity and nature of the scent seem to matter little, as long as they aren't offensive. However, it should also be distinctive and congruent with product offerings, and managers need to pay attention to costs—diffusion methods can be expensive, as can the scents themselves.[17]

A brand manager of a hotel group in Las Vegas, Nevada, discussed olfactory stimuli as a motivator for consumers to interact with the hotel, noting, "[The] Mirage has a beautiful smell . . . it's calming, you go in and you wanna get more. People want to explore."[18] A recent study suggests combinations of scent and music can actually enhance each other and increase arousal level, and scent and loud music in the same store seemed to produce the stronger pleasure effects for young female fashion shoppers.[19]

Touch Customers often need to touch merchandise. But the desire to touch also extends to the environment as a whole. Again, Las Vegas provides an example: "Sculptures, artworks, statues, and other architectural details . . . are primarily designed to be touched by consumers to provide a higher level of connection between the consumer and the context in many Las Vegas settings."[20]

Taste All our other senses interact with the sensation of taste. For example, we have little ability to differentiate varieties of products (such as coffee and red wine) without using our sense of smell as well as taste. We even use sound as an aid in tasting—would celery be celery without the crunch? And while consumers don't literally taste stores, they associate restaurants, hotels, and bars with memories of good (or bad) meals and other tastes.[21]

Sight As Apple's product designers know very well, design is a critical visual characteristic not only of products and their packaging but also of the store environment and the way it uses space. The spatial arrangements in a retail store have important consumer-behavior effects:

1. Space modifies and shapes consumer behavior.
2. Space affects consumers by stimulating the senses.
3. Retail stores, like other aesthetic surroundings, affect customer perceptions, attitudes, and images.
4. Space can be designed to create desired customer reactions.[22]

Atmospherics in Service Settings

In a service setting, the physical and social surroundings may become a part of the service itself. For example, the nature of a concert or play is shaped largely by lighting, the design of the set, the way sound is produced, and the characteristics of the people who are sharing the experience. Other examples could include medical offices, spas and salons, Apple Stores, and restaurants, each of which provides a social surrounding that enhances (or detracts from) the customer's experience.

SOCIAL SURROUNDINGS

Have you ever bought something, or decided not to buy it, based on who was shopping with you? The study of **social surroundings**, which we'll discuss further in Chapter 12, deals with the effects other people have on a consumer in a consumption situation. For example, the presence of a group can result in conformity pressures on a consumer; high school and college students often feel pressured to purchase particular brands of beverages, clothing, and even automobiles because their friends do so. Knowing you're buying something other people will use also dramatically influences purchase actions. You may buy a higher-quality beer or wine for a special evening with friends, for instance, or low-fat or vegetarian dishes for guests with food preferences or restrictions. For example, people tend to buy light or salty snacks partly as something to have around the house if friends should drop by.[23]

Other people can also influence the impact of communications on the consumer. For example, the presence of others in a room likely reduces our attention to advertisements that cross the screen. In a personal-selling situation, the presence of a friend can lower the impact of the sales presentation. Research on conformity has found subjects conformed to the views of a group even when they objectively knew the group was wrong. However, if at least one other member of the group concurred with the subject in the experiments, the group conformity effect was lost.[24] Thus, in a sales encounter, a friend who supports your resistance to the sales message will likely reduce its impact compared to what it would be if you were alone.

Social motives sometimes even explain why people go out and shop. Shopping can be an important social experience in which consumers meet new people and possibly make friends with them. In one study, researchers recorded the social interactions of one hundred randomly selected individuals who entered a large mall alone.[25] In 51 percent of the cases, the interpersonal interactions were informational, such as when the subjects asked someone where to find an item. Another 23 percent of the interactions were perfunctory, in which the subject acknowledged another person's presence. In 26 percent of the cases, however, social interactions and conversations took place between the subject and someone else. The studies' authors interpret these results as indicative of the importance of social interaction in the shopping experience. They even suggest the rebirth of central business districts and older malls lies in their new social significance.

A new retail venue that crosses the frontier between shopping with friends and with strangers is the shopping social network. In this digital consumer experience, photo sharing and real-time commentary from other shoppers, fashion insiders, and friends are combined. The best known site is Pinterest. Other sites with similar general features are Pose and Feyt.

Retailers are usually wise to encourage the social aspects of shopping. A shopper who's with others both visits more stores and makes more unplanned purchases.[26] In fact, many products wouldn't exist unless people gathered into social groupings. A small industry exists to provide party supplies, such as noisemakers, napkins, specialized mixers, and so on. Even a beverage such as beer is consumed in contexts that are often social in nature. In an inventory of beer-drinking situations, half the contexts dealt with social situations, including entertaining close friends at home, attending a social event for which people bring their own beverages, going to a bar after work, going to a restaurant on Friday or Saturday night, or taking a camping trip, beach trip, or extended picnic.[27] We turn now to the task definition.

THE TASK DEFINITION

We buy and consume products and services for many reasons at many times and places, all of which together form what we call the task definition, or our situational reason for buying or consuming. For instance, one common task definition is the need to give a gift for a holiday, birthday, graduation, or wedding. The task definition when we buy a beverage could be to satisfy thirst, to relax and socialize, or to stay awake. In fact, the number of task definitions is probably infinite. It's up to the skilled marketing manager to identify those buying reasons that aren't adequately met by existing products.

Closely related to the task definition is the usage situation. **Usage situations** form the context in which a product is used and influence the product characteristics the consumer seeks. For example, the usage situation of camping presents unique requirements for eating utensils, food packaging, bedding, and shelter. These requirements center on the need for lightweight, portable, and durable goods. The task definition of going camping, therefore, suggests a usage situation that may influence the consumer's choice of products. Those who choose the situation of living outdoors for short periods of time can become a heavy-spending market segment, as outdoor products maker Coleman has discovered.

Occasion-Based Marketing Opportunities

A problem for marketers is that a product can become locked into one usage situation, limiting its market potential. Consumers may come to use a product habitually in a particular situation and consider it inappropriate for other situations. Orange juice is a good example. By convention, orange juice has become associated with breakfast. Although nutritious and tasty, the beverage hasn't been adopted by consumers as a thirst-quenching beverage the way soft drinks have. The orange juice trade association has spent millions trying to redefine the task definition of the beverage. A campaign based on the theme "Orange juice isn't just for breakfast anymore" brought national attention to its thirst-quenching qualities, while a second attempt to redefine the task definition of orange juice focuses on a health appeal. The trade association has teamed with the American Cancer Society to explain the relationship between oranges and cancer prevention and with the March of Dimes to promote the idea that increasing expectant mothers' folic acid intake by drinking orange juice can help prevent birth defects.

Many other companies have worked to change their products' usage situations. Turkey growers have attempted to persuade US families to eat the big birds on occasions other than Thanksgiving and Christmas. The seasonal demand for turkey causes production problems for them. Another example is beef. Although beef held a three-to-one market-share advantage over poultry after World War II, poultry consumption now well exceeds that of beef.[28] In an attempt to broaden the situational usage of the product, the beef trade association has sponsored commercials suggesting that beef makes a good breakfast meat.

The ability to recognize new or overlooked usage situations can lead marketers to profitable new market segments. The forerunner of the Internet (the ARPANET) existed for many years as a tool for scientists and intellectuals, but using it was clumsy. In 1988, a Frenchman decided to write a front end to make it easier to get into and maneuver around the Internet. Thus, the prototype for the web browser was born. Later, as the Internet rose in popularity, companies began designing ever more sophisticated browsers. Innovators such as Google have vastly increased Internet usage and, at the same time, made their shareholders wealthy.

Gift Giving

An important ritual in most societies, and a particularly common task definition for consumers, is the giving of gifts. People build reciprocal relationships by engaging in the ritual pattern of giving, receiving, and giving back. Gifts reflect status hierarchies, denote rites of passage (e.g., graduation and marriage), and influence the socialization of children through the formation of gender roles (i.e., toys often confirm societal expectations of male and female children). Gift giving has strong symbolic qualities; with their choice of presents, givers convey who they are, who the receiver is, and the nature of their relationship. For example, the failure of a gift-giver to remove a price tag from a gift violates the symbolic notion that gifts are nonmonetary expressions of affection.[29]

Gift giving also has important economic consequences, and retailers take full advantage of the many gift occasions prescribed by many societies. Historically, some 30 percent of sales, and as much as 50 percent of annual profits, are booked during the Christmas season. So powerful is the social effect of the holiday season that consumers will even purchase gifts for difficult people—that is, those who don't want or need gifts, are likely to be unappreciative of a gift, or are very different from the purchaser.[30]

The type of gift situation, of course, influences a consumer's degree of engagement in the purchase. For example, people usually devote greater search efforts and spend more money on gifts celebrating a rite of passage (a low-frequency, large-scale event, such as the wedding of a close friend) than for gifts intended for a rite of progression (a high-frequency, small-scale event, such as a birthday).[31] Researchers have found people are more socially conservative when buying gifts for their spouses than for themselves, buying safe, traditional goods.[32] One possible reason is they perceive much greater risk in buying for their spouses than for themselves.

Why do people give gifts? We can analyze their reasons. There are essentially two gift types—voluntary and obligatory. Voluntary gifts are those made with a minimum of outside pressures forcing the action. In contrast, obligatory gifts are the result of strong social norms pressuring the person into action. An example might be a gift for a niece graduating from high school. One measure of the difference is the degree to which self-interest influences the gift. In cases of low self-interest, the giver has few ulterior motives for giving. When high self-interest exists, ulterior motives play a predominant role in the gift giving.

When the gift is voluntary and low self-interest is present, an altruistic motive exists for the action. For instance, you might give a friend a small present completely out of the blue to cheer him or her up. In contrast, when the gift is voluntary and high self-interest exists, the motive is frequently to create an obligation. Giving someone an expensive present with the hope he or she may reciprocate is an example.

On the other hand, low-involvement ritual gifts occur when an obligation exists but the giver has low self-interest in the exchange. Giving presents to acquaintances at Christmas, birthdays, and graduations fits this category. Finally, when an obligation exists and the person has a high self-interest in the exchange, high-involvement reciprocity occurs. In such instances, there are strong pressures to give. The exchange relationship may be highly important to the person, and love or friendship may be involved. You might purchase an anniversary present for your spouse because forgetting the event would lead to dire consequences. For example, 53 percent of women in 2015 polled said they'd end their relationship if they didn't get something for Valentine's Day.[33]

Consumers not only give gifts to others; they also purchase gifts for themselves. Indeed, many of the situational variables that influence purchasing gifts for others also motivate consumers to buy for themselves. **Self-gifts** are premeditated, indulgent, relevant to the self, and influenced by context. They may be purchased to reward an accomplishment (e.g., getting a high grade on a consumer-behavior test), to serve as therapy for a disappointment (e.g., failing to get a coveted job), or to commemorate a holiday or life transition (e.g., a birthday).[34] Self-gifts can range from a doughnut to a new car. Consumers higher in the personality trait of materialism tend to purchase self-gifts more frequently, particularly as a means to manage their moods. These individuals appear to associate buying with happiness. Sometimes, they buy to avoid resentment:

> *I don't think I could bear seeing something I loved on a friend or family member, knowing I had bought it for them but wanted it for myself. The resentment would be corrosive. I self-gift to avoid having nasty little thoughts about people I love.[35]*

In a series of four studies, a researcher found strong evidence gift givers should take great pains to wrap their offerings nicely. Wrapping a gift results in more positive attitudes toward owning the product and appears to place recipients in a better mood state, allowing them to enjoy the entire process more. However, a more recent study suggests the opposite:

> *One of the interesting findings was that if you wrap a gift, you raised people's expectations and the liking of the same gift goes down. If you wrap a gift that, you know, is really just meant to be a little something, it might behoove you not to wrap it—or if you are going to wrap it, to not wrap it so nicely.[36]*

TIME AS AN ENVIRONMENTAL INFLUENCER

In his *Advice to a Young Tradesman*, Ben Franklin wrote, "Remember that time is money." Since then, some authors have suggested time may be the most important variable in consumer behavior because it plays a role in so many areas.[37] As we discussed earlier, definitions of brand loyalty should specify the period of time over which we're looking at a particular buying behavior. Similarly, studies of the diffusion of innovation require us to consider how rapidly a new product or service is adopted. Behavioral learning theory (see Chapter 5) tells us rewards must be given in close temporal proximity to a behavior to be effective. These examples represent only a few of the cases in which time is an important consumer behavior variable.

We can analyze time from three perspectives—as a resource, as a product, and as a situational variable. Let's explore each of these perspectives.

Time As a Resource

At the individual level, we use our time in four ways—for work, necessities, housework, and leisure.[38] We usually have little control over when and for how long we work. We have somewhat more control over necessities, such as how long we sleep and when we eat. The effort we spend on housework is even more variable, with dual-earner families spending less time on "household production." Finally, we have the most discretion over how we use what's left, our leisure time.

If we think of time as a resource, the way people choose to spend it says a great deal about them. For instance, we can categorize the activities in which consumers engage as either substitutable or complementary based on their relationship to time.[39] **Substitute activities** are separate activities that satisfy the same need for the consumer; but they are also mutually exclusive (i.e., they can't occur together). For example, given limited leisure time, playing handball and racquetball are substitute physical activities. **Complementary activities** are those that can both take place. Thus, you may garden and mow the grass to fulfill your need to have a beautifully landscaped home; you don't have to choose between them. Nor do complementary activities have to occur simultaneously. They can take place over a period of time, such as a week or a month. Consumer choices about the way they use their time says a great deal about their lifestyles.

Various constraining factors influence the substitutability and complementarity of activities. For example, the employment status of spouses and the presence or absence of children may strongly influence the way husbands and wives spend their time. (Chapter 12 discusses these issues in more detail.) In fact, evidence exists that marital satisfaction is influenced by the extent to which couples share views on the complementarity and substitutability of activities. Those who jointly participate in activities have greater marital satisfaction.[40]

The way individuals view time is even influenced by their culture.[41] North Americans and Western Europeans tend to run on linear separable time: the past, present, and future all exist; time is divided up and allocated; and there's a future orientation. Time can be lost or wasted. Many businesspeople run on linear time. Time doesn't stretch into the future for those on circular traditional time. They tend to do today only what has to be done today. People on linear separable time often find it frustrating to deal with those on circular time because the latter may not see a relationship between time and money.

Finally, those who keep procedural traditional time are governed by the task rather than the time. For them, meetings begin when the time is right and end when they are over. The idea of wasting time is irrelevant, and completing the task is the key. Native American cultures often reflect this view of time. Some evidence exists that Asians are also on procedural time.[42] Medical doctors run on procedural time as well, creating conflicts with exasperated patients (and possibly insurance providers) who are thinking in terms of linear time.

Time As a Product

Of course, time can also be a type of product. We make many purchases to buy time, including takeout and prepared foods and appliances such as microwave ovens and garbage disposals. Fast-food restaurants have flourished because consumers want to eat on the go.

Because time acts as a product attribute, advertisers use time-oriented appeals in their promotional materials. A study investigated the changing use of time-oriented appeals between 1890 and 1988 by analyzing ads in the *Ladies' Home Journal*. The authors found the proportion of ads that used time as the primary appeal increased dramatically. In 1890, less than 5 percent of the ads appealed predominantly to time. By the late 1980s, nearly 50 percent of the ads included a time-oriented appeal as a major component. An example is an ad for Hunt's Manwich headlined, "When it's dinner time and time is tight."[43]

Time As a Situational Variable

In addition to recognizing time as a product, we should also understand it as a **situational variable**. Generally, the situational characteristic of time that influences consumers is its availability. The amount of time a consumer has available to complete a task, such as buying a product, will influence the strategy he or she uses to select and purchase the product. For example, researchers have found that, as time pressure increases, consumers spend less time searching for information. They also use information less and give more weight to negative information when time pressures are severe.[44]

A number of shopping apps for smartphones and tablets attempt to save the customer time or combine more than one activity. For example, Amazon's Dash Buttons allow one-touch reordering of certain kitchen, bath and laundry products using your home's Wi-Fi. An experiment was conducted to directly assess the impact of time pressure on grocery shopping. Actual grocery shoppers were assigned to either a control group with no time pressure or to the experimental group, which was asked to complete their shopping in one-half the participants' expected shopping time. The time-pressured group more frequently failed to purchase intended products and made fewer unplanned purchases. Time pressure also caused a decrease in the total number of purchases. Finally, time pressures caused greater problems when the respondents were shopping in unfamiliar stores.[45] The managerial implication of the study is that retailers should create a shopping environment that makes it easy to locate desired products to facilitate shopping by time-pressed consumers.

Time may also interact with other variables to influence purchase behavior. For example, the length of time since a shopper's last meal has been shown to influence how much he or she will buy at a grocery store. As noted by the researchers, a person who shops while hungry may find his or her "imagination readily places potatoes and onions around roasts and transforms pancake mix into a steaming, buttered snack."[46]

Interestingly, a situation-consumer interaction was found in the research on hunger and grocery shopping. The food buying of shoppers classified as overweight was not affected by how long they had gone since their last meal. The effect of buying more when hungry occurred mainly for people of average weight. The authors interpreted the results as indicating overweight consumers fail to use internal cues to determine their hunger. Rather, they use the presence of food to determine how much to buy and consume.[47]

Time of day is an important situational variable that can be used as a means of segmenting products. For example, food products may be marketed for use in the morning (breakfast foods) or the evening (dinner foods). In the 1980s, the beer company Anheuser-Busch created an entire advertising campaign with the slogan "The Night Belongs to Michelob."

Time can influence distribution strategy as well. Consumers experiencing a shortage of time want to obtain products quickly and with minimal effort. The drive-through windows at fast-food restaurants exemplify a distribution system that allows customers to obtain burgers, fried chicken, and other foods rapidly. Mail-order, telephone-order, and computer-ordering systems for products have been developed so consumers don't have to take the time to go to a brick-and-mortar store to make a purchase.

ANTECEDENT STATES

Antecedent states are those temporary physiological and mood states a consumer brings to a consumption situation. Physiological states include hunger, thirst, and fatigue. **Mood states** are temporary variations in our emotions, which range from very positive to very negative feelings. (Chapter 4 discussed in some detail the effect of mood on consumers' information processing.)

Temporary physiological states can influence buying through two means. First, they may lead to problem recognition. For example, the gnawing hunger pangs in a person's stomach may bring recognition that a problem needs to be solved. Second, physiological states can influence consumers by changing the feeling component of the hierarchy of effects. (Chapter 7 discussed hierarchy-of-effects models). For example, when a person is hungry, the presence of food is likely to create highly positive feelings concerning consumption. Thus, a hungry person who enjoys red meat will have very positive feelings when he or she sees a porterhouse steak. These positive feelings may then lead to an increased likelihood of purchasing the steak. Similarly, if a shopper is thirsty while in a store, that physiological state is likely to create positive feelings about thirst-quenching beverages. Let's look next at mood states.

The Effects of Temporary Mood States on Consumers

Mood states have also been found to influence consumer behavior. In one survey, people were asked why they shopped. Two of the reasons given were wanting to alleviate either depression or loneliness.[48] In such instances, consumers expressed the idea they used the shopping and purchasing experience to influence their temporary mood state.

Psychologists have investigated the effects of mood on gifts to charities, to others, and to themselves. After creating either positive or negative moods in their subjects, the researchers measured how strongly changes in mood state affected behavior. In one study, a group of second- and third-grade children were asked to think of something that made them very happy. Another group was asked to think of something that made them feel very sad. A third group, the control group, was asked to not think of anything in particular. After their mood was influenced, the children were given a chance to help themselves to candy from a treasure chest. Those with either a positive or a negative mood took more candy than those in the control group.

The mood study shows people tend to reward themselves when they feel either good or bad. The mediator of the phenomenon appears to be the affective component of attitudes—the same concept suggested as the explanation for why hungry people buy more in a supermarket. As the authors of the mood study explained, "When one is feeling good, one tends to be more generous to oneself." The phenomenon extends beyond self-generosity: People are also more generous to others when they're in a positive mood state.[49]

Why did the children in sad moods also indulge themselves more than those in the control group? The reason seems to be to make themselves feel better. Significantly, the impact of negative moods seems to extend to how much one person will help another. Research suggests people over the age of six will help others more when they're feeling bad, as well as when they're feeling good, than when they're in a neutral mood state. Again, the motivation seems to be that people derive good feelings from helping others. When a person feels bad, he or she may seek out ways to feel better and consequently help others more.

Evidence suggests temporary mood states may influence consumer reactions to advertisements. In one experiment, half of the subjects read an uplifting story that placed them in highly positive moods. All respondents then evaluated a print advertisement. Results revealed those placed in a positive mood state had more favorable brand attitudes and fewer counterarguments to the ad than subjects who didn't read the story. The study's author suggested those in positive mood states engaged in less cognitive processing, which would cause fewer counterarguments to occur. In addition, a positive mood state tended to cause subjects to process information peripherally. Thus, those in good moods were less affected by central cues, such as argument quality, and more influenced by peripheral cues, such as source attractiveness.[50]

Research on the effects of mood on consumer behavior is still in its infancy. We can't be sure mood influences the buying of products in the same way it affects, say, the taking of candy or the distribution of coupons to obtain a prize.[51] But evidence indicates mood states may be particularly effective in influencing consumer buying behavior in retail settings, particularly at the point of purchase.

USAGE SITUATION, PERSON, AND PRODUCT INTERACTIONS

We can view the buying act as either a two-way or a three-way interaction. In a two-way interaction, consumer situations interact with personal factors (a situation-person interaction) or with the type of product or service being offered (a situation-product interaction). A three-way interaction takes place between person, product, and situation variables.[52]

An **interaction** occurs when two or more factors combine to cause consumers to behave in a different manner than they would have otherwise. In a situation-product interaction, consumers view two products as useful in different situations. For example, most of us would see Gatorade as appropriate in situations when we've worked up a thirst, such as after a tennis match, whereas drinking Canada Dry Ginger Ale after a workout sounds perfectly awful. In contrast, Gatorade has little appeal as a mixer at a party, while Canada Dry Ginger Ale would be quite appropriate there. Thus, the type of product and the type of situation interact so the type of product favored is determined by a situational context. Figure 11.4 diagrams these interactions.

FIGURE 11.4
Situation-Product Interaction

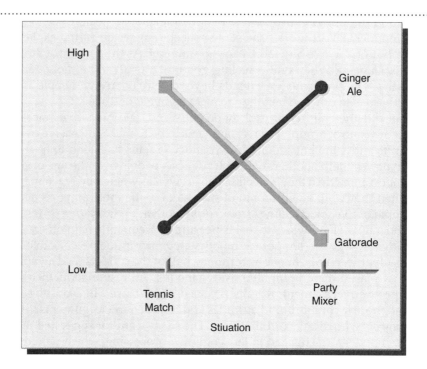

Situation-product interactions form the basis for benefit segmentation. That is, marketers create different products to offer specific benefits relevant in different situations. For example, diving watches were developed to allow users to tell time while underwater and know when their air was about to run out. In contrast, formal watches were created as ornaments. Their benefit is their expensive and luxurious look.

An example of a situation-product interaction is illustrated by a study developed to probe how purchase agents react to lunches in fancy restaurants versus ordinary restaurants. In the study, the fanciness of the restaurant represents the type of product and the reason for the lunch represents the situational factor (specifically, the reason for the lunch is a task-definition factor). The researchers found the buyers evaluated the suppliers' position more favorably in ordinary restaurant meetings than in fancy restaurant meetings. However, if the reason for the lunch had been a celebration for closing a contract, the fancy restaurant may have been more appropriate than the ordinary restaurant. The authors interpreted the results as indicating sales representatives should be extremely careful in staging business lunches in fancy restaurants. They argued the restaurant context should fit the business context.[53]

MANAGERIAL IMPLICATIONS OF SITUATIONAL INFLUENCES

The principles and concepts derived from the study of situational influences have applications to RESPonsive elements.

Research

Marketing research is required to identify situational influences we can use to develop positioning strategies. Research may also indicate which consumer situations presents opportunities for new products, for example, laptops developed, in part, as a means of allowing those on the road to do work comparable to what they could perform in their offices. Laptops, tablets, and smartphones enable a person to perform the task definition of working away from the office.

Environment

Because the entire chapter focuses on the environment, we don't discuss this RESPonsive element separately.

Segmentation

If we can divide markets into groups of consumers who are homogeneous in terms of a particular situational influence, we can develop products that may present a solution to a problem or enhance that situation. For example, one result of the increased number of women working outside the home has been that more males need to do their own gift purchasing (i.e., instead of the wife making the purchase). This created opportunities to devise gift services to appeal to these males.

Positioning

Situational influences—physical and social surroundings, time, task definition, and antecedent states—offer many opportunities for marketers to position and differentiate their products. A clear situational differentiator, for example, is time-saving features. Apple originally marketed its iMac without a floppy drive—it was clearly optimized for working in a time-saving Internet environment. Apple has also typically emphasized the capability of its computers for tasks, such as publishing, where graphics are important, and for music recording and composing, where sound cards and digital-recording capabilities are critical.

In 1998, seventy McDonald's restaurants in northern California experimented with the use of one line for serving, as opposed to multiple lines. Although multiple lines actually move people faster, having multiple lines is more stressful for customers. Jumping from line to line, or watching someone who arrived after us move toward the front faster, creates stress. McDonald's was investigating whether this point of differentiation—single versus multiple lines—would help position McDonald's restaurants favorably versus those of competitors. But McDonald's now typically has several lines in its restaurants.

On the other hand, self-checkout lines in supermarkets may be going away. One of the reasons cited is customers want human interaction, which probably actually slows down the checkout process.[54]

What do we mean by consumer situations?

Consumer situations are temporary environmental circumstances that form the context within which a consumer activity occurs. Situational factors that influence consumers include physical and social surroundings, task definition (the occasion for which a product is bought), time, and consumers' temporary physiological and mood states (antecedent states). These situations may influence consumers when they receive communications about a good or service, when they make a purchase, and when they use the product of service.

What are five types of situational influences?

Consumer situations consist of the temporary environmental factors forming the context in which a consumer activity occurs. These five factors define the time and place of the action, explain why the action takes place, and influence consumer behavior. They're the physical surroundings, social surroundings, time, task definition, and antecedent (physiological) states

What are the elements of physical surroundings that influence behavior?

Store layout, atmospherics, crowding, music, and store location are all factors in the physical environment that can affect consumers. Social motives influence why people shop, their involvement in the purchase, and their conformity to the tastes and preferences of others. Task definition identifies the reason we seek a product or service, which might be a situation such as a gift occasion, a party, or a meal. Usage situations are also a potent segmentation tool.

How do our social surroundings influence our behavior?

Social surroundings deals with the effects other people have on a consumer in a consumption situation. Knowing you're buying something other people will use also dramatically influences purchase actions. You may buy a higher-quality beer or wine for a special evening with friends, for instance, or low-fat or vegetarian dishes for guests with food preferences or restrictions.

What are the characteristics of gift-giving situations?

People build reciprocal relationships by engaging in the ritual pattern of giving, receiving, and giving back. Gifts reflect status hierarchies, denote rites of passage (e.g., graduation and marriage), and influence the socialization of children through the formation of gender roles (i.e., toys often confirm societal expectations of male and female children). Gift giving has strong symbolic qualities; with their choice of presents, givers convey who they are, who the receiver is, and the nature of their relationship.

How does time influence consumption activities?

Time can be a resource, a product characteristic, and a situational variable. We can segment consumers on the basis of their perception and use of time as a resource. Many products and services have been created and positioned on the basis of their ability to save time, making time a product characteristic. As a situational variable, the availability of time influences consumer actions, especially during information search.

KEY WORD

antecedent states	density	situational variable
atmospherics	interaction	social surroundings
complementary activities	marketing triad	store layout
consumer environment	mood states	substitute activities
consumer situations	physical surroundings	task definition
crowding	self-gifts	usage situations

REVIEW QUESTION

1. Define the concept of consumer situation. What are the five types of situation identified in the chapter?

2. Give an example of a person-situation interaction. Give an example of a situation-product interaction.

3. The effect of music on shoppers is one example of how physical surroundings can influence buying. Identify five other means by which the physical environment can influence buying. Do you think music can influence Internet shopping? Why or why not?

4. What are the effects of location on a consumer's choice of store?

5. Draw the model of how atmospherics influences shopping behavior (see Figure 11-4). What are the components of store atmosphere?

6. How can the presence of other people influence the consumption situation, the purchase situation, and the communications situation?

7. Define task definition.

8. Identify five categories of gift-giving situations and give four reasons for gift-giving.

9. Identify and give examples of three ways in which time can influence consumption activities.

10. How might a company use information to lower consumer dissatisfaction with delays in service?

11. Different cultures define time in different ways. Discuss the views of time held in various cultures.

12. Define the concept of the antecedent state. What are two types of antecedent states and how might each influence consumption?

DISCUSSION QUESTION

1. The shoe industry is segmented largely by usage situation. Identify as many usage situations as you can for which shoe producers have created different types of shoes.

2. The consumer situation can interact with the type of person and the type of product. Give an example of each type of interaction. Think about your own characteristics and preferences and about those of someone else who's quite different from you. Compare the way each of you responds to various types of situations and products.

3. Draw a diagram of the grocery store with which you are most familiar. Identify the specific physical features of the store that are designed to move customers in specific patterns and encourage them to purchase specific products.

4. Recall from your own experiences two consumer behavior situations in which large numbers of people were present. To what extent did the presence of people enhance the overall experience? When might large numbers of people detract from the consumption experience?

5. Draw a map of your community, freehand or using a map app. Place the locations of your residence and college on the map. Next, draw in or locate the retailers you most frequently patronize. Is there any relationship between the locations of the retailers and the location of your residence and college?

6. Considering all the components that help establish a store's atmosphere, describe the atmosphere of two popular eating or drinking establishments you patronize. To what extent do you think the atmosphere of these establishments was consciously created?

7. List all the gifts you've given over the past year. What occasion prompted the giving of each? In which instances did you purchase a gift that was designed specifically to be given as a gift?

8. Identify several products or services that differentiate themselves from their competitors on the basis of saving or using up time. How do these products communicate this benefit to consumers? Can you identify a product or service that could be marketed as saving time for college students? How much of a market is there for products and services that help you use up time?

9. Suppose you're an advertising executive charged with developing a campaign for a company that sells exotic coffees. The campaign is to be based on the idea people drink coffee because of their good or bad mood. Develop an Internet ad carrying out this task.

ENDNOTES

[1] Yongjian Wang, Michael S. Minor, and Wei Jie, "Aesthetics and the Online Shopping Environment: Understanding Consumer Responses," Journal of Retailing 87, no. 1 (2011): 46–58.

[2] Ronald E. Milliman, "Using Background Music to Affect the Behavior of Supermarket Shoppers," Journal of Marketing 46 (Summer 1982): 86–91; Ronald E. Milliman, "The Influence of Background Music on the Behavior of Restaurant Patrons," Journal of Consumer Research 13 (September 1986): 286–289.

[3] James J. Kellaris and Robert J. Kent, "The Influence of Music on Consumers' Temporal Perceptions: Does Time Fly When You're Having Fun?" Journal of Consumer Psychology

1, no. 4 (1992): 365–376. But see also Sylvie Droit-Volet, Danilo Ramos, José L. O. Bueno, and Emmanuel Bigand, "Music, Emotion, and Time Perception: The Influence of Subjective Emotional Valence and Arousal?" Frontiers in Psychology (2013): 417, accessed January 7, 2016, doi: 10.3389/fpsyg.2013.00417.

[4] James J. Kellaris, Susan Powell Mantel, and Moses B. Altsech, "Decibels, Disposition, and Duration: The Impact of Musical Loudness and Internal States on Time Perceptions," in Advances in Consumer Research, vol. 23, ed. Kim P. Corfman and John J. Lynch, Jr. (Provo, UT: Association for Consumer Research, 1996), 498–503.

[5] Charles S. Areni and David Kim, "The Influence of Background Music on Shopping Behavior: Classical versus Top-Forty," in Advances in Consumer Research, vol. 20, ed. Leigh McAlister and Michael L. Rothschild (Provo, UT: Association for Consumer Research, 1993), 336–340.

[6] G. Harrell, M. Hutt, and J. Anderson, "Path Analysis of Buyer Behavior under Conditions of Crowding," Journal of Marketing Research 17 (February 1980): 45–51.

[7] Robert East, Wendy Lomax, Gill Willson, and Patricia Harris, "Decision Making and Habit in Shopping Times," European Journal of Marketing 28, no. 4 (1994): 56–71.

[8] Black Friday Death Count, accessed January 8, 2008, http://blackfridaydeathcount.com/.

[9] Jonah Lehrer, "When We're Cowed by the Crowd," Wall Street Journal, May 28-29, 2011, C18; Joseph P. Simmons, Leif D. Nelson, Jeff Galak, and Shane Frederick, " Intuitive Biases in Choice versus Estimation: Implications for the Wisdom of Crowds," Journal of Consumer Research 38 (June 2011): 1–15; Cindy Waxer, "Asking the Crowd to Make Something," Technology Review (July 19, 2011), accessed January 8, 2016, http://www.technologyreview.com/business/38066/?nlid=nldly&nld=2011-07-20; Sarah E. Needleman and Lora Kolodny, "Site Unseen: More 'Angels' Invest via Internet," Wall Street Journal, January 23, 2013, accessed February 4, 2013, http://online.wsj.com/article/SB10001424127887323301104578258651038480358.html.

[10] R. Mittelstaedt, W. Curtis, S. Grossbart, and R. Rogers., "Psychophysical and Evaluative Dimensions of Cognized Distance in an Urban Shopping Environment," in Combined Proceedings, ed. R. C. Curhan (Chicago: American Marketing Association, 1974), 190–193. See also Priya Raghubir and Aradhna Krishna, "As the Crow Flies: Bias in Consumers' Map-Based Distance Judgments," Journal of Consumer Research 23 (June 1996): 26–39.

[11] David J. Burns, "Image Transference and Retail Site Selection," International Journal of Retail and Distribution Management 20 (September–October 1992): 38–43; Jean-Charles Chebat, M. Joseph Sirgy, and Valerie St-James, "Upscale Image Transfer from Malls to Stores: A Self-Image Congruence Explanation," Journal of Business Research 59 (November 2006): 1288–1296, accessed January 8, 2016, doi:10.1016/j.jbusres.2006.09.007.

[12] Paul Kelly, "Reorganizing the Store," Progressive Grocer, March 1996, 21.

[13] Paul Tarricone, "Real Estate: Airports Can Be a Launching Pad for Revenue," Facilities Design and Management, February 1996, 26.

[14] Philip Kotler, "Atmospherics as a Marketing Tool," Journal of Retailing 49 (Winter 1973–1974): 48–64.

[15] Robert Donovan and John Rossiter, "Store Atmosphere: An Environmental Psychology Approach," Journal of Retailing 58 (Spring 1982): 34–57.

[16] Cited by Mary Jo Bitner, "Consumer Responses to the Physical Environment in Service Settings," in Creativity in Services Marketing: What's New, What Works, What's Developing, ed. M. Venkatesan, Diane Schmalensee, and Claudia Marshall (Chicago: American Marketing Association, 1986), 89–93.

[17] Eric R. Spangenberg, Ayn E. Crowley, and Pamela W. Henderson, "Improving the Store Environment: Do Olfactory Cues Affect Evaluations and Behaviors?" Journal of Marketing 60 (April 1996): 67–80: See also Deborah J. Mitchell, Barbara E. Kahn, and Susan C. Knasko, "There's Something in the Air: Effects of Congruent or Incongruent Ambient Odor on Consumer Decision Making," Journal of Consumer Research 22 (September 1995): 229–238.

[18] Ebru Ulusoy Akgun, "Consumer Experience Intensity: Towards a Conceptualization and Measurement" (PhD diss., University of Texas-–Pan American, 2011), 155.

[19] Michael Morrison, Sarah Gan, Chiris Dubelaar, and Harmen Oppewal, "In-Store Music and Aroma Influences on Shopper Behavior and Satisfaction," Journal of Business Research, 64, no. 6 (2011): 558-594.

[20] Ebru Ulusoy Akgun, "Consumer Experience Intensity: Towards a Conceptualization and Measurement" (PhD diss., University of Texas–Pan American, 2011), 154.

[21] Aradhna Krishna and Ryan S. Elder, "The Gist of Gustation," in Sensory Marketing: Research on the Sensuality of Products, ed. Aradhna Krishna (New York: Routledge, 2010).

[22] Ron Markin, Charles Lillis, and Chem Narayana, "Social-Psychological Significance of Store Space," Journal of Retailing 52 (Spring 1976): 43–54.

[23] Russell Belk, "An Exploratory Assessment of Situational Effects in Buyer Behavior," Journal of Marketing Research 11 (May 1974): 160.

[24] Solomon E. Asch, Social Psychology (Upper Saddle River, NJ: Prentice-Hall, 1952).

[25] Richard Feinberg, Brent Scheffler, and Jennifer Meoli, "Social Ecological Insights into Consumer Behavior in the Retail Mall," in Proceedings of the Division of Consumer Psychology, ed. Linda Alwitt (New York: American Psychological Association, 1987), 17–19; Christina Binkley, "One Old Mall Fights Back," Wall Street Journal, May 26, 2011, accessed January 8, 2016, http://online.wsj.com/article/SB10001424052702304066504576343770327812028.html.

[26] Donald H. Granbois, "Improving the Study of Customer In-Store Behavior," Journal of Marketing 32 (October 1968): 28–33.

[27] William Bearden and Arch Woodside, "Consumption Occasion Influence on Consumer Brand Choice," Decision Sciences 9 (April 1978): 275.

[28] "Per Capita Consumption of Poultry and Livestock, 1965 to Estimated 2016, in Pounds," National Chicken Council, accessed January 8, 2016, http://www.nationalchickencouncil.org/about-the-industry/statistics/per-capita-consumption-of-poultry-and-livestock-1965-to-estimated-2012-in-pounds/.

[29] Mary Finlay, "Motivations and Symbolism in Gift-Giving Behavior," in Advances in Consumer Research, vol. 17, ed. Marvin E. Goldberg, Gerald Gorn, and Richard W. Pollay (Provo, UT: Association for Consumer Research, 1990), 699–706. 30. For holiday sales 2000-2015, see http://www.statista.com/statistics/243439/holiday-retail-sales-in-the-united-states/ accessed January 14, 2016.

[30] Cele Otnes, Young Chan Kim, and Tina M. Lowrey, "Ho, Ho, Woe: Christmas Shopping for 'Difficult' People," in Advances in Consumer Research, vol. 19, ed. John Sherry, Jr. and Brian Sternthal (Provo, UT: Association for Consumer Research, 1992), 482–488.

[31] This distinction is noted in David Cheal, The Gift Economy (New York: Routledge, 1988), cited in Mary Finley Wolfinbarger and Mary C. Gilly, "An Experimental Investigation of Self-Symbolism in Gifts," in Advances in Consumer Research, vol. 23, ed. Kim P. Corfman and John G. Lynch Jr. (Provo, UT: Association for Consumer Research, 1996), 458–462.

[32] "Valentine's Day Statistics," Statistic Brain, accessed January 8, 2016, http://www.statisticbrain.com/valentines-day-statistics/.

[33] Eileen Fischer and Stephen J. Arnold, "More Than a Labor of Love: Gender Roles and Christmas Gift Shopping," Journal of Consumer Research 17 (December 1990): 333–343.

[34] David Glen Mick and Michele DeMoss, "Further Findings on Self-Gifts: Products, Qualities, and Socioeconomic Correlates," in Advances in Consumer Research, vol. 19, ed. John Sherry, Jr. and Brian Sternthal (Provo, UT: Association for Consumer Research, 1992), 140–146.

[35] "Self-Gifting: Who's at the Top of Your Holiday Shopping List? You," Globe and Mail, December 7, 2012, accessed January 8, 2016, http://www.theglobeandmail.com/life/holiday-guide/holiday-survival-guide/self-gifting-whos-at-the-top-of-your-holiday-shopping-list-you/article6036488/.

[36] Daniel J. Howard, "Gift-Wrapping Effects on Product Attitudes: A Mood-Biasing Explanation," Journal of Consumer Psychology 1, no. 3 (1992): 197–223; Lauren Laborde, "The Science of Gift-Wrapping," December 23, 2011, accessed January 8, 2016, http://www.bestofneworleans.com/blogofneworleans/archives/2011/12/23/the-science-of-gift-wrapping.

[37] F. M. Nicosia and R. Mayer, "Toward a Sociology of Consumption," Journal of Consumer Research 3 (September 1976): 65–76.

[38] Laurence Feldman and Jacob Hornik, "The Use of Time: An Integrated Conceptual Model," Journal of Consumer Research 7 (March 1981): 407–419.

[39] Morris Holbrook and Donald Lehmann, "Allocating Discretionary Time: Complementarity among Activities," Journal of Consumer Research 7 (March 1981): 395–406.

[40] Ibid.

[41] Robert Graham, "The Role of Perception of Time in Consumer Research," Journal of Consumer Research 7 (March 1981): 335–342.

[42] Jay D. Lundquist, Sara Tacoma, and Paul M. Lane, "What Is Time? An Explanatory Extension toward the Far East," in Developments in Marketing Science, vol. 16, ed. Michael Levy and Dhruv Grewel (Coral Gables, FL: Academy of Marketing Science, 1993), 186–190.

[43] Barbara L. Gross and Jagdish N. Sheth, "Time-Oriented Advertising: A Content Analysis of United States Magazine Advertising, 1890–1988," Journal of Marketing 53 (October 1989): 76–83.

[44] Anthony D. Miyazaki, "How Many Shopping Days until Christmas? A Preliminary Investigation of Time Pressures, Deadlines, and Planning Levels on Holiday Gift Purchases," in Advances in Consumer Research, vol. 20, ed. Leigh McAlister and Michael L. Rothschild (Provo, UT: Association for Consumer Research, 1993), 331–335. See also Peter Wright, "The Harassed Decision Maker: Time Pressures, Distractions, and the Use of Evidence," Journal of Applied Psychology 59 (October 1974): 555–561; Frank Denton, "The Dynamism of Personal Lifestyle: How We Do More in Less Time," in Advances in Consumer Research, vol. 23, ed. Chris T. Allen and Deborah Roedder John (Provo, UT: Association for Consumer Research, 1994), 132–136.

[45] C. Whan Park, Easwar S. Iyer, and Daniel C. Smith, "The Effects of Situational Factors on In-Store Grocery Shopping Behavior: The Role of Store Environment and Time Available for Shopping," Journal of Consumer Research 15 (March 1989): 422–433.

[46] R. E. Nisbet and D. E. Kanouse, "Obesity, Food Deprivation, and Supermarket Shopping Behavior," Journal of Personality and Social Psychology 12 (August 1969): 289–294.

[47] Ibid.

[48] E. M. Tauber, "Why Do People Shop?" Journal of Marketing 36 (October 1972): 47.

[49] D. L. Rosenhan, B. Underwood, and B. Moore, "Affect Moderates Self-Gratification and Altruism," Journal of Personality and Social Psychology 30 (October 1974): 546–552; B. Moore, B. Underwood, and D. L. Rosenhan, "Affect and Altruism," Developmental Psychology 8 (January 1973): 99–104.

[50] Rajeev Batra, "The Role of Mood in Advertising Effectiveness," Journal of Consumer Research 17 (September 1990): 203–214.

[51] D. Kenrick, D. Baumann, and R. Cialdini, "A Step in the Socialization of Altruism as Hedonism," Journal of Personality and Social Psychology 37 (May 1979): 747–755.

[52] S. Ratneswar and Alan G. Sawyer, "The Use of Multiple Methods to Explore Three-Way Person, Brand, and Usage Context Interactions," in Advances in Consumer Research, vol. 19, ed. John Sherry, Jr. and Brian Sternthal (Provo, UT: Association for Consumer Research, 1992), 116–122.

[53] Paul Schurr and Bobby Calder, "Psychological Effects of Restaurant Meetings on Industrial Buyers," Journal of Marketing 50 (January 1986): 87–97.

[54] Richard Gibson, "Merchants Mull the Long and the Short of Lines," Wall Street Journal, September 3, 1998, B1, B4; Brad Tuttle, "Three Changes to Look for at the Checkout Line," Time, July 12, 2011, accessed January 8, 2016, http://moneyland.time.com/2011/07/12/3-changes-to-look-for-at-the-checkout-line/.

12

Social Influences: Group, Dyadic, and Diffusion Processes

Learning Objectives:

1. Why do consumers submit to social pressure?

2. What's gained from membership in a brand community?

3. How does the family influence decision making?

4. How is social media changing our buying behavior?

5. How does information influence behavior?

6. How can managers use information to influence loyalty and sales?

How Do Groups Influence Our Buying Behavior?

Groups strongly impact consumer behaviors. We find numerous examples of how groups influence our buying decisions in sports marketing. Fans often purchase team paraphernalia due to group pressure to fit in. Additionally, consumers often participate in rituals at sporting events as part of group collective behavior. An example is shaking one's car keys prior to the kickoff of a football game.

The objects we buy have symbolic meaning.[1] When a sports spectator wears a Boston Red Sox hat, he's telling the social world about his specific **in-group** and **out-group**.[2] By wearing the hat, he's telling the social world he's part of Red Sox Nation, the team's fan club (in-group), and he isn't part of the rival New York Yankees (out-group). Clearly,

consumers often purchase items and/or alter their behavior based on social influences.

In the college arena, a number of schools are well known for their highly identified fan base. Schools such as Texas A&M, the University of Florida, and Kansas State University are known for their devoted fan bases. For example, Texas A&M holds midnight yell practice the night before home games. Some twenty thousand students regularly attend this ritual. Such group behavior and commitment isn't common across all college sports teams. So, what encourages some groups to unite while others don't? This chapter will explore the influence of groups on our behavior.

GROUP PROCESSES

A **group** is a set of individuals who interact with one another over some period of time and who share a common need or goal. The group itself typically serves as a means to achieving a goal. Consumers belong to numerous groups, each of which has some impact on buying behavior. For example, college students are likely to be members of families, sororities or fraternities, dorms, sports teams, or clubs. While membership in a group is often a precursor to group influence, formal membership isn't required for group influence to exist.[3] For example, a person may feel psychologically connected to a group (e.g., Harley-Davidson owners, Republican or Democratic Party, etc.), but he or she doesn't actively interact with other group members. Membership may actually take place virtually (i.e., online), such as a Disney fan who interacts on-line with other Disney fans.. Simply feeling this **psychological closeness** may affect their buying habits.[4]

Groups influence buying in two general ways. First, they may influence the purchases made by individual consumers (e.g., a sports fan may buy a team jersey with the name of the team's superstar or a favorite player on the back). Consumers may be influenced into a purchase behavior simply by observing other people using a brand.[5] On a day-to-day basis, we observe hundreds of people, often strangers, using brands. These exposures are similar to a product placement in the context of the exposures appearing natural in the scene. However, they're unlike product placement in the context of the user is traditionally not paid any compensation. You may change your future purchase decisions when you run across someone carrying a Starbucks cup of coffee. A recent study found consumers do, indeed, select brands more frequently after viewing a stranger consuming a product.[6]

The second way groups influence buying decisions is in group decision making. For example, a student club may have to decide where to hold a party and what refreshments to purchase.[7] Group decision making can often be a laborious process because each individual may have his or her own goals. As a result, coming to a consensus may be difficult.

The study of group processes is relevant to decision making within companies. The buying center within a company usually consists of several individuals who jointly make purchase decisions. Also, employees often form groups to decide where to have parties, which restaurant to go to for a celebration, and which radio station to listen to as background music.

Types of Groups

Sociologists have developed a variety of terms to describe the different types of groups a person may belong to, aspire to join, or avoid.[8] Table 12.1 provides a brief definition of the various groups, which include reference groups, primary and secondary groups, and formal and informal groups. The most important of these groups is the reference group.

Reference Groups   The term **reference group** is broad and encompasses a number of more specific types of groups. The common factor among the types of reference group is that each is used by the consumer as a point of reference to evaluate the correctness of his or her actions, beliefs, and attitudes.

TABLE 12.1
Types of Groups

- *Reference.* This is a group whose values, norms, attitudes, or beliefs are used as a guide for behavior by an individual.
- *Aspiration.* This is a group to which an individual would like to belong. If membership in it proves impossible, it becomes a symbolic group for the person.
- *Dissociative.* This is a group with which the person doesn't wish to be associated.
- *Primary.* This is a group of which a person is a member and with which that person interacts on a face-to-face basis. Primary groups are marked by intimacy among their members and by a lack of boundaries for the discussion of various topics.
- *Formal.* This is a group whose structure is defined in writing. Examples are labor unions, *and* universities.
- *Informal.* This is a group that has no written organizational structure. Informal groups are often socially based, such as a group of friends who meet frequently to play golf, have lunch, or party together.

One type of reference group is the aspiration group. An **aspiration group** is a set of people with whom a consumer identifies. One can see the effects of aspiration groups on college students in the spring of their senior year, when they're interviewing for jobs. Their aspiration group has suddenly changed and, along with it, so has their clothing—from shorts and flip flops to business attire.

A **dissociative group** is another type of reference group. The dissociative group is still a point of reference; however, the consumer wants to avoid being associated. For example, some people are very loyal to either Ford or Chevrolet, but not both. The rivalry between the two loyal groups is often expressed with disparaging bumper stickers about the other brand. Sports fans are notorious for demonstrating their allegiance while also showing they're not part of the rival group. For instance, in the related picture, two Colorado State University fans wear their green and gold to the annual Rocky Mountain Showdown. The Showdown is the rival game between Colorado State University and the University of Colorado. By wearing these colors, they men are demonstrating their allegiance as well as their disconnect with the rival school.

Colorado State University students show their allegiance by dressing in the school colors

BRAND COMMUNITY GROUPS

Consumers often form groups that share a deep-seeded devotion to a brand. These groups are called **brand communities**.[9] Many consumers develop a psychological sense of brand community prior to ever interacting socially with other brand enthusiasts.[10] While many members of a brand communities interact socially with fellow members, brand communities can involve a psychological brand community, where they don't actually interact with other members. Figure 12.1 is a simplification of work by Carlson, Suter, and Brown[11] As you can see, consumers first feel identification with the brand. When a consumer identifies with the brand, his or her self-schema overlaps with the brand's identity. Once **identification** occurs, the individual can feel psychologically connected to a community of followers. Finally, the brand benefits from a number of positive outcomes, such as increased attendance, increased brand preference, and positive word-of-mouth.

FIGURE 12.1
The Psychological Sense of
Brand Community Model

Identification
with Brand → Psychological Sense
of Brand Community → Attendance

Brand Preference

Word-of-Mouth

Numerous brand communities exist for tangible brands, including Jeep, Harley-Davidson, and Apple. Brand communities also exist for intangible brands, such as Harry Potter, Star Trek, Disney, and the Chicago Cubs. A question remains as to why groups form around a brand. The answer may have to do with the psychological benefits each member feels.[12] Community members gain psychological satisfaction by sharing their brand experiences with other brand followers. When a Harley rider discusses his religious-like devotion to the brand, the community members who hear the story feel a deeper connection to the brand. They're living vicariously through the storyteller.

Sports fans often express their identity through their attire.

The brand, in turn, benefits from this visceral connection brand community members exhibit in three key areas. First, brand community members are loyal. They tend to buy the brand more often than others. Second, they're missionaries in their willingness to recruit others to the brand. Finally, they're less likely to switch brands.[13] Firms that cultivate these brand relationships may benefit from the enthusiasm of its members. Harley-Davidson, for instance, embraces the Harley Owners Group (HOG) by interacting with HOG members at rallies to gain product insight.[14]

The Harley-Davidson Rally in Sturgis, South Dakota is an example of a brand community at work.

One way to explain the brand community phenomenon is through **social identity theory**. Social identity theory suggests our identity partially derives from the social categories to which we belong.[15] The social categories define our place in the social world. As mentioned in the opening vignette, consumers demonstrate their group membership by purchasing items related to the group. When a twelve-year-old wears an Oklahoma State University hoodie, she tells the world about her aspirational group while she demonstrates her dissociative group (the University of Oklahoma). Clearly, brand communities are an important group to firms. The companies that embrace and cultivate these groups may be able to reap enormous benefits.

Managerial principle 12.1
To increase brand loyalty, you can encourage consumers to join a brand community focused on your brand.

How Groups Influence Consumers

Groups affect consumers through five basic means: group-influence processes, the creation of roles within the group, the development of conformity pressures, social-comparison processes, and the development of group polarization. We'll address these next.

Group-Influence Processes The type of group having the most impact on consumers is the reference group. Reference groups affect people through norms, via information, and through the value-expressive needs of consumers. A **norm** is a behavioral rule of conduct agreed upon by a majority of the group in order to establish behavioral consistency within the group. Norms are rarely written down but are, nonetheless, generally recognized as standards for behavior by group members. Norms represent shared value judgments about how things should be done by members of the group. **Normative influence** occurs when norms act to influence behavior. For example, the effects of unwritten corporate dress codes illustrate the impact of normative influence on the clothing purchased by employees. Similarly, norms can influence what and how much a person eats or drinks at a party and even the type of car a consumer purchases.

Groups can also influence consumers by providing them with information and encouraging the expression of certain types of values. **Informational influence** affects individuals because the group provides highly credible information that influences the consumer's purchase decisions. A reference group's values and attitudes toward consumption exert **value-expressive influence** on consumers. Because the person wishes to be a part of the group and to be liked by its members, he or she may act in ways that express these values and attitudes.

Reference-group influence may vary depending on the type of product purchased. Some have suggested reference-group influence is higher for "public" products, such as smartphones and automobiles, than for "private" products, such as refrigerators and mattresses.[16]

Roles A role consists of the specific behaviors expected of a person in a given position. When a person takes on a role, normative pressures exert influence on the person to act in a particular way. An important role in consumer behavior is that of the decider. This person makes the final decision concerning which brand to choose. In organizational buying settings, identifying the decider is crucial. Often, an individual outside of the purchasing department is actually responsible for the buying decision; reaching this individual with the promotional message can make the difference in whether a sale is made.

The term **role-related product cluster** has been given to the set of products necessary to play a particular role. For marketing managers, identifying those products that match the roles of consumers can be useful. For example, the role-related product cluster of a successful skate boarder might include a "girl" skateboard, a pair of DC shoes, and a DC ball cap. An advertising campaign for the skateboard could symbolically tie its product to the rest of the product cluster as necessities for the skateboard enthusiast.

Conformity Pressures **Conformity** may be defined as a "change in behavior or belief toward a group as a result of real or imagined group pressure."[17] Marketers have recently used group pressure to increase sales volume. Groupon is a website that offers discounts as much as 50 to 80 percent off the regular price of a good or service. The site encourages shoppers to motivate their friends to buy the products. Consumers earn the large discounts only if enough people buy the discounted item within a limited time period.[18] This online strategy taps into conformity pressure by encouraging others to buy.

Managerial principle 12.2
To get a large participation rate, create brand promotions that are contingent upon many individuals participating in the promotion.

Two types of conformity can be identified. The first is simple **compliance**, in which the person merely conforms to the wishes of the group without really accepting the group's dictates. The second is **private acceptance**, in which the person actually changes his or her beliefs in the direction of the group. A number of factors may increase the groups' conformity pressures.

Factors Within the Group that Lead to Conformity Three aspects of groups may act to increase the conformity pressures felt by its members. One aspect is cohesiveness, which refers to how closely knit a group is. A group whose members have a high degree of loyalty and identification can exert greater influence on its members.

The expertise of the group also affects conformity pressures. Because consumers are members of many groups, several different groups may have input into a particular purchase decision. The group whose members have more expertise relevant to the decision will have greater influence on the purchase.

The third group aspect that's been found to influence decisions is size, particularly when the group is of a transient nature. In a classic series of experiments, the psychologist Solomon Asch had people judge which of the series of lines on one card matched the length of a line on another card. The task was quite simple, and when done alone, the subjects made almost no errors. However, in the experiment, Asch also used confederates (i.e., researchers playing a role) who systematically made incorrect estimates and who succeeded in inducing wrong answers. The impact of the group varied with the number of confederates. The likelihood of the subjects agreeing with the confederates increased until the size of the group reached about four people. After the group size got to four people, the impact of adding more individuals to the group was minimal.[19]

Factors Within the Person that Lead to Conformity The ability of a group to make a person conform depends on the nature and the needs of the person as well as the properties of the group. One such personal factor is the amount of information the person has available for a decision. When little information is available or when the information is ambiguous, the group has more impact on the person's decision.

The attractiveness of the group and the person's need to be liked by the group often work together to create conformity pressures. In most cases, the more the person wants to be part of the group, the more he or she also wishes to be liked by its members. In such circumstances, the individual tends to conform to group norms and pressures in order to fit in as well as possible.

Type of Decision The type of decision is a final factor that may influence the amount of conformity pressure felt by the person. When a product is highly salient and conspicuous to others, conformity pressures increase.

Perhaps the buying situation that best illustrates the impact of group conformity pressures involves home shopping parties. Pampered Chef is a brand sold via home shopping parties. The host invites friends for an evening meal and a demonstration of the kitchen items used to prepare the meal. Nearly everyone who attends purchases something. In effect, strong friendship ties create a type of moral economy in which buying is expected.

Social-Comparison Processes Another way in which groups influence consumers involves people's need to assess their own opinions and abilities by comparing themselves with others. The process through which people evaluate the "correctness" of their opinions, the extent of their abilities, and the appropriateness of their possessions has been called **social comparison**.[20] In addition to using groups to obtain factual information, consumers use groups to determine where they stand in terms of their opinions, abilities, and possessions.

It's important to note people typically compare themselves to others who are at about the same level on the given attributes rather than to someone who shows great differences. Social comparison, however, isn't limited to contrasting oneself with peers. The idealized images of how one should look that come from advertising can also influence one's self-image. One study reported a series of experiments on the topic. In one of these experiments, college women viewed magazine ads that used either highly attractive models or no models. After being exposed to the highly attractive models in the ads, subjects were less satisfied with their own physical appearance. Thus, advertising does cause social comparison to occur, and these comparisons can affect our feelings about ourselves.[21]

Another study looked at the social influences on food consumption. In the study, the researchers measured the number of candies chosen from a bowl after a confederate chose a small or large number of candies. The consumers altered the number of candies taken depending on the number of candies taken by the confederate and the size of the confederate. Specifically, consumers chose fewer candies when the confederate chose a small portion, unless the confederate was obese.[22] The findings of this study demonstrate how social influences play a role in our quest for impressions management.

Group Polarization For several decades, psychologists have studied a highly perplexing phenomenon—**group polarization**. Group polarization is the tendency of groups to make decisions that are more extreme than initial inclinations of the members. In studies, researchers have provided groups and individuals with decision dilemmas and compared their choices. Although they first found groups tended to select the riskier alternative, later research found conservative and risky shifts could occur.[23]

The study of group polarization is particularly relevant to organizational sales. If a group decision to purchase an industrial product or service is made, the salesperson needs to recognize that risky or conservative shifts may occur. Because the dominant culture of most companies is toward financial conservatism, organizational sellers should probably tailor the marketing mix based on this dominant value.

FAMILIES AND HOUSEHOLDS

The term family is actually a subset of a more general classification—household. A **household** is all the people occupying a living unit. Examples of households include roommates living in an apartment, unmarried couples living together, a husband and wife with children, two couples sharing the same house, and a husband, wife, children, and grandparents living under one roof. The key similarity among all the examples is the group must live in the same residence. Using this definition, a husband, wife, and children who live together are a household as well as a family.

Multiple types of families exist. The **nuclear family** consists of a husband, a wife, and their offspring. The **extended family** consists of the nuclear family plus other relatives, such as the parents of the husband or the wife. Although many societies expect a husband and wife to reside with one or the other of their parents, in the United States and Canada, children from middle-class families tend to strike out on their own to form families away from their parents. Such a trend has been called the **detached nuclear family**.

Over the past two decades, major changes have occurred in the United States and Canada in the nature of households and families. New living arrangements profoundly affect the number and size of households and families. Many of these changes are discussed in the next section.

The Demographics of Households

Two general types of household can be identified—family and nonfamily. Data from the US Census Bureau indicate household growth has outpaced population growth. Since 1970, the average household size has fallen from 3.14 to 2.61 persons, and average family size has fallen from 3.58 to 3.20 persons. Currently, 66 percent of people in the United States are family households, down from 81percent in 1970. The trend toward smaller households lies in an increasing divorce rate, decisions of young people to leave home prior to marriage, and the tendency of older people to maintain their own homes after other family members are gone.[24]

Later marriage is another factor linked to the decreasing size of households. In 1966, the average male was 22.8 years old and the average female 20.5 years old at the time of first marriage. By 2010, the age for first marriage for males and females had risen to 27.7 and 26.0, respectively.[25]

The trend toward later marriage has a number of implications. First, it suggests more people will remain single. Second, it implies fertility rates will decrease because older couples simply have more trouble conceiving than do younger couples. By remaining single longer, young people have more time to invest in themselves by pursuing educational and work goals. Marketers may have an opportunity to market different products to this group. For instance, people in the age range of twenty to thirty years may be more interested in visiting Las Vegas than Disneyland if they're still single and childless. On the other hand, courtship has changed dramatically as many couples are meeting through dating sites such as eHarmony, Christian Mingle, and Match.com. A recent study found as many as 25 percent singles are meeting through dating websites.[26]

Divorce is a fact of life for couples today. In the late 1970s, it was estimated that 35 percent of new marriages would end in divorce. That estimate is now about 49.3 percent.[27] One result of the higher divorce rate is a large increase in the number of single men and women caring for children 18 years of age or younger. Between 2000 and 2008, the percentage of male households with no wife present increased from 49.1 to 57.7 percent. The percentage of female households with no male present increased from 18.9 to 68.9 percent. On a more positive side, since the mid-1980s, divorce rates have declined slightly, from about 5.3 per one thousand population in 1981 to 4.2 in 1999 and 3.6 in 2007.[28]

Another major trend in family composition over the past decade is the increased frequency of "boomerang kids," which are adult children who left home to attend college or to start a career and moved back home. According to the Pew Research Center, 13 percent of adult children have moved back into their parents' homes.[29] This may be largely due to economic conditions. Clearly, this change in household structure may also have some dynamic changes in the demand for some products and services.

Changes in family demographics can influence buying habits in a number of ways. For example, parents with boomerang kids may choose to travel less or dine out less frequently so they can include their adult children in their activities. Marketers must determine the role of the extra household member in the buying decisions and target such households accordingly.

The change of US households plays a role in the marketing mix in a variety of ways. For example, the rapid increase in the number of working women has dramatically changed the way marketers attempt to reach this group. Back in 1970, women made up just 37.97 percent of the workforce, but by 2010, women accounted for 47.21 percent of the workforce. Further, many of these women are holding professional jobs. In 2010, sixty percent of the accountants were women.[30] A result of the increasing tendency of women to work is men are taking over more purchasing responsibility, including shopping online, which men are now outpacing women. Men in the top 20 percent income bracket spent $3,970 on Internet purchases in the fourth quarter of 2009, while women in this same income category, only spent $1,958.[31]

Family Decision Making During the course of everyday living, family members make thousands of decisions. The study of family decision making is quite difficult for three reasons. First, as in organizational buying units, the decision maker may not be the user or maintainer of the product. Second, families come in many different configurations. A family with a working mother, stay-at-home dad, and two small children will employ very different decision-making processes than a single mother living on welfare with two teenage sons. A third problem concerns the reliability and validity of the information obtained. For example, a general tendency exists among some couples for either the husband or the wife to systematically overestimate his or her influence, participation, and authority in household decisions.

A number of issues in family decision making are discussed in this section. These include determining which family members have the most influence on various household decisions and identifying the role of children in family decision making.

Relative Influence of Decision Makers   A key question in studying family decision making concerns who in the family has the most influence on various types of decisions. An early effort to identify the relative influence of family members on household decisions was conducted in Belgium.[32] The classic study identified the following four role-specialization dimensions in the buying of products:

* Wife-dominated decisions: The wife is largely independent in deciding what to buy.
* Husband-dominated decisions: The husband is largely independent in deciding what to buy.
* Autonomic decisions: Decisions of lesser importance that either the husband or wife may make independently of the other.
* Syncratic decisions: Decisions in which the husband and wife participate jointly.

Research conducted in the United States has found similar patterns. One study investigated the decision patterns of financially secure middle-aged couples.[33] In this study, husband-dominated decisions tended to focus on the details of automobile purchases (e.g., where to purchase the car). Wife-dominated decisions tended to involve the detailed aspects of kitchen and laundry purchases, such as what brand the new washer and dryer should be. Syncratic decisions appeared to predominate in the study. Areas in which syncratic decisions were found included vacations, home appliances, home selection, when to purchase the next car, and when to purchase new furniture.

Influence in the Family   Researchers have looked specifically at the ability of members of the family to influence decisions. Three factors strongly influence a member's family influence: financial resources of the family member, importance of the decision to the family member, and gender-role orientations of the family members.[34] Researchers have found that, as a member's financial contribution to the family unit increases, the member's influence also increases. Similarly, the importance of the decision to a family member also increases that person's influence on a particular decision.

The third factor affecting the amount of influence is the gender-role orientation of the spouses. Gender role relates to the extent to which a member of the family follows traditional normative conceptions of how males and females should behave. Research on the effects of gender role suggests families that are less traditional in their gender-role orientation have a greater tendency to use a joint decision-making style. In general, gender-role orientation is instrumental in defining the decision-role responsibilities of husbands and wives.[35]

Finally, there's a change over the life of the family. Across a wide range of decisions (e.g., automobiles, vacations, electronic devices, furniture, and appliances), the influence of the wife tends to increase over time, peaking in the retirement years. The startling exception is groceries, where the wife's influence decreases as the couple ages.[36]

The Role of Children in Family Decision Making   Children clearly make a difference in family decisions (Chapter 16 also discusses this issue). Even when children don't dominate the decision process, they have the potential to form alliances with either the father or the mother to produce a majority decision.

The influence of children on household decisions increases as the children grow older. One study of adolescents and their parents found, as the adolescent's age increased, his or her influence on the various decision stages also increased. Another major finding was peer communication was related to mentioning and discussing purchases with parents. These results demonstrate the large impact peer groups have on adolescents' product preferences. The study also found, because adolescents increasingly earned money outside of the home, they had more input in purchase decisions.[37] A more recent study found adolescents used bargaining, such as money deals (i.e., offers to pay for all or part of the cost), reasoning, and direct requests most effectively in dealing with their parents about family decisions. On the other hand, begging, whining, and declaring "everyone else" was doing something were least effective.[38]

In other research, adolescents' and mothers' perceptions of their influence on family purchase decisions were compared. As one would expect, the adolescents believed their influence was greater than the mothers rated it. Similarly, the mothers rated their own influence as greater than the adolescents believed. The study did show adolescents are active participants in family purchase decisions, even for products not for their own use. For example, even in the purchase of the family car, both adolescents and mothers indicated the young person had some impact on the decision.[39] Marketers recently used this fact to their advantage in advertising. An advertisement for the Toyota Highlander shows a boy approximately twelve years old declaring parents don't have to drive a "lame" car.

Managerial principle 12.3
When you design a product message, be sure to consider the role each family member may play in the decision.

Childhood Consumer Socialization

One reason for the family's importance is its role as a socialization agent. Socialization is the process by which individuals acquire knowledge, skills, and dispositions that enable them to participate as members of society.[40] This general concept can be narrowed to that of **childhood consumer socialization**, which refers to the processes by which children acquire the skills and attitudes relevant to functioning as consumers.

Understanding how individuals are socialized into consumers is important for several reasons. First, knowledge of the factors influencing consumer socialization can provide information to marketers that may be useful in designing marketing communications. Children are potent consumers. It's estimated children younger than 12 years directly spend nearly $27.5 billion a year in the United States.[41] Second, public-policy decisions concerning the regulation of the marketing of products to children should, in part, be based on an understanding of the consumer socialization process.

A Model of Consumer Socialization

Figure 12.2 presents a simple model of consumer socialization. It suggests consumer socialization is based on three components.

FIGURE 12.2
A Model of Consumer
Socialization

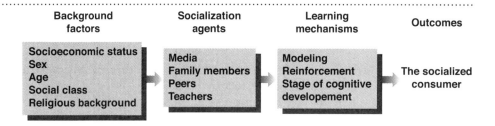

Background factors	Socialization agents	Learning mechanisms	Outcomes
Socioeconomic status Sex Age Social class Religious background	Media Family members Peers Teachers	Modeling Reinforcement Stage of cognitive developement	The socialized consumer

Socialization background factors include variables such as socioeconomic status, sex, age, social class, and religious background. Socialization agents are those individuals directly involved with the consumer who have influence because of their frequency of contact, importance, or control over rewards and punishments given to the consumer. Examples of socialization agents include parents, siblings, peers, teachers, the media, the Internet, and media personalities, such as athletes, movie stars, and rock stars.

Researchers have investigated the impact of background factors and socialization agents on consumer socialization. In an important early study that analyzed the factors of family, mass media, newspaper readership, school, peers, age, social class, and gender, researchers found the family was crucial for teaching the "rational" aspects of consumption.[42] However, the influence of parents is situation specific. Their impact varies across the stages of the decision process, across various types of products, and across various personal characteristics (e.g., age, socioeconomic class, and sex of the child). Researchers have also suggested children's perceptions of their parents' life satisfaction and financial skills contribute strongly to the willingness of the child to accept parents as consumption role models. Where parents were perceived as unsuccessful or unskilled, children turned elsewhere for role models.[43]

Researchers also found peers were an important socialization agent. Peers contributed particularly to the expressive element in which one buys for materialistic or social reasons (e.g., buying to keep up with the neighbors). For teenagers, buying to impress or be like others was clearly important. The teenage years are a critical time that helps the child form a unique identity that's different from his or her parents. Teens are often influenced by peers who may have very different preferences in music, movies, and so on than adults.

BUYING BEHAVIOR AND SOCIAL NETWORKS

In recent years, social media has grown exponentially. While we're still learning how social media impacts our buying decisions, it undoubtedly touches many lives. Social networking accounts for 22 percent of all time spent online in the United States, and there are more than one billion Facebook users. So, what are the consumer behavior implications of social media? Social media has changed the market place to a more interactive exchange. Communication is no longer a one-way street with marketers sending messages to the consumer and the consumer simply absorbing the information. Social media allows the consumer to be engaged.

Social media impacts consumers by creating another, more intimate, touch point. As Figure 12.3 illustrates, consumers are touched by a number of points: the store and/or web page, social media, promotion, and customer service. The social media piece of this model is the touch point where the consumer is most engaged.

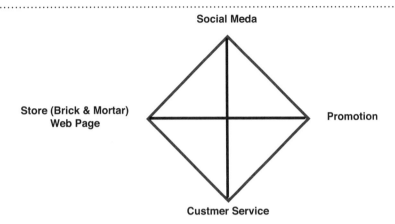

FIGURE 12.3
A Model of Consumer Touch Points

This immediacy is another key consumer behavior aspect of social media. Society has changed due to the immediacy of communication. For example, in the past, college students often planned social gatherings weeks in advance just to get the word out. In August 2011, a few students at Colorado State University sent out a message on Facebook regarding a pool party at a local apartment complex. They were planning on around one hundred students showing up. Nearly three thousand students attended the event after the message was forwarded hundreds of times. By the time the event broke up, there were four arrests and ten students sent to the hospital.[44] This example demonstrates the immediate and effective power of social media.

Managerial principle 12-4
Firms that are willing to engage with customers via social media can develop products that better meet customer needs.

Social Media

Red Robin Embraces Social Media

Red Robin, a family-oriented restaurant chain, offers a great example of using social media to the firm's advantage. Red Robin encouraged its frontline employees to participate in the social network of Yammer, a "Facebook for business." The employees were encouraged to exchange information on Yammer. Prior to this experiment, employees felt that their input to supervisors was not relayed to upper management.

In 2012, the brand introduced a new sandwich, the Tavern Double burger. After frontline employees posted concerns they heard from customers, management was able to tweak the sandwich in a short period of time. This was a dramatic change for the brand as it traditionally takes six to twelve months to make changes to menu items. Thereafter, sales of the sandwich improved. Consequently, social media allowed for quicker, if not immediate, changes to product offerings.[45]

DYADIC EXCHANGES

Dyadic exchange takes place when two individuals transfer resources between each other. We focus on two important types of dyadic exchange—word-of-mouth communications and the service encounter.

Word-of-Mouth Communications

Word-of-mouth (WOM) communication refers to an exchange of comments, thoughts, or ideas between two or more consumers, none of whom represent a marketing source.[46] WOM communications have an extremely strong impact on consumer purchase behavior.

Some estimates suggest referrals from others accounted for three times as many purchases as did advertising.[47] One study found 90 percent of customers trust recommendations from acquaintances and friends and 70 percent trust online WOM communication.[48] With the development of online communities (e.g., Facebook), WOM recommendations may spread even faster than in prior years.

WOM can be used instead of advertising. Hastens, a mattress brand from Sweden, relies exclusively on WOM promotion. The brand sells upscale mattresses at a high price of up to $99,900. The mattresses are made with horse hair and each requires more than 180 hours of manual labor to produce. One store in San Jose, California, relies entirely on its wealthy clientele to promote the brand.

Hastens promotes it $99,900 mattress to an elite clientele

Why is WOM communication so salient? One reason may be because WOM information comes directly from another person, who describes his or her own experiences, and information tends to be more credible because the individual doesn't have a vested interest in the product. The result is more weight behind WOM.

A **negativity bias** operates in WOM communications. One piece of negative information about a product or service influences a consumer more than one, two, or even three items of positive information. A likely explanation for the disproportionate influence of negative information is, because most products are pretty good, negative information is rather rare. When such information does occur, it takes on greater importance because of its high saliency.

Urban Legends   One interesting form of WOM communication is the urban legend, which is a fictional story that contains a plot and employs an ironic twist.[49] In a recent study, we found when the twist involved negative information, which is the central character was punished in some way, respondents were more likely to spread the legend.[50]

So, what are the consumer behavior ramifications of urban legends? Urban legends often spread when new products roll into the market.[51] For instance, the following urban legend spread shortly after microwaves were created:

An elderly widow treated her poodle like it was her child. Each Saturday, she gave the dog a bath and then dried the pooch on her opened oven door. One Christmas, her children gave her a microwave. Unfortunately, she cooked the dog from the inside out.[52]

While there's no proof this incident actually occurred, the story may have warned consumers against the dangers of the microwave. Ironically, there were similar negative stories about ovens when they first entered the market.

Why WOM Communication Occurs   The omnipresence of WOM communication results from the needs of both the receiver and the sender of the information. The receiver may desire information because he or she fails to believe the advertisements and sales messages received in the marketplace. Also, the receiver may be seeking additional information in order to decrease anxiety about a risky purchase. When receivers are highly involved in a purchase decision, they tend to go through a longer search process for a product or service. In these high-involvement situations, personal influence is increasingly important.

The process of influencing others fulfills the needs of senders of information. The ability to provide information and to sway others in their decisions provides a person with feelings of power and prestige. Influencing others can also help influencers erase doubts about their own purchases. In addition, by providing information to others, a sender can increase his or her involvement with a group. Thus, providing information acts to increase social interaction and the general cohesion of the group.[53] Finally, people can engage in WOM communications in order to derive some benefit. That is, by giving someone else information, based on the norm of reciprocity, they should at some point return the favor.

Opinion Leadership   The study of WOM communication shows some people provide information more frequently than others. Individuals who share information more often may become **opinion leaders**, defined as those consumers who influence the purchase decisions of others.

Opinion leadership does not appear to be a general trait held by specific individuals who influence others across a broad range of categories. Rather, opinion leadership is specific to the product category and the situation. Within a single product category, such as appliances or household furnishings, an opinion leader may influence others across a number of different products.

Characteristics of opinion leaders   Attempts to find demographic and personality characteristics that pinpoint opinion leaders haven't been very successful. The most clear-cut finding is opinion leaders are involved with the product category. They're interested in the product category, tend to read special-interest magazines about it, may write a blog about the product category, and are knowledgeable about it. Some evidence exists that opinion leaders may be more self-confident and socially active than followers. Opinion leaders may also have a somewhat greater social status than followers; however, they do belong to the same peer group as followers. Finally, they tend to be more innovative in their purchases than followers, but they aren't the consumers who are product innovators.[54]

Comparing opinion leaders and product innovators   Opinion leaders and product innovators are similar in a variety of respects. Product innovators are the small set of people who are the first to buy new products. The innovator may be described as an adventurer who strikes off on his or her own to buy new products. In contrast, the opinion leader is like an editor who can influence others but who can never be too far away from the goals, values, and attitudes of those whose opinions are being influenced. Innovators are less integrated into social groups and feel freer to break group norms by adopting new products very early in their life cycle. In contrast, opinion leaders are more socially integrated and exert their influence, in part, because they don't espouse beliefs that are widely divergent from those of the group.[55]

A group of researchers has found those most ready to use new technology demonstrate many of the characteristics of product innovators. They describe technology readiness as composed of four dimensions—optimism (belief in the benefits of technology), innovativeness, comfort level (feeling of control over technology), and assurance.[56]

Mavens and Surrogates   In addition to opinion leaders and product innovators, researchers have identified two other sources of personal influence—the market maven and the surrogate consumer. **Market mavens** are "individuals who have information about many kinds of products, places to shop, web sites, and other facets of markets, and initiate discussions with consumers and respond to requests from consumers for market information."[57] These individuals play a broader role in personal influence than do opinion leaders. The expertise of market mavens isn't product specific. Rather, it's based on more general market expertise. Market mavens may seek to obtain marketplace information in order to be useful to others in social exchanges and to provide a basis for conversations.[58]

The second type of influencer that has been identified is the surrogate consumer. A **surrogate consumer** is a person who acts "as an agent retained by a consumer to guide, direct, and/or transact marketplace activities."[59] He or she can play a wide variety of roles, such as tax consultant, wine steward, interior decorator, stock broker, or car buyer. The surrogate consumer tends to be used in high-involvement purchases in which the consumer desires to surrender some control to a capable external agent. The consumer abdicates to the surrogate many of the functions that take place in the consumer-decision process. Table 12.2 summarizes the characteristics of the four types of influencers discussed here.

Influencer Type	Basis for Expertise	Charateristics
1. Opinion leader	Enduring involvement in product category.	Enduring involvement, higher status, integrated into social group.
2. Product innovator	Purchase of innovative product.	Less integrated into social groups than opinion leaders.
3. Market maven	General market knowledge.	Demographic characteristics unknown; enjoys having general knowledge abut the marketplace
4. Surrogate consumer	Knowledge specific to product category.	Frequently a paid professional.

TABLE 12.2
Characteristics of Four Types of Consumer Influencers

Service Encounters

The **service encounter** is a personal interaction that occurs between a consumer and a marketer. A service encounter can occur in pure service contexts, such as a physician's examination, having a massage, or ordering a meal at a restaurant. Service encounters also occur in mixed service contexts. For example, consider your involvement with your car. Certainly, automobiles are goods. However, a number of service encounters will have occurred during and after your purchase. That is, when you bought it, you interacted with the seller. When having it serviced or repaired, you encounter additional company representatives. In sum, during the service encounter, a consumption experience is occurring. During the service encounter, the consumer and the marketer act as though they're on a stage reading from a common service script that creates expectations on both actors' parts. To the extent that either violates the script in a negative manner, dissatisfaction may result. Thus, if the service provider violates expectations (e.g., by being too pushy), the consumer will be dissatisfied. Conversely, if the consumer violates expectations (e.g., by being overly demanding), the service provider will be dissatisfied.

The use of theater as a metaphor to describe the service encounter provides a vocabulary for understanding the exchange process. Figure 12.4 depicts the service encounter as theater.[60] Like any production, there's a stage where the play takes place. In addition, there are front and back regions for both the consumer and the firm. In the front region, both parties reveal impression management and defensive practices. The back region is like a backstage area, where rehearsal occurs, secondary support exists (i.e., people who help the production), and management functions reside.

An example of theater in a service encounter can be seen at Disney entertainment. Disney is famous for training its employees to act accordingly to the script and remain in character. Imagine an eight-year-old noticing Snow White behind a building smoking a cigarette. Disney's "magic" likely would vanish for the child if this performance ever happened. Clearly, Disney understands the art of theater in a service setting.

Managerial principle 12-5
You can increase customer satisfaction by motivating your service personnel to follow the service script. However, give employees the freedom to deviate from the script in order to meet customer needs.

Managerial principle 12.6
You can enhance consumer's service experience by creating theater. Be wise and use theater only when appropriate.

FIGURE 12.4
A Model of the Service
Encounter as Theatrical
Performance

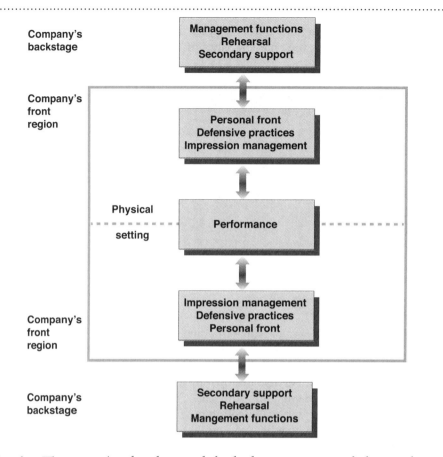

Service Themes As already noted, both the consumer and the employee follow scripted roles during the service encounter. Researchers have identified three themes that may occur for each party in the encounter.[61] The three themes for consumers are autonomy, mutuality, and dependence. They depict the nature of the relationship the consumer desires to form with the service provider. Consumers desire autonomy when they believe they have the information they need and seek to engage in self-service. Those who purchase relatively low-involvement goods from retail stores frequently desire autonomy. Consumers may also have a high degree of expertise and, as a result, seek autonomy. The sophisticated investor who purchases stocks from a discount brokerage exemplifies this case. As product involvement increases and as consumer expertise decreases, consumers may seek either mutual cooperation or dependence in the relationship with the employee. Examples of mutual cooperation might include purchasing expensive clothing, original art, or stocks and bonds by a consumer with some knowledge of the risks and benefits involved. In contrast, if the consumer has limited knowledge or expertise, total dependence may be placed on the employee. In such instances, the consumer wants the employee to take an active role and participate fully in the service encounter. At the extreme, the employee becomes a surrogate consumer.

The roles are not static, however. For example, in an extended service encounter (e.g. between a guide and a client in a rafting expedition), the customer is in a more dependent state at the beginning, with mutuality occurring as the encounter progresses. By the end of the trip, the two are usually—at least temporarily—friends.[62]

During these transactions, employees also have themes that may, however, conflict with the customer's themes. The three employee themes are indifference, cooperation, and dominance. If the customer wants mutual cooperation, the employee should provide it without attempting to become dominant. The indifference theme, however, is tricky. Generally, consumers who want autonomy don't want indifferent service providers. Rather, they desire providers who leave them alone until they need attention to complete the transaction.

DIFFUSION PROCESSES

Generally speaking, the term *diffusion* refers to the idea substances or even ideas can gradually spread through a medium and reach a state of equilibrium. In a consumer-behavior setting, **diffusion** refers to the process by which innovative ideas, products, and services spread through the consumer population.

Two types of diffusion processes are of concern to marketers. The first is information diffusion and alternative models of information transmission. The second involves the diffusion of innovations. This section identifies the factors that influence how consumers adopt innovative products.

Transmission Processes

A question of importance to marketers and sociologists concerns how communications flow within the consumer environment. Researchers have proposed several models of how information is transmitted from the mass media to the general population. The **trickle-down theory** holds that trends—particularly fashion trends—begin with the wealthy. The wealthy adopt styles of clothing and attitudes that distinguish themselves from lower classes. The non-wealthy may attempt to emulate the wealthy by copying their actions. In this way, the fashions and behaviors of the wealthy trickle down.

One problem with the trickle-down theory is relatively little communication actually occurs between the classes. Most communications occur between people in the same social class. Second, in a mass-communication culture, information about fashion is transmitted almost instantaneously. Information transmission is much more like a flood than a trickle.

The approach that appears to represent the flow of personal influence much better is the **multistep flow model**. In this approach, the mass media transmits information to four distinct sets of people—lead users, opinion leaders, gatekeepers, and followers.[63] Each type of person is viewed as having the capability of providing information to the other categories of people. Lead users are those individuals who lead the way on important market trends. This group often develops radically new product concepts and solutions.[64] Opinion leaders influence other consumers by giving advice and verbal direction for the search, purchase, and use of a product.[65] Gatekeepers have the ability to decide whether others in a group will receive information. However, a gatekeeper's opinions may or may not influence the others in a group. Followers are those who are influenced by the opinion leader or by the information provided by the gatekeeper.

The multistep flow model recognizes a number of important pieces of information:

1. Mass communications can directly reach nearly everyone in the population.
2. Lead users are the first people to use new prototypes and products.
3. Opinion leaders are able to influence a group of followers. However, for different products, the role of opinion leaders and followers may be reversed.
4. Gatekeepers can choose whether or not to provide information to opinion leaders and followers.
5. Communications can be transmitted back and forth between the four groups.

The Diffusion of Innovations

The study of the adoption of new products is important for marketers. In order to grow, a company must continually improve existing products and periodically develop new products for the changing marketplace. The study of product adoption is also important because of the relatively low success rate of new products. The overall cost of introducing a new product has been estimated to be in the millions of dollars, and less than half of these products succeed.

One study proposed a simple model of the diffusion process, identifying six key factors that influence the nature and extent of the diffusion of an innovation.[66] First, diffusion occurs within a social system or market. Second, diffusion depends on the individual adoption decisions of thousands or even millions of consumers. The individual adoption process is synonymous with individual consumer decision making, discussed earlier. The decisions of individuals are influenced by three factors—the characteristics of the innovation, the characteristics of innovators, and the personal-influence process. These three factors make up the third, fourth, and fifth elements of the diffusion process. The final element is the nature of the diffusion process, which results from the influence of the five preceding elements. The following subsections discuss in greater detail the elements of the diffusion process.

The Social System   The study of the social system in which products are diffused is closely related to the analysis of the impact of cultural and subcultural processes on consumers. Evidence indicates that the speed of diffusion is influenced by several aspects of the social system. First, the greater the compatibility between the innovation and the values of the members of the social system, the quicker the rate of diffusion is. Second, the more homogeneous (i.e., nonsegmented) the social system, the faster the diffusion process is. The diffusion of innovations across cultures is dependent upon the distance between the countries and the social similarity of the cultures.[67]

Characteristics of the Innovation   One approach to distinguishing the innovation characteristics of products and services concerns the technological aspects of the innovations versus the symbolic aspects.[68] A symbolic innovation communicates a different social meaning than it once did because of the acquisition of new intangible attributes. An example of a symbolic innovation is the diffusion of new hairstyles or fashion. A technological innovation results from a change in the characteristics of a product or service through the introduction of a technological change. Two examples of a technological innovation are Blu-ray and 3-D television.

Characteristics of Innovators   One of the important challenges faced by marketers of innovative products is identifying the characteristics of people who buy the product early in its life cycle. People who are innovative tend to have higher incomes, higher levels of education, greater social mobility, higher opinion leadership in the product category, and more favorable attitudes toward risk.

Factors Influencing the Diffusion Pattern   Figure 12.5 identifies the normal pattern of innovative product diffusion. Note that the curve describing the diffusion process is somewhat S-shaped. During the introductory phase, the percentage of consumers adopting the product is small and advances slowly. As the product moves into the growth stage, the percentage accelerates, and the curve bends upward rapidly. During maturity, growth slows until it turns negative, marking the beginning of decline.

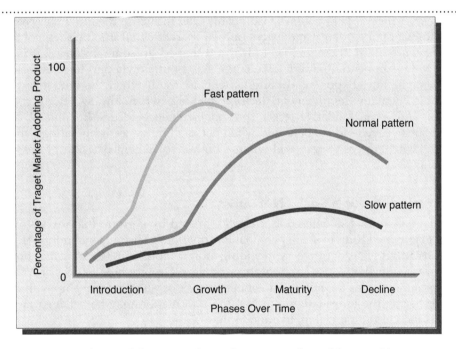

FIGURE 12.5
A Model of Product Diffusion

The exact shape of the curve depends on a number of factors. If consumers adopt the innovation is very quickly, the fast pattern in Figure 12.5 results. If the adoption rate is slow, the pattern becomes much flatter and more drawn out, as shown in the slow pattern. Three factors affect the rapidity with which an innovation is adopted and, as a consequence, the shape of the curve: characteristics of the product, characteristics of the target market, and extent of the marketing effort.

Characteristics of the product   The same factors that influence the likely success of an innovation also influence the rapidity with which it's adopted. To the extent it fulfills a need, is compatible, has a relative advantage, has low complexity, has observable positive features, and is easily tried, the product will be adopted more quickly.

Characteristics of the target market   Products targeted to different groups will exhibit divergent adoption patterns. For example, products that appeal to younger, more highly educated, change-oriented individuals are often adopted quickly, but they also run the risk of moving into decline quickly. Many websites fit into this category, such as the Chive. The Chive claims the average fan of the website is 28 years old, college-educated, makes $60,000 a year, and likes to drink beer. The site has become the Internet version of the Maxim magazine.[69]

One personality trait that appears to influence an individual's adoption of a product is his or her need for uniqueness—that is, the need to be different relative to others, for the purpose of enhancing one's self-image and social image.[70] Findings of a study show those consumers with a high need for uniqueness are more likely to adopt a product when they learn about the product from an impersonal source, such as the media, rather than a social source, such as a friend.[71]

Managerial principle 12-7
To increase the adoption speed of a new product, pick the right product characteristics, know the target market, and use marketing wisely.

Extent of the marketing effort   Companies can influence the growth curve of a product by the quality and extent of their marketing effort. The shape of the diffusion pattern, therefore, isn't always S-shaped. In some instances, it may show an exponential pattern—the curve starts out slowly and then increases at a rapid rate. Exponential patterns tend to result when the innovation is adopted via low-involvement decision making, when low switching costs exist, and when a relative lack of personal influence occurs. In contrast, the S-shaped curve tends to be found when personal influence is operating, when high switching costs exist, and when a high-involvement decision process is taking place.[72]

Diffusion through Social Networks

Social networking is defined as websites created by a group that invites others to join the group to share personal information.[73] The personal information often contains lists of interests, including music, books, movies, and affiliations such as a university or social club. Social networks are credible sources of WOM communication as the network members have a personal relationship with the one sharing the information. Further, the information may be believed more due to a noncommercial motivation to share.

Social networking sites have grown dramatically in popularity over the past few years. Facebook gets more than 133 million unique visitors per month followed by, Twitter's 23 million, and LinkedIn's 15 million. Businesses have chosen to capitalize on this opportunity by creating active Facebook pages. More than 40 million businesses now have an active page on Facebook alone.[74]

Consumers are increasingly using these social networking sites to make buying decisions. In one study, 20 percent of consumers reported being influenced in their buying decisions by social media. In addition, those who used social networking sites spent an average of 40 percent more than those who didn't use the sites.[75] These findings suggest marketers have discovered a means to use the Internet to market without paying the large expense associated with television and radio advertising. In fact, the fastest growing segment of the advertising market is the Internet.

MANAGERIAL IMPLICATIONS

The preceding discussion of groups, dyadic exchanges, and diffusion adds a number of new concepts to our understanding of the consumer. Applications to the RESPonsive Marketing concepts are summarized in the following sections.

Research

Through research into the diffusion process, the marketing manager can get a feel for the likely growth curve of the product. Will the product be a slow starter that must be nurtured for a substantial length of time, or will a strong marketing effort allow it to start fast?

Research also offers insight to companies on the potential to embrace a brand community. In many cases, the brand community wants an "authentic" experience that doesn't involve being sold to. Firms can use research to better understand customers' needs without stepping on their toes with commercial motives.

Environmental Analysis

Monitoring information transmission processes is also important for marketing managers. Marketing research should be employed to identify exactly what a company's customers are communicating to others about its products or services. It's crucial for companies to track customer satisfaction and then take quick steps to remedy problems that may occur.

Segmentation

Managers can segment the market based on group membership. Naturally existing groups of consumers make outstanding target markets for companies because they're readily identifiable and reachable. For example, numerous companies target military veterans, public teachers, government workers, church groups, the National Rifle Association, and so on.[76] Product and service offerings can be developed specifically for the members of the groups. Promotional strategy can be built around the concept that the product or service is positioned as being offered specifically to the members of the group.

Positioning

The discussion about opinion leaders suggested they're rather different than followers and one should position an innovative product so it's of interest to opinion leaders. Firms can then position the product as necessary to account for the differences between leaders and followers. For example, although new high-technology devices (e.g., computers) are often introduced to companies via opinion leaders (in this case, technology enthusiasts), these enthusiasts seldom have the authority to make the purchases, and a different appeal may be necessary—probably one that relies more on the ability of innovations to improve the bottom line and less on the cool technology.

Marketing Mix

Knowledge of diffusion processes is important to managers, particularly those involved in marketing new products and services. Product managers need to investigate the extent to which an innovation has a relative advantage over competitors and is compatible with the values and lifestyle of the target market. Furthermore, the manager needs to assess the product's complexity, trialability, and observability.

For consumer markets, it's worthwhile to consider the addition of promotional items that will attract children and make use of their ability to influence family decisions. For example, in late 1999, Burger King introduced fifty-seven new Pokémon toys, each available with the purchase of a children's meal. It was reported at the time that parents were "bracing their stomachs for two months of hamburgers."[77] Although few parents may agree to eat hamburgers for fifty-seven days, many families probably visited Burger King more than usual during this promotion to avoid the whining of their kids.

SUMMARY

Why do consumers submit to social pressure?

This chapter focused on the social influences we face in marketing. Obviously, we're tempted and/or encouraged to buy and experience many things by those around us. A group is a set of individuals who interact and share a common goal. Ironically, an individual doesn't need to be a formal group member to be influenced by the group. For instance, a Red Sox fan in Phoenix may not be a member of the team's fan club, but he could still be encouraged to purchase team paraphernalia to show his loyalty.

Groups influence our purchase behavior in two ways. First, we often buy products after observing others using the brand. These noncommercial exposures may, in fact, motivate us more than a standard commercial because they may appear as being unbiased and authentic. The second way groups influence our buying decisions is in group decision making. Groups such as student clubs or a small klatch of friends periodically make buying decisions. These buying decisions can often become laborious as each person interjects his or her own preferences.

What's gained from membership in a brand community?

One type of group that's been recently introduced in the marketing literature is the brand community. Brand communities can develop around any number of brands. We can see brand communities focused on sports teams, Jeeps, Harley-Davidson, Disney, Apple, and Star Wars, to name a few. Individuals who are part of a brand community find pleasure by gathering to share their brand experiences with like-minded people. Firms that regularly cultivate the relationship between their brand and the community can benefit in a number of ways. These firms often gain loyalty and missionaries, and they decrease the level of brand switching.

Why do individuals identify with a brand? One theory, social identity theory, suggests we obtain our own identity partially through group membership. For instance, if someone has a desire to be viewed as tough and rugged, he might be inclined to identify with Harley-Davidson. Once the individual identifies with the brand, he often increases his brand purchases.

Groups affect purchase behavior through a number of processes. Group norms, or rules of conduct, can encourage the individual regarding what product to buy. A related concept, conformity pressure, can influence behavior through compliance as well as private acceptance. Further, if the person views the group as attractive, conformity pressure increases.

How does the family influence decision making?

Families and households have a unique influence on our buying decisions. As statistics demonstrate, the average household composition has changed dramatically since the 1970s. With 27 percent of people living alone today, households are much smaller than in previous decades. This change, along with the divorce rate, suggests more buying decisions are being made in isolation rather than as a group.

Organizational buying behavior is different than individual buying behavior. While individuals within the organization can influence buying decisions, just as individuals can affect household buying decisions, organizations will often engage in competitive bidding for products. Individuals and households are less likely to do so. Two key elements that affect both individuals and organizations are trust and commitment.

How is social media changing our buying behavior?

Social media has changed our shopping habits. It has also changed sellers' habits. Around 20 percent of consumers now use social media to assist them in making a buying decision. Firms are changing as they learn to engage with consumers on a regular basis. Social media gives firms an opportunity to interact with the consumer. By transforming the communication into an interactive exchange, firms are better positioned to create the products consumers want.

How does information influence behavior?

One of the most influential factors in buying decisions is WOM. As mentioned, referrals are three times more impactful than commercial advertising. This fact alone suggests any negative information may permanently damage a brand's reputation. One area where WOM is often central to future buying decisions is the service encounter. Because there isn't a tangible product to show others, consumers use WOM to express their satisfaction or dissatisfaction.

Besides WOM, researchers often investigate how information diffuses through society. The trickle-down theory suggests trends begin with the wealthy and then trickle down to lower classes. The multistep flow model, however, contends information is transmitted via mass media to four groups at the same time: lead users, opinion leaders, gatekeepers, and followers. Overall, social influence is a huge factor in shaping the purchases consumers make. Firms will be better served as they increase their understanding of how groups interact and transmit information.

How can managers use information to influence loyalty and sales?

Diffusion in a consumer-behavior setting is the process by which ideas, products, and services spread through the consumer population. As many companies are now embracing social media, they're creating opportunities to develop a relationship with consumers. Social networks are powerful tools for spreading WOM. Consumers use these networks to discover what their friends and family recommend to buy. In fact, consumers who used social media to research product information spent 40 percent more than those who didn't use these sites.

KEY WORD

aspiration group
brand communities
childhood consumer socializa-
    tion
compliance
conformity
detached nuclear family
diffusion
dissociative group
dyadic exchange
extended family
group
group polarization

household
identification
informational influence
in-group
market mavens
multistep flow model
negativity bias
norm
normative influence
nuclear family
opinion leaders
out-group
private acceptance

psychological closeness
reference group
role-related product cluster
service encounter
social comparison
social identity theory
socialization background factors
surrogate consumer
trickle-down theory
value-expressive influence
word-of-mouth

REVIEW QUESTION

1. What are the two general ways in which groups influence buying decisions?

2. What do brand managers gain from studying aspirational groups?

3. What does a consumer gain from joining a brand community?

4. How can a firm benefit when a brand community is created around its brand?

5. What are some examples of normative influence on you in your daily life?

6. Define the two types of conformity pressure.

7. What leads some individuals to conform to social pressure and others to not conform?

8. List ten factors in US demographics that have influenced the decision-making process.

9. In what purchase decisions do husbands, wives, and children have the most influence?

10. How are children socialized on buying-decision behaviors?

11. Describe the model of consumer socialization presented in the chapter.

12. How can firms use WOM to their advantage?

13. How can firms incorporate Facebook and Twitter to influence opinion leaders?

14. How do you foresee Facebook and Twitter evolving in the next five years as a marketing tool?

1. Write down ten products your family has a heavy influence on your purchase decision and ten different products your friends have a heavy influence on your decision. Are there categorical differences between the lists?

2. Make a list of products for each of the four role-specialization dimensions in product purchase: wife-dominated decision, husband-dominated decision, autonomic decision, and syncratic decision.

3. Identify five advertisements that target children as a decision maker. What are the main selling points in each ad the advertiser is conveying to children?

4. Watch at least one hour of television tonight. Keep track of all commercials that are targeted to an aspirational group of yours, writing down the brand and the specific aspirational group.

5. This chapter discussed a number of brand communities. Write down all the benefits a consumer gains from being in a brand community. What brand community would you most likely join and why?

6. Think about a group to which you currently belong and are an active member. What are some normative influences that reside within the group?

7. Describe a situation where WOM influenced your buying behavior. What type of relationship do you have with the person who gave you the information? Was the person an expert on the topic?

8. Describe the details of a service encounter you recently experienced. What kind of theater was involved in the encounter?

9. Social networking has grown exponentially in recent years. Pick a brand and develop a short plan for using Facebook, Twitter, and LinkedIn to target a group of your choice.

ENDNOTES

[1] Douglas B. Holt, "How Consumers Consume: A Typology of Consumption Practices," *Journal of Consumer Research* 22 (June 1995):1–16.

[2] D. Todd Donavan, Swinder Janda, and Jaebeom Suh, "Environmental Influences in Corporate Brand Identification and Outcomes," *Journal of Brand Management* 14, no. 1–2 (September–October 2006):125–136.

[3] Michael G. Pratt, "To Be or Not to Be: Central Questions in Organizational Identification," in *Identity in Organizations: Building Theory Through Conversations*, ed. David A. Whetten and Paul C. Godfrey (Thousand Oaks, CA: Sage, 1998), 171–207.

[4] Brad D. Carlson, Tracy A. Suter, and Tom J. Brown, "Social versus Psychological Brand Community: The Role of Psychological Sense of Brand Community," *Journal of Business Research* 61 (2008): 284–291.

[5] Rosellina Ferraro, James R. Bettman, and Tanya L. Chartrand, "The Power of Strangers: The Effect of Incidental Consumer Brand Encounters on Brand Choice," *Journal of Consumer Research* 35 (2009): 729–741.

[6] Ibid.

[7] James C. Ward and Peter H. Reingen, "Sociocognitive Analysis of Group Decision Making among Consumers," Journal of Consumer Research 17 (December 1990): 245–262.

[8] Michael S. Olmstead, The Small Group (New York: Holt, Rinehart & Winston, 1962). For a fascinating discussion of group influence on decision making, see Irving L. Janis, Victims of Groupthink (Boston Houghton Mifflin, 1972).

[9] J. H. McAlexander, J. W. Schouten, H. F. Koenig, "Building Brand Community," Journal of Marketing 66 (2002): 38–54.

[10] Brad D. Carlson, Tracy A. Suter, and Tom J. Brown, "Social versus Psychological Brand Community: The Role of Psychological Sense of Brand Community," Journal of Business Research 61 (2008): 284–291.

[11] Brad D. Carlson, Tracy A. Suter, and Tom J. Brown (2008), "Social Versus Psychological Brand Community: The Role of Psychological Sense of Brand Community," Journal of Business Research, 61 (4), 284-291.

[12] J. H. McAlexander, J. W. Schouten, H. F. Koenig, "Building Brand Community," Journal of Marketing 66 (2002): 38–54.

[13] Ibid.

[14] Sam Hill and Glenn Rifkin, Radical Marketing: From Harvard to Harley, Lessons from Ten that Broke the Rules and Made It Big (New York: Harper Business, 1999).

[15] C. O'Reilly III and J. Chatman, "Organizational Commitment and Psychological Attachment: The Effects of Compliance, Identification, and Internalization on Prosocial Behavior," Journal of Applied Psychology 71 (1986): 472–499.

[16] Francis Bourne, "Group Influence in Marketing and Public Relations," in Some Applications of Behavioral Research, ed. R. Likert and S. P. Hayes (Basil, Switzerland: UNESCO, 1957). For a study that tested these ideas, see William Bearden and Michael Etzel, "Reference Group Influence on Product and Brand Purchase Decisions," Journal of Consumer Research 9 (September 1982): 183–194.

[17] Charles A. Kiesler and Sara B. Kiesler, Conformity (Reading, MA: Addison-Wesley, 1969), 7.

[18] Rachel Emma Silverman, "Holiday Shopping with Daily-Deal Sites," Wall Street Journal, November 28, 2010, accessed January 10, 2016, http://blogs.wsj.com/juggle/2010/11/28/cyber-monday-holiday-shopping-with-daily-deal-sites/.

[19] Solomon E. Asch, Social Psychology (Upper Saddle River, NJ: Prentice Hall, 1952).

[20] Leon Festinger, "A Theory of Social Comparison Processes," Human Relations 7 (May 1954): 117–140.

[21] Marsha L. Richins, "Social Comparison and the Idealized Images of Advertising," Journal of Consumer Research 18 (June 1991): 71–83.

[22] Brent McFerran, Darren W. Dahl, Gavan J. Fitzsimons, and Andrea C. Morales, "I'll Have What She's Having: Effects of Social Influence and Body Type on the Food Choices of Others," Journal of Consumer Research 36 (2010): 915–929.

[23] R. E. Knox and R. K. Safford, "Group Caution at the Race Track," Journal of Experimental Social Psychology 12 (May 1976): 317–324.

[24] Jonathan Vespa, Jamie M. Lewis, and Rose M. Kreider US Census Bureau, Population Characteristics, (2013).

[25] US Census Bureau, "Median Age at First Marriage, 1890–2010," Infoplease, accessed January 10, 2016, http://www.infoplease.com/ipa/A0005061.html.

[26] Eli J. Finkel, Paul W. Eastwick, Benjamin R. Karney, Harry T. Reis, and Susan Sprecher, "Online Dating: A Critical Analysis from the Perspective of Psychological Science," Psychological Science in the Public Interest 13, no. 1 (January 2012): 3–66.

[27] Centers for Disease Control and Prevention, "National Marriage and Divorce Rate Trends," CDC, accessed January 10, 2016, http://www.cdc.gov/nchs/nvss/marriage_divorce_tables.htm.

[28] US Department of Commerce, Statistical Abstract of the United States, 1995 (Washington DC: US Government Printing Office, 1995), 61; US Department of Commerce, Statistical Abstract of the United States, 1998 (Washington DC: US Government Printing Office, 1998), 76; Centers for Disease Control and Prevention, National Vital Statistics Reports 48, no. 2 (March 9, 2000); Centers for Disease Control and Prevention, "National Marriage and Divorce Rate Trends," CDC, accessed January 10, 2016, http://www.cdc.gov/nchs/nvss/marriage_divorce_tables.htm.

[29] Wendy Wang and Richard Morin, "Recession Brings Many Young People Back to the Nest: Home for the Holidays…and Every Other Day," Pew Research, accessed November 24, 2009, http://pewresearch.org/pubs/1423/home-for-the-holidays-boomeranged-parents.

[30] Mehroz Baig, "Women in the Workforce: What Changes Have We Made?" Huff Post Business, January 14, 2016, accessed January 14, 2016, http://www.huffingtonpost.com/mehroz-baig/women-in-the-workforce-wh_b_4462455.html.

[31] Ray A. Smith, "Wanted: Guy Shoppers for Fashion Sites," Wall Street Journal, July 22, 2010, accessed January 10, 2016, http://www.wsj.com/articles/SB10001424052748704684604575381022669942964.

[32] Harry L. Davis and Benny P. Rigaux, "Perception of Marital Roles in Decision Processes," Journal of Consumer Research 1 (June 1974): 51–62.

[33] Alvin Burns, "Husband and Wife Purchase Decision-Making Roles: Agreed, Presumed, Conceded, and Disputed," in Advances in Consumer Research, ed. William Perreault (Atlanta: Association for Consumer Research, 1977), 50–55.

[34] William Qualls, "Household Decision Behavior: The Impact of Husbands' and Wives' Sex Role Orientation," Journal of Consumer Research 14 (September 1987): 264–279.

[35] Ibid.

[36] Cynthia Webster and Samantha Rice, "Equity Theory and the Power Structure in a Marital Relationship," in Advances in Consumer Research, vol. 23, ed. Kim P. Corfman and John G. Lynch, Jr. (Provo, UT: Association for Consumer Research, 1996), 491–497.

[37] George Moschis and Linda Mitchell, "Television Advertising and Interpersonal Participation in Family Consumer Decisions," in Advances in Consumer Research, vol. 13, ed. Richard Lutz (Provo, UT: Association for Consumer Research, 1986), 181–185.

[38] Kay M. Palan and Robert E. Wilkes, "Adolescent–Parent Interaction in Family Decision Making," Journal of Consumer Research 24 (September 1997): 159–169.

[39] Ellen Foxman and Patriya Tansuhaj, "Adolescents' and Mothers' Perceptions of Relative Influence in Family Purchase Decisions: Patterns of Agreement and Disagreement," in Advances in Consumer Research, vol. 15, ed. Michael Houston (Provo, UT: Association for Consumer Research, 1988), 449–453.

[40] For a review of the literature on socialization, see Gregory M. Rose, "Consumer Socialization, Parental Style, and Developmental Timetables in the United States and Japan," Journal of Marketing 63 (July 1999): 105–119.

[41] Richard Tomkins, "Selling to a Captivated Market," Financial Times, April 23, 1999, 10.

[42] George Moschis and Roy Moore, "Decision Making Among the Young: A Socialization Perspective," Journal of Consumer Research 6 (September 1979): 101–112.

[43] Elizabeth S. Moore-Shay and Britto M. Berchmans, "The Role of the Family Environment in the Development of Shared Consumption Values: An Intergenerational Study," in Advances in Consumer Research, vol. 23, ed. Kim P. Corfman and John G. Lynch, Jr. (Provo, UT: Association for Consumer Research, 1996), 484–490.

[44] Sarah Jane Kyle, "Social Media Alters Party Scene," Fort Collins Coloradoan, August 29, 2011.

[45] David Lavenda, "How Red Robin Transfored its Business with Yammer," captured 1-14-2016, http://www.fastcompany.com/3025396/work-smart/how-red-robin-burgers-got-yummier-with-yammer

[46] This definition is based, in part, on one developed by Paula Fitzgerald Bone, "Determinants of Word-of-Mouth Communications during Product Consumption," in Advances in Consumer Research, vol. 19, ed. John F. Sherry, Jr. and Brian Sternthal (Provo, UT: Association for Consumer Research, 1992), 579–583.

[47] Stephen P. Morin, "Influentials Advising Their Friends to Sell Lots of High-Tech Gadgetry," Wall Street Journal, February 28, 1983, 30.

[48] Jonah Bloom, "The Truth Is: Consumers Trust Fellow Buyers before Marketers," Advertising Age (February 13, 2006): 25.

[49] J. H. Brunvand, "Some News from the Miscellaneous Legend Files," Western Folklore 49 (January 1990): 111–120.

[50] D. Todd Donavan, John C. Mowen, and Goutam Chakraborty "Urban Legends: The Word-of-Mouth Communication of Morality through Negative Story Content," Marketing Letters 10, no. 1 (1999): 23–34.

[51] Ibid.

[52] J. H. Brunvard, The Vanishing Hitchhiker, Norton & Company, 1981.

[53] Ernst Dichter, "How Word-of-Mouth Advertising Works," Harvard Business Review 44 (November–December 1966): 148.

[54] Everett M. Rogers, Diffusion of Innovations, 4th ed. (New York: Free Press, 1995). See also William H. Redmond, "Contemporary Social Theory and the Bass Diffusion Model," in Enhancing Knowledge Development in Marketing, vol. 7, ed. Cornelia Dröge and Roger Calantone (Chicago: American Marketing Association, 1996), 176–181.

[55] Thomas Robertson and James Myers, "Personality Correlates of Opinion Leadership and Innovative Buying Behavior," Journal of Marketing Research 6 (May 1969): 168. For an extended application of similar notions to high-technology adoptions, see Geoffrey A. Moore, Inside the Tornado: Marketing Strategies from Silicon Valley's Cutting Edge (New York: Harper Business, 1995).

[56] A. Parasuraman and Charles Colby, "A Scale for Measuring Customers' Technology Readiness: Replication, Refinement, and Implications for Service Organizations" (paper, Fourth Vanderbilt/AMA Frontiers in Services Conference, September 24–26, 1998).

[57] Lawrence Feick and Linda Price, "The Market Maven: A Diffuser of Marketplace Information," Journal of Marketing 51 (January 1987): 83–87. See also Linda Price, Lawrence F. Feick, and Audrey Guskey, "Everyday Market-Helping Behavior," Journal of Public Policy and Marketing 12 (Fall 1995): 255–266.

[58] Todd A. Mooradian, "The Five-Factor Model and Market Mavenism," in Advances in Consumer Research, vol. 23, ed. Kim P. Corfman and John G. Lynch Jr. (Provo, UT: Association for Consumer Research, 1996), 260–263. See also Michael T. Elliott and Anne E. Warfield, "Do Market Mavens Categorize Brands Differently?" in Advances in Consumer Research, vol. 20, ed. Leigh McAlister and Michael Rothschild (Provo, UT: Association for Consumer Research, 1993), 202–208; Terrell E. Williams and Mark E. Slama, "Market Mavens' Purchase Decision Evaluative Criteria: Implications for Brand and Store Promotion Efforts," Journal of Consumer Marketing 12, no. 3 (1995): 4–21.

[59] Stanley C. Hollander and Kathleen M. Rassuli, "Shopping with Other People's Money: The Marketing Management Implications of Surrogate-Mediated Consumer Decision Making," Journal of Marketing 63 (April 1999): 102–118.

[60] Stephen J. Grove and Raymond P. Fisk, "The Service Experience as Theater," in Advances in Consumer Research, vol. 19, ed. John F. Sherry, Jr. and Brian Sternthal (Provo, UT: Association for Consumer Research, 1992), 455–461.

[61] Michael Guiry, "Consumer and Employee Roles in Service Encounters," in Advances in Consumer Research, vol. 19, ed. John F. Sherry, Jr. and Brian Sternthal (Provo, UT: Association for Consumer Research, 1992), 666–672.

[62] Linda L. Price, Eric J. Arnould, and Patrick Tierney, "Going to Extremes: Managing Service Encounters and Assessing Provider Performance," Journal of Marketing 59 (April 1995): 83–97. See also Linda Price and Eric J. Arnould, "Commercial Friendships: Service Provider–Client Relationships in Context," Journal of Marketing 63 (October 1999): 38–56.

[63] Jan Kratzer and Christopher Lettl, "Distinctive Roles of Lead Users and Opinion Leaders in the Social Networks of Schoolchildren," Journal of Consumer Research 36 (2009): 646–659; Henry Assael, Consumer Behavior and Marketing Action (Boston: Kent, 1983).

[64] Christopher Lettl, Hans Georg Gemunden, and Christoph Hienerth, "Exploring How Lead Users Develop Radical Innovation: Opportunity Recognition and Exploitation in the Field of Medical Equipment Technology," IEEE Transactions on Engineering Management 55, no. 2 (2008): 219–233.

[65] Leisa Rienecke Flynn, Ronald E. Goldsmith, and Jacqueline K. Eastman, "The King and Summers Opinion Leadership Scale: Revision and Refinement," Journal of Business Research 31, no. 1 (1994): 55–64.

[66] Hubert Gatignon and Thomas Robertson, "A Propositional Inventory for New Diffusion Research," Journal of Consumer Research 11 (March 1985): 849–867.

[67] Ibid. See also Kristiaan Helsen, Kamel Jedidi, and Wayne S. DeSarbo, "A New Approach to Country Segmentation Utilizing Multinational Diffusion Patterns," Journal of Marketing 57 (October 1993): 60–71.

[68] Elizabeth Hirschman, "Symbolism and Technology As Sources of the Generation of Innovations," in Advances in Consumer Research, vol. 9, ed. Andrew Mitchell (Provo, UT: Association for Consumer Research, 1981), 537–541.

[69] Claire Suddath, "The Chive's Smut With a Smile," Bloomberg Business, October 17, 2013, captured 1-16-2016, http://www.bloomberg.com/bw/articles/2013-10-17/the-chives-founders-john-and-leo-resig-master-millennial-marketing

[70] Kelly Tepper Tian, William O. Bearden, and Gary L. Hunter, "Consumers' Need for Uniqueness: Scale Development and Validation," Journal of Consumer Research 28, no. 1 (2001): 50–66.

[71] Caglar Irmak, Beth Vallen, and Sankar Sen, "You Like What I Like, but I Don't Like What You Like: Uniqueness Motivations in Product Preferences," Journal of Consumer Research 37 (2010): 443–455.

[72] Hubert Gatignon and Thomas S. Robertson, "A Propositional Inventory for New Diffusion Research," Journal of Consumer Research 21 (1985): 849–867.

[73] Michael Trusov, Randolph E. Bucklin, and Koen Pauwels, "Effects of Word-of-Mouth versus Traditional Marketing: Findings from an Internet Social Networking Site," Journal of Marketing 73 (2009): 90–102.

[74] "Facebook Says There Are Now 40 Million Active Small Business Pages, captured 1-14-2016, http://techcrunch.com/2015/04/29/facebook-40-million/#.ium11nz:ff9d

[75] "ForeSee Results Debuts Social Media Value Benchmark," Business Wire, accessed January 10, 2016, http://www.businesswire.com/news/home/20101117005664/en/ForeSee-Results-Debuts-&r=&bc=.

[76] For an interesting examination of an unusual group, Harley-Davidson motorcycle enthusiasts, see John W. Schouten and James H. McAlexander, "Subcultures of Consumption: An Ethnography of the New Bikers," Journal of Consumer Research 22 (June 1995): 43–61.

[77] Stephen Lynch, "Pokémon Provides the Blueprint for the Perfect Pre-Teen Fad," McAllen Monitor, November 25, 1999, 1D.

chapter

13

Pop Culture

Learning Objectives:

1. What are the components of culture?

2. What is the role of consumer goods in culture?

3. What are rituals?

4. What is fashion and what are the characteristics of fashion trends?

Using Makeup

One rite of passage for girls, which then becomes a ritual over most of their life, is putting on makeup. This ritual is influenced by both the mother and peers. The relationship with the mother seems to be complex. On the one hand, mothers are models of this ritual. On the other, they perform a gatekeeping function. As an informant told one of the authors of this book, "[I] wasn't allowed to wear makeup until ninth grade unless for special occasions, i.e. family photos, which,

if approved, was applied by the mother figure." When asked if other girls were starting earlier, the informant replied, "Oh, yes."

Peer influence is important, but it becomes a mostly-private practice as the ritual stabilizes. However, especially for younger women, the web has influenced this ritual. A variety of online games, how-to demonstrations, and virtual make-overs allow greater experimentation than before.

THE COMPONENTS OF CULTURE

As we'll see, rituals such as makeup application are one component of culture. Let's turn first to the general subject of culture.

Culture has been defined in a variety of ways. One classic definition states that **culture** is a set of socially acquired behavior patterns transmitted symbolically through language and other means to the members of a particular society.[1] Cultures may be distinguished in terms of their regulation of behavior, the attitudes of the people, the values of the people, the lifestyle of the people, and the degree of tolerance of other cultures.[2] Another perspective comes from the symbolic interactionists, who view culture as composed of a set of competing images transmitted through media via important signs and symbols.[3]

Broadly speaking, culture is a way of life. It includes the material objects of a society, such as clothing, footballs, autos, religious texts, forks, and chopsticks. It's also composed of ideas and values. For example, most endorse the belief people have a right to choose between different brands of products. Culture consists of a mix of institutions that includes legal, political, religious, and even business organizations. Some may even symbolically represent a society—for example, McDonald's, Mexican tequila, or French champagne. The ways we dress, think, eat, and spend our leisure time are all components of our culture.

A number of additional ideas are necessary to gain an overall understanding of culture. A culture is learned—it's not present in our genes. Culture is transmitted from generation to generation, influencing future members of the society. The process of learning one's own culture is called **enculturation**. The difficult task of learning a new culture is called **acculturation**. Researchers have distinguished the level of acculturation from the level of **cultural identification**, which refers to the society in which a person prefers to live. Cultural identification is attitudinal in nature. In contrast, the level of acculturation is behavioral, referring to the extent to which the actions of a visitor conform to the norms and mores of a culture.[4]

A culture is also adaptive. It changes as a society faces new problems and opportunities. In other words, just as organisms evolve, so do cultures. They take on new traits and discard old ones to form a new cultural base. There's considerable evidence that attitudes toward those leading a more open LBGT lifestyle are changing. In addition, the recent series of shootings over the last few years (e.g., San Bernardino, California; Charleston, South Carolina; Newtown, Connecticut), may be leading to a change in our cultural views on gun possession and control.

Finally, culture satisfies needs. By providing **norms**, or rules of behavior, a culture gives an orderliness to society. It provides **values**, delineating what's right, good, and important. People need to know what's expected of them, what's right and wrong, and what they should do in various situations. Culture fulfills such societal requirements.

Culture is so pervasive and automatically accepted that identifying the elements of one's own culture is difficult. In fact, it's been suggested that understanding one's own culture requires knowing something about another culture, which provides the perspective needed to realize other people really do things differently.[5] For example, by international standards, some think Americans are fanatics concerning personal hygiene and cleanliness. Oddly enough, this was a result of a cleanliness campaign during the Civil War, as handwashing had been found to dramatically decrease military mortalitiy.[6]

Managerial principle 13.1
Scan the environment for signs of emerging changes in cultural behavior.

Scholars use a number of key concepts to describe cultures. As noted earlier, each culture has a set of values denoting the end states people should strive to attain. When comparing and contrasting cultures, one sees the relative importance of various values differs.

All societies have a distinctive set of norms. Norms are more specific than values and dictate acceptable and unacceptable behaviors. Two general types of norms exist. **Enacted norms** are expressed explicitly, sometimes in the form of laws. An example is which side of the road you drive a car. Sometimes, norms are absolutely imperative. In the United States, people drive on the right side, but in Great Britain, Australia, Kenya, Japan, and elsewhere, people drive on the left side.

The second type of norm is embedded in the culture and learned only through extensive interaction with the people of the culture. Called **cresive norms**, they include three types: customs, mores, and conventions.[7]

Customs are handed down from generation to generation and apply to basic actions such as what ceremonies are held and the roles played by the sexes. Sometimes, we obey customs without really knowing why. Along the border with Mexico, Cinco de Mayo is an important holiday, but some know only that it means May 5 and drinking is called for (it actually celebrates the defeat of the French by the Mexican Army in 1862).

Mores are customs that emphasize the moral aspects of behavior. Frequently, mores apply to forbidden or regulated behaviors, such as the exhibition of uncovered skin in fundamentalist cultures.

Conventions describe how to act in everyday life, and they frequently apply to consumer behavior. For example, yard landscaping varies widely from society to society. In the United States, yards are regularly very large and covered with grass. In Germany, yards often feature neat flower gardens. In Japan, yards are small, elaborately planted with bushes, and frequently feature the sound of bubbling water.

Another element of culture is the myths held by its people. **Myths** are stories that express key values and ideals of a society. For example, in the United States, a popular mythological character is Superman. He displays important values within US culture, such as great strength and a mild-mannered exterior. Superman fights crime and injustice. As one authority on the topic has noted, myths help explain the origins of existence, reveal a set of values for the society, and provide models for personal conduct.[8]

The creation of myths is extremely important to marketers. The Superman myth was created via a comic book. Other consumer myths include fictional characters, such as Santa Claus, the Phantom, E.T., the Green Lantern, and the Easter Bunny. In addition, cultural myths may also be based on real people, such as George Washington cutting down the cherry tree and refusing to lie about it. More recent cultural icons of near-mythic proportions are Nelson Mandela, the first president of post-apartheid South Africa, and Steve Jobs, the legendary technology figure.

Each culture also has its own set of symbols, rituals, and values to which marketers can tie their products and services. For example, in the United States, the eagle is a symbol representing strength, courage, and patriotism. Companies wanting to create such an image may use the eagle in their advertising or packaging. Commercials for Miller beer, for example, often feature an eagle. In Australia, the koala is an important symbol companies use companies to link themselves symbolically to the country.

Managerial principle 13.2
Be careful about transferring cultural symbols from one culture to another.

Various rituals are also important to culture. In late January or early February of each year, millions of people in the United States gather in small groups, sit in front of a television set, and eat fattening foods while watching the Super Bowl.

To increase interest in similar rituals abroad, the National Basketball Association (NBA) targeted Asia. NBA games can now be seen in most countries in the area, and Southeast Asia and many others areas have formed a professional basketball league.[9] Similarly, the National Football League (NFL) plays exhibition games in Japan, Europe, and Mexico, with the Jacksonville Jaguars playing one "home" game per year in London, England, through 2020.

Cultural rituals may be borrowed from one country and spread to another. For example, the *quinceañera* is a coming-out ceremony for fifteen-year-old Hispanic girls that has been introduced into the United States. Other borrowings are less fortunate—the numeral 39 somehow came to symbolize prostitution in Afghanistan, and cars in that country with license plates including 39 (and cell phones with 39) dropped sharply in value.

Values vary widely across cultures. As an example, in the United States, the freedom to own guns is deeply ingrained. From 2001 to 2011, female participation in shooting sports increased by 51.5 percent, and the number of female-only gun clubs, with names such as A Girl and a Gun and She Can Shoot, have proliferated.[10] Other countries have less liberal laws for gun possession (e.g., in Poland, only about 1 percent of citizens owns a gun), and these laws reflect a different set of values about owning guns.

The Cultural Matrix

The cultural matrix shown in Figure 13.1 depicts three important sets of factors that compose a culture: values, institutional-social environment, and material environment. The intertwining of these sets creates the overall cultural fabric of a society. As shown in the figure, the material environment consists of factors such as the technical-scientific level of the society, the extent and type of natural resources present, the geographical features of the society, and the society's degree of economic prosperity. The institutional-social environment includes the legal, political, religious, business, and subcultural institutions and groups that compose the society. Subcultures are subdivisions of a national culture centered on some unifying characteristic, such as social class or ethnicity (Chapter 14 discusses subcultures further).

A culture is also influenced by the dominant values of the society. Values will be discussed in a separate section in the chapter. In US culture, key values include individualism, freedom, and achievement. Culture can be affected by additional factors, such as natural disasters and wars, and even technical advances. The likely influx of robots into the family home over the next few years may have an impact on relationships between people, and robots and people For example, the care of elderly parents may become a responsibility of robotic aides.

As time passes, changes occur in the external environment, social institutions, and values found within the cultural matrix. In addition, a constant interplay of movements and countermovements takes place within the matrix. As a result, new ideas and trends are constantly bubbling to the surface. These ideas and trends form popular culture, or simply pop culture. Popular culture is constantly changing, bringing variations in fashion and lifestyles. These changes may lead to corporate catastrophes or marketing opportunities. For example,

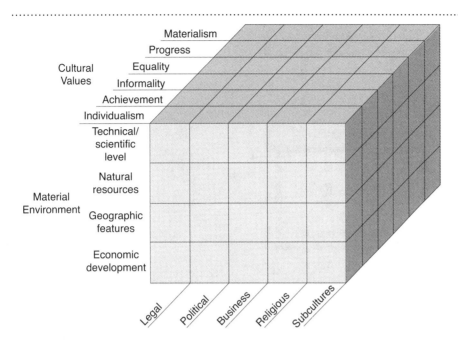

FIGURE 13.1
The Cultural Matrix

Zumba has exploded in popularity as a fitness program, and the popular franchise Zumba Fitness announced a 37 percent revenue increase in 2012 over the previous year.[11] A variety of sports, including mixed martial arts (MMA), lacrosse, roller derby, pickleball, and rugby, have laid claim to being the fastest-growing sport recently.[12] The challenge to marketers in the exercise and sports industries is to anticipate these trends.

In this chapter, we focus on culture and its impact on consumer behavior. We now turn to analyzing the role of consumer goods within a culture. We then relate core American values to the cultural meanings consumers hope to attach to themselves. We follow by presenting information on cultural rituals and symbols. We close by discussing **popular culture**, which represents the shorter trends that occur within the overall fabric of a society.

THE ROLE OF CONSUMER GOODS IN A CULTURE

Consumer behavior researchers have long been interested in the role consumer goods play in a culture. Figure 13.2 diagrams the relationship among individual consumers, consumer goods, and the culturally constituted world. The significance of goods lies in their ability to carry and communicate cultural meaning.[13] **Cultural meanings** refer to these values, norms, and shared beliefs that are communicated symbolically. They're transferred from the culturally constituted world to consumer goods and from these goods to individuals.

The culturally constituted world is the lens through which individuals interpret the world around them. It's made up of the values, mores, and norms that define a particular society. It forms a kind of blueprint designating how people should act and behave. As shown in Figure 13.2, the transfer of meaning from culture to object may occur through advertising and fashion systems, while the transfer of meaning from consumer goods to individuals may take place through various rituals, including possession, exchange, grooming, and divestment.

FIGURE 13.2
Communicating Cultural
Meaning
Source: Reproduced with
permission from Grant
McCracken, "Culture and
Consumption: A Theoretical
Account of the Location
of Meaning Structure and
Movement of the Cultural
Meaning of Consumer
Goods," *Journal of Consumer
Research* 13 (June 1986):
71–84.

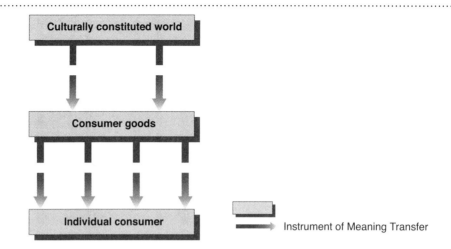

Managerial principle 13.3
Product positioning imbues a
product with meaning. Position products and services
to reflect desired meanings
you want associated with the
product.

Advertising is a conduit through which meaning pours from the culturally constituted world to consumer goods. By positioning a product, the advertiser imbues it with meaning. For example, BMW has used the slogan "The
Ultimate Driving Machine" extensively. The company's goal is to position the
brand as exciting and nimble. Through this positioning process, meanings are
drawn from the culturally constituted world and transferred to the automobile
through the advertisements.

The fashion system is a broader, more diffuse set of agents of transfer. It
includes magazines, the Internet, opinion leaders, and others. The characters in
television shows often give meaning to various products and services. Television programs such as *What Not to Wear* and *Say Yes to the Dress* have acted to
transfer meaning to new types of clothing and accessories.

Figure 13.2 depicts consumer goods and services as transferring cultural
meanings to individuals. In essence, people use goods to link cultural meanings
to themselves. If the meaning we attach to our material objects is understood by
others, we successfully portray who and what we are to others. As one authority has stated,

> *What can be said of clothing can be said of virtually all other high-involvement
> product categories and several low-involvement ones. Clothing, transporta-
> tion, food, housing exteriors and interiors, and adornment all serve as media
> for the expression of the cultural meaning that constitutes the world.*[14]

Some have argued rituals are used to transfer meanings of objects to the
individual. A ritual is a symbolic series of actions that link the person to the
material good. The exchange of gifts at birthdays and Christmas illustrates such
rituals. Gifts possess symbolic properties that act to transfer cultural meanings
(e.g., love) from one person to another. We'll discuss rituals in more detail later
in the chapter.

Core Values

Values are enduring beliefs about ideal end states and modes of conduct. In
general, values tend to be few in number. They're more abstract than attitudes

and serve as standards to guide actions, attitudes, and judgments. Specific attitudes about objects tend to reflect and support a person's values. Within a society, **cultural values** represent the shared meanings of ideal end states and modes of conduct. Thus, cultural values depict a shared meaning of what's important and what end states of existence people should seek.[15]

The values that make up the culturally constituted world in the United States have a variety of sources. One important source of our culture, of course, is the European heritage of the early settlers of the United States and Canada. The flight from religious persecution and authoritarian monarchies indelibly etched into the American culture the values of individualism and freedom. Some have argued the frontier created the values of rugged individualism, informality, equality, and diligence.[16] Certainly, the Judeo-Christian heritage of early Americans also influenced what were to become core American values.[17]

A number of authors have developed lists of core American values. Frequently mentioned values include beliefs in the importance of individualism, youthfulness, progress, materialism, activity, achievement, efficacy, informality, equality, and distrust of government. Other values sometimes mentioned include freedom, external conformity, humanitarianism, authority, respect for institutions, mastery of the environment, and religion. The so-called Protestant ethic also influences values relating to work and frugality. Such themes are sometimes used by advertisers. It has also been proposed that one advantage of pioneer brands is the notion of being a pioneer is a manifestation of the values of innovation and progress.[18]

In every society, there are also countercurrents to the traditional cultural values. For example, in the United States, respect for institutions has been steadily falling for several decades. As noted earlier, culture is adaptive, and one should expect to occasionally see movements that are inconsistent with the traditional values of a culture.

Consumer Research on Cultural Values

One important research issue concerns how cultural values influence specific consumption decisions. Figure 13.3 shows the sequence of moving from global values to domain-specific values to evaluations of product attributes.[19] **Global values** consist of enduring beliefs about desired states of existence.

Domain-specific values are beliefs pertaining to more concrete consumption activities. Examples include beliefs that manufacturers should give prompt service, guarantee their products, help eliminate environmental pollution, and be truthful. Evaluations of product attributes are highly specific beliefs about individual products. For example, how well does a Corvette handle? Is it easy to repair?

Researchers have found people with different global values also exhibit divergent domain-specific values and product evaluations. Indeed, individual differences in global values translate to markedly different product preferences. For instance, people whose global values emphasize logic, an exciting life, and self-respect tend to prefer compact cars and outdoor recreation, whereas those whose global values emphasize national security and salvation are more attracted to standard-sized cars and television.

Figure 13.3 exemplifies what are called **means-end-chain models**, identify the linkages between consumer desires for specific product features with increasingly abstract concepts, such as benefits desired and values that are important to an individual. For example, consider a person who desires to purchase a car with a small, fuel-efficient engine. Three major benefits result from this feature—good gas mileage, lower purchase and operating costs, and protection of the environment. In turn, these benefits lead to a frugal lifestyle. Finally, a frugal lifestyle leads to the terminal value of a clean environment. In sum, the purchase of a car with the attribute of a small, fuel-efficient engine acts as a means to reach the desired end state of a cleaner environment. The process of probing to identify the linkages between means (i.e., attributes) and terminal values (i.e., end states) is called **laddering**.[20]

FIGURE 13.3

Individual's Belief System Organization of the value-attitude system.

Source: Adopted by permission from Donald E. Vinson, Jerome Scott, and Lawrence Lamont, "The Role of Personal Values in Marketing and Consumer Behavior," *Journal of Marketing* 41 (April 1977): 46.

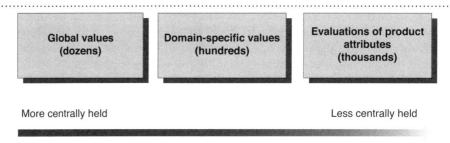

As we'll see later in the chapter, values are closely connected to social change. As the culture of a society changes, so do the values of the individuals that make up the society. Changes in values can directly influence managerial strategy. Consider Stouffer's, which recognized the values of many female grocery shoppers were shifting from emphasizing their roles as "providers for the family" and moving toward self-fulfillment. Acting on this recognition, the company successfully introduced a line of frozen entrees that were positioned as fulfillment oriented. Later on, Stouffer's re-emphasized a family orientation with the "Let's Fix Dinner" challenge, linking family dinners to parental concerns about drug use, body image, and other issues. On the other hand, males are now doing about one-third of the cooking in recently-established US households, resulting in increased male input on desired kitchen items and other housewares. Crystal glassware is out for wedding gifts, although remote-controlled party coolers may not quite have made it onto these lists yet.

Research on the List-of-Values Scale An index developed specifically for consumer research on values is called the list-of-values (LOV) scale. One study using the scale investigated how values in the United States changed between 1976 and 1986.[21] The researchers conducted a national survey of consumers in 1976 and again in 1986. Overall values were quite stable over the time span. Between the 1976 and 1986 figures, the correlation ratio was 0.91 for males and 0.77 for females. These high correlations indicate only small changes in values. Note, however, the correlation for females was lower than that of males, indicating a greater change in women's values. An analysis assessing the change in values by age showed the most change occurred among people younger than thirty.

LOV-scale research has shown people's values influence their attitudes, which affect behavior. One study investigated the characteristics of those who shop for natural foods. The results revealed people who emphasize internal values (i.e., self-fulfillment, excitement, sense of accomplishment, and self-respect) like and purchase natural foods more than do people who emphasize external values (i.e., sense of belonging, being well respected, and having security).[22] A following study suggested a "role-relaxed" person began to appear in the 1990s. The role-relaxed consumer was less concerned with appearing "normal" and more driven by internal values. Consistent with this notion, role-relaxed baby boomers scored lower on the importance of being well respected than the 1986 sample. However, in recent years, the importance of being well respected has increased, while there is less emphasis on a sense of security.[23]

Research on the Value of Materialism   Perhaps the value with the greatest impact on consumer behavior is materialism. We've already discussed materialism as an individual difference variable in Chapter 6. A number of researchers have attempted to identify whether the emphasis on the cultural value of materialism has changed in the United States. They approached the question by content analyzing popular literature, such as comic books and popular novels. (Content analysis involves coding the themes of written material into various categories.) One study investigated the frequency with which materialistic themes appeared in several comic books, such as *Archie*, *Uncle Scrooge McDuck*, and *Richie Rich*. As the researcher explained, a 1965 edition of *Archie* has an example of a materialistic theme: "Veronica tells Archie that having everything she wants bores her, and Betty convinces Archie to go out with her instead so that Veronica feels challenged. It works, but Veronica wins, thanks to her new outfits that catch Archie's eye."[24]

After examining the time period from the 1940s to the mid-1980s, the author of the study reported finding little evidence of changes in materialistic themes over the forty-year period. Interestingly, he argued the comic books may have a positive socializing influence on children. The values portrayed in them were generally positive. The stories indicated wealth can be either good or bad. When the role models acted poorly, they experienced bad fortune. The wealthy characters in the stories were encouraged not to flaunt their riches, and the deserving poor were portrayed as honest and intelligent (i.e., they were people who lacked only the opportunity to be wealthy).

Considering sources other than comic books, however, one does find evidence of changes in materialism as a value. One study, for example, investigated the frequency with which brand names were mentioned in popular novels.[25] It found a more–than-fivefold increase in the usage of brand names between 1946 and 1975. Some critics charge that the manner in which companies name products is making the "sacred profane." For example, True cigarettes and First Romance novels can be viewed as taking sacred words and symbols and making them profane by connecting them with products. Indeed, the charges seem to have some merit. The word *truth* could be considered tainted by an association with a cigarette brand because tobacco companies long avoided telling consumers about the harmful effects of smoking.

When one looks at themes in advertisements, one gains another perspective on materialism in American society. Some authors have distinguished two types of materialism—instrumental and terminal. **Instrumental materialism** involves obtaining a material good in order to perform some activity. Instrumental materialism is viewed as benign because the good is an instrument for the accomplishment of something else. In contrast, **terminal materialism** involves the possession of a good as an end in itself. Terminal materialism is viewed as potentially destructive because it leads to unbecoming traits such as envy, possessiveness, selfishness, and greed.[26]

One study investigated two thousand print advertisements having to do with the interior or the exterior of houses. The ads, spanning the years 1901 through 1979, were content analyzed to determine the frequency with which material goods were cast in terms of their theme. The results revealed utilitarian themes, in which the product's benefits were described in terms of practicality and efficiency, decreased in frequency over the time span. In contrast, themes involving luxury increased dramatically, indicating an increase in materialistic themes. However, although luxury themes have increased substantially over time, the underlying themes of such ads have more frequently been of an instrumental nature. As the authors explained,

> *It is also evident that this materialistic emphasis has been more involved with instrumental themes of using the advertised items than with terminally materialistic themes of having the product for its own sake. If we have become a culture of consumption, it does not yet appear that this consumption is an end rather than a means to other ends.*[27]

Do men or do women exhibit greater amounts of materialism? A study investigated the materialism and sharing behavior of men and women in Germany and Canada. Across both nationalities, women were found to be more sharing, generous, nurturing, and caring than men. One explanation suggested by the authors was that material goods mean different things to men than to women. For men, material goods help establish power and competitive relations, whereas they're part of social relations for women. Of course, one alternate explanation is that women generally have more of the so-called "cuddle chemical," oxytocin.[28]

We usually think of the United States as a clearly materialistic society, but how does it compare in this respect to other industrialized nations? One study compared the degrees of materialism in the United States and the Netherlands—countries whose prosperity is about equal.[29] Members of middle-class households in both countries completed questionnaires. The results indicated levels of materialism were highly similar between the two nations across the various scales. The only difference was the sample in the Netherlands revealed slightly higher levels of possessiveness toward material goods than US consumers.

In another study, researchers compared materialistic values among consumers in Europe, the United States, and Turkey.[30] Results revealed Turkish consumers were simultaneously more materialistic and more generous than US and European consumers. In explaining the results, the authors suggested factors unique to the Turkish culture may account for the surprising findings: Turkey has an ancient history of prosperity, a cultural legacy that may have accustomed the Turks to the idea they can afford to be generous.

Cross-cultural comparisons of materialistic values suggest one must avoid simple statements about why people are materialistic. Clearly, a variety of factors influence materialistic values, including a nation's overall prosperity and its particular cultural history. The research on materialism as a value in the United States has yielded mixed results. Some studies find little evidence of an increase in materialism, whereas others find ample evidence. As the housing advertisement study suggested, the answer may lie in the type of materialism studied. Americans do seem to have a mistrust of owning things for their own sake. An emphasis on terminal materialism is inconsistent with American values that emphasize practicality and efficiency. Nonetheless, there's overwhelming evidence the United States is a materialistic society. As one author noted, "The findings indicate the pervasiveness of a consumer culture . . . and suggest that the baby boom generation, reared in material abundance, may be unabashedly materialistic."[31] Even certain genres of music seem to encourage materialism more than others. At least one hip-hop commentator and financial advisor thinks so and has a Twitter account (ThisIsWhyUBroke) in which he rails against the materialism of big-time rappers.

RITUALS

Cultural rituals are socially standardized sequences of actions that are periodically repeated, provide meaning, and involve the use of cultural symbols. Rituals can be public or private. They vary from large-scale civic rituals, such as the Super Bowl, to private rituals, such as prayer. Ritual behaviors are scripted, so they're formal and prescribed by convention, and in many cases, they involve the consumption and use of products.

These characteristics of rituals are embodied in its formal definition. The term *ritual* refers to an expressive, symbolic activity constructed of culturally sanctioned behaviors that occur in a fixed, episodic sequence and tend to be repeated over time. Ritual behavior is dramatically scripted and acted out and is performed with formality, seriousness, and inner intensity.[32]

Rituals should be distinguished from habits. Habits are also repetitive, last over time, and can have inner intensity. For example, most of us have a sequence of actions we follow to go from home to work or school. Such sequences of actions are considered habits rather than rituals. Rituals differ from habits on three criteria. First, rituals are prescribed by society rather than by the individual. Second, people are more consciously aware of what takes place in a ritual than they are of what's going on in a habit. Third, rituals have greater symbolic meaning than habits and have more affect attached to them.[33]

Table 13.2 presents a typology of ritual experience. As evident in the table, rituals exist at various levels of abstraction. At their most abstract—as in religious, magic, and aesthetic rituals—they have cosmological value. At their most concrete—as in the grooming and mating rituals of animals—rituals are determined biologically. The types of rituals shown in the table also point out the functional value of rituals. For example, the cultural rituals of graduation and marriage act as rites of passage that symbolically denote a change in a person's status. Similarly, rituals can serve to pass on knowledge and create bonds within groups. Thus, holiday celebrations, the exchange of birthday gifts, and office luncheons are enacted in order to fulfill specific goals within groups.[34]

Rituals commonly have four elements: artifacts, scripts, performance roles, and an audience. Consider, for example, the various aspects of a college basketball game. One can identify in this ritual the artifacts (i.e., basketballs, pompons, beer, etc.), the script (i.e., the rules of the game), performance roles (i.e., players, referees, coaches), and the audience. Of course, rituals vary in formality and in the extent to which each of the four elements is present.

TABLE 13.2
A Typology of Ritual
Experience

Primary Behavior Source	Ritual Type	Examples
Cosmology	Religious	Baptism, meditation, mass
	Magic	"Healing," gambling
	Aesthetic	Performing arts
Cultural values	Rites of passage	Graduation, marriage
	Cultural	Festivals, Valentine's Day, Groundhog Day, Super Bowl
Group learning	Civic	Memorial Day parade, elections, trials
	Small group	Pancake Day, fraternity initiation, business negotiations, office luncheons
	Family	Mealtime, bedtime, birthday and holiday celebrations
Individual aims and emotions	Personal	Grooming, household rituals
Biology	Animal	Greeting, mating

Source: Dennis Rook, "The Ritual Dimenison of Consumer Behavior," *Journal of Consumer Research* 12 (December 1985), 251-64. Reprinted with Permission.

At the cultural level, researchers have identified four types of rituals: exchange, possession, grooming, and divestment.[35] **Exchange rituals** involve the exchange of gifts, information, goods, or money. **Possession rituals** involve acts in which a person engages to lay claim to, display, and protect possessions. For example, housewarming parties and zealous car waxing can be viewed as possession rituals. **Grooming rituals** act to ensure the special perishable properties of clothing, hairstyles, and looks are present. In some cases, the grooming ritual isn't performed on the consumer but on a possession or product. An example is the constant grooming of lawns by many homeowners. **Divestment rituals** may help us leave behind important and symbolic items. They may be performed to erase the meaning associated with the previous owner of the good. For example, after buying an older house, new homeowners will frequently engage in cleaning and redecorating behaviors in order to lay claim to the possession. Similarly, a divestment ritual may occur when a person disposes of a personalized item, such as a special coat, car, or house. When one of the authors sold a prized Camaro and asked the new owner for a ride to work, for example, the new owner asked if he wouldn't like to drive it one last time. She provided him with an additional opportunity for a divestment ritual.

The list of consumption-related rituals is long. They include rites of passage (e.g., weddings, baby showers, and funerals), religious ceremonies, holiday festivities (e.g., Christmas and Thanksgiving), family activities (e.g., television viewing at prescribed times, summer vacation, and Sunday dinner), and large-scale public rituals (e.g., singing the national anthem, watching parades, and attending sports events).[36] The ritual of Christmas has an unwritten "tree rule" that dictates married couples with children should put up a Christmas tree. Some of these rituals have both a religious element and an added, commercial element. For example, Easter has both religious and secular significance.

For manufacturers and retailers, success often lies in recognizing the importance of culturally prescribed consumer rituals and tying the company's products to these rituals. By identifying ritualistic patterns of behavior, marketers can design and promote products that might serve as artifacts in the activities. For example, the beauty ritual involves a long series of steps for many women. Some adroit marketers (e.g., Clinique) have attempted to lengthen the ritual by adding new steps and products, such as using an astringent to close facial pores after washing. Donna Karan, Zirh, Neutrogena, and others have assembled similar multistep skin-care systems for men and are beginning to have some success.[37] The idea is to change grooming habits into rituals prescribed by the firm by promising to provide the important consumer benefit of more-attractive skin.

A final point of interest to retailers and service providers is the notion of rituals as catalysts for consumers to construct "small worlds"—that is, to develop and maintain social relationships. Although the rituals may differ (e.g., male bonding occurs at sports events, whereas women might socialize at an arts performance), the end result is similar. If facilities and events facilitate the development of small worlds of interconnected consumers, perhaps including a sense of belonging may enhance the value provided. For example, some participants have noted they attend certain events more for social purposes than for the value of the actual performance or event.[38]

Cultural Symbols

In addition to values and rituals, cultures have symbols. **Symbols** are entities that represent ideas and concepts.[39] Chapter 3 discussed semiotics, a field that investigates the meaning of symbols. As noted there, symbols are important because they communicate complex ideas rapidly with a minimum of effort. If an American company wants to communicate the concept of patriotism, a useful symbol is the US flag. By adroitly using symbols, companies and advertisers can tie cultural values to their products or services, enhancing their attractiveness to consumers. It can be argued that people "consume" symbols.[40] That is, products may be evaluated, purchased, and consumed based, in part, on their symbolic value. For a product to have symbolic value, it must have a shared reality among consumers, meaning large numbers of consumers must have a common conception of the product's symbolic meaning. For example, in order for an automobile to have prestige value, others in the relevant social group must view it in the same manner as the buyer.[41]

Companies frequently symbolize the characteristics of their products via the names chosen for them. One expert insists names must express the "soul" of the product, as well as strike an emotional chord with consumers.[42] For example, auto manufacturers have been fond of naming their products after swift and agile animals. Perhaps the most-famous example is the Ford Mustang. More recently, automobiles have begun to sport names with a more high-tech theme.

Numerous symbols exist in American culture. The symbol of money—and occasionally power or greed—is the dollar sign ($). One symbol to denote Christian spiritual meanings is the cross. A smoking pipe might be used to symbolize contemplation. Similarly, wearing glasses can indicate intelligence and, possibly, physical weakness—à la Clark Kent, Superman's alter ego. Planting a tree suggests permanence, and so forth.

Colors also have symbolic value. In the United States, black can have a variety of symbolic meanings depending on the context. When worn at funerals, it indicates mourning. In contrast, black bustiers and garter belts suggest high levels of sex appeal. Blue indicates coolness—for example, Ice Blue Aqua Velva.

White means purity, as in wedding dresses. Pink is feminine, and for babies, blue is masculine.

Clothing also has important symbolic meaning for consumers. Table 13.3 identifies a variety of functions clothing may have for consumers, as well as the potential symbolic value of such clothing. One function of clothing is to act as an emblem of group membership. The popularity of T-shirts and handbags that possess a logo illustrates the symbolic nature of clothing. Clothing with designer logos faded after great popularity in the 1980s, but these logos came back in big, oversized versions in the 1990s.[43] Now, the very wealthy may have tired of being identified as such by labels from luxury designers and may prefer a small label or even none at all.

TABLE 13.3

Clothing: Its Functional Uses and Symbolic Meanings

Function	Use	Symbolic Meaning	Example
Camouflage	Hide the body	Sexually conservative	Robe
	Cover blemishes or injuries		Cosmetics, patches
Display	Reveal body parts	Sexually explicit	Tight or skimpy dress
Utilitarian	Protect the body	Down-to-earth, practical	Some jeans, raincoats
Aesthetic	Beautify or enhance the body	Love of beauty	Jewelry
Souvenir	Reminder of the past	Love of family or experience	Charm bracelet
Emblematic	Group membership	Show membership in a group	Fraternity jacket
	Connotative	Reveal social class or wealth	Expensive jewelry

Source: Adapted, in part, from a table in Rebecca Holman, "Apparel As Communication," in *Symbolic Consumer Behavior*, ed. Elizabeth Hirschman and Morris Holbrook (Ann Arbor, MI: Association for Consumer Research. 1980). 8.

Although all cultures use symbols, they may be more important in some cultures than in others. For example, Japan has been called the empire of signs. This statement is true both literally and figuratively. Japan's urban landscape is cluttered with signs, some flashing incessantly and others meticulously lettered. Figuratively, the Japanese culture engages in a large number of symbolic activities. The practice of exchanging business cards (*meishi*) has a symbolic function. The great care taken in wrapping and packaging plays a role in the spiritual and cultural life of the country.

The Japanese are also fond of using foreign words in promotional materials that may have several symbolic meanings. The foreign words may connote something new or modern, indicate a Western influence, and symbolize prestige. One researcher attempted to count the number of English loanwords in a Japanese dictionary but gave up after recording seven thousand instances. Examples of such loanwords include *botsu* (boots), *tobako* (cigarette), and *kitchin* (kitchen).

Two researchers spent a summer in Japan investigating the use of English loanwords by Japanese companies. They observed Japanese beverage companies frequently include English prose in their advertising. For example, one ad

Managerial principle 13.4
Carefully consider the use of language, especially in foreign contexts. One of the authors once discussed the difference between the English words *ashamed* and *embarrassed* with a Mexican woman. She said she couldn't use *embarrassed* even though she knew the difference, because it was too similar to the word for "pregnant" in Mexico.

for Kirin beer was written in English: "The legendary KIRIN is a symbol of good luck. Open up KIRIN today, and you'll see what it is all about." Japanese promotional messages may use similes and metaphors that could sound very strange. One beverage, called Pokka White Sour, featured a promotional message in English: "Pokka White Sour is refreshing and white like Alpine snow. Its sour taste of yogurt will extend on your tongue softly and be a sweetheart."[44]

We frequently assume symbols are universal, when, in fact, they aren't. For example, a picture of a snake may represent sex, evil, medicine, energy, or other ideas, depending on the culture. In the United States, a cross is typically a religious symbol. In Taiwan, crossing your fingers at right angles represents the number ten.

POPULAR CULTURE

In a recent article, South Korea lauded its pop culture exports.[45] What is pop culture? Many definitions have been proposed. For the purposes of understanding its impact on consumer behavior, the most appropriate definition of pop culture is "the culture of mass appeal." Pop culture has the following characteristics:

1. It taps into the experiences and values of a significant portion of the population.
2. It doesn't require any special knowledge to understand it.
3. It's produced in such a way that large numbers of people have easy access to it.
4. It most frequently influences behavior that doesn't involve work or sleep.[46]

To understand popular culture, one must distinguish it from high culture. **High culture** is exclusive in style, content, and appeal. It frequently harks back to the old masters of art, theater, music, and literature. To the advocates of high culture, pop culture frequently appears loud, brassy, and even immoral. The lifestyles of rock and hip-hop stars are frequently used as an illustration.

As many scholars have noted, however, the distinction between high culture and pop culture can be hazy and distinctions can change over time in either direction. For example, when Walt Disney produced *Fantasia*, he borrowed from high culture the music of great classical composers, such as Beethoven. A huge success, *Fantasia* has become part of pop culture even though it employs elements of high culture. However, Shakespeare's works originated as pop culture by appealing to mass audiences who sought entertainment in the working-class theaters of his day. Similarly, Paul McCartney and Eric Clapton, once considered rather mindless British pop musicians, are now part of the music world's cultural establishment.

Managerial principle 13.5
Note that foreign popular culture can also migrate to the United States. Korean pop music, or K-pop, has swept Asia and is becoming influential in the United States. Gangnam style may be only the beginning.

Examples of Pop Culture

Because pop culture involves anything that has mass appeal and is used in nonwork activities, the range of subject matter encompassed by the term is extremely large.

Advertising   Advertising becomes pop culture when its images, themes, and icons become embraced by the mass public. Examples of figures from advertising that have achieved pop culture status include Ronald McDonald, Dos Equis's "Most Interesting Man in the World," the muscled "Old Spice guy" Isaiah Mustafa, and the Aflac duck.

Television   Television has certainly acted to create popular culture. Indeed, one scholar has argued television "has become preeminently *the* popular culture and a primary purveyor of values and ideas."[47] Researchers have found television viewing affects consumers' views of the world. For example, people whose viewing is considered heavy have been found to overestimate both the amount of violence and the degree of affluence in the United States.[48] As a result, a rating system has been devised for television shows to help parents monitor the amount of violence their children are seeing.

The changing face of TV   Several phenomena point to changes in the role of television. First, although spending on TV ads continues to account for 42 percent of all advertising spending, its dominance decreases annually (in the UK, digital advertising pulled in front as early as 2009). The same is true for print ads.

Second, although much ink has rightfully been spilled about the spread of "American" culture through US television shows, this is no longer a one-way street. For example, a handful of shows in the United States are actually copies or adaptations of series from other cultures. *Homeland* is based on the Israeli TV show *Hatufim*, *Survivor* is adapted from Sweden's *Expedition Robinson*, *Ugly Betty*" was based on Columbia's *Betty La Fea*, *Big Brother* first aired in the Netherlands, and *Telenovela* is a play on the Mexican TV genre.

Third, tablets and smartphones have changed how and when we watch TV. A surge in online TV came in 2014 and now much of TV is online. Some thinking is that, because we now watch television when traveling—even just commuting—perhaps shorter shows along the lines of many Youtube videos will appear .[49]

Music   Music can also shape pop culture. The phenomenon of hip-hop, or rap, music illustrates the enormous impact of music on the consumer behavior of a generation. The beginnings of hip-hop music can be traced to 1968, when it was invented in the Bronx section of New York City. The first hip-hop label was established in 1979. In 1985, MTV began a rap program. By 1993, rap moved into mainstream popular culture when Coca-Cola employed hip-hop in its advertising with performers dressed in the baggy fashions associated with the music phenomenon.

FASHION

The concept of fashion can be defined either narrowly or broadly. According to the narrow interpretation, fashion is identified with clothing, costumes, and bodily adornment. For example, the practice of body piercing for the purpose of adornment exemplifies fashion in pop culture.

The broader definition of fashion extends the concept to include any use of products to express one's self-image or role position. **Fashion**, then, is a set of behaviors temporarily adopted by a people because the behaviors are perceived to be socially appropriate for the time and the situation.[50] From this perspective, fashion involves the adoption of symbols to provide an identity. The symbols may include clothing, jewelry, automobiles, housing, artwork, and any other socially visible object that communicates meaning within the popular culture.

Fashion Trends

Fashion is inherently dynamic as it constantly changes over time. One can't over-emphasize the importance of the symbolic value of fashion. Indeed, symbolic value may overwhelm any utilitarian value. One merely has to look at the pain endured by wearing corsets and high-heeled shoes to understand the relative weight people give to symbolic versus utilitarian value of the consumer behavior. Of course, men have their own fashions and, like women, endure physical discomfort to look good—witness hair transplants. Indeed, men dressed about as fashionably as women until the "so-called masculine renunciation of lavish dress in the mid-eighteenth century."[51]

Fashion trends have a number of characteristics, including type of trend, speed of trend, fashion turning points, and the degree of individual-level adherence to the trend.[52] Let's look at each of these.

Type of Trend   Two basic types of fashion trends have been identified. In the **cyclical fashion trend**, members of a society adopt styles that are progressively more extreme in one direction or another. Examples include skirt lengths and tie widths. In the **classic fashion trend**, particular looks become "classic," such as the blue pin-striped suit.

Speed of Trend   The trend may be very fast or slow. Some trends are simple fads and come and go quickly. An example would be dyeing one's hair with Kool-Aid. A long-lasting trend is shaving of facial hair by many men and of underarm hair by most women in the United States.

Fashion Turning Points   Within cyclical fashion trends, a turning point eventually occurs because a technological or cultural barrier has been reached. For example, in the late eighteenth century, the hoopskirt became progressively wider until women could no longer move through doorways. Similarly, in the early 1970s and again in the 1990s, miniskirts headed upward until a cultural barrier was reached in the form of preserving some modesty. Perhaps the same thing will happen with body piercing, as convenient locations of the body for piercing are increasingly "occupied."

The Degree of Individual-Level Adherence to the Trend   Although fashion trends can be discerned in the overall society, at the individual level, each person appears to behave in an almost random manner regarding the trend. Indeed, some people will take delight in dressing or behaving in exactly the opposite manner prescribed by the trend. In turn, these countertrends may become the basis for new fads.

Managerial principle 13.6
Understand the risks of following trends that may be short-lived or are nearing the end of their cycle.

How Pop Culture Develops

As noted earlier, there are numerous trends and countertrends within the overall cultural matrix of a society. These arise from the interplay of changes in the material environment, the institutional-social environment, and cultural values. The shorter-term trends that bubble up from the cultural matrix come and, in most cases, go. Fashion trends were once set by designers, but now many trends

SOCIAL MEDIA

How Has Social Media Changed the Fashion Industry?

Social media has changed the fashion industry in at least two ways. First, the traditional fashion weeks in New York, Paris, Milan, and elsewhere are beginning to fray at the edges. There are now too many fashion weeks, and too many shows per week, for an individual to physically visit. Fashion shows are also beginning to move online. Although this trend is only about five years old, it can be expected to expand.

Second, fashion media has moved online. Tom Fitzgerald of Tom and Lorenzo.com, explained, "You need to produce a ton of content. It is multiple times a day, multiple points being made in your own voice without being repetitive, so that the first time a person comes to your blog, they'll think, 'Oh, I'm going to come back tomorrow."

Source: Elizabeth Holmes, "How to Make It in Fashion's New Media World," *Wall Street Journal*, February 5, 2013, accessed January 13, 2016, http://www.reuters.com/article/2013/02/11/net-us-fashion-newyork-socialmedia-idUSBRE91A0K420130211.

start with teenagers. Specialized market research firms find "cool kids" and pay them hundreds of dollars to interview their friends on camera. This sort of research led to Reebok's introduction of shoes in pastel colors and Burlington Industries' introduction of jeans in darker shades of blue.[53] While these mass trends last, they may influence tens of millions of people in their everyday lives.

As popular culture trends arise from the cultural matrix, media and opinion leaders must begin to communicate the symbols that carry the meanings of the trend. The media include the Internet, television, radio, print, movies, theater, and so on. Important mass-opinion leaders include performers, songwriters, journalists, advertisers, sports celebrities, and various editors, although other important people can act as opinion leaders as well.

In sum, the diffusion of popular culture occurs through a process that mimics the spread of innovations (discussed in Chapter 12). The spread of popular culture can be fast or slow. It diffuses through a process that closely approximates the multistep diffusion model. It has a life cycle that can be short (i.e., a fad) or very long (e.g., the Rolling Stones continue to be popular after decades). But its impact can't be underestimated. Marketers who want to link their products to the fads and fashions that push the hot buttons of masses of people should develop an advanced understanding of pop culture.

MANAGERIAL IMPLICATIONS OF POPULAR CULTURE

The consumer behavior concepts that emerge from investigations of culture and popular culture can be applied to each of the RESPonsive Marketing concepts. The following sections summarize some of the possibilities.

Research

Marketing research can help managers gain an understanding of how cultural values change in a society. For example, changes in values—such as increased desires for pleasure, excitement, and fun—could influence how products are named, what their colors are, and how they are designed. In advertising, such values would influence the underlying tone of the message and the choice of models. We can see this happening through changes in advertising for established products such as Coca-Cola, whose themes have included "Delicious, Refreshing, Exhilarating" (1886), "The Pause That Refreshes," "Things Go Better with Coke," "Have a Coke and a Smile," "I'd Like to Give the World a Coke," "It's the Real Thing," "Coke Is It," and "Always Coca-Cola." As an indication of how cultural values change, The Gap clothing brand seems to have "lost its cachet" with buyers recently. Several high-end designers have fallen back on freelancing, are taking a breather, or have gone in different directions (e.g., Christian Lacroix went bankrupt as a clothier and is remaking himself as a furniture designer).[54]

Environmental Analysis

Culture and popular culture are, of course, both creatures of the external environment. Environmental scanning is therefore critical to understanding changes and how those changes should be incorporated into company offerings.

A major result of political changes in Eastern Europe in the early 1990s was the introduction of consumerism and consumer values into this large region of the world. Numerous companies were able to take advantage of this rapid change to introduce their products and services. Perhaps the next area of the globe where dramatic changes may be in the offing is Africa. A company wishing to take advantage of such changes will need to have a keen understanding of the cultures and pop cultures of this vast area, in particular, the leading economies of Nigeria and South Africa.

Segmentation

One of the tasks needed to successfully use segmentation is identifying segments of consumers who respond well to a certain product and positioning strategy. Often, these segments are assumed to break out along demographic lines (e.g., young females), but other bases may be important here as well. For example, among young females, there are differences based on popular culture and the lifestyles of popular culture icons. Julia Gnuse, who is named "the world's most tattooed woman" by Guinness World Records, may be an icon for some. On the other hand, an expanding segment of the population of young people finds Latin music attractive: Shakira, for example, might be a more appealing cultural icon for this segment of the population. Using popular culture icons is always somewhat risky because fads can change quickly.

Positioning and Differentiation

Brands can be positioned and differentiated based on important cultural values. Only one brand, of course, can hold the position as largest of the competing brands. Although Coca-Cola is the world's largest soft drink company, Dr. Pepper successfully made an appeal to the more iconoclastic, against-the-grain aspect of our cultural makeup by positioning itself as "One of a Kind." This both strengthened the position of Dr. Pepper in consumer minds and appealed to our cultural propensity to engage in a little risky behavior.

Marketing Mix

When developing the marketing mix, companies should analyze core values of every culture involved, as well as the culture to which the product is being marketed. This strategy works both for US firms marketing in other countries and for foreign firms marketing in the United States. For example, Anheuser-Busch used Native Americans in an ad to sell Budweiser in Britain. It became Budweiser's most popular campaign ever there, with viewers requesting photos of the primary actor. Brand awareness rose to an all-time high, and sales increased 20 percent. For Britons, the Native American expressed "genuine American values," explained Louis Blackwell, editor of the UK advertising publication *Creative Review*. However, other Native Americans in the United States got wind of the ad and asked that it be withdrawn. In Britain, the ad managed to represent US values well. For Native Americans, the ad called attention to the fact their population has an alcoholism rate about five times that of the general US population. On both sides of the Atlantic, the ad involved core values, but it led to different results.

SUMMARY

What are the components of culture?

A culture is composed of the socially acquired behavior patterns transmitted to the members of a society. Culture, as way of life, consists of the learned values, norms, rituals, and symbols of a society, which are transmitted through both the language and the symbolic features of the society. Cultural values consist of the shared views of a society concerned with desired states of existence and the appropriate economic, social, religious, and other behaviors in which its members engage. Cultural norms are the rules of behavior people are expected to follow. Three types of cultural norms are customs, mores, and conventions.

Cultural symbols are concrete objects that represent abstract concepts. Symbols can be utilized by managers in naming their products and in designing promotional materials. Cultural rituals are periodically repeated patterns of behavior. Tying products to rituals can be a successful marketing strategy. Cultural myths are stories that express the key values and ideals of a society.

We learn our own culture through the enculturation process and about a another culture through acculturation. Three sets of factors compose culture and make up the cultural matrix: the institutional/social environment, the material environment, and cultural values.

What is the role of consumer goods in culture?

Consumer goods help transfer meaning from the culturally constituted world to consumers. Goods are way stations of meaning. The culturally constituted world acts as a lens through which we interpret the world around us. Meaning is transferred from the culturally constituted world to goods through the advertising and fashion systems. Meaning is transferred from goods to people through various types of rituals.

What are rituals?

Cultural rituals are standardized sequences of actions that are periodically repeated. Rituals are dramatically scripted and acted out with formality, seriousness, and intensity. They serve to symbolically link the meaning of a product to an individual. Rituals are composed of four elements: artifacts, scripts, performance roles, and audience. Four types of consumer rituals have been identified: exchange, possession, grooming, and divestment. Examples of rituals that have a strong impact on consumer behavior are Christmas, graduations, and weddings.

What is fashion and what are the characteristics of fashion trends?

Fashion is a set of behaviors temporarily adopted by a people because the behaviors are perceived to be socially appropriate for the time and the situation. From this perspective, fashion involves the adoption of symbols to provide an identity. The symbols may include clothing, jewelry, automobiles, housing, artwork, and any other socially visible object that communicates meaning within the popular culture. Characteristics of fashion trends include the type of trend (i.e., cyclical versus classic), the speed of the trend, fashion turning points, and the degree of individual adherence to the trend.

KEY TERMS

acculturation
advertising
classic fashion trend
cresive norms
cultural identification
cultural meanings
cultural rituals
cultural values
culture
cyclical fashion trend

divestment rituals
domain-specific values
enacted norms
enculturation
exchange rituals
fashion
global values
grooming rituals
high culture
instrumental materialism

laddering
means-end-chain models
myths
norms
popular culture
possession rituals
symbols
terminal materialism
values

DISCUSSION QUESTIONS

1. Define the concept of culture. What are its basic characteristics?
2. What's the role of consumer goods in a culture? What translates the meaning of culture to consumers?
3. What are several core American values that have been identified?
4. Consumers may be regarded as having belief systems that include global values, domain-specific values, and evaluations of product attributes. Define these terms and indicate how they're related.
5. Define the concept of cultural symbol. Give some examples of clothing that are symbols to consumers.
6. What is pop culture? What are its characteristics?
7. Identify four examples of pop culture.
8. How is pop culture formed?

DISCUSSION QUESTIONS

1. Some commentators have argued movies and television shows produced in the United States are teaching children to be violent. Instances of children ages nine to twelve actually murdering other children have been cited to support the point. To what extent do you think the media influence cultural values?

2. Two popular television shows released in fall 2015 were *Blindspot* and *Supergirl*. Compare and contrast the cultural values these two shows portray.

3. Global values, domain-specific values, and evaluations of product attributes are often related. Consider the attributes you prefer in automobiles. How do these preferred attributes reflect your domain-specific values and global values?

4. Describe a ritual you go through consistently in your everyday life. It could be a religious ritual, some type of grooming ritual, or even one involving the preparation of food, among other things. To what extent is this ritual shared by others?

5. Go through a magazine and look at the advertisements. Identify as many cultural symbols as you can. In each case, state what you think the advertiser is attempting to do by using the symbol.

6. Consider the pop singer Rihanna. What's the symbolic function of the clothing she wears?

7. Identify a current cultural trend that's influencing the behavior of students at your college campus. From where did this trend emerge? What values are transmitted by this trend? How long do you think its life cycle will be?

8. In 2012, shoemaker Skechers USA signed an endorsement deal with Meb Keflezighi, who had just won the New York City Marathon and is an Olympic medalist. However, Keflezighi was thirty-six years old at the time and nearing the end of his career. Discuss the extent to which this was a risky move for Skechers.

ENDNOTES

[1] Melanie Wallendorf and M. Reilly, "Distinguishing Culture of Origin from Culture of Residence," in *Advances in Consumer Research*, vol. 10, ed. Richard Bagozzi and Alice Tybout (Ann Arbor, MI: Association for Consumer Research, 1983), 699–701.

[2] David Tse, Kam-hon Lee, Ilan Vertinsky, and Donald Wehrung, "Does Culture Matter? A Cross-Cultural Study of Executives' Choice, Decisiveness, and Risk Adjustment in International Marketing," *Journal of Marketing* 52 (October 1988): 81–95.

[3] This comment was made by the sociologist Chuck Edgley, who made numerous other helpful comments for this chapter.

[4] Sunkyu Jun, A. Dwayne Ball, and James W. Gentry, "Modes of Consumer Acculturation," in *Advances in Consumer Research*, vol. 20, ed. Leigh McAlister and Michael L. Rothschild (Provo, UT: Association for Consumer Research, 1993), 76–82. See also James W. Gentry, Sunkyu Jun, and Patriya Tansuhaj, "Consumer Acculturation Processes and Cultural Conflict: How

Generalizable Is a North American Model for Marketing Globally?" *Journal of Business Research* 32 (February 1995): 129–139.

[5] Henry Fairchild, *Dictionary of Sociology* (Totawa, NJ: Littlefield, Adams, 1970).

[6] Katherine Ashenburg,"Why do Americans Cherish Cleanliness? Look to War and Advertising," accessed January 18, 2016, http://www.nytimes.com/roomfordebate/2013/05/27/are-americans-too-obsessed-with-cleanliness/why-do-americans-cherish-cleanliess-look-to-war-and-advertising.

[7] George J. McCall and J. L. Simmons, *Social Psychology: A Sociological Approach* (New York: Free Press, 1982).

[8] Joseph Campbell, *Myths, Dreams, and Religion* (New York: E. P. Dutton, 1970).

[9] Warner Warner, "Basketball Thrills Koreans as NBA Dribbles into Asia," *Wall Street Journal*, May 17, 1996, B9; *ASEAN Basketball League*, accessed January 13, 2016, http://aseanbasketballleague.com/.

[10] Robert Farago, "Female Gun Ownership on the Rise. Or Not." *Truth about Guns*, accessed January 16, 2016, http://thetruthaboutguns.com/2010/03/robert-fargo/female-gun-ownership-on-the-rise-or-not; Erica Goode, "Rising Voice of Gun Ownership Is Female," *New York Times*, February 10, 2013, accessed January 13, 2016, http://www.nytimes.com/2013/02/11/us/rising-voice-of-gun-ownership-is-female.html?_(November&_r=0.

[11] Matthew Handrahan, "Zumba Fitness 2 Drives Revenue Growth for Majesco," *Games Industry*, accessed November 21, 2015, http://www.gamesindustry.biz/articles/2012-03-13-zumba-fitness-2-drives-revenue-growth-for-majesco.

[12] See, for example, "What Is the Fastest Growing Sport in the World?" *Answers*, accessed January 16, 2016, http://wiki.answers.com/Q/What_is_the_fastest_growing_sport_in_the_world.

[13] Much of the discussion of the cultural meaning of goods is based on Grant McCracken, "Culture and Consumption: A Theoretical Account of the Structure and Movement of the Cultural Meaning of Consumer Goods," *Journal of Consumer Research* 13 (June 1986): 71–84.

[14] Ibid., 78.

[15] For an interesting discussion of the definition of values, see L. J. Shrum, John McCarty, and Tamara Loeffler, "Individual Differences in Value Stability: Are We Really Tapping True Values?" in *Advances in Consumer Research*, vol. 17, ed. Marvin Goldberg and Gerald Gorn (Provo, UT: Association for Consumer Research, 1990), 609–615.

[16] Theodore Wallin, "The International Executives' Baggage: Cultural Values of the American Frontier," *MSU Business Topics* 24 (Spring 1976): 49–58.

[17] Cora DuBois, "The Dominant Value Profile in American Culture," *American Anthropologist* 57 (December 1955): 1232–1239. See also Janet T. Spence, "Achievement American Style: The Rewards and Costs of Individualism," *American Psychologist* 40, no. 12 (December 1985): 1285–1295.

[18] Frank H. Alpert and Michael A. Kamins, "An Empirical Investigation of Consumer Memory, Attitude, and Perceptions toward Pioneer and Follower Brands," *Journal of Marketing* 50 (October 1995): 34–45.

[19] D. E. Vinson, J. Scott, and L. Lamont, "The Role of Personal Values in Marketing and Consumer Behavior," *Journal of Marketing* 41 (April 1977): 44–50.

[20] Thomas J. Reynolds and David B. Whitlack, "Applying Laddering Data to Communications Strategy and Advertising Practice," *Journal of Advertising Research* 35 (July–August 1995): 9–17; Charles E. Gengler and Thomas J. Reynolds, "Consumer Understanding and Advertising Strategy: Analysis and Strategic Translation of Laddering Data," *Journal of Advertising Research* 35 (July–August 1995); Gerald Zaltman and Robin Higie Coulter, "Seeing the Voice of the Consumer: Metaphor-Based Advertising Research," *Journal of Advertising Research* 35 (July–August 1995): 35–51.

[21] Lynn Kahle, Basil Poulos, and Ajay Sukhdial, "Changes in Social Values in the United States during the Past Decade," *Journal of Advertising Research* 28 (February–March 1988): 35–41.

[22] Pamela Homer and Lynn Kahle, "A Structural Equation Test of the Value–Attitude–Behavior Hierarchy," *Journal of Personality and Social Psychology* 54 (April 1988): 638–646.

[23] Lynn Kahle, "Role-Relaxed Consumers: A Trend of the Nineties," *Journal of Advertising Research* 35 (March–April 1995): 66–67; "Social Values 2007.m4v," YouTube video, 1:30, posted by "UOregon," June 8, 2010, http://www.youtube.com/watch?v=02BQIowj1gM.

[24] Russell Belk, "Material Values in the Comics: A Content Analysis of Comic Books Featuring Themes of Wealth," *Journal of Consumer Research* 14 (June 1987): 26–42.

[25] Monroe Friedman, "The Changing Language of a Consumer Society: Brand Name Usage in Popular American Novels in the Postwar Era," *Journal of Consumer Research* 11 (March 1985): 927–938.

[26] Russell Belk and Richard Pollay, "Materialism and Magazine Advertising during the Twentieth Century," in *Advances in Consumer Research*, vol. 12, ed. Elizabeth Hirschman and Morris Holbrook (Provo, UT: Association for Consumer Research, 1985), 394–398.

[27] Ibid., 397.

[28] Floyd W. Rudmin, "German and Canadian Data on Motivations for Ownership: Was Pythagoras Right?" in *Advances in Consumer Research*, vol. 17, ed. Marvin Goldberg and Gerald Gorn (Provo, UT: Association for Consumer Research, 1990), 176–181. See also Linda Geddes, "Our Happy Hormone Wedding: Couple Test Themselves for 'Cuddle Chemical' Before and After Ceremony," *Daily Mail*, March 27, 2010, accessed January 12, 2016, http://www.dailymail.co.uk/health/article-1261236/Our-happy-hormone-wedding-How-levels-love-hormone-oxytocin-ceremony--intriguing-results.html.

[29] Scott Dawson and Gary Bamossy, "Isolating the Effect of Non-Economic Factors on the Development of a Consumer Culture: A Comparison of Materialism in the Netherlands and the United States," in *Advances in Consumer Research*, vol. 17, ed. Marvin Goldberg and Gerald Gorn (Provo, UT: Association for Consumer Research, 1990), 182–185.

[30] Guliz Ger and Russell Belk, "Measuring and Comparing Materialism Cross-Culturally," in *Advances in Consumer Research*, vol. 17, ed. Marvin Goldberg and Gerald Gorn (Provo, UT: Association for Consumer Research, 1990), 186–192.

[31] Susan Spiggle, "Measuring Social Values: A Content Analysis of Sunday Comics and Underground Comix," *Journal of Consumer Research* 13 (June 1986): 100.

[32] This definition is based, in large part, on Dennis Rook, "The Ritual Dimension of Consumer Behavior," *Journal of Consumer Research* 12 (December 1985): 251–264. We have added the idea that rituals are culturally mandated in order to help distinguish the idea of a ritual from that of a habit.

[33] These ideas were developed by Mary A. Stanfield Tetreault and Robert E. Kleine III, "Ritual, Ritualized Behavior, and Habit: Refinements and Extensions of the Consumption Ritual Construct," in *Advances in Consumer Research*, vol. 17, ed. Marvin Goldberg and Gerald Gorn (Provo, UT: Association for Consumer Research, 1990), 31–38.

[34] Dennis Rook, "The Ritual Dimension of Consumer Behavior," *Journal of Consumer Research* 12 (December 1985): 251–264.

[35] Grant McCracken, "Culture and Consumption: A Theoretical Account of the Structure and Movement of the Cultural Meaning of Consumer Goods," *Journal of Consumer Research* 13 (June 1986): 71–84.

[36] Ray Brown, *Rituals and Ceremonies in Popular Culture* (Bowling Green, OH: Popular Press, 1980). For a discussion of funerals and other aspects of death, see James W. Gentry and Cathy Goodwin, "Social Support for Decision Making during Grief Due to Death," in *Marketing and Consumer Research in the Public Interest*, ed. Ronald P. Hill (Thousand Oaks, CA: Sage, 1996), 55–68; Terrance G. Gabel, Phylis Mansfield, and Kevin Westbrook, "The Disposal of Consumers: An Exploratory Analysis of Death-Related Consumption," in *Advances in Consumer Research*, vol. 23, ed. Kim P. Corfman and John G. Lynch Jr. (Provo, UT: Association for Consumer Research, 1996), 361–367.

[37] In late 2015, a search for "men's makeup tips" yielded some 5.2 million results, including from such well-known brands as Sephora and from *Men's Fitness*.

[38] Brenda Gainer, "Ritual and Relationships: Interpersonal Influences on Shared Consumption," *Journal of Business Research* 32 (March 1995): 253–260.

[39] Charles Morris, *Signs, Language, and Behavior* (New York: George Braziller, 1946).

[40] Elizabeth C. Hirschman, "Comprehending Symbolic Consumption: Three Theoretical Issues," in *Symbolic Consumption Behavior*, ed. Elizabeth Hirschman and Morris Holbrook (Ann Arbor, MI: Association for Consumer Research, 1981), 4–6. See also Morris Holbrook, *Consumer Research: Introspective Essays on the Study of Consumption* (Thousand Oaks, CA: Sage, 1995).

[41] Objects can, however, possess symbolic value independent of their value as viewed by others. For example, a person is unlikely to swap wedding rings even when the alternative offered is of better quality. See Marsha L. Richins, "Valuing Things: The Public and Private Meanings of Possessions," *Journal of Consumer Research* 21 (December 1994): 504–521.

[42] Cacilie Rohwedder, "Name-Finders Save New Products from Fiascos in Global Market," *Wall Street Journal*, April 11, 1996, B5.

[43] Teri Agins, "Signs of the Times: Logos on Clothing Are Back and They're Bigger Than Ever," *Wall Street Journal*, February 22, 1996, B1, B9. But logos are also getting smaller: see Young Jee Han, Joseph C. Nunes, and Xavier Drèze, "Signaling Status with Luxury Goods: The Role of Brand Prominence," *Journal of Marketing* 74 (July 1, 2010): 15–30.

[44] This section was based on an article by John Sherry and Eduardo Camargo, "May Your Life Be Marvelous: English Language Labeling and the Semiotics of Japanese Promotion," *Journal of Consumer Research* 14 (September 1987): 174–188.

[45] "Korea Becomes a Nation of Cultural Exports," *Korea IT Times*, February 13, 2012, accessed January 13, 2016, http://www.koreaittimes.com/story/19796/korea-becomes-nation-cultural-exports.

[46] This definition, as well as the characteristics of popular culture, was taken from Michael J. Bell, "The Study of Popular Culture," in *Concise Histories of American Popular Culture*, ed. M. Thomas Inge (Westport, CT: Greenwood Press, 1982), 443.

[47] Robert S. Alley, "Television," in *Handbook of American Popular Culture*, ed. M. Thomas Inge (Westport, CT: Greenwood Press, 1982), 1368.

[48] Thomas C. O'Guinn and L. J. Shrum, "The Role of Television in the Construction of Consumer Reality," *Journal of Consumer Research* 23 (March 1997): 278–294. See also L. J. Schrum, ed., *The Psychology of Entertainment Media: Blurring the Lines between Entertainment and Persuasion* (New York: Routledge, 2012).

[49] Amy Chozick and Joshua Mitnick, "Coming to America." *Wall Street Journal*, March 11, 2011, D1, D2. Mark Sweney, "Internet overtakes Television to Become Biggest Advertising Sector in the UK," *The Guardian*, September 29, 2009, accessed January 13, 2016, http://www.guardian.co.uk/media/2009/sep/30/internet-biggest-uk-advertising-sector.

[50] George B. Sproles, *Fashion: Consumer Behavior toward Dress* (Minneapolis, MN: Burgess, 1979).

[51] Craig J. Thompson and Diana L. Haytko, "Speaking of Fashion: Consumer's Uses of Fashion Discourses and the Appropriation of Countervailing Cultural Meanings," *Journal of Consumer Research* 24 (June 1997): 15–42.

[52] These characteristics were originally developed by Christopher M. Miller, Shelby H. McIntyre, and Murali K. Mantrala, "Toward Formalizing Fashion Theory," *Journal of Marketing Research* 30 (May 1993): 142–147.

[53] Roger Ricklefs, "Marketers Seek Out Today's Coolest Kids to Plug into Tomorrow's Mall Trends," *Wall Street Journal*, July 11, 1996, B1, B2.

[54] Christina Binkley, "Wanted: A Second Chance," *Wall Street Journal*, June 9, 2011, D1.

14

Subcultures and Demographics

Learning Objectives:

1. How do subcultures differ from demographic groups?

2. What are the dominant types of subcultures within the United States?

3. Do the elderly process information differently than young adults?

4. What makes the African-American and other subcultures important markets?

"Hello:" As Adele Ages

When British pop singer Adele's sophomore album, *21*, debuted, the name of the album owed something to that of her first album, *19*, which was, in Adele's words, "about being between 18 and 19 and being in love."[1] It likely escaped no one's attention that the titles may also happen to appeal to a certain age group. Will these consumers stay with Adele now that she has released *25*?

Incidentally, somewhat-older mothers ages twenty-five to forty-four make up a good portion of her fan base. Adele has herself decided not to use her age in her titles in the future, but that doesn't diminish the importance of age as a demographic factor.

THE MANY CULTURES OF THE US

Within the overall culture of North America, subgroups retain a varying mix of the values, beliefs, and symbols of their culture of origin. These groups form subcultures that can become important target markets for marketers. For example, the need of Jews to have kosher food makes them an attractive target for marketers willing to adequately control the preparation of food products. Meanwhile, mainstream marketers such as ConAgra Foods have begun to market kosher foods because consumers are attracted to the wholesome image of the food products. Indeed, some 85 percent of the sales of Hebrew National's frankfurters goes to non-Jewish customers.[2]

In addition to originating from immigration, subcultures can also develop from naturally occurring subdivisions within a society. All societies contain such subgroups, which may be based on age, social class, and regional differences. In each case, some factor causes differences in values and lifestyles sufficient to create a subculture. For example, a combination of retirement, common physical problems, and similar housing needs has resulted in the development of the elderly subculture.

A **subculture** may be defined as a subdivision of a culture based on some unifying characteristic, such as social status or nationality, whose members share similar patterns of behavior that are distinct from those of the national culture.[3] Numerous demographic characteristics have been used to identify subcultures, including the following:

- nationality (e.g., Italian, Polish)
- race (e.g., African American, Native American, Asian American)
- region (e.g., New England, Southwest)
- age (e.g., elderly, Generation Alpha)
- religion (e.g., Catholic, Muslim)
- gender
- social class (e.g., upper class, lower class)

Subcultures and Demographic Groups

The concepts of subcultures and demographics are closely related. **Demographic variables** describe the characteristics of populations. There are a variety of demographic variables, including the following:

- nationality
- marital status
- age
- income
- religion
- region
- gender
- ethnicity
- occupation
- education

Of course, many of these demographic variables also describe subcultures. Within the demographic category of religion, for example, one can identify a number of distinct subcultural groups in the United States, including Jews, Christians, and Muslims.

When one speaks of cultures or subcultures, the focus is on the group's values, customs, symbols, and actions. Demographic features merely describe the characteristics of a population of people. The reason a marketer might speak of an African-American subculture is this demographic characteristic conveniently describes a group of people who may have similar behavior patterns.

Changes in age and ethnic distribution, as well as attitudes toward gays and lesbians, have had a major impact on marketing strategy. For example, with the changing nature of the social classes, retailers have either had to go upscale or appeal to the lower end. Companies such as Sears, which traditionally focused on the middle class, lost market share to specialty stores on the upper end and discount department stores on the lower end. During the recession of nearly a decade ago, however, many people went to down-market purchases to save money, resulting in the growth of Dollar General and Family Dollar stores. Although that recession is over, some of these customers aren't returning to the higher-end stores they once patronized.

In this chapter, we'll discuss certain key subcultural groups. Let's begin with the important topic of age subcultures.

AGE SUBCULTURES

As consumers move through their life cycle, predictable changes in values, lifestyles, and consumption patterns occur. A five-year-old has a completely different set of needs than a twenty-year-old, who has different needs than a seventy-year-old. Because various age cohorts of consumers have similar values, needs, and behavioral patterns, they form subcultures that may constitute important market segments. Furthermore, changes in the number of people in age categories due to variations in birthrates create new marketing opportunities.

An analysis of age trends is also important to marketers because highly accurate projections of the future age composition of the population can be made more easily than for other demographic factors, such as income or occupation. These projections allow marketers to recognize potential marketing opportunities years in advance, which greatly simplifies the planning process.

Perhaps as profound as the changing ethnic population of the United States is its changing age composition and income distribution. The number of children under eighteen years of age living below the poverty line was estimated at 27 percent by the Kaiser Family Foundation. However, poverty among people older than sixty-five was measured at only 14 percent—a lower poverty rate than among either children or the working-age population, which is 18 percent.

One factor that influences the age distribution of the population is immigration. Immigrants tend to be younger, and immigrant women tend to have higher birthrates. Because of the youth of the immigrants and their higher fertility rates, immigration is the single most important factor retarding the aging trend of the US population.

Four age groups of critical importance to marketers are discussed in this section—baby boomers, Generation X, millennials, and the elderly.

The Baby Boomers

Although some debate may exist as to whether the **baby-boom generation** actually forms a subculture, sufficient lifestyle similarities exist among the huge group of Americans born between 1946 and 1964 that the group has a large impact on marketers and the economy as a whole. The United States is currently experiencing fundamental changes in the age characteristics of its population. The major reasons for the shifts in the average age of Americans over the next forty years lie in the dramatic changes in birthrates over the last half century. During the Great Depression (1929–1939), a **baby bust** occurred. The number of children born to the average woman during her lifetime (i.e., the **fertility rate**) dropped to the replacement level of two.1 births. The total number of births dropped 25 percent.[4]

The Depression "birth dearth" was followed by the post–World War II baby boom. The fertility rate shot past 3.8, and the total number of births increased by one-third over Depression levels. The baby boom lasted through 1964. It was followed, however, by another baby bust. Caused by changes in the technology of birth prevention (e.g., the birth-control pill) and the emergence of the working woman, this baby bust sent fertility rates plunging to as low as 1.8 in 1976—a rate far below replacement level.5 Another baby bust came during the Great Recession of 2007–2009.

This series of changes in the birthrate created a huge bulge of 77 million people (over half again as large as the previous generation). As time passes and the boomers grow older, the bulge moves through the population like a melon being digested by a boa constrictor.[6] Legions of boomers have reached retirement age each year since 1995. Boomers tend to be affluent, with a new set of product needs and wants—now focused on medicines and retirement.

Implications for Marketing Strategy One of the prime marketing requirements for consumer-goods companies is the tracking of the baby-boom generation. Indeed, a marketing law might be phrased as "Those who live by the baby boom shall die by the baby boom." For example, with their traditional target market of five- to seventeen-year-olds declining by more than one-half million during the 1980s, McDonald's was threatened with both a possible decline in revenues and the loss of their primary workforce—teenagers. To navigate the changing age demographics, the company hired retired people to work behind the counters.

Other companies had to make adjustments as well. In 1981, Levi Strauss was the world's largest clothing manufacturer, when jeans production peaked at 560 million pairs. However, by the mid-1980s, profits began to drop dramatically and were down 20 percent by 1988. One of the company's strategic responses was to move into roomier khaki and chino pants, which fit the middle-aged spread of the baby boomers better than jeans. Levi's now sells about $1 billion per year of Dockers slacks. Sales were also helped by the fact that younger males who might prefer jeans still need at least one pair of dressier pants, and Dockers fit the bill. On the other hand, sagging waistlines have become such a fashion statement that "sagging pants" legislation was passed in Ocala, Florida, in 2014 and was being considered in Alabama and elsewhere in late 2015.[7]

Likewise, although dental care improvements have decreased the number of cavities needing to be filled (in 1984, *Forbes* forecast the end of the dental profession), boomers' concern with continuing to look good led to a 20 percent increase in the number of dentists and a near-doubling of dentists' average income between 1987 and 1996.[8]

Not all is positive for the baby-boom generation, however. Because of their large numbers, baby boomers had major problems finding jobs. Many are chronically underemployed. One result was the dependence of some boomers on their parents for financial support even in their forties.[9] These boomers were called RYAs (returning young adults who move back in with relatives) and IL-YAs (incompletely launched young adults who aren't financially independent).

Generation X

Born between 1965 and 1980 (opinions differ on when Gen X ends), the number of **Generation Xers**, or Gen Xers, is small, but the group possesses $125 billion of discretionary income. Given a variety of names, such as "after-boomers" and "flyers" (i.e., fun-loving youth en route to success), the group is noted for valuing religion, formal rituals (e.g., proms), and materialism, as well as more negative attitudes toward work and getting ahead than the boomers.[10] Because of the group's small size, employers must compete for them in the job market. The US Army began its Army College Fund to attract enlistees, allowing them to save up to $25,200 during their term of service for college. One research group calls Generation Xers in the United States and northern Europe the "new realists," who have resigned themselves to the possibility they'll never achieve the affluence of their parents' generation.[11]

On television, Fox Broadcasting Company—home of *The Simpsons*—and MTV specifically targeted Xers. Advertising managers are particularly concerned with how to reach this market. A slew of Generation X magazines was launched, but they're remarkably similar, focusing on music, celebrities, and lifestyle. Among those that fell shortly after launch are *Real*, *Forehead*, the *Nose*, and *Hypno*.[12]

In the food realm, Heinz launched a $50 million advertising program in 1999 to lure teenagers back to ketchup, using references to acne, angst, alienation, and irony as an appeal. One example is the dollop of ketchup that will never come out of the bottle because, the advertisement says, it "has issues."[13]

Now past acne and ketchup, the group has moved into the time span when its members can purchase nicer cars, larger houses, and other big-ticket items. The vice president and general manager of Nissan USA noted that Generation X now accounts for 25 to 30 percent of its automobile sales. He added, "As they age and move up in income, they'll grow in importance. We want to make a good first impression."[14] And they may share global similarities. For years, international marketers have noticed people in different countries with similar educational and income backgrounds seem to act in much the same way. The Xers may have become the first generation to share even closer commonalities—many surf similar social media, watch the same television shows, and view the same videos. This tying together via a worldwide media net may mean Gen Xers everywhere are leading "parallel lives," which means cross-national marketing opportunities are much greater than ever before.[15]

Millennials

The next cohort to appear on the horizon consists of the 72 million children of the baby boomers, who are now reaching adulthood. They represent 28 percent of the current population, rivaling the baby boomers' 30 percent.

Like Generation Xers, **millennials** are more heterogeneous in racial and socioeconomic terms than boomers. For example, the original boomers were 75 percent non-Hispanic white, whereas the millennials are 67 percent non-Hispanic white. They are the first to have significant numbers (about one in thirty-five) of

Managerial principle 14.1
The "global teens" notion can be pushed too far. Chinese teens don't eat ketchup, and changing their mind may be "a 50-year journey," in the words of a Heinz executive.

mixed race, making the traditional racial categories nearly obsolete. Although the first half of the boomers were born in the era of segregation, this isn't true of any of the millennials. Baby boomers learned Father knows best, but for millennials, Dad isn't home. In 1970, 12 percent of children lived in a one-parent household, but in 2011, only 60 percent of millennials reported growing up with both parents.[16] One group of millennials was particularly in demand. There were only 7.4 million twelve- to fifteen-year-old girls, the prime babysitter pool—and 35 million families with newborns to eleven-year-olds who needed sitters.[17]

The millennials hark back to the political activism of their baby-boomer parents. As in 1968, French students in 1998 took to the streets to protest crowded and poorly equipped schools. Unlike the situation between baby boomers and their parents in the 1960s and 1970s, both the boomers and the millennials are environmentalists. Manufacturers are appealing to millennials by noting they don't use rabbits to test cosmetics, a theme that appeals as well to former 1960s activists.[18]

The Elderly

A fourth major age trend in the United States is the "graying of America" (and of Japan, Germany, and a host of other countries). The aging of the population will be one of the most dominant demographic factors for the foreseeable future. Barring global war or other disasters, the population of those under thirty will never again be as large as it was in 1983. By the year 2020, those over sixty-five will outnumber teenagers two to one.

A number of factors (e.g., birthrates, mortality rates, and immigration rates) influence the projected population and its characteristics in the years ahead. Unfortunately, each is difficult to predict accurately. Birthrates are influenced by the technology available to prevent births as well as by cultural values and lifestyle patterns. **Mortality rates** have been falling since the 1970s. Life expectancy increased by three years during the 1970s and another two to three years in the 1980s. Men born in 1995 will live, on average, 72.5 years, and women, 78.5 years. Because of the striking difference in the life expectancy of men and women, an aging population means more women. Of those over eighty-five years old, there are about six women to every four men. Elderly women will increasingly form an important segment for marketers to target.

AGE AND INFORMATION PROCESSING

Just who is the **mature consumer**? No specific age is associated with becoming mature or reaching one's golden years. However, a series of events occurs between the ages of fifty-five and sixty-five that sets the aging consumer apart from younger people. During this period, retirement has either occurred or is anticipated. In all likelihood, income becomes relatively fixed after retirement, making inflation more of a threat than before nearing or reaching retirement. Health concerns become more important at about this age, and close friends begin to pass away.

Many mature consumers are well off financially. Although only 23 percent of American consumers are fifty-five or older, they control 75 percent of the nation's wealth and about half of its discretionary income.[19] Mature consumers also have a great deal of free time. In 1900, 60 percent of all men older than sixty-five were still working. In 1940, the figure was 40 percent. In 2010, about 21 percent of men older than sixty-five were working, although the recession tended to delay retirements a bit.[20]

Mature consumers—here defined as age fifty-five or older—differ from younger people in two major aspects. First, in certain ways, mature consumers process information differently. In particular, their visual, hearing, and taste senses decrease in acuity. One study found information-processing differences limit the extent to which the elderly are able to use nutritional information about cereals. As compared with younger consumers, the elderly were less able to search intensely for nutritional information on packages and select an appropriate cereal.[21] From a public-policy perspective, the results suggest, although nutritional information is more readily available to consumers on packages, the elderly may not be able to make appropriate use of it. The changes in information-processing abilities indicate marketers should be concerned with how much time the elderly are given to make a decision. Providing additional time for information processing—for instance, making an advertisement longer or having a salesperson proceed more slowly—may assist older consumers.

A second way mature consumers differ from younger consumers is in motor skills. As people age, their ability to walk, write, talk clearly, and drive a car can gradually deteriorate. In many cities, companies are now providing a variety of services to the elderly to help them overcome these age-related obstacles. Examples of such services include in-home food delivery, yard and house cleaning, fix-up services, and nursing care. In Japan, with a larger aging problem than the U.S., self-driving cars are being developed to help older citizens continue to be mobile. Japan is also developing robots to attend the elderly. Table 14.1 identifies other ways the consumption habits of the elderly differ from those of younger consumers.

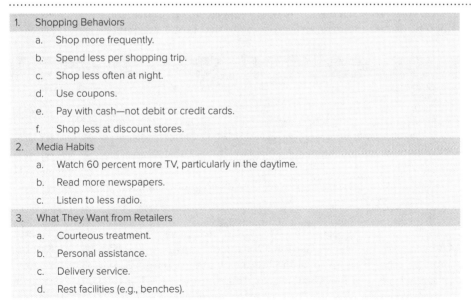

TABLE 14.1
Consumption Habits of Mature Consumers Compared with Younger Consumers

1. Shopping Behaviors
   a. Shop more frequently.
   b. Spend less per shopping trip.
   c. Shop less often at night.
   d. Use coupons.
   e. Pay with cash—not debit or credit cards.
   f. Shop less at discount stores.
2. Media Habits
   a. Watch 60 percent more TV, particularly in the daytime.
   b. Read more newspapers.
   c. Listen to less radio.
3. What They Want from Retailers
   a. Courteous treatment.
   b. Personal assistance.
   c. Delivery service.
   d. Rest facilities (e.g., benches).

Sources: Adapted from K. L. Bernhardt and T. C. Kinnear, "Profiling the Senior Citizen Market," in *Advances in Consumer Research*, vol. 3, ed. B. B. Anderson (Ann Arbor, MI: Association for Consumer Research, 1976), 449–452; Zarrel Lambert, "An Investigation of Older Consumers' Unmet Needs and Wants at the Retail Level." *Journal of Retailing* 55 (Winter 1979): 43.

One major finding concerning the elderly is that they're cautious consumers. They don't tend to risk being wrong for the sake of acting quickly.[22] In addition, the higher the perceived risk, the less likely the elderly are to try a product.[23]

Another phenomenon that occurs as people grow older is an increase in the amount of time spent watching television. The elderly especially use the television both for entertainment and for obtaining information. The importance of the television increases, in part, because elderly people tend to have fewer social contacts.[24]

Managerial principle 14.2
Remember lifestyle profiles (see Chapter 6) aren't necessarily the same as a subculture profile. African Americans, for example, are found in a range of lifestyles.

In addition, the elderly may also be somewhat more vulnerable to scams and fraud, perhaps due to their differences in information processing and motor skills. On the other hand, marketers find that attitude, more than age, defines the mature marketplace. The elderly generally feel younger than they actually are.[25] One implication for managers is that promotional materials should focus on portraying the elderly at the age they feel rather than at their chronological age. Furthermore, as the US government's de facto definition of "retirement age" (i.e., full Social Security benefit eligibility) creeps up from sixty-five to sixty-seven, we may find our own working definitions of "elderly" will change.

ETHNIC SUBCULTURES

Another demographic variable frequently used to describe subcultures is ethnicity. Although used in a variety of ways, **ethnicity** generally refers to a group bound together by ties of cultural homogeneity. Such a group is linked by similar values, customs, dress, religion, and language. Ethnicity is frequently closely linked to nationality or region of origin. One may speak of Mexican Americans and Chinese Americans as ethnic groups because each shares a common national or geographic ancestry as well as a similar culture. Table 14.2 provides population sizes for several ethnic groups between 2010 and 2015. In this section, we'll discuss the African-American, Hispanic, and Asian-American subcultures and their importance as potential target markets.

TABLE 14.2
US Population for White, Black, Asian, and Hispanic Groups, 2010 and 2015

	Total	White	Black	Asian	Hispanic*
2010	310,233	246,630	39,909	14,415	49,726
2015	325,540	256,306	42,137	16,527	57,711

*Persons of Hispanic origin may be of any race. This is may change with the 2020 census.
Source: "Statistical Abstract of the United States: 2012," *US Census Bureau*, accessed February 1, 2016,
http://www.census.gov/library/publications/2011/compendia/statab/131ed/population.html

RACE AS A SUBCULTURE

A number of factors shape the African-American subculture, which represents 14.3 percent of the US population. One major contributor is income deprivation. About 30 percent of low-income families were Hispanic, 22 percent were African American, and 6 percent were "other nonwhite." Thirty-seven percent of African-American households had incomes of less than $15,000. In contrast, 30 percent of Hispanic and 14 percent of white households had incomes this low.[26] Other factors influencing the subculture are educational disparities, a young and highly mobile family structure headed by a high proportion of females, and a concentration of its population in central cities.

Despite these disadvantages, the African-American subculture is growing in importance as a market segment. As shown in Table 14.3, it has impressive buying power, is increasing in size faster than the general population, and is rising in socioeconomic status. The African-American subculture is also marked by the importance of religious and social organizations. African Americans disproportionately belong to fundamentalist Protestant groups and to the Democratic political party. There's also a recognized speech pattern, known as African American Vernacular English (AAVE) or African American English (AAE), that 80 percent of the African-American population uses to some extent. This dialect appears frequently in television programs, but its use in written or spoken advertising is quite limited.[27]

1.	*Average annual household income.* $51,425.
2.	*Youth.* Median age is thirty years as compared with thirty-six for the total population.
3.	*Geographic concentration.* Sixty-five percent of African Americans live in the top fifteen US markets.
4.	*Unique tastes and preferences.* Spend far more than whites on boys' clothing, rental goods, and cognac. African Americans are among the heaviest users of the mobile web.

TABLE 14.3
Factors that Make African Americans an Important Market Segment

Sources: http://www.prlog.org/10077453-new-report-forecasts-african-american-buying-power-to-hit-1-1-trillion-by-2012.html; US Census Bureau Fact Sheet 2005–2009; "The African-American Market," Allied Media Corp., accessed January 16, 2016, http://www.allied-media.com/Publications/african_american_publications_.htm; Aaron Smith, "Mobile Access 2010," Pew Research Center, accessed January 16, 2016, http://www.pewinternet.org/Reports/2010/Mobile-Access-2010.aspx.

We should note the African-American subculture is not homogeneous. For example, different groups of African-American consumers have divergent views of hip-hop music. While the sound is popular with lower-class blacks and youths, older individuals in the middle class may respond negatively to it. National advertisers who employ hip-hop to reach black audiences may, in fact, be offending the very people they're attempting to reach, according to the authors of one study. The researchers noted that national advertisers perhaps should follow the lead of an Atlanta radio station that plays "songs you grew up on, and no rap."[28]

A critical issue marketers face in the promotion of products to black consumers involves liquor and cigarette advertising. Blacks spend relatively more of their income on liquor and cigarettes than whites, and advertising that specifically targets the group frequently draws fire from public-interest groups. For example, Heileman attempted to launch PowerMaster, a new brand with a high-alcohol content that was targeted to urban blacks. After a public outcry, the company backed off the brand. The next year, the company was again criticized when it sought to bring out Crazy Horse malt liquor—another high-alcohol brand. Later, Heileman began a repositioning effort for its Colt 45 malt liquor with an ad in which a young black college graduate gives advice to a younger friend. One official with the Institute on Black Chemical Abuse said, "[I]t's in poor taste. It's inaccurate to portray someone like the gentleman, with this sense of mission, yet acting as a proponent of malt liquor right there on the street."[29]

The Hispanic Subculture

Hispanics are the largest minority in the United States (see Table 14.2). It's been estimated that Mexican admissions alone represented 23 percent of all documented immigration into the United States between 1971 and 1990, although Mexican immigration has slowed in recent years and there may now be a net outflow.[30]

The **Hispanic subculture** is based on a number of factors that bind the group together. A common language unites most Hispanics: the primary language of 82 percent of US Hispanic households is Spanish.[31] A common religion, Catholicism, also imparts a sense of commonality to Hispanics (over 85 percent of Hispanics are Catholic). Hispanics also tend to live in metropolitan areas. Sixty-three percent of Hispanics live in urban areas (compared with 85 percent of the African-American population).[32] Because Hispanics share a similar language and religion and are concentrated geographically, they may make an outstanding target market.

The Hispanic subculture is also marked by a constant influx of new members through immigration, while others return home. A circular pattern exists. Many Hispanics enter the United States, stay for a length of time, and then leave. It has been estimated that about as many returned home as came into the United States between 2005 and 2010, which may be why American products sell so well in our southern neighbor nation.[33]

Hispanics reveal a highly conservative value structure. They're more likely than whites to express traditional American values concerning the importance of hard work, they're optimistic regarding their future standard of living, and they seek the "good life."[34] Hispanics tend to be more family oriented than Anglos, live more for the present, and be somewhat less competitive. Table 14.4 presents a number of important facts about the Hispanic market.

Managerial principle 14.3

The approximate stabilization of Hispanic immigration and possible current outflow still leave a very large subculture to target, including new immigrants. The cycle of returning Mexicans may also present opportunities to introduce products in Mexico that recent returnees have become accustomed to in the United States.

TABLE 14.4

Some Key Characteristics of the Hispanic Subculture

1.	Mexican Americans make up two-thirds of US Hispanic households.
2.	The average annual household income is nearly $41,000.
3.	Thirty-one percent of Hispanic households have an income of more than $50,000.
4.	On average, Hispanics spend more on in-home food preparation than non-Hispanics. They also outspend non-Hispanics in children's clothing and fashion.
5.	Over 80 percent of Hispanics watch Spanish-language TV—a percentage that's been rising in recent years.

Sources: "The 2011 Statistical Abstract," *US Census Bureau*, accessed January 22 2016, http://www.census.gov/compendia/statab/cats/income_expenditures_poverty_wealth.html; " Bouree Lam, "Black, White Asian, Hispanic: The Disparities in Household Income," accessed January 22, 2016, http://www.theatlantic.com/business/archive/2014/09/black-white-asian-hispanic-the-disparities-in-household-income/380314/

Hispanic Segmentation Despite some similarities, an important aspect of the study of Hispanics is recognizing they're not one homogeneous group. Speaking of a single Hispanic market segment is inappropriate.[35] At least four distinct groups (i.e., segments) exist—Mexican Americans (65.2 percent of US Hispanics), Central and South Americans (14.3 percent), Puerto Ricans (9.6 percent), and Cubans (4.3 percent). Among the four Hispanic groups, there are differences in the way Spanish is spoken, in food preferences (e.g., generally speaking, Mexicans eat refried beans, Cubans eat black beans, and Puerto Ricans eat red beans), and in political attitudes.

Each of the Hispanic groups is also geographically concentrated. Los Angeles, where 2.1 million Hispanics live, is considered the prime target area for reaching Mexican Americans. Similarly, Miami contains the largest concentration of Cubans (Miami is 62 percent Hispanic), and New York City has the largest number of Puerto Ricans.[36]

One other point of differentiation is the degree of acculturation. Hispanics range from new arrivals to tenth-generation (or more) descendants of immigrants. In addition to length of stay, fluency in English and general contact with the majority culture also influence the degree of preference for US products. Some products, such as clothing, are largely free of any language barrier and are easily adopted. Others, such as debit cards—obtaining and using—require more learning and adjustment. One study found Mexican Americans consumed more white bread, highly sugared cereals, and other unhealthy foods than either Anglos or Mexicans. It's been suggested this was due to a time-lag effect: Mexican immigrants had assimilated a version of the Anglo-American lifestyle that didn't reflect contemporary health concerns.[37]

Problems in Marketing to Hispanics   A number of problems exist in trying to market to the Hispanic subculture. As already noted, marketing to Puerto Ricans isn't the same as marketing to Cuban Americans or to Mexican Americans. Moreover, cultural differences may exist within each segment. One advertising executive declared, if the United States and Mexico went to war, Hispanics in California would likely fight for Mexico, while those in Texas would fight for the United States.[38]

A second problem in marketing to Hispanics is the differences in the type of Spanish spoken. The word for "earring," *pantella*, can mean "television screen" or even "lamp shade" to some Hispanics. In some areas of the United States, a bodega is a small, Hispanic-owned grocery, but in south Texas, it's a warehouse.[39]

The Asian-American Subculture

In the 1980s, over 40 percent of all immigrants to the United States came from Asia. Some estimate that, by the year 2050, the number of Asian Americans will nearly equal the number of Hispanics in the United States, who will be the largest minority by then. Asian Americans are already becoming a potent economic and intellectual force. The percentage of Asian Americans who graduate from college is nearly twice that of white Americans. In addition, family incomes of Asian Americans are higher than those of all other major ethnic groups in the US. To a greater degree than the differences that separate Hispanics, Asian Americans differ in language and culture of origin. Chinese, Vietnamese, Japanese, and Korean are the most common Asian languages spoken in the United States and are significantly different. Incomes also differ. The median household income for Asian Indians in the United States is $69,470, compared with only $43,850 for Cambodian, Hmong, or Laotian families.[40]

Comparing Anglo, African-American, and Hispanic Consumption

One study surveyed Anglo, African-American, and Hispanic consumers in order to compare the groups on a variety of consumption characteristics.[41] The results were inconsistent with a number of stereotypes concerning the groups. First, no evidence was found for differences in brand loyalty among the groups (Hispanics are often assumed to be very brand loyal). For brand loyalty, only an age effect occurred (respondents older than fifty-five reported being more brand loyal). No differences were found among the groups regarding coupon proneness, impulse buying, shopping for generic products, or the tendency to shop for specials. Both African Americans and Hispanics showed a greater tendency to shop for bargains. Overall, however, the results didn't reveal large differences among the groups on any of the variables.

Managerial principle 14.4
Avoid assuming stereotypes of ethnic subcultures are accurate. Marketing strategy should be based on sound marketing research and environmental analysis.

Portraying Minorities in Advertisements

One issue of concern to many has been the degree to which ethnic groups appear in advertising and commercials. Given their proportion in the US population, African Americans are slightly underrepresented in magazine advertisements, but Hispanics are even more underrepresented, whereas Asian Americans are slightly overrepresented. In addition, Hispanics and Asian Americans are more likely to be depicted in a major role in advertisements than are African Americans.[42]

On a final note, it's important to realize notions of race and ethnicity are becoming increasingly fluid. For example, one of the common assumptions about Chinese society is it developed in isolation from the West. But an archaeologist found 3,000-year-old corpses with European features and blond hair in western China, wearing textiles of a Celtic tartan style.[43] Again, caution is needed when using ethnicity or nationality as a marketing segmentation variable.

REGIONAL SUBCULTURES

Another major subcultural variable of interest to marketers concerns how populations locate themselves in the regions of the United States. Measuring and predicting the demographic patterns of **regional subcultures** is important to marketers for two reasons. First, different regions have distinct lifestyles resulting from variations in climate, culture, and the ethnic mix of people. Consequently, different product preferences exist. For example, there are regional preferences for foods and beverages. Some coffee manufacturers blend their coffee differently for the various regions—heavier in the East, lighter in the West, and with chicory in Louisiana.

A second reason for studying regional subcultures is their growth rates and size may vary dramatically. For many types of goods, it's important to shorten the distribution channel as much as possible. New production facilities, therefore, should be built in areas experiencing the greatest population growth. In addition, companies looking for new growth opportunities should possibly focus on regions expected to experience population increases.

Dramatic changes are occurring in the populations of the regions of the United States. In the past, the Northeast and North Central regions were the most heavily populated. But currently, three of the five most populated states (California, New York, Texas, Illinois, and Florida) are in the lower half of the United States. As a result of shifting demographics, corporations are changing their marketing emphasis—and in many cases, their corporate headquarters—to better focus on emerging markets. Political changes also occur. The 2010 census allocated eleven more Congressional seats to states in the South and the West, with states in the Northeast losing these seats.[44]

Regional population shifts occur for several reasons. One factor that affects these shifts is the search for jobs. During the severe recession of 1980–1982, for example, many workers moved from the North Central states to the West and Southwest in search of employment. People also move for lifestyle reasons. Florida has grown rapidly because of the huge influx of retirees seeking the sun in their retirement years. Although Northeastern states like Maine and New Hampshire have the highest median age population, Florida is the nation's "oldest" large state, with an average age of 41.[45]

A third reason for regional population shifts is a difference in birthrates. These differences take longer to manifest themselves, but over a period of ten to twenty years, the variations become meaningful. In general, the West is younger than the Northeast and North Central regions. The median age in the Northeast is greater than 30, whereas in the West it falls dramatically. For example, Alaska's median age is 28.3. Utah is the "youngest" state, with a median age of 25.5. In Utah's case, a confluence of demographic factors accounts for the state's youthfulness. The Mormon population and influence in Utah is large. A central focus of the religion is the importance of the family and of childbearing, which, in turn, keeps median age relatively low.

The combination of a net inflow of migration and a youthful population portend future above-average growth in the West. The youthful population there will tend to have higher birthrates than the older populations found in states in the Northeast and North Central regions.

Geodemographics

An area of study that's having major impact on marketing research is geodemographics. **Geodemographics** takes as its unit of analysis census blocks (i.e., the neighborhood) and obtains demographic information on consumers within neighborhoods. Census blocks found to contain people with similar demographic characteristics are clustered together to form potential target markets for companies. This process of identifying groups of neighborhoods with households that are demographically similar is called **cluster analysis**. One basic concept of geodemographics is individuals within a neighborhood have similar demographic characteristics, buying patterns, and values. A second important concept is neighborhoods may be placed into similar categories, even when they're widely separated.[46]

Geodemographic analysis can be an important managerial tool. In particular, geodemographics is a vital component of direct marketing. By contacting consumers directly with similar geodemographic profiles, companies can precisely target a market segment. The result is a much more efficient use of a company's resources. A number of national firms offer geodemographic analysis, such as ACORN in the United Kingdom and Nielsen PRIZM in the United States.

Geodemographic analysis is a marketing research technique used in segmenting the marketplace, repositioning brands, and designing the marketing mix. Neighborhoods identified as being in the same cluster then become market segments.

L.L.Bean was one of the early users of geodemographic analysis to segment the marketplace. Because the company mails expensive catalogs to potential customers, it had to find a cost-effective way of identifying "L.L.Bean types." PRIZM was hired to develop a geodemographic profile of the market segment L.L.Bean should target. Catalogs were then sent to zip codes possessing a high percentage of L.L.Bean-type neighborhoods. The company slowly built a database that not only identified where their clients lived but also what magazines they read, the television shows they watched, and even the products they owned.[47]

Geodemographic analysis can assist managers in designing the marketing mix by providing a detailed profile of where customers live, what they buy, and what their demographic characteristics are. In particular, the location of stores and the selection of merchandise for stores can be guided by geodemographics. Recently, market researchers have used geodemographic analysis to identify good locations for new golf courses. By determining where golf courses are

Managerial principle 14.5
Consider using a national firm for geodemographic analysis. Large firms with data-mining capabilities may find they can do their own analysis.

currently located and identifying a demographic profile of golfers and where they live, researchers can pinpoint areas of the United States that have a surplus of golfers in relation to the number of courses available. Figure 14.1 presents a map that depicts the concentrations of golfers in the Michigan area, with dark areas representing high concentrations of golfers. The map was drawn to assist managers in deciding whether to build a new golf resort, called Sugar Loaf. Based on the map, do you think the resort would be successful?

FIGURE 14.1

A Geodemographic Map Showing the Concentrations of Golfers in Michigan Near a Resort—Sugar Loaf

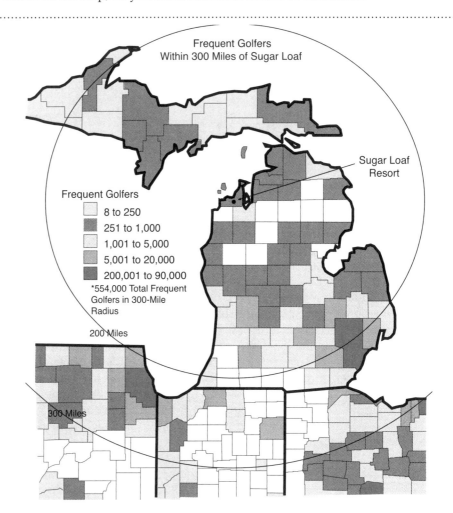

Should Companies Segment by Geography?

The question of whether companies should segment by geographical areas is similar to the question of whether global companies should standardize their products across all markets or adapt their offerings to local conditions. There's little doubt a national marketing effort is less expensive than a region-based strategy. As one consultant succinctly put it, "Breadth of choice equals complexity; complexity equals increasing costs."[48] For example, when Campbell's divided the country into twenty-two regions, it had to promote eighty-eight employees to brand sales managers, retrain its sales force, and make major changes in production—all costly moves. In addition, an effort to target a specific region frequently brings retaliation from local companies. When Campbell's introduced its Spicy Ranchero Beans into the Southwest, the area's dominant marketer of beans, Ranch Style Beans, retaliated with heavy advertising and sales promotions.

Despite the problems related to developing regional marketing strategies, many companies have begun using regional segmentation. For example, the thirty-two teams of the National Football League present a dilemma for store chains selling league merchandise. Although a few teams, such as the Dallas Cowboys, have a national following, in many cases, regional teams draw the largest interest. A national chain such as Footlocker, therefore, must consider the appropriate mix of "national" versus "regional" teams to feature in its stores.[49]

....

SOCIAL-CLASS SUBCULTURES

Social classes may be defined as the relatively permanent strata in a society that differ in status, wealth, education, possessions, and values. All societies possess a hierarchical structure that stratifies residents into classes of people. Both actual and perceptual factors distinguish the groups. In concrete terms, classes differ in occupations, lifestyles, values, friendships, manner of speaking, and possessions. In perceptual terms, individuals perceive that different classes have diverging amounts of prestige, power, and privilege. Finally, members of a class tend to socialize with each other rather than with members of other classes. As one theorist observed, social classes are multidimensional.

Three primary factors differentiate the social classes: economic status (e.g., occupation, wealth, and house type and location), educational credentials, and behavioral standards (e.g., community participation, aspirations, and recreational habits).[50]

In the relatively egalitarian culture of the United States, discussions of social class may make people uncomfortable. When answering an interviewer's question about social class, one woman said, "It's the dirtiest thing I've ever heard of."[51] Despite its unpleasant connotations, the study of social class has important managerial implications for marketers. Therefore, despite the discomfort, we discuss it.

In comparison with how the term is used by sociologists, marketing managers interpret the concept of social class narrowly. Marketers are concerned with how the buying patterns of social classes differ rather than with the political, institutional, and cultural reasons for their existence. For marketers, the social classes are seen as subcultures with distinct lifestyles, buying patterns, and motivations.[52] Thus, they view the social classes as potential market segments possessing divergent needs, wants, and desires for products and services.

Table 14.5 provides a social-class hierarchy scheme and summarizes some of the characteristics of the social classes. The descriptions given in the table have proved quite accurate for at least the last fifty years in the United States. Recent trends, however, are creating some subtle changes. One trend is a new group of people who could be placed in the lower-upper class. These are professionals who marry and form two-career families. Because of their high incomes and need to juggle two careers, these families have become a separate target market. For example, when one spouse must move because of job relocation, the other spouse may need help finding employment comparable to the current position, and businesses have sprung up to cater to this need.[53]

TABLE 14.5
The Social-Class Hierarchy

What Are the Social Classes?
A. Upper-Class Americans
Upper-upper (0.3%). The world of inherited wealth and old family names. Working is a matter of choice, and members often serve on the boards of directors of major corporations. Members of this class serve as a reference for lower classes. Not a major market segment because of its small size.
Lower-upper (1.2%). The newer social elite, drawn from current professionals and corporate leadership. May be extremely wealthy, but the money is relatively new. Is an achieving group and will spend money to show its wealth. Will guard its social-class position because of insecurity. Is a major market for specialized luxury goods, such as Mercedes automobiles.
Upper-middle (12.5%). The rest of college-graduate managers, intellectual elite, and professionals. Lifestyle centers on private clubs, causes, and the arts. Collegiate credentials expected. Housing is extremely important to this group, particularly where the house is located. The quality and appearance of products are also important.
B. Middle-Class Americans
Middle class (32%). White-collar workers and their blue-collar friends. Live on "the better side of town," try to "do the proper things." Have white-collar friends and acquaintances. Respectability is a key idea for this group. Home ownership, high moral standards, and focus on the family are important ideals. They tend to have high-school educations or some college but don't reach high levels in their organizations.
Working class (38%). Blue-collar workers. Lead "working-class lifestyle" whatever their income, school background, and job. Jobs tend to be monotonous, although affluence is possible if they have a union job. Tend to stay close to their parents and relatives and live in older parts of town. Do have money for consumer products and, with the middle class, represent the market for mass consumer goods.
C. Lower-Class Americans
Upper-lower (9%). Working, not on welfare. Living standard is just above the poverty level. Behavior judged as "crude" and "trashy." Tend to be unskilled workers.
Lower-lower (7%). On welfare, visibly poverty stricken, usually out of work (or have the "dirtiest jobs"). Some are bums, common criminals. This group has become separated from the upper-lower group because it exists mainly on government transfer payments. With the upper-lower class, accounts for only 6%–7% of disposable income.

Source: Data adapted from Richard P. Coleman, "The Continuing Significance of Social Class in Marketing." *Journal of Consumer Research* 10 (December 1983): 265–280.

Differences between social classes are evident in their communication patterns. One study found people can identify an individual's social class simply by hearing him or her read something.[54] Social classes differ in their speech cadence, voice modulation, and fluency of speech. The choice of words also varies among the social classes.[55] Lower classes describe the world in more concrete terms than do the middle and upper classes. If asked where he or she obtained bubble gum, a lower-class child would likely state a person's name. An upper-class child would provide a more general answer and state simply, "From the grocery store."

Although most marketers agree social class is an important concept, published examples of its use in marketing are sparse because there are a number of problems in using social class as a segmentation variable. One problem in measuring social class is the measures assume an individual's social class is an average of his or her position on several dimensions of status. The consistency with which an individual reveals a particular social class across a number of dimensions is called **status crystallization**. Some have argued those who have low crystallization are more prone to express liberal ideas and advocate changes in the social order.[56] An example of low crystallization might be a Hispanic attorney whose parents were laborers.

Social Class and Buying Behavior

Because of the problems of the social-class concept, one must use caution in interpreting the findings of studies investigating its impact on buying behavior. One finding of importance to marketers is the reasons for shopping differ among the social classes. The upper classes tend to shop not only out of necessity but also for pleasure.[57] Higher-class women tend to favor stores with a high-fashion image, such as the Neiman Marcus chain, whereas lower-class women favor mass merchandisers and stores with price appeal. The shopping patterns of the upper class reveal the importance of maintaining a certain social image. Products that reflect differences in class, such as furniture, are viewed as "socially risky." Upper-class consumers tend to purchase such products from specialty shops and department stores geared to providing personal service in an upscale atmosphere. For low-risk products, such as toasters, the upper-class shopper is perfectly willing to buy a brand-name product from a discounter. The relationship between income and willingness to buy store-brand rather than national-brand merchandise may be curvilinear: low-income and higher-income shoppers are less likely to buy store brands than those in between.[58]

The social classes also differ in the amount and type of information search behavior done prior to and during shopping. Middle- and upper-class consumers tend to engage in more information search prior to making a purchase. For example, before buying appliances, they may read newspapers, brochures, and test reports. In contrast, lower-class consumers are more apt to rely on in-store displays and salespeople.[59] In general, lower-class consumers have less product information. They are less informed about product prices and are no more likely to buy products on sale than are upper-class consumers. Upper-class consumers are also less likely to use price as an indicator of quality. They tend to judge the quality of products on their merits rather than on their price.

Managerial principle 14.6 Note that shopping behavior can be affected by wide environmental trends. During the Great Recession, Walmart found itself serving more upscale customers than usual. Income had dropped for some, but others were becoming more cost-conscious and the effect generalized to those whose high income was stable or even rising.

Psychological Differences among the Classes

Many of the differences noted in the consumption behaviors of the social classes can be explained by differences in the way each views the world. Members of the middle classes tend to focus on the future. They're generally self-confident, are willing to take risks, believe they can control their fate, and see their horizons as broad. In contrast, the lower classes focus on the present and the past. They're concerned with security, their family, and themselves.

Psychological differences in the social classes were demonstrated in a study that investigated how groups of consumers differed in their perception of the symbolism of products.[60] Lower-class individuals tended to believe owners of big houses and nice cars obtained them because of good luck. In contrast, consumers with higher social status attributed the ability to purchase status symbols to the self-motivation of the owner. Such results indicate a more fatalistic view of life among the lower classes. These psychological and lifestyle differences are summed up by the following quotation:

> For twenty years researchers have found that "working-class life styles have been almost impervious to change in their basic characteristics—i.e., the limited horizons, the centrality of family and clan. The chauvinistic devotion to nation and neighborhood have been little altered by the automobile, telephone, or television. The modernity—and change—that these people seek is in possessions, not in human relationships or 'new ideas.'"[61]

Social Class and Lifestyles

As a macroenvironmental force, social class strongly influences consumer lifestyles. Four generalizations can be made concerning the impact of social class on consumer lifestyles: social class influences lifestyle, social class is predictive of resources owned, goods may be purchased as status symbols, and consumption of status symbols is a skill.

Social Class Influences Consumer Lifestyles   Perhaps the most important contribution of social class to the understanding of consumer behavior is it strongly influences lifestyle. Max Weber was perhaps the earliest researcher to link social class and lifestyle, although he viewed lifestyle as more closely linked to status than to class. Some consumer researchers have even argued lifestyle is the "essence of social class."[62] The style of consumption (i.e., lifestyle) may be viewed as an expression of a particular social class. How consumers live is directly influenced by their education, household income, occupation, and type of house. Level of education tends to influence a person's activities, interests, opinions, values, and beliefs. Household income influences the capacity to purchase consumer goods and to express other interests. Occupation influences the type of people with whom a person associates as well as the types of products and services a person purchases to play the occupational role. As noted in Chapter 12, the products and services a person must have in order to engage effectively in a particular role are called a role-related product cluster.[63] A stereotypical view of the role-related product cluster of a successful young attorney or stockbroker might include an Armani suit, a luxury car, and a vacation home.

Social Class Is Predictive of Resources Owned   Four resource dimensions have been identified as influenced by social class—financial, social, cultural, and time. First, those in higher social classes tend to have greater financial resources because of their occupations or inherited wealth. Second, as one moves higher in social-class level, opportunities for social participation increase, and associations are made with those of higher social standing. The level of social participation generally rises as social status increases. Social skill and social standing appear to be closely linked.[64] Third, those in higher social classes tend to be familiar with cultural matters. In addition, higher-education credentials provide "cultural capital" for individuals. Finally, those in higher social classes tend to have a broader time horizon than those in lower social classes. The higher social classes require people both to have longer time horizons and to delay gratification while building personal skills through education. Those in higher social classes frequently have less free time but have more flexibility in choosing the activities on which to spend their time.

Goods May Be Purchased As Status Symbols   Products and services may be purchased as a means of showing membership in a particular social class. Goods and services may represent social-class standing because of restrictions that make it difficult for individuals not in the social class to own them. These restrictions tend to arise because individuals in lower social classes lack the resources to purchase or effectively use these status symbols. For example, in the United States, owning a BMW or Mercedes-Benz has come to represent membership in the lower-upper class for many individuals. Similarly, a high level of educational resources is required to read and enjoy certain magazines, such as the *New Yorker*, that are indicative of upper-middle-class standing.

It has long been recognized that, in order to depict social status, people must display appropriate material items. This is because we frequently encounter individuals who are strangers, and the only way to ascertain a person's status is through visual cues. There's a problem, however, in portraying social class through material goods. If the ownership of a material symbol is diffused across levels of the class hierarchy, it becomes a **fraudulent symbol**.[65] That is, if members of different social classes display the same symbol of status, it won't accurately depict the meaning desired. For a material item to adequately symbolize social-class standing, accuracy is required in both the encoding and decoding stages.[66]

Ownership of the material item must be homogeneous within a single social class in order for accurate encoding to occur. Thus, people within the class should consistently possess the good. In addition, there must be wide agreement that possession of the item symbolizes a particular social-class standing. When a shared status meaning is attached to a material good by society at large, accuracy in decoding occurs. Examples of material symbols individuals decode in a consistent manner are clothing, health care, automobiles, and housing.[67] Another material symbol people accurately encode and decode is the possession of hired household help. The presence of chauffeurs, cooks, and gardeners is indicative of an individual in the upper classes.

Managerial principle 14.7
Consider the strategy of Louis Vuitton (LV). As more downscale customers wanted the company's products, its "starter" items began to display the brand name in very large letters. But the most upscale LV products carry no brand name at all. Only a haute couture client can now recognize the most-upscale LV items.

Consumption of Status Symbols Is a Skill   The adroit purchase of goods and services can be used to solidify or help advance an individual's social-class standing. Individuals who fail to represent their social class via the "correct" visible symbols risk scorn and the disrespectful title of "nouveau riche." Learning to make the correct purchases is a type of skill. The problems associated with moving rapidly from one class to another have been grist for Hollywood movie makers. In *The Princess Diaries*, for example, Anne Hathaway plays an ordinary girl who becomes a princess overnight.

An argument can be made that a great deal of status anxiety currently exists in the United States. The number of consumption guides, fashion experts, interior decorators, and real estate professionals suggests great concern about appropriate consumption. People wouldn't hire these surrogate consumers if the accurate display of symbolic material goods were unimportant. The need to purchase the "correct" goods and services to support or help advance status has created an entire class of surrogate consumers.

OTHER SUBCULTURES

Because space limitations restrict a full discussion of all the various subcultures available for target marketing, only a few are outlined here. One geographically based subculture is represented by the increase in population of rural areas. From 1990 to 1995, three-quarters of the rural counties in the United States grew in population, reversing the pattern of the 1980s. This movement was spearheaded by those looking for retirement living or recreational uses. The rise in telecommuting and long-distance driving may be allowing more workers to move into rural areas as well. Another subculture is made up of the some 56.7 million living in the US who are disabled in some way, a segment of the population that offers additional marketing opportunities. [68]

THE MANAGERIAL IMPLICATIONS OF SUBCULTURES AND DEMOGRAPHICS

Subcultures have application to each of the RESPonsive Marketing strategy concepts. First, marketing researchers can conduct studies to identify the subcultural-difference variables that motivate consumers to action. Second, if different groups within the target market share similar subcultural characteristics, they can become segments that may be targeted. Third, by developing an understanding of a target market's subcultural and demographic characteristics, promotional messages can be developed that will tap into the group's needs and wants. Finally, companies can position brands based on a subcultural- or demographic-difference characteristic of a target market. These ideas are discussed more fully below.

Research

Market research can identify the unmet needs of various subcultures. However, attention also needs to be paid to the possibility that "representative samples" may, in fact, not be representative. As discussed in this chapter, there are a number of divisive elements within the Hispanic and Asian-American subcultures (e.g., country of origin) that can prevent a sample from representing the subculture as a whole. At the extreme, a third-generation Hispanic attorney from Houston who graduated from Harvard Law School and drives a BMW may have less in common with new immigrants from Central America than she does with other big-city attorneys. Although this case isn't typical, marketing mistakes are possible if attention isn't paid to the forces that divide, as well as unite, a particular subculture.

Environmental Analysis

Marketing managers should conduct environmental analyses in order to track changes in the size of a market for any product or service. Segments of appropriate size and buying power can then be identified and specific products developed and promoted for the target groups.

In addition to carefully analyzing age trends, marketers should conduct broader-scale demographic analyses. Environmental analyses should be conducted to identify changes in the ethnic composition of the population, which may reveal new consumer segments to be targeted.

Segmentation

An example of a manufacturer using ethnic subculture appeals as a segmentation device is Mattel. The company now offers the Barbie doll (born on March 9, 1959, she's a baby boomer) as representative of a variety of ethnic and national subgroups. There is, for example, a Puerto Rican Barbie, and Spanish, Swedish, and Northwest Coast Native American Barbies In addition to segmenting along ethnic lines, Mattel also offers a wheelchair Barbie, a WiFi and speech recognition- equipped Barbie that can converse, and in 2016, four new realistic body types.

Positioning and Differentiation

One method of positioning a product is to differentiate it vis-à-vis competitors by making special appeals to subgroups or subcultures. As an example, the appeal of the popular music industry has continued and even increased due to ever-finer positioning of music to narrower targets. "Rock" music is now subdivided into "light," "punk," "industrial," and other forms. At the same time, musical "products" once targeted to small subcultural markets are now finding opportunities to mainstream themselves. For example, both country and Latin music have expanded well beyond their subcultural roots.

Marketing Mix

Differences between age cohorts, ethnic groups, regions, and social classes have implications for differences in promotional, product, and pricing strategies. Multiple examples (e.g., Levi's, Sears) demonstrate the need to respond to changes in age cohorts. The makers of Pokémon face the issue of how to retain interest in new cohorts of preteens; the conventional wisdom is that this fad will soon end, and preteens will move on to a new fantasy world. Nintendo has built a $6 billion empire whose survival depends on the outcome. The makers are counting on a synergy between collectible elements (e.g., Beanie Babies, Cabbage Patch Dolls, and baseball cards), a complete mythology (e.g., Power Rangers), and a raft of websites (starting with www.pokemon.com), shows, and games to keep interest flowing for years to come. One can even buy sheet music to teach the Pokémon theme to budding pianists and guitar players.

SUMMARY

How do subcultures differ from demographic groups?

A subculture is a group of people who make up a subdivision of a national culture. One or more features distinguish a subculture, whose member share patterns of behavior distinct from those found in the larger culture. Demographic characteristics, such as age and religion, are often used to identify subcultures.

What are the dominant types of subcultures within the United States?

Age groups particularly important for marketers in the twenty-first century are the baby-boom generation and the elderly (increasingly, these groups are becoming the same). The 72 million children of the baby boomers— millennials— are now entering their peak earning years.

African Americans and Hispanics are the major ethnic subcultures in the United States. The increase in immigration from Mexico now about equals the number of Mexicans leaving the United States to return home, a process aided by the slow growth in jobs in the United States and better opportunities in Mexico over the past few years.

Another basis for classification of subcultures is region of the country. A region may develop a distinct subculture for a number of reasons. Differences in the religion, ethnicity, and nationality of the people who settle in an area can make for a distinct set of values and behavior patterns. For example, Utah has a distinct subculture largely because of the influence of the Church of Jesus Christ of Latter-Day Saints, or Mormons. Southern Louisiana is another example of a distinct regional subculture, as is deep South Texas, which blends Mexican and American cultures.

Social classes also represent distinct subcultures. A variety of factors distinguish the social classes, including occupation, wealth, education, possessions, values, housing, and associations. A market may be segmented along the lines of social class.

Perhaps the most important social-class factor for understanding consumer behavior is social status influences lifestyles. Social-class membership is often predictive of resources. In addition, many goods and services are bought for their symbolic value in representing a particular social class. The "correct" consumption of status symbols is a skill. Consumers who are uncomfortable with their skill level may locate surrogate consumers to assist them in making the "correct" purchases.

Do the elderly process information differently than young adults?

The aging of the population will be one of the most dominant demographic factors for the future. By 2020, those over sixty-five will outnumber teenagers two to one. Mature consumers differ from younger people in two major aspects. First, in certain ways, mature consumers process information differently. Second, mature consumers may differ from younger consumers in motor skills.

What makes the African-American and other subcultures important markets?

The African-American culture is large and possesses great spending power, is increasing in size faster than the general population, and is rising in socioeconomic status. The subculture is also younger than the general population. A majority of the African-American population is urban and lives in large cities.

KEY TERMS

baby bust	demographic variables	fraudulent symbol
baby-boom generation	ethnicity	Generation X
cluster analysis	fertility rate	geodemographics

Hispanic subculture

mortality rates

status crystallization

mature consumer

regional subcultures

subculture

millennials

social classes

REVIEW QUESTIONS

1. Identify six different types of subcultures in the United States.
2. Define the term *subculture*.
3. Describe the baby-boom generation. Discuss the impact of this group on two industries.
4. Identify three ways in which the elderly process information differently from the rest of the adult population.
5. Four segments of the Hispanic subculture have been identified based on ancestry. Identify these segments and give their relative sizes.
6. What are some of the reasons for regional shifts in population?
7. Define the concept of social class.
8. Provide two examples of how upper and lower social classes differ in their shopping patterns and leisure activities.
9. What's the correlation between social class and income?
10. Identify the ways social class may influence consumer lifestyles.

DISCUSSION QUESTIONS

1. Subcultures can be found in most large collections of people. Identify as many subcultures as you can within the university or college you are attending. Describe the norms, values, and behaviors of those subcultures that set them apart from one another.
2. Because of the long lead times required for planning and bringing new products to market, managers must often look five to ten years into the future. What marketing opportunities and problems might the baby boomers present to managers between 2016 and 2026?
3. You're the marketing manager for an investment group that's developing a shopping center targeted to the elderly market. What types of services, stores, and amenities would you attempt to provide in the shopping center? What problems might you encounter in targeting a shopping center specifically for the elderly?
4. You're the marketing director for a company planning to establish a chain of new department stores targeted to customers with incomes greater than $150,000. What considerations would influence your decisions as to where to locate the stores geographically?

5. Identify a product for which the marketing mix must be varied across the geographical regions of the United States. Explain why the marketing mix should be varied for the product.

6. Identify the various department stores in your region of the country and the social classes that each of these stores appears to target.

7. Just as we assign people to social classes, we also rank institutions of higher education by prestige. Identify two institutions that can be placed into each of the following classifications: highest prestige, moderately high prestige, middle prestige, and low prestige. What criteria determine how the universities are classified?

8. Why is it that people in the United States (including the authors of this text) tend to be uncomfortable discussing the topic of social class?

9. Do you think social-class mobility is increasing or decreasing in the United States.? What are the primary means of upward mobility today?

10. Conduct a quick survey among ten of your acquaintances designed to identify the types of goods and services they consider status symbols. Provide the results.

11. Men's grooming products are the fastest growing segment of the skin-care industry. How would you target this demographic segment?

ENDNOTES

[1] "Adele Biography," *Adele*, accessed January 14, 2016, adele.com and Hannah Karp, "Adele's Most Fervent Fans: Soccer Moms," *Wall Street Journal*, November 19, 2015 accessed January 31, 2016, http://www.wsj.com/articles/adeles-most-fervent-fans-soccer-moms-1447963361

[2] "Hebrew National—Answering to a Higher Authority," *Tori Avey*, accessed January 14, 2016, http://toriavey.com/toris-corner/2012/06/hebrew-national-answering-to-a-higher-authority/.

[3] D. O. Arnold, *The Sociology of Subcultures* (Berkeley, CA: Glendasary Press, 1970).

[4] R. T. Reynolds, B. Robey, and C. Russell, "Demographics of the 1980s," *American Demographics* (January 1980), 11–19.

[5] "Americans Change," *Businessweek*, February 20, 1978, 64–80.

[6] Campbell Gibson, "The Four Baby Booms," *American Demographics* (November 1993), 37–40.

[7] "Saggy Pants Ban," *Huffington Post*, January 14, 2016, accessed January 14, 2016, http://www.huffingtonpost.com/news/saggy-pants-ban/.

[8] David Plotz, "Defining Decay Down: Why Dentists Still Exist," *Slate*, August 18, 1999, accessed January 14, 2016, http://www.slate.com/articles/briefing/articles/1999/08/defining_decay_down.html.

[9] Christina Buff, "Passing the Bucks: Aging Boomers Cut the Cord but Can't Let Go of the Wallet," *Wall Street Journal*, July 8, 1996, A1, A5.

[10] Ronald Alsop, "Busters May Replace Boomers as the Darlings of Advertisers," *Wall Street Journal*, November 12, 1987, 35; Chris Manolis, Aron Levin, and Robert Dahlstrom, "A Generation X Scale: Conceptualization, Measurement, and Nomological Validity," *Marketing Theory and Applications*, vol. 7, ed. Edward Blair and Wagner A. Kamakura (Chicago: American Marketing Association, 1996), 435–436.

[11] Diane Summers, "A View of the X-Files," *Financial Times*, January 20, 1996, 11.

[12] Jennifer DeCoursey, "Growing Pains Plague Generation X Magazines," *Advertising Age*, November 5, 1995, S24.

[13] Richard Tomkins, "Shaking Out the Last Dollop of Growth," *Financial Times*, June 12–13, 1999, 7.

14 Raymond Serafin and Cleveland Horton, "X Marks the Spot for Car Marketing," *Advertising Age*, August 9, 1993, 8.

15 Cyndee Miller, "Teens Seen As the First Truly Global Customers," *Marketing News*, March 27, 1995, 9.

16 Susan Mitchell, "The Next Baby Boom," *American Demographics*, October 1995, 22–31; "Missing Mom or Dad," *Pew Research Center*, March 22, 2010, accessed January 14, 2016, http://pewresearch.org/databank/dailynumber/?NumberID=969.

17 Emily Nelson, "Why Teenage Sitters Have So Much Power," *Wall Street Journal*, September 26, 1996, B1, B7.

18 Gerald Celente, "Sons and Daughters of Woodstock Say 'Hell, No,'" *Financial Times Weekend Supplement*, January 2–3, 1999, 3.

19 Rick Christie, "Marketers Err by Treating Elderly as Uniform Group," *Wall Street Journal*, October 31, 1988, B1, B3.

20. Fabian Linden and Paul Ryscavage, *How We Live: Then and Now* (Washington, DC: US Bureau of the Census, 1986); US Department of Commerce, *Statistical Abstract of the United States, 1995* (Washington, DC: US Government Printing Office, 1995), 399 and Braedyn Kromer and David Howard, "Labor Force Participation and Work Status of People 65 Years and Older,".accessed January 21, 2016, http://r.search.yahoo.com/_ylt=AwrBT_w7iqJWFFwAkllXNyoA;_ylu=X3oDMTEyMGxxcXRsBGNvbG8DYmYxBHBvcwM3BHZ0aWQDQTAyMDBfMQRzZW MDc3I-/RV=2/RE=1453521596/RO=10/RU=http%3a%2f%2fwww.census.gov%2fprod %2f2013pubs%2facsbr11-09.pdf/RK=0/RS=aBd8z3jbCeAnfZDNn3TKKaosvGg-

21 Catherine A. Cole and Siva K. Balasubramanian, "Age Differences in Consumers' Search for Information: Public Policy Implications," *Journal of Consumer Research* 20 (June 1993): 157–169.

22 Jack Botwinick, *Aging and Behavior: A Comprehensive Integration of Research Findings*, 2nd ed. (New York: Springer, 1978).

23 L. G. Schiffman, "Perceived Risk in New Product Trial by Elderly Consumers," *Journal of Marketing Research* 9 (February 1972): 106–108.

24 Rose L. Johnson, "Age and Social Activity As Correlates of Television Orientation: A Replication and Extension," *Advances in Consumer Research*, vol. 20, ed. Leigh McAlister and Michael L. Rothschild (Provo, UT: Association for Consumer Research, 1993), 257–261.

25 Gabrielle Sandor, "Attitude (Not Age) Defines the Mature Market," *American Demographics* (January 1994): 18–21; Benny Barak and Leon Schiffman, "Cognitive Age: A Nonchronological Age Variable," in *Advances in Consumer Research*, vol. 8, ed. Kent B. Monroe (Ann Arbor, MI: Association for Consumer Research, 1981), 602–606; Robert E. Wilkes, "A Structural Modeling Approach to the Measurement and Meaning of Cognitive Age," *Journal of Consumer Research* 19 (September 1992): 292–301.

26 Margaret Simms, Karina Fortuny, and Everett Henderson, "Racial and Ethnic Disparities among Low-Income Families," Urban Institute, accessed January 14, 2016, http://www.urban.org/research/publication/racial-and-ethnic-disparities-among-low-income-families.

27 Jennifer Edson Escalas, "African-American Vernacular English in Advertising: A Sociolinguistic Study," in *Advances in Consumer Research*, vol. 21, ed. Chris T. Allen and Deborah Roedder John (Provo, UT: Association for Consumer Research, 1994), 304–309.

28 Lydia A. McKinley-Floyd, J. R. Smith, and Hudson Nwakanma, "The Impact of Social Class on African American Consumer Behavior: An Interdisciplinary Perspective," in *Marketing Theory and Applications*, vol. 5, ed. C. Whan Park and Daniel C. Smith (Chicago: American Marketing Association, 1994), 384–389.

29 Laura Bird, "Critics Shoot at New Colt 45 Campaign," *Wall Street Journal*, February 17, 1993, B1.

30 Karthick Ramakrishnan, "Mexican Migrants are Heading Back Home—and That's Bad News for the US Economy," *Los Angeles Times*, November 27, 2015, accessed January 14, 2016, http://www.latimes.com/opinion/op-ed/la-oe-1127-ramakrishnan-net-outflow-20151127-story.html.

31 Lisa A. Yorgey, "Cultured Creative," *Target Marketing* (November 1995): 22–28.

32 Daniel McQuillen, "Cities of Gold," *Incentive* (February 1996): 38–40. Other estimates place the number of Hispanics living in urban areas at up to 88 percent. See Lisa Peñaloza, *"Atravesando Fronteras*: Border Crossings: A Critical Ethnographic Exploration of the Consumer Acculturation of Mexican Immigrants," *Journal of Consumer Research* 21, no. 1 (June 1994): 32–54.

33 B. G. Yovovich, "Cultural Pride Galvanizes Heritages," *Advertising Age* (February 15, 1982): M9, M44; Miriam Jordan, "Tide Turns on Border Crossing," *Wall Street Journal*, April 23, 2012,

accessed January 14, 2016, http://online.wsj.com/article/SB1000142405270230345900457736222
11298534158.html.

[34] B. A. Brusco, "Hispanic Marketing: New Application of Old Methodologies," *Theme* (May–June
1981): 8–9.

[35] Joel Saegert, Francis Piron, and Rosemary Jimenez, "Do Hispanics Constitute a Market
Segment?" in *Advances in Consumer Research*, vol. 19, ed. John Sherry and Brian Sternthal
(Provo, UT: Association for Consumer Research, 1992), 28–33.

[36] Marilyn Lavin, "Acculturating the Hispanic Consumer: The Grocery Shopping Experience,"
Marketing Theory and Applications, vol. 6, ed. David W. Stewart and Naufel J. Vilcassim
(Chicago: American Marketing Association, 1995), 359–364.

[37] Melanie Wallendorf and Michael R. Reilly, "Ethnic Migration, Assimilation, and Consumption,"
Journal of Consumer Research 10 (December 1983): 292–302. Cited in Lisa Peñaloza, "*Atravesando
Fronteras*: Border Crossings: A Critical Ethnographic Exploration of the Consumer
Acculturation of Mexican Immigrants," *Journal of Consumer Research* 21, no. 1 (June 1994):
32–54.

[38] John Sugg, "Miami's Latino Market Spans Two Continents," *Advertising Age* (February 15, 1982):
M9, M44.

[39] Additional problems occur when companies are politically incorrect in a foreign language.
Microsoft accidentally released a Spanish-language thesaurus suggesting Indians can be
equated with man-eating savages and offering "bastard" as a synonym for those of mixed race.
Don Clark, "Hey, #@*% Amigo, Can You Translate the Word 'Gaffe'?" *Wall Street Journal*, July
8, 1996, B6.

[40] US Census Bureau, "Income and Poverty Status of Americans Improve, Health Insurance
Coverage Stable, Census Bureau Reports," press release, September 26, 1996; "Socioeconomic
Statistics and Demographics," *Asian Nation*, accessed January 14, 2016, http://www.asian-
nation.org/demographics.shtml.

[41] Robert E. Wilkes and Humberto Valencia, "Shopping-Related Characteristics of Mexican
Americans and Blacks," *Psychology and Marketing* 3 (1986): 247–259. See also Francis J. Mulhern
and Jerome B Williams, "A Comparative Analysis of Shopping Behavior in Hispanic and Non-
Hispanic Shopping Areas," *Journal of Retailing* 70 (Fall 1994): 231–252.

[42] Charles R. Taylor, Ju Yung Lee, and Barbara B. Stern, "Portrayals of African, Hispanic, and
Asian Americans in Magazine Advertising," in *Marketing and Consumer Research in the Public
Interest*, ed. Ronald P. Hill (Thousand Oaks, CA: Sage, 1996), 133–150; Leon E. Wynter,
"Business and Race," *Wall Street Journal*, November 6, 1996, B1.

[43] Gale Eisenstodt, "Myths and Mummies," *Financial Times Weekend Supplement*, August 28–29,
1998, 1.

[44] "US Population Shift Accelerates to South, West States, 2010 Census Shows," *Bloomberg*,
December 21, 2010, accessed January 14, 2016, http://www.bloomberg.com/news/2010-12-22/u-
s-population-shift-accelerates-to-south-west-states-2010-census-shows.html and "Median age
of U.S. population in 2014, by state, " accessed February 2, 2016, http://www.statista.com/
statistics/208048/median-age-of-population-in-the-usa-by-state/.

[45] US Department of Commerce, *Statistical Abstract of the United States, 1995* (Washington, DC: US
Government Printing Office, 1995), 33.

[46] David J. Curry, *The New Marketing Research Systems: How to Use Strategic Database Information for
Better Marketing Decisions* (New York: Wiley, 1993).

[47] Ibid.

[48] Alix M. Freedman, "National Firms Find That Selling Local Tastes Is Costly, Complex," *Wall
Street Journal*, February 9, 1987, 17.

[49] Andrew Gaffney and Andy Bernstein, "Jim Connelly," *Sporting Goods Business* (February 1996):
62–65.

[50] Richard Coleman, "The Continuing Significance of Social Class in Marketing," *Journal of
Consumer Research* 10 (December 1983): 265–280.

[51] R. H. Tawney, *Equality* (London: Union Books, 1981).

[52] James Carmen, *The Application of Social Class in Market Segmentation* (Berkeley, CA: Institute of
Business and Economic Research, 1965).

[53] Bill Leonard and Roger D. Sommer, "Relocating the Two-Income Family," *HR Magazine* (August
1995): 55–58.

[54] Dean Ellis, "Speech and Social Status in America," *Social Forces* 45 (March 1967): 431–437.

[55] Leonard Schatzman and A. Strauss, "Social Class and Modes of Communication," *American Journal of Sociology* 60 (January 1955): 329–338.

[56] The classic reference is Gerhard Lenski, "Status Crystallization: A Non-Vertical Dimension of Social Status," *American Sociological Review* 21 (August 1956): 458–464.

[57] Stuart Rich and Subhash Jain, "Social Class and Life Cycle as Predictors of Shopping Behavior," *Journal of Marketing Research* 5 (February 1968): 43–44.

[58] Alan Dick, Arun Jain, and Paul Richardson, "Correlates of Store Brand Proneness: Some Empirical Observations," *Journal of Product and Brand Management* 4, no. 4 (1995): 15–22.

[59] V. Kanti Prasad, "Socioeconomic Product Risk and Patronage Preferences of Retail Shoppers," *Journal of Marketing* 39 (July 1975): 42–47.

[60] Russell Belk, Robert Mayer, and Kenneth Bahn, "The Eye of the Beholder: Individual Differences in Perceptions of Consumption Symbolism," in *Advances in Consumer Research*, vol. 9, ed. Andrew Mitchell (Ann Arbor, MI: Association for Consumer Research, 1981), 523–529.

[61] Cited in Richard Coleman, "The Continuing Significance of Social Class in Marketing," *Journal of Consumer Research* 10 (December 1983): 265–280.

[62] J. H. Myers and Jonathan Guttman, "Life Style: The Essence of Social Class," in *Lifestyle and Psychographics*, ed. William Wells (Chicago: American Marketing Association, 1974), 235–256.

[63] Another group of authors has called this the "standard package" for both different occupational groups and for different cultural groups (e.g., Asian Americans). See Cecelia Wittmayer, Steve Schulz, and Robert Mittelstaedt, "A Cross-Cultural Look at the 'Supposed to Have It' Phenomenon: The Existence of a Standard Package Based on Occupation," in *Advances in Consumer Research*, vol. 21, ed. Chris T. Allen and Deborah Roedder John (Provo, UT: Association for Consumer Research, 1994), 427–434.

[64] Much of this section is based on ideas suggested by James Fisher, "Social Class and Consumer Behavior: The Relevance of Class and Status," in *Advances in Consumer Research*, vol. 14, ed. Melanie Wallendorf and Paul Anderson (Provo, UT: Association for Consumer Research, 1987), 492–496.

[65] Erving Goffman, "Symbols of Class Status," *British Journal of Sociology* 2 (December 1951): 294–304.

[66] Russell Belk, "Developmental Recognition of Consumption Symbolism," *Journal of Consumer Research* 9 (June 1982): 887–897.

[67] Scott Dawson and Jill Cavell, "Status Recognition in the 1980s: Invidious Distinction Revisited," in *Advances in Consumer Research*, vol. 14, ed. Melanie Wallendorf and Paul Anderson (Provo, UT: Association for Consumer Research, 1987), 487–491.

[68] Scott Kilman and Robert L. Rose, "Population of Rural America Is Swelling," *Wall Street Journal*, June 21, 1996, B1, B4: Matthew W. Brault, "Americans with Disabilities: 2010,": accessed January 22, 2016, http://www.census.gov/prod/2012pubs/p70-131.pdf

chapter

15

Consumer Neuroscience

Learning Objectives:

1. What is consumer neuroscience?

2. What are the techniques being used in consumer neuroscience?

3. What are some ethical issues in consumer neuroscience studies?

4. What are some unique contributions of consumer neuroscience studies?

Exploring Consumers' Subconscious Preferences

A phenomenon that has plagued researchers for a very long time is the observation that many consumers are either unable or unwilling to tell why they do the things they do. For instance, urban-dwelling consumers may purport purchasing large vehicles, such as sport utility vehicles (SUVs), for practical reasons such as extra space or the low probability they may go "off-roading," even when they hardly ever utilize the space or drive on rugged terrain. Indeed, despite the plethora of advertisements showing these massive cars going up steep hillsides and through muddy streams, only about five percent of SUV owners ever go off-road driving.[1]

A classic case of consumers' hesitancy to state their true feelings on a particular product dates back to observations by marketers of Nescafé instant coffee in the 1940s. Struggling to figure out why Nescafé's early sales were so low, consumers were asked directly to state how they felt about the brand. Consumers who reported disliking Nescafé often cited disliking the flavor of the coffee as their reason, but in blind taste tests where consumers did not know the brands of the coffees they were tasting, they would report enjoying Nescafé's flavor. This apparent contradiction in consumers' stated preferences guided marketers to discover that it was more than just flavor that was driving consumers' perceptions about this brand. Closer investigation using **projective techniques**, which are research tools used to uncover the true underlying motivations, feelings, or opinions of consumers when they are unable or unwilling to express them directly, exposed that those responsible for purchasing coffee for their households felt they would perceive themselves or be perceived by others as "lazy" as a result of buying instant coffee for their family members.[2] This information was valuable to marketers of Nescafé, who went on to emphasize in

415

the positioning of their product that the convenience of instant coffee saved homemakers time to focus greater devotion to more important household activities.[3]

Projective techniques are a category of qualitative research techniques that seek to uncover true feelings or tendencies produced in a consumer's **subconscious**, the part of the mind that the consumer is not directly aware of having influence over her or his feelings, opinions, or actions. Since the times of the Nescafé and similar projective research, marketers have discovered that applying neuroscientific techniques to investigate marketing phenomena also has the ability to reveal subconscious motivators of consumers. For instance, an experiment by Frito-Lay, the owner of the Cheetos brand of cheese puffs, gathered neurological data about consumers' brain activities and discovered they had strong feelings described as "giddy subversion" about the orange residue their snack food left on fingers during consumption.[4] As a result, Cheetos brand advertising campaigns emphasize subversive, or rebellious, activities using the cheese puffs.

CONSUMER NEUROSCIENCE

Neuroscience is a broad term referring to the systematic study of the structure or function of the nervous system, including the brain. The recent development of new tools and techniques has led to an eruption of brain research and significant findings, such as mirror neurons, which may help explain our tendency to imitate others. If you've ever bought a soft drink because someone else in your group did so first, perhaps your mirror neurons were involved!

While neuroscience has traditionally been a discipline of biology, other sciences and social sciences have since adopted its scientific methods to explore phenomena within diverse fields, inspiring subdisciplines such as neuroeconomics, neurofinance, neurosociology, neurolaw, and neuromarketing, among many others.[5] The last term, **neuromarketing**, is sometimes used interchangeably with the term **consumer neuroscience**, although a conceptual distinction between the two terms is beginning to arise among marketing scholars and practitioners. Whereas neuromarketing is coming to be regarded as the application of neuroscientific methodologies and instruments toward the systematic study of *market* phenomena, consumer neuroscience is the application of neuroscientific methodologies and instruments toward the systematic study of *marketing* phenomena.

Understanding the distinction between **market research** and **marketing research** holds the key to understanding the distinction between the neuromarketing and consumer neuroscience terms presented in this chapter. Market research involves studies seeking to investigate marketing practitioner phenomena. Examples of market research questions include: Do consumers prefer the T-Mobile location at the mall or the stand-alone store on Tenth Street? Why hasn't Drake's new single appealed to the usual target consumers of his music? Is the new Tide advertising campaign increasing brand awareness among consumers who own high-efficiency washing machines? In other words, market research seeks to address problems that are specific to a particular business or brand. The results of market research may or may not be generalizable to other businesses or brands, as such studies are not motivated by the desire to be generalizable, but rather, they are motivated only by the need to address a specific practitioner-related issue. Neuromarketing is a methodology to help market researchers study such issues. Neuromarketing has been practiced in-house by many large companies and by market research firms such as Nielsen Consumer Neuroscience.

Alternatively, marketing research involves studies seeking to investigate general phenomena in the scientific discipline of marketing. Examples of marketing research questions include: Under what conditions and product contexts would consumers prefer to shop at mall locations versus stand-alone locations? What are the determinants of creating and maintaining consumer loyalty toward musicians? How can brand awareness be measured? Studies seeking answers to these questions would be designed with the intent of being able to **generalize**, or be statistically reproduced, in many different product-, geographical-, and consumer-characteristic contexts. Unlike market research studies, marketing research studies have a primary objective of being able to be applied generally. Marketing research studies that use neuroscientific methodologies and instruments to accomplish this objective would be referred to as consumer neuroscience studies.

Experimental Design in Consumer Neuroscience

Consumer neuroscientific studies are based on the responses of a consumer's brain toward marketing **stimuli**, which are things or occurrences that provoke a particular physiological or psychological reaction within the subject being studied. For instance, if we are studying the effect of different types of music on sales in a retail setting, the stimuli to which we would expose consumers would be the different kinds of music they hear while they are shopping (e.g., jazz, classical, soft rock). These stimuli are purposefully designed and managed in an experimental setting in order to isolate a consumer's specific reaction to just that stimuli. In other words, marketing experiments and the marketing stimuli being studied in them are purposefully planned to minimize any **experimental noise**, which are interferences and reactions to stimuli that are not the focus of the intended research.

Experimental noise can be **systematic** or **random**. Systematic sources of interference are not a problem for the researcher, because they can be measured and controlled. When interferences or reactions are systematic, it means they are methodical and, thus, can be measured. For instance, let's say that we are studying consumers' neurological reactions to an advertising campaign for a particular political candidate's platform on renewable energy sources. We are interested in investigating what sorts of neurological reactions using the particular terminology of "global warming" versus "climate change" elicits. So, the stimulus to which we expose the consumers in our study is the particular terminology in the advertising campaign. During our experiments, we notice that whether the **experimental subject**, the voluntary participant providing data toward answering our research question, is left-handed or right-handed has a systematic effect on our data output. Thus, while we are not interested, specifically, in studying the handedness of consumers, collecting the systematic data on whether they are left- or right-handed will allow us to separate out in our data the effects of handedness from the effects of our focal stimulus of terminology.

Managerial principle 15.1
Beware of the possible effects of noise—systematic or random—on results from consumer neuroscience investigations.

Unfortunately, every experiment will also contain some random experimental noise that the researcher is unable to systematically determine the source of and, therefore, control. Good experimental design will control for as much systematic noise as possible while acknowledging that the data will, to some degree, be affected by random error as well.

A Quick Primer on the Brain

In order to hypothesize about neurological reactions of the brain to marketing stimuli, consumer behavior researchers must understand, to some degree, the basic functioning of and processes within the human brain, which is the main organ of the human nervous system. The human brain contains four lobes, as shown in Figure 15.1: frontal (closest to the forehead), parietal (in the top middle region of the skull), temporal (the lower region of the brain), and occipital (in the back of the skull). The basic structure of the human brain is similar to that of other mammals, except the human brain has a larger **cerebral cortex**, which is the outermost layer of neural tissue and is responsible for functions such as attention, awareness, memory, perception, and language, among others. Knowledge of the cerebral cortex is particularly relevant to consumer neuroscientific studies that distinguish neurological data according to the two **cerebral hemispheres**, or left and right sides, of the brain. One such method will be described in the next section of this chapter.

FIGURE 15.1
The Cerebral Lobes and Hemispheres
Sources: http://www.appsychology.com/Book/Biological/cerebral_cortex.htm, https://en.wikipedia.org/wiki/Cerebral_hemisphere

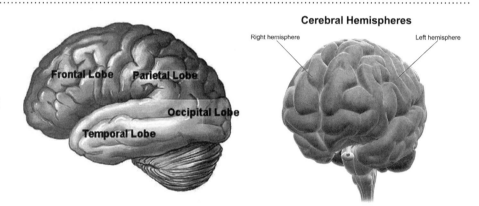

The brain is composed of two types of cells: **neurons** and glial cells. Neurons are nerve cells that produce and transmit electrical and chemical signals through connections known as **synapses**. There are approximately one hundred billion neurons in a human brain. The glial cells provide support and protection for the neurons as the neurons perform their main function of **neurotransmission**, which is communication with other neurons through their chemical and electrical synapses. There are approximately one hundred trillion synapses in a human brain. Neuroscientific techniques, some of which will be described in the next section, measure the activities of these synapses, which can range from excitatory to inhibitory. The excited, inhibited, or other reactions of neurons depend on the internal and external stimuli to which they are exposed either naturally (i.e., as part of their lives), or contrived in an experimental setting.

TECHNIQUES USED IN CONSUMER NEUROSCIENCE

There are several types of neuroscientific technologies that can be used to study the brain's structure and the reactions and processes that occur within it. **Magnetic resonance imaging (MRI)** uses magnetic fields and radio waves to produce two- or three-dimensional images of the brain. **Functional magnetic resonance imaging (fMRI)** produces images of a brain's active regions by detecting excess blood supply within those regions. Positron emission tomography (PET) is an imaging technology that shows functional processes in the body, including the brain, through the insertion of a radioactive chemical into the body. Diffuse optical tomography (DOT) inserts infrared light into an experimental subject's body and measures the parts of the brain containing hemoglobin in the blood that have absorbed this light, indicating activity in specific neural regions. Event-related optical signal (EROS) also uses infrared light but measures the diffusion of the light through the neurons rather than the hemoglobin. **Electroencephalography (EEG)** records the frequency levels of electrical activity in the brain, with both specific and broad interpretations of those frequency levels to the mental state of the experimental subject. Magnetoencephalography (MEG) measures miniscule changes in the magnetic field of a brain, allowing it to detect the location of brain signals from outside of the brain. Because both consumer neuroscience and neuromarketing have predominantly applied fMRI and EEG techniques, the remainder of this section will focus on only these two.

fMRI

fMRI detects the active regions in a brain by identifying the excess blood oxygen levels present in those regions. Like MRI, fMRI produces high-quality two- and three-dimensional images of the brain. Unlike MRI, which produces images of the physical structure of the brain, fMRI produces images of activity in the brain. Thus, the two techniques can be differentiated according to their objectives, with MRI revealing anatomical structure and fMRI revealing specific regions of brain activity through the detection of the metabolic function of the blood oxygen levels in those regions. fMRI machines, such as the one pictured in Figure 15.2, are very large and expensive to operate. Using a fMRI machine can cost researchers approximately $1,000 per hour, and considering that fMRI experiments utilize approximately twenty to thirty experimental subjects, using fMRI can be prohibitively expensive for most academic and many market researchers.[6] While fMRI machines are able to produce high-resolution pictures of

FIGURE 15.2
An fMRI Machine and Sample Output
Sources: https://en.wikipedia.org/wiki/Functional_magnetic_resonance_imaging, http://www.nhs.uk/conditions/mri-scan/pages/introduction.aspx

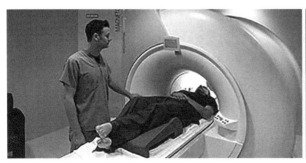
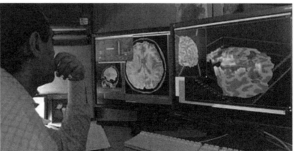

specific brain location activity, they also produce a great deal of auditory noise for the experimental subject, who is already exposed to a relatively claustrophobic and unnatural experimental environment. As a result, fMRI data must be closely monitored for effects of experimental noise.

Marketing researchers prefer fMRI over other neuroscientific techniques when the objective of a study is to determine the precise location of activity within a brain. For instance, a series of fMRI-based studies revealed the part of the brain that is active when an experimental subject is in an altruistic mindset (i.e., the *posterior superior temporal sulcus*) is not physiologically capable of being active when the part of the brain responsible for focus on financial gain or self-interested pleasure (i.e., the *nucleus accumbens*) is active.[7] This could explain why, for example, donations to charities are lower when consumers are presented with the option of receiving a gift in return for a donation or experimental subjects perform with less effort when they are rewarded for their participation with a monetary reward rather than the opportunity to just do a good deed. That is, we have discovered through fMRI studies that humans cannot have a compounding effect of altruistic and self-interested motivations—they can be either philanthropists or consumers, but they cannot be both at the same time.

The application of fMRI in marketing research contexts is growing, with consumer neuroscience studies often supplementing neuroscientific methodologies with traditional research methodologies to demonstrate the reliability of the interpretation of the neurological techniques. For instance, in a recent study investigating salespersons' characteristics and motivations, researchers used data from fMRI scans in tandem with answers from self-reported surveys given to experimental subjects as well as collection of genetic material.[8] The researchers showed that there is a genetic variant that can predict neurological processes in the brain that are associated with empathy as well as aligned with a salesperson's self-reported characterization of her or his customer orientation. In other words, there are both biological markers as well as parts of the brain that "light up" in a way to predict empathetic responses in a salesperson who is customer oriented (i.e., makes an effort to fulfill his or her customers' needs and build long-term relationships).

In another example, researchers were able to show that when a consumer sees a price, it will affect the way a consumer evaluates the product.[9] In this study, the researchers used self-reported survey data on consumers' preferences for a product as well as fMRI scans to discover that the timing of price information shown to a consumer, in relation to when the product information is shown, will affect how the consumer feels about purchasing the product. Studies like this not only advance marketing researchers' knowledge of neuroscientific techniques and consumer behavior, they also have the potential to affect practical marketing management in the real world. For instance, in this last study, there is the potential to affect the design of online retailers, who have some control over the order of the pricing and product information they show to shoppers.

One of the most interesting consumer behavior experiments using fMRI involved studying a group of consumers who reported liking and drinking wine. Researchers asked these voluntary experimental subjects to sample five types of cabernet sauvignon wines, which were given to them with labels indicating fake prices of the wine. In reality, they sampled only three types: two samples of a $5 bottle being realistically labeled at $5 and deceptively labeled at $45, two samples of a $90 bottle being realistically labeled at $90 and deceptively labeled at $10, and one sample of a $35 bottle labeled at its real price. The experimental subjects reported that they could taste five distinct wines in the sample. They also reported the wines labeled as more expensive as tasting better. Moreover, the neural imaging scans from the fMRI showed particular activity in the brain when subjects were drinking what they were deceived into thinking was more expensive wine. In other words, they were actually experiencing better tasting wines in their heads because of the expectations they formed based on their perceptions of price prior to drinking it.

EEG

EEG measures the frequency levels of electrical activity in the brain through electrodes strategically placed in various positions on the scalp. These positions are reported in summaries of EEG experiments according to the **International 10-20 System**, an internationally recognized way of describing the application of EEG electrodes on the scalp. Each locational description uses a letter and a number to identify the lobe (e.g., frontal, parietal, and occipital) and cerebral hemispheric location, respectively. Figure 15.3 illustrates these locations.

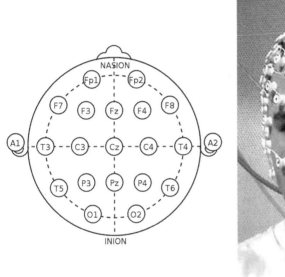
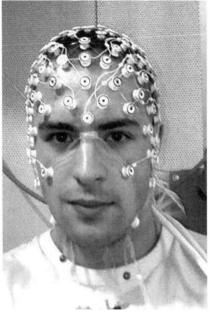

FIGURE 15.3
EEG Electrode Locations
Source: https://en.wikipedia.org/wiki/10-20_system_%28EEG%29

The most popular categorization of brainwaves from EEG measurement are the delta, theta, alpha, beta, and gamma waves, each of which is associated with various interpretations as to the mental state of the experimental subject producing those waves. Table 15.1 summarizes the **frequency**, or the rate at which the waves are repeated over a period of time, of each of these wavelengths. The frequency measurements are reported in **hertz (Hz)**, which is defined as cycles per second.

Consumer behavior researchers may prefer EEG over fMRI technology for several reasons. An immediate reason is it is significantly less costly to gain access to and operate EEG technology as compared to neuroimaging technology. A more experimentally relevant reason is EEG equipment can be used in more

TABLE 15.1
EEG Frequency Levels

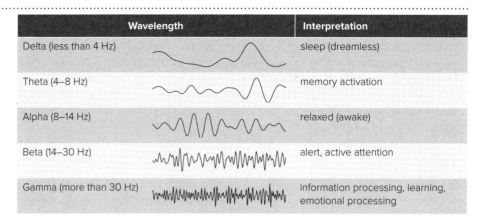

Wavelength		Interpretation
Delta (less than 4 Hz)		sleep (dreamless)
Theta (4–8 Hz)		memory activation
Alpha (8–14 Hz)		relaxed (awake)
Beta (14–30 Hz)		alert, active attention
Gamma (more than 30 Hz)		information processing, learning, emotional processing

natural settings that are less restrictive and uncomfortable to the experimental subject, allowing the potential for less experimental noise in EEG experiments relative to fMRI experiments. Essentially, an fMRI subject must lie flat on his or her back and be perfectly still inside a large magnetic "doughnut" that bangs continually. In comparison, EEG subjects can sit upright in a chair or even be mobile when wireless headsets are used. A third reason is electrical changes are registered by EEG in fractions of a second, whereas changes in blood flow, which is what fFMI devices measure, introduces a time lag of about six seconds. However, a key disadvantage of EEG is, while it can detect reactions to stimuli, it cannot provide researchers information regarding from which part of the brain the reaction originated. Depending on the requirements of the specific type of equipment used, it may also take a longer time to prepare an experimental subject for EEG testing. In general, an experimental subject may be more quickly placed into a fMRI setting than he or she could be outfitted with EEG electrodes that must be placed in precise positions. However, recent advances in EEG equipment fabrication have made this time lag less of a problem. With practice, researchers have managed to achieve placement of a fourteen-electrode apparatus in less than ten minutes per subject.

Managerial principle 15.2
The objectives of the research should drive the selection of the neuroscientific methods and instruments used.

As with the decision to choose any experimental methodology, the main motivator for experimenters in using an EEG methodology would be because it is best suited to answer the research question. For instance, one EEG technique is hemispheric lateralization (or hemispheric asymmetry), which involves the measurement of asymmetries, or differences, in alpha wave frequency bands across the left and right frontal lobes of the brain. Prior research has found such asymmetries are associated with a subject's approach or avoidance response to external stimuli. Specifically, significantly higher alpha band power in the left hemisphere, relative to the right hemisphere, is indicative of an approach response. Conversely, significantly higher alpha band power in the right hemisphere, relative to the left hemisphere, is indicative of an avoidance or withdrawal response. Marketing researchers have used this technique to accurately predict, for example, consumers' intentions to purchase products based on different consumer and product characteristics, such as brand familiarity, product price, and perceived quality.[10] Increasingly, researchers are using hemispheric lateralization, along with other EEG sub-methodologies, to accurately predict product preferences and consumer perceptions of promotional campaigns, among other consumer behavior phenomena.[11]

Why Use Consumer Neuroscience?

So, why should consumer behavior researchers use consumer neuroscience methodologies to answer research questions at all? In other words, what does consumer neuroscience add to our knowledge of consumer behavior that traditional marketing techniques cannot? One advantage of neuroscientific research to investigate marketing issues is, as such methods continue to evolve in instrumentation and methodology, they are becoming cheaper and faster than the traditional methods of, for example, consumer surveys, focus groups, and consumer observations. Neuromarketing experiments can also produce data that contain less experimental noise than conventional methods. Indeed, since neurological data is gathered from consumers' subconscious reactions to stimuli, there is less chance of intentional or accidental error on the part of the consumer. As a result, consumer neuroscience studies require significantly smaller **sample sizes**, the number of experimental subjects or observations in a study, in order to achieve experimental accuracy. Finally, as indicated in the introduction to this chapter, consumers are often unable or unwilling to accurately report their preferences when asked directly. Moreover, prior research has indicated that the process of overtly asking consumers to report preferences may even bias the outcome of the study in unintended ways. Indeed, consumers are not always consciously aware of why they choose certain things over others—brain data has the potential to gather this information without the need to compel conscious recollection and explicit statements from consumers. fMRI, in particular, has already demonstrated increased accuracy over survey results in predicting consumer behavior—a valuable discovery when considering fMRI requires a small fraction of the sample size required by survey research.[12]

ETHICAL ISSUES IN CONSUMER NEUROSCIENCE STUDIES

In 2011, the *New York Times* published an editorial by a popular brand consultant and media columnist describing a fMRI experiment that found that experimental subjects' brain activities when responding to the sound of their phones mimicked the sort of brain activity that occurs around significant others and family and is associated with feelings of love and compassion.[13] The data and methodological processes from this experiment were never published in any peer-reviewed publications and received some public condemnation by academic neuroscientists, but the experiment did underscore to the general public the notion that marketers may now be able to determine the subconscious feelings that are produced by consumers when they interact with brands and products.[14]

More recently, the online social networking giant Facebook and dating website OKCupid came under fire for intentionally manipulating their services to conduct consumer behavior experiments on users without their knowledge.[15] The Facebook experiment manipulated the number of negative versus positive posts seen in the unknowing experimental subjects' "newsfeeds." Facebook found users who were intentionally exposed to less positive posts by others tended to make more negative posts themselves. Users who had their negative posts reduced, produced more positive posts. Facebook apologized for the poor communication of the experiment that was intended to manipulate users' emotions. OKCupid's cofounder admitted to intentionally misleading subscribers about their compatibility percentages with other subscribers, finding in this experiment that users were more likely to send a message to those whom they perceived as having higher compatibility ratings. Unapologetically, OKCupid cited its user agreement as justification for being able to conduct these experiments, even though they contained some deception.[16] Beyond the notion that both companies' experiments intentionally manipulated their users' emotions, these publicized cases brought the issue of experimental subject consent out of academia and into the minds of the general public.

Consent, Privacy, and Confidentiality

Consent is permission given by someone for something to happen to that person. In experimental settings, subjects give **informed consent** before engaging in the experiment, meaning the researcher informs the subject fully of the possible consequences and benefits of being an experimental subject and the subject, having considered those benefits and consequences, freely agrees to be a part of the experiment. Generally, the researcher will ask the experimental subject to sign a consent form stating that he or she understands the possible experimental risks. This consent form will likely have been approved by an **institutional review board (IRB)**, which is a committee federally mandated by US law to approve and monitor research involving human subjects. Other countries have similar ethical committees and legislation for human subject research.

Managerial principle 15.3
Private firms conducting neuroscientific research on human experimental subjects should seek out guidance from private firms providing IRB services.

With only a few exemptions, all research involving human experimental subjects must have their experimental processes approved by their institutional or an independent IRB before proceeding. Exemptions include research involving the analysis of data that is already publicly available (e.g., stories about people written in newspapers), the collection of data from humans that are publicly available in a way that the experimental subjects cannot be identified (e.g., taking notes on how customers act in a supermarket checkout line without interacting with them), certain experiments involving testing classroom strategies (e.g., testing "clickers" in a large class and then asking students to fill out a feedback form about their experience with them), and experiments to assess certain publicly provided goods and services (e.g., government solicitation of perceptions of consumers about a new government program). All other human experiments, including those performed in a university setting, must demonstrate to an IRB that they have met its ethical guidelines. These guidelines include fully disclosing any physical or emotional risks of the experiments, minimizing deception during an experiment, and revealing any deception necessary to the experiment to subjects after the conclusion of the experiment. For instance, if we wanted to conduct an experiment using fMRI to assess consumers' neurological reactions to truthful and dishonest advertising, we would have to disclose to our voluntary experimental subjects any possible risks of the fMRI experimental setting, gain their official informed consent to participate in the experiment, and reveal to them at the conclusion of the experiment that some of the scenarios to which they were exposed contained dishonest advertising clais.

Having a plan to approach the specific **privacy** needs of experimental subjects and the **confidentiality** of any data gathered from them is necessary for IRB approval. Privacy refers to the notion that the experimental subject should maintain full control over any physical, behavioral, or emotional information shared with researchers, including providing full informed consent for how that information is accessed by researchers. Confidentiality refers to how data gathered from experimental subjects is treated, with the expectation that, in experimental settings, any information shared with researchers will not be divulged in a way that identifies the experimental subject to others to an extent and in a way that was not previously agreed upon in the consent disclosure.

Consent, privacy, and confidentiality seem relatively straightforward in traditional marketing research utilizing, for example, survey data. The subject understands he or she will take a survey, may opt out of answering any questions, can quit the survey at any moment, and is assured her or his or her true identity will not be reported in tandem with the survey results. However, in the case of consumer neuroscientific experiments, consent, privacy, and confidentiality have the potential to raise ethical questions that are not present with traditional experimental methods. For instance, to what extent can a subject provide consent and maintain control over the information revealed by the subconscious portions of the mind? While a survey taker can refuse answers to direct questions, an experimental subject wearing an EEG cap, for example, cannot refuse the brainwaves he or she creates as subconscious neurological reactions to experimental stimuli. An IRB may approve an experiment where the subjects acknowledge that subconscious information will be collected and reported as part of the study, but the informed consent form and accompanying explanations from the study's researchers would need to explain this point to experimental subjects explicitly.

Protection of Consumer Interests and Autonomy

The use of experiments to gain insight into the feelings and motivations of consumers in a commercial context is not new, as demonstrated by the multitude of examples in this textbook alone of marketing and other research that use scientific methodology to do so. The use of neuroscientific technology as a means to these ends, however, has raised concerns in academia as well as the general public.

Although the classic marketing tale of manipulating consumers to buy more popcorn and drinks in a movie theater through subliminal messaging may have been based on a hoax, the public reaction to the suggestion of being manipulated through covert means indicates the degree to which consumers prioritize the maintenance of **autonomy**, which is the independent ability or free will of a person to act in her or his own greatest welfare, and protection from exploitation by commercial interests.[17] Some researchers argue that businesses acting on data gathered through consumer neuroscientific methods have the potential to work against the interests of consumers, including their autonomous will to make purchase decisions.[18] For instance, knowing how brains subconsciously react to the manipulation of various senses (e.g., vision, smell, and hearing) could give marketers the power to elicit certain neurological reactions in consumers that cause them to purchase at levels higher than they would in the absence of stimuli that manipulate those senses. Of course, consumer behavior researchers have long been studying the effects of changing various sensations to affect consumers. However, in traditional research, marketers observed or asked directly for the reactions of their human experimental subjects and produced interpretations of those reactions to guide their managerial decisions. Moreover, in such research and such manipulations, the consumer has the potential to become aware of the stimuli to which he or she is being exposed. For example, if a researcher finds certain smells in a store increase sales and, thus, managers employ those smells in their stores, the consumer still has the ability to consciously detect changes to what he or she is smelling. In consumer neuroscientific research, however, marketers gain information on how to produce neurological reactions of which the consumer is likely not consciously aware. Researchers now have the ability to discover that certain stimuli activate particular neurological responses which, thus, cause certain consumer reactions. If managers, in practice, were able to elicit subconscious reactions that encourage spending, to what degree can we still assert that the consumer is capable of making autonomous decisions of her or his own free will anymore? Will consumer neuroscience provide opportunities for marketers to better address consumers' existing needs, or does it have the potential to manipulate purchases from consumers that they would not want otherwise? While the application of neuroscience to marketing research is increasing in its potential to inform scholars and practitioners about consumer behavior, the ethical issues and questions surrounding this emerging discipline in the field of marketing are proliferating, as well.

CONTRIBUTIONS OF CONSUMER NEUROSCIENCE STUDIES

In 2013, it was reported that approximately thirty university business schools contained faculty researchers applying neuroscience to business-related topics.[19] With the increase of the number of academic conferences such as the Interdisciplinary Symposium on Decision Neuroscience, academic journal articles and special issues, and non-academic marketing and managerial practices devoted to neuroscientific approaches in business, it is likely this number has increased significantly since then.

Consumer neuroscience research has resulted in some findings that have grown our knowledge of consumer processes and motivations in ways that have not been possible with traditional marketing research methods. Consider the Pepsi Challenge. This classic promotional challenge has taken place in shopping malls since the 1970s, with Pepsi asserting that volunteers preferred the taste of Pepsi over Coca-Cola in taste tests where they did not see a label on what they were drinking. Subsequent research found that brand perceptions and not just biological taste buds could affect taste, however. Early research that also used taste tests with self-reported data found that consumers were highly influenced on how their cups were labeled.[20] Specifically, labeling a bottle with Coca-Cola led those who stated a preference for Coca-Cola to say they liked the beverage in that bottle better—even though there was Pepsi in it! The same occurred for volunteers who stated they generally preferred Pepsi. That is, in taste tests where they were drinking Coca-Cola in bottles labeled Pepsi, subjects stated preferring the Pepsi-labeled bottles. This early research illustrated the power of branding over participants' stated reasons for preference, but consumer behavior researchers only new that this power existed and could not yet explain what was causing it—until neuroscience was applied to this phenomenon.

Recently, a team of researchers used fMRI to find that knowledge of the brand activates parts of the brain that are independent from the part of the brain that functions when they are given only sensory information (e.g., taste).[21] When brand is known ahead of time, the power of the brand and all the cultural

Managerial principle 15.4
In addition to gaining information on what is happening, managers should consider whether their current data collection is providing information on why it is happening.

connotations the brand carries was found to exist in prior experiments, but the neuroscientific experiments explained the source of this poer.

Neurological measures not only help explain consumer behavior, as exemplified in the example above, but they also help make valuable predictions. For instance, a recent study used EEG to predict the commercial success of movies with more accuracy than verbalized preferences.[22] That is, the brain waves of participants more accurately matched up with box-office sales data than data on what they said about how much they would be willing to pay to see the movie. This is significant for marketing, especially considering consumers' verbalized intentions do not often enough match up with their behavior. A problem that has plagued consumer behavioral researchers for a long time is that consumers surveyed frequently report levels of willingness to do something, such as purchase a product, and do not actually do it. Thus, looking at neurological data presents researchers a way to solve the classic problem that consumers' reported intentions do not always translate into purchase actions. Nevertheless, researchers still find it prudent to gather self-reported and other non-neurological data to supplement and validate neurological data, as such data is usually not difficult to gather in tandem with neurological data.

MANAGERIAL IMPLICATIONS OF CONSUMER NEUROSCIENCE

The principles and concepts of consumer neuroscience have application to each of the five RESPonsive Marketing concepts. These are discussed below.

Market Research

Marketers should consider conducting research using consumer neuroscience techniques after they have familiarized themselves with some level of understanding of the brain, the techniques, and their applications. A question to answer is whether the firm should attempt to do this research in-house, retain an outside consultant who can help the firm get started, or identify outside firms that specialize in these techniques. Well-known brands such as Hyundai, Google, Disney, Microsoft, Chevron, and Frito-Lay, among many others, use neuromarketing consultants to guide their product designs and promotional messages.[23]

Issues with consumer neuroscience research include cost and the artificiality of an experimental setting that is intended to study natural consumer behavior. As discussed in this chapter, fMRI studies in particular are relatively costly and take place in very unnatural settings.

Environmental Analysis

When marketing a brand, managers must carefully examine the communication and competitive environments. If the communications environment is cluttered with advertisements (and it usually is), possible serial position effects, the tendency of a consumer to recall things based on their orders, and other characteristics of advertisements can be studied via EEG.

Segmentation

Different messages and potentially even different products can be targeted to consumers with divergent knowledge levels. EEG might be used to examine the arousal level occasioned by subjects representing different market segments and various advertising forms. Or, as an experiment summarized in this chapter illustrated, fMRI can be deployed to study the orientations of a sales force that was already segmented by other characteristics.

Positioning and Differentiation

EEG can be used to study the arousal levels accompanying different advertisements, jingles, and other promotional elements. fMRI can be used to approach this task in a different way, such as investigating localization of brain responses to such marketing stimuli. Organizations can identify and evaluate the way their target markets react to the brand names of products, as well as the name of the organization, similar to the modern neurological Pepsi-versus-Coke "taste" tests described in this chapter.

Marketing Mix

The concepts in this chapter are particularly relevant to the product development and promotional strategy elements of the marketing mix. EEG brain lateralization studies can detect approach motivation versus avoidance motivation. Event-related potential studies (not discussed here, but another capability of EEG) have been used to measure whether brand attributes fit well or poorly with the brand name. EEG techniques used to study new product innovations include approach-avoidance and memory activation. Moreover, the finding that fMRI provides significant predictive power over traditional marketing surveys unlocks a great deal more potential for predicting consumer behavior than marketers were able to do with prior methods.[24]

SUMMARY

What is consumer neuroscience?

Consumer neuroscience is the application of neuroscientific methodologies and instruments to study marketing phenomena. It differs from the concept of neuromarketing in that consumer neuroscience studies marketing phenomena while neuromarketing studies market phenomena. Consumer neuroscientific studies are based on the responses of experimental subjects' brains toward marketing stimuli in experiments designed to isolate specific reactions stimuli of interest while minimizing experimental noise. The human brain is unique from other animals in its advanced development of the cerebral cortex, which is composed of the left and right cerebral hemispheres. Neuroscientific methodologies collect data generated by synaptic connections, known as neurotransmission, from the responses of neurons to external or internal stimuli.

What are the techniques being used in consumer neuroscience?

There are several types of neuroscientific technologies that can be used to study the brain's structure and the reactions and processes that occur within it. The most relevant technologies and methodologies for the study of consumer behavior are fMRI and EEG. Each has its own distinct advantages and disadvantages. In general, consumer neuroscience techniques are increasingly able to help address marketing issues in ways that are more efficient and effective than conventional marketing research techniques. These advantages include being cheaper and faster in collecting data, providing data that contain less experimental noise, requiring smaller sample sizes, and gathering consumers' true preferences in contexts where consumers are either unable or unwilling to be completely truthful.

What are some ethical issues in consumer neuroscience studies?

In experimental settings, researchers must obtain informed consent from experimental subjects before engaging in experiments. Researchers inform voluntary experimental subjects of the possible consequences and benefits of participating in an experiment as well as assure the subjects of privacy and confidentiality. In the United States, all human experiments are legally required to be approved and monitored by an IRB, which may be an institutional or private committee. The use of neuroscientific technology as a means to investigate and affect consumer behavior has raised ethical issues for both researchers and the general consuming public, namely concerns regarding protecting consumer interests and maintaining consumer autonomy in purchasing decisions.

What are some unique contributions of consumer neuroscience studies?

Consumer neuroscience research has resulted in some findings that have grown our knowledge of consumer processes and motivations in ways that have not been possible with traditional marketing research methods. Using neural techniques, consumer behavior researchers are now able to explain phenomena that they had only been able to observe as existing in prior studies. Neurological measures also help make valuable predictions, and they are often supplemented with traditional data such as self-reported answers on surveys.

KEY TERMS

autonomy
cerebral cortex
cerebral hemispheres
confidentiality
consumer neuroscience
electroencephalography (EEG)
experimental noise
experimental subject
frequency
functional magnetic resonance
   imaging (fMRI)

generalize
hertz (Hz)
informed consent
institutional review board (IRB)
International 10-20 System
magnetic resonance imaging
   (MRI)
market research
marketing research
neuromarketing
neurons

neuroscience
neurotransmission
privacy
projective techniques
random
sample size
stimuli
subconscious
synapses
systematic

REVIEW QUESTIONS

1. What are projective techniques, and under what circumstances might a researcher choose to employ them? Without using an example already discussed in this chapter, think of a product and research question

related to it where a projective technique may be necessary to figure out consumers' true feelings or opinions.

2. How does market research differ from marketing research? Come up with your own unique example of a research question for each.

3. What is experimental noise, and why does it matter to an experiment?

4. What are neurons, synapses, and neurotransmissions? How are they all related?

5. What is MRI, and how does it differ from fMRI?

6. Name and briefly explain at least two advantages and two disadvantages of using fMRI in an experiment. Do the same for an EEG experiment.

7. Describe how consumers could "taste the price of wine" in the fMRI experiment described in this chapter.

8. Explain why consumer neuroscientific experiments often require smaller sample sizes than traditional marketing experiments that use self-reported or physically observed consumer data?

9. What is informed consent and why is it important to obtain in research experiments?

10. What is an IRB and why is it significant to consumer neuroscience research?

11. How is the concept of privacy different from the concept of confidentiality? Explain how each is significant to research involving human experimental subjects?

12. What is the notion of consumer autonomy, and why is it an ethical issue for both (a) consumer neuroscience researchers and (b) the general public?

13. What sorts of knowledge are researchers able to obtain using neuroscience that they were not able to obtain before? Provide examples to supplement your answers to this question.

DISCUSSION QUESTIONS

1. Are researchers "tricking" consumers when they use projective techniques? In your educated opinion, is the use of such techniques ethical? Answer these same questions for consumer neuroscience studies.

2. Marketing stimuli are things or occurrences that provoke a particular physiological or psychological reaction within the experimental subject being studied. Think of a consumer behavior experiment you would like to conduct and identify the stimuli to which your experimental subjects would be exposed. Are there any sources of experimental noise for which you would need to control?

3. Develop three separate research questions that would best be tested using each of the following: (a) MRI, (b) fMRI, and (c) EEG? Be sure to provide a justification for each method.

4. The researcher who tested for tasting the price of wine anticipated being criticized by others on the grounds that he only used casual wine drinkers and not professional wine connoisseurs in his sample. He also stated that he expects professionals would show a greater effect of tasting price than his sample "because they really care about it."[25] Explain why you believe this may or may not be true.

5. The chapter reading states, "Consumers are not always consciously aware of why they choose certain things over others." Can you think of an example of a type of purchasing decision that consumers may engage in without entirely conscious thought. What sort of research questions related to this purchasing behavior could a neuroscientific experiment help to investigate?

6. Marketing researchers have always sought to gain more information on why consumers make certain purchase decisions. Why is it more of an ethical concern when neuroscientific techniques are used to investigate this?

7. Make up a hypothetical experimental scenario where you would collect data on a consumer behavior issue. Describe how you would gather data to answer your main research question, including how you would maintain privacy and confidentiality of research subjects.

8. What do you think about the Facebook and OKCupid experiments described in this chapter? Argue a case that they were ethical experiments that should not require IRB oversight. Next, write a counterpoint arguing that the experimental topics or experimental procedures were unethical.

9. Some researchers in the social sciences criticize the IRB approval requirements as being inappropriate for social sciences research. Such critics state the IRB requirements are often overly burdensome for or misunderstanding of social sciences research methods and intentions because they were originally created with medical and therapeutic applications in mind. Do you agree? Why or why not? Create arguments both in favor of and against the need for IRB requirements in human subject research of consumer behavior.

10. This chapter observed that, while the application of neuroscience to marketing research is increasing in its potential to inform scholars and practitioners about consumer behavior, the ethical issues and questions surrounding it are also proliferating. What do you think? Will consumer neuroscience provide opportunities for marketers to better address consumers' existing needs, or will it manipulate purchases from consumers that they would otherwise not want?

11. What is the difference between explaining consumer behavior and predicting consumer behavior? Why would both types of information be important to researchers? Finally, come up with two research questions: one where the answer would explain some sort of consumer behavior and one where the answer would predict some sort of consumer behavior.

ENDNOTES

[1] Rebecca Leung, "The Thrill of the SUV: Owners Believe Bigger Is Always Better," *CBS News*, July 11, 2003, accessed January 18, 2016, http://www.cbsnews.com/news/the-thrill-of-the-suv/.

[2] Mason Haire, "Projective Techniques in Marketing Research," *Journal of Marketing* 14, no. 5 (April 1950): 649–656.

[3] Mark Batey, *Brand Meaning* (New York: Routledge, 2008).

[4] Adam L. Penenberg, "Neurofocus Uses Neuromarketing to Hack Your Brain," *Fast Company* (September 2011).

[5] José Morais, "Dyslexia and Poor Reading: Cognitive and Ethical Issues," in *Applied Psycholinguistics: Positive Effects and Ethical Perspectives*, vol. 1, ed. Giuseppe Mininni and Amelia Manuti (Milan, Italy: FrancoAngeli, 2012), 46–60.

[6] Carmen Nobel, "Neuromarketing: Tapping into the 'Pleasure Center' of Consumers," *Forbes*, accessed January 17, 2016, http://www.forbes.com/sites/hbsworkingknowledge/2013/02/01/neuromarketing-tapping-into-the-pleasure-center-of-consumers/#2715e4857a0b6f6ea7721430.

[7] Ori Brafman and Rom Brafman, *Sway: The Irresistible Pull of Irrational Behavior* (New York: Broadway Books, 2008).

[8] Richard P. Bagozzi, Willem J. M. I. Verbeke, Wouter E. van den Berg, Wim J. R. Rietdijk, Roeland C. Dietvorst, and Loek Worm, "Genetic and Neurological Foundations of Customer Orientation: Field and Experimental Evidence," *Journal of the Academy of Marketing Science* 40, no. 5 (September 2012): 639–658.

[9] Uma R. Karmarkar, Baba Shiv, and Brian Knutson, "Cost Conscious? The Neural and Behavioral Impact of Price Primacy on Decision Making," *Journal of Marketing Research* 52, no. 4 (August 2015): 467–481.

[10] Niklas Ravaja, Outi Somervuori, and Mikko Salminen, "Predicting Purchase Decision: The Role of Hemispheric Asymmetry over the Frontal Cortex," *Journal of Neurosciences, Psychology, and Economics* 6, no. 1 (March 2013): 1–13.

[11] Giovanni Vecchiato, Jlenia Toppi, Laura Astolfi, Fabrizio De Vico Fallani, Febo Cincotti, Donatella Mattia, Francesco Bez, and Fabio Babiloni, "Spectral EEG Frontal Asymmetries Correlate with the Experienced Pleasantness of TV Commercial Advertisements," *Medical and Biological Engineering and Computing* 49, no. 5 (May 2011): 579–583; Rumen Pozharliev, Willem J. M. I. Verbeke, Jan W. Van Strien, and Richard P. Bagozzi, "Merely Being with You Increases My Attention to Luxury Products: Using EEG to Understand Consumers' Emotional Experience with Luxury Branded Products," *Journal of Marketing Research* 52, no. 4 (August 2015): 546–558; Ariel Telpaz, Ryan Webb, and Dino J. Levy, "Using EEG to Predict Consumers' Future Choices," *Journal of Marketing Research* 52, no. 4 (August 2015): 511–529.

[12] Dan Ariely and Gregory S. Berns, "Neuromarketing: The Hope and Hype of Neuroimaging in Business," *Nature Reviews Neuroscience* 11, no. 4 (April 2010): 284–292; Maarten A. S. Boksem and Ale Smidts, "Brain Responses to Movie Trailers Predict Individual Preferences for Movies and Their Population-Wide Commercial Success," *Journal of Marketing Research* 52, no. 4 (August 2015): 482–492; Vinod Venkatraman, Angelika Dimoka, Paul A. Pavlou, Khoi Vo, William Hampton, Bryan Bollinger, Hal E. Hershfield, Masakazu Ishihara, and Russell S. Winer, "Predicting Advertising Success Beyond Traditional Measures: New Insights from Neurophysiological Methods and Market Response Modeling," *Journal of Marketing Research* 52, no. 4 (August 2015): 436–452.

[13] Martin Lindstrom, "You Love Your iPhone. Literally." *New York Times*, September 30, 2011, accessed January 17, 2016, http://www.nytimes.com/2011/10/01/opinion/you-love-your-iphone-literally.html?_r=0.

[14] Yu-Ping Chen, Leif D. Nelson, and Ming Hsu, "From 'Where' to 'What': Distributed Representations of Brand Associations in the Human Brain," *Journal of Marketing Research* 52, no. 4 (August 2015): 453–456.

[15] Jonathan Bacon, "Neuroscience and Marketing: What You Need to Know," *Marketing Week*, August 6, 2014, accessed January 17, 2016, https://www.marketingweek.com/2014/08/06/neuroscience-and-marketing-what-you-need-to-know/.

[16] Molly Wood, "OKCupid Plays with Love in User Experiments," *New York Times*, July 28, 2014, accessed January 17, 2016, http://www.nytimes.com/2014/07/29/technology/okcupid-publishes-findings-of-user-experiments.html?_r=0.

[17] Stuart Rogers, "How a Publicity Blitz Created the Myth of Subliminal Advertising," *Public Relations Quarterly* 37 (Winter 1992–1993): 12–17.

[18] Emily Murphy, Judy Illes, and Peter B. Reiner, "Neuroethics of Neuromarketing," *Journal of Consumer Behaviour* 7 (July–October 2008): 293–302.

[19] Ale Smidts, Ming Hsu, Alan G. Sanfey, Maarten A. S. Boksem, Richard B. Ebstein, Scott A. Huettel, Joe W. Kable, Uma R. Karmarkar, Shinobu Kitayama, Brian Knutson, Israel Liberzon, Terry Lohrenz, Mirre Stallen, and Carolyn Yoon, "Advancing Consumer Neuroscience," *Marketing Letters* 25, no. 3 (September 2014): 257–267.

[20] Mary E. Woolfolk, William Castellan, and Charles I. Brooks, "Pepsi versus Coke: Labels, Not Tastes, Prevail," *Psychological Reports* 52, no. 1 (February 1983): 185–186.

[21] Samuel M. McClure1, Jian Li, Damon Tomlin, Kim S. Cypert, Latané M. Montague, and P. Read Montague, "Neural Correlates of Behavioral Preference for Culturally Familiar Drinks," *Neuron* 44, no. 2 (October 2004): 379–387.

[22] Maarten A. S. Boksem and Ale Smidts, "Brain Responses to Movie Trailers Predict Individual Preferences for Movies and Their Population-Wide Commercial Success," *Journal of Marketing Research* 52, no. 4 (August 2015): 482–492.

[23] Laurie Burkitt, "Neuromarketing: Companies Use Neuroscience for Consumer Insights," *Forbes*, accessed January 17, 2016, http://www.forbes.com/forbes/2009/1116/marketing-hyundai-neurofocus-brain-waves-battle-for-the-brain.html.

[24] Vinod Venkatraman, Angelika Dimoka, Paul A. Pavlou, Khoi Vo, William Hampton, Bryan Bollinger, Hal E. Hershfield, Masakazu Ishihara, and Russell S. Winer, "Predicting Advertising Success Beyond Traditional Measures: New Insights from Neurophysiological Methods and Market Response Modeling," *Journal of Marketing Research* 52, no. 4 (August 2015): 436–452.

[25] Lisa Trei, "Baba Shiv: How a Wine's Price Tag Affects Its Taste," *Insights*, accessed December 1, 2015, http://www.gsb.stanford.edu/insights/baba-shiv-how-wines-price-tag-affect-its-taste.

16

The Dark Side of Consumer Behavior

Learning Objectives:

1. What current corporate behaviors seem to be driving the dark side of consumer behavior?

2. What dark-side behaviors do consumers engage in?

3. What is the role of corporate social responsibility?

4. How should firms deal with rumors?

Vapes

Since 2004, e-cigarettes, or e-cigs (often called "vapes"), have been the new disruptive technology in the tobacco industry. E-cigs are battery-powered devices in various shapes containing a heating element that rapidly warms flavored oil, generating a vapor for inhaling. Vaping devices are designed in a variety of shapes but can generally be classified into three categories: a pen-like design similar to a large cigar (called eGo), a box design held in the palm of the hand, and less-expensive models resembling paper rolled tobacco called cig-a-likes. The more serious the user, the higher the probability he or she will use the box design.

For the box design, there are many product variations, numerous manufacturers, and a number of settings, allowing users to create their own sensory experience. The oils burn flavors that fall into four major categories: tobacco, menthol, fruits, and desserts. Some of the more popular flavors include vanilla custard, Fruity Pebbles cereal, and tropical fruit mix. The oils may also contain a predetermined level of nicotine, most often varying from none to 30 milligrams (mg), so users can adjust their nicotine intake from zero to a level exceeding the 12 mg typical of a rolled cigarette. In addition to selecting a flavored oil and the nicotine content, buyers may choose the color of their devices, select from a number of accessories like drip tips (the mouth piece), select the power of the battery (fixed or variable wattage), as well as the coils (in Ohms of resistance) used to heat the oil. In general, lower Ohm resistance and higher wattage produce larger clouds of exhaled vapor. The box models and eGo's have a push button allowing for vaping on demand. They are sold primarily in specialty stores (vape shops). In contrast, cig-a-likes are sold through traditional cigarette outlets, are disposable, and much less expensive.

E-cigarette sales have been driven by rapid consumer adoption of commercial products, with $820 million in US sales in 2009 growing to $2.47 billion in 2014. Despite advertising and promotional claims that e-cigs were safer than cigarettes, studies show a wide variability in the experience delivered and in the quality of devices. From 2013 to 2014, use of e-cigs by middle- and high-school students tripled. This has brought on calls for more control within the industry by regulatory agencies. As a consequence, the US Food and Drug Administration (FDA) tried to regulate the sale of vapes. The FDA still isn't authorized to regulate the industry, although rules are expected in early 2016.

In this chapter, we consider that consumer behavior has a "dark" side. Companies can prey on consumers through unscrupulous behavior. As the opening story shows, however, consumers may also engage in negligent behavior. Examples include actions that harm themselves, such as the consumption of drugs such as steroids and cocaine. As one method of decreasing the likelihood that such activities might occur, as well as the harm that results, the government regulates the buying and selling of goods and services.

CORPORATE BEHAVIORS AND THE DARK SIDE OF CONSUMER

Companies can engage in deceptive advertising, advertising to children, and unfair pricing, among other behaviors. Let's explore some less-than-honorable corporate practices.

Deceptive Advertising

Advertisements can be deceptive when they're literally false or potentially misleading. Some ads are easy to evaluate. For example, "guaranteed to last ten years" is a statement that's either true or false. Potentially misleading ads are more difficult to assess because consumer interpretation of the ad is relevant. When ads are interpreted incorrectly, the result is miscomprehension due to the inferences made by consumers

The possibility of miscomprehension is rather large. One study showed, on average, consumers had a miscomprehension rate of 30 percent for television advertisements. A second study by the same authors concerning print advertisements indicated 21.4 percent of the meanings in magazine advertisements were misunderstood, and in a further 15.5 percent of cases, the consumers didn't comprehend the message at all.[2] While the precise rate of miscomprehension and non-comprehension is somewhat controversial, the potential for miscomprehension of advertisements is clearly significant. From a marketing manager's standpoint, the phenomenon of miscomprehension means a certain proportion of the audience is likely to miscomprehend the advertising message.

The Federal Trade Commission (FTC) is charged with regulating deceptive advertising rather than dealing with the issue of miscomprehension. One example of FTC action on deceptive advertising involved Kraft Singles individually wrapped cheese slices. Losing market share to imitation-cheese products, Kraft launched a campaign positioning its Singles as containing as much calcium as 5.0 ounces of milk. Because about 30 percent of the calcium was lost in processing, however, the actual calcium remaining was equal to 3.5 ounces of milk. The FTC determined this ad was deceptive and ordered Kraft to desist from making

Managerial principle 16.1
For vape manufacturers, advertisers and most other businesses, the possibility of new regulations is always present. Someone in the company needs to be paying attention to possible regulatory changes of the industry.

this claim. One of the controversies in the Kraft case was whether the difference between the calcium in 5.0 or 3.5 ounces of milk was material. That is, did Kraft want consumers to make their decision based on the fact that Singles had more calcium than its artificial competitors or was the actual amount of increased calcium important? The FTC and consumer researcher David Stewart argued for the latter position, while analyst Jacob Jacoby argued for the former.[3] As you can see, what constitutes deceptive advertising isn't always clear-cut.

The FTC has issued a series of advertising guidelines and enforcement policy statements on advertising claims, which range from product specific (e.g., metallic watchbands and hosiery) to general (e.g., environmental marketing claims and use of the word *free* in advertising).[4] A recent aspect of the FTC's activity has been regulatory cases involving deceptive advertising on the Internet. Many of the early cases involved offers by small companies to repair consumer credit records.[5]

Unfair Advertising

In 1976, the FTC attempted to rule that all advertising aimed at children was unfair. In this case, the issue wasn't deception but whether such advertising was unfair because children might not be able to understand the messages. This led to a fourteen-year battle between US Congress and the advertising industry over a legal definition of what was "unfair." During this period, the FTC could use the idea of "unfairness" in individual cases but couldn't issue industry-wide rules. As a result, unfairness played only a minor role in FTC actions in the 1980s and early 1990s. Agreement on a definition was finally reached in 1994. More recently the FTC turned its attention to children and internet usage, revising the Children's Online Privacy Protection Rule in 2013. [6]

Corrective Advertising

In response to the increased attention given to deceptive advertising tactics in the 1960s and early 1970s, the FTC began to order corrective measures from some of the guilty parties. The incident that sparked the idea of corrective advertising involved Campbell's soup advertisements in which clear marbles were placed in the bottom of a soup bowl, forcing the vegetables to the surface. Consumers believed the soup contained more vegetable pieces than it actually did. The FTC issued a cease-and-desist order that banned this practice.[7]

Perhaps the most famous of all corrective advertising cases involved Warner-Lambert's claim that Listerine mouthwash could prevent or lessen the severity of colds and sore throats. The company began manufacturing Listerine in 1879 and advertising the product in 1921: Warner-Lambert had been making this claim for more than half a century. In 1975, the FTC ordered that the company must attempt to correct misimpressions that its advertisements had created. Between 1978 and 1980, Warner-Lambert spent more than $10 million on corrective advertising. Nearly 95 percent of this money was devoted to television commercials.[8]

Children's Advertising

Both marketing managers and public-policy makers have reacted to criticisms of advertising directed at children. As noted in Chapter 12, children are influential in family decision making. They also directly control a significant amount of purchases. Children younger than twelve have a combined annual income of $27.5 billion in the United States and influence some $188 billion in US purchases, about $1.87 trillion worldwide. Professor James Neal has coined the term *filiarchy* (like patriarchy or matriarchy) to describe children's growing spending power within the family.[9]

In addition, children prefer nationally labeled brands, which are often more profitable than private-label brands. Whereas 70 percent of adults have become major buyers of private-label store brands, only 7 percent of children would even consider the stuff. They want brand-name gifts and designer clothes. Brands offer children a common commercial language, something that identifies them as part of a group.[10]

Marketing managers and public-policy makers have benefited from consumer behavior research and theory that examines children's responses to advertising. Some key issues researchers have investigated include the following:

- Can children tell the difference between commercials and programming?
- Do children understand the selling intent of commercials?
- Do commercials make children want products that aren't good for them?

The need for continued concern regarding children's exposure to television and web material is related to the influence television has on children. The influence of television may have slipped in recent years as techniques such as children's membership clubs, catalog-marketing programs, and marketing to children on the Internet have flourished.[11] One other reason the influence of television may have declined is that children may be seeing fewer commercials. In 1990, the Children's Television Act limited the advertising children would see during children's television programs—no more than 10.5 minutes per hour on weekends and no more than 12 minutes per hour during the week. A more recent agreement (i.e., 1996) commits television stations to carry at least three hours of educational children's shows a week.[12]

Finally, Nintendo warned even before releasing its 3DS game player that children younger than six years shouldn't play games in 3-D mode on the device. Nintendo suggested prolonged staring at 3-D images could inhibit eyesight development. "We are being proactive about informing our customer, even though it may not necessarily be positive for our sales," explained Satojru Iwata, Nintendo's president. Now, 3-D is morphing into virtual and augmented reality, and products such as the Oculus Rift and the Oculus-powered VR headset from Samsung are within consumer price ranges. Gatorade, the North Face, Marriott and others have already ventured into this new immersive medium by making VR "experiences" available to consumers. For example, Gatorade will allow you to try to hit a 90 mph fastball thrown by a major league pitcher.

DARK-SIDE BEHAVIORS CONSUMERS ENGAGE IN

Most of us would agree that seat belts save lives, smoking is hazardous to your health, and drinking and driving don't mix. Still, many consumers, in some manner or another, exhibit what might be termed negligent behavior. **Negligent behavior** is composed of those actions and inactions that may negatively affect the long-term quality of life of individuals and society. This type of behavior can occur in two contexts. The first form of negligent behavior occurs because the consumption of a product in and of itself presents a hazard of some sort. The consumption of cigarettes and certain drugs are two examples that fall into this category. A second form of negligent behavior occurs when the consumer uses a product in an unsafe manner or fails to use safety features and follow safety instructions. Failure to use seat belts and not following dosage instructions for over-the-counter drugs are examples of this type of negligent behavior.[14]

There are two common approaches to induce people to act in a safer manner. One involves legislation that creates laws that force consumers to wear seat belts, ban the advertising and sale of cigarettes, and impose stiffer penalties for drunk driving. A second approach involves the use of marketing techniques to encourage more appropriate consumer actions. Consumer behavior research and theory provide insight into how marketers and public-policy makers can influence consumers to behave in a safer manner.

Product Misuse

Many of us would never think of using a blow dryer in the shower or a lawn mower to trim the hedges. Consumers' misuse of products in just such a fashion, however, has prompted marketers and public-policy makers alike to exert special precautions in the design and testing of products. In fact, the majority of product-related injuries result not from a flaw in the product itself but through misuse of an otherwise safe product.[15] As one individual put it, "The most dangerous component is the consumer, and there's no way to recall him."[16] Table 16.1 shows various possible explanations for consumer misuse of "safe" products.

TABLE 16.2
Consumer Misuse of "Safe" Products: Potential Explanations

1. *Action slip.* A performance error resulting from faulty cognitive processing. This is particularly likely when the consumer is focusing on desired end results rather than the more mundane actions necessary to arrive at the desired state.
2. *Error proneness.* The tendency not to be vigilant, especially during activities performed routinely.
3. *Reinforcement.* The consumer takes a risk but doesn't suffer any consequences. Each successive trial that doesn't result in harm reinforces the proneness to risky behavior.
4. *Hedonic goals.* Consumers focused on fantasy, fun, and feelings are less likely to calculate the risks involved in their behavior.
5. *Ritual/socially sanctioned misuse.* Campus beer bashes may represent quasi-sanctioned product misues.
6. *Individual irrationality.* The actions of obsessive, compulsive, or addictive personalities.
7. *Advertising.* Advertising representations may be partially responsible for unsafe behavior because they encourage extreme forms of product use.

Source: Adapted from Jeffrey Stoltman and Fred Morgan, "Psychological Dimensions of Unsafe Product Usage," in *Marketing Theory and Applications*, vol. 4, ed. Rajan Varadarajan and Bernard Jaworski (Chicago: American Marketing Association, 1993), 143–150. For a discussion of irrationality, see Dan Arielv's books and videos at danarielv.com..

As mentioned earlier, one method of inducing people to act in a safer manner is legislation. In addition to regulating consumer behavior, this might involve setting government safety standards for almost every type of industry. If a company's products fail to meet such standards, the products are subject to recall. However, it's been estimated that "no more than 20 percent of all consumer product related injuries can be addressed by feasible regulation of the production and distribution of consumer products."[17]

We also noted earlier that a second method of preventing product misuse lies in increasing consumer information. However, this second alternative has been called into question. There's a practical limit to the amount of information that can be presented on a label, and inserts and manuals are usually discarded early in the life of products such as power tools. Even experience may not be helpful because novices are often more careful and vigilant than the experienced user.

The argument has been made that a third alternative is needed that relies on product design. From this perspective, we need more study of how products are actually used in order to incorporate into a design an increased level of safety: "[T]he actual hazard arises in the kitchen or in the hedgerow, not in the store."[18] For example, the oval-shaped Ford Taurus instrument panel was a departure from previous designs. It was, in part, the result of customer complaints that previous panels had too many small buttons that were too close together and were too difficult to manage while driving.[19] At the same time, some have begun to think that we are overdoing consumer protection and becoming a nation of wusses.

Drinking and Driving

Alcohol-related traffic fatalities declined by one-third between 1988 and 1998, to a still-substantial 15,935.[20] In the 1980s, increased attention was given to the issue of drinking and driving, partly because of the efforts of the national organization Mothers Against Drunk Driving (MADD), which was founded in 1980. Public-policy makers could make greater use of consumer behavior research concerning this area. This subsection describes some of the methods currently used, along with their strengths and weaknesses.

Informing and Educating   Using the approach of informing and educating assumes individuals act rationally in an effort to further their self-interest. Thus, the public should be presented with objective information about the hazards of driving drunk.[21] When developing such information campaigns, advertisers have frequently used a fear-inducing message appeal.

Social Controls   The majority of liquor advertisements portray the beverage in question as a drink consumed in the presence of others and as a means of heightening one's acceptability. The strategy of social controls plays on the understanding that individuals are influenced by the actions and attitudes of those around them. The dominant theme employed in this tactic is to have social influencers disapprove driving drunk. Examples of this strategy include campus meetings of the Students Against Drunk Driving (SADD) organization or commercials showing family or friends taking car keys away from the person who overindulged.

Economic Incentives   Using concepts derived from behavior modification theory, one approach might be to reward individuals for demonstrating the desired behavior. Insurance companies currently use this approach by providing reduced rates to individuals who agree not to drink and drive. Some restaurants give a free meal to a designated nondrinking driver who will drive his or her friends who are drinking home. The limitation of this approach is that some individuals may refrain from drinking and driving only if they perceive the benefits as outweighing the costs.

Economic Disincentives Rather than rewarding individuals for not drinking and driving, the use of economic disincentives punishes them. This punishment could occur directly (e.g., through fines, car repair costs, and high insurance premiums) or indirectly (e.g., through an excise tax on alcohol that would result in higher liquor prices). However, consumers may continue to drink and drive if they feel the benefits of their behavior still outweigh the costs.

Compulsive Behavior

Some negligent behaviors are the consumption of products that are hazardous in and of themselves, as discussed in the previous section. Many of these behaviors become compulsive or addictive over time. Other behaviors aren't harmful in moderation but become harmful when the behavior becomes compulsive. Let's explore some compulsive behaviors.

Smoking Until the late 1960s, consumers were exposed to nearly three thousand cigarette commercials per week, representing thirty-eight different brands. Concern over the health hazards of cigarette smoking had begun in the 1950s. However, it wasn't until the issuance of the US surgeon general's report in 1964 that policy makers began to exert considerable efforts to alter the public's smoking behavior. The US Department of Health and Human Services used such tactics as bumper stickers that read "Smoke, Choke, Croak" and endorsements from athletic stars proclaiming, "I don't smoke." In general, the approach was to depict smokers as distraught coughers, whereas nonsmokers were portrayed as happy and healthy.[22]

Thirty years later, the campaign was still in full swing. During the mid-1990s, the negative publicity concerning smoking and the actions of cigarette manufacturers grew in intensity. In particular, the advertising campaign employing Joe Camel, a cartoon character, was attacked for targeting the youth of America. In 1994, *Advertising Age* and the Roper organization conducted a national poll that found 68 percent of Americans believed cigarette ads influence children and teens to smoke. The results further revealed two-thirds of Americans, including half of all smokers, wanted the US government to increase restrictions on cigarette advertising. Over 50 percent of those polled wanted all cigarette advertising banned.[23]

In 1996, the federal government introduced a series of new restrictions on cigarette advertising and sales with the aim of halving tobacco use by children and adolescents. The new guidelines ban vending machines and self-service displays except where those younger than eighteen also aren't allowed, require photo identification for anyone under the age of twenty-seven buying cigarettes, ban billboards near schools and playgrounds, limit billboards and advertisements in magazines with a young readership to black-and-white text only, and restrict the distribution of promotional items (e.g., clothing).[24]

The increased antismoking activity hasn't led to a continuing decline in cigarette consumption. Although smoking dropped from the 1960s through 1992, the percentage of adult smokers remained at 24.7 percent from 1995 to 1997. Smoking has now declined to 16.8 percent of adults in 2014, and only about 9 percent of high schoolers report that they have smoked in the last 30 days.[25] However, one study indicated adolescents are three times more responsive to cigarette ads than adults, leading the study's authors to conclude, "Cigarette advertising for market share is primarily a battle of brands for consumption by the young."[26] So the battle over the issue is by no means over. Some researchers argue poor communications strategies by antismoking groups are partly to blame, but the root causes are the strong social reward for smoking in some circles (e.g., among teenagers) and certain deeply held cognitive positions. In fact, consumer awareness of the major health effects of smoking is now quite high. Researchers have found smokers now actually overestimate, rather than underestimate, the risk of lung cancer from smoking. These results suggest many smokers simply tune out or develop counterarguments for antismoking messages.[27]

Another new group of actors in the antismoking arena are makers of products such as nicotine gums and patches. The drug companies attempt to switch smokers to their products, which are available as over-the-counter drugs. Because these manufacturers are well versed in consumer advertising, their antismoking message may be successful in ways public-interest commercials couldn't be.

Compulsive Drinking   The decline in alcohol-related deaths on the road, mentioned earlier, may be part of an overall decline in alcohol consumption. The National Institute on Alcohol Abuse and Alcoholism reports that, in 1991, drinking per capita fell to its lowest mark since 1965, with hard liquor intake declining to near-1949 levels.[28] In 1995 alone, consumption of hard liquor dropped 1.6 percent. This created interest among distillers such as Jack Daniels and Bacardi in developing beers under their labels. As further evidence of the downward trend, a decades-old voluntary moratorium on television advertising by makers of hard liquor ended with Seagram's airing of commercials in 1996. Another uptick in liquor advertising began in about 2010, with brands like Skinnygirl Cocktails leading the charge [29]

Despite the decrease in sales of hard liquor, there are at least three disturbing trends in alcohol consumption. First, one of the newer drinking fads involves alcoholic soft drinks ("alcopops"), which taste like colas or fruit juices but may contain more alcohol than beer. Going under such names as Cola Lips, Two Dogs, Mrs. Puckers', Hooper's Hooch, Lemonhead, and Moog in Britain, where they were first introduced, products such as Mike's Hard Lemonade (vodka-based) and Smirnoff Ice (with an added stimulant) are established in the United States. Second, binge drinking, which is consuming more than five drinks at a time, has increased dramatically. Forty-two percent of college students have engaged in binge drinking, and 35 percent of college women now drink to get drunk—over three times the average found in 1977. Surprisingly, binge drinkers ages 65 and older binge more often than young adults, those ages eighteen to thirty-four.[30] Third, the gender gap in alcohol use by teenagers is disappearing. By age 15, 17.4 percent of girls and 16.1 percent of boys have engaged in some alcohol use.[31]

Gambling   Gambling is a form of addictive consumption that affects an estimated eight to twelve million people. Although a compulsive gambler is most likely to make less than $25,000 a year, many are high-income professionals.

Like drug users, compulsive gamblers may exhibit a high while engaging in the activity, followed by depression when they stop.[32]

We often think of gambling in connection with casinos, which have spread from landlocked locations in Nevada and New Jersey to such locales as riverboat gambling. In addition, a majority of states now have state-run lotteries, which make it easy to gamble with nothing more than a visit to the local convenience store. Internet gaming is also of concern. A recent study found that Internet gaming addiction may lead to physical changes in the brain.

Gambling exists in many countries. In Japan, 17.8 billion yen a year, equal to one-fourth of the national government's budget and more than the Japanese car industry's production revenues, is spent on pachinko, a game that appears to be addictive for the Japanese. The game is played on an upright pinball-like machine, where steel balls drop through formations of nails. Pachinko is even more convenient to play than the state lotteries in the United States because pachinko parlors can be found on virtually any busy street, with more than 12,000 parlors in operation.[33]

Other countries with gambling include Taiwan and Nepal. In China, lotteries are run under the name of "social welfare projects" to avoid government prohibitions. Gambling on horse racing is called an "intelligence competition"— participants guess which horse is "smart enough" to finish first or in an "intelligence trifecta" (i.e., guessing first, second, and third place correctly).[34]

Compulsive Shopping As described in Chapter 6, compulsive buying is a major societal problem. Compulsive buyers use shopping the way some addicts use alcohol or drugs. Like other addicts, compulsive shoppers seek the experience to protect their self-image, but when they end the experience, they feel more self-loathing and are subject to the disapproval of others, which, in turn, produces guilt. They attempt to escape this self-loathing by engaging in the experience again. According to some psychologists, this type of experience isn't pleasurable even while the addict is engaged in the activity.[35] Perhaps surprisingly, certain drugs have been found to relieve compulsive shopping.[36]

It has also been suggested that compulsive shopping may be hereditary. Ten percent of the relatives of compulsive shoppers are compulsive shoppers themselves, whereas only 2 to 3 percent of the entire population suffers from this compulsion.[37]

Other Compulsions Other forms of compulsive consumption are shown in Table 16.3. One of the more interesting compulsions is overwork. A Japanese court ordered Dentsu, the world's largest advertising agency, to pay $1.2 million to the survivors of Ichiro Ishima, who, during his last eight months of employment by Dentsu, had worked from early in the morning to 2:00 a.m. for 105 days and beyond 4:00 a.m. for 49 days. His family said he averaged only two to four hours of sleep a night.[38]

Prior to the 1980s, perspectives on compulsive behavior emphasized sociological and psychological influences. However, research on compulsive behavior since then has evolved in two directions. One is based on the possibility that various forms of addiction may have physical—even genetic—roots and may be due to neurochemcial imbalances. That certain addictive tendencies seem to be inheritable (e.g., evidence that alcoholism runs in families) suggests physical causes.[39]

TABLE 16.2
Examples of Compulsive Consumption

Substance abuse	Alcoholism
	Stimulants, sedatives, cannabis, opioids, cocaine, hallucinogens
Eating disorders	Anorexia, bulimia
Impulse-control disorders	Compulsive gambling, exercise, tanning, compulsive buying, compulsive sexuality

Sources: Based on Elizabeth C. Hirschman, "The Consciousness of Addiction: Toward a General Theory of Compulsive Consumption," *Journal of Consumer Research* 19 (September 1992):155–179; Ronald J. Faber et al., "Two Forms of Compulsive Consumption: Comorbidity of Compulsive Buying and Binge Eating," *Journal of Consumer Research* 22 (December 1995): 296–304; various episodes of the television shows *My Strange Addiction* and *Buried Alive.*

The other new direction of research suggests several forms of compulsive behavior may be driven by the same forces. In other words, they may occur together. A study, for example, found compulsive buyers also tended to suffer from binge eating. In fact, compulsive buyers were more likely to suffer from a range of eating disorders, substance abuse or dependence (i.e., alcohol, sedatives, cocaine, etc.), and other disorders, such as gambling and kleptomania.[40]

Future research on compulsive consumption will add to our knowledge base. These new directions, as well as sociologically-, psychologically-, and even genetically-oriented studies, may one day enable us to more completely understand the dark-side aspects of consumer behavior. These behaviors may actually be more widespread than currently thought when one considers that much research on compulsive behaviors depends on self-reporting. Because these attitudes and behaviors aren't socially desirable, respondents may be unwilling to report—or at least to report completely—on their behavior.[41]

AN APPROPRIATE ROLE FOR THE CORPORATION

Prior to the 1960s, most individuals generally accepted the idea that a business's primary objective was to obtain economic profit. This thinking began to change as social values in the United States changed. Today, 95 percent of Americans believe companies have responsibilities to employees and communities beyond making profits.[42]

Managerial principle 16.3
A recent trend in cause-based marketing is to reward altruism with a "gift" such as a T-short or coffee mug. In this case, cause-related marketing becomes even more like conventional product marketing. The effectiveness of this strategy isn't well understood.

Many companies exert much energy, time, and money to portray themselves as good corporate citizens who act in a socially responsible manner—companies spend considerably more than $1 billion annually in cause-related marketing alone. **Corporate social responsibility** refers to the idea that business has an obligation to help society with its problems by offering some of its resources. Several arguments support the notion that developing a positive image in terms of social responsibility is important for companies.

Succeeding in the Long Run

One argument for being socially responsible involves a long-term rather than a short-term perspective. A business's self-interest could be advanced if the business embraced a long-run view. This position would permit expenditures in support of socially responsible activities and provide future benefits in the form of consumer approval and loyalty. A focus on short-run profits would discourage expenditures devoted to societal problems. For example, in 1996, the nation's largest waste company, WMX Technologies, secretly sponsored an engineering study for an environmental group, the North Valley Coalition of Concerned Citizens. The coalition, which was underfunded, needed sophisticated evidence that would support its efforts to keep the second-largest waste management company, Browning-Ferris, from reopening its Sunshine Canyon Landfill in the Los Angeles area.[43] In the longer term, such behavior may invite additional regulation.

Acquiring a Positive Public Image

Companies can create a positive public image by acting in socially responsible ways. For example, one study revealed customers are less likely to blame the company for accidents when the product has safety standards that exceed, rather than simply meet, those of the government. Also, consumers are less likely to blame the manufacturer when products include safety warnings.[44]

Another way companies may reveal socially responsible behavior is by making speedy product recalls. A product recall could even be seen as a corporate opportunity in that the situation allows the company to show its ability to act professionally in a pro-consumer fashion.[45] A series of studies by John Mowen, one of the authors of this text, examined the impact product recalls could have on consumer impressions of a company. These studies found consumers perceived a familiar company as significantly less responsible for a product defect than an unfamiliar company; consumers viewed companies who reacted to product defects prior to intervention by the Consumer Product Safety Commission as less responsible for the defects; and consumer impressions of the company were influenced by the speed with which it initiated a product recall.[46] Table 16.3 gives an overview of the implications of these findings.

TABLE 16.3
Overview of Product-Recall Implications

Companies should strive to maintain a highly visible positive corporate image. Such a company is less subject to a negative consumer response when a recall is initiated.

Companies should establish a recall plan that can be quickly implemented should disaster strike. Consumers have a more favorable impression of companies that react quickly in a product-safety situation.

When a problem is first discovered, it may be best to overstate the problem to the public. Consumers will subsequently develop more favorable impressions of the company when they hear the problem isn't as severe as first expected. If the company displays the reverse behavior—that is, minimizes the problem, only to later discover the difficulty is worse than first announced—the result can be negative consumer impressions.

Companies should endeavor to manufacture the safest products possible. The safer the products, the less likelihood of severe injuries, negative consumer opinions, and product liability awards.

Companies shouldn't shy away from press coverage of product recalls. Information from independent sources such as the media, especially when the company is described as behaving in a socially responsible manner, can generate favorable consumer impressions.

Source: Adapted from Joshua Wiener and John C. Mowen, "Product Recalls: Avoid Beheading the Messenger of Bad News." *Mobius* 4 (1985): 18–21.

Finally, it's important to note the influence the perceived corporate responsibility of a company may have on product evaluations isn't direct. That is, perceptions of corporate social responsibility affect the overall corporate image. This image then has an effect on product evaluations.[47] But an improved image doesn't directly improve product evaluations.

DEALING WITH RUMORS

A positive public image can also be affected by the diffusion of rumors. Rumors periodically plague both large and small companies. They are a kind of group contagion that results from fears and anxieties. For example, national hysteria over the possibility of an Ebola epidemic in 2014 spawned many incorrect rumors.

Rumors have caused problems for all types of companies. In 1979, Procter & Gamble (P&G) began to be plagued by the rumor the firm embraced satanism. Flyers circulated among fundamentalist Protestant congregations noted the P&G symbol contained a sorcerer's head and thirteen stars—a purported sign of Satan. McDonald's has also been hit by rumors alleging satanism. Even more disturbing has been the fiction that the company added ground worms to its hamburger meat. Rumors have spread that subliminal sexual references were included in the Disney movies *Aladdin*, *The Lion King*, and *The Little Mermaid*.[48] The K (for kosher) sign that appears on bottles of Snapple has been interpreted as meaning the company supports the Ku Klux Klan. A rumor once circulated that Liz Claiborne stated on *The Oprah Winfrey Show* that she didn't want African Americans wearing her clothes, a rumor that persisted despite the host's own insistence that she has never interviewed Claiborne.[49] Since the first Tylenol poisoning incident in 1982, the FDA has logged some five hundred tampering complaints per year, reaching a peak of more than 1,700 complaints in 1986.[50]

Types and Causes of Rumors

Sociologists and psychologists have identified a number of types of rumors. **Pipe dream rumors** represent wishful thinking on the part of the circulators. They are positive hopes concerning something that might happen, such as the size of the Christmas bonus given by a corporation.

The **bogie** is a fear rumor that spooks the marketplace. This is the type of rumor that's plagued McDonald's and P&G. A bogie demolished the first king-sized menthol cigarette, Spud, in the 1940s.[51] A rumor spread that a leper worked in the plant where the brand was packaged. In six months, the cigarette had disappeared.

Rumors can also be **self-fulfilling rumors**. In this case, the rumor is based on a perception of what could happen if something else were to occur. Bank runs are examples of self-fulfilling rumors. It's true that if all of the depositors in a bank suddenly withdraw their money, any bank will fail. In bad times, this knowledge can spook people and result in the very behavior that's the source of the fear.

Premeditated rumors are spread by individuals with something to gain, hoping the rumors may help them financially or otherwise. Premeditated rumors can spread through the stock market and cause short-term shifts in the value of companies, from which unscrupulous individuals can make a profit. P&G believed its Satan rumors resulted, in part, from the salespeople of a competing firm distributing flyers describing P&G's supposed satanic activities. P&G has had a particularly hard time with Amway distributors. It has sued Amway distributors six times for statements linking the company to satanism.[52]

Finally, rumors can be **spontaneous rumors** when people seek explanations for unusual events. One author suggested the ground-worm rumors striking McDonald's may have begun when a consumer found tubular matter in a hamburger.[53] Such matter could easily be a small blood vessel not ground up well. In order to explain the material, the consumer leapt to the conclusion that the tube must have been a worm.

The right environment is required for rumors to be nourished to the point they can move through the population. The two factors that seem to be required are uncertainty and anxiety. Rumors generally occur and spread most rapidly when times are bad and people are uncertain about their future. It's not surprising the rumors that struck McDonald's and P&G were at their worst during the severe recession between 1980 and 1983.

In addition to uncertainty and anxiety, researchers have found the importance and the ambiguity of a rumor influence its spread. A formula expresses the relationship:[54]

$$Rumor = Ambiguity \times Importance$$

Urban legends, a phenomenon related to rumors, are realistic stories about incidents that are reputed to have occurred. They diffuse through the population like rumors and often appear to have a local connection. One legend has a groom mounting a chair at his wedding party, announcing the marriage was going to be annulled and the reason was underneath everyone's dinner plate. When the stunned guests flipped their plate, there was the bride in flagrante delicto with the best man. This story has been set in New York City and Schenectady, New York, New Hampshire, and Medford, Massachusetts. A similar version set in St. Paul, Minnesota, has the groom consorting with the maid of honor. University of Utah folklorist Jan Harold Brunvand has written some thirteen books filed with urban legends. Nearly everyone "knows" that alligators prowl New York sewers. Many may have heard about the Good Samaritan who approaches a woman slumped in her car. She moans that she's been shot in the head and shows grey matter oozing from the wound. She's actually been hit in the head by the tin at the end of a tube of Pillsbury biscuits that exploded in the heat, and the supposed brain matter is biscuit dough.[55]

Managers should monitor the environment for the spread of rumors about their company. One expert suggested companies should go through a series of actions if a rumor strikes them:

- Step 1. Ride out the rumor.
- Step 2. Trace its origins.
- Step 3. Treat it locally.
- Step 4. Rebut it with facts, but don't deny the rumor before the public hears about it.[56]

Rumors, however, are rarely eradicated completely. P&G's Satan rumor resurfaced in the mid-1990s, some sixteen years after it began. P&G was awarded approximately $19 million in 2007 because Amway's distributors had spread the rumor.

In fact, rumors can jump from company to company. The worms-in-hamburger rumor struck Wendy's prior to jumping to McDonald's. There's a potential problem with using refutation strategies to eliminate the spread of rumors. A study investigated the worm rumor and McDonald's hamburgers.[57] The authors found the negative impression of McDonald's remained when the rumor was refuted with facts (e.g., red worms cost $5 per pound and couldn't possibly be used). When a refutation strategy mentions the rumor, the consumer is reminded of the negative information. One way around the problem may be to give the facts without mentioning the rumor. McDonald's did this with a major promotional campaign advertising the fact the hamburgers are made with 100 percent pure beef. No mention of the rumor was made in the advertising campaign.

After Toyota was fined a record $1.2 billion in 2014 for misleading consumers about recalls in 2000 and 2010 and after General Motors was shown to have misled consumers about faulty ignition switches, Toyota, perhaps as a preemptive measure, announced its own recall of 6.34 million cars worldwide.[58]

Avoiding Government Regulation

Managerial principle 16.4
The evidence leans strongly in favor of immediately recognizing a company mistake and taking immediate, visible action to deal with the problem. Such actions should be announced by the highest-ranking company official possible.

A final reason to act in a socially responsible manner is to avoid government regulation. Given current societal values, if a business doesn't respond to societal demands on its own, consumer groups may exert pressure on governments to intervene.

All business functions concern themselves to some degree with social responsibility. However, the burden falls mostly to the marketer. Indeed, when a company is perceived as acting unethically or in an irresponsible fashion, marketing is the function most likely to be blamed.[59] Marketers can best avoid this label by following the strategies suggested previously—namely, maintain a positive initial corporate image and respond quickly when difficulties arise.

MANAGERIAL IMPLICATIONS

The consumer behavior concepts that emerge from the study of the dark side of consumer behavior have a number of managerial applications identified within the RESPonsive Marketing principles.

Research

Along with environmental scanning, market research should be used to determine how consumers view the company. In particular, it may be important to monitor the degree to which the public's view of the company's approach to corporate social responsibility is accurate.

Market research may also need to be used to determine whether customers are using a company's product in a novel, unplanned manner that may be unsafe or have other negative consequences.

Environmental Analysis

It's clearly important to ensure a company's actions are in compliance with laws and regulations. This is particularly true for start-ups. Perhaps equally important is that the company is seen as socially responsible. Enhanced perceptions of corporate social responsibility lead directly to increased company image and indirectly to enhanced product evaluations.

Segmentation

Some segments of the population are more concerned with issues of corporate social responsibility than are other segments. As an example, we suggested millennials are politically active and perhaps more interested in social issues than has been the case since the 1960s and 1970s. This may present opportunities for marketing managers to segment the market into groups of the more, and less, socially involved. Because the more socially involved are also of a certain age group, targeted campaigns may be useful.

Positioning and Differentiation

The concept of corporate social responsibility has direct implications for the positioning of a company. Efforts to create a "good-citizen" image help position a company as one that puts customers first. *Corporate Responsibility* magazine creates an annual "100 Best Corporate Citizens" list and ranks seven categories as critical: environment, climate change, employee relations, human rights, governance, finance, and philanthropy. Companies that were in top positions in the 2015 list include Microsoft, Hasbro, Johnson & Johnson, Xerox and Sigma-Aldrich Corp.

European companies in particular have tried to position themselves as responsible corporate citizens by adopting the notion of **product stewardship**, which emphasizes responsibility for the end of the product life cycle. It may be that the opportunity exists to use product stewardship as a point of differentiation with competitors in the United States as well.

Marketing Mix

Pricing, promotion, product development, and distribution should be undertaken in a socially responsible manner. Management should ensure these actions are communicated through the firm's public relations activities.

Pricing can be an issue of contention. Medical advances have presented pharmaceutical companies with a dilemma. When "big pharma" develops a drug with significant health benefits, the company's right to a good return on the investment may conflict with corporate social responsibility. Certainly, the company deserves to profit from taking the risk to develop the drug, but pricing a drug to quickly recoup investment may restrict availability to the well-off. Some companies have introduced programs to provide prescription drugs to those who can't afford them, aimed at blunting this criticism.

SUMMARY

What current corporate behaviors seem to be driving the dark side of consumer behavior?

Certain issues and groups are of particular importance in our society, and, as a result, receive a good deal of regulatory attention. One such issue is deceptive advertising. Because of the potentially large impact on consumers, legislators have passed laws making it illegal to mislead consumers. A group of consumers that regulatory agencies particularly seek to protect is children. Whenever companies market products to children, they must take special care to ensure they're acting responsibly. A third sensitive area is environmental protection.

What dark-side behaviors do consumers engage in?

Another problem area in public policy is negligent consumer behavior, a term that refers to actions and inactions that negatively affect long-term quality of life of individuals or of society in general. Failure to wear seat belts, smoking, drunk driving, and product misuse are a few examples of negligent consumer behavior. It's often difficult to draw the line between individual freedom and the public-policy interest in restricting the negligent actions of consumers.

Compulsive behavior, whether drug abuse, kleptomania, gambling, or other compulsions, may actually be increasing. Gambling, for example, is becoming more accessible as the number of venues increases. The introduction of Internet gaming may result in an increase in the activity. Current research on compulsive behavior is investigating possible physical, psychological, and social factors.

What is the role of corporate social responsibility?

Corporate social responsibility is clearly an important concept. In general, the more socially responsible corporations are, the less need there is for consumer-oriented law and regulations. Acting in a socially responsible manner can help a company survive in the long run, improve its public image, and decrease the likelihood of government intervention in corporate affairs.

How should firms deal with rumors?

Several types of rumors exist: Pipe dreams, bogies, self-fulfilling, premeditated, and spontaneous. Closely related are urban legends. Although companies sometimes succumb to the temptation to ignore rumors, companies who deal quickly and openly with rumors, and take immediate action if needed, experience the best results.

KEY WORDS

bogie
compulsive consumption
corporate social responsibility
negligent behavior

pipe dream rumors
premeditated rumors
product stewardship
self-fulfilling rumors

spontaneous rumors
urban legends

REVIEW QUESTIONS

1. High prices have often ranked as one of the most important consumer concerns. What do you think is the primary consumer concern today?
2. What categories of deceptive advertising has the FTC considered in the past?
3. To what extent can children tell the difference between commercials and programming?
4. To what extent do commercials tend to make children desire products that aren't good for them?
5. What is the definition of negligent consumer behavior?
6. Identify four examples of negligent consumer behavior.

7. What are the primary methods now being used to attack the problem of drunk driving?

8. What's meant by the idea of corporate social responsibility? Give four examples of how companies can act in a socially responsible manner.

9. Identify the reasons for and against businesses actively attempting to portray themselves as socially responsible.

10. According to the text, what factors influence consumer reactions to companies that issue product recalls?

11. What are some ways companies might be able to make children's advertising more acceptable to parents?

DISCUSSION QUESTIONS

1. Which consumer issues do you think are most important–deceptive advertising, drunk driving, or some other problem area? Do you believe corporate treatment of consumers has improved or worsened over the past five years?

2. What do you think of the notion of product stewardship? Should a manufacturer's responsibility for a product extend through product disposal?

3. From an attributional perspective, describe the possible effect of Listerine's corrective ad, which read, "While Listerine will not help prevent colds or sore throats or lessen their severity, breath tests prove Listerine fights onion breath better than Scope."

4. Political commercials have been called the most deceptive advertisements of all. Discuss the types of deception you've seen or heard in political advertisements. Give specific examples of each type of deception.

5. Discuss the distinction between deceptive ads, miscomprehension of ads, and noncomprehension of ads. What can management do to reduce the incidence of each of these three problems?

6. Watch Saturday morning cartoons and observe the advertising directed at children. What types of advertising appeals are being used? To what extent are cartoon characters being featured in the advertising? What sort of guidelines do you think companies that advertise to children should follow?

7. variety of approaches may be taken to control negligent consumer behavior. Discuss the alternative means through which public-policy makers can attempt to reduce drunk driving. Which approaches do you consider to be most effective?

8. Two different viewpoints exist concerning the social responsibility of corporations. One is that the only responsibility of a company is to make a profit for its stockholders (provided, of course, the company is acting legally), and the other holds that businesses have a responsibility to help improve society. Identify and defend your viewpoint on this issue.

ENDNOTES

[1] "Electronic Cigarette Statistics," *Statistic Brain*, accessed January 19, 2016, http://www.statisticbrain.com/electronic-cigarette-statistics/. This discussion is largely taken from William H. Locander, Michael S. Minor William B. Locander, "Kicking a 'Bad' Habit: The Role of Multi-Sensations and Embodied Co-Creation in Adopting Electronic Cigarettes." Working paper, January 2016.

[2] Jacob Jacoby and Wayne D. Hoyer, "Viewer Miscomprehension of Televised Communication: Selected Findings," *Journal of Consumer Research* 15 (March 1989): 434–443. See also Jacob Jacoby and Wayne D. Hoyer, "The Miscomprehension of Mass-Media Advertising Claims: A Re-Analysis of Benchmark Data," *Journal of Advertising Research* 30 (June–July 1990): 9–16.

[3] Jacob Jacoby and George J. Szybillo, "Consumer Research in FTC versus Kraft (1991): A Case of Heads We Win, Tails You Lose?" *Journal of Public Policy and Marketing* 14, no. 1 (Spring 1995): 1–14; David M. Stewart, "Deception, Materiality, and Survey Research: Some Lessons from Kraft," *Journal of Public Policy and Marketing* 14, no. 1 (Spring 1995): 15–28; Seymour Sudman, "When Experts Disagree: Comments on the Articles by Jacoby and Szybillo and Stewart," *Journal of Public Policy and Marketing* 14 (Spring 1995): 29–34.

[4] Arent Fox, "FTC Advertising Guidelines," *Web.com*, accessed June 11, 1998, http://www.webcom.com/lewrose/guides.html.

[5] "Sellers Beware Online," *Sales and Marketing Management* (December 1994): 16; Arent Fox, "FTC Tackles Fraud on the Information Superhighway, Charges Nine Online Scammers," *Web.com*, accessed April 28, 1996, http://www.webcom.com/lewrose/article/ftc-net.html.

[6] Ivan L. Preston, "Unfairness Developments in FTC Advertising Cases," *Journal of Public Policy and Marketing* 14 (Fall 1995): 318–320. and "Children's Privacy," accessed January 27, 2016 https://www.ftc.gov/tips-advice/business-center/privacy-and-security/children's-privacy

[7] For an account by an advertising executive involved in the controversy, see Dick Mercer, "Tempest in a Soup Can," *Advertising Age*, October 17, 1994, 25–29.

[8] William L. Wilkie, Dennis L. McNeill, and Michael B. Mazis, "Marketing's 'Scarlet Letter': The Theory and Practice of Corrective Advertising," *Journal of Marketing* 48 (Spring 1984): 11–31.

[9] Richard Tomkins, "Selling to a Captivated Market," *Financial Times*, April 23, 1999, 10. See also Martha C. White, "American Families Increasing Let Kids Make Buying Decisions, *Time*, April 11, 2013,, accessed January 27, 2016, http://business.time.com/2013/04/11/american-families-increasingly-let-kids-make-buying-decisions/

[10] Kyle Pope, "Better to Receive: How Children Decide on Gifts They Want, and Plot to Get Them," *Wall Street Journal*, December 24, 1993, A1, A5.

[11] For an example, view opportunities to shop for Barbie dolls at websites such as Sandi Holder's Doll Attic, accessed November 8, 1999, http://www.dollattic.com.

[12] Elizabeth Jensen and Albert R. Karr, "White House, TV Industry Compromise on Educational Programs for Children," *Wall Street Journal*, July 30, 1996, B14.

[13] Cindy Long, "Agencies Join Forces to Combat Billions of Dollars Lost from Telemarketing Fraud," *McAllen Monitor*, November 19, 1999, 1C–12C.

[14] Thomas C. Kinnear and Cynthia J. Frey, "Demarketing of Potentially Hazardous Products: General Framework and Case Studies," *Journal of Contemporary Business* 7 (1978): 57–68.

[15] Richard Staelin, "The Effects of Consumer Education on Consumer Product Safety Behavior," *Journal of Consumer Research* 5 (June 1978): 30–40. For a philosophical view of why safety devices lead to complacency and similar paradoxes, see Edward Tenner, *Why Things Bite Back: Technology and the Revenge Effect* (New York: Knopf, 1996).

[16] Walter Guzzardi, "The Mindless Pursuit of Safety," *Fortune*, April 9, 1979, 54–64.

[17] Richard Staelin, "The Effects of Consumer Education on Consumer Product Safety Behavior," *Journal of Consumer Research* 5 (June 1978): 30–40.

[18] Jeffrey J. Stoltman and Fred W. Morgan, "Expanding the Perspective on Consumer Product Safety," in *Marketing and Consumer Research in the Public Interest*, ed. Ronald P. Hill (Thousand Oaks, CA, Sage, 1996) 177-198.

[19] John Pierson, "Ford Labors over Tiny Buttons and Dials in Quest for a Driver-Friendly Dashboard," *Wall Street Journal*, May 20, 1996, B1, B7.

[20] See the website of the National Drunk and Drugged Driving (3D) Prevention Coalition, accessed April 7, 2000, http://www.3dmonth.org/idf.htm.

21 Janet R. Hankin, Ira J. Firestone, James J. Sloan, and Joel W. Ager, "The Impact of the Alcohol Warning Label on Drinking during Pregnancy," *Journal of Public Policy and Marketing* 12 (Spring 1993): 10–18.

22 Thomas C. Kinnear and Cynthia J. Frey, "Demarketing of Potentially Hazardous Products: General Framework and Case Studies," *Journal of Contemporary Business* 7 (1978): 57–68.

23. Steven W. Colford and Ira Teinowitz, "Teen Smoking and Ads Linked," *Advertising Age*, February 21, 1994, 1, 36.

24 Richard Tomkins, "Advertising Curb May Lift Tobacco Industry Profits," *Financial Times*, August 26, 1996, 4. See also Tara Parker-Pope, "Tough Tobacco-Ad Rules Light Creative Fires," *Wall Street Journal*, October 9, 1996, B1, B6.

25 Centers for Disease Control and Prevention, "Current Cigarette Smoking Among Adults in the United States," accessed January 27, 2016, http://www.cdc.gov/tobacco/data_statistics/fact_sheets/adult_data/cig_smoking/index.htm and "Youth and Tobacco Use", accessed January 27, 2016, http://www.cdc.gov/tobacco/data_statistics/fact_sheets/youth_data/tobacco_use/index.htm

26 Richard W. Pollay, S. Siddarth, Michael Siegel, Anne Haddix, Robert K. Merritt, Gary A. Giovino, and Michael P. Eriksen, "The Last Straw? Cigarette Advertising and Realized Market Shares among Youths and Adults, 1979–1993," *Journal of Marketing* 60 (April 1996): 1–16. See also Cornelia Pechmann and Chuan-Fong Shih, "Smoking Scenes in Movies and Antismoking Advertisements before Movies: Effects on Youth," *Journal of Marketing* 63 (July 1999): 1–13.

27 John E. Calfee and Debra Jones Ringold, "The Cigarette Advertising Controversy: Assumptions about Consumers, Regulations, and Scientific Debate," in *Advances in Consumer Research*, vol. 19, ed. John F. Sherry Jr. and Brian Sternthal (Provo, UT: Association for Consumer Research, 1992), 557–562.

28 Tim W. Ferguson, "Calm Down: Risk Is Not All Around," *Wall Street Journal*, December 14, 1993, A17; Judith Valente, "Scotch Makers Tell Youth It's Hip to Be Old-Fashioned," *Wall Street Journal*, December 29, 1993, B1, B5.

29 Yumiko Ono, "Some Liquor Makers Are Happy if You Switch to Beer—As Long as It's Theirs," *Wall Street Journal*, May 23, 1996, B1, B5; Sally Goll Beatty, "Seagram Flouts Ban on TV Ads Pitching Liquor," *Wall Street Journal*, June 11, 1996, B1, B6. Ron Dicker, "TV Liquor Advertising Binge Begins, Led by Skinnygirl, Jagermeister," accessed January 27, 2016, http://www.huffingtonpost.com/2012/05/23/tv-advertising-hard-liquor_n_1540123.html

30 J. Craig Andrews and Richard G. Netemeyer, "Alcohol Warning Label Effects: Socialization, Addiction, and Public Policy Issues," in *Marketing and Consumer Research in the Public Interest*, ed. Ronald P. Hill (Thousand Oaks, CA: Sage, 1996); "Fact Sheets—Binge Drinking," *Centers for Disease Control and Prevention*, accessed January 19, 2016, http://www.cdc.gov/alcohol/fact-sheets/binge-drinking.htm.

31 National Institute on Alcohol Abuse and Alcoholism , "Underage Drinking," accessed January 25, 2016, http://pubs.niaaa.nih.gov/publications/UnderageDrinking/UnderageFact.htm.

32 Bob Smith, "Compulsive Gamblers: In Over Their Heads," *HR Focus*, February 1992, 3.

33 Martin Fackler, "To Draw in New Crowds, an Industry Bets on Itself: Pachinko Parlors Court Japan's Youth, " *The New York Times*, September 6, 2014, accessed January 25, 2016, http://www.nytimes.com/2014/09/07/world/asia/to-draw-in-new-crowds-the-pachinko-industry-bets-on-itself.html?_r=0 and Bum Seok Jeong, ,Doug Hyun Han, Sun Mi Kim, Sang Won Lee and Perry F. Renshaw, "White matter connectivity and Internet gaming disorder," *Addiction Biology* (April 2015)accessed January 26, 2016, http://onlinelibrary.wiley.com/doi/10.1111/adb.12246/full

34 "Gambling on the Rise in China," *China News Daily*, June 27, 1996.

35 Gerhard Scherhorn, "The Addictive Trait in Buying Behavior," *Journal of Consumer Policy* 13 (1990): 33–51; Elizabeth C. Hirschman, "The Consciousness of Addiction: Toward a General Theory of Compulsive Consumption," *Journal of Consumer Research* 19 (September 1992): 155–179; Elizabeth C. Hirschman, "Cocaine As Innovation: A Social-Symbolic Account," in *Advances in Consumer Research*, vol. 19, ed. John F. Sherry Jr. and Brian Sternthal (Provo, UT: Association for Consumer Research, 1992), 129–139.

36 For information on pharmacological treatments for compulsive shopping, see, for example, Christopher Pittenger and Michael H. Bloch, "Pharmacological Treatment of Obsessive-Compulsive Disorder, *Psychiatric Clinics of North America* 37, no. 3: 375–391, accessed January 20, 2016, http://www.ncbi.nlm.nih.gov/pubmed/25150568.

37 "Compulsive Shopping Could Be Hereditary," *Marketing News*, September 14, 1998, 31.

[38] Emiko Terazono, "Suicide of Employee Who Worked Excessive Hours Costs Japanese Company $1.2 Million," *Financial Times*, March 30–31, 1996, 3; "Compulsive Work Addiction," *Bridgewater Landing,* accessed January 20, 2016, http://www.brightwaterlanding.com/compulsive-work-addiction/.

[39] Elizabeth C. Hirschman, "Professional, Personal, and Popular Culture Perspectives on Addiction," in *Marketing and Consumer Research in the Public Interest*, ed. Ronald P. Hill (Thousand Oaks, CA: Sage, 1996), 33–53; Ning Wang and Michael S. Minor, "Genes, Social Behavior, and Consumer Behavior" (working paper, September 2015).

[40] Ronald J. Faber, Gary A. Christenson, Martina de Zwann, and James Mitchell, "Two Forms of Compulsive Consumption: Comorbidity of Compulsive Buying and Binge Eating," *Journal of Consumer Research* 22 (December 1995): 296–304.

[41] David Glen Mick, "Are Studies of Dark Side Variables Confounded by Socially Desirable Responding? The Case of Materialism," *Journal of Consumer Research* 23 (September 1996): 106–119.

[42] Nancy Dunne, "Portrait of an American Dilemma," *Financial Times*, June 17, 1996, 1.

[43] Jeff Bailey, "The Dump's Foe Is Indignant and Has Money for a Fight," *Wall Street Journal*, June 7, 1996, A1, A4.

[44] Mitch Griffin, Barry J. Babin, and William R. Darden, "Consumer Assessments of Responsibility for Product-Related Injuries: The Impact of Regulations, Warnings, and Promotional Policies," in *Advances in Consumer Research*, vol. 19, ed. John F. Sherry Jr. and Brian Sternthal (Provo, UT: Association for Consumer Research, 1992), 870–878.

[45] G. Fisk and R. Chandran, "How to Trace and Recall Products," *Harvard Business Review* (November–December, 1975): 90–96.

[46] John C. Mowen, "Further Information on Consumer Perceptions of Product Recalls," in *Advances in Consumer Research*, vol. 7, ed. Jerry Olson (Ann Arbor, MI: Association for Consumer Research, 1980), 519–523; John C. Mowen, David Jolly, and G. S. Nickell, "Factors Influencing Consumer Responses to Product Recalls: A Regression Analysis Approach," in *Advances in Consumer Research*, vol. 8, ed. Kent Monroe (Ann Arbor, MI: Association for Consumer Research, 1981), 405–407.

[47] Tom J. Brown and Peter A. Dacin, "The Company and the Product: Corporate Associations and Consumer Product Responses," *Journal of Marketing* 61, no. 1 (January 1997): 66–84.

[48] Lisa Bannon, "Bazaar Gossip: How a Rumor Spread about Subliminal Sex in Disney's *Aladdin*," *Wall Street Journal*, October 24, 1995, A1, A6.

[49] Dorothy Rabinowitz, "Race and Rumor," *Wall Street Journal*, April 29, 1996, A20.

[50] John Stockmeyer, "Brands in Crisis: Consumer Help for Deserving Victims," in *Advances in Consumer Research*, vol. 23, ed. Kim P. Corfman and John G. Lynch Jr. (Provo, UT: Association for Consumer Research, 1996), 429–435.

[51] Robert Levy, "Tilting at the Rumor Mill," *Dun's Review*, July 1981, 52–54.

[52] Zachary Schiller, "P&G Is Still Having a Devil of a Time," *Businessweek,* September 11, 1995, 46.

[53] James Esposito and Ralph Rosnow, "Corporate Rumors: How They Start and How to Stop Them," *Management Review* (April 1983): 44–49.

[54] G. W. Allport and L. Postman, *The Psychology of Rumor* (New York: Holt, Rinehart & Winston, 1947).

[55] Neal Gabler, "The Lure of Urban Myths," *Playboy* (August 1996): 70–153.

[56] Robert Levy, "Tilting at the Rumor Mill," *Dun's Review*, July 1981, 52–54. Problems with aggressive approaches to crisis management are discussed in John Stockmeyer, "Brands in Crisis: Consumer Help for Deserving Victims," in *Advances in Consumer Research*, vol. 23, ed. Kim P. Corfman and John G. Lynch Jr. (Provo, UT: Association for Consumer Research, 1996), 429–435.

[57] Alice Tybout, Bobby Calder, and Brian Sternthal, "Using Information Processing Theory to Design Marketing Strategies," *Journal of Marketing Research* 18 (February 1981): 73–79.

[58] James R. Healey, "First Take: Big Toyota Recall Could Avoid GM Situation," accessed January 25, 2016, http://www.usatoday.com/story/money/cars/2014/04/09/gm-toyota-recall-regulators-fine/7501327/

[59] Patrick Murphy and Gene Laczniak, "Marketing Ethics: A Review with Implications for Managers, Educators, and Researchers," in *Review of Marketing*, ed. Ben M. Enis and Kenneth J. Roering (Chicago: American Marketing Association, 1981), 251–266.

INDEX

A

A&E television network, 9
abasement, 117
Abercrombie & Fitch, 208
Absolut Vodka, 65, 213
absolute threshold, **61**–62, 64
Accenture, 95
acculturation, **362**
Ace of Cakes, 272
achievement motivation, **125**
achievement, 117
ACORN, 399
acquisition phase, **3**
Activia, 152
activities, 316
  complementary, 316
  substitute, 316
actual product performance, **280**, 283
actual self, 153
actual state, **236**
actualizers, 158
adaptation, **66**
adaptation level, **66**
Adele, 387
adjustment and anchoring, **243**
adolescents, 339
Adolph Coors Company, 74
advertisement(s), 193, 369
  attitude toward, 187–190
  bookend, 94
  direct comparative, 215
  humorous, 217
  indirect comparative, 215
  soap opera, 100
advertising, 43, 44, 91, 121, 161, 171, 243, 280, 342, **366**, 375–376
  comparative, 40, 215
  corrective, 437
  deceptive, 436–437
  to children, 437–438
  unfair, 437
advertising clutter, **87**, 102
advertising wearout, **221**
Advice to a Young Tradesman, 316

aesthetics, **68**, 70, 71, 77, 277, 278, 279
  and perceptual organization, 70–71
  making products aesthetically
    pleasing, 68–71
  needs, 117
affect, **101**, **114**
affect and CS/D, **283**
affective feelings, **172**
affect-referral heuristic, **254**–255
affiliation, 117, 133
  need for, 117–118
African-American consumption,
  comparing, 397
African American English (AAE), 395
African-American subculture, 394–395
African American Vernacular English
  (AAVE), 395
African Americans, 408
age, 36, 388, 407, 408
  and information processing, 392–394
  subcultures, 389–392
aggression, 117
aggressive drivers, 149
AIO statements, **156**
  AIO inventories, questions in, 156,
    157
  and psychographics, 156–157
airlines, 37, 282, 284
Aldersen, Wroe, 9
Aleve, 215
Almond Joy, 91
alternative evaluation, **241**–249
  stage of generic decision-making
    model, 232
altruistic marketing, **5**–6
Amazon.com, 1, 29
ambiguity, tolerance for, 36
American Association of Retire
  Persons, 286
American Cancer Society, 313
American culture, 367
American Express Corporation, 154,
  155
American Marketing Association, 9
American Medical Association, 111

American Red Cross, 6
Americans, 402
  lower-class, 402
  middle-class, 402
  upper-class, 402
ammonia hydroxide, 83
Amp, 170
Amway, 446, 447
anchoring and adjustment, **243**
anger, 114
Anglo consumption, comparing, 397
Anheuser-Busch, 318, 380
antecedent states, 36, **318**–319
anthropology, 8
anti-meth campaign, 184
antismoking, 441
Apple, 1, 33, 62, 70, 98, 213, 231, 232,
  233, 249, 291, 308, 321
  iPod, 206
applied behavior analysis, **131**
apps, 33
Aquafresh, 42
Archie, 369
Arm & Hammer, 271
Armstrong, 9
arousal, 57, 65, 118–119, 149
  physiological, 114
  psychodynamic theory of, 65
ARPANET, 314
Asch, Solomon, 334
Asian-American subculture, 397
aspiration group, **331**
associationist school of psychology,
  93, 104
AT&T, 95
atmospherics, **309**, 310
  and shopping behavior, 310
  elements of store atmosphere,
    309–311
  in service settings, 311–312
**ATSCI (attention to social
  comparison interaction)**, **143**, 150
attention, **56**, 63
  involuntary, 56, 58, 77
  selective 58

attention, *(continued)*
  voluntary, 56–58, 77
attention stage of perception, **53**
  and information processing, 56–60
attitude, 172, 175, 176, 180, 185, 192,
    193, 219
  belief, behavior formation, and
    change, 169–200
  consumer, 192
  formation process, 42
  forming, 173–176
  hierarchies of, 175
  persuasion, belief, and behavior
    change, 181
  when it predicts behavior, 180
attitude toward the ad, 187–190
attitude-toward-the-object model,
    177–179, 180, 193
  algebraic formula, 178
attracting voluntary attention, 57
attractiveness,
  of the source, 206–208
  physical, 188, 223
attribute importance, 171
attributes, 170
attribution(s), 123, 283
  external, 123
  internal, 123
attribution error, fundamental, 124
attribution theory, 122, 123, 205,
    282–283
Audi, 56, 96, 97
augmentation-discounting model,
    123–124
augmenting principle, 124
auto industry, US, 51
autonomic decisions, 338
autonomy, 117, 346, **425**
  protection of, 425–426
availability heuristic, 243–244
awareness set, 237

B

baby-boom generation, 369, 371,
    389–391, 408
  marketing strategy of, 390–391
baby bust, 390
Bacharach, Burt, 206
Bain & Company, 285
balance theory, 185–187
balance-theory framework, cognitive
    elements in, 185
balanced and imbalanced states, 186
Baldwin, Alec, 123
Barbie, 407
barriers, 120

Barrymore, Drew, 210
Barter Kings, 9
bases for segmentation, 35
BBC, 1
Becker, Betina, 245
behavior(s), 35, 130, 219
  and intentions to behave, 172–173
  change, 181
  compulsive, 441–444
  consumption, 192
  creating directly, 174–175
  formation and change, 169–200
  forming, 173–176
  hierarchies of, 175
  learning and motivation, 111–141
  motivated, 112–113
  negligent, 438, 439
  usage, 37
behavior category of the person
    segmentation variable, 36, 37
behavior intentions, 172
behavior segmentation, 37
behavioral activation system (BAS), 59
behavioral economics, 30, **31,** 32
behavioral freedom, motivation to
    maintain, 119–120
behavioral influence hierarchy, 175,
    176
behavioral influence perspective, 8,
    125, 234, **235**–236, 260
behavioral influence techniques, 188
behavioral inhibition system (BIS), 60
behavioral intentions model, 180, 184,
    193
behavioral learning, 134
  and consumer behavior, 125–132
beliefs, 73, 97, 175, 176, 183, 192, 219,
    365, 366, 404
  attitude, behavior formation, and
    change, 169–200
  consumer, 170–173
  forming, 173–176
  hierarchies of, 175
  persuasion, attitude, and behavior
    change, 181
  salient, 177
believers, 158
benefit segmentation, 37, 191
benefits, 170
  consumers seek, 36, 37
Better Business Bureau, 286
Betty Crocker, 67, 272
Beyoncé, 88
bias, negativity, 343
Big Brothers Big Sisters of America, 6
biotechnology, 33

Black and Decker, 76
Black Friday, 308
Black, Jack, 206
Blackwell, Louis, 380
Bloomberg Businessweek, 5
Blue Bell Ice Cream, 120
BMW, 41, 51, 92, 96, 97, 366
body resources, need for, 149
bogie, 446
Bohemia, 62
bookend ads, 94
boomerang kids, 337
Boston Beer Company, 271
Bowman, Doug, 71
boycotts, 286
brain, primer, 418
brand(s), 1, 2, 125, 127, 133, 152, 193,
    379
  awareness, effects of, 255
  equity, 278, 279
  indifference, 290
  knockout, 244–245
  loyal consumers, identifying,
    291–292
  personality, 152, 292, 293
  personality traits, 152
  secondary, 40
  switching, spontaneous, 66
brand commitment, 291
brand communities, 291–292, **331,**
    352
  groups, 331–336
  model, psychological sense of,
    332
brand experience, 292, 293
  model, 293
brand knowledge, 96
brand loyalty, 36, 38, **289**–293, 295
  attitudinal measures of, 290–291
  behavioral approaches to, 290
Bridalplasty, 2
Britain, 30
Brosnan, Pierce, 127
Brown, Tom J., 331
Browning-Ferris, 445
Brunvand, Jan Harold, 447
Budweiser, 43, 56, 100, 217
Buick, 40, 41, 102
Burger King, 191, 352
butterfly curve, 66, **67**
buyers, 282
buying behavior,
  and social class, 403
  and social networks, 340–341
  groups influence on, 329
buying units, 3, 15, 17

C

Cadillac, 40, 41, 188
Cake Boss, 272
calm, 114
Camel, Joe, 441
Campbell Soup Company, 62, 400–401, 437
CampusLive, 205
Cap'n Crunch Berries Cereal, 89
Capital One, 123
Carlson, Brad D., 331
Cat's Pride, 217
categories of brands, 238
causality, motivation to attribute, 122–123
celebrities, 187, 201, 206, 209, 210, 211
celebrity endorsers, 124, 205, *see also* endorsers
central cues, 182
central route to persuasion, 182
cerebral cortex, 418
cerebral hemispheres, 418
channel surfing, 55
charity, 190
Charmin, 191
Chevrolet, 40, 41
Chicago Business Press, 29
Chick-fil-A, 174–175
Chieftain Cement, 217
childhood consumer socialization, 339
children, 340, 352, 389, 437, 438, 449
role in family decision making, 339
advertising to, 437–438
Children's Online Privacy Protection Rule, 437
Children's Television Act, 438
China, 32
Chive, 350
choice, 249–254
among noncomparable alternatives, 257
among stores, 257–258
compensatory models of, 250
low-involvement, 251
non-compensatory model of, 251
overload, 249
under high- and low-involvement conditions, 249–250
which models consumers use, 253–254
choice stage of generic decision-making model, 232
Christian Mingle, 337
Chronicle of Higher Education, 73
Churchill, Winston, 310

circular time, 317
circular traditional time, 316
Claiborne, Liz, 446
Clarkson, Kelly, 211
classes,
psychological differences among, 403–404
social, 408
see upper class, middle class, lower class, consumer(s), and Americans
classic fashion trend, 377
classical conditioning, 125–128, 132
paradigm, 126
perspective, 173
Close-Up (toothpaste), 42
clothing, 374, 376
cluster analysis, 399
clutter, advertising, 87, 102
Coca-Cola, 23–24, 45, 56, 169, 173, 202, 215, 294, 376, 379, 426
cognition, need for, 36, 150, 183
cognitive consistency, 185
cognitive learning, 84, 92
and memory, managerial implications of, 101–104
cognitive responses, 27, 182, 206
cognitive understanding, 117
cohesiveness, 334
Cold Stone Creamery, 274, 295
color, 59, 73, 74, 306, 373
Columbia University, 303
comic books, 369
commodities, 272
communication, 203
persuasive, see persuasive communications
via symbolic products, 155
communications model, 203–204
communities, brand, 331
comparative advertising, 40, 215
comparative message, 214–215
comparator, 112
compensatory models of choice, 249, 250, 254
competitive marketing environment, 30
competitive positioning, 40
competitors, 75, 215
complaint(s), and exit behavior, 288
complaint actions, types of, 286
complaint behavior, factors influencing, 287
complementary activities, 316
complex exchange, 11
compliance, 334
compound traits, 147, 150

comprehension stage of perception, **53**
comprehension, 77
compulsive behavior, 441–444, 450
buying, 151–152
other compulsions, 443
shopping, 443
compulsive consumption, 443, 444
ConAgra Foods, 388
concept testing, 42
conclusions, drawing, 214
concrete message, 214
conditioned response (CR), 126, 127
conditioned stimulus (CS), 126, 127, **134**
conditioning, 125–134
classical, 125–128, 132
operant, 125, 132, 134
Conference Board, 31
confidence, consumer, 31
confidentiality, 424–425
confirmation, expectant, 280
conformity, 334
group factors that lead to, 334
person factors that lead to, 335
pressure, 334, 353
conjunctive rule, 251–252, 254
connectedness, 36, 151
consent, 424–425
consideration set, 87, 238, 239
consumer(s), 9, 14, 117, 182, 183
adaptation, 66
analyzing, 5
and the environment, reciprocity between, 34
attitudes, 172, 192
complaints, corporate reactions to, 287–288
confidence, 31
consumption habits of mature, 393
dark-side behaviors, 438–444
emotions, 114–116
ethical issues in, 13–15
groups influence, 333–336
influences, characteristics of, 345
influencing without their knowledge, 63–66
interest, maintaining, 66–68
interests, protection of, 425–426
keeping them from forgetting, 98–101
lifestyles, 155–156
lower-class, 403
middle-class, 403
misbehavior, 5
motivation, and perceived risk, 120–121

consumer(s), *(continued)*
  post-acquisition process, model, 270
  process, 249–255
  psychoanalytic theory, 145–146
  psychological needs, 116–125
  research, 26
  responses to communications, 84–91
  responses, shaping, 130
  risks, types of, 121
  role-relaxed, 369
  satisfaction or dissatisfaction, model
    of, 276
  segments, predicting attitudes of,
    178
  socialization, model of, 340
  touch points, model of, 341
  upper-class, 403
consumer behavior, 3, 172
  and behavioral learning, 125–132
  concepts, managerial application
    areas of, 25
  dark side, 435–454
  developing marketing strategy,
    23–50
  economic environment, 30–32
  environmental analysis, 29–34
  history of, 3–4
  in market segmentation, 34–40
  in marketing mix development,
    41–45
  introduction to, 1–22
  marketing research, 25–29
  marketing strategy, developing,
    23–50
  model, 15
  natural environment, 32
  negligent, 449
  organizing model of, 15–19
  perspectives of, 7–9
  phases of, 3–4
  product positioning and
    differentiation, 40–41
  technology environment, 33–34
  theories, 7
  understanding, 4–7
  using to solve marketing problems,
    45–47
consumer beliefs, 170–173
**consumer complaint behavior,
  285**–288
consumer decision making, 232
  alternative perspectives on, 233–236
  decision processes, 231–268
consumer environment, 304
consumer involvement, 57, 77
  types of, 57
consumer knowledge, 92, 91, 103

  and brand perception, 91–98
  memory, and information
    processing, 83–110
consumer marketing, 14
consumer neuroscience, 415, 416–434
  ethical issues, 423–426
  experimental design in, 417–418
  managerial implications of, 427–428
  studies, 426–427
  techniques, 419–423
  why use, 423
consumer performance, 273
  types of, 273
Consumer Product Safety
  Commission, 445
consumer satisfaction, 275, 282–283
  measuring, 284–285
consumer search behavior, 237–241
consumer situations, 304, 305, 322
  types of, 305
Consumers Union, 286
consumption,
  behaviors, 192
  compulsive, 443
  habits of mature consumers, 393
  hedonic, 119
  performance, 272–273
  related rituals, 372
consumption amount, 271
consumption experience, 270, 273–274
  and mood states, 275
  satisfying, 270–275
consumption frequency, 271
consumption phase, 3
consumption purpose, 271
consumption visions, 236
content analysis, 27
contentment, 114
context, 258
**contingencies of reinforcement,
  130**–131
contracted performance, 273
convenience, 278–279
conventions, 363
cooperation, mutual, 346–347
Coors beer, 99
core values, 366–367
corporate behaviors, and dark side of
  consumer, 436–438
corporate reactions to consumer
  complaints, 287–288
Corporate Responsibility magazine, 449
corporate social responsibility, 444,
  450
corporation, appropriate role for,
  444–445
corrective advertising, 437

Corvette, 96, 97
counteraction, 117
Covergirl, 210
Crayola crayons, 119
Creative Review, 380
creativity, 93, 97
credence services, 240
credibility, 205–206, 223
cresive norms, 363
Crest (toothpaste), 40, 42, 191
cross-cultural environments, 304
Crowd Management Strategies, 308
crowding, 307–309
cues,
  central, 182
  peripheral, 182
  retrieval, 90, 91
cultural, 90–91, 182
  environments, 304
  matrix, 364–365
  myths, 380
  norms, 380
  symbols, 373–375, 380
cultural identification, 362
cultural meanings, 365
  communicating, 366
cultural rituals, 371–373, 380
cultural values, 367
  consumer research on, 367–371
culture, 38–39, 161, **362**, 380
  acculturation, 362
  American, 367
  and subculture environment, 30
  components of, 362–365
  enculturation, 362
  high, 375
  identification, 362
  marketing environment, 30
  pop/popular, 361–386, see also
    popular culture
  role of consumer in, 365–371
  segmentation basis, 36, 38–39
  US, 388–389
Curtis, Jamie Lee, 152
customer,
  loyalty, 269, 293
  satisfaction, 282, 295
  service, 269
cyclical fashion trend, 377

D

Da Vinci Code, The, 71
Dali, Salvador, 71
dating, online, 12
De Beers, 59
deceptive advertising, 436–437

decider, 334
decision(s), 335–338
    autonomic, 338
    husband-dominated, 338
    syncretic, 338
    type of, 335
    wife-dominated 338
decision making,
    approach to attitude change,
        181–183
    hierarchies, 175–176
    influence of decision makers, 338
    perspectives on, 234
decision-making perspective, 77,
    233–235, 260
Deepwater Horizon, 32
defendance, 117
deference, 117
Dell, 95
demographic(s),
    and subcultures, 387–414
    marketing environment, 30
demographic characteristics of the
    people segmentation variable, **35**
demographic variables, **388**
density, **307**, 308
Dentsu, 443
dependence, 346
depression, 114
depth interviews, **27**, **145**, 146
desired state, **236**, 259
detached nuclear family, **336**
development, new-product, 42
Deviant Art, 33
difference threshold, **61**–62, 64
differentiation,
    and positioning, 76, 102, 133, 161,
        379, 407, 428, 449
    product, 40, 47
diffuse optical tomography (DOT), 419
diffusion, **347**
    information, 347
    of innovations, 347–350
    pattern, factors influencing, 349
    processes, 347–351
    through social networks, 350–351
direct comparative advertisements,
    215
disabled subculture, 406
discounting principle, **123**
discrete exchange, **12**
discriminative stimuli, **129**–130
    operation of, 130
disease, 32
Dish Network, 55
disjunctive rule, **252**

Disney, 1, 245, 291, 345, 375, 446
disposition phase, **3**
dissatisfaction, 279
    emotional, 280
dissociative group, **331**
distribution strategy, 234
    and pricing applications, 44–45
distributive justice, 282
divestment rituals, **372**
divine proportion, **71**
divorce, 337
domain-specific values, **367**
dominance, 117, 347
Domino's Pizza, 237
door-in-the-face technique, **189**–190
Doritos, 56
Downey, Robert, Jr., 54
drama, **218**
dramas versus lectures, 218
dramatistic performance, **273**–**274**
drawing conclusions, **214**
DRD4 dopamine receptor gene, 147
Drillman, Paula, 146
drinking, compulsive, 440, 442
driving habits, bad, 141, 440
Drucker, Peter, 5
Duckhorn Vineyards, 98
Duncan Hines, 272
Duncan, Tim, 209
durability, 277, 278, 279
Durant, Kevin, 205
dyadic exchange, **342**–347
Dyson, 171

E

E! network, 2
E.T. (movie), 363
eagle, 363
ear worms, 91
Earnhart, Dale, Jr., 210
Easter Bunny, 363
eating disorders, 444
e-cigarettes, 435, 436
economic disincentives, 441
economic environments, 304
    and consumer behavior, 30–32
    marketing environment, 30
economic incentives, 440–441
economic status, 401
economics, 7
    behavioral, 30
ecstasy, 114
education, 35, 36, 388, 401, 404, 440
EEG, 421–422
effects and alternative evaluation,
    hierarchies of, 242

ego, **144**
ego-defense function, **172**, 193
eHarmony, 337
elaboration likelihood model (ELM),
    181, 182, 183
elasticity, 36, 37
elderly, 392, 408
electroencephalography (EEG), **419**
elemental traits, **147**, 150
eliciting stimulus (UCS), 126, 127
elimination behaviors, 129
elimination-by-aspects heuristic, **252**
emotional dissatisfaction, **280**
emotional satisfaction, **280**
emotions, 101, **114**, 283
    consumer, 114–116
employee interactions, 278, 279
enacted norms, **363**
enacted performance, **273**
encoding, **84**, 89–90, 103, 205, 206, 209,
    211
enculturation, **362**
endorser, expert, 206
    trustworthy, 206
    untrustworthy, 206
    see also celebrity endorsers
enduring involvement, **57**, 77
Energizer Bunny, 68
energy drink, 169, 171
enjoyment and fun, 159
environment,
    and consumers, reciprocity between,
        34
    physical, 174
environmental analysis, 17, 24–25,
    29, 46, 75, 102, 132–133, 161, 191,
    222, 258, 294, 351, 379, 406–407,
    427, 448
Environmental Defense Fund, 44
environmental influencers, **17**
episodic memory, 88
equity theory, **281**
    and consumer satisfaction, 280–282
Eskimo Joes, 72
ESPN, 55
esteem needs, 117
ethical dilemma, **14**
ethical exchange, **14**
ethical issues,
    in consumer relations, 13–15
    in exchange, relational, 11
ethics, **13**, 18
    professional, 15
ethnic subcultures, 394
ethnicity, 35, 36, 388, **394**
ethnographic research, **27**
Europe, 370

even-a-penny-will-help technique, **190**
evolutionary psychology, needs for material and body resources, 149–150
exchange, 3, **9**, 18
  benefits of, 9–10
  complex, 11
  discrete, 11
  ethical, 11
  external, 11
  formal, 11
  informal, 11
  internal, 11
  relationships, dimension of, 11–13
  restricted, 11
exchange processes, **3**
exchange rituals, **372**
excitement, 159
exhibition, 117
exit behavior, **288**
  and complaints, 288
expectant confirmation, **280**
expectant disconfirmation model (disconfirmation paradigm), 279–280
expectations, **73**
  and the price-quality relationship, 74–75
  product, 280
  role of, 73–74
experiences, 158, **272**
experiential perspective, **7**
experiential (impulse) purchase, **176**
experiential choice processes, 154
experiential hierarchy, 175, **176**
experiential path to attitude change, 185
experiential perspective, 234, **235**, 260
experiential services, 240
experiment, **28**
experimental noise, **417**
experimental subject, **417**
expertise, 334
exposure stage of perception, **53**
  and information processing, 54–56
exposure, 76
  selective, 54
expressive needs, **116**
extended family, **336**
external attribution, **123**
external exchange, **11**
external search, **237**, 239, 260
  degree of, 240
  measuring, 239–240
external stimuli, **113**
extinction, **129**

F

Facebook, 1, 33, 55, 56, 60, 88, 171, 212, 256, 292, 340, 350, 423
Faison, Ebony, 119
Fallon, Jimmy, 88
families and households, 336–340, 353
  size, 35, 36
  decision making, 337–338
  detached nuclear, 336
  extended, 336
  influence in, 338–339
  nuclear, 336
Farve, Brett, 202, 210
fashion, **376**–378, 381
  industry, 378
  trends, 377
  turning points, 377
fear appeal, **216**
Federal Trade Commission (FTC), 215, 436, 437
Federer, Roger, 206
feelings, 10
  affective, 172
  and memory, 101
Ferrari, 40, 41
fertility rate, **390**
Feyt, 312
Fibonacci series (of numbers), 71
figure-ground principles, 70
filiarchy, 438
financial perceived risk, 121
Fishbein attitude-toward-the-object model, 177, 179, 249, 251
Fishbein, Martin, 180
Fitzgerald, Tom, 378
flashbulb memory, **101**
Flickr, 71
flowers, 347
flush factor, 54
focus groups, **27**, **146**, 245
Foot Locker, 120
foot-in-the-door technique, **189**
Ford Motor Company, 36, 88
  Mustang, 52, 90, 96, 97, 170, 171, 177, 178, 179, 180
forgetting, and time, 100
formal exchange, **11**
Fox Broadcasting Company, 391
framing, **247**
  and prospect theory, 247–249
Franklin, Benjamin, 316
fraudulent symbol, **405**
free riding, **14**–15
frequency heuristic, **253**
frequency, **421**
  consumption, 271

Freud, Sigmund, 144
  structure of the personality, 144–145
Frito-Lay, 29
fulfilleds, 158
Full Throttle, 169, 170
full-scale production, 43
fun and enjoyment, 159
functional magnetic resonance imaging (fMRI), **419**–421
fundamental attribution error, **124**

G

Galaxy S 3 smartphone, 113
gambling, 442–443
gaming, 443
garbage, 289
gatekeepers, 347, 348
Gatorade, 95, 201, 202
Geico, 206, 213
gender, 291, 388
gender-role orientation, 388, 339
General Electric (GE), 59
General Mills Inc., 67, 157, 271
General Motors (GM), 40, 51, 52, 448
generalize, **417**
Generation Xers, **391**
Generation Y, 43
generic decision-making model, **232**, 233
genes, SKTT and DRD4, 147
geodemographics, **38**, 45, **399**–400
geography,
  segmentation basis, 36, 38
  companies segment by, 400–401
Georgia-Pacific, 219
Gestalt, **68**, 70, 278
  principle of contrast, 59
Gestalt psychologists, **68**, 69, 70, 92, 93, 104
Gestalt psychology, 69
  approach to knowledge, 92–93
Ghost Whisperer, 27
gifts, 248, 249, 322, 366
  giving, 314–315
  obligatory, 314
  self-, 314
  voluntary, 314
Gillette, 95, 201, 202
Gilmore, James H., 272
glial cells, 418
global attitude measure, **179**
  versus attitudes toward the object, 179–180
global values, **367**
Gnuse, Julia, 379
Go Daddy, 173

golden ratio, 71
golden rule, 15
goodness or badness, 245–246
goods, 10, **272**
    purchased as status symbols, 405
Google, 1, 33
Got Milk? (commercial), 97
government regulation, avoiding, 448
great recession of 2007–2009, 30, 31, 51
Great Wolf Lodge, 3
Green Lantern, 363
grooming habits, 373
grooming rituals, 372
group(s), 330, 352
    aspiration, 331
    brand community, 331–336
    dissociative, 331
    factors that lead to conformity, 334
    in-, 329
    norms, 353
    out-, 329
    processes, 330–331
    reference, 330–331, 333
    size, 334
    subcultures and demographic,
        388–389
    therapy, 146
    types of, 330–331
group polarization, 335–336

H

habits, 371
    grooming, 373
halo effect, 171, **207**
Hanes, 206
Harley-Davidson, 72, 291, 333
    Harley Owners Group (HOG), 333
harm avoidance, 117
Hasbro, 449
Hastens, 342
Hathaway, Anne, 405
Hayek, Salma, 183
Head & Shoulders, 90, 95
hedonic consumption, 119
Heider, Fritz, 186
Heileman, 395
Heinz, 129, 391
hertz (Hz), 421
heuristic,
    affect-referral, 254–255
    availability, 243–244
    elimination-by-aspects, 252
    frequency, 253
    lexicographic, 252
    representativeness, 244
Hewlett-Packard, 95

hierarchical models of choice, 251
hierarchies of effects, 173, 175
hierarchy,
    behavioral influence, 176
    experiential, 176
    high-involvement, 175
    low-involvement, 176
high culture, 375
high involvement, 176
    effects of, 57–58
    choice, 250
    decision processes, 234
    decisions, 234
high-involvement hierarchy, 175, 233
Hilton, Paris, 211
hindsight bias, 243
Hispanic(s), 394, 395, 408
    consumption, comparing, 397
    problems marketing to, 397
    segmentation, 396–397
Hispanic subculture, 395, 396–397
hobbies, dangerous, 111
Hollister, 208
Hopper, 55
households and families, 336–340, 353
    demographic of, 336–337
humor in messages, 216–218
    effect on product evaluation, 218
humorous ads, 217
Hurley (brand), 292
husband-dominated decisions, 338
hypothetical value function, 246, 247
Hyundai Motor Company, 41, 75

I

IBM, 34, 98
IcyHot, 6
id, 144
idea generation, 42
identification, 331
iDrive, 92
ILYAs (incompletely launched young
        adults who aren't financially
        independent), 391
image transference, 309
imbalanced states, and balanced, 186
immigrants, 389
impersonal threats, 120
impulse buying, 256
impulse-control disorders, 444
impulse (experiential) purchase, 176
impulse purchase, 255–258
impulse-seeking purchases, 8
income, 35, 36, 388, 404
incremental effects theory, 65
Index of Consumer Sentiment, 31

indifference, 347
**indirect comparative advertisements,
    215**
individual difference variables, 142
individual influence factors, 17
industrial marketing, 14
inelastic, price, 37
inept set, 238
inert set, 238
infavoidance, 117
influence factors, individual, 17
influencers, 343
    environmental, 17
influencing behavior, 128
informal exchange, 11
information, 10, **52**
    diffusion, 347
    search, 403
    semantic, 88
    verbal and pictorial, 89
    vivid versus abstract, 213–214
information overload, 85, 86
information processing, 52, 76
    and age, 392–394
    and exposure stage of perception,
        54–56
    attention stage of perception,
        56–60
    memory and consumer knowledge,
        83–110
    overview of, 52–60
    perceptual processes, 51–82
    system, 53
information salience, 99
informational influence, 333
informed consent, 424
informing, 440
ingratiation, 188–189
in-group, 329
innovation, 348–349
    diffusion of, 347–350
    product, 344
    symbolic, 348
    technological, 349
inputs, 281
Institute on Black Chemical Abuse,
    395
institutional review board (IRB), 424,
    429
instrumental materialism, 369
instrumentality of search, 240
Intel, 95
intentions to behave, and behaviors,
    172–173
interaction, 320
interaction set, 258
interactional justice, 282

Interdisciplinary Symposium on Decision Neuroscience, 426
interface,
    proactive, 98
    retroactive, 98
internal attribution, **123**
internal exchange, **11**
internal search, **237**–239, 260
internal stimuli, **112**
International 10–20 System, **421**
Internet, 314
interpretation process, **71**
    of information phase, 73
interpretive research methods, **8**
interrupt, **112**
interviews, depth, 27, 145, 146
involuntary attention, **56**, 58, 77
    attracting, 58–60
    how to elicit, 60
involuntary risks, **121**
involvement response, **57**
involvement, **53**
    consumer, 77
    enduring, 77
    level, 58
    situational, 77
iPod, 231
Ishima, Ichiro, 443
Ivory Soap, 68, 214
Iwata, Satojru, 438

J

Jackson, Michael, 24
Jacoby, Jacob, 437
Jaguar, 52, 90
James, William, 149
Japan, 40, 374, 393, 443
Jeep, 178, 179, 291
Jennings, Greg, 217
jingles, 91
JMD, 63
JND, 62, 63
Jobs, Steve, 363
Johnson & Johnson, 202, 449
Johnson, Magic, 202
Jolie, Angelina, 210
Jordan, Michael, 6, 120, 127, 187, 201, 202, 206
joy, 114
just meaningful difference, 62
just noticeable difference (JND), **61**
justice, 282
    distributive, 282
    interactional, 282

K

Kaiser Family Foundation, 389
Kansas State University, 329
Kant's categorical imperative, 15
Karan, Donna, 373
Katona, George, 31
Kelley, Harold, 123
Kennedy, John, 204
KFC, 244, 245
Kia, 40, 41
kids, boomerang, 337
Kinect, 24
KitchenAid, 76
knockoffs, 245
knockout brands, 244–245
knowledge,
    consumer, 92, 103
    objective, 91
    of others, 91, 92
    subjective, 91
knowledge role, **172**
Koch Jim, 271
Kotler, Philip, 9, 310
Kraft Foods, 54, 436, 437

L

L.L. Bean, 399
laddering, **368**
Larry the Cable Guy, 183
Las Vegas Convention Bureau, 154
law of contiguity, **95**
layout, effects of, 309
Le Bon, Gustav, 308
lead users, 347–348
leaders, opinion, 347–348, 351
leadership, opinion, 343–344
Lean Cuisine, 95
learning,
    behavioral, 134
    cognitive, 84, 92
    observational, 131, 135
    paired-associate, 95
    serial, 93
    vicarious, 131, 135
learning through education, **92**
learning through experience, **92**
lecture, **218**
    versus dramas, 218
legends, urban, 343
    see also urban legends
Lenova, 95
Levi Strauss, 390
lexicographic heuristic, **252**
lexicographic model, 254
Lexus, 41

LG, 1
libido, **145**
life themes, **219**, 220
lifestyle, **142**, **155**, 156, 162
    and social class, 404–407
    consumer, 155–156
    psychographic analysis, and marketing strategy, 155–160
lighting, 305, 306
likability, 208–211, 223
likelihood,
    and goodness or badness, 242
    judging, 242–243
Likert scales, 284
Lincoln Motor Company, 36, 56, 88
linear time, 316
LinkedIn, 33, 160, 350
List of Values (LOV) scale, 157, **159**, 368
    research on, 368–369
Listerine, 183
lists versus narratives, 221
Little Richard, 206
logos, 73
Lohan, Lindsey, 205
long-term memory, 84, **86**, 87, 88 91
looking glass self, 154
love belongingness, 117
lower-class Americans, 402
lower-class consumers, 403
low-involvement choice, 251
low-involvement decision processes, 234
low-involvement hierarchy, 175, **176**, 235
low-involvement products, 45
loyalty,
    brand, 36, 295
    customers, 293
    identifying brand-loyal consumers, 291–292
    switch, 290
    undivided, 290
    see also customer loyalty and brand loyalty
loyalty and satisfaction, 269–302
    comparing, 293
    predicting, 292–293

M

M&M/Mars, 62
macro-segmentation, 39
Madden, John, 202
Madonna, 67
magnetic resonance imaging (MRI), **419**

magnetoencephalography (MEG), 419
makers, 158
managerial applications analysis, 132–135
managerial implications of,
  attitudes, beliefs, and behavior formation and change, 190–192
  consumer neuroscience, 427–428
  groups, dyadic exchanges, and diffusion, 351–352
  memory and cognitive learning, 101–102
  motivation, 132–133
  perceptual processes, 75–76
  personality and psychographics, 160–161
  persuasive communications, 222–223
  popular culture, 378–379
  post-acquisition processes, 293–294
  responsive marketing, 258–259
  situational influences, 321–322
  subcultures and demographics, 406–407
  the dark side of consumer behavior, 448–449
Mandela, Nelson, 363
Manning, Peyton, 206, 210
maps, perceptual, 40
March of Dimes, 313
marital status, 35, 36, 388
market embeddedness, **13**, 18
market mavens, **344**
market research, 101–102, 243, **416**, 427
market segmentation, **34**, 46
market testing, **42**
marketer, 15–16
marketing, **5**
  altruistic, 5–6
  consumer, 14
  effort, extent of, 350
  environments, 30
  industrial, 14
  opportunities, occasion-based, 313–314
  problems, using consumer behavior to solve, 45–47
  RESPonsive, see RESPonsive marketing
  to Hispanics, 397
marketing concept, **3**
marketing mix, **16**–17, **25**, 76, 102, 133, 152, 161, 191–192, 223, 259, 294, 352, 380, 407, 428, 449
  development, 46, 47
  consumer behavior in 41–45

high- and low-involvement product purchases, 234
marketing research, **25**–26, 46, **416**, 417
  consumer behavior in, 25–29
marketing solutions analysis, **45**
marketing strategy, **16**, **24**
  and consumer behavior, developing, 23–50
  and self-concept, 153–155
  lifestyle and psychographic analysis, 155–160
  of baby-boom generation, 390–391
marketing strategy cycle, **24**
marketing triad, **304**
marriage, later, 336–337
Martha Stewart Living (magazine), 85
Mary Kay, 13
Maslow's hierarchy of needs theory, 117, 133, 158
Match.com, 12, 337
match-up effect, **207**
material resources, need for, 149
materialism, 369, 370
  instrumental, 369
  research on value, 369–371
  terminal 370, 371
Mattel, 407
mature consumer, **392**
mavens and surrogates, 344
McCann-Erickson ad agency, 146
McClelland, David, 117, 118
McClelland's theory of learned needs, 117–118, 132
McConaughey, Matthew, 204
McDonald's, 60, 68, 191, 321, 376, 390, 446, 447, 448
means-end-chain models, **367**
Medium (TV show), 27
Meetup, 33
meishi, 374
memory, **53**, 84–91
  and cognitive learning, 101–104
  and feelings, 101
  consumer knowledge, and information processing, 83–110
  episodic, 88
  flashbulb, 101
  long-term, 84, 86, 87, 91
  multiple-store model, 84
  picture, 103
  semantic, 96–98, 103
  sensory, 84
  short-term, 84, 85, 86, 87
  verbal, 103
  working, 84, 85
memory-control processes, **89**

men, 337, 370, 392, 393
Mercedes, 41, 292
mere exposure phenomenon, **173**, 181
message(s),
  characteristics and structure, 220–224
  comparative, 214–215
  concrete, 214
  construction, 211
  one-sided versus two-sided, 216
message complexity, **213**
message content, **211**, 212
  and message characteristics, 211–220
  developing, 212
message structure, **220**
Mexicans, 395, 408
Mexico, 32
MFC, 245
Michelli, Joseph, 269
micro-segmentation, 39
Microsoft, 1, 24, 55, 288, 449
middle-class Americans, 402
middle-class consumers, 403
millennials, 43, 117, **391**–392, 448
Miller Brewing Company, 74
Miller, George, 85
Miller's law, **85**, 103
minorities, in advertising, 398
Mirage, 311
miscomprehension, 436
modalities, using multiple, 99–100
model, **131**
money, 10
Monster, 169, 170
Montana, Joe, 202
mood, **101**, 236, 275
mood states, **256**, **318**, 319
  and the consumption experience, 275
  effects on choice, 256–257
  consumers, effects of temporary, 318–319
mores, 363
mortality rates, **392**
Mothers Against Drunk Driving (MADD), 440
motivated behavior, 112–113
motivation, 43, **112**, 118, 134
  and behavior learning, 111–141
  managerial implications of, 124–125
Mounds (candy bar), 91
Mountain Dew, 161
movement, 59
Mowen, John, 445
MSN.com, 55
MTV, 376
Mulally, Alan, 88

multiattribute models, **177**
  and decision-making path to
    persuasion, 183
  predicting consumer attitudes,
    176–187
multiattribute perspective, 184
multiple-store memory model, 84
multistep flow model, 347, 353
Murray's social needs, 117
music, 91, 126, 275, 376, 407
  effects of, 306–307
Mustang (Ford), 52, 90, 96, 97, 170, 171,
    177, 178, 179, 180
mutual cooperation, 346–347
mutuality, 346
Myspace, 33
myths, 363
  cultural, 380
  Superman, 363

N

Nabisco, 54
narratives versus lists, 221
National Basketball Association, 364
National Football League, 55, 364, 401
National Institute on Alcohol Abuse
    and Alcoholism, 442
nationality, 35, 36, 388
Native Americans, 380
natural environment, 30
  and consumer behavior, 32
  marketing environment, 30
Nature Company, 159
Neal, James, 438
need(s), 35
  aesthetic, 117
  esteem, 117
  expressive, 116
  Maslow's hierarchy of needs theory,
    117, 158
  McClelland's social needs, 132
  McClelland's theory of learned,
    117–118
  Murray's social, 117
  physiological, 117
  safety, 117
  utilitarian, 117
need for achievement, 117
need for affiliation, 117–118
need for body resources, 149
need for cognition, 36, **150**, 183
need for material resources, 149
need for power, 118
need for uniqueness, 118
need recognition, 112
negative reinforcer, 128

negativity bias, 343
negligent behavior, 438, 439, 449
Nescafé, 415, 416
Netherlands, 370
networking, social, *see* social
    networking
neurological measures, 427
neuromarketing, 416, 417, 428
neurons, 418
neuroscience, 29, 416
  consumer, 415–434
  experimental design in, 417–418
  techniques, 419–423
  why use, 423
neuroscience studies, 426–427
  ethical issues, 423–426
neurotransmission, 418
neutral stimulus, 125
Neutrogena, 373
new-product development process, 42
news gathering, 212
Nicholson, Jack, 141
Nielsen PRIZM, 399
Nike Inc., 99, 120, 147, 151, 171
Ning, 33
Nintendo, 407, 438
Nissan, 96, 97, 391
Nixon, Richard, 204
noise, 306, 418
  experimental, 417
**non-compensatory models of choice,
    251**
nongovernment organizations
    (NGOs), 44
norm(s), 333, **362**, 363, 365
  cresive, 363
  cultural, 380
  enacted, 363
  group, 353
norm of reciprocity, 189
normative influence, 333
**North American Standard Industrial
    Classification System (NASIC),
    39**
North Valley Coalition of Concerned
    Citizens, 445
NOS, 170
novelty, 117
nuclear family, 336
*Nudge: Improving Decisions about
    Health, Wealth, and Happiness*, 32
nudity, 208

O

O'Connor, Arthur, 256
O'Donnell, Rosie, 205

O'Neal, Shaquille, 6
objective knowledge, 91
objects, 170
obligatory gifts, 314
observational learning, 131, 132, 135
observational research, 27
occupation, 35, 36, 388
occurrence, 273
Ogilvy & Mather, 211
Ohio State University, 303
OKCupid, 423, 424
Oklahoma, 205
Old Spice, 217
Olestra, 26
Oliver, Richard, 293
ongoing search, 237
online dating, 12
online quantitative data, 29
operant conditioning, 125, **128**–131,
    132, 134
opinion leaders, 343–344, 347–348, 351
  characteristics of, 344
  comparing product innovators, 344
opponent-process theory, 115–116,
    134
opportunity loss perceived risk, 121
Optimist International Junior World,
    201
optimum stimulation level, 118–119
order, 117
Oreos, 206
organization, perceptual, 68–70, 77
orientation reflex, 58
outcomes, 281
out-group, 329
overload, information, 85, 86
overwork, 443

P

paired-associate learning, 95
Palmer, Arnold, 202
Pampered Chef, 13, 335
paradox, 213
parents, 340
Parthenon (in Greece), 71
Pavlov, Ivan, 125, 126
Peabody Hotel, 295, 274–275
peers, 340
Peller, Clara, 213
Pentagon, 71
Pepsi, 23, 88, 169, 202, 426
perceived risk, 120
  and consumer motivation, 120–121
  how to reduce, 122
perceived value, 74, **75**
perception, 53

of risk, factors influencing, 121–122
stages of, 53
subliminal, 77
perceptual maps, 40–41
of automotive brand, 41
perceptual organization, 68–70, 77
and aesthetics, 70–71
rules of, 69
perceptual processes, information
processing, 51–82
performance, 278, 279
dramatistic, 273–274
enacted, 273
perceived risk, 121
peripheral cues, 182
peripheral route to persuasion, 182
person, 319–322
factors that lead to conformity, 335
personal influence, ethical
implications of, 190
personal selling, 43–44
personal value, 6
personality, 38, 43, **142**, 143, 162
and psychographics, managerial
implications of, 160–163
brand, see brand personality
category of characteristics of the
person segmentation variable, 36,
38
psychoanalytic theory of, 144
self-concept and lifestyle, 142
and psychographics, 141–168
traits, use of scales measuring
152–153
understanding, 143–153
persuasion, 181
and attitude-toward-the-object
model, 183–184
attitude, belief, and behavior
change, 181
central route to, 182
communications, 201–230
peripheral route to, 182
Pew Research Center, 337
Phantom, 363
phased strategy, 253
physical,
attractiveness, 223
environment, 174
perceived risk, 121
physical surroundings, 36, 305, **306**
store environment, 306–312
physiological arousal, 114
physiological needs, 117
pictorial information, 89
picture memory, 103
piecemeal report strategy, 253

Pike Place Fish Market, 3
Pine, Joseph B., 272
Pinterest, 33, 292, 312
pipe dream rumors, 446
Pitt, Brad, 210
Pizza Hut, 56, 239
Planters Peanuts, 54
plastic surgery, 2
play, 117
Playtex, 208
pleasure principle, 144
polarization, group, 335–336
political marketing environment, 30
pollution, 32
popular culture, 361–364, **365**, 366–386
examples, 375–376
how it develops, 377
managerial implications of, 378–380
population, US, 394
Porsche, 69, 96, 97
Pose, 312
positioning, 16, 24, 25, 46, 76, 102, 133,
152, 161, 191, 223, 259, 294, 321–
322, 351, 379, 407, 428, 449
and segmentation strategies, 17
competitive, 40
product, 40, 47
specific, 40
positive reinforcer, 128
positron emission tomography (PET),
419
possession rituals, 372
possible selves, 153
post-acquisition processes, 269–270
satisfaction and dissatisfaction,
275–285
evaluation stage of generic decision-
making model, 232
post-purchase satisfaction, 42
power, 117
need for, 118
preattention, 63, 64, 77, 84
premeditated rumors, 446
prepurchase search, 237
previously neutral stimulus (CS), 126,
127
price(ing), 75, 259, 420, 449
and distribution applications, 44–45
change, 248
JND, problems with, 62
strategies, 74, 234
price elasticity, 37
price inelastic, 37
price-quality relationship, 74–75
Prilosec, 183
primacy effect, 220
primary effect, 94

priming, 98, 116, 134
privacy, 424–425
private acceptance, 334
proactive interference, 98
problem recognition, 236
stage of generic decision-making
model, 232
problem solving, 93
Procter & Gamble Co. (P&G), 26, 83,
191, 202, 287, 446, 447
product(s), 42, 47
adoption, 348
attributes, 192
characteristics of, 349–350
development, 42–43
diffusion, model of, 349
disposition, 288–289
failure, 282–283
innovators, 344
comparing opinion leaders, 344
interactions, 319–322
low-involvement, 45
making aesthetically pleasing, 68–71
misuse, 439–440
performance, actual, 280, 283
performance, evaluating, 277–279
price or features, changing, 60–63
recall implications, overview, 445
symbolism and self-concept, 154
product differentiation, 40, 41, 47
product expectations, 280
product positioning, 40, 47
product quality, 277
product stewardship, 449
product use, 271
production, full-scale, 43
projective techniques, 415
promotional strategy, 76, 161, 234
and psychoanalytic theory, 145
and self-concept, 154–155
based on type of consumer, 176
implications, 43–45
propensity for taking risks, 36
proportion, divine, 71
proportion-of-purchases method, 290
prospect theory, 246
protection, of consumer interests and
autonomy, 425–426
proximity,
sensory, 214
spatial, 214
time, 214
psychoanalytic theorists, 145
**psychoanalytic theory of personality,
144**–145, 162
and consumer research, 145–146
and promotional strategy, 145

psychodynamic theory of arousal, **65**
psychographic analysis, **142**
  lifestyle, and marketing strategy,
    155–160
  traditional perspectives, 156
psychographics, 36, **38**, 43, **156**, 162
  and AIO statements, 156–157
  and personality, managerial
    implications of, 160–163
  category of characteristics of the
    person segmentation variable, 38
  personality, and self-concept,
    141–168
psychological closeness, **330**
psychological needs, consumer,
  116–125
psychological perceived risk, 121
psychologists, Gestalt, *see* Gestalt
  psychologists
psychology, 7, 8
  associationist school, 93
public image, acquiring positive, 445
public policy, **5**
public relations, 44
punisher, **114**, 125, 128, 129
purchases,
  impulse, 8, 255–258
  variety-seeking, 8, 256
Pure Salmon campaign, 44

Q

Q Score, 201, 202, 209
qualitative research methods, **26**
quality, dimensions of, 277–278
quantitative data, online, 29
quantitative methods, **26**–29
questionnaire, **28**
questionnaire scales, **28**
quiet set, 258

R

race, 388
  subculture, 394–398
rage, 114
random, **417**
raw materials, 32
reactance, **119**, 120
reality principle, **144**
rebates, 248, 249
recall, 87, **208**
  implications, 445
recall task, 86
recency effect, 94, **220**
recognition, 87
recognition task, 86

recycling, 289
Red Bull, 146, 152, 169, 170, 176
Red Robin, 341
Reebok, 188, 378
reference group, **330**–331, 333
referrals, 342
refund, 285
region, 388, 408
regional subcultures, **398**–401
regulatory environments, 304
rehearsal, **85**, 86, 90
Reichheld, Frederick, 285
reinforcement, 129
  behavior, 128
  contingencies of, 130–131
  schedules of, 129
reinforcer, **114**, 125, 128, 129, 130
  negative, 128
  positive, 28
  secondary, 128
rejection, 117
relational exchange, **12**
  characteristics of, 12–13
  key findings, 13
relationships with others, 159
relative influence of decision makers,
  338
reliability, **146**, 277, 278, 279
religion, 35, 36, 388
Rembrandt (mouth rinse), 42, 183
repeat purchase behavior, **290**
repetition effects, 221
representativeness heuristic, **244**
research, 24, 25, 46, 75, 132, 152, 160,
    191, 222, 258, 294, 321, 351, 378–
    379, 406, 448
  consumer, 26
  ethnographic, 27
  marketing, 46, 243, see also
    marketing research
  observational, 27
  categories of, 10
research methods,
  interpretive, 8
  qualitative and quantitative, 26–27
response generation, **90**, 91
responsibility, social, *see* social
  responsibility
RESPonsive marketing, **24**, 25, 46,
    75, 101, 132, 152, 190–194, 222,
    258–261, 293, 379, 406, 427, 448
restricted exchange, **11**
retrieval, **84**, 103
retrieval cues, **90**, 91
retroactive interference, **98**
reward, 128
rhetorical devices, 213

rhetorical figures of speech, 212
Rice, Jerry, 202
Ripkin, Cal, Jr., 202
risk,
  avoidance, 133
  financial perceived, 121
  involuntary, 121
  opportunity loss perceived, 121
  perceived, 120–122
  perception, 242
  performance perceived, 121
  physical perceived, 121
  propensity for taking, 36
  psychological perceived, 121
  reduction strategies, 122
  social perceived, 121
  time perceived, 121
  voluntary, 121
ritual(s), 35, 363, 364, 366, 371–375, 381
  divestment, 372
  consumption-related, 372
  cultural, 371–373, 380
  exchange, 372
  grooming, 372
  possession, 372
ritual experience, typology of, 372
Ritz Carlton Hotel, 3, 269, 272, 294
Rockstar, 169, 170
role-related product cluster, **334**
role-relaxed consumer, 369
roles, 334
Roper organization, 441
Rotex Explorer, 35
Ruffles, 26
rules, 362
  of perceptual organization, 69
rumors, 446, 447, 450
  actions to take, 447
  dealing with, 446–448
  pipe dream, 446
  premeditated, 446
  self-fulfilling, 446
  spontaneous, 446
  types and causes, 446–448
rural subculture, 406
Ryan, Nolan, 202
RYAs (returning young adults who
  move back in with relatives), 391

S

S&P 500 Index, 202
Sacrament of the Last Supper, The
  (painting by Dali), 71
safety, 117, 306
sales promotion, 44
salience, information, 99

salient attributes, 179, 183
salient beliefs, **177**
sample sizes, **423**
Samsung, 113, 131, 438
San Antonio Spurs, 209
Santa Claus, 363
satisfaction, 295
    and loyalty, 269–302
        predicting, 292–293
    customer, 295, see also customer
        satisfaction
    development of, 279
    emotional, 280
    post-purchase, 42
    to delight, 285
    trap, 285
satisficing, **251**
scales, use of measuring personality
    traits, 152–153
schedules of reinforcement, **129**
schema, **97**, 98
search,
    by consumers, 240–241
    external, 237, 239, 260
    instrumentality of, 240
    internal, 237–239, 260
    ongoing, 237
    prepurchase, 237
    stage of generic decision-making
        model, 232
search processes, **237**, 260
Sears, 95, 389
secondary brands, 40
secondary reinforcer, **128**
secondary sources, **29**
security, 159
segmentation, 16, 25, 46, 75–76, 102,
    133, 152, 161, 191, 223, 258–259,
    294, 321, 351, 379, 407, 427–428,
    448–449
    and positioning strategies, 17
    bases for, 35
    behavior, 37
    benefit, 37, 191
    market, 34, 46
segmentation basis, 38
    characteristics of person as a, 35–38
    geography as, 38
segmenting, 24
    business markets, 39
    consumer markets, 35
selective attention, **58**
selective exposure, **54**
    and social media, 56
selectivity, **205**, 206
self,
    actual, 153

actualization, 117
    and symbolic interaction, 153–154
    looking glass, 154
    possible, 153
    social, 153
self-concept, **142**, **153**, 162, 171
    and marketing strategy, 153–155
    and product symbolism, 154
    and promotional strategy, 154–155
    dimensions of, 153
    personality, and psychographics,
        141–168
self-congruity effect, 154
self-fulfilling rumors, **446**
self-fulfillment, 159
self-gifts, **315**
self-prophecy effect, 181
self-respect, 159
selling, personal, *see* personal selling
semantic information, 88
semantic memory, **96**, 103
    networks, 96–98
    network for sports cars, 97
semiotics, **72**, 73, 76, 78
sensation, **61**, 77
sense of accomplishment, 159
sense of belonging, 159
sensory memory, 84
sensory proximity, 214
sentience, 117
sentiment connections, **185**
separateness, 36
separateness-connectedness, **151**
serial learning, **93**
serial position effect, **93**–94
service, *see* customer service
service encounter, **345**–347
service themes, 346–347
service/product quality, consumer's
    evaluation of, 279
services, 10, **272**
sex, 35, 36, 117
sexually suggestive ads, impact of, 208
shame, 114
shaping, **130**
Shearson Lehman Brothers, 59
shopping, 312, 403
    compulsive, 443
short-term memory, **84**, **85**, 86, 87, 103
Showgirls, 72
Shrek movies, 68
sight, 311
Sigma-Aldrich Corp., 449
sign(s), **72**, 73, 76, 78, **203**
situation-product interaction, 320
situation segmentation basis, 36
situational factors, 322

situational influences, 303–328
    managerial implications of, 321
situational involvement, **57**, 77
situational traits, **148**, 150
situational variable, **317**
Six Flags Mountain theme park, 245
SKTT gene, 147
Skype, 292
smell, 311
smoking, 441–442
Snapple, 446
soap opera ads, 100
social classes, 388, **401**, 408
    and lifestyles, 404–407
    buying behavior, 403
    influences consumer lifestyles, 404
    predictive of resources owned,
        404–405
social comparison, **335**
social controls, 440
social identity theory, **207**, **333**, 352
social influences, group, dyadic, and
    diffusion processes, 329–360
social media, 1, 2, 88, 160, 205, 212,
    232, 256, 272, 341, 350, 353, 353,
    378
    and selective exposure, 56
    tracking behavior with, 171
    websites, 33
social needs, McClelland's, 132
social network(s), 353
    and buying behavior, 340–341
    diffusion through, 350–351
    use, 160
social networking, 340, 350
social perceived risk, 121
social responsibility, 448, 449
    corporate, 450
social self, 153
social status, 408
social surroundings, **36**, 305, **312**–**313**,
    322
social system, 348
social threats, **120**
social-class hierarchy, 401–402
social-class subcultures, 401–405
social-comparison processes, 335
socialization,
    agents, 340
    childhood consumer, 339
socialization background factors, **340**
socially responsibility, corporate, 444
sociology, 8
sounds, 59
source, **205**
    attractiveness model, 209
    meaningfulness, 209–210

source, (continued)
   secondary, 29
source characteristics, 205
source credibility, 205–206, 223
source effects,
   impact of, 211
   managerial implications of, 211
source expertise, 205, 206
source likability, 208–211
source trustworthiness, 205
spatial proximity, 214
specific positioning, 40
Splenda, 90
spokesperson, trustworthy, 207
spontaneous brand switching, 66
spontaneous rumors, 446
stages of generic decision-making
   model, 232
Stanford Research Institute (SRI), 157
Starbucks, 3, 8, 40, 193, 271, 295
status, 10
status crystallization, 403
status symbols,
   consumption as a skill, 405
   goods purchased as, 405
stewardship, product, 449
Stewart, David, 437
stimuli, 417
   conditioned, 126, 134
   discriminative, 129–130
   eliciting, 126
   external, 113
   internal, 112
   neutral, 125
   previously neutral, 126
   unconditioned, 134
store layout, 309
store location, effects of, 309
Stouffer's, 368
strategy,
   marketing, see marketing strategy
   pricing, 74
   promotional, 76, 161
strivers, 158
strugglers, 158
Student City, 133
Students Against Drunk Driving
   (SADD), 440
subconscious, 416
subcultural, 304
subculture, 35, **38**–39, 161, 388, 407,
   408
   African-American, 394–395
   and demographic groups, 388–389
   and demographics, 387–414
      managerial implications,
      406–407

as a segmentation basis, 38–39
   Asian-American, 397
   disabled, 406
   ethnic, 394
   Hispanic, 395–397
   marketing environment, 30
   other, 406
   race as, 394–398
   rural, 406
   social-class, 401–405
subjective knowledge, 91
subjective norm (SN), 180
subliminal advertising, 64, 65
subliminal perception, 64–66, 77
substance abuse, 444
substitute activities, 316
succeeding, in the long run, 444–445
succorance, 117
Sumba Fitness, 365
Super Bowl, 43, 54, 56, 88, 94, 100, 188,
   193, 216, 364
superego, 144
Superman myth, 363, 373
Superstorm Sandy, 32, 34, 133
surface traits, 148, 150, 152, 155
surrogate consumer, 344
surrogates and mavens, 344
surroundings, 305
   physical and social, 36
Sustein, Cass, 32
Suter, Tracy A., 331
sweepstakes, 249
switch loyalty, 290
symbol, fraudulent, 405
symbolic innovation, 348
   and the self, 153–154
symbolic interactionism, 153
symbols, 3, 74, 76, 133, **145**, 153, 363,
   373, 374
   cultural, 373–375, 380
   effects of, 71–75
synapses, 418
syncretic decisions, 338
systematic, 417

T

target market, characteristics of, 350
task definitions, 36, **305**, 313–315
taste, 311
technological marketing environment,
   30
   and consumer behavior, 33–34
technological innovation, 349
television, 376
   remote-control devices, 55
terminal materialism, 369–371

Tesla, 42
testing, concept, 42
testing, market, 42
Texas A&M, 329
T-groups, 146
Thaler, Richard, 32
thematic apperception tests (TATs),
   145
theorists, psychanalytic, 145
theory, 7
theory of reasoned action, 180
threats,
   impersonal, 120
   social, 120
3M, 287
**3M model of motivation and
   personality, 147**, 149, 150, 152, 155,
   161, 162
   and traits, 146–149
threshold,
   absolute, 61–62, 64
   difference, 61–62, 64
Thurstone, L. L., 172
time, 36, 305, 322, 404
   and forgetting, 100
   as a product, 317
   as a resource, 316–317
   as a situational variable, 317
   as environmental influencer, 316–318
   circular, 317
   circular traditional, 316
   linear, 316
   perceived risk, 121
   proximity, 214
timeliness, 278–279
tolerance for ambiguity, 36
toll-free numbers, 288
Tom and Lorenzo.com, 378
Toshiba, 95
tough, 311
Tower of Terror in Queensland,
   Australia, 119
Toyota, 41, 52, 448
   Prius, 178
traditional decision-making
   perspective, 234
trait(s), 146, 147, 162
   approach, 162
   compound, 147, 150
   elemental, 147, 150
   how they are organized, 150–151
   location in the 3M model, 150
   predictors of distracted driving, 148
   situational, 148, 150
   source credibility, 206
   surface, 150, 152, 155
   theory, 146

3M model of motivation and personality, 146–149
tranquil, 114
transfer meaning model, 210
transformational advertising, **219**
transmission processes, 347–348
Transport Canada, 158
Travelers insurance, 58
trend(s), 377
    classic fashion, 377
    cyclical fashion, 377
    individual-level adherence, 377
    speed of, 377
trickle-down theory, **347**, 353
Troyer, Verne, 206
Trublend, 210
trustworthiness, 206
    and expert endorser, 206
truth effect, **183**
Tumblr, 55
Turkey, 370
TV test, 15
tweets, 205
Twitter, 1, 29, 33, 55, 56, 71, 88, 171, 212, 350, 371
two-factor theory, **221**, 222
2010 Winter Olympics, 44
Tylenol, 215, 446

U

unconditioned response, **134**
unconditioned stimulus, 127, **134**
Under Armour, 205
Underhill, Paco, 174, 271
understanding, 117
undivided loyalty, 290
unfair advertising, 437
unique ads, creating, 99
unique selling proposition, **157**
uniqueness, 117
    need for, 118
unit relation, **186**
United States, 31, 32, 51, 370, 398
    cultures of, 388–389
United Way, 6
University of Florida, 329
University of Michigan Survey Research Center, 31
untrustworthy endorsers, 206
upper-class Americans, 402
upper-class consumers, 403
urban legends, 343, **447–448**
US Army, 391
US Department of Agriculture (USDA), 83

US Department of Health and Human Services, 441
US Food and Drug Administration (FDA), 26, 436
US population, 394
usage behavior, **37**
usage rate, 36
usage situations, **313**, 319–322
users, lead, 347–348
utilitarian function, **172**
utilitarian needs, **117**

V

validity, **146**
VALS lifestyle classification scheme, **157**, 163
VALS 2, 158, 159, 163
    consumer segments, 158
valuation of gains and losses, **246**–247
value-expressive function, **172**
value-expressive influence, **333**
values, 35, **362**, 363, 364, 365, 366, 367, 368, 404
    core, 366–367
    cultural, 367
    domain-specific, 367
    global, 367
    perceived, 74
    personal, 6
vapes, 435–436
variety seeking, **256**
    purchases, 8, 256
Veblen, Thorstein, 3
verbal information, 89
verbal memory, 103
vicarious learning, **131**, 135
Victoria's Secret, 208
Villanova University, 73
Viper, 90
vivid messages, **213–214**
vivid versus abstract information, 213–214
Volkswagen, 41
voluntary attention, **56**, 58, 77
voluntary gifts, 314
voluntary risks, **121**
Volvo, 133
von Restorff effect, **99**, 102, 103

W

Walmart, 44, 308, 310
Walt Disney Company, *see* Disney
Warner-Lambert, 437
Washington, George, 363

water, 32
weather, 32
Weber, E. H., 61
Weber, Max, 404
Weber's law, **61**, 62, 63, 76
Wendy's, 213, 447
Wheaties, 157
Whirlpool, 287
White, Shaun, 209
wife-dominated decisions, 338
Wikipedia, 33
Wilson Research Strategies, 159
Wines That Rock (WTR), 4
Winfrey, Oprah, 205
WMX Technologies, 444
women, 337, 370, 389
Woods, Tiger, 95, 201, 202
word-of-mouth (WOM), 1, 123, 245, 286, **342**, 353
word-of-mouth communications, 342–345
    why it occurs, 343
working memory, 84, **85**
Wrangler Jeans, 210

X

X6 crossover vehicles, 51
Xbox, 24
Xerox, 449
Xyience Xenergy, 170

Y

Yammer, 341
YouTube, 1, 33, 51, 88

Z

zapping, **55**, 188
Zeigarnik effect, **100**, 102, 103
Zeigarnik, Bluma, 100
Zielske, Hubert, 100
zipping, **55**, 188
Zirh, 373